MW01015816

Tax Havens of the World
(7th edition)(1999/2,000)
(2nd printing)
Tax Haven Reporter
by Thomas P. Azzara
Publisher • Author • Investment Adviser
• Deeds of Trust • Offshore Incorporations •

54 Sandy Port Drive • P.O. Box CB 11552 • Nassau, Bahamas

• telephone (242) 327-7359 • cellular (242) 359-1132

e-mail • taxman@batelnet.bs

http://www.bahamasbahamas.com/

http://www.endtaxes.com/

ISBN: 1-893522-02-4

i

"Over and over again the courts have said that there is nothing sinister in so arranging one's affairs as to keep taxes as low as possible. Everyone does so, rich or poor, and all do right, for nobody owes any public duty to pay more tax than the law demands; taxes are enforced extractions, not voluntary contributions." **- Judge Learned Hand**

"The art of taxation consists in so plucking the goose as to obtain the largest possible amount of feathers with the smallest amount of hissing." **- Jean Babtiste Colbert** (French Statesman: *Minister of Finance* - 1619 - 83)

"They have no right to put their hands in my pockets." **- General George Washington** (1732 - 99)

"The absence of income or significant corporate income taxes, along with political stability, is the bedrock on which foreign investment in The Bahamas has been built." - **Embassy of the United States (Nassau, Bahamas) (April, 1990)**

"One of the most effective applications of offshore trusts is in an ownership combination with a limited company." - **Richard Graham-Taylor, partner Ernst & Young, Grand Cayman (January 1990)**

"The legal right of a taxpayer to decrease the amount of what otherwise would be his taxes, or to altogether avoid them by means which the law permits, cannot be doubted." - **United States Supreme Court,** *Gregory v. Helvering,* 293 U.S. 465 (1934)

"There is one difference between a tax collector and a taxidermist - the taxidermist leaves the hide." **- Mortimer Caplin**

"Taxation is theft." - **Unknown author**

AN ENGLISH TAX COLLECTOR is shown being chased by an irate colonial woman from a New England farm in pre-Revolutionary days.

Dedication

This book is being respectfully dedicated to:

The good people of the Bahamas, and....

my daughter, LeeAnn

and wife, Linda

- Thomas P. Azzara

A LITHOGRAPH OF THE REVOLUTIONARY ERA entitled "The Bostonians Paying the Excise Man, or Tarring and Feathering." The background shows the dumping of tea in the harbor and the Liberty Tree.

Preface

Tax Havens of the World (7th edition • 2nd printing) has been revised and rewritten seven times since our first edition in 1985. This book is a composite of many hours of search and research. The source of this investigation includes the **Internal Revenue Code of 1986** (including TAMRA and the Revenue Reconciliation Act of 1993), the Prentice-Hall and Commerce Clearing House Federal Treasury Regulations, and other books and treatises supplied by the tax haven governments, reputable international tax attorneys, college law professors and authors writing on the subject.

Tax havens are used by many thousands of American and foreign businessmen alike. Often, they are used in complete disregard for the U.S. tax law, i.e., income tax evasion. Other times, they are used legitimately to legally avoid U.S. income taxes. For example, under the U.S. tax Code, there are no income taxes owed on the offshore rents accruing to an American owned foreign company, even if the American owns all the shares in the company. Manufacturing profits, and consulting profits - when the services are performed in the tax haven itself - are 100% tax free under U.S. tax law too.

Other legal tax loopholes

Offshore banks and companies are not subject to U.S. capital gains taxes on their publicly traded Wall Street type stock, bond, and commodity trades. The United States has never taxed the capital gains of the non-resident alien, unless the foreigner was "doing business within the U.S.". "Doing business within the United States", generally means operating through a U.S. office or permanent establishment from within the U.S. However, the U.S. tax code even exempts a non-resident company from U.S. capital gains taxes even when it does have an office and staff inside the U.S., if all the company's business amounts to merely trading in the Stock Market. From his home or office on Fifth Avenue in New York, or the Sears Tower in Chicago, or from Beverly Hills, any person working for an offshore company could call his broker at Merrill Lynch or Paine Webber and day trade NYSE, NASDAQ or AMEX listed securities 1,000 times a week, and no tax on the profits would be owed the U.S. Treasury.

Today, nearby tax havens like the Cayman Islands, Panama, Barbados, and The Bahamas rival the industrial cities including London, Tokyo and New York for business. The pint sized Cayman Islands now boast more commercial banks (594) in the commercial registrar than in all California. The dollars on deposit in these Cayman banks exceeds $500 billion, which is also more than all the commercial banks in California. The Bahamas, just 50 miles off the coast of Florida, was once the third largest financial center in the world next to New York and London. Today, the Bahamas ranks in the top ten as a financial center, just behind the Cayman Islands. There are more than 390 banks and trust companies registered here in Nassau.

The Bahamas, the Cayman Islands, Turks & Caicos Islands, Anguilla and Bermuda have no personal income taxes, no corporate income taxes, no capitol gains taxes, no withholding taxes, no estate, gift or inheritance taxes, no sales taxes, no employment taxes, no death duties, and no probate fees. Guarantees against future taxes are provided by these governments for periods up to 50 years. Exempt trusts can receive guarantee up to 100 years.

Unfortunately, the American taxpayer easily cannot qualify for the aforementioned tax exemptions allowed nonresidents, unless he can avoid both the Controlled Foreign Corporation provisions enacted during the Kennedy Administration and the Passive Foreign Investment Company provisions enacted in 1986. Most tax attorneys and big 8 accounting firms will probably tell you that is not possible. This is not to imply that U.S. taxpayers don't attempt to secure the above tax exemption afforded foreigners anyway. They do.

The bottom line is, while the foreign investor can get a complete tax exemption from U.S. capital gains taxes from the U.S. government on its publicly traded stock, bond and commodity transactions, the U.S. person operating in an almost identical manner is taking risk.

The investment banking firm of Warburg, Dillion Read (on Park Ave. N.Y.) have offices in 39 foreign countries - including the Bahamas, the tiny Cayman Islands, Hong Kong and the Channel Islands. Makes you wonder why, doesn't it? And, Warburg, Dillion Read are not the only large U.S. investment firms offshore. The list of U.S. companies with operations in the tax havens is too long to name here, but include Brown Brothers/Harriman & Company (Cayman), Solomon Brothers (Bahamas), CitiCorp Bank & Trust (Bahamas), Chase Manhattan (Cayman Islands).

Types of tax havens

Tax havens (also called *financial centers* and *fiscal paradises)* are independent countries with very low or no tax rates. [1.] With the exception of the United States Virgin Islands (USVI), all these countries are located outside the Continental United States and outside the USA's tax jurisdiction. Many tax havens are members of the British Commonwealth of Nations, thus favorite tax shelters for British businessmen. These include the Bahamas, Cayman Islands, Bermuda, the Channel Islands, Mauritius (Indian Ocean), Isle of Man (also called Manx), Hong Kong, Vanuatu (South Pacific), Cook Islands, Gibraltar, Anguilla, Montserrat, and Barbados. You may be surprised to learn that although these nations fall under British domain, some of these tax havens are more geared to attract the U.S. businessman. The Cayman Islands and the Bahamas, because of their close proximity to the United States, are actually the home of more U.S. corporate concerns than British. In fact, it can be said that only three of the above thirteen havens are in the main British financial centers - those being Gibraltar, the Isle of Man and the Channel Islands (Sark, Jersey, Guernsey and Alderney). The rest are used by citizens from all the industrial nations - anywhere high taxes are imposed.

"Low-tax" and "No-tax" Havens

The Caribbean has an abundance of what writers call "no-tax" and "low-tax" haven nations. The governments of these countries have lowered or eliminated their tax rates for corporations or individuals doing business there.

Countries like The Caymans, The Bahamas, Bermuda, Panama, the Netherlands Antilles, Barbados and the British Virgin Islands (B.V.I.s) derive substantial revenues from their tax haven status. [2.] Start-up incorporation fees, annual filing fees, the issuing of bank and insurance licenses, and stamp duties add up to big bucks for these under-industrialized countries in rather remote places. The Dutch "Antilles" government derived over $90 million dollars in revenue as a result of their tax haven status in 1986. These dollars could not have been attracted otherwise. Moreover, the revenue that passes onto the private sector - to lawyers, hostelers, accountants, banks, businessmen for office rental space, and the tourist trade - becomes a larger part of the Antilles local economy. Most knowledgeable professionals familiar with these fiscal paradises say the chances of these nations imposing taxes anytime soon is highly unlikely.

The strategies for successful offshore tax planning are complex and involved. There is a mountain of legislation (both foreign and U.S.) that must be dealt with. Making matters even more inane, some authors have written books suggesting there is "nothing" to be gained from using tax havens unless you like flirting with the law. This view is not correct at all because tax havens can and are being used successfully every day. Professor Marshall J. Langer, in his book *Practical International Tax Planning* ($150/copy), says there are over 100 incorporations a month in the Cayman Islands alone. Only a few fail because of mismanagement.

	Corporate Tax Rates	
	1985	**1999**
Canada	46%	38%
France	50%	33%
Germany	56%	36%
Italy	46%	36%
Japan	43%	37.5%
United Kingdom	45%	34%
United States	46%	34%
Australia	46%	33%
Source: Revised Data based on National Tax Journal September 1987 and Price Waterhouse Corporate Taxes (1999).		

1. Some tax havens (including the Cayman Islands, Isle of Man and the Channel Islands) are "colonies" or "possessions" (not independent nations) of the United Kingdom while others are neo-havens and "territories" of the United States.

2. The Cayman Islands, Bermuda, the Bahamas are "no tax havens". Panama and Hong Kong do not tax "foreign source incomes". International Business Companies incorporated in the Netherlands Antilles, Barbados and the BVI pay some tax, but rates are very low - under 3%.

Corporate Tax Rates		
	1985	**1999**
Bermuda	0%	0%
Cayman Islands *	0%	0%
Channel Islands *	0%	0%
Isle of Man *	0%	0%
Barbados **	1% to 2-1/2%	1% to 2-1/2%
Vanuatu *	0%	0%
Bahamas **	0%	0%
B.V.I. **	0%	0%
Anguilla *	0%	0%
Nevis **	0%	0%
Hong Kong Σ	0%	0%
Panama Σ	0%	0%
Gibraltar Σ*	0%	0%

* "Exempted Companies"
** "International Business Corporations" (IBC)
Σ no tax on "foreign source incomes"
Source: Tax Haven Reporter (1999)

Tax Havens like to be called financial centers

The Central Banks and governments of the world's tax havens agree on one thing - they much prefer to be called *financial centers* than *tax haven*. The word *tax haven* congers up the notion of tax evasion, money laundering, and illegal drug profits, none of which a respectable tax haven wants to be associated with. But, by whatever name you choose to call them, tax havens, financial centers or fiscal paradises are a part of the economic scene we live, work and hopefully prosper in.

Even some of the foremost scholars writing about the world's fiscal paradises have had to redo their thinking on occasion. Marshall J. Langer (adjunct professor of law at Miami University, graduate *summa cum laude* from the Wharton School of Finance and Syracuse Law School) changed the title of his much acclaimed book, *Practical International Tax Planning* at least once. Formerly, Langer's memoir was titled *"How to use tax havens"*, obviously a much to venturesome title for an American law professor's textbook. What might Congress, the U.S. Treasury Department, and the IRS have to say about a U.S. law professor whose book prompts and promotes legal tax avoidance? Marshall Langer's publisher - the **Practicing Law Institute** (Manhattan, N.Y.) - might be running a real reputation risk too. The **PLI** is the oldest publisher of legal works in the United States, dating back to the time when Thomas Jefferson was President.

The Paradox

What we have is a paradox. For while industrial nations like the U.S., Canada, West Germany and the UK continually cry foul the abusive use of the fiscal paradises by their own citizenry (along with the loss in tax revenues), their own tax laws perpetuate and foster the colossal growth of these fiscal haciendas.

By its nomenclature, a *tax haven* is a location which offers a low-tax or no-tax environment for which businessmen can operate. Falling into this category are such recognizable havens as Bermuda, the Cayman Islands, the Bahamas, Liechtenstein, and Switzerland, to name a few. Additionally, high tax nations like the U.S. and UK offer tax haven benefits to foreign investors to attract funds into London and New York. The English, with urbane euphemism, class these as *invisible earnings*.

The United States is a tax haven for the foreign investor trading shares on any one of the U.S. stock exchanges because U.S. tax law allows trades by non-resident individuals, foreign corporations and foreign trusts to be executed free from U.S. capital gains taxes. And while the foreign investor is limited in his trading position to no more than 5% of the outstanding float of the publicly traded U.S. company, there is no exemption or relief for the U.S. citizen at all. [3]

Moreover, foreign investors can trade directly U.S. corporate and Treasury bonds free from capital gains taxes in any quantity, from $100,000 to $1,000,000,000,000. And if this wasn't incentive enough to buy United States bonds, Congress recently repealed the 30% interest withholding tax on bonds issued after July 18, 1984. Today, the foreign investor can receive his U.S. bond interest free from U.S. income, withholding and estate taxes, if he lives in a tax haven or organizes a holding company in one.

According to the London *Times,* half the world's money now moves around in an *offshore environment.* It's a simple fact that penal taxation by the host nation encourages its citizenry to trade in their neighbor's houses to gain a more

---

3. See IRC §897(c)(3) - Exception for Stock Regularly Traded on Established Securities Markets.

favorable tax climate. Today, all the industrial nations offer tax incentives similar to those offered foreign investors investing in the U.S. The trend to export money will continue so long as home country tax rules remain favorable.

Yet the paradox continues. The U.S. and the other industrial nations simply cannot advertise the fact that they are a splendid tax haven for foreigners. Such revelations would cause dissent among the local citizenry.

Tax haven governments lower incorporation costs to attract foreign investors

Throughout the 1970's and 80's, and for most of the 1990's, the costs to register an offshore holding company in most any of the world's tax havens were continually on the rise. One celebrated tax haven writer remarked that if the Cayman Islands continued to raise their government registration fees any higher, they would price themselves out of the market. The Cayman Islands (a *no-tax* haven) got to be one of the biggest banking and financial centers in the world by offering lower registration costs than any of its competitors (i.e., Bermuda, the Bahamas, British Virgin Islands, Netherlands Antilles, Barbados). Today, the costs to form an exempt or ordinary company in Cayman range from $1,500 to $2,500, but that's significantly higher than the costs to form a similar company in the Bahamas, the British Virgin Islands, the Turks & Caicos Islands, Panama or Nevis.

240,000 IBCs registered in British Virgin Islands

Over the last fourteen years the BVI has moved up to rank right behind Cayman and the Bahamas (and ahead of Bermuda) as the premier offshore banking and financial center in the Caribbean. Ironically, it was an incident in 1983 - the termination of the **U.S.-BVI Tax Treaty** by the U.S. Treasury Department - that led to the BVI's phenomenal growth. Only after the U.S. government canceled the BVI-U.S. tax treaty did the BVI government decide to institute new and competitive tax haven legislation (i.e., the **International Business Companies Ordinance of 1984**) to attract foreign investors. [4]

In 1987, 2,000 IBCs were registered in the BVI, but by the end of 1988 the figure had soared to 7,000. Incorporation levels during 1990 reflect an almost 50% increase over 1989, a year in which slightly more than 11,000 IBCs were registered. Today there are about 240,000 IBCs registered in the BVIs. The BVIs can now claim to have more offshore companies in their registrar than the Caymans have in theirs ($\approx$ 50,000). [5]

The Caymans - #1 offshore banking center

The Cayman Islands are three specks of tropical greenery in the Caribbean Sea about 450 miles south of Miami and just south of Cuba. The main island of Grand Cayman harbors the capital city George Town which lies on the western shore. Practically all commercial banking activities are carried-on in George Town.

As of January 1, 1999 the number of bank and trust companies licensed in the Cayman Islands passed the 594 mark, representing over 50 countries, and including 60 with their own local operations. The benefits of doing business in the Islands are reflected in the total of over 30,000 companies registered in the Government registrar, including more than 350 offshore insurance companies. Forty-three of the world's top 50 banks maintain subsidiaries or branches in Cayman. Many of the remaining 470+ banks are said to be privately owned, set up for a restricted clientele.

Banks are closely regulated by the Government's Inspector of Banks. In the past 20 years there have been just three bank failures, none of which were of inter-banking significance. [6]

---

4. The old *B.V.I. - U.S. Income Tax Treaty* reduced U.S. withholding taxes and contained many lucrative tax breaks for BVI companies investing in the United States. With the treaty benefits taken away, the BVI government believed the BVI would become far less popular as an offshore financial center, and subsequently passed the **IBC Ordinance of 1984** to attract new foreign investors. In July of 1987, the U.S. Treasury Department canceled another important tax treaty with a known tax haven - the Netherlands Antilles. Almost immediately the Netherlands Antilles government passed new IBC legislation to make itself competitive with the Cayman Islands, BVI, Bahamas, and Panama.

5. From *Offshore Investment Magazine* (Number 14, pg 9) - *British Virgin Islands - An Ill Wind Blows Somebody Some Good,* by Peter Cohen.

6. From a Cayman Islands Government Information Services booklet - *Advantages of the Cayman Islands as an Offshore Financial Center.*

Bank deposits in Cayman's 594 banks now exceed $500 Billion

Timothy Ridley of the accounting firm of Maples & Calder on Grand Cayman wrote the editor of *Offshore Investment Magazine* in the summer of 1988 to rebuke a report that claimed the total bank deposits in Cayman was US$200 billion instead of the more nearly correct figure of US$250 Billion. Mr. Ridley went on to say that total bank deposits in Cayman were expected to exceed US$275 BIL by the end of 1988. But, today's statistics show the 594+ Cayman Island banks have more than $500 billion dollars on deposit - substantially more than all the commercial banks in the State of California. It's no wonder George Town on Grand Cayman has earned the nick-name - *little Wall Street*.

No corporate or individual income taxes. No taxes of any kind!

Caymanians have historically had a distaste for taxation and this has provided a natural setting for the system of laws and regulations dating back to the 1960's, which have created and encouraged the growth of the Islands as an offshore financial center. The Caymans are what lawyers refer to as a no-tax haven. Taxes or all types simply do not exist in this country.

Like the other zero-tax havens (i.e., the **Bahamas,** Bermuda, Anguilla, Vanuatu and Nauru (in the South Pacific), the Caymans have traditionally enjoyed a complete absence of direct taxation. There are no corporate income taxes, no personal income taxes, no capital gains taxes, no withholding taxes, no estate, gift or inheritance taxes, no sales taxes, no probate fees, no property taxes and no employment taxes. The only form of direct taxation the Caymans ever imposed was a $10 a year tax on adult males, but this was abolished in 1985.

Exempt & Ordinary Companies

There are two types of companies you can form in Cayman - an **ordinary company** and an **exempt company.** An exempt company is the one most often chosen by North Americans, as it can receive a guarantee against the imposition of future taxes from the Governor in Council for up to 30 years. An exempt company is also relieved from some of the rules and regulations that an ordinary company must comply with under the Cayman's Commercial Code - **Companies Law.**

Today, there are about 2,000 new incorporations each year in Cayman. The laws governing these businesses are derived from English "Common-Law" statutes, which are the foundation for the companies law of the United States too. Other entities, such as partnerships, mutual funds, and joint ventures are permitted in this Caribbean no-tax haven that time seems to have forgotten.

Exempted & Ordinary Trusts

An **exempted trust** can be formed in Cayman and can receive a guarantee against future taxation for up to 50 years from the date the exempted trust is created. An application is sent to the *Registrar of Trusts s*tating that the beneficiaries do not include, and are not likely to include, any person resident or domiciled in the Islands. A registration fee of CI$200 (about US$250) is payable the Registrar, and the documents containing the trust's powers are lodged with the Government. An additional fee of CI$100 must be paid the trustees in March of each year, and the trustees must file accounts, minutes and other information at this time. These documents are open to inspection by the Government and trustees, but are not open to public inspection.

Trusts other than exempted trusts can be formed in Cayman upon payment of a stamp tax of CI$40. There is no requirement for public recording or registration of an **ordinary trust**. An **ordinary trust** is usually assigned a bank or trust company to act as trustees, and it is customary to use local entities for this function. Neither the *settlor* (grantor) or the *beneficiaries* have to be physically present within Cayman, and the trust's assets may be kept outside the islands.

The Bahamas lower incorporation costs

To regain some of its lost glory (The Bahamas were once the third largest financial center in the world behind New York and London), the Bahamas government introduced its own **IBC Act** in January of 1990. The Bahamas **IBC Act (1990)** mimics the BVI **International Business Companies Ordinance of 1984** almost to the letter. Over 90,000 IBCs have been registered since the first year (1990) of the Act. [7]

---

7. *"A Bahamas base - in just 24 hours."* **Offshore Adviser**, pg. #4 (November, 1990)

Total costs to form an IBC in Nassau, Bahamas are today slightly less than the costs to register an IBC in the British Virgin Islands. There are other advantages the Bahamas now have over the BVI, Caymans, Bermuda, Panama, or the Turks & Caicos Islands.

1) The Bahamas are a **zero tax haven** like the Cayman Islands, Bermuda and the Turks & Caicos Islands. Resident individuals and companies doing business within the Bahamas are not liable to any income taxes. The BVIs and Panama have domestic tax systems with high tax rates for resident individuals and resident companies doing business within the country (i.e., profits drawn from the local economy).

2) The Bahamas, just 50 miles off the coast of Florida, is the closest tax haven to the United States. Direct flights from London, New York, Ft. Lauderdale, Palm Beach and Miami arrive and depart daily. Round trip air fare from Ft. Lauderdale to Nassau is just $150. Air travel time is only 55 minutes.

3) The Bahamas are 5,300 sq. miles in size. That is to say, the Bahamas are approximately 500 times bigger in land area than the Cayman Islands; 2,500 times bigger than Bermuda; 1,000 times the size of the BVI; and 30 times the size of the Turks & Caicos Islands. Land prices on some out-islands are not inflated as are real estate prices in the Caymans and Bermuda.

4) The Bahamas receive more tourist each year from more parts of the world than any Caribbean tax haven. Over 3.5 million Americans, Canadians, Asians, South Americans, and Europeans visit the Bahamas each year.

5) The Bahamas have a well tested **Bank Secrecy Code** protecting the foreign investor against unauthorized disclosure of financial information to outsiders (including IRS agents, lawyers, foreign and domestic courts, etc.). Criminal and civil penalties, including fines and imprisonment, can result if bank officials and others with fiduciary responsibilities breach this law. The Cayman's Bank Secrecy Code was copied from the Bahamas Bank Secrecy Code in the early 1960's. It paved the way for the Caymans colossal growth as an offshore banking center. Bermuda does not have a written bank secrecy code.

Domicile of Trust Act (1991)

The Bahamas government introduced a new **Domicile of Trust Act** in 1991. Under prior law, the life of an offshore trust domiciled in the Bahamas was limited to 21 years beyond the life of the existing beneficiary named in the Trust. This rule was amended to allow for the trust to exist for 80 or 100 years. The new Domicile of Trust Act is designed to safeguard trusts from attack by other jurisdictions.

Turks & Caicos lowers fees for offshore asset holding companies.

Drafting legislation unmistakenly similar to that enacted in the Cayman Islands, the Turks & Caicos government look to capture their share of the offshore tax haven business by offering lower incorporation fees than in Cayman. Both **exempted** and **ordinary** companies can be formed in the Turks for about 1/2 what you would spend for a similar company in the Cayman Islands. Government registration fees are $275 for ordinary companies and $325 for exempted companies. Annual fees are $300.

Total costs (including lawyers, trust companies, agents and a registered office) are right about $1,400. Note, this is slightly higher than in the Bahamas. Unfortunately, few airline companies have direct flights into the Turks and air fare is substantially higher than a flight to Nassau.

Currently there are some 12,000+ exempted companies in the TCI. In addition, 1,000 captive insurance companies have been registered since the enactment of the **Insurance Ordinance 1989.**

Non-resident foreign companies, trusts, banks and individuals can trade stocks, bonds, commodity contracts and options 100% free from U.S. capital gains taxes.

Under the U.S. Tax Code, only when a foreign company, foreign trust or nonresident alien individual takes up permanent residence within the United States will he be subject to U.S. capital gains taxes in the same way as domestic taxpayers. For a corporation permanent residence would be a U.S. office or warehouse. Capital gains realized by foreign corporations and other nonresidents "not engaged in a trade or business **within** the United States" are exempted from tax under IRC §871 and IRC §881 & IRC §897(c)(3). Moreover, U.S. Treasury Regulations §864-2(C)(1) & (2) provides an exception for what embodies being "engaged in a *trade or business within* the United States". Under U.S. regulations, a nonresident's Stock Market transactions carried-out through a U.S. stock broker, independent agent, or an employee are **not** considered to cause the nonresident to be "engaging in a *trade or business within* the United States".

12.

Table of Contents

Chapter 5 • The Cayman Islands & other Caribbean tax havens   85

Chapter 6 • Panama & other shipping havens   159

Chapter 7 • Switzerland & the European tax havens   181

Introduction

In the United States broad taxing powers have been delegated to the IRS to be sure. But, as far reaching as the IRS's authority is, their right to tax is certainly not unlimited. A U.S. citizen must, according to Code-Section 61, include in the calculation of his gross income *"all income from whatever source derived"*. This means a citizen who receives dividends or interest from foreign investments (including bank accounts) must include them with all his other income. Similarly, all domestic corporations are taxed on their world-wide income unless a tax treaty, exemption or credit mitigates the tax.

Treaties, tax credits, exemptions

Tax treaties reduce the tax on passive incomes such as interests, dividends, royalties, and capital gains on the sale of stocks or securities. The United States maintains a network of some 42 or so bi-lateral income tax treaties with other nations. By and large, the purpose of these agreements is to reduce and eliminate the possibility of *"double taxation"* of income by the two countries a party to the treaty agreement. If two countries both have the right to levy their full rate of tax on a particular item of income, the resultant tax liability for the unfortunate taxpayer could exceed 100% of income.

For example, absent the income tax treaty between the Netherlands and the USA, if a Dutch citizen invests $1,000,000 in a NYSE stock with a dividend yield of 12% pa, he might receive a gross dividend from his investment of $120,000 by years end, and would pay a 30% U.S. withholding tax on the $120,000 dividend amounting to $36,000. In addition, Dutch income taxes at rates ranging up to 72% would be imposed on the $120,000 dividend for a total tax liability of about $122,400 (more than the dividend itself!). This assumes the Dutch individual was in the highest tax bracket for 1988, and no credit or deduction for foreign taxes paid was permitted. Under the U.S.-Netherlands tax treaty, the U.S. dividend withholding tax rate is **reduced** from 30% to 15%, and to 5% when a Dutch company has a "substantial holding" in the U.S. company

paying the dividend. A "substantial holding" is 10% of the U.S. company's stock. [1]

Tax Treaties are "reciprocal agreements". Under the U.S.-Netherlands tax treaty, the regular Dutch dividend withholding rate of 25% is reduced to 15%, with a further reduction to 5% if the U.S. recipient corporation owns at least 25% of the voting stock of the Dutch company paying the dividend, or if the U.S. recipient and another U.S. company together own at least 25%, and each owns at least 10% of the voting stock of the Dutch company.

Another mechanism used to stop double taxation is the allowance of a **tax credit** for foreign taxes paid. [2] In still other cases, a special **exemption** might allow certain kinds of profits to go untaxed altogether. As a result of all of the above, most businesses generally pay one tax not two. [3]

Offshore Holding Companies

In this world of legal complexities there are certain entities that the IRS really doesn't have the power to tax under current U.S. law. One such entity is the **foreign corporation** *not engaged in a trade or business within the United States*, and not **controlled** by U.S. persons. [4]

The reason a **foreign corporation** might not be subject to U.S. taxation is not necessarily because it is incorporated in another tax jurisdiction, because the IRS can and does have

1. The Dutch allow a "tax credit" under their tax treaties, but only permit a "tax adjustment" against foreign taxes paid absent a treaty. Generally, under the U.S. tax system a full tax credit against foreign taxes paid is allowed the US resident taxpayer. The U.S. "foreign tax credit" system is a whole different area of tax management calling for specialized tax planning techniques. It will not be discussed in this book.

2. See footnote #1 supra.
3. Under the US-Swiss Income Tax Treaty the US cannot tax the "foreign source incomes" of a Swiss-US branch if the contracts are signed outside the USA, and a foreign office plays a material role in the contract negotiations. Since the exporting of U.S. inventory by a nonresident is considered "foreign source income" under the **Code**, you could defer and accumulate these profits in the branch ad-infinitum. Since the Swiss do not levy **any tax** on the **foreign branch profits** of a Swiss incorporated entity, unless remitted back to Switzerland, US exporting profits can go 100% tax free.
4. IRC §7701(a)(1)

the power to tax profits of some foreign corporations (or the U.S. shareholders of that corporation).[5.] The reason some foreign corporations often pay no taxes (U.S. or other) is likelier to hinge upon the following criteria:

• "source of income" of that foreign corporation's profits. If the income is drawn from outside the United States it is usually not subject to U.S. taxation.
• capital share structure of the foreign corporation and the amount of stock "controlled" by **"U.S. shareholders"**. (see Chapter 2 - Controlled Foreign Corporations). Does the foreign corporation have a "U.S. Shareholder" as defined under IRC §951(b)? If not, no tax!
• tax jurisdiction where the foreign company is incorporated, i.e. a no or low tax haven.

If the foreign corporation has no source of income from the U.S., and is not actively engaged in a trade or business within the U.S., and is not **controlled** by a U.S. taxpayer, than the IRS cannot tax it. [6.]

The Tentacles of the Pentapus

Professor Harvey P. Dale of the N.Y.U. School of Law uses a descriptive analogy to explain to his students the five areas of the Internal Revenue Code that can cause an international tax plan to fail. These five categories [or tentacles of a pentapus, as Professor Dale chooses to call them] are as follows:

1. A **Personal Holding Company** described under Code-Section §541-47;
2. A **Foreign Personal Holding Company** under Code §551-58;
3. A **Controlled Foreign Corporation** under Code §951-64;
4. **Foreign Investment Company** under Codes §1246-47; [7.]
5. A company subject to the **accumulated earnings tax** under Code-Section §531-37.

As any well-schooled international tax practitioner will tell you, if any of these legislative laws can be made to apply to your business the taxes owed the U.S. Treasury would be large.

Ironically, the **Tax Reform Act of 1986** canceled the effect of the foreign investment company provisions for IRC §1246 by ending the preferential treatment for long term capital gains. But, the legislators came up with a substitute "tentacle" for the pentapus when they enacted new Code-Section 1291 thru 1297 **(Passive Foreign Investment Companies)**. We will discuss the *tentacles of the pentapus* later in this book.

To pay (taxes), or not to pay (taxes)? That is the question.

In 1981 the single U.S. taxpayer with taxable income of $100,000 would have owed the U.S. Treasury $50,054 in taxes because the Federal tax rate was a whopping 70% of taxable income. In 1988 a taxpayer living in California or New York with $100,000 in capital gains will pay federal and state taxes totaling about $34,000. By the same token, a foreign corporation domiciled in the Bahamas, or the Cayman Islands (there are approximately 40,000 registered investment holding companies in these two no-tax havens alone) would pay no U.S. capital gains taxes in 1988, because the Internal Revenue Code exempts a foreign corporation from tax on its <u>gains</u> from stocks and bonds provided it is not *engaged in a trade or business within the United States,* and does not have a U.S. office. [8.] T. Regulation §1.864-2(c)(1) allows the foreign company to effect its stock trades over a "U.S. Securities Exchange" through a U.S. "broker" or employee without incurring U.S. tax. Moreover, since the **Tax Reform Act of 1984** <u>repealed</u> the 30% interest withholding tax on "portfolio interest" on U.S. obligations issued <u>after</u> July 18, 1984, a Cayman or Bahamian holding company can receive U.S. corporate or treasury bond interest free of ALL taxes, both U.S. and foreign.

U.S. Treasury's Gordon Reports - proof of prodigious taxpayer folly

The United States does not condone the use of tax havens by its citizens openly, but the **Internal Revenue Code** contains numerous

---

5. IRC §957(a); IRC §541; IRC §951.
6. See IRC §861(a); IRC §951 to §958.
7. IRC §1246 turned long term capital gains into "ordinary income" taxable at ordinary rates under pre-**Tax Reform Act of 1986** law. Since the preferential tax treatment for long term capital gains has been removed under our new laws, the problems caused by IRC §1246 are no longer of consequence.

8. See IRC §881 (Corporations) and IRC §871 (nonresident individuals).

provisions fostering the existence and growth of these havens, regardless. The Caymans received over 400,000 tourists and businessmen in 1987 while the Bahamas claim over 3,000,000 visitors pa, most all arrivals coming from the USA and Canada. Haven watchers now say the 500 registered Cayman banks now hold over $500 billion dollars on deposit, surpassing Switzerland banks in deposit dollars. But it's the USA's *Gordon Reports* that are most interesting.

According to the U.S. Treasury's own *Gordon Reports,* during the period between 1970 and 1979... (1) the increase in direct investment in tax havens was more pronounced in some better known havens, with a 5-fold increase in the Bahamas, and a 39-fold increase in Bermuda; (2) the level of increase in assets of U.S. controlled corporations outpaced that of those in non-havens by 5 to 3; (3) banking deposits grew from $11 billion in 1968 to $358 billion in 1978; (4) gross dividend, interest and other payments to tax haven residents from U.S. sources constituted 42% (1978) of all such payments to nonresidents.

The second U.S. Treasury *"Gordon Report of 1984"* concluded.... (1) U.S. direct investment in Caribbean countries other than the Netherlands Antilles increased by over 43% from 1978 to 1982, and (2) financial activity through the "Antilles" increased with net U.S. borrowings from affiliates growing from $1 billion to $16 billion. [9.]

Favorite Japanese Tax Havens

It isn't just the American taxpayer that is using the offshore tax havens to escape home country tax rates. According to the Japanese Ministry of Finance, the three most popular tax havens for the Japanese are Panama, Hong Kong and Liberia. Investment in these three tax havens increased 4-fold between 1978 and 1983, whereas the total Japanese direct foreign investment increased by only 80% during the same period. Together, these havens accounted for 1/4 of all Japanese direct foreign investment in 1983.

No tax havens & low tax havens galore

Tax lawyers generally bunch the tax havens into two or three categories. The **no-tax havens**,

which include the Bahamas, Bermuda, the Cayman Islands, Vanuatu, Nauru, the Turks & Caicos Islands and Anguilla, have no personal income tax, no corporate income tax, no capital gains, no employment taxes, no estate, gift or inheritance taxes, no probate fees, no sales taxes, and no property taxes. Except for some menial "stamp duties" these havens are devoid of all forms of taxation.

Panama, Hong Kong, Costa Rica, Singapore and Gibraltar have a **territorial system of taxation**. These havens impose taxes on the local economies at rates from 18% to 50%, but allow "foreign source incomes" to go completely untaxed. It should be pointed that Singapore will tax "foreign source income" if it is remitted back to Singapore. McDermott International (Panama) and Seagate Technologies (Singapore) are two U.S. companies that have headquarters in tax havens.

The third category of tax haven is the **low-tax haven**. Low-tax havens include the Netherlands Antilles Barbados and Switzerland. Aside from low-tax rates, these havens have important tax treaties or tax agreements with the United States. Top corporate tax rates range from 9.8% (Switzerland) to 1% in Barbados and the Netherlands Antilles.

In 1987 the Antilles tax treaty was terminated. The United States signed a similar tax treaty with Barbados, and the Barbados agreement got ratified by the U.S. Senate in February, 1986. Under Article 10 (Dividends) of the Barbados-U.S. treaty, dividends enjoy a reduced withholding tax rate of 15%, and a further reduction to 5% if the Barbados parent owns at least 10% of the voting stock of the U.S. subsidiary. Absent a U.S. tax treaty, the U.S. withholds 30% at the source on dividends paid to foreign investors.

International Business Corporations (IBCs)

IBCs or International Business Corporations are another type of business company peculiar to the Caribbean nations. Antigua, Nevis, Barbados, St. Kitts, and the British Virgin Islands (B.V.I.s) all have enacted legislation promoting the use of the IBC. IBCs must be owned or controlled by nonresidents, and generally cannot carry on any local business or invest in local securities. Except for Barbados' low IBC tax rate

---

9. *International Tax Report*, pg. 3. (September, 1987)

of 1% to 2-1/2%, the IBCs organized in these Caribbean countries do not pay any taxes whatsoever.

Today, under the British Virgin Island's **IBC Ordinance of 1984** there are 240,000 registered corporations, with 1,500 new companies being formed each month. Briefly, here are some of the advantages IBCs enjoy in the BVIs.

- low company formation fees of under $1,000.
- a minimum requirement of one shareholder and one director is all that is needed to form a BVI company.
- board meetings can be conducted anywhere in the world, even by telephone.
- no annual returns or accounts need be filed with the Government Registrar.
- information concerning shareholders & directors are not a matter of public record and can be kept confidential.

Fascinating history of the United States Federal Income Tax [10.]

For the first 137 years since the signing of the *Declaration of Independence* the United States functioned without an income tax. During the Civil War an income tax was imposed for two years. In 1894 the Civil War tax was re-imposed, but the Supreme Court ruled a year later that the tax was unconstitutional. Up until 1913 it was not legally possible for the United States to levy an income tax on individuals. But, in that year the 16th Amendment to the Constitution was ratified, and Congress enacted an income tax at a rate of 1% on net taxable income up to $20,000 per year, and a "supertax" of from 2% to 6% on higher amounts. The maximum rate of 6% did not apply unless the taxpayer's taxable income exceeded $500,000 per year, a lot of money in those days.

Walace E. Olsen, president of the **American Institute of CPAs**, wrote an article in the *Wall Street Journal* in October 1973 saying:

A fear expressed by a number of opponents back in 1913 was that the proposed law, with its low tax rates, was the camel's nose under the tent. Once a tax on incomes was enacted, rates would tend to rise.

Senator William Borah of Idaho was outraged by such anxieties and derided a suggestion that the rate might eventually climb as high as 20%. "Who", he asked, could impose such socialistic, confiscatory rates?" Only Congress. And how could Congress the representatives of the American people be so lacking in fairness, justice and patriotism?"

During WWII the USA's income tax for individuals reached a maximum of 90%. In the 1970's State and Federal taxes combined put the U.S. individual tax rate at over 80%. Moreover, corporate earnings are taxed first at the corporate level, before they are passed onto the shareholder (where they are taxed again). On a million dollars of corporate profit, as little as $100,000 gets to be spent by the U.S. shareholder when rates are this confiscatory. If Francis Scott Key, author of the *"Star Spangled Banner"* (written during the War of 1812), were alive today I have to wonder if he would still consider America the *"land of the FREE and home of the brave"* be it that the Congress, the Senate and the Presidents of more recent vintage have been so bold (AKA brave) to impose Federal income tax at rates to 70% (1981) on America's middle-class. [11.]

Imagine no capital gains taxes?

If Idaho Senator William Borah was outraged about the possibility of a 20% Federal Income Tax someday, back in 1913, think how mad he would get if he learned that the U.S. now taxes its citizens at a rate of 28% on long term capital gains, and moreover that many nations of the free world do not tax capital gains at all, or only tax them marginally.

Below is a list of the nations (industrial and tax haven alike) that either impose no capital gains taxes at the corporate or individual levels, or only tax gains in certain circumstances at low rates.

---

11. The *War of 1812* was fought to get rid of once and for all that infamous British tax collector - King George III. King George III was the British monarch who's tea tax, molasses tax and other tariffs were so adamantly opposed by the American colonists during the struggle for independence. Ironically, King George III was responsible for the tax haven status of the Cayman Islands. He abolished taxes in the Caymans forever. Americans that manage to incorporate in the Cayman Islands might do best to thank King George for that!

---

10. Abridged from Marshall Langer's **Practical International Tax Planning**

Trinidad & Tobago - has no capital gains tax on assets held over 12 months. This applies to corporations and individuals and foreigners. Gains on the disposal of assets within 12 months are subject to tax at the standard rates. Any security can always be sold tax free.

South Africa - Industrial nation with no capital gains tax at the corporate and individual levels. Investment income from outside South Africa is not subject to tax in certain circumstances.

Barbados - no corporate or individual capital gains taxes.

Channel Islands - no capital gains taxes on offshore companies (Exempted Companies).

Costa Rica - no capital gains taxes on the sale of land or buildings.

Denmark - no capital gains taxes on shares held over 3 years by a company.

Cayman Islands - no capital gains taxes or any kind of taxes.

Bahamas - no capital gains taxes, no any kind of taxes.

Dominican Republic - no capital gains taxes.

Ecuador - capital gains on certain security transactions taxed at 8%. Same for individuals as for companies.

Egypt - for corporations, capital gains are exempt from tax if the proceeds of the sale are used to purchase another capital asset within 2 years. Capital gains on the sale of securities are not taxed.

Hong Kong - no capital gains taxes.

Jamaica - no capital gains taxes.

Kenya - no capital gains taxes. Abolished June 14, 1984.

Malaysia - no capital gains tax on security transactions, but a 2% share transfer tax applies to amounts over M$ million in an unlisted land-based company. Land & buildings are taxed.

New Zealand - Through January 1, 1988 there had been no capital gains tax legislation.

Japan - capital gains on the sale of portfolio securities by individuals are usually tax exempt. However, income from continuous trading in securities and/or income from the transfer of at least 200,000 shares (with a par value of 50¥) of one corporation during a year is taxable.

Nicaragua - Effective January 1, 1985 capital gains on the sale of property and other fixed assets, or shares in corporations, are taxed at 1% on the first $100,000 to a maximum of 15%.

Singapore - no capital gains taxes.

Taiwan - no capital gains tax on sale of listed security by non-investment oriented companies. Individuals are subject to capital gains tax.

Bermuda, Montserrat, the Netherlands Antilles, Anguilla, Vanuatu, Turks & Caicos, Nauru, the British Virgin Islands, Western Samoa, and Gibraltar have no capital gains taxes.

In 1985 the IRS estimated that the net capital gains shown on the 101.7 million returns received totaled $66.7 billion dollars. This amount exceeded dividend income on those same returns by $11.3 billion dollars.

There are very few avenues left for the U.S. **individual** taxpayer to legally avoid U.S. capital gains taxes. The United States taxes its citizens on their worldwide incomes. However, with proper planning a foreign corporation organized with foreign shareholders [like the ones in Chapter 2 (**Controlled Foreign Corporations**)] can trade in U.S. stocks and other securities 100% tax free.

Bahamas compared with other well known tax havens

	Bermuda	Turks & Caicos Islands	Bahamas [2]	Saint Vincent
Accessibility from New York	2 hours	4-1/2 hours	1 hours (from Miami)	6 hours
Size	21.4 sq. miles	166 sq. miles	5,382 sq. miles	150 sq. miles
Population	65,000	7,000	200,000	124,000
Language	English	English	English	English
Political Stability	very good	excellent	very good	very good
Corporate tax rate	0%	0%	0%	0% to 45%
Resident Individual's tax rate	0%	0%	0%	0% to 45%
Yearly company maintenance costs	US$5,000	US$500	US$350	US$380-$800
Initial Costs to	**US$4,000**	**US$1,000**	**US$1,100**	**US$1,000** Incorporate
Annual Government	US$1,200+	US$300 (exempt companies)	$250 - $350	US$190 tax *International Companies*
Tax on bank deposits	none	none	none	no
Bearer Shares	No	Yes	Yes	Yes
Trusts laws	Yes	Yes	Yes	Yes
Resident Agent Req.	No	Yes	Yes	Yes
Time to Incorporate	3 weeks	24 hours	24 hours	Few days
Location of Shareholder meetings	Anywhere	Anywhere in World	Anywhere	Anywhere
Location of Board Meetings	Anywhere	Anywhere in World	Anywhere	Anywhere
Exchange Controls	None	None	**No** if non-resident Co.	None
Financial Statements for Shareholders	Required	Yes	Yes	Yes
Filing annual return with Government	for Companies - Yes	No	No (Central Bank)	No
Minimum number of shareholders to form company	One	One	Two	One
Tax Treaties	**limited US treaty**	**None**	**None**	**Many**
Capital gains taxes	No	No	No	**No**
Estate/Inheritance taxes.	No	No	No	Yes [1]

1. Non- residents and *International Companies* are are not subject to estate or inheritance taxes.
2. The new *International Business Companies Act of 1989* went into effect in early 1990.

CHAPTER 1 • The Bahamas

The Commonwealth of the Bahamas, as they are officially known, is made up of some 700 islands and 2,500 cays or islets scattered over 750 miles of the Atlantic Ocean. This 100,000 sq./mile archipelago begins about 50 miles due east of West Palm Beach, Florida, where Freeport on the island of Grand Bahama is located, and extends lazily some 500 miles southeastward, finally ending among the Turks & Caicos Islands [another Caribbean no-tax haven, geographically (but not politically) part of the Bahamas].[1] Only about 25 of the Bahama islands are inhabited, and three-fourths of the people reside on just two islands - New Providence (where Nassau the Capital is located) and Grand Bahama Island (Freeport).

The Bahamas - the perfect no-tax haven

The Bahamas have one of the largest volumes of tax haven business in the world. There is no personal or corporate income tax, no capital gains tax, no withholding tax, no business tax, no estate tax, no gift tax, no inheritance tax, no death duties, no employment taxes, no sales taxes, and no probate fees in the Bahamas. Corporations, individuals, partnerships, trusts, and estates (including nonresident controlled Bahamian corporations) all enjoy this immunity. The principal source of revenue for the government comes from company registration fees and customs duties.

> *"While a Bahamian company may offer tax advantages to non-Bahamian beneficial owners under certain circumstances, it is essential that the laws of their own country be carefully considered before action is taken. Unless adequate planning is undertaken, the tax advantages may ultimately be lost to the owner. Consideration must be given to the ultimate disposition of accumulated funds."* - **Touche Ross International (Bahamas).** [2]

Economic Overview - Tourism and Banking

Some of the information that follows was provided by Curtis M. Stewart, Consul for the **Embassy of the United States of America** in Nassau.

---

1 The Turks & Caicos Islands are a British Colony. The Bahamas are an independent nation and member of the British Commonwealth.
2. from **Tax & Investment Profile Bahamas** (October 1987), printed in the UK.

Islands of The Bahamas

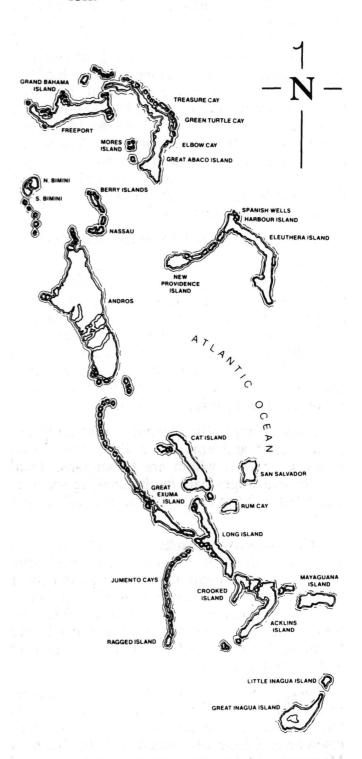

The Bahamas is one of the most prosperous countries in the Caribbean. Both inflation and external debt are low, the government's budget balanced, and the people enjoy one of the highest per capita incomes ($9,000) in the region.

Tourism and **banking** form the backbone of the economy accounting for two thirds of the total gross domestic product (GDP) and representing the primary source of hard currency in the economy. Tourism alone accounts for 50% of the GDP and employs about half the Bahamian work force of about 140,000. In 1988, tourism earnings totaled about $1.14 billion dollars. About 80% of the tourists are Americans. Because the number of American tourists is large, the Bahamian economy is closely linked to the U.S. economy. A Bahamian $ is freely exchangeable into one U.S. $.

Bank and Financial Services Industry

Financial services are the economy's second most important sector. The Bahamas' status as a tax haven and its bank secrecy laws have led to its growth as an international banking center. Of the 404 banks and trust companies licensed in the Bahamas, about 75% actually have an office and staff in the country. Most of these banks manage assets for wealthy individuals, as well as for offshore companies and trusts.

Banking typically accounts for roughly 8% of the GDP and employs a little over 3,000 persons, 95% of whom are Bahamians. Total salaries and wages paid by the banking sector is estimated to be in the region of $60 million per year.

The majority of banks and trust companies are nonresident or offshore companies that generate no Bahamian dollar earnings and cover all their expenses for administration costs, utilities, maintenance and other overhead by bringing in foreign exchange. Total expenditures for these items by the banks is in the region of $120 million per year.

During 1988, several American and Canadian banks either sold all or part of their business in the Bahamas or moved part of their operations elsewhere. Chase Manhattan and the Bank of Montreal sold their retail business in Nassau, and the Bank of America and the Bank of Boston moved parts of their operations to Grand Cayman and Luxembourg.

One of the reasons Chase Manhattan, Bank of America and the Bank of Boston decided to sell their offshore retail banking centers probably had to do with the U.S.A.'s new sub-part F provisions brought on by the **Tax Reform Act of 1986.** Prior to the '86 Act, offshore U.S. subsidiary banks that were **controlled** by the U.S. parent could solicit customer deposits without the subsequent profits being categorized as sub-part F income. Sub-part F profits are imputed back to the U.S. shareholders (parent) and federal income taxes are due. Under pre-**Tax Reform Act of 1986** law, there was no imputation of profits back to the parent company in the USA. Before 1986, offshore banking operations in any tax haven could be run tax free.

The new U.S. tax law now inhibits most offshore retail banking operations in tax havens and other foreign countries if the offshore bank is a **Controlled Foreign Corporation** under IRC §957(a) (i.e., more than 50% of its voting or value shares are owned by **U.S. shareholders**).

Public & Private Banking in the Bahamas

Back in the 17th century, pirates ruled the seas and land around the Bahamas Islands. Banking back then was a matter of digging a hole and sketching a treasure map where "X" marked the spot. Owing to its colored history, The Bahamas was the first international banking center to be established offshore (long before the Cayman Islands), and it is still considered to be setting the standard for other offshore centers even today. [3.]

Banking in the Bahamas is a bit more sophisticated today. There are currently about 404 banks registered in the Bahamas. About 107 of these financial institutions are non-active or restricted operations, with persons specified in the license. The remaining 284 banks are financial institutions dealing with the general public, some of them being privileged under the Exchange Control Regulations to deal in any currency.

---

3. When the Cayman Islands decided to make itself a full-fledged and reputable tax haven they needed a bank secrecy code to protect investors. Instead of drafting a Code from scratch, the Cayman government decided to copy The Bahamas Bank Secrecy Code, then adopted it as their own.

Fees paid by banks and trust companies vary between $1,000 and $160,000 annually, depending on the type of license.

Banks dealing with the public

Of the 284 or so licensed financial institutions, only about 9 are authorized to deal in "gold and foreign currencies". Seven of these banks are clearing banks. A further 10 trust companies are authorized agents, and act as custodians and dealers in foreign currency securities.

These 19 authorized dealers and agents include three branches and three wholly owned subsidiaries of the largest Canadian banks, two branches and three subsidiaries of the largest U.S. banks, two branches and two subsidiaries of four of the largest U.K. banks, one Luxembourg branch, a subsidiary of a Swiss bank and one Cayman subsidiary. The remaining institution is a Bahamian based company.

According to Hans C. Weber of the Foreign Commerce Bank in Zurich, Switzerland... *"Every investor who can afford some diversification should have a foreign bank account."*

Bank Secrecy Laws

The secrecy attached to relations and transactions between financial institutions has been another essential factor in attracting business to Nassau. The statute law of the Bahamas super-imposed upon the wisdom of the English law has strengthened the inviolability of secrecy and confidentiality in the tax haven.

The Bahamian secrecy laws are imposed on all Bank and Trust Companies, their directors, officers, and employees, attorneys, and auditors. Only with an order from the Supreme Court can a third party acquire information, in criminal matters, about any account. Tax evasion in one's home country is not a criminal matter in the Bahamas. Any offshore account in The Bahamas is protected by this strict bank secrecy law.

The Bahamas is not a party to any tax or fiscal information-sharing agreements (i.e., tax treaties) with any other country. Once you open an account in the Bahamas, you are the only one who has the privilege to access it.

With these secrecy laws, you would think that the banks could be used to hide illegal money (like drug money). Any persons using the banks in an illegal manner will find that the secrecy laws do not apply to them and all the information about their account will be turned over to the proper official upon request of the Bahamas Supreme Court (based on the agreement of Mutual Assistance in Drug Matters with the United States).

> *Tax evasion is not illegal in the Bahamas, since we do not have income, capital gains or inheritance taxes. Tax evasion is not considered suitable grounds for ordering access to information about an account. -* from ***Welcome Bahamas, - Our #2 Industry Banking,*** pg 71.

The banking community thinks that the secrecy laws governing banks and trust companies should be tightened further, with a view of giving more confidence to the investor. But, foreign investors from high tax jurisdictions have no need to worry. Neither the IRS, Revenue Canada, or the British Inland Revenue can obtain information about a bank account you may have in the Bahamas.

One word of caution to those citizens of high tax jurisdictions. Understating ones income by not reporting the interest income from an offshore bank account is a crime (felony) in the U.S., Canada, the United Kingdom, and most other industrialized nations. Proper tax planning and the use of holding companies and trusts can often relieve the foreign investor from breaking the tax laws of his home country.

Bahamian bankers will gladly open a bank account for you. It's up to you whether you report the interest income or don't. Bankers here will not disclose any information to any foreign revenue service under any circumstances.

The Offshore Banking Industry, part of the #2 industry in the Bahamas, provides individual investors with the opportunity to invest in the European fashion 50 miles off the U.S. coast. While you are on your sunny Bahamian vacation, stop by and see what the offshore bankers can do for you.

Confidentiality and Anonymity.

Anthony J. R. Howorth is a banker-writer and British citizen. Formerly with NatWest International Trust Corporation (Bahamas), Ltd., Anthony has 25 years of banking and trust company experience. Educated at Oxford's New

College, Howorth has lived in Barbados, the Cayman Islands, Panama and now the Bahamas.

When asked to explain the reasons for the scores of private banks in the Bahamas, Howorth responded.

"English trust law, no capital gains or income taxes, acceptable regulations, professional services, instant money transfer systems, FAX, S.W.I.F.T., Reuters, and other communications."

In addition, the Bahamas is located in the New York time zone. There is representation of all major banks, a very acceptable climate and an international standard of living without any of the frustrations of traveling in and out of other major financial centers.

The private banks tend to specialize in discretionary management of large funds for selected private clients...they make healthy returns for their owners and their clients. They retain the utmost confidence from their clients and give the highest forms of confidentiality and anonymity."

It's an $8 trillion dollar market and taxes are a big obstacle

According to Keith Sjogren of Canadian Imperial Bank of Commerce, Toronto. "The size of the market is estimated at $8 trillion dollars! Each year over $16 billion is handed down by the wealthy to their offspring.

One word of advice to the foreign investor. Foreign investors contemplating investing in the US markets should consider using a Bahamian IBC instead of investing directly in their own name. The United States can subject your U.S. investments to U.S. estate taxes when you invest in your own name. However, U.S. estate taxes do not apply to an offshore Bahamian IBC even if its sole asset holding is U.S. real estate, and all the shares are owned by a nonresident alien individual. Foreign investors who need advice should contact the **Tax Haven Reporter, P.O. Box CB 11552, Nassau, Bahamas** Telephone 242-327-7359 or 242-359-1132.

Another profitable business for private banks is the partnership programme in a U.S. brokering business without fear of capital gains taxes."

U.S. tax law allows foreign banks, nonresident aliens and foreign companies to trade in the U.S. stock and bond markets with a U.S. stock broker without incurring a capital gains taxes.

Numbered Bank Accounts

As in Switzerland, there is a Code of Ethics which calls for bankers to know who they are dealing with - to prevent illegal activities. There is no such thing as a "secret" account. The bank client is known by bankers in charge of his or her account. Basically, one has a numbered account.

If you are a famous person, you might prefer to be a number instead of a name, but your identity definitely will be information available to bank officials.

If you need more anonymity open a ciphered bank account, in Panama or try a "chop" account in Hong Kong. A "chop" account comes with your own personal seal. Only when the seal appears on your drafts can a check be cashed.

International Business Companies (IBCs) of the Bahamas

At one time the Bahamas were ranked third in the world as a banking/financial center, just behind London and New York. Today, the Bahamas still rank in the top ten, but have slipped down the list behind the Caymans and the British Virgin Islands. To regain some of its lost prestige, a new Companies Act was passed in 1990, and on January 15, 1990, the *International Business Companies Act of 1989* went into effect. The Act simplifies the requirements for incorporation and reduces the costs of forming an offshore company in the Bahamas. This new law signaled the beginning of a new era for the Bahamian financial sector. In the first few hours, on the day the Act went into effect, 100 new companies were formed.

Michael L. Barnett, president of the Bahamas Bar Association, said at the 1990 Eighth Bahamas International Financial Conference... *"new (banking) legislation, together with the traditional features of the Bahamas (no taxes), which has made it a registrar financial center, has caused much excitement. I commend the International Business Companies Act, 1989 to your favorable consideration."*

An IBC is a company which is restricted from carrying on business with persons resident in the Bahamas, and cannot invest in real property situated in the Bahamas, other than by holding a lease of property for use as an office. An IBC cannot carry on any banking, trust, insurance or reinsurance business, or provide a registered office for other companies. Essentially, an IBC operates internationally, investing in stocks and bonds, trading oil, gas, commodities, what have you. An IBC is not taxed in the Bahamas.

An IBC can open bank accounts, retain local professional services, prepare and keep its books and records, hold directors and shareholders meetings in the Bahamas. This is not considered carrying on a business in the Bahamas under the Act.

An IBC can also hold the shares or debt obligations of other companies incorporated in the Bahamas, and an IBC's shares may be held by residents of the Bahamas.

An IBC is formed by lodging a Memorandum and Articles of Association with the Registrar's Office. There is no fixed authorized capital requirements, nor is there a maximum limit on authorized capital. For an authorized share capital of $5,000 or less the annual license fee is $100. Where the authorized capital is more than $5,000 but less than $50,000, the fee is $300. Where the authorized capital exceeds $50,000 the license fee is $1,000 a year.

An IBC may be incorporated within 24 hours with two subscribers. The IBC may issue shares with or without par value, bearer or shares registered in someone's name. An IBC has an option of stating in its Memorandum whether it will issue share certificates. IBC shares can be repurchased, redeemed or otherwise acquired, but only out of surplus or in exchange of a newly issued shares.

At least one director must be elected to manage the IBC, and the director can be a corporation or individual, and need not be a resident of the Bahamas. The company must keep proper books and records at its registered office in the Bahamas, but these records are not open to public inspection, and no annual return has to be filed with The Registry.

An IBC must keep a share register, minutes of all directors and shareholders meetings, copies of all resolutions, a register of directors and officers, and books and records that reflect a fair assessment of the company's financial position. It is also required that an imprint of the company seal be kept at the company's registered office. While the company records are not open to public inspection, they are open to inspection by other shareholders, and even then the right to inspection is curtailed to be "only in the furtherance of a proper purpose".

For more information on registering an IBC in the Bahamas write:

The Registrar General's Department
Registry of Companies
P.O. Box N-532
Nassau, Bahamas
Tele:242-322-3316/7/8
Fax line: 242-322-5553

The Bahamas Trusts (Choice of Governing Law) Act of 1989

The Bahamian concept of trust law and administration is derived from England.

In 1989 the government of the Bahamas, in an effort to make the Bahamas a more favorable jurisdiction for the formation of trusts by foreign investors, sent the following summary which represents the primary gambit of the Commonwealth of the Bahamas' **Trust (Choice of Governing Law) Act, 1989.**

"This **Act** seeks to create a legislative basis whereunder persons who wish to create Trusts in respect of property, whether such property is located in the Bahamas or elsewhere, may choose the laws of The Bahamas as the governing law of such trusts; whether or not they are resident in the Bahamas.

Its provisions include, inter alia, that;

(i) "A term if a trust expressly declaring that the laws of the Bahamas shall govern the trust is valid, effective and conclusive regardless of any other circumstances."

(ii) "All questions arising in regard to a trust which is governed by the laws of The Bahamas or in regard to any deposition or property upon trust thereof including... questions as to: -

(a) the capacity of the Settlor;
(b) any aspect of the validity of the trust or disposition or the interpretation or effect thereof;
(c) the administration of the trust....
shall be determined in accordance with the laws of The Bahamas without reference to

the laws of any other jurisdiction with which the trust or disposition may be connected."

It must be recognized that this new law does not validate, inter alia, the disposition of property which is not owned by the Settlor.

(iii) "No trust governed by the laws of The Bahamas and no disposition of property to be held on trust that is valid under the laws of the Bahamas is void, voidable liable to be set aside or defective in any manner by reference to a foreign law; nor is the accuracy of the Settlor to be questioned by reason that: -

(a) the laws of any foreign jurisdiction prohibits or do not recognize the concept of a trust; or

(b) the trust or disposition avoids or defeats rights, claims or interest conferred by foreign law upon any person by reason of a personal relationship to the settlor or by way of heirship rights...."

There is no requirement to register a Bahamian trust with the government, nor is it necessary to file a copy of the trust indenture with any Government authority, unless it is a unit trust offering shares to the public.

Bahamas Fraudulent Dispositions Act, 1991

Following the Bahamas **Trust (Choice of Governing Law) Act, 1989,** the Parliament of the Bahamas enacted into law an *Act to Amend the Law Relating to Dispositions made with an Intent to Defraud.* The new law is now officially called the **Fraudulent Dispositions Act, 1991.**

Bahamas Trustee Act, 1998 ("the Act")

Scores of persons from around the globe create trusts in the Bahamas to retain wealth and pass it on. the Bahamian government regards trusts as an important element in The Bahamas' financial services sector, which accounts for an estimated 15 percent of the nation's gross domestic products.

On July 27th, 1998, the Bahamas, at long last, introduced its much awaited Trustee Act, 1998. The Act introduces sweeping changes and much needed reform to the Trustee Act, 1893 (which was based on the English Act of the same date - 1893). Below we highlight the most important provisions of the Act, with help from the a Nassau newspaper - *The Punch,* and *Focus* - a newsletter of Higgs and Johnson (Attorneys at law - Nassau, Bahamas).

The Trustee Act, 1998, completely revises the law of trusts in the Bahamas, overtaking the antiquated Trustee Act of 1893, and creating a new, modern trust regime.

Retention of Powers by the Settlor

The retention by the settlor of certain powers expressly declared not to render a trust invalid or to cause a trust created inter vivos to be characterized as a testamentary disposition [S.3]. The powers include the power of revocation, powers of appointment over any part of the trust property, powers of amendment, powers of addition or removal of trustees, protectors or beneficiaries and powers to direct the trustees in connection with the exercise of any of their powers and discretions.

Section three of the Trustee Act seeks to come to grips with a problem created when a settlor (the creator of a trust) seeks to retain too much control of assets placed in a trust.

A notable case of this nature was the so called "Rahman" case in Jersey, where a Lebanese settlor set up a trust in which he was given an extraordinary degree of control over the administration of the trust assets, and was allowed to dictate to his trustees what he wanted them to do. The court held that the trust was a sham, and never existed.

On the death of the Lebanese, his funds went to the persons entitled to receive them under the forced heirship rules of the state of Lebanon instead of the persons who he had intended should receive them.

Section three [S.3] of the new Act specifically provides that even if a settlor retains a number of power, the trust remains valid. These include powers to revoke and amend the trust and alter its terms, to make a deed of appointment, to nominate people to receive benefits, or to give trustees directions with respect to how the trust should be run.

Investment Powers of the Trustee

The old concept of "Trustee Investments" in the sense of eligible investments which are broadly classified is entirely discarded. A trustee has the same powers of investment as the individual owner absolutely entitled to the trust property.

The prudent investor rule is introduced and the trustee must have regard to the purpose, distribution requirements and other circumstances of the trust. Nevertheless, a special onus is put on the trustee who professes to have or ought to have special skills or expertise to use such skills or expertise. A trustee may obtain advise prior to exercising any powers of investment and is absolved from liability with respect to any action taken pursuant to such advice.

The 1998 Act deals with an age-old problem relating to investments by trustees.

In an effort to prevent trustees from investing in speculative assets that might ultimately prove worthless and cause great hardship to beneficiaries under the trust, the 1893 Act spelt out a broad list of types of investments. Most of these have ceased to exist or are totally irrelevant in today's world.

The present Act recognizes that people are living in an age of computers, rapidly advancing technology and ever-changing investment vehicles, and adopts a radically new approach in keeping with modern thought.

The old idea of specifying a list of investments has been totally abandoned and replaced by the "prudent investor" concept.

This means that in making, retaining and changing investments, trustees must exercise reasonable care and caution, and the skill of an ordinary person. They must also regard the suitability of investments not in isolation, but in the context of the trust property as a whole with a view to obtaining an overall balance of risk and return reasonably suited to the trust.

Trustees must also have regard to the need for diversification so that they do not have all their eggs in one basket.

They are required to take into account inflation, the size of the trust property as a whole, and general global economics conditions.

A higher standard of skill is expected of professional trustees than that required of lay trustees. Section six deals with a related matter- the need for advice in considering investments.

Under prior law, a trustee was not empowered to obtain advice on the suitability of investments and charge it to the trust fund, but he can under the 1998 Act.

The advice must come from people thought to be qualified to give advice as a result of their ability and practical experience.

Under section 8 of the Act, trustees are permitted to lend money on security, but they must first get a valuation of the property from the knowledgeable person.

General Powers of Trustees and Personal Representatives

A Trustee is given wide powers, including those to effect transactions, to contract, to sell, manage, mortgage, repair and maintain real estate.

A Trustee is given significant powers to insure (even against personal liabilities which they may incur in the execution of trusts)[S. 24].

Trustees are now given extensive powers to employ and pay agents [S. 30]. A novel provision permits the trustee, if permitted by the trust instrument, to delegate the execution or exercise of all or any trust powers and discretions vested in him [S. 31]. A prohibition against delegation has existed for centuries but the Parliament of the Bahamas has caused it to yield to the demands of modern commerce.

Section 31 seeks to resolve a difficulty enshrined in the old law relating to the delegation of trustee powers, which has long been prohibited.

Under the new Act, however, "A trustee may, notwithstanding any rule of law or equity to the contrary but only if expressly so permitted by the trust instrument, by power of attorney or any other written instrument, delegated to any person outside The Bahamas or to any person in The Bahamas while the trustee is absent therefrom the execution or exercise of all or any trusts, powers and discretions vested in him as such trustee either alone or jointly with any other person."

Again this is a feature that has been introduced to enable trustees to cope with modern business. The reasoning behind this change is that today seldom does one find, for example, a father who creates a trust and his beneficiaries all living in the same country.

Business today is conducted at a fast pace across many borders, and it is necessary for trustees to appoint agents in many jurisdiction, and confer on them a greater degree of authority than was required in the last century.

Trustee's Indemnities

The trust instrument need not necessarily contain the lengthy indemnities for the protection of the trustee. From a practical standpoint, a useful innovation is that a trustee may require (upon ceasing to be a trustee for any reason whatsoever) a release and indemnity and may withhold such trust property as the trustee in good faith considers necessary to pay outstanding liabilities or to satisfy the indemnity.

Such indemnity and right to withhold trust property does not extend to liabilities arising out of a breach of trust [S. 32-36].

Maintenance on Alienation Permitted

This will avoid the need for the use of drafting techniques to circumvent these restrictions [S. 40].

Advice on Directions from the Court

Without commencing an action a trustee may apply by a written statement for the opinion, advice or direction of the court [S.77].

Protectors

The office of the protector received legislative sanction. further, the exercise by the protector of certain powers will not cause him to be deemed the trustee. Unless, otherwise specifically provided in the trust instrument, the protector will be liable to the beneficiaries for any bona fide exercise of his powers [S. 81].

Disclosure of information to Beneficiaries can be kept secret (even from them!)

A very innovative aspect of the Act restricts the right of certain beneficiaries (whether in interest or possession) to information in respect of the trust property for example, beneficiaries who are objects of appointment and discretionary beneficiaries. The trustee is vested with significant discretion to withhold information and is under no obligation to disclose the existence of the trust to contingent beneficiaries, discretionary beneficiaries or objects of power. Significantly, a new class of privileged document is created in that documents relating to the exercise of a trustee's discretions and **letters of wishes** are not discoverable in litigation [S.83].

> Significantly, a new class of privileged document is created in that documents relating to the exercise of a trustee's discretions and letters of wishes are not discoverable in litigation [S.83].

The same section stipulates the beneficiaries who are entitled to information, namely beneficiaries who have vested interests.

The new Act also makes better provision for the maintenance advancement and protection of beneficiaries.

Under prior law, if any man dies and leaves funds in a trust in his will for his children and other people who are not of full age, they will not normally receive the funds until they come of age, and unless the will specifically give authority there is no automatic assistance for them in the meantime.

For example, if emergencies occur before they reach the required age they can expect little help from the trust.

Under sections 37 and 38, however, power to look after children and take care of their needs is deeply entrenched.

Section 39, an allied part of the Act, deals with protective trusts, designed specifically to protect mostly young people who may be unable to manage their affairs properly.

If a young beneficiary finds himself in this position, a trustee has the right to retain the assets and look after them, doing funds out carefully so that they are not used unwisely.

Similarly, in a section dealing with "restraints against alienation," the Act prevents certain beneficiaries from selling out their interests.

The rule in Saunders v. Vautrier Abolished

This rule which permits a beneficiary or beneficiaries who is or are solely interested in the trust property to terminate or modify a trust will not have effect if this would defeat a material purpose of the trust unless the settlor is alive and consents to such termination [S. 87].

Incorporation of Administrative Powers by Reference

It will now be possible to incorporate standard administrative powers by reference to the First Schedule to the Act [S.90]. Significantly, the First Schedule contains what is commonly referred to as a "Special Company" clause which permits the trustee to allow others to manage companies (typically those with more risky assets) and indemnifies him/her from the need to monitor such management [Cl. 8].

Application of the Act

The Act will apply generally to trusts and estates constituted or created before or after its coming into force although there are a number of exceptions.

Purpose Trusts

Early drafts of the Bill for the Act included a section on non-charitable purpose trusts. This has been deleted from the Act and it is purposed that a new act dealing only with these trusts will be introduced in due course.

Ship Registrations

The Bahamas also has a comprehensive procedure for ship registration through the **Merchant Ship Act of 1976.** Foreign owned ships are eligible to be registered in the Bahamas if they are less than 12 years old at the time of registry and are ocean going vessels of 1,600 or more net-registered-tons and are engaged in *foreign-going trade.* Ships of less than 1,600 tons or older than 12 years may be registered with the expressed permission of the Minister of Transport.

Initial fees to register a ship of 5,000 tons or less are $1.20 per net registered ton, and $1.10 per ton on ships above that size, plus an annual fee equal to 10% of the initial fee, plus $900. For example, the registration fee for a 5,000 ton vessel would be $7,500 ($6,000 initial fee + 10% of initial fee or $600 + $900).

Ship owners who wish to transfer registry of existing ships to the Bahamas will not be required to have their vessels re-surveyed if the ship has valid safety and tonnage certificates.

The United States has an *Exchange of Note Agreement (EON)* with the Bahamas which allows Bahamian registered ships to enter and leave U.S. ports for destinations outside the USA free of federal income taxes. IRC §883(a) limits the *EON* exemption to ships where 50% or more of the value of the stock in the shipping company is owned by individuals who are resident of the Bahamas, and to certain other shipping companies where the stock is regularly traded on a U.S. or foreign stock exchange.

Foreign Investment Opportunities

Perhaps the most promising sector for foreign investment in the Bahamas is agriculture which, together with the fisheries industry, accounts for about 5% of the country's revenues and employs about 5% of the labor force. Despite the fact that the Bahamas import over 80% of its food, agriculture production increased by 7.6% in 1989, with an estimated value of $34.38 million.

There are 238,000 acres of prime agriculture land which remains uncultivated. The Bahamian Department of Agriculture has identified the following areas as potentially the most profitable for investors:

1 - beef cattle production and processing,
2 - pork production and processing,
3 - tree food crops,
4 - dairy production and processing,
5 - winter vegetable crops,
6 - aquaculture and mariculture.

Biggest no tax havens - in terms of size

The Bahamas are the closest tax haven to the United States. As far as tax havens go, the Bahamas are one of the largest in land area. With over 700 islands and cays (pronounced *"keys"*) totaling 5,400 square miles, only Panama, Vanuatu and Switzerland are bigger. The Bahamas are only slightly smaller than the state of New Jersey (7,400 sq. miles), and actually larger than Long Island, N.Y. (1,401 sq. miles - population over 10,000,000).

From the businessman's point of view, the Bahamas are a **zero tax haven.** Like the Cayman Islands, Bermuda and Vanuatu (in the South Pacific), the Turks & Caicos Islands and Anguilla, the Bahamas are devoid of all direct and indirect taxation. There are no corporate or personal income taxes, no estate, gift or inheritance taxes, no sales, withholding or capital gains taxes in any of these no-tax havens. Like the pillars of antiquity were a symbol of democracy, freedom and power, modern Bahamians enjoy more freedom and democracy than found in either Greek or Roman societies. No excise men needed here.

Largest tax havens by land area		
	area (sq. miles)	population
Panama	29,000 sq. miles	1.8 million
Switzerland	16,000 sq. miles	6.4 million
Vanuatu	5,700 sq. miles	112,304
Bahamas	5,400 sq. miles	245,000
Western Samoa	1,133 sq. miles	152,000
Luxembourg	999 sq. miles	364,000
N. Antilles	403 sq. miles	241,000
Hong Kong	391 sq. miles	5,000,000
Isle of Man	221 sq. miles	50,000
Cayman Islands	93 sq. miles	17,000
Cook Islands	89 sq. miles	22,000
Channel Islands	78 sq. miles	136,000
Liechtenstein	62 sq. miles	26,000
B.V.I.	58 sq. miles	12,000
Bermuda	21 sq. miles	67,000
Nauru	8 sq. miles	6,000
Gibraltar	2.5 sq. miles	30,000

Exchange Controls

Approval from the Central Bank to conduct business in any currency other than the Bahamian dollar is required of nonresidents, but is easily obtained from the Exchange Control Department.

Bank Secrecy Code in the Bahamas

The Bahamas bank secrecy law is a carbon copy of the Cayman Islands Bank and Trust Companies Regulation of 1966. When the Cayman government went hunting for bank secrecy laws to bolster their status as a tax haven, they merely copied the secrecy laws of the Bahamas, than adopted them as their own.

Government • Political Stability

Until 1973 the Bahamas were a colony of Britain, but on July 10, 1973 Britain ended its 300 years of colonial rule and the Bahamas became the Commonwealth's 33rd independent member. Black prime minister Lynden O. Pindling, who led the drive for independence, was easily elected by the House of Assembly with the help of the black majority which make up 85% of the 250,000 people living in the Bahamas. Assembly members are elected by universal suffrage and they appoint the Prime Minister.

The transition from colony to independent nation was a peaceful one and the new government has made it clear that it does not intend to disrupt the Bahamas tax haven status with its fragile financial infrastructures.

Today, the Commonwealth of the Bahamas is a constitutional monarchy with Queen Elizabeth II of Great Britain the official head of state. Under the 1973 Constitution, the British Monarch appoints a Governor-General who ceremoniously appoints other members to the 17 member Senate. Effectively, the black majority which control the Assembly now control the white minority in the matters of political affairs in the Bahamas.

In regards to political stability, you have to rate the Bahamas as one of the most stable tax havens in the world. With strong ties to Britain, protection from a foreign aggressor is practically guaranteed by the British Royal Navy. On the negative side, the Bahamas still have a serious unemployment problem among it's 200,000 black inhabitants. Outbreaks of civil unrest have happened in other tax havens. [5.]

Foreign investors flocking to the Bahamas

Superstar Michael Jordan of the Chicago Bulls, has purchased the Bahamian island known as Crab Cay for $3.9 million. Mr. Jordan who has been the most valuable player in the U.S. National Basketball Association for a number of years, flew to The Bahamas some weeks ago to inspect the property. Crab Cay is a 181 acre island located in the Harbour of George Town Exumas next to Miriah Harbor, which is also part of Elizabeth Harbour.

Confirming the sale was Percy Fox of Ocean View Realty of George Town who is co-brokering the sale along with Mr. Peter Galanis. the former Member of Parliament for Pinedale, who is also a licensed real estate broker.

The sale of Crab Cay was consummated some five weeks ago when Jordan offered to

5. In 1973 in Bermuda black revolutionaries caused riots and disturbances which culminated in the murder by assassins of Governor Sir Richard Sharpes and his aid and the police chief. Two blacks were tried and hung for the murders but the hanging led to more riots in December 1977 with an estimated $5 million dollars in damage. Although the Bermuda government is biracial it is the white minority (which make up 40% of the total population) that effectively dominate both politically and economically.

purchase the island. It was listed by the owner Ernst Lubner of Germany for $2.8 million but the price went up to $3.9 million when Mr. Lubner discovered that Jordan was eager to make the purchase.

Mr. Fox told *The Journal* that many foreign investors are now expressing an interest in the Examas. This was confirmed by Mr. George Damianos of Damianos Realty Company in Nassau. According to Mr. Damianos, there is a resurgence in the real estate market, especially in the Family Islands. [6.]

He said five years ago you couldn't get $500 for same land you are now getting $5,000 an acre today. There is now a strong interest of foreign investor for second homes or primary homes in The Bahamas. Once you have foreign investors buying homes, it spurs on the Bahamian to buy exclusive homes or premier properties, said Mr. Damianos.

"Some Bahamians are buying real estate in the Abacos and elsewhere, holding onto it and are watching the value increase.

The interest in the Family Islands is fascinating to me, said the gleeful realtor. There is no question that there has been significant growth in the Bahamian economy in the last few years. Within a week after the '97 general election on March 14th there were announcements of the sale of the old Atlantis Hotel on West Bay Street and the Sheraton British Colonial Hotel to foreign inventors. The Bahamian developer told *The Journal*, in addition to the foreigners, white Bahamians who had their money parked in bank accounts are now participating in major business deals. Businesses are being realigned and the sale of real estate is now at an unprecedented level. In eight weeks, more homes have changed hands than it did in the last 25 years," said the businessman.

"Whereas in '92 white Bahamians were not sure that Hubert Ingraham was their man, they were not sure that Sir Lynden Pindling was finished. The effect of March 14th is that they are convinced that Ingraham was their man and there was no way that Pindling would come back. They are now in deals like crazy," related the developer. "There are some powerful

dynamics taking place and the purchase of Colina Insurance by a Bahamian businessman speaks volumes of the new confidence" he said.

A general election candidate of the Progressive Liberal Party told *The Journal*, "all of this is combining to make it increasingly difficult for the black Bahamian businessman, who in part would have had an affirmative action-type of support from the previous government and what did not have to face the clout of white Bahamians dealing with politicians."

The former PLP candidate reasoned, "tomorrow if something should change, the white Bahamians don't have to be afraid as they were in '67."

---

6. Bahamas Business Journal (1997).

From Blackbeard to Donald Trump to the New Atlantis Hotel Casino on Paradise Island - the Bahamas have a colorful history

The recorded history of the Bahamas began on October 12, 1492 when Christopher Columbus landed on San Salvador (Watling Island) and claimed it for Spain. Here Columbus took six Indians from the island and proceeded to Rum Cay and Long Island, two other Bahamian islands 50 miles to the southwest. The Spaniards that followed Columbus were not interested in these rocky islands, and never established settlements.

In 1647 the Eleutherian Adventurers Company was formed in London to colonize the islands. Drawing members from England, Bermuda and the Carolinas, they settled at Governors Harbour on the Island of Eleuthera. With the blessings of Oliver Cromwell they later settled in Nassau, on the island of New Providence. In 1703 the settlement in Nassau was destroyed in a Spanish raid thereby allowing the pirates to strengthen their position. Captains Avery and Edward Teach (the famous Blackbeard), and two pirate woman Anne Bonny and Mary Read are among the famous pirates that based in New Providence. It is estimated that as many as 2,000 pirates were resident in New Providence at one time. In 1720 the royal governor Captain Woodes Rogers was forced to ally himself with the pirates to fend off another Spanish attack.

After the American Revolution some 3,000 American loyalists and their slaves settled in the Bahamas. When slavery was done away with in 1834, the islands declined into economic recession, and many people moved away. During the American Civil War the blockade-runners gave new life to the economy. Later, during Prohibition, many rum-runners set up headquarters in the Bahamas, using speedboats to deliver their contraband liquor to the Atlantic States.

It wasn't until the late 20th century that the Bahamas evolved into an important financial center and tax haven for entrepreneurs such as N.Y. real estate tycoon Donald Trump. Trump was owner of a luxury Paradise Island hotel and casino, until he sold out to Merv Griffin. Griffin later sold out to a South African investor who pumped over $600,000,000 into the properties, renaming it **Atlantis.** Many visitors claim this new hotel/casino is more luxurious than even the top Las Vegas establishments.

For more information on **doing business** in the Bahamas write:

> The Secretary
> **The Bahamas Chamber of Commerce**
> P.O. Box N-665
> Nassau, Bahamas

Nassau and Freeport in the Bahamas. Nearest tax havens to the United States.

In the early 1990's, I left Ft. Lauderdale at 2:15 on a Friday afternoon on a Delta airline flight. Forty-five minutes later our plane touched down in Nassau - one of several zero tax havens in the Caribbean. I'm a tax planner specializing in the use of tax havens. My journey to Nassau was a career move - to experience first hand. The fact that Nassau in the Bahamas is a tourism Mecca in a tropical paradise surrounded by some of the most beautiful beaches in the world was only a secondary inducement to my trip. The fact that the Bahamas were once ranked third in the world as a financial center, behind New York and London, and the fact that companies can be registered here for around $1,000, and companies can trade stocks and bonds on the U.S. and World stock exchanges free from capital gains taxes - that's enough to whet anyone's appetite.

One cannot discount the magnificent beauty of these tropical islands surrounded by *Shallow Seas* - called *Baja Mar* in Spanish. When the astronauts were asked what was the most beautiful view on earth from outer space, they chose the emerald, blue, topaz and mauve *Baja Mar* encircling the Bahamas. And it's no wonder. From your plane window the Bahamas look like nothing you have seen before. Fascinating, breathtaking, unforgettable. 6.

Freeport on Grand Bahama Island

Nassau on the island of New Providence is the seat of the Government of the Bahamas, but Nassau is certainly not the only place where one

---

6. *Baja Mar* was corrupted in translation by the English settler and later gave way to the very name for the Nation of Th *Bahamas.*

34.

can conduct offshore business. Grand Bahama Island 70 miles to the north of Nassau is a splendid tropical oasis strategically located just 60 miles off the coast of Florida. Grand Bahama possesses virtues no other Caribbean island can boast, planned development and tax benefits offered in the Freeport/Lucaya area.

Freeport began as the brainchild of Wallace Groves, an American businessman who dreamed of building a planned community from the pine forests of Grand Bahama. After realizing Grand Bahamas potential, he signed the Hawksbill Creek Agreement with the Bahamas Government and the British Crown in 1955 wherein a company, The Grand Bahama Port Authority, agreed to develop a large area of Grand Bahama Island for industrial and commercial use, dredge a deep water harbor an construct an airport, build schools and hospitals and other basis community needs. In return, the Government granted the **Grand Bahama Port Authority** 150,000 acres of land (230 square miles - twice the land area of the Cayman Islands) known as the Port area, and gave it exclusive rights to grant and administer business licenses.

The Hawksbill Creek Agreement also allowed for many attractive tax benefits, including freedom from corporate and individual tax.

In 1961, the Port Authority growth momentum experienced a resurgence with the involvement of Sir Charles Hayward, a wealthy British industrialist. Today the **Port Authority Group of Companie**s is owned, controlled and managed by Sir Charles's son, Sir Jack Hayward and by Mr. Edward St. George, who acquired an ownership position in 1976. I had the good fortune to meet with Mr. St. George in his office at the Port Authority building while on a business trip to Freeport in February. I was very impressed with their organization. These businessmen own and operate the Intercontinental Airport where I landed, the island's water and electric company, the Port facilities for ships, and built the roads on Grand Bahama. Recently, they sold the telephone company to the Bahamas Government.

About 40,000 people live in Grand Bahama, of which about 15% are expatriates. The local currency is the Bahamian dollar which is at parity with the U.S. dollar. It is unnecessary therefore to convert US$ to B$ upon entry into the country.

Freeport on Grand Bahama, like Nassau, has unparalleled advantages for the potential investor including (1) excellent banks with very strict non-disclosure laws and with the ability to conduct business from a warm tropical Caribbean island, (2) close proximity to U.S. mainland (25 minutes from Miami), (3) good transportation facilities with U.S. Immigration and Customs pre-clearance, (4) stable economic and political climate, (5) excellent communication facilities.

Enquires to:

Grand Bahama Port Authority
P.O. Box F-2666
Freeport, Bahamas
242-352-6711
Fax 242-352-9864
Telex: 30020 Callback: PORTAUTH

Management Trustee Companies - offshore quarterbacks

Taking a cab from the Nassau International Airport you pass through the famous Cable Beach area. Further on down West Bay Street, on the right hand side, you'll come upon the old, established NatWest/Coutts building, a most impressive layout - covering 10 acres or more of prime real estate. Housed in this office building, which looks more like an upstate New York's socialites mansion than an office building, are the books and records of thousands upon thousands of offshore companies and trusts belonging to wealthy clients from all around the globe. Coutt's clients (now owned by SG Hambros Bank & Trust - another offshore banking giant) come from Saudi Arabia, the United States, Great Britain, France, West Germany, Canada, Mexico, Columbia, Argentina, Brazil - anywhere there are high taxes. Coutts also has clients from other tax havens like the Cayman Islands, Channel Islands, Panama, Bermuda, Hong Kong and Singapore.

While local lawyers and accountants can expedite the incorporation and day to day affairs for the client's holding company, it is the management trustee companies that often handle the business of the very rich and famous. Minimum opening deposit to establish a relationship with SG Hambros is said to be $500,000. As would be expected, fees are much higher at these larger institutions.

Offshore advisors, in conjunction with local lawyers, accountants, banks and trust companies, by and large, can handle all the formalities of 35. forming and running a client's offshore company or trust in the Bahamas. They can provide a registered office and mailing address, a secretary and management team, accountants and bookkeepers for the company's books and records, and much more. Often these people will run the day to day affairs of offshore companies for foreign investors.

Typically bank and trustee companies in the Bahamas provide the following services:

- Company formation and management,
- Personal trustee and executorship services,
- Offshore Banking services,
- Mutual funds and unit trusts,
- Estate planning/personal wills,
- Custodian and safekeeping,
- Registrar and transfer agents
- Registered office facility,
- Accounting and administrative services,
- Portfolio Management,
- Offshore Bank Management
- Captive Insurance,
- Corporate trustee,
- Pension funds,
- **Nominee**, attorney and agency services,
- Bond and stock trading facilities,
- Ship registration services,
- Foreign sales corporation services,
- International trading companies,
- Multi-currency time deposits,

Tax planning, not tax evasion should be your goal.

For the U.S. taxpayer finding the right people to form and run your offshore company (or trust) is as important as what to invest in the first place. Only nonresident aliens (naturalized Bahamians or other foreigners) should be employed as bookkeepers and trustees. The reasons are basic.

The U.S. courts generally will not subpoena a nonresident alien to appear before a U.S. grand jury to answer questions under oath about a U.S. taxpayer's offshore activities. On the other hand, U.S. courts and the IRS can and will subpoena a U.S. citizen who is a bookkeeper or trustee or director for an offshore company or trust. Ordinarily, the IRS will initiate an investigation only when the offshore operation is run in violation of U.S. tax law, or when a U.S. tax liability exists. It is very important that you employ only offshore managers who are nonresident aliens to run your tax haven operations.

In an inquiry, the IRS will approach the U.S. citizen taxpayer simply to ask questions and gather financial information about his offshore company or trusts. The **<u>Tax Reform Act of 1986</u>** granted the IRS much broader powers to gather information from U.S. citizens with operations in the foreign sector.

Since the IRS has no jurisdiction in the Bahamas or any other tax haven, it cannot direct its questions to SG Hambros or any other Bahamian based lawyer, bank or management trustee company. In their information gathering process the IRS might seek to:

1. Establish whether the offshore company is a **Controlled Foreign Corporation (CFC)**. If it is not, no tax liability generally exists for the U.S. taxpayer (shareholders), and he is free to go about his business.[7]

2. Establish whether a U.S. person owns **10% or more** of the **voting** stock in the offshore company. If no U.S. person owns the requisite 10% voting stock, no U.S. tax liability can result under the CFC provisions. The U.S. taxpayer is free to go on with his affairs (untaxed!).

3. Determine whether the offshore company has **Sub-part F income** (i.e., passive incomes such as capital gains, interest from foreign bank accounts, dividends, royalties) for the current fiscal year, or prior fiscal years. For the IRS to make a proper determination, it must have access to the books and records of the foreign corporation.[8]

The **Tax Reform Act of 1986** gave the U.S. courts and the IRS special powers to secure offshore books and records by more or less allowing the IRS to twist the arm of the U.S. shareholder who resides in the United States to furnish the info. Relying on Bahamian Bank Secrecy Laws alone is not always the wisest recourse. The directors of a properly managed offshore company should easily be able provide

---

7. IRC §957(a) defines a "Controlled Foreign Corporation" as any foreign corporation where (1) more than 50% of the total combined voting power of all classes of stock of such corporation entitled to vote, or (2) 50% of the total value of all the stock (voting and nonvoting), are owned alone or collectively by U.S. shareholders. 8. IRC §951(b) defines a "U.S. Shareholder" as a U.S. person who owns 10% or more of the **voting** stock in the foreign corporation. Note: U.S. persons that do not own 10% or more of the voting stock are not counted in when making the determination whether the foreign corporation is a CFC. Furthermore, U.S. persons that do not meet the 10% ownership test cannot have any of the offshore profits (i.e., subpart F incomes) imputed to them. No tax liability under IRC §951 will develop to shareholders who are not "U.S. shareholders.
8. The different types of Subpart F incomes are outlined under IRC §954.

the IRS with enough information to squelch further investigation (satisfy the IRS that no tax liability exists), thus avoid a tax or legal problem for the U.S. investor.

It takes good tax planning and a talented offshore team to make a plan work. You should contact the *Tax Haven Reporter* at the address below in the Bahamas if you need to recruit competent managers. Many management trustee companies and lawyers do not possess adequate in-house tax planners conversant with the U.S. tax laws. It's often up to you to see that it's done right.

My business partners include a Bahamian law firm and two reputable banks here in Nassau. The law firm has over 30 years of experience. Accountants, lawyers and trust companies typically charge about $1,500 or more to register an IBC (no trusts, no tax planning, no advice).

If a client wants to form a company through the mail in 48 hours he should UPS a bank cashiers check (or money orders) for $2,100 to my address here in Nassau. We'll prepare all the documents, and forward the appropriate fees to the Government Registrar, etc. A company can be registered without the client even coming to Nassau. It takes only 24 hours for the Bahamian Government to stamp and return to us the Memorandum and Articles for a company.

When the client is ready he should contact me at 242-327-7359 and I'll tell you exactly how to send the money. I've formed more than 1,000 IBCs within the last 9 years.

Investors will be able to open a bank and security account for their IBCs so they alone have signature authority over the accounts - and that's the way most clients want it. We have arrangements with several of Nassau's major banks. We can provide you with the bank's application forms, signature cards, bank brochures etc., so you can open your account without physically flying into the Bahamas. You will need a reference letter from your local banker, but these are easy to obtain.

These Bahamian banks have been in operation here in Nassau for over 30 years. These bank have subsidiaries in all the other tax havens, including the Caymans, Hong Kong, Monaco, Zurich, Gibraltar, the British Virgin Islands and Jersey in the Channel Islands. One is a giant British bank - like Chase Manhattan - with more than 2,000 offices worldwide. One of the banks has no offices inside the United States. You can choose whichever bank you want. With either of these banks clients can open broker's accounts anywhere in the world and trade under the guise of the Bank's name. The client's IBC does not appear on the stock certificates, and his anonymity is totally preserved.

Masking a client's Stock Market trades is a traditional way of doing business here in the Bahamas and in the other tax havens. It's done by most all the major bank and trust companies. Banks in the Bahamas do not have to file tax returns with the IRS.

The *Bahamian Bank Secrecy Code* forbids any bank executive or advisor from giving information to any outside tax collector, attorney or foreign court.

The costs to form an IBC *(International Business Company)* is $2,100.

Costs to form IBC (includes Government and other Formation fees)	=	$850
Cost for registered agent (i.e., our lawyer); registered office (P.O. Box # and telephone #) trustees for trusts ...	=	$600pa
Trust instruments (2 deeds)	=	$450
Our advice for steering you to the right people, coordinating your company formation & providing you with bank application forms.......	=	$200
Total costs (first year)	=	$2,100

Annual maintenance costs

(registered office/agent, P.O. Box, telephone #) (Paid to NPP, Ltd. when Government annual fees become due (April 30th of each year)		= $500 pa
Annual government fee for $5,000 authorized capital for IBC		= $250 pa
Trustee fee		= $300 pa
Total cost (2nd year)		=$1050 pa

Mailing Address for Tax Haven Reporter
Thomas P. Azzara *Tax Haven Reporter* **P.O. Box CB 11552** **Nassau, Bahamas** Phone: 242-327-7359 Cellular: 242-359-1132 e-mail taxman@batelnet.bs

Newsletter Subscription rates:

Tax Haven Reporter: $150/Yr/12 issues • Back issues and special reports cost $10/each, but order 5 back issues at a time and the cost is only $5/apiece. Orders are shipped the day a customer's check or money order arrives. Book, *Tax Havens of the World,* is free with newsletter subscription.

Working with the Controlled Foreign Corporation & the "new" PFIC provisions.

It's nice to dream about tax havens and no taxes (one of God's original gifts to mankind!), but U.S. citizens should study their Federal tax laws before jumping in feet first. If a **U.S. Shareholder** [as defined under IRC §951(b)] owns shares in a Bahamian company that is a **Controlled Foreign Corporation** [as defined under IRC §957(a)], the **Sub-part F** income (as defined under IRC §954) of that Bahamian CFC will be **imputed** to the U.S. taxpayer. When sub-part F income of a Bahamian CFC is imputed to the U.S. shareholder, the shareholder <u>must</u> include it on his tax return and pay taxes on it. Sub-part F incomes include dividends, interests, capital gains, and a host of other types of incomes, but exclude "**rents** and royalties" from the active conduct of a trade or business in the haven. [9]

There are constructive ownership rules under IRC §958 that can make a U.S. shareholder own shares directly and indirectly through other foreign corporations, trusts and partnerships. In the example below, if a U.S. shareholder owned 25%% of the shares in Z, and Z owned 100% of the shares in Y, then the U.S. shareholder would be considered to **indirectly** own 25% of the shares of Y by virtue of Z's 100% stock ownership in Y.

The Controlled Foreign Corporation Provisions (CFC) are covered in greater detail in Chapters 2 of this book. The **CFC** provisions under IRC §951 to §958 account for most of the U.S. tax planners problems, but four other sections of the **Internal Revenue Code** can lead to other adverse tax problems. Without going into a full discussion, these other provisions include (1) the "new" **Passive Foreign Investment Company** provisions (IRC §1291-97); (2) **Accumulated Earnings Tax** (IRC §532); (3) the **Foreign Personal Holding Company** provisions (IRC §551); and the **Personal Holding Company** provisions (IRC §541). A more detailed discussion is provided in chapters, 3, 4 and 5.

Example #1: Twenty U.S. Investors own all the shares of Bahamian CFC **Z**. **Z** owns a Bahamian hotel costing $10,000,000 that has after expense profits of $1,500,000 from **rentals** (rents are **not** sub-part F income) in 1989. Company **Z** also owns 29% of the shares in a 2nd Bahamian company **Y** which owns $5,000,000 in U.S. stocks and Treasury bonds issued after July 18, 1984. **Y's** interest income from bonds was $1,000,000 (passive interest is **Sub-Part F** income).

For purposes of determining the U.S. taxpayer's tax liability, only **U.S. shareholders** (persons that own 10% or more of Z's voting stock) are subject to imputation of **Z's** sub-part F income. However, if **Z** does not have any Sub-part F income, no imputation of offshore profits can happen.

But what about the **sub-part F** income of Bahamian investment company **Y**? Because all of Y's 1,000 shares of voting stock are owned by Bahamian **Trust X**, there will be no **U.S. Shareholders** of company **Y**. Sub-part F income of **Y** will not be imputed to the U.S. shareholders of **X**, because with respect to Y, **there are no U.S. shareholders.** Only U.S. shareholders that own 10% or more of the **voting stock** of Y [directly or indirectly thru the stock ownership rules of IRC §958(a) & (b)] can have sub-part F income **imputed** to them under the CFC provisions. Consequently, Y's $1,000,000 in passive profits can be accumulated tax free offshore.

The *Tax Reform Act of 1986* added the "new" **Passive Foreign Investment Company** (PFIC) provisions to U.S. tax Code. IRC §1291-97 can subject the U.S. shareholder of an offshore company to a special "penalty tax rate" and "add-on interest penalty" under IRC §1291 if the offshore company is a PFIC. A company is a PFIC if more than 50% of its assets are passive in nature or more than 75% of its income is passive income. Again, attribution rules through other foreign entities are applied to make the PFIC determination. [10]

In the above example, Bahamian Company Y is a PFIC because more than 75% of its income is passive (i.e., from interest, dividends or capital gains). Bahamian Company Z is not a PFIC because less than **50%** of all Z's **assets** (which include Z's proportionate share of Y's <u>assets</u>) are passive type **assets** (29% of Y's $5,000,000/$11,450,000 or **12.7%**), and less than **75%** of **Z's** income is derived from passive investments (29% of Y's passive income of $1,000,000 belongs to Z for purposes of determining Z's total income ($1,500,000 [rents] + $290,000 from Y). Z's percentage of passive income is 16.2%. Since this is below the 75% allowed under the U.S. regulations, Z is not a PFIC.

In the example above, Y's passive income might actually have amounted to $20,000,000 before Z's proportionate share of Y's income would cause Z to exceed the 75% passive income limit. (i.e., 29% of $20,000,000 = $5,800,000 attributed to Z makes Z's passive income ratio $5.8 mil/$7.3 (total income = $5.8 Y income + $1.5 Z rents = $7.3 mil.) or 79.5%.

---

9. See Code §954(c)(1)(A)

10. See IRC §1296 for the definition of Passive Foreign Investment Company. See IRC §1296(c).

Working with U.S. Controlled Foreign Corporation and Passive Foreign Investment Company provisions.

Investment Holding Company Y

1. Can trade in U.S. stocks & bonds free of all capital gains taxes.
2. Is not a Controlled Foreign Corporation under US CFC rules (see §IRC 951-58)(see "Tax Havens of the World" - Chapter 2).
3. Owns 29% of Y non-voting stock owned by parent Z.
4. Y is a PFIC under IRC §1291, thus not subject to Accumulated Earnings Tax. See IRC §532(b).
5. Uses 2 classes of stock as spoken about in the U.S. Treasury Regulations. Not an uncommon practice when using tax havens. See T.Reg. §958-1(d) Ex. #(1).

Bahamian Grantor Trust X
(Trust laws are well established in Bahamas)

Bahamian Investment Holding Company Y
(Resident Company)

Bahamian Grantor Trust X

1. Grantor Trust X owns 71% of Y's nonvoting stock + 100% of Y's 1,000 shares of voting stock. A Bahamian bank & trust company can act as your trustee.

2. Grantor Trust X (a non-resident alien) keeps Company Y from being classified a Controlled Foreign Corporation under IRS's own attribution of ownership rules. See IRC §958(a) and (b).
   Apply the Treasury's "examples" yourself. Controlled? or Not Controlled??

Bahamian RE Company Z

1. Z owns luxury hotel/motel or condos in Bahamas. Z has no sub-part F incomes.

2. Z is owned by U.S. investors exclusively...

3. No current U.S. taxes even if Z is a CFC corporation under IRC §951 because incomes from rents from unrelated customers is not Foreign Personal Holding Company income. Only Sub-part F or Foreign Personal Holding Company Income can be imputed to "U.S. Shareholders" of a Controlled Foreign Corporation. See IRC §954(c).

Bahamian Real Estate Company Z
(Resident Company)

Planning & Limitations

1. To avoid new PFIC classification gross income from passive investments cannot exceed 75% of all of Z's gross income.
2. Income of Y can be imputed to Z under IRC §1296(c).
3. U.S. tax law will consider Z as earning. its proportionate share (29%) of Y's profits. Z will also own 29% of Y's assets for purposes of determing if Z is is a PFIC..
4. At least 50% of Z's assets must be non-passive type assets (i.e., hotels, casinos, office equipment., condos) to avoid the PFIC classification.

Only U.S. persons who own 10% or more of Z's voting stock will be subjected to "imputation" of Z's Sub-Part F earnings, and then only if Z is a CFC.

U.S. INVESTORS

DEMONSTRATION

39.

CONTROLLED FOREIGN CORPORATIONS

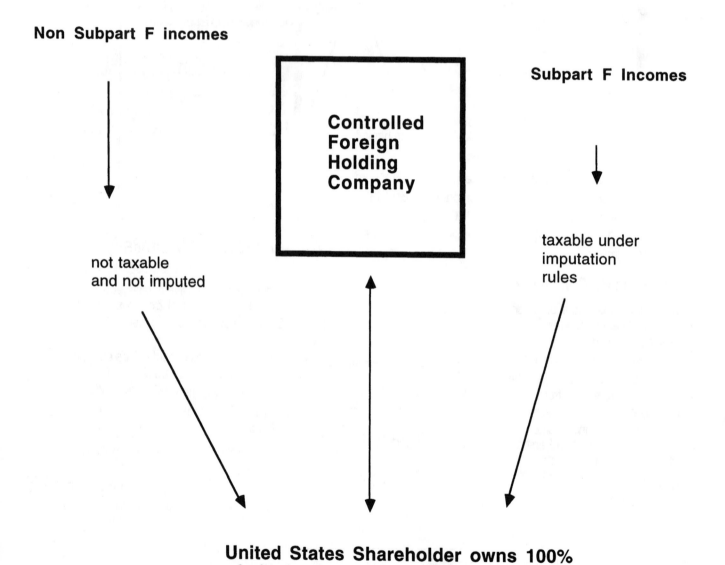

Non Subpart F incomes

not taxable
and not imputed

**Controlled
Foreign
Holding
Company**

Subpart F Incomes

taxable under
imputation
rules

**United States Shareholder owns 100%
of single class of outstanding stock**

CHAPTER 2 • The Controlled Foreign Corporation

The Internal Revenue through its Codes and Treasury Regulations are empowered with a series of perplexing laws used to determine whether a foreign corporation is "Controlled" by the U.S. taxpayer. Generally, a corporation that is formed outside the continental United States falls into one of two categories that being a foreign corporation **not** controlled, or a **Controlled Foreign Corporation** (CFC). The difference between the two is pivotal. Certain American owners (defined as **United States Shareholders** under IRC §951(b)) of a controlled foreign corporation are taxed currently on certain kinds of offshore profits (called **sub-part F** incomes) as they are earned. These **sub-part F** incomes are imputed to the U.S. Shareholders indirectly, and it's immaterial whether the foreign corporation distributes its earnings as a dividend. But, U.S. Shareholders of a foreign corporation that is not a CFC are not subject to the imputation rules, and will only be taxed on the offshore profits when they are remitted as a dividend, or in a liquidation.

If a foreign corporation is a **CFC** certain incomes must be tested to see if they are sub-part F incomes. The following lists six types of incomes that are classified sub-part F income.

1. Income from services performed outside the tax haven country.
2. income from sales to affiliated companies.
3. Passive incomes such as dividends, interests, capital gains, and rents from related parties.
4. Income from U.S. insurance risks.
5. Most types of shipping incomes.
6. Income of a CFC engaged in a U.S. trade or business, if the income is exempt by treaty from direct taxation.

"U.S. Shareholders" as defined under IRC §951(b)

For purposes of the Controlled Foreign Corporation provisions the term **U.S. Shareholder** has it's own distinctive definition. Under IRC §951(b) a U.S. Shareholder is a U.S. person [as defined in Section 957(d)], who **owns** [within the meaning of section 958(a), or is considered as owning by applying the rules of ownership of section 958(b)], **10% or more** of the total **combined voting power** of all classes of stock entitled to vote of such foreign corporation.

Remember. U.S. persons that own **under 10% of the voting stock** are not counted in when making the determination whether the foreign corporation is **"Controlled"**. Moreover, only U.S. persons that fit the definition of **U.S. Shareholders** can have **sub-part F income** imputed to them.

What is a Controlled Foreign Corporation (CFC)?

If you want to avoid the **CFC** status you must first know what a CFC is. IRC §957(a) defines a CFC as any foreign corporation of which **more than 50% of its value or voting stock is owned** [within the meaning of IRC §958(a), or is considered as owned by applying the rules of ownership of IRC §958(b)], **by United States shareholders** on any day during the taxable year of such foreign corporation. Remember, for purposes of determining the **more than 50%** limit, U.S. persons that own less than 10% of the voting stock will not be considered.

Example #1: If U.S. shareholder **A** owns 50% of the voting stock of foreign corporation X, and U.S.shareholder **B** owns 11% of the voting stock, while the remaining 39% is owned by foreign shareholder **D**, then foreign corporation X is a CFC because **more than 50%** of the voting stock (61% in the example) would be considered to be owned by U.S. Shareholders (A & B).

However, if all the facts in the above example are the same except U.S. shareholder **B** held only 6% of the voting stock, and the other 5% was held by U.S. person **C**, then foreign corporation **X** would not be a CFC because only 50% of the total outstanding voting stock is owned by a **U.S. shareholders** (A) under IRC §957(a) and IRC §951(b), and 50% is not **"more than 50%"**.

The Controlled Foreign Corporation provisions were added to the *Code* with the Revenue Act of 1962 during the Kennedy Administration. The **Tax Reform Act of 1986** made one material change to the **CFC** provisions. For years beginning after January 1, 1987, **"value shares"** as well as **"voting shares"** will be used to make the determination whether the foreign corporation is a CFC. In years before 1986, only voting stock was considered. It should be further pointed out that the definition for **U.S. Shareholder** was not amended by the TRA '86, and turns solely upon the basis of the percentage of "voting stock" **owned** by a U.S. person.

Example #2: Eleven U.S. persons each own exactly 9% of the total outstanding voting stock (and value stock) of foreign corporation T. Although 99% of the foreign corporation is owned by U.S. persons, foreign corporation T is not a Controlled Foreign Corporation because no U.S. Shareholders exist to own the requisite "more than 50" of the voting and value shares in foreign corporation T.

However, had five (5) of the above 11 U.S. persons owned 12% (each) of the voting stock (or 60% of the voting stock) of foreign corporation T, then such foreign corporation would be a CFC, and each of the 5 U.S. persons holding 12% of the stock would be taxable on foreign corporation T's sub-part F incomes, whether distributed to them or not.

The remaining 6 U.S. persons who do not qualify as U.S. Shareholders (because they do not own 10% or more of the voting stock) will not be subject to the imputation rule on the sub-part F incomes of foreign corporation T.

It is important that you know whether your foreign corporation is a CFC, and whether you are considered a **U.S. shareholder** of a CFC under U.S. tax law. Even if the foreign company is a CFC, there are still certain types of offshore profits that are not categorized as sub-part F income.

The following is a list of incomes the IRS does not deem to be sub-part F income. A foreign corporation can **accumulate** these **types** of profits free from federal income taxes. Further, even if the foreign company is **controlled** by **U.S. Shareholders** no imputing of offshore profits would be called for under current U.S. tax rules.

1. Income from manufacturing in the tax haven - including exporting profits back to the United States or overseas.
2. Trading or selling, if the tax haven company buys from an unrelated party and sells to an unrelated party outside the United States, and its foreign office plays a material part in the sales activity.
3. Drilling and mining.
4. Insurance or reinsurance of foreign risks.
5. Certain off-shore banking profits are not sub-part F incomes.

The **Tax Reform Act of 1986** severely curtailed the types of activities a controlled offshore bank (in the Caymans or the Bahamas) could engage in without being subject to the sub-part F rules. Prior TRA '86 law allowed an offshore CFC bank to make loans to related and unrelated customers, and trade in securities (stocks and Eurodollars). Such activities did not generate sub-part F income. Under the **Tax Reform Act of 1986**, such profits are **sub-part F** income. [1]

Another U.S. Treasury Regulation test for *Control*

The problem of "control" for purposes of the CFC provisions is not resolved yet because in all cases United States Shareholders will be found to own the requisite percentage of total combined voting power with respect to such foreign corporation if any of the following conditions of Treasury Regulation 1.957-1(b)(1) are satisfied.

(i) If they have the power to elect, appoint or replace a **majority** of the body of persons exercising, with respect to such foreign corporation, the powers ordinarily exercised by the board of directors of a domestic corporation.

(ii) If **any person** or persons elected or designated by such shareholders have the power, where such shareholders have the power to elect **exactly one-half** of the members of such governing body of such foreign corporation, either to cast a vote deciding an evenly divided vote of such body, or for the duration of any deadlock that may arise, to exercise the powers ordinarily exercised by such governing body; or

(iii) If the powers which would ordinarily be exercised by the board of directors of a domestic corporation are exercised with respect to such foreign corporation by **a person** whom such shareholders have the power to elect, appoint or replace.

The following example might be used to circumvent the CFC enigma of T. Regs. 957-1(b)(1) cited above.

Let's assume you are the only U.S. Shareholder with voting stock, and that you hold exactly 50% of all the stock entitled to vote. A citizen of the Bahamas owns the remaining 50% of voting stock. According to the corporation's "Articles" (by-laws) two directors are to be elected by the shareholders who hold voting stock, and one additional director is to be appointed by a U.S. director (if any) to help run

---

1. *Sup-part F* income is also called *Foreign Personal Holding Company* income by the tax writers. See IRC §954(a).

the company. Thus, the company has three directors in all.

> Care must be taken not to collaborate your votes with other voting stockholders as that can cause the corporation to be viewed as a CFC by the IRS. A simple show of hands (votes) at the shareholders meeting would be enough when electing directors to run the company.

Let's assume the voting stock was apportioned as follows:

a) 50% of the voting shares (i.e., 1,000 shares) will be held by founder **F**, a U.S. citizen.
b) The remaining 50% of the voting stock (1,000 shares in all) is held by well-to do-citizen **B** of a foreign country (we'll say he's from the Bahamas, but he could be from any foreign country).

Next, at the annual meeting of shareholders you (U.S. citizen F) and foreigner B should nominate and elect two directors. It shouldn't be too difficult for you (U.S. citizen F) to get yourself elected as one of the managing directors, because you have 50% of the voting stock. Remember, the law allows you this percentage without being in-control. At this point the foreign corporation is not a CFC.

After the **election** of the two directors, a **third** director might be appointed by the U.S. director if such appointment is specified in the by-laws. Note, there is a real power struggle to get to the top, and once you're there, you'll have to share power somewhat. But, look a bit closer.

The regulations really don't force you to surrender control of your enterprise although it may appear that way on the surface. All the decision making can remain essentially in your hands if you really want it to because you're the most powerful of the three directors. Why are you the most powerful? Because you can appoint or replace the "third" director.

Hopefully, the appointed director will vote with you on important matters, but even if he doesn't, you have the power to replace him. You can't under any circumstances tell him how he must vote. Under the above conditions you would be in compliance with T.Reg. §957-1(b) because the U.S. shareholders don't have the power to elect, appoint or repl**ace most** of the directing body. They will not be able to elect and single director outright, thus cannot elect a majority of the directors by any means. Further,

the U.S. elected director (also the voting U.S. shareholder) cannot **replace** or **appoint** more than a third of all the directors, and a third is not a **majority** by any means. [2]

There is nothing in the regulations that say you cannot appoint or replace a non-elected director. The regulations only forbid U.S. voting shareholders (you as a director would meet this qualification) from appointing or replacing **most** of the body of persons exercising the powers ordinarily exercised by a board of directors of a domestic company. In the above example, U.S. shareholders with voting power cannot elect a director alone. They only have the power to force a deadlock.

> Note: T. Regulation §957-1(b)(1)(i) and (ii) and (iii), is only applicable when there is a **U.S. Shareholder** (i.e., a U.S. person who owns 10% or more of the voting stock). See the chart on page #47 for the situation when there are **no** U.S. Shareholders.

Legal Tax Avoidance or Illegal Tax Evasion. What is the difference?

It would be prudent to mention something about tax avoidance and tax evasion from a U.S. tax planner's perspective. Authors Jon E, Bischel (Professor of Law at Syracuse University College of Law) and Robert Feinschreiber propose in their book, *Fundamentals of International Taxation*, *"The exact scope of the term evasion or avoidance of federal income tax is unclear. In this regard, however, utilization of the statutorily provided benefits is outside the scope of this rule."* To put it another way, if you are in compliance with the regulations, tax avoidance is not an issue.

We can apply the this rule to T. Regulation §957-1(b)(2), where it states....

"Any arrangement to shift the formal voting power away from **U.S. Shareholder**s of a foreign corporation will not be given effect if in reality voting power is retained. The mere ownership of stock entitled to vote does not by itself mean that the shareholder owning such stock has the voting power of such stock for purposes of Section 957. For example, if there is **any**

---

2. Is it mere coincidence that the rules allow you to own no more than 50% of the voting stock for the CFC determination, and likewise impart a 50% percentile limit on the "number of directors" you can appoint or replace under T.Reg. 957-1(b)(ii), i.e., "exactly one half of the members"?

arrangement, whether expressed or implied that any shareholder will not vote his stock, or will vote it only in a specific manner, or that the shareholders owning stock having not more than 50% of the total combined voting power will exercise voting power normally possessed by a majority stockholder, then the nominal ownership of the voting power will be disregarded in determining which shareholders actually hold such voting power, and the determination will be made on the basis of such agreement."

As you can see, the importance of the foreign shareholder voting his own stock independently cannot be over emphasized. Any formal agreement would be calamitous. If the IRS should disregard the foreigner's voting stock, the U.S. shareholder in our example who owns 50% of the voting stock would be found to own 100% of the voting stock. Beware that the IRS cannot shift the formal voting power back to you under these provisions.

Attribution of Ownership Rules IRC §958(a)

Aside from stock owned directly, a U.S. stockholder can own an interest in a foreign corporation in two other ways. The first is called the **Chain of Ownership** rule and it is explained under IRC §958(a). The second is called the **Constructive Ownership** rule and it is located under IRC §958(b).

Under the **Chain of Ownership** rules, stock owned directly or indirectly, by or for a foreign corporation, foreign partnership, foreign trust or foreign estate shall be considered as owned **proportionately** by its shareholders, partners or beneficiaries. Thus, stock in a foreign corporation will be considered owned by a person by reason of the application of the preceding sentence, if he owns stock in a foreign entity that also owns stock in the foreign corporation, or stock in another entity that owns stock in the foreign corporation. This is a limited form of stock attribution, as the rule only applies to stock owned through foreign entities. Under T.Regs. §958-1(b) attribution stops with the first United States person in the chain of ownership running from the foreign corporation. Here is an example from Treasury Regs. §958-1(d) of Example (1). Remember, this is the U.S. Treasury's own explanation.

(1) United States person A and B own 25% and 50%, respectively, of the one class of stock in foreign corporation M. Corporation M owns 80% of the one class of stock in foreign corporation N, and N corporation owns 60% of the one class of stock in foreign corporation P. Under paragraph (b) of this section, M corporation is considered as owning 48% (80% of 60%) of the stock in P. corporation; such 48% is treated as actually owned by M corporation for the purpose of again applying paragraph (b) of this section. Thus, A and B are considered to own 12% (25% of 48%) and 24% (50% of 48%), respectively, of the stock in P corporation.

Constructive Ownership Rules

The **Constructive Ownership** rule is more encompassing than the **chain of ownership** rule. Under the constructive ownership statutes, an individual shall be considered as owning stock owned directly or indirectly, by or for his spouse, his children, his grandchildren, and his parents. Moreover, stock owned directly or indirectly by or for a partnership or estate shall be considered as owned proportionately by its partners or beneficiaries. Stock owned by a trust shall be considered as owned proportionately by its beneficiaries in proportion to their actuarial interest of such beneficiaries in such trust. Stock owned by a trust for any person who is the owner or grantor will be considered as owned by that person.

In addition, if 10% or more of the value of stock in a corporation is owned directly or indirectly, by or for any person, such person shall be considered as owning the stock owned directly or indirectly by or for such corporation, in that proportion which the value of the stock which such person owns bears to the value of all the stock in such corporation. [3]

Important Point: Under the **constructive ownership** tests, if U.S. person A owns 8% of the stock of foreign corporation B, which owned 100% of the stock in foreign corporation C, U.S. person A would not be considered to own any stock in corporation C under the constructive ownership rules, yet under the **chain of ownership** rules (T.Regs. §958-1(a)(2) he would be considered to own 8% of foreign corporation C, but only if corporation B was also a foreign corporation. According to the **Code**, you are to use the larger percentage when making the ownership determinations.

---

3. T.Regs.§958-2(c)(1)(iii); IRC §958(b)(3).

The U.S. Treasury Regulations provide the taxpayer with an abundance of good illustrations. The following Treasury Regulation example coordinates the two attribution rules we have just discussed. [4.]

Example (1) (a). United States person A and B, and domestic corporation M own 9%, 32% and 10%, respectively, of the one class of stock in foreign corporation R. A also owns 10% of the one class of stock in M corporation. For purposes of determining whether A is a **United States Shareholder** with respect to R corporation, 10% of the 10% interest of M corporation in R corporation is considered as owned by A. See paragraph (c)(1)(iii) of this section. Thus, A owns 10% (9% plus 10% of 10%) of the stock in R corporation and is a **United States Shareholder** with respect to such corporation. Corporation M and B, by reason of owning 10% and 32%, respectively, of the stock in R corporation are U.S. Shareholders with respect to such corporation.

(b) For purposes of determining whether R corporation is a **controlled foreign corporation**, the 1% of the stock in R corporation directly owned by M corporation and considered owned by A cannot be counted twice. Therefore, the total amount of stock in R corporation owned by U.S. shareholders is 51%, determined as follows.

Stock Ownership in R Corporation

A..	9%
B..	32%
M corporation......................	10%
Total..................................	51%

Comments and Overview

Had corporation M held only 9% of the stock in foreign corporation R, U.S. person A would have been considered to own none of foreign corporation R through foreign corporation M. A would then been attributed with owning only 9% of foreign corporation R, and foreign corporation R would not have been a controlled foreign corporation because A's 9% and M's 9% are not taken into account. [5.]

Complete Control of a Foreign Corporation

Most tax haven authors writing today suggest that to avoid the USA's CFC provisions you either need a foreign partner who can own

50% of the company, or you need 11 or so U.S. partners, or some combination of the above. One writer even provides several names for prospective partners - (Manny, Moe, Jack, Bonnie, Clyde, Abbott, Costello, Burns, Allen and Harpo!!). All very suitable names, I suppose, for your "nominees, but this writer believes you can launch a Cayman or Bahamian foreign corporation all by yourself, if you really want to.

Beware, the IRS does not recognize the use of nominees in a tax plan. Better to work with their Treasury Regulations, then to use nominee shareholders.

According to IRC §951(b), when making the determination whether a foreign corporation is a CFC only **U.S. Shareholders** are to be considered in the count. A U.S. Shareholder is a U.S. person [as defined in Section 957(d)] who **owns** [within the meaning of section 958(a), or is considered as owning by applying the constructive ownership rules of section 958(b)], **10% or more of the total combined voting power** of all classes of stock entitled to vote of such corporation. To reiterate, you have to **own** 10% or more of the voting stock to be classified as a U.S. Shareholder for purposes of this section of law. If there are no U.S. Shareholders after applying Section 958(a) and (b), a foreign corporation cannot be a **Controlled Foreign Corporation**.

Of course, what good is a foreign corporation to a U.S. person (investor or entrepreneur) if he has no control over its functions? The answer to this question is obviously not very much. Luckily, there is a way to arrange the affairs so the U.S. person can still more or less exercise control, without **owning** the requisite amount of voting stock.

Example #3: Referring to the chart on pg. #43, let's assume U.S. **founder F**, on the same day he incorporates his foreign Cayman corporation, distributes all 100% of the voting stock of the Cayman holding company to a wholly owned Cayman (grantor) trust. If the trust agreement appoints F as one of the three trustees (we'll say the other two trustees are Cayman entities), and delegates the **power to vote** the voting stock **owned** by the trust at shareholder meetings to F, then F will be able to indirectly elect the Cayman holding company directors. T.Regs. §957-1(b)(1) only prohibits **U.S. Shareholders** (and F is not a U.S. Shareholder because he **owns** not a share

---

4. T. Regs.§ 958-2(f)(2).
5. T. Regs.§951-1(g).

voting stock) from electing, appointing or replacing the directors of a foreign corporation. Refer to T.Reg. §957-1(a) & (b) on page #50. [6]

> **Real Ownership:** The United States and the United Kingdom (and most Commonwealth nations) have what lawyers call a **common law system of taxation.** The use of trusts both foreign and domestic is well-recognized in both jurisdiction. All the courts acknowledge that a foreign trust can be the legal owner of an asset. The conveyance of property to a trust is common practice in the U.S.A. and is an oft employed tax planning technique to reduce one's domestic tax liability. If a foreign trust is the legal **owner** of the voting stock of a foreign corporation, there should be no argument from the IRS or the U.S. courts over who the real owner is. The real owner is the trust. [7]

To repeat, the distinction between **U.S. Shareholder** and **U.S. person** is an important one. Only U.S. Shareholders are restricted from electing, appointing or replacing foreign directors, and then only a majority of those directors. T.Regs. §951-(g)(2) supplies some guidelines to follow to see if a **U.S. person** is in fact a **U.S. shareholder** too. The nomenclature and terminology is the key to understanding this provision. The law says when a foreign corporation has more than one class of stock outstanding, and one or more **U.S. persons** OWN (ownership is the key word under this law) shares of any class of stock which possesses the power to appoint, elect or replace a person or persons of the foreign corporation that exercises the powers ordinarily exercised by a member of the board of directors of a domestic corporation, then such **U.S. person would be a U.S. Shareholder too.**

Since founder **F owns** not a single share of voting stock, he can't be made to qualify as a U.S. Shareholder. As far as the IRS is concerned, F is just another plain and simple U.S. person, unless he can be made to own **10% or more** of the voting power of the Cayman company, directly or indirectly, **or** unless he can appoint, elect or replace at least one director with the stock he does own. [8]

Shifting of Formal Voting Power

We need to maneuver past one last stumbling block to be free of the IRS's tax tentacles over our foreign company. The IRS is not in the blind to any arrangements to shift the formal voting power away from the U.S. taxpayer. However, even if the IRS were to apply the first part of paragraph (b)(2) (marked **"Y"** on page 50, supra), the worst scenario would be that the voting stock owned by the trust would be **disregarded**. Because there are no other U.S. stockholders that own any voting stock, **disregarding** the stock won't increase the percentage held by some other U.S. person. Carefully reading part "Y" (up to "Moreover, where.....") and you can readily see that if there was an agreement to vote the Cayman holding company stock in a specific manner, the "nominal" ownership of that voting stock would be **disregarded**. But, disregarding (or not counting) the voting stock held by the foreign trust would not have any adverse effect. **F** could still vote the shares as trustee. F is not a **U.S. shareholder!** In a like manner, disregarding the trust's voting stock will not have a damaging effect on the status of the Cayman company as a non-controlled foreign company because there are no other U.S. shareholders or persons who hold (own) **any** of the voting stock left outstanding that could be attributed to them.

> The Controlled Foreign Corporation provisions are now over 25 years old. That the original engineers of these tax laws took the trouble to painstakingly distinguish between non-voting and voting shareholders is clear. Isn't it odd that the lawmakers would construct a maze of elaborate rules, using voting vrs. non-voting stock, yet not expect tax planners would develop strategies using voting and non-voting stock? Read the Treasury's regulations on page 50 and the **Code**'s design will become clearer.

Reading the last part of this paragraph (marked X) and you find that where there are U.S. Shareholders who hold one class of stock, and another class of voting stock outstanding is voted on behalf of any person or persons, then that person or persons will be deemed the **real owners** of the stock. [9] Again,

---

6. The foreign trust should have only the foreign corporation as a beneficiary. See IRC §679(c).

7. *"One of the most effective applications of offshore trusts is in an ownership combination with a limited company."* - Richard Graham-Taylor, partner Ernst & Young, **Grand Cayman (January 1990).**

8. In the example, F **owns** only non-voting (value) stock. Non-voting stock cannot elect or appoint or replace a director under any circumstances. It is an investment in the profitability of the company hence the term "value shares" often provided by the Treasury Regulations.

---

9. This is probably the only occurrence in the entire Internal Revenue Code and T. Regulations where you will find ownership of stock being stripped away from one owner and shifted to another - in this case a trustee. Note, that this paragraph applies when there are "U.S. Shareholders" [10% or more owners of voting stock as defined by IRC §951(d)], and appears not to be applicable if say there were no U.S. shareholders for the foreign company in the first place.

Cayman Holding Company and Trust

Cayman Trust (owns 71% or 14,200,000 non-voting stock of Cayman Company + 2,000 shares of voting stock)

Cayman Holding Company

20,000,000 non-voting shares + 2,000

voting shares authorized in "Articles

of Incorporation"

U.S. Stockholders (corporation or individual(s) owns 29% or 5,800,000 non-voting stock of Cayman Holding Company directly and 20.59% indirectly. Total ownership: 49.59%

Important Attributes

1. Avoids Controlled Foreign Corporation (CFC) Status (IRC §957)
2. Avoids Foreign Personal Holding Company Status (IRC §554)
3. Avoids Personal Holding Company Status (IRC §544)
4. Avoids Foreign Investment Company Status (IRC §1246)
5. Only one U.S. person needed to founder company.
6. One time filing of Form 5471 may be all that is required for IRS.
7. Not required to file any information returns about Foreign Trust IRC §679(c)(2)(A). Forms 3520 and 3520A need not be filled out.

(See appendix in back of book)

under the rules, if there are no U.S. shareholders that own the one class of stock that is owned by U.S. persons, it is not possible for the voting stock to be owned by F, even if he votes them on behalf of the Cayman trust for himself.

> **Caveat:** If the Cayman holding company issues another class of voting stock representing 10% of the voting power outstanding to U.S. person **D**, founder **F** would be deemed to own the other 90% (held by the trust) of voting stock if he voted them for himself.

Code-Section §956 - Another problem for U.S. Shareholders of Controlled Foreign Corporations

Investments by a Controlled Foreign Corporation in *United States property* of certain types will be treated as a dividend distribution to the U.S. Shareholders, regardless whether any dividend is actually received. This special <u>imputation</u> rule can have adverse tax consequences because it applies even if the **CFC** has no sub-part F income.

Only the increase in earnings invested in U.S. property is subject to tax. The earnings of a CFC invested in U.S. property is the aggregate amount of the property held by the corporation at the close of the taxable year, to the extent that this amount would have constituted a dividend if it was distributed. The increase in U.S. property for the taxable year is generally determined by subtracting the amount of U.S. property on hand at the close of the preceding taxable year from the amount at the close of the taxable year in question.

Example #1: U.S. citizen Y owns 100% of the single class of stock of Bermuda company **BZ**. In 1987 **BZ** has earnings from the operation of a Bermuda resort of $100,000. In 1987 BZ invests these earnings in U.S. real estate. Because Y is a U.S. shareholder in a CFC, the $100,000 U.S. investment is treated as a dividend paid to Y, though Y has received no money.

Example #2: Baron von Lipper of Liechtenstein is the sole stockholder of Bermuda company **BL**. **BL** has worldwide earnings of $10,000,000 in 1987. **B L** invests $5,000,000 in an oil lease in West Texas. None of this $5,000,000 is treated as a taxable dividend to Baron von Lipper under IRC §956 because the CFC provisions apply only to U.S. Shareholders in CFCs. Baron von Lipper is a non-resident alien individual, not a U.S. shareholder.

For some mysterious reason the U.S. Treasury Department does not consider all property in the United States to be U.S. property for purposes of applying Code-Section 956 rules. Excepted from the definition of U.S. property under T.Regs. §1.956-2(a)(2) are the following types of properties:

(1) Obligations of the United States such as Treasury bonds and treasury bills.
(2) Money or currency.
(3) Certain deposits with persons carrying on the banking business.
(4) Investments in stock or obligations of an unrelated domestic company. For purposes of this subdivision, an unrelated domestic company is a domestic corporation which is neither a U.S. Shareholder (as defined under IRC §951(b)) of the Controlled Foreign Corporation making the investment, nor a corporation 25% or more of whose total combined voting power of all classes of stock entitled to vote is owned or is considered as owned after applying the constructive ownership rules of §958(b) by United States shareholders of the Controlled Foreign corporation.
(5) For years after December 31, 1985, movable drilling rigs or barges and other movable exploration or exploitation equipment (other than vessels or aircraft) when used on the Continental Shelf (as defined in IRC §638).
(6) Any aircraft, railroad rolling stock, motor vehicle, or vessel purchased for use mainly outside the United States.
(7) Products purchased for export to foreign countries.

Example #3. Bermuda company **BZ** in Example #1 (above) purchases $100,000 in Exxon stock at $50/share. By virtue of exception #4 under T.Reg. §1.956-2(a)(2), BZ has not made an investment in U.S. property. Thus while U.S. citizen Y would be classified a U.S. Shareholder in a CFC, **Y** would not be required to include the U.S. stock purchase made by BZ as a dividend distribution includible on his U.S. income tax form.

U.S. Treasury rejects the use of nominees

If you think you can dodge the regulations under §956 by using another foreign corporation or trustee to buy the U.S. property on your behalf, think again. T.Reg. §956-1T(b)(4)(i) states that for purposes of this subsection... "A controlled foreign corporation will be considered to hold indirectly (A) the investment in United States property held on its behalf by a **trustee or nominee** or (B) at the discretion of the District Director (of the IRS), investments in U.S. property acquired by any other foreign corporation that is *controlled* by the controlled foreign corporation, if one of the principal purposes for creating, organizing or funding (through capital contributions or debt) such foreign company is to avoid the application of section 956." For purposes of determining *control*, the foreign company need only be a tad related to the controlled foreign corporation.

Voting (and non-voting) stock attribution through foreign trusts and foreign companies.

The Treasury Regulations under §958-1 & 2 provide several examples of how stock can be owned constructively and indirectly, by and through foreign entities (i.e., foreign trusts, foreign corporations, foreign partnerships). These Treasury Regulations (a.k.a. *"Regs."*) speak repeatedly and often of the usage of **one and two classes of stock** having **voting and non-voting power.**

Regs. §1.958-1(d) EXAMPLE (3): Foreign Trust Z was created for the benefit of U.S. persons D, E, and F. Under the terms of the trust instrument, the trust income is required to be divided into three equal shares. Each beneficiary's share of the income may either be accumulated for him or distributed to him in the discretion of the trustee. In 1970, the trust is terminated and there is to be paid over to each beneficiary the accumulated income applicable to his share and 1/3rd of the corpus. The corpus of the trust is composed of 90% of the **one class** of stock in foreign corporation S. By the application of this section, each of D, E, and F is considered to own 30% (1/3 of 90%) of the stock in S. Corporation.

Regs. §1.958-2(c)(ii) From Trusts-(a) **To beneficiaries**. Stock owned, directly or indirectly, by or for a trust shall be considered as owned by its beneficiaries in proportion to the actuarial interest of such beneficiaries in such trust. **(b) To owner**. Stock owned directly or indirectly, by or for any portion of a trust of which a person is considered the owner under sections 671-78 (relating to grantors and others treated as substantial owners) shall be considered as owned by such person.

Comments and Conclusions: For purposes of determining stock ownership and CFC status, few tax professionals would argue that Foreign corporation S in example # 3 (above) is a **CFC**, and beneficiaries D, E and F are **U.S. shareholders.** It can easily be surmised too (by **reversing the reasoning**) that **Foreign trust Z** (in the Treasury's example #3) is **not** a grantor type trust. Accordingly, one could deduce that income distributed from trust **Z** to U.S. beneficiaries D, E, and F could be received via **Rev-Rul. 69-70** free of all U.S. taxes **if Trust Z** had been a legitimate foreign grantor type trust in the first place. See **(b)** above for case where

stock in **S** is deemed owned by a foreign grantor. [10.]

Is technical compliance with the law enough?

The tax committees in Congress are aware U.S. taxpayers might try to circumvent the CFC perplexity if they plan painstakingly. In **Committee Report on P.L. 99-514** (issued after the **Tax Reform Act of 1986**) the committee stated...

*We (the committee) are concerned that the present controlled foreign corporation rules can be manipulated by taxpayers to avoid the provisions of sub-part F. since U.S. control is defined solely in terms of voting power, taxpayers can structure their investments to avoid sub-part F by ensuing that they hold no more than 50% of the voting power of a corporation, even when they hold the majority of the value of the corporation in the form of **nonvoting** stock.*

Technical compliance with the stock attribution and constructive ownership rules under T.Regs. §958-1&(2) should be the tax planners first line of defense. Referring to the chart on page #47 note **(1)** that under the stock attribution and constructive ownership rules the most <u>nonvoting</u> stock U.S. person(s) can own indirectly is 20.59%, with another 29% being owned directly. Total U.S. ownership in the Cayman company cannot possibly exceed 49.59%, as it is a mathematical impossibility, **(2)** that all (100%) of the voting stock of the Cayman Company is owned by a foreign trust (which also owns 71% of the nonvoting stock too), thus <u>technically</u> U.S. person(s) cannot be made to own **any** voting stock of the Cayman company, and it follows that no U.S. person can be made-out to be a *U.S. Shareholder,* **(3)** that the stock attribution of ownership procedures for both **Foreign Personal Holding Companies,** PHCs and FICs are successfully circumvented, making these provisions a non-problem for the tax practitioner. Is this the way it was meant to be? Have we uncovered some sort of *master design, or are we treading on thin ice?* [11.]

---

10.   Revenue Ruling 69-70 states that *foreign source income* from a **foreign grantor trust** received by U.S. beneficiaries is **not** taxable income. See Chapter 12 (Foreign Trusts).

11. By definition the *Internal Revenue Code* is just that, a *"Code"* of decipherable literature, written to be construed and mulled over by U.S. taxpayers, professors, students, lawyers and tax judges. It is more by design then by accident that it reads at

and 7701(a)(7). For the classification of a member in an association, joint-stock company, or insurance company as a shareholder, see section 7701(a)(8).

(b) **Percentage of total combined voting power owned by United States shareholders—(1) Meaning of combined voting power.** In determining for purposes of paragraph (a) of this section whether United States shareholders own the requisite percentage of total combined voting power of all classes of stock entitled to vote, consideration will be given to all the facts and circumstances of each case. In all cases, however, United States shareholders of a foreign corporation will be deemed to own the requisite percentage of total combined voting power with respect to such corporation—

(i) If they have the power to elect, appoint, or replace a majority of that body of persons exercising, with respect to such corporation, the powers ordinarily exercised by the board of directors of a domestic corporation;

(ii) If any person or persons elected or designated by such shareholders have the power, where such shareholders have the power to elect exactly one-half of the members of such governing body of such foreign corporation, either to cast a vote deciding an evenly divided vote of such body or, for the duration of any deadlock which may arise, to exercise the powers ordinarily exercised by such governing body; or

(iii) If the powers which would ordinarily be exercised by the board of directors of a domestic corporation are exercised with respect to such foreign corporation by a person whom such shareholders have the power to elect, appoint, or replace.

(2) **Shifting of formal voting power.** Any arrangement to shift formal voting power away from United States shareholders of a foreign corporation will not be given effect if in reality voting power is retained. The mere ownership of stock entitled to vote does not by itself mean that the shareholder owning such stock has the voting power of such stock for purposes of section 957. For example, if there is any agreement, whether express or implied, that any shareholder will not vote his stock or will vote it only in a specified manner, or that shareholders owning stock having not more than 50 percent of the total combined voting power will exercise voting power normally possessed by a majority of stockholders, then the nominal ownership of the voting power will be disregarded in determining which shareholders actually hold such voting power, and this determination will be made on the basis of such agreement. Moreover, where United States shareholders own shares of one or more classes of stock of a foreign corporation which has another class of stock outstanding, the voting power ostensibly provided such other class of stock will be deemed owned by any person or persons on whose behalf it is exercised, or, if not exercised, will be disregarded if the percentage of voting power of such other class of stock is substantially greater than its proportionate share of the corporate earnings, if the facts indicate that the shareholders of such other class of stock do not exercise their voting rights independently or fail to exercise such voting rights, and if a principal purpose of the arrangement is to avoid the classification of such foreign corporation as a controlled foreign corporation under section 957.

(c) **Illustrations.** The application of this section may be illustrated by the following examples:

Example (1). Foreign corporation R has two classes of capital stock outstanding, 60 shares of class A stock, and 40 shares of class B stock. Each share of each class of stock has one vote for all purposes. E, a United States person, owns 51 shares of class A stock. Corporation R is a controlled foreign corporation.

Example (2). Foreign corporation S has three classes of capital stock outstanding, consisting of 60 shares of class A stock, 40 shares of class B stock, and 200 shares of class C stock. The owners of a majority of class A stock are entitled to elect 6 of the 10 corporate directors, and the owners of a majority of the class B stock are entitled to elect the other 4 of the 10 directors. Class C stock has no voting rights. D, a United States person, owns all of the shares of the class C stock. He also owns 31 shares of class A stock and as such an owner can elect 6 members of the board of directors. None of the remaining shares of class A stock, or the 40 shares of class B stock, is owned, or considered as owned, within the meaning of section 958, by a United States person. Since, as owner of 31 shares of the class A stock, D has sufficient voting power to elect 6 directors, D has more than 50 percent of the total combined voting power of all classes of stock entitled to vote, and S Corporation is a controlled foreign corporation.

Example (3). M, a United States person, owns a 51-percent interest in R Company, a foreign company of which he is a member. The company, if it were domestic, would be taxable as a corporation. The remaining interest of 49 percent in the company is owned by seven other members none of whom is a United States person. The memorandum of association of R Company provides for only one manager, who with respect to the company exercises the powers ordinarily exercised by a board of directors of a domestic corporation. The manager is to be elected by unanimous agreement of all the members. Since M owns 51 percent of the company, he will be deemed to own more than 50 percent of the total combined voting power of all classes of stock of R Company entitled to vote, notwithstanding that he has power to elect a manager only with the agreement

That the plan offered on page #47 is **technically** in compliance with the CFC provision so as not to trigger CFC status is not the question. Few would argue that the Cayman company in the diagram is a CFC, or that there exists a U.S. Shareholder [as defined under IRC §951(b)] who could have **sub-part F** income imputed to him. However, some courts have found mere technical compliance not to be enough. Moreover, the regulations tell us... *where there is a expressed or implied agreement* that the foreigner (in this case the trustee of the grantor trust), who **owns** voting stock, will vote that stock in a particular way, then the IRS **might** disregard the voting power ostensibly owned by the foreigner (i.e., the trust), and rule the foreign company to be a CFC. [12].

> Only U.S. persons that own 10% or more of the voting stock are deemed *U.S. Shareholders,* and only stock owned by *U.S. shareholders* is consider when making the determination as to whether the foreign corporation is a Controlled Foreign Corporation. See IRC §957(a) & 951(b).

Regs. §957-1(c) EXAMPLE (7).. Foreign corporation **A** authorized to issue 100 shares of **one class** of capital stock, issues, for $1,000 per share, 45 shares to domestic corporation M, 45 shares to foreign corporation B, and 10 shares to foreign corporation C. Corporation C, a bank, lends $3 million to finance the operations of A corporation. In the course of negotiating these financial arrangements, D, an officer of C corporation, and E, an officer of M corporation, orally agree that C corporation will vote its stock as M corporation directs. By virtue of such oral agreement M corporation possesses the voting power ostensibly owned by C corporation, and A corporation is a controlled foreign corporation.

Literal Interpretation of T.Regs. §957

A quick reading of T.Regs. §957-(1)(b)(1) clearly requires the existence of a **U.S. Shareholder** before the provisions of (i), (ii) and (iii) become applicable. This part of the law needs no interpretation. On the other hand, while T.Regs.§957-1(2)*(Shifting of formal voting power)* appears to require the presence of at least one U.S. shareholder for the shifting of control to take effect, only a very **literal** interpretation of these provisions can lead you to that conclusion.

---

times like ancient hieroglyphics, with its meanings buried under volumes of unearthly prose decipherable, but elusive too. To be useful, however, it must also provide logical answers and practical conclusions; otherwise neither taxpayer or IRS will prevail.

12. See T.Regs.§ 957-1(b)(2).

In fact, the regulations are not precise enough to draw any conclusion, and need be reworked and clarified for both taxpayers, courts, and the IRS.

In the diagram depicted on page #47 there can be no doubt that the U.S. courts will recognize the foreign trust as the legitimate owner of the *voting stock* of the Cayman company. To rule otherwise would be to go against all the attribution of ownership and constructive ownership rules of the Code and regulations.

Nevertheless, it would be prudent, indeed wise, for planners to use discretion and good judgment when taking advantage of offshore confidentiality (bank secrecy) laws. Keep the **trust powers** a secret known only to your most trusted bankers, lawyers and offshore managers. An IRS challenge is not likely if you employ adequate offshore management.

Dating back to their inception (i.e., the **Revenue Act of 1962**) it has been the contention of Congress and the U.S. Treasury that the main ingredient necessary for *"control"* would be **voting control** by *U.S. shareholders*. When in 1961 Treasury Secretary Dillon was asked by Congressman Byrnes to define *control* for purposes of the new law Dillon affirmed...

Mr. Byrnes: *"But it is a foreign corporation in which American have the principal investment as far as stock ownership?"*

Secretary Dillon: *"That is right. They manage and control it."*

Mr. Byrnes: *"Your definition now is 51 percent?"*

Secretary Dillon: *"Over 50%.... We feel that the ownership tests relates to U.S. persons who still maintain effective control.... We thought 10% (the Kennedy Administrations phase-in proposal) was reasonable considering the form which new foreign investments have been taking."*

Under Code §957(a), a foreign corporation is a **CFC** if *"more than 50% of its voting (and value) are owned by U.S. shareholders."* The **value** criteria being added with the **Tax Reform Act of 1986.** Moreover, as proclaimed by Secretary Dillon, only U.S. persons that own **10% or more** of the voting stock in the foreign corporation will be at risk [current IRC §951(b)]. U.S. persons that own less than the threshold amount (10%) will not be considered U.S. shareholders and will not be looked-at in determining if the FC is controlled.

There are a myriad of structures and schemes that can be crafted by the U.S. taxpayer to avoid the CFC status. Neither IRS, U.S. tax judge, law professor or Congressional tax committee would argue that none exist. The laws, by their own design, created many of these loopholes and gaps.

Perhaps the most widely accepted scheme, offering the least likelihood of IRS challenge, is the case where 11 U.S. persons each own exactly 9% of the stock in a foreign corporation. Virtually every book and thesis on CFCs contain this enormously impractical plan, including such luminary publishers as **Prentice-Hall** - their legal tax writing staff, (2) Midas Malone - author of *Tax Free*, and (3) Tax Management Inc., - a subsidiary of The Bureau of National Affairs, Inc. in Washington DC, who's lawyers and writers advise Congressional tax committees on how and what to adopt into law. Example #2 below outlines the scenario..

Example #2: 11 unrelated U.S. persons each own 9% of the one class of outstanding stock in Bahamian Company A. By virtue of this information alone, Bahamian company A is not a CFC because no U.S. person owns "more than 10% of the voting stock" in A. Thus, there are no U.S. **shareholders** who own "more than 50%" of the stock in a foreign corporation.

Bahamian Company A realizes $100,000 in capital gains from U.S. stocks transactions in 1989. In addition, Bahamian company A receives $300,000 in rents from an office building (or condominiums) located in the Caymans. Total 1989 income of A is $400,000.

Result: Since Bahamian company A is not a CFC, none of the 11 U.S. persons [who **are not** U.S. shareholders pursuant to IRC §951(b)] will have any sub-part F income ($100,000 in U.S. capital gains) imputed to them.

Problem: Suppose 2 of the 11 U.S. persons redeem their Bahamian company shares. Now there will be 9 U.S. persons who own 11% of A's single class of stock. Bahamian company A will become a CFC, and each of the 9 U.S. persons will become **U.S. shareholders** (persons that own **more than 10%** of a foreign company). **Result**: All the sub-part F income of A ($100,000) will be taxable to the 9 U.S. shareholders in 1989, the year it is earned. However, the $300,000 in rents from the Cayman office building is **not** sub-part F income, and not imputed to the U.S. shareholders. All non sub-part F income of A can be accumulated offshore under current U.S. tax laws. [13]

---

13. No reference to the new **Passive Foreign Investment Company** (IRC §1291-96) provisions were provided for in this example, but planners should take note that none of the 11 US

Offshore Confidentiality Laws

Now we get to the part that's sticky. In virtually all the offshore tax havens, including the Cayman Islands, Liechtenstein, Bahamas, Switzerland, Panama, Vanuatu, Hong Kong, Channel Islands and Isle of Man, there is some semblance of **bank secrecy laws** (also called Confidentiality laws) in place. All the major banks in these havens must abide by the host country secrecy laws formulated by the local government to protect foreign depositors and investors. There are often criminal sanctions imposed for unauthorized disclosures. You, as a managing director or executive of an offshore company or trust, have a fiduciary duty to obey the host country bank secrecy laws, the same as anyone else. Should we conclude that because you are an American you are exonerated from these foreign laws and can turn over private documents, offshore trust instruments, and the like to nosy IRS agents on the lamb? The answer is positively not.

During the IRS' **Operation Tradewinds** and **Project Havens** over a decade ago, word was rumored that an IRS informant arranged female companionship for a Bahamian banker visiting Miami so IRS intelligence agents could examine the contents of his briefcase, which allegedly contained names of *prominent Americans* who had numbered accounts at a bank in Nassau. Whatever the truth behind the allegations that IRS agents are roaming the Caribbean suborning bank employees to violate local secrecy legislation, and otherwise violate the letter and spirit of the law, there is serious doubt whether such evidence obtained abroad in violation of foreign law would be allowable in a criminal proceeding here in the USA.

According to Professor Marshall Langer, *"the real problem is akin to the doctrine of the **fruit of the poisonous tree** in constitutional law., ... "Many attorneys in this field are of the opinion that so much of the Service's information is*

---

stockholders would suffer any adverse tax consequences upon the disposition of their stock because Bahamian company A is not a PFIC. Capital gain on the foreign stock would receive the same tax treatment as gain on shares in any domestic company.

tainted in its inception that if it were held to the standards required of American companies doing business abroad its investigations would collapse."

Custom and Tradition

In addition to bank secrecy laws, many tax havens, including the Caymans, the Bahamas and Liechtenstein, permit shareholder nominees to own shares and sign *side-agreements* with/for the real owners. It is here where major differences of opinion between the IRS and these offshore jurisdictions manifest themselves. The IRS **will not** recognize a nominee as the real owner of a foreign corporation under any circumstances.

On the other hand, a document signed by a *stand-in* nominee shareholder giving authority to own or receive shares in a company **after** the start-up and registration phase (i.e., place the nominee' name on the **Government's Registry** to disguise the real stock ownership) to the real owners is a tradition in many offshore havens. Cayman courts, indeed the foreign courts in all these tax havens, fully endorse such secretly signed agreements and will uphold such *side-agreements* in their local courts too.

Combined **State** and **City** income tax rates can boost the overall tax rate of upper and upper-middle-class Americans to 50% or better. Below are the top combined state and local income tax rates for the 48 largest U.S. cities.

City	Top Tax Rate	City	Top Tax Rate
New York	11.275%	Los Angeles	9.3%
Chicago	3.%	Houston	none
Philadelphia	7.06%	Detroit	7.6%
San Diego	9.3%	Dallas	none
San Antonio	none	Phoenix	8%
Baltimore	7.5%	San Francisco	9.3%
Indianapolis	3.4%	San Jose	9.3%
Memphis	6%	Washington	9.5%
Jacksonville	none	Milwaukee	6.93%
Boston	5% to 10%	Columbus	8.9%
New Orleans	6%	Cleveland	8.9%
Denver	5%	El Paso	none
Seattle	none	Nashville	6%
Austin	none	Oklahoma City	6%
Kansas City	7%	Fort Worth	none
St. Louis	7%	Atlanta	6%
Portland	9.6%	Pittsburgh	6.1%
Miami	none	Tulsa	6%
Honolulu	10%	Cincinnati	8.9%
Albuquerque	8.5%	Tucson	8%
Oakland	9.3%	Minneapolis	8%
Charlotte	7%	Omaha	5.9%
Toledo	9.15%	Virginia Beach	5.75%
Buffalo	7.9%	Sacramento	9.3%

Source: *The Wall Street Journal*

Most Offshore Cities in tax havens impose **no** income or estate taxes on resident and non resident companies, trusts and individuals doing business or living there. Below is a list of cities in some of the top tax havens. Note, some havens will impose estate (£) and/or income taxes (√) on investors that take up permanent residence, or are doing business within the country deriving profits from the local economy.

City	Country/Island	Top Tax Rate
Nassau,	Bahamas	0%
Georgetown	Grand Cayman	0%
Freeport	Grand Bahama Island	0%
Douglas	Isle of Man	20%√£
St. Helier	Jersey (Channel Islands)	20%√£
St. Peter Port	Guernsey (Channel Is.)	20%√£
British Virgin Islands	Road Town (Tortola Is.)	√ £
Hamilton	Bermuda	£
Avarua	Rarotonga Is (Cook Islands)	£ √
Panama City	Panama	√
Hong Kong	Hong Kong Island	√ £
Vaduz	Liechtenstein	√ £
Luxembourg	Luxembourg	√ £
Lugano	Switzerland	9.8%√£
Campione	Italian enclave	0%
Bridgetown	Barbados	√ £
Zurich	Switzerland	9.8%√ £
Gibraltar	Gibraltar	√ £
Geneva	Switzerland	9.8% £
Vila	Vanuatu (Efate Is.)	0%
Apia	Western Samoa (Upolu Is.)	√ £
Willemstad	N. Antilles (Curacao Is.)	√ £

Source: *The Tax Haven Reporter*

Countries with CFC regimes

There are currently 15 industrial countries with controlled foreign corporation (CFC) regimes. Most all of them followed the U.S., which was the first country to enact the CFC rules during the Kennedy administration.

While I have not reviewed all the CFC rules for all the countries below, the ones I have reviewed rely on the 50% ownership criteria as the threshold for taxation.

New Zealand has no capital gains tax as yet.

United States (1962)   Sweden (1990)
Canada (1972)   Norway (1992)
Germany (1972)   Denmark (1994)
Japan (1978)   Spain (1995)
France (1980)   Portugal (1995)
UK (1984)   Finland (1995)
New Zealand (1988)   Brazil (1996)
Australia (1990) Korea (1997)

Foreign Corporations not "Controlled" by U.S. Shareholders

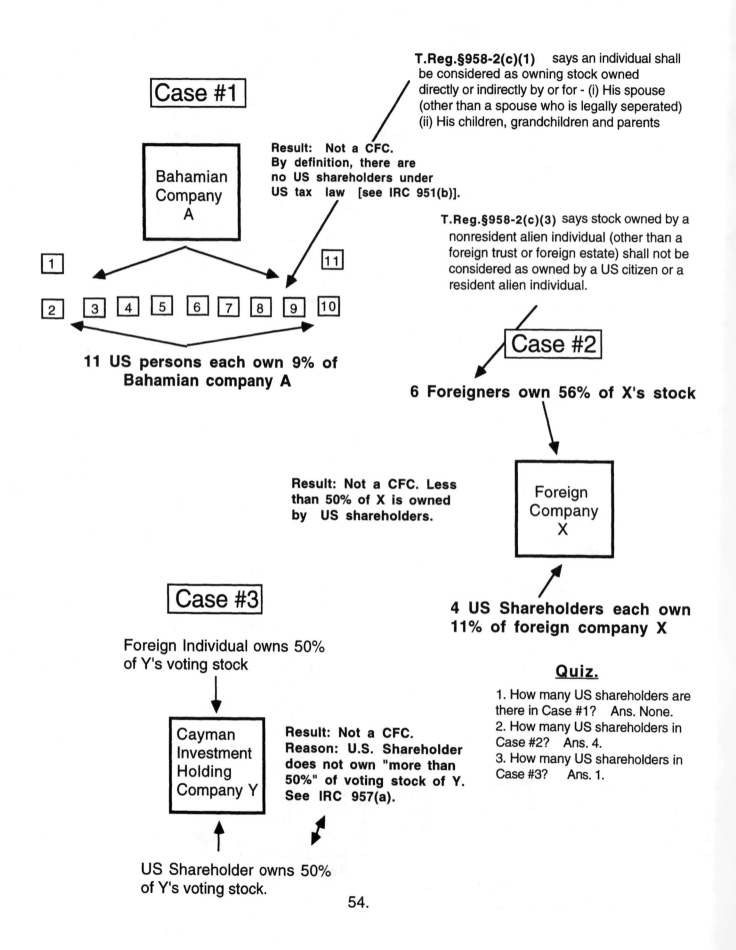

Case #1

Bahamian Company A

1

2 3 4 5 6 7 8 9 10

11

11 US persons each own 9% of Bahamian company A

Result: Not a CFC. By definition, there are no US shareholders under US tax law [see IRC 951(b)].

T.Reg.§958-2(c)(1) says an individual shall be considered as owning stock owned directly or indirectly by or for - (i) His spouse (other than a spouse who is legally seperated) (ii) His children, grandchildren and parents

T.Reg.§958-2(c)(3) says stock owned by a nonresident alien individual (other than a foreign trust or foreign estate) shall not be considered as owned by a US citizen or a resident alien individual.

Case #2

6 Foreigners own 56% of X's stock

Result: Not a CFC. Less than 50% of X is owned by US shareholders.

Foreign Company X

4 US Shareholders each own 11% of foreign company X

Case #3

Foreign Individual owns 50% of Y's voting stock

Cayman Investment Holding Company Y

Result: Not a CFC. Reason: U.S. Shareholder does not own "more than 50%" of voting stock of Y. See IRC 957(a).

US Shareholder owns 50% of Y's voting stock.

Quiz.

1. How many US shareholders are there in Case #1?   Ans. None.
2. How many US shareholders in Case #2?   Ans. 4.
3. How many US shareholders in Case #3?   Ans. 1.

54.

Diagrams for United States Treasury Regulation Examples

CONSTRUCTIVE OWNERSHIP TESTS
(See examples pages 44 and 45

CHAIN OF OWNERSHIP TESTS
(see Treasury Regulation
§1.958-1(d), Example 1)

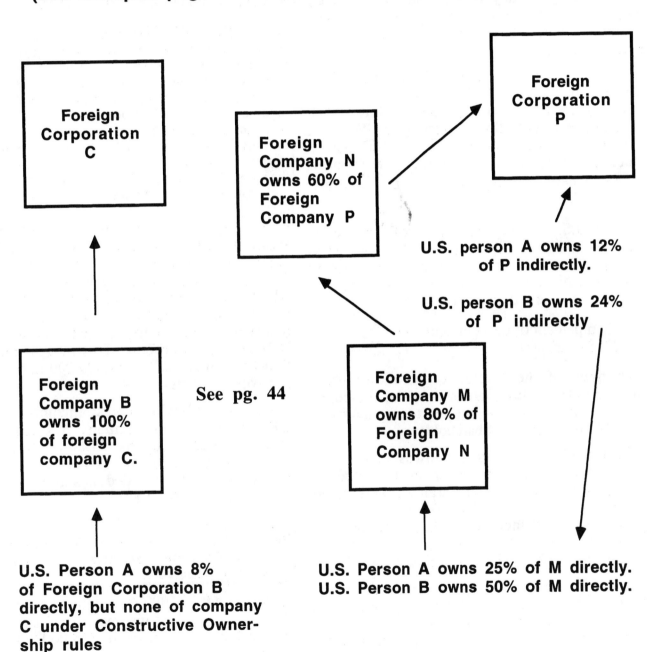

Foreign Corporation C

Foreign Company N owns 60% of Foreign Company P

Foreign Corporation P

U.S. person A owns 12% of P indirectly.

U.S. person B owns 24% of P indirectly

See pg. 44

Foreign Company B owns 100% of foreign company C.

Foreign Company M owns 80% of Foreign Company N

U.S. Person A owns 8% of Foreign Corporation B directly, but none of company C under Constructive Ownership rules

U.S. Person A owns 25% of M directly.
U.S. Person B owns 50% of M directly.

The *De Minimis Tax Haven Rule*. A loophole for citizens who want to use tax havens but avoid an IRS challenge.

Internal Revenue Code §952(a) provides the statutory definitions for **sub-part F** incomes of a Controlled Foreign Corporation (**CFC**). Sub-part F incomes include dividends, interests, annuities, capital gains, gains from commodity transactions, foreign currency gains, rents and royalties from **related** entities, most offshore insurance company profits, most offshore banking profits, foreign base company sales income, foreign base company services income, foreign base company shipping income, and foreign base company oil related income.

If a U.S. person (corporation, individual, estate or trust) owns 10% or more of the voting power of a CFC, he will be classified as a **U.S. Shareholder**. U.S. Shareholders in a CFC must report their *pro-rata* share of the sub-part F incomes to the IRS in the year it is earned; <u>unless</u> he can escape taxation under the **De Minimis Rule** explained below.

The U.S. Treasury Regulations state in Temp. Reg. §1.954-1T(b)(ii) that **if** the sum of the gross foreign base company income and gross insurance income of a controlled foreign corporation is less than the lesser of:

(1) 5 percent of gross income, **or**
(2) $1,000,000.

then none of the foreign corporation's gross income will be classified as Sub-Part F income, thus no income will be subject to imputation to any 10% or more U.S. Shareholders.

Example#1: U.S. person X owns 60% of the voting stock in Bahamian company Y. Y receives $500,000 in interest from Barclay's Bank in the Bahamas. Absent the De Minimis rule, U.S. person X would include $300,000 (his pro rata share of $500,000 profit) on his U.S. income tax return because X is a U.S. Shareholder in a CFC.

Not all offshore incomes are categorized Sub-Part F under the U.S. statutes. Income from manufacturing in the tax haven, rents from unrelated entities, and royalties gotten from the active conduct of a trade or business are **not** labeled sub-part F incomes.

Example #2: In 1989 Bahamian holding Company Y has $45,000 in sub-part F insurance and foreign personal holding company income, **plus** $950,000 in **non-sub-part F income** from the operation of a Bahamian hotel. The $45,000 in sub-part F income is not taxable income, and U.S. Shareholder X does not have to include his **pro rata** share of this $45,000 on his tax return. The $45,000 represents only 4.7% of Bahamian Company Y's total gross income and is under $1,000,000 limit of the de minimis rule.

> *De minimis* **tax haven rule** - Sub-part F income from a Controlled Foreign Corporation is not taxed if the sum of the corporation's sub-part F <u>foreign base company incomes</u> (and gross <u>insurance income</u>) are less than the lesser of (1) 5% of the corporation's gross income or (2) $1,000,000. In addition, post **Tax Reform Act of 1986 rule**s require all of a foreign corporation's income to be treated as sub-part F insurance income or foreign base company income if the **sum** of its sub-part F foreign base company income and insurance income exceeds **70%** of all its gross income. [15].

Example #3: U.S. citizen BW owns 100% of the stock in Bahamian real estate company Y. Bahamas company **Y** owns 4 condominiums which it sublets to tourists receiving $1,000,000 in rents from unrelated persons. Y company also receives $250,000 in interest income from a Bahamian bank account. This interest income **is** Sub-Part F income. The $1,000,000 in rents **is not** sub-part F income.

Since $250,000 interest income represents 20% of Bahamian company Y's **total** gross income ($1,250,000), the "5% de minimis rule" cannot be relied upon. **Here,** the $250,000 would have to be included as sub-part F income and reported to the IRS.

> The IRS refer to **Sub-part F income, Foreign Base Company Income**, and **Foreign Personal Holding Company Incomes** by the same name. They are interchangeable.

Example #4: In 1990 Bahamian Company Y has $760,000 in interest income from Barclay's bank in the Bahamas. It takes in $25,000,000 in rents from its condominiums.

---

15. See IRC 954(a)(3)(A) for the **De Minimis Rule.** Added by the *Tax Reform Act of 1986*.

Exploit the "De Minimis Rule" & beat the IRS at their own game

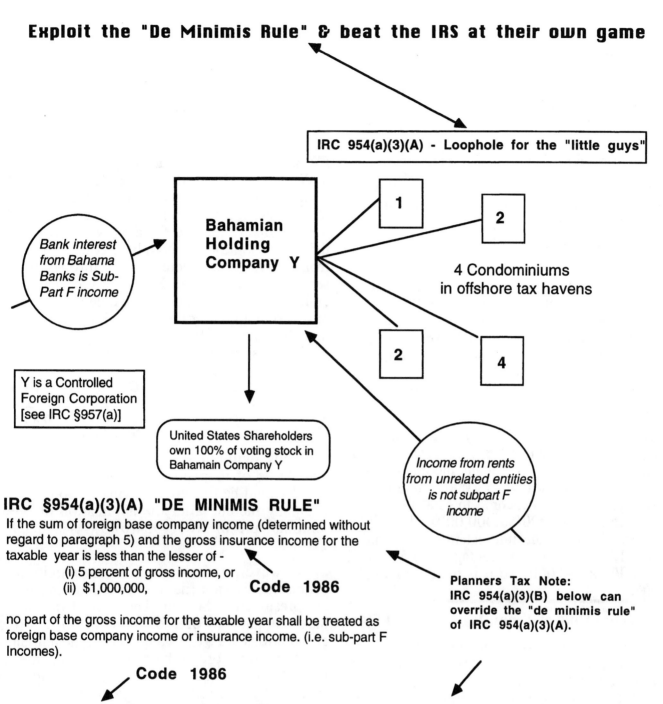

IRC 954(a)(3)(A) - Loophole for the "little guys"

Bank interest from Bahama Banks is Sub-Part F income

Bahamian Holding Company Y

1

2

2

4

4 Condominiums in offshore tax havens

Y is a Controlled Foreign Corporation [see IRC §957(a)]

United States Shareholders own 100% of voting stock in Bahamain Company Y

Income from rents from unrelated entities is not subpart F income

IRC §954(a)(3)(A) "DE MINIMIS RULE"

If the sum of foreign base company income (determined without regard to paragraph 5) and the gross insurance income for the taxable year is less than the lesser of -

  (i) 5 percent of gross income, or

  (ii) $1,000,000, **Code 1986**

no part of the gross income for the taxable year shall be treated as foreign base company income or insurance income. (i.e. sub-part F Incomes).

Code 1986

Planners Tax Note:
IRC 954(a)(3)(B) below can override the "de minimis rule" of IRC 954(a)(3)(A).

IRC 954(a)(3)(B) FOREIGN BASE COMPANY AND INSURANCE INCOME IN EXCESS OF 70 PERCENT OF GROSS INCOME - If the sum of the foreign base company income (determined without regard to paragraph 5) and the gross insurance for the taxable year exceeds 70 percent of gross income, the entire gross income for the taxable year shall, subject to the provisions of (4) and (5) be treated as foreign base company income or insurance income (whichever is appropriate).

Committee on Ways and Means (House of Representatives) said this in P.L. 99-515
"Under the conference agreement, none of a CFC's gross income for a taxable year is treated as foreign base company income (another name for sub-part F) or tax haven insurance income if the sum of the corporation's gross foreign base company and gross tax haven insurance income for the year is less than the lesser of 5% of its gross income, or $1 million." - from Tax Management, Inc. (12/19/89)

Because Y's **sub-part F** income ($760,000) does not exceed 5% of all its gross income ($25,760,000) for 1990, none of Y's income will be categorized Sub-part F income. The $760,000 in interest income can be accumulated offshore tax free. Y's sub-part F income is 3% of total gross income and that's less than $1,000,000.

Marshall J. Langer and Rufus Thulen Rhoades translate the 5% de minimis rule in their book *Income Taxation of Foreign Related Transactions* (pg 3-88) and provide this example:

EXAMPLE #1: Robert Rho, a California resident, owns all the stock Rho Pacific S.A., a Panama corporation. Rho Pacific generates $8 million of gross income from home sales and $350,000 from interest earned on installment paper taken from customers. In 1989, Rho Pacific earns $12 million in gross income and its interest doubles to $700,000.

The result is that the interest even though it is FPHC income earned in 1988 is disregarded - that is, it is not foreign base company income because the number is less than $1,000,000 and the percentage of interest income to total income is 4.2% (i.e., $350,000/$8,000,000). In 1989, however, although the interest income remains below $1,000,000, the percentage is 5.5% (i.e., $700,000/$12,000,000), so it is treated as FPHC income.

Anti-Abuse Rule of Temp.Regs. §1.954-1T(4)

To prevent you from using two or more foreign corporations to keep your sub-part F incomes below the $1,000,000 threshold and below the 5% of gross income limitation, and to prevent you from spreading-out your foreign base company incomes to avoid the 70% **full inclusion rule** of IRC §954(a)(3)(B), the Temp. Regs. provide an anti-abuse rule that <u>aggregates</u> the incomes of all your offshore companies so as to treat them as income from a single corporation.

The Treasury will presume that two or more controlled foreign corporations have been organized, acquired or maintained to avoid the effect of the de minimis and full inclusion requirements if the corporations are related to each other through another **corporation,** a **partnership**, or a corporate **branch**. See T.Reg. §1.954-1T4(iii).

The Treasury illustrates the **anti-abuse rule** with this example:

Example: P is the sole United States shareholder of three controlled foreign corporations CFC1, CFC2 and CFC3. The Three CFC are partners in FP, a foreign entity classified as a partnership under IRC §7701(a)(2) and §301.7701-3 of the regulations. For their current taxable years each of the CFCs gets all its income other than foreign base company income from activities conducted through FP, and its foreign base company income from activities conducted jointly through FP and separately without FP. Based on the facts in the table below, for the current taxable years, foreign base company income derived by each CFC, including income derived from FP, is less than 5% of the gross income of each CFC and less than $1,000,000.

	CFC1	CFC2	CFC3
Gross income..	$4,000,000	$8,000,000	$12,000,000
5% of gross income..	$200,000	400,000	$600,000
FBHC income....	$199,000	$398,000	$597,000

Thus, without the application of the anti-abuse rule of this subparagraph, each CFC 1, 2 and 3 would be treated as having no foreign base company income after the application of the de minimis rule of IRC §954(b)(3)(A) and §954-1T(b)(1).

However, under these facts the requirements of this subdivision [i.e. (i) of the anti-abuse rule] are presumed to be met. The sum of the foreign base company income of the controlled foreign corporations are **$1,194,000.** Thus, the amount of adjusted gross foreign base company income will not be less than the amount of gross foreign base income by reason of the de minimis rule of Section 954(b)(3)(A) and this paragraph (b).

The Treasury's Temp. T.Regs. §1.954-1T(4) look through business entities such as partnerships corporations or corporate branches, and then consolidate their incomes for purposes of the **de minimis rule exemption**. Notably left-out are foreign trusts. Under the current rules, use of a foreign trust to hold and accrue sub-part F passive type investment incomes, to allow a controlled foreign corporation to meet the requirements for the 5% de minimis rule exemption or circumvent the 70% full inclusion rule is not forbidden. The likelihood that foreign trusts will be included with other foreign entities when the Temporary Regs. are finalized remains a possibility however.

Comments & Conclusions

We have briefly reviewed a loophole in our U.S. tax **Code [1986]** that actually confers a tax exemption up to $1,000,000 to U.S. taxpayers of offshore companies. However, exploiting the *de minimis tax haven rule* (This phrase was coined by *Commerce Clearing House's* tax writers), may not always insulate you from the other IRS rules and taxes that a foreign company might incur under other sections of the Code.

Under IRC §552, if five or fewer U.S. shareholders own more than 50% of a foreign corporation's voting or value stock they must include any *Undistributed Foreign Personal Holding Company Income* on their U.S. income tax returns.

For these reasons, it is advisable that U.S. taxpayers venturing offshore use a plan similar to the one depicted on page #47 as a first line of defense, then build around it.

Highlights of President Clinton's Revenue Reconciliation Act of 1993

The just-passed Revenue Reconciliation Act of 1993 (the Act) raises taxes across the board for U.S. taxpayers. Under prior law there were three statutory tax rates for individuals - 15%, 28% and 31%. The top statutory rate of 31% was effective for taxable income (i.e., income after all allowable deductions) exceeding the following amounts:

- $53,500 (single)
- $76,400 (head of household)
- $89,150 (married filing jointly)
- $44,575 (married filing separately)

Long term capital gains were taxes at a maximum rate of 28%.

The new Revenue Reconciliation Act of 1993 adds two new tax brackets. A fourth bracket of 36% applies to taxable income exceeding the following amounts:

- $115,000 (single)
- $127,500 (head of household)
- $140,000 (married filing jointly)
- $70,000 (married filing separately)

In addition, a 10% surtax applies to certain high income taxpayers. The new surtax is computed by applying a 39.6% rate (i.e., a 5th

bracket) to taxable income over the following amounts:

- $250,000 (single)
- $125,000 (married filing separately)

Long term capital gains continue to be subject to a maximum rate of 28%.

Example: George Steinbrenner is the president of a Florida shipbuilding company and also the president of the New York Yankees. George is married but files a separate tax return. In 1993, George is paid a salary of $125,000 by the Florida shipbuilder, and $875,000 by the New York Yankees.

Assuming Mr. Steinbrenner has few substantial business expenses, Mr. Steinbrenner will pay $346,500 in Federal income taxes on his $875,000 Yankee salary. On his first $125,000 in income, Mr. Steinbrenner will pay about $30,000 in federal income taxes.

While Florida (and Miami) has no income taxes, New York State and New York City both will expect George to pay income taxes there on his N.Y. Yankee salary. New York City and N.Y. State's combined income tax is approximately 11%. George Steinbrenner and anyone with a taxable salary of $1,000,000 could be paying almost 50% in income taxes this year. The tax rates above are retroactive for 1993, which means they apply from January 1, 1993.

Provisions Affecting Offshore Operations and Multinational Corporations

Generally, under prior law, the Code did not tax income earned by a foreign corporation until the earnings were repatriated to the United States as a dividend. An exception was made if a U.S. person owned 10% or more of the *voting stock* (defining him as a *U.S. shareholder)* in a *Controlled Foreign Corporation* (CFC). Such a *U.S. shareholder* was required to put his pro-rata share of the CFC's *sub-part F* income (i.e., passive incomes, such as capital gains, interests and dividends) on his tax return. Other income that was not sub-part F income was not subject to U.S. taxes and could be accumulated offshore - in many cases tax free.

New CFC Rules [16.]

The new tax law does not change the definition of *U.S. Shareholder* or *Controlled Foreign Corporation*. Consequently, under the new changes you would need to own 10% or more of the voting stock in a CFC for the new changes to take effect.

The new law calls for 10% voting stock shareholders in CFCs to include in income currently their pro rata share of a specified portion of the CFC's current and accumulated earnings. The provision would generally apply to a CFC holding passive assets representing 25% or more of the total assets of the CFC. The portion of the current and accumulated earnings subject to the inclusion would be the lesser of (1) total current and accumulated earnings and profits accumulated in tax years beginning after September 30, 1993, or (2) the amount of the excess passive assets.

The amount of excess passive assets would equal the amount by which the average amount of passive assets held by a CFC as of the close of each year exceeds 25% of the average of the CFCs total assets held at the end of each quarter. For this purpose, passive assets would be defined as under PFIC rules (Passive Foreign Investment Companies - see IRC §1291). Includible earnings would be adjusted to account for earnings previously taxed. [17.]

Look thru rules for CFC's were added so you can't use a chain of foreign CFCs to dilute your passive offshore holdings.

If a CFC group has excess passive assets, the aggregate excess passive asset amount will be allocated among the CFCs in the CFC group on the basis of each CFC's related earnings. A CFC group means one or more chains of CFCs connected through stock ownership of a top-tier CFC if:

• The top-tier CFC owns directly more than 50% (by vote or value) of the stock of at least one of the other CFC's; and

• More than 50% (by vote or value) of the stock of each of the CFC's (other than the top-tier) is owned directly or indirectly by one or more other members of the group.

Editor's comments and advice: The new tax law was aimed mainly at the larger multinational corporations that have wholly owned subsidiaries in foreign countries. If you don't own more than 10% of the voting stock in the offshore company, the changes mentioned here do not apply to you. Also, take notice that the CFC and PFIC rules do not apply to foreign trusts. In some cases, passive assets could be owned by a foreign trust and avoid application of the new rules.

New PFIC provision

Certain leased property will be treated as assets held by a foreign corporation for purposes of the PFIC (Passive Foreign Investment Company) asset test. The rule will apply to tangible personal property with respect to which the foreign corporation is the lessee under a lease with a term of at least 12 months.

Suggested Readings

The entire U.S. Internal Revenue Code and Treasury Regulations can be found in any good public or college law library. These books can be purchased in a condensed form at a reasonable price (considering they're over 10,000 pages in length) from the following publishers.

References:

Federal Income Tax Regulations (4 volumes set @ $30), and **Internal Revenue Code of 1986** (2 book set costs about $19.95).

Commerce Clearing House or Prentice-Hall,
4025 W. Peterson Ave. Englewood
Chicago, Illinois 60646 Cliffs, NJ 07632

"A Complete Guide to the Omnibus Budget Reconciliation Act of 1990"

Commerce Clearing House
4025 W. Peterson Ave.
Chicago, Illinois 60646

---

16. See new IRC §956A
17. .From "Guide to the NEW TAX LAW", by Ernst & Young (1993)

CHAPTER 3 • The Pentapus

Professor Harvey Dale of the New York School of Law (also Counsel to Cadwalader, Wickersham & Taft - NYC, Washington D.C., Palm Beach) is credited with coining the term "Pentapus". The "Pentapus" represents 5 sections of the Internal Revenue Code that cause the most problems for international tax planners. We discussed one arm of the tentacles of the pentapus in Chapter 2 (Controlled Foreign Corporations). In this chapter we will take a closer look at the others.

The five arms of the pentapus [or tentacles, as Professor Dale chooses to call them] are as follows:

1. A **Personal Holding Company** described under Code-Section §541-47;
2. A **Foreign Personal Holding Company** under Code §551-58;
3. A **Controlled Foreign Corporation** under Code §951-64;
4. **Foreign Investment Company** under Codes §1246-47;
5. A company subject to the **accumulated earnings tax** under Code-Section §531-37.

When the PFIC were introduced with the *Tax Reform Act of 1986*, Professor Dale and Roy Albert Powell (also with Cadwalader, Wickersham and Taft) indicated that with a sixth tentacle, the term pentapus should become "sexapus". After consulting with a classical scholar, Dale determined that the term should be either "hexapus" (the Greek) or "sexipede" (the Latin). Stanley I. Rubenfeld (Sherman & Sterling) in a paper to the Tax Club opted for sexapus. Other legal writers have developed their own terms - "hexapede", "novepede" (includes three more tentacles - 30% withholding tax; effectively connected income; and the new branch profits tax).

Foreign Personal Holding Company

The **Foreign Personal Holding Company** (FPHC) provisions were enacted by Congress in 1937 to curb the abusive use of foreign corporations for strictly tax avoidance purposes. International tax practitioners always try to steer clear of this menacing section of law because if the FPHC provisions apply the United States shareholders of the company will be taxable on their pro-rated share of the undistributed FPHC income.

For purposes of Section §552(a) a **Foreign Personal Holding Company** is any foreign corporation whose gross income consists of dividends, interests, royalties, annuities, gains from the sale of stock or securities, certain rents, and moneys received under personal service contracts in such amounts so as to exceed **60%** of all company earnings, and whose shares are held by no fewer than **5 U.S. Individuals** who together hold **more than 50%** of either the value or voting stock outstanding. For the FPHC provisions to apply, both the **gross income test** (IRC §552(a)1) and the **stock ownership test** (IRC §552(a)(2) must be breached. [1]

The FPHC tax seldom applies because planners take whatever remedy they have at their disposal to avoid it. For example, a foreign corporation could move its FPHC assets (stocks, bonds and other FPHC items) into a foreign trust. This would insulate the foreign company from the FPHC status by reducing its FPHC income to a safe level.

Another perfectly legal way to avoid the FPHC problem is to distribute as a dividend the **undistributed FPHC income** to the U.S. shareholders. IRC §561 (a) allows the foreign corporation to deduct the dividends paid during the taxable year when computing its FPHC income.

Still, another avenue available to avoid FPHC status by satisfying the **stock ownership** tests of IRC §552(a)(2).

Stock Ownership Tests

For a foreign corporation to be considered a FPHC more than 50% of either its voting power or value of its outstanding stock must be owned, directly or indirectly, by no more than 5 individual U.S. citizens or residents (called the **United States Group** by the Code).

---

1. The term "U.S. Individuals" is misleading because all types of U.S. shareholders (including domestic corporations, partnerships, estates, and trusts) are taken into account when making the determination whether a foreign company is a FPHC.

IRC §554(a) provides that shares can be attributed to an individual from his family, thus a U.S. shareholder can constructively own more shares then he actually owns. For example:

Example #1: If U.S. individual A owns 6% of Cayman corporation X directly, and his brother, sister, wife, partner own an additional 3% each, A constructively owns 18% of Cayman company X. Moreover, if A owned 100% of domestic corporation D, which in turn owned 10% of Cayman company X, A would be considered to own a total of 28% of Cayman company X for purposes of determining whether X was a FPHC.

Under IRC §554(a)(5) stock ownership rules stock can be attributed more than one time.

Example #2: A's wife in the above example would be considered to own 13% of Cayman company X because of A's indirect ownership of Cayman company X through domestic corporation D. However, if A's wife was considered to own the 10% of Cayman company X, A could not be made to own any stock in Cayman company X, as the rules of constructive ownership don't apply to make the stock count more than once.

In addition, stock in Cayman company X can be attributed to A, A's wife, brother, or partner, depending on which attribution will produce the greater concentration of stock ownership. In the above example, A would be attributed the 10% stock in Cayman company X held by domestic corporation D, and A's wife would be attributed none of the Cayman stock through domestic company D. [2]

Gross Income Test

When a foreign corporation's gross income consists of at least 60% of passive type incomes (interest, dividends, capital gains, royalties), it is said that the company has FPHC income. When arriving at the 60% threshold, no distinction is made between foreign source income and U.S. source income. Both types are counted when adding up the taxable amount to be included in the gross income of the U.S. shareholder(s).

It should be pointed out, the U.S. shareholder is taxable on the FPHC income of a foreign corporation that is undistributed to him, thus the shareholder pays a current tax, even though he or she has not received the income from the FPHC, and later may be taxed again on the dividends withdrawn and paid by the foreign company. This is double taxation of profits at its zenith.

Undistributed FPHC Income

Tax relief from the FPHC penalty tax can be gotten by distributing as a dividend the **undistributed FPHC income** to the U.S. shareholders. Unfortunately, if your goal is to accumulate profits offshore in a no-tax haven, you'll not want to distribute your company profits every year.

Personal Holding Companies (IRC §541)

Another *tentacle of the pentapus* similar to the Foreign Personal Holding Company statute is the **Personal Holding Company** provision. Under IRC §542(a) a corporation is a personal holding company if at any time during the last half of the taxable year more than 50% in value of its outstanding stock is owned, directly or indirectly, by no more than 5 individuals. In addition, at least 60% of the corporation's "adjusted ordinary gross income" must consist of passive investment income (dividends, interests).

When computing the personal holding company's taxable income several adjustments are allowed. Net long term capital gains are excluded, the "regular income tax paid" is deducted, and the 80% dividends-received deduction is added back.

The FPHC tax applies to the U.S. shareholders of the foreign company, The personal holding company tax is levied against the foreign company itself.

The **PHC** tax under President Clinton's new *Revenue Reconciliation Act of 1993* is 39.8%. It is imposed on the **undistributed personal holding company income**. The tax applies to foreign and domestic companies alike, and is in addition to the regular corporate tax.

Banks, insurance companies, foreign personal holding companies and passive foreign investment companies are not subject to the PHC tax.

---

2. Theodore Ness and Eugene Vogel, **Closely Held Corporations**, pg. 6-13.

Side-step the PHC & FPHC Problems Simultaneously

Investors can purge the PHC and the FPHC problems from an offshore plan by using a two tier structure. Such methods are unquestionably permissible under the law. See chart on page 47.

Example #3: Suppose U.S. shareholder **T** owns 29% of the total outstanding single class of stock of foreign corporation **B**. The remaining 71% of B is owned by foreign trust **C**. Under the constructive ownership rules for both **personal holding companies** and **foreign personal holding companies**, U.S. shareholder T will own no more than 49.59% of the stock in offshore company B. T owns 29% of B directly, and 20.59% of **B** indirectly through attribution from foreign trust **C**.

Since fewer than 5 U.S. individuals do not own "more than 50%" of all the outstanding value and voting shares in foreign corporation B, neither the PHC nor the FPHC tax will be applicable, assuming foreign trust C does not sell any of the shares in B.

Accumulate Earnings Tax

Another arm of the Pentapus is the **Accumulated Earnings Tax (AET)** of IRC §532(a). This tax is applicable to foreign corporations (but not foreign trusts) which were formed for avoiding tax with respect to its shareholders by allowing earnings and profits to **accumulate,** instead of being distributed as a taxable **dividend** to the shareholders. The **AET** applies to domestic and foreign corporations, but only income that has a U.S. source is considered when determining the tax. The tax under President Clinton's new *Revenue Reconciliation Act of 1993* is 39.8%. The AET can be avoided if the foreign corporation passes a dividend equal to the accumulated taxable income.

---

3. *"Doing Business in the United States"* by Price Waterhouse, pg 165; see T.Regs. §541-1(b) too.

The Foreign Investment Company Tentacle

Like the Controlled Foreign Corporation legislation, the **foreign investment company** provisions were enacted with the Revenue Act of 1962 during the Kennedy Administration. Its aim was to send more tax dollars to the U.S. treasury, in this case at the expense of the shareholders by restricting the use of foreign corporations as strictly passive investment vehicles. By converting long term capital gains on the sale of foreign investment company stock into ordinary income, taxable at a higher tax rate, the U.S. shareholder was penalized for investing outside the United States.

It's ironic but the **Tax Reform Act of 1986** nullified the effectiveness of the Foreign Investment Company (FIC) legislation because for years after July 1, 1987 U.S. capital gains would be taxed as ordinary income anyway. To make up for this unintended windfall to the taxpayer, Congress legislated new rules to augment the suddenly ineffective FIC provisions. This new legislation is the **Passive Foreign Investment Company** provisions of IRC §1291 to 1297.

It should be pointed out that the Bush Administration is seeking to restore a lower capital gains tax rate which, if passed by Congress and codified into law, would bring the dormant **FIC** provisions back to life. The FIC provisions of IRC §1246 were never repealed, and should a new system for taxing capital gains be enacted, it is highly probable they will be a force for offshore operations to reckon with. We'll will skip over the FIC rules, and discuss the more important "new" rules for **Passive Foreign Investment Companies** (PFICs).

Passive Foreign Investment Companies (PFICs)

Under current U.S. tax law, capital gains (except for certain real estate gains on USRPIs described under IRC §897) of a nonresident alien company, trust or individual are exempted from U.S. tax under IRC §881 and IRC §871. Thus, the stock and bond capital gains of foreign mutual funds often go 100% tax free.

To discourage U.S. citizens from investing in offshore mutual funds that generate passive

Avoiding Passive Foreign Investment Company status

Bahamian Trust Z

1. Foreign trusts (that have no U.S. beneficiaries) are useful for avoiding the PFIC, CFC, PHC, and FPHC provisions. Only a foreign company can be classified a PFIC or CFC, or FPHC.
2. If trust Z holds $500,000 in U.S. interest and dividend bearing instruments, Company Y will have no PFIC passive investment income or assets accruing into it. See example #5 and #6 on page 67.
3. A management fee of $10,000 paid to Company Y would not produce passive income for Company Y. If Company Y's only income was this $10,000 fee, Y would not be a PFIC because less than the 50% of its assets and less than 75% of its income would be from passive investments.

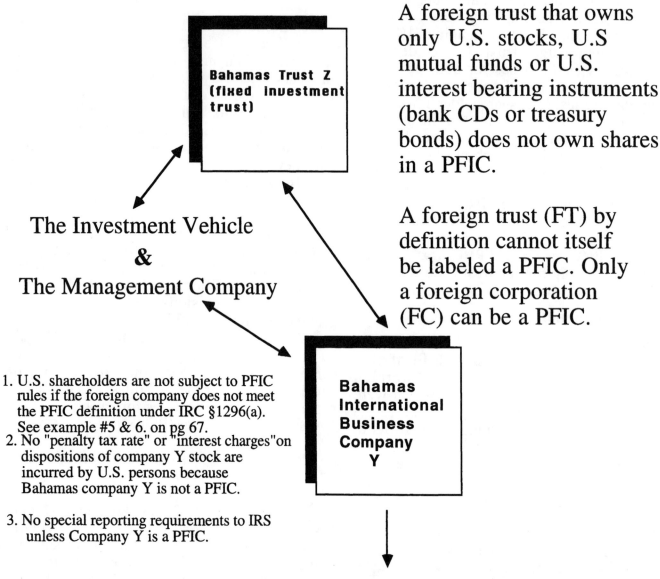

Bahamas Trust Z (fixed investment trust)

A foreign trust that owns only U.S. stocks, U.S mutual funds or U.S. interest bearing instruments (bank CDs or treasury bonds) does not own shares in a PFIC.

The Investment Vehicle
&
The Management Company

A foreign trust (FT) by definition cannot itself be labeled a PFIC. Only a foreign corporation (FC) can be a PFIC.

Bahamas International Business Company Y

1. U.S. shareholders are not subject to PFIC rules if the foreign company does not meet the PFIC definition under IRC §1296(a). See example #5 & 6. on pg 67.
2. No "penalty tax rate" or "interest charges" on dispositions of company Y stock are incurred by U.S. persons because Bahamas company Y is not a PFIC.

3. No special reporting requirements to IRS unless Company Y is a PFIC.

UNITED STATES SHAREHOLDER(S)

incomes (i.e., capital gains, interest, dividends, royalties), yet pay little or no taxes in the host country where they are organized (effectively deferring taxes for their shareholders until the profits are distributed), Congress enacted the PFIC provisions.

The **Tax Reform Act of 1986** added new Code-sections §1291 thru §1297 for PFICs. Without proper planning the tax problems brought about by these new tax laws are nothing less than diabolical.

With the removal of the favorable tax treatment for long term capital gains by the **TRA of 1986**, foreign investment companies would be doubly attractive to the U.S. investor, because the U.S. investor could defer his Federal income tax liability indefinitely by simply choosing a foreign fund or unit trust over a comparable domestic U.S. mutual fund.

Investment companies incorporated in places like the Cayman Islands, the Channel Islands and Bermuda can accumulate their profits offshore tax free for their foreign investors, deferring the shareholder's tax liability until the year in which the shares are disposed of at a profit.

Example #1: U.S. individual **X** invests $100,000 in Channel Island Unit Trust **Y** in 1981. In June of 1985, **X** sells the units of Channel Island Unit Trust **Y** through his stockbroker for $200,000. X realizes a $100,000 long term capital gain, and pays federal income taxes on 40% ($40,000) of the $100,000 gain, because 60% of the gain was exempt from tax under **pre-1986 Tax Reform Act tax** law. For the 4 years U.S. individual X held onto his investment, **X** did not have had to pay **any** federal income taxes**,** provided no dividends were distributed by the Channel Island Fund.

Since the IRS cannot tax the profits of a foreign investment company domiciled in foreign countries like the Channel Islands, the Caymans, Bermuda or the Bahamas, because the IRS's jurisdiction is limited to entities organized within the United States, offshore foreign funds like Channel Island Unit Trust **Y** were paying little or no taxes to the U.S. Treasury. [4.]

Passive Foreign Investment Companies - Defined

Not all offshore companies organized in tax havens will be PFICs. A foreign corporation is a PFIC only if 75% or more of its gross income for the tax year is **passive income**, or at least 50% of the average value of its assets produce or are held for the production of passive income. **Passive Income** is defined under IRC §904(d)(2)(A) and includes dividends, interests, passive rents (but not rents from unrelated parties), royalties, annuities, gains from the disposition of stocks and bonds, commodity trading gains, and currency gains. **Passive income** does not include manufacturing profits, most service related incomes, and rents from unrelated parties. [5.]

Example #1A: Jill, a U.S. citizen, acquires 50 shares of a Bahamian luxury hotel operator **Z** for $100,000 in 1988. 80% of Bahamian company **Z's** assets are from rents received from tourists visiting the island. 20% of Z's assets are invested in the U.S. stock markets. In 1988 90% of Bahamian company Z's earnings came from the operation of its Bahamian hotels, and 10% came from its investments in the U.S. stock markets. Since Z i**s not** by definition a PFIC, Jill does not hold shares in a PFIC, and IRC §1291-97 does not apply to any sale she might make of Z stock. Moreover, Bahamian company Z can sell it's U.S. stocks **free** of all capital gains taxes.

Furthermore, all Z's profits from the operation of its hotels **plus** any gain realized on its investments in the U.S. stock markets will not be taxed by the Bahamian government, as the Bahamas have no corporate income taxes.

In 1999, **50%** of Bahamian company Z's assets and earnings come from the operation of its hotels, and 50% of its assets and earnings come from **passive** investments in U.S. stocks and bank accounts. Jill sells her 50 shares for $500,000. Her $400,000 capital gain will be taxed just like any other capital gain she might have in 1999, as Bahamian company **Z** is still not a PFIC by definition.

---

interests to their shareholders annually or force the fund to pay tax on these profits if retains. U.S. Investment Companies cannot defer taxes for their shareholders, as can a Cayman or Bermuda or Channel Island fund, where no taxes are levied on the profits or accumulations by the host foreign governments.
5. See IRC 954(c)

---

4. U.S. tax laws force domestic investment companies and mutual funds to pass on their capital gains, dividends and

Note, over the 11 year period Bahamian company Z has managed to **accumulate** its profits offshore **tax free** for Jill. The U.S. does not penalize Jill for investing in a non-PFIC.

Under the post **TRA '86** rules, the gain recognized by the U.S. shareholder on the disposition of PFIC stock, or on the receipt of an "excess distribution" (i.e., dividends) from a PFIC, is considered earned pro-rata over the U.S. shareholder's holding period and is treated as ordinary income and taxed at the taxpayer's **highest rate of tax** applicable to the tax year which it is allocated. This **super tax** is then increased by an *interest charge* that is calculated by using Code-Section 6621 rates and methods for underpayments. While U.S. persons are subjected to these rules, a non-resident alien (NRA) or foreigner would not be.

Example #2: Jill, a U.S. citizen, owns 1,000 shares in a publicly traded Channel Island (CI) investment company (called a Unit Trust), which is classified as a PFIC on January 1, 1987. If Jill purchased the CI units on December 31, 1984 for $10,000 and disposed of them on December 31, 1989 for $20,000, the $10,000 gain would be **allocated** ratably ($2,000 apiece) over Jill's 5 year holding period. Under the rules, the amounts allocated to 1985 and 1986 will be treated as earned in 1989 (because the amounts are allocated to taxable years prior to January 1, 1987) and are not subject to the *interest charge*. The $2,000 allocated to 1987 will be taxed at 38.5% (the highest rate of tax in 1987), and the interest will be added onto the amount from April 15, 1988, the due date for 1987 tax return. The $2,000 allocated to 1988 will be taxed at 28% (the highest rate of tax for 1988), but an interest charge will be added onto that amount from April 15, 1989 to the date of the 1988 return. The $2,000 allocated to 1989, the year of sale, as well as the $4,000 allocated to 1985 and 1986 will be included in Jill's income for 1989 and taxed accordingly. [6.]

In effect, the new PFIC rules can wipe-out the tax deferral, including the accumulated profits, for the unwary investor.

---

6. This example was abridged from a memorandum by Richard J. Melnick, Esquire, writing for TAX MANAGEMENT INTERNATIONAL (1987).

Is there a way of legally avoid PFIC status?

Not all offshore companies will be able to meet the asset and income tests to avoid PFIC status, but there are still some avenues you can pursue to shield your company from the PFIC provisions.

Number one, only companies are vulnerable to the PFIC provisions of IRC §1291 thru §1297. A foreign trust, nonresident alien individual or foreign partnership, by their very nature, cannot be PFICs. [7.]

Secondly, only U.S. persons that are direct or indirect shareholders in a PFIC are subject to the PFIC rules. Foreign investors (including foreign companies, trust beneficiaries and partners) are exempt entirely.

U.S. treasury regulation §1.1292-1(b)(7) defines a shareholder as a U.S. person that directly owns stock of a PFIC, or that is an indirect shareholder.

U.S. treasury regulation §1.1292-1(b)(8) defines an indirect shareholder of a PFIC as a U.S. person that indirectly owns stock in a PFIC. A person indirectly owns stock if it is treated as owning stock of a corporation owned by another person (the actual owner).

Treasury regulations under §1.1292-1(b)(8)(ii) says... A person that owns 50% or more in value of the stock in a foreign corporation that is not a PFIC is considered to own a proportionate amount (by value) of any stock owned directly or indirectly by that foreign corporation.

Example #3: U.S. person A owns 60% of nonPFIC X organized in the Bahamas which owns 10% of PFIC Y (unit trust in the Channel Islands). U.S. person A is considered to own 6% (60% of 10%) of PFIC Y.

Example 3a: U.S. person A owns 49% of nonPFIC X organized in the Bahamas. Bahamas company X owns 10% of PFIC Y (unit trust in the Channel Islands). U.S. person A is considered

---

7. Similarly, the Controlled Foreign Corporation provisions of IRC §957 apply only to companies. By definition, foreign trusts and partnerships cannot be CFCs or PFICs, and are not subject to the provisions under IRC §951 thru 958 or IRC §1291 thru 1297.

to own none of PFIC Y because he doesn't own 50% or more of non-PFIC X.

Treasury regulation §1.1292-1(b)(8)(ii)(B) says "A person that directly or indirectly owns stock of a PFIC is considered to own a proportionate amount (by value) of any stock owned directly or indirectly by the PFIC." Thus, even if you own 2% of the stock in PFIC X, you will be considered to own a proportionate share of PFIC stock owned by PFIC X.

Example #4: U.S. person owns 2% of the stock in PFIC X which owns 50% of the stock in PFIC Y. U.S. person will be considered to own indirectly 1% (2% times 50%) of PFIC Y.

Note, the PFIC stock ownership rules apply only to determine the amount of PFIC stock directly or indirectly owned by a U.S. person. A foreign trust that holds PFIC stock on behalf of a foreign company would be considered to be holding that PFIC stock for the U.S. shareholder, the same as if it were a foreign corporation, but the foreign trust itself cannot (by definition) be a PFIC.

Example #5: U.S. person A owns 10% of PFIC X which is the beneficiary of foreign trust Z. Foreign trust Z's assets include $1,000,000 of a U.S. mutual funds traded on Wall Street + 10% of a PFIC Y (traded in the Channel Islands).

Using the PFIC attribution rules, U.S. person A is deemed to own a 1% interest (10% X 10%) in PFIC Y by reason of foreign trust Z's 10% ownership of PFIC Y.

In example #5 above, U.S. person A would not be deemed to own any of the $1,000,000 in U.S. mutual funds owned by the foreign trust Z for two reasons. First, the $1,000,000 in U.S. mutual funds is not an interest in a PFIC, and second, foreign trust Z cannot be a PFIC.

How to avoid PFIC status by holding a timely directors meeting

If the offshore company cannot meet the asset or income test to avoid being tagged a PFIC, you should ask the directors of the company to move the passive income producing assets into a foreign trust.

Example #6: On January 1, 1992, U.S. person A purchases 2% of Bahamian company X.

Bahamian X's only asset is $500,000 in U.S. stock. Bahamian company X is a PFIC by reason of its passive investments.

On July 2nd 1993, the directors of Bahamian company X hold a directors meeting and move the $500,000 U.S. stock account into Bahamian trust Y. After July 1993, Bahamian company X will no longer meet the PFIC asset test, thus the U.S. person will not be a shareholder in a PFIC.

The U.S. PFIC rules allow you one full year to avoid the PFIC problem, so don't wait too long to move vulnerable passive assets into a safe vehicle. Under Section §1297(b), "a corporation will not be treated as a PFIC during its start up year if it will not be a PFIC in either of the 1st 2 taxable years following the start-up year, even if the offshore company is a PFIC in the first year."

Subsection IRC §1296(c)

For purposes of determining whether a foreign corporation (**FC**) will be classified as a PFIC, IRC §1296(c) says if a FC owns at least 25% (in value) of the stock of another corporation, for purposes of determining whether such FC is a PFIC, such FC shall be treated as if it (1) held its **proportionate** share of the assets of such corporation, and (2) received directly its **proportionate** share of the income of such other corporation.

Example #7: Cayman company **X** owns 25% of Cayman company **Y**. All Y's earnings in 1988 amounting to $100,000 came from passive assets ($1,000,000 in offshore bank accounts). Cayman company X will be considered to own its **proportionate** share ($25,000) of Y's earnings, and 25% of Y's assets ($250,000 in bank accounts).

Note, if Cayman company **X** owns under 25% of the stock in **Y** (Y is a PFIC) it will not be considered to own any of Y's assets or earnings under IRC §1296(c).

Look-thru provisions for foreign trusts, nonresident alien individuals and foreign partnerships are provided only for purposes of determining how much PFIC stock the foreign trust or partnership holds on behalf of the U.S. person. No stock ownership rules exist that turn a foreign trust into a PFIC. See example #5 above.

IRC §1296(c) & 1297(a) stock attribution & look through rules

IRC §1297 (a) attribution rules apply to treat stock of a PFIC actually owned by a foreign corporation (or person) as owned by the U.S. person. For example, a U.S. person owning 50% of the stock in a non-PFIC foreign corporation which owns all the stock in a PFIC would be treated as owning 50% of the shares of the PFIC. If the U.S. person owns less than 50% of the stock of the non-PFIC, then the U.S. person would not be treated as owning any of the stock in a PFIC. If, on the other hand, U.S. person owned 10% of the stock in a PFIC which owned 100% of the stock in another PFIC, then the U.S. person would be treated as owning 10% of the 2nd PFIC too. Under the law, if shares in the 2nd PFIC are sold by the first PFIC, the U.S. investor would be liable to the **super tax** and the **interest charges**, as though he had held the stock in the 2nd PFIC himself.

Qualified Electing Fund (IRC §1295)

IRC §1295 provides the tax planner with an election under IRC §1295(b) that a PFIC can take that will relieve the U.S. stockholders from the unfavorable tax treatment (highest tax bracket + an interest charge) that apply to shareholdings in PFIC stock. IRC §1293 says every U.S. person who owns stock in a Qualified Electing Fund at any time during the taxable year of such fund shall include in gross income, 1) as ordinary income, his pro-rata share of the ordinary earnings of such fund, and 2) as long term capital gain, the pro-rata share of the net capital gain of such fund for the current taxable year.

Boiling it all down, tax practitioners after December 31, 1986 have only a few formats to follow as a recourse.

1) Form another **downstream** investment holding company (PFIC) in a treaty nation like Barbados or the Bahamas and use it as the investment vehicle to invest in U.S. treasuries, U.S. stocks, et cetera. Acquire the shares in this company.

2) Make the election under IRC §1295 and stop paying dividends, interests or royalties to the **Qualified Electing Fund**.

By using the **Qualified Electing Fund** as a **shell company** (to hold non-interest and dividend paying investments), no income will accrue to it, and no income will be present to for distribution to the U.S. shareholders. Earnings and profits can be accumulated and reinvested while taxes are deferred in a 2nd downstream holding company. The Tax Reform Act of 1986 even provides you with an exemption from the **Accumulated Earnings Tax** for such a downstream PFIC under IRC §532(b).

Assets of Offshore Mutual Funds managed by Sir John Templeton top US$20 Billion dollars.

John Templeton was once a U.S. citizen taxable on all his worldwide income. About 15 years ago, Mr. Templeton abandoned his U.S. citizenship in what has to be viewed as a tax move. Now, Templeton's estate (estimated by some to be as large as $1 billion - with most of it offshore) is free from U.S. estate taxes. Templeton recently sold his offshore fund empire to California based Franklin funds for an estimated $920,000,000.

Headquartered in Nassau in the Bahamas, John Templeton's mutual fund empire had grown to mammoth proportions. Worldwide assets under management increased 26% in 1989 to $20+ billion dollars. Templeton, Galbraith and Hansberger (the management company for the funds) boast 750,000 clients worldwide. Pre-tax profits for the management company rose 31% to $63,800,000. Much, if not all, of the profits earned by Templeton's management company are tax free. U.S. tax law does not tax foreign source management company earnings unless the offshore management company has an office in the U.S.

Templeton's U.S. source capital gains from trading in stocks, bonds or options *of a publicly traded* U.S. company are exempt from taxes, unless the offshore fund owns **more than 5%** of the outstanding stock of the U.S. company [(see IRC §897(c)(3)]. Templeton can engage a U.S. stockbroker (i.e., FAX machines, telephones) to facilitate his trades. These activities will not result in a U.S. tax liability for the funds. Templeton's management company is incorporated in the Cayman Islands.

There's no question that fees received from Templeton's **foreign clients** can be received in the Bahamas 100% tax free. What should be inspiring to all *ye humble souls and plutocrats* is that fees paid by his **U.S. clients** (or by their offshore companies) can probably be received in the Bahamas tax free too.

Whether the U.S. will tax the **personal service incomes** of a foreign corporation depends on several factors. Number one, if the foreign corporation has a U.S. office or operates through its agents or employees, it will be taxed the same as any domestic U.S. company "doing a trade or business within the United States". But, according to Boris Bittker and J. Eustice in *Federal Income Taxation of Corporations and Shareholders* .. .. "The source of income from the **performance of personal services** depends upon the place of performance of the services. If the foreign company does not have a U.S. office and performs the services outside the USA in the foreign country itself, the income will be considered **foreign source income,** even though it might be paid by a U.S. based entity or client." **Foreign source incomes** are not subject to the U.S. 30% withholding tax. Most **U.S. source incomes** are. [8., 9.]

IRS Revenue Rulings provide some guidance

Some Revenue Rulings dealing with the performance personal services are interesting, because revenue rulings are followed by the courts and the IRS investigators, and can be relied on by the U.S. taxpayer in a tax case. Note that in (25) the "broker's commissions" were considered to be from **U.S. sources**. A management fee for managing money in the Bahamas would be from **foreign sources,** since the services were performed strictly in the Bahamas. See Rev.Rul. 80-64 and (30) below.

(25) Services performed by agent - Nonresident alien commodity broker sent orders from foreign customers to his agent in U.S. for execution by other brokers through U.S. exchange. His commissions were **U.S. source**. His services were "personal" although performed by agent not by taxpayer himself. *Helvering v Boekman* (2 Cir;1939), 107 Fd2 388, 23 AFTR 890, rev'g 38 BTA 541

(30) Compensation in kind. - Foreign corp. operated sugar mill in Philippines, retained part of planters' sugar for its milling services and then sold it in the U.S. Sugar was **foreign-source income** - it was compensation for services outside U.S., not proceeds of property produced outside and sold in U.S. *Comm. V Hawaiian Philippines Co.* (9 Cir;1939), 100 F2d 988, 22 AFTR 378, cert den 5-22-39, aff'g 35 BTA 173. *Comm. V San Carlos Mining Co., Ltd.* (9 Cir;1933), 63 F2d 153, 12 AFTR 152, af'g 24 BTA 1132.

RevRul 60-55, 1960-1 CB 270: Foreign Corp. received commissions from U.S. corp. for promoting and securing purchase orders from foreign customers. Commissions were **foreign-source income** (not subject to 30% U.S. withholding tax, i.e., tax free) to extent reasonable allowance for services rendered.

Foreign Corp. had temporary war-time arrangement with U.S. co. to have its foreign customers send orders direct to U.S. co. that shipped goods direct to buyers FOB U.S., collected price and gave foreign corp. 20%. Commissions **were foreign** source **inco**me for sale activities abroad; situs of sales in U.S. not determinative although compensation was measured by amount of sales. *British Timkin, Ltd.* 12 TC 880.

(45) Continental shelf - Income of foreign corp. from exploratory drilling in outer continental shelf of U.S. is **income from U.S. sources.** *RevRul 80-64*, 1980-1 CB 158

---

8. See pg. 17.02.
9. See T.Regs. §861-4(a) for "US source of income" rules.

Comparing the Caribbean offshore financial centers

	Anguilla	Antigua	Bahamas	Barbados	Bermuda	BVI	Caymans	Netherlands Antilles	Panama	Turks & Caicos Islands
CORPORATE COSTS										
Incorporation	US$650	US$975	US$880	US$2,000	US$2,525	US$925	US$2,100	US$1,650	US$500	US$1,220
Annual - Registered Office	US$400	US$475	US$600	US$1,000	N.A.	US$350	US$1,070	X	US$300	US$500
- Incl Directors Fees	US$900	US$975	US$1,100	US$1,250	US$2,000	US$1,000	US$2,070	US$1,650	US$450	US$1,000
CORPORATE TAXES	None	None	None	2-1/2% to 1% for IBCs	None	None	None	2.4% to 3%	None	None
LAWS										
Exchange Control	No	Limited to local	Not for IBCs	Yes	Yes	No	No	No	No	No
Bank Secrecy	Yes	Yes	Yes	Yes	Yes	Yes	Yes	Yes	Yes	Yes
Forced Inheritance	No	Yes	Yes	No	Yes	No	Yes	No	No	Yes
Protection for Trusts	Yes	No	Yes	Yes	Yes	No	No	No trust law	No	No
Trust Perpetuity Law	No	Yes	Yes	No	No	Yes	Yes	No trust law	Yes	Yes
Company Mobility	No	Yes	Yes	Yes	Yes	Yes	Yes	Yes	Yes	Yes
Ownership disclosure	Yes	No	No	No	Yes	No	No	For banks	No	No
Annual Return required	Yes	Yes	No	No	Yes	No	No	No	No	No
Share Register available for public inspection	Yes	Yes	No	Yes	Yes	No	No	No	No	No
COMMUNICATIONS										
Air	Poor	Fair	Excel	Good	Excel	Fair	Excel	Good	Good	Fair
Mail	Fair	Fair	Excel	Good	Good	Good	Good	Good	Good	Fair
Telephone/Fax	Good	Fair	Excel	Good	Good	Good	Good	Fair	Good	Fair
SERVICES										
Accounting	Poor	Good	Good	Good	Good	Good	Good	Good	Good	Fair
Banking	Poor	Good	Good	Good	Good	Good	Good	Good	Good	Good
Legal	Fair	Good	Good	Good	Good	Good	Good	Good	Good	Good
Trust	None	Good	Good	Good	Good	Good	Good	Fair	NA	Good
Corporate	Good	Good	Good	Good	Good	Good	Good	Good	Good	Good
Insurance	Poor	Fair	Good	Fair	Good	Good	Good	Good	Good	Fair
Investor Protection	None	None	None	None	None	None	None	None	Fair	None
POLITICAL STATUS	BCC	Ind.	Ind.	Ind.	BCC	BCC	BCC	KoN	Ind. Republic	BCC

Source: International Money Marketing (March 1992)

BCC = British Crown Colony   Ind. = Independent   KoN = Kingdom of the Netherlands

CHAPTER 4 • Foreign Investment in the United States

According to the U.S. Department of Commerce, foreign direct investment in the United States reached a grand total of $261.9 billion by the end of 1987 while U.S. direct investment abroad reached a total of $308.8 billion. These statistics include only direct investments, i.e., holdings of 10% or more by a foreign investor, as contrasted with *"portfolio"* type investments and other assets. By way of comparison, total U.S. assets abroad rose by $96.4 billion in 1987, reaching a total of $1,167.8 billion at the end of 1987. Total foreign assets in the United States rose $195.4 billion (more than twice the USA's 1987 foreign investments), reaching a total of $1,536 billion. [1]

While the numbers reveal a rather sobering story, a recent IRS survey of some 12,000 foreign owned corporations operating inside America tells a much more intriguing if not inspiring tale. According to the IRS study, in the majority of cases these foreign owned U.S. companies are paying an effective tax rate of just 1% on their U.S. profits, while thousands are paying no tax at all. Moreover, the number of U.S. companies owned by foreign interests has been steadily on the rise, increasing from 6,000 in 1972 to 38,000 in 1983. [2]

According to the international accounting firm of Price Waterhouse **(PW),** through the end of 1987 the leaders in direct foreign investments in the United States were the U.K. ($76 billion); the Netherlands ($47 billion); Japan ($32 billion); Canada ($20 billion); W. Germany ($19 billion); Switzerland ($16 billion), France ($12 billion); and the Netherlands Antilles ($11 billion). The top three leaders for the period of 1986 to 1987 were the U.K. ($9 billion); Japan ($7 billion) and the Netherlands ($8.5 billion).

How foreign owned U.S. companies are structured so to reduce their U.S. income tax liability to near zero, while simultaneously exploiting various tax haven jurisdictions, will be the focus of our discussion.

Interest Stripping?

Knowledge is power. We've all heard that repeated to us since childhood. Several years ago, Price Waterhouse sent me a guide titled *Tax Planning for Acquisitions in the United States,* by Peter J. Hart, Vice Chairman - PW Tax Services. Price Waterhouse was and stil is one of the largest international accounting firm in the world with offices in 100 countries and territories. The PW guide superseded **Rev.Rul. 87-89** (back-to-back loans) and **Rev.Ruls. 84-152** and **84-153** (lending through Netherlands Antilles Finance Subsidiaries), so those rulings were taken into account when PW issued their tax planning guide.

The guide deals with the wide-spread practice of *interest stripping.* The guide's importance revolves around a handful of charts outlining various *schemes* a foreign investor might use to significantly lower his exposure to U.S. tax. Of particular interest are **PW**'s charts urging clients and staff to exploit: [3]

• the old **U.S.-Netherlands Income Tax Treaty** to avoid the 30% U.S. interest withholding taxes. *(a.k.a. interest stripping)*

• a Netherlands finance company to channel U.S. interest income offshore, while securing the interest deduction for the U.S. company, thus reducing the U.S. subsidiary's U.S. tax liability.

• a second non-Dutch parent (offshore) company to act as the ultimate receiver of the interest income since the Dutch do not impose any interest withholding taxes even when moneys are remitted to tax haven jurisdiction such as the Caymans or Bahamas. See chart on page #73.

While there have been a myriad of new tax changes made by the U.S. tax writers since 1989, interest stripping remains one of the biggest tax planning tools left for big international business.

---

1. From *Tax Planning for Acquisitions in the United States* by Price Waterhouse (January 1, 1989), pg. 2.
2. From *Have Powers will Travel - IRS,* **Offshore Advisor** (June, 1988), pg 16.

3. PW's **Information Guide**, *Tax Planning for Foreign Investment in US Real Property,* by Richard M. Hammer (Chairman of PW's International Tax Service Panel).

The Netherlands generally require a 0.0625 to 0.25 percentage point profit on the reloaning of borrowings where the finance subsidiary assumes no risk of currency fluctuation (e.g., where borrowings and reloanings are denominated in the same currency). The minimum interest rate will depend on the size of the loan and whether the funds have been borrowed from an unrelated party. The Netherlands subsidiary's interest expense can be offset against income in determining its taxable base under the Dutch tax system. - **PW Information Guide (1989)**

The question of adequate capitalization has been the subject of much litigation, and is determined on criteria other than solely the debt to equity ratio. The IRS will not issue a ruling as to whether or not a corporation is adequately capitalized. Under IRC §385 of the Code, the IRS is authorized to prescribe regulations for determining whether an interest in a corporation has the character of debt or equity. While proposed regulations were issued and later withdrawn, no regulations currently exist. **Source: Price Waterhouse (January 1989)**

Adequate Capitalization

Price Waterhouse warns against inadequate capitalizations of both the U.S. subsidiary and the Netherlands Finance company. If the Internal Revenue Service (IRS) determines that the corporation is inadequately or *thinly* capitalized, loans would be treated as being in substance share capital. Thus, interest payments would be nondeductible; both interest payments and repayments of principal would be regarded as dividends (subject to dividend withholding tax) to the extent the paying company had available earnings and profits. According to PW.. *Although the IRS **cannot** arbitrarily disregard the legal form of a transaction, there is sufficient case law to support the principle that **substance takes precedence over form** in certain circumstances. A cautious approach is therefore advisable.*

Some of the factors to be considered when judging whether debt will be treated as debt and not equity are:

1. Whether there is a **written** unconditional promise to pay on demand or on a specified date a certain sum of money, and to pay a **fixed rate of interest**.
2. Whether the debt is subordinate to other debts.
3. The ratio of debt to equity of the corporations. In this regard, debt-to-equity ratios of 1: 1, 2: 1 and 3: 1 have been safe harbors in the past. Although ratios as high as 9: 1 have been respected by the U.S. courts and IRS, it is not advisable that you structure your operations with this much debt.
4. Whether the debt is convertible into stock of the corporation. In this regard, the planner should refrain from issuing convertible stock.
5. The relationship between holdings of stock in the corporation and holdings of the interest in question.

To draw a clearer picture of what set-ups might be respected by the IRS, let's insert a few names and numbers to the reproduced PW chart that appears on page #73. For purposes of our illustration, the foreign parent company depicted in the PW chart will be a non-controlled [non **CFC** as defined under IRC §957(a)] Bahamian company. The U.S. subsidiary will be 100% owned by the U.S. parent company, consequently it can pay dividends to its parent 100% tax free. We will assume the financed U.S. subsidiary will reinvest the loan proceeds in either a hotel, an office building, a N.Y. **condo,** or an expansion manufacturing plant.

Example #1: Non-Controlled Bahamian company B capitalizes Netherlands Finance Company N with $1,000,000 cash (paid-in capital), in exchange for 100% of N's single class of stock. **N** subsequently borrows $3,000,000 from 4 foreign lenders (private trusts in Caymans, Bahamas, Isle of Man and Bermuda), agreeing to pay interest at a fixed rate of 10% **pa**. U.S. subsidiary **X** has a paid-in capital of $1,000,000. **X** borrows $3,000,000 from the Netherlands Finance Company **N**, agreeing to pay interest at a rate of 10.5% pa (or $315,000 annually). Debt-to-equity ratio = 3:1.

In 1990 X's taxable income (before deducting the interest expense on the foreign loan) from its U.S. operations amounts to $615,000. Absent the annual interest deduction, X's U.S. Federal income tax liability would amount to about $165,000. However, deducting the interest expenses reduces X's taxable income to $300,000. Thus, X will have only $300,000 in taxable income, and pay $76,750 in U.S. income taxes in 1990.

Netherlands Finance Company **N** will pay a flat 42% Dutch corporate income tax on its *"net"* interest income. Since N **pays** $300,000 in

Finance Company Established By Foreign Parent

(reproduced from charts provided by Price Waterhouse)

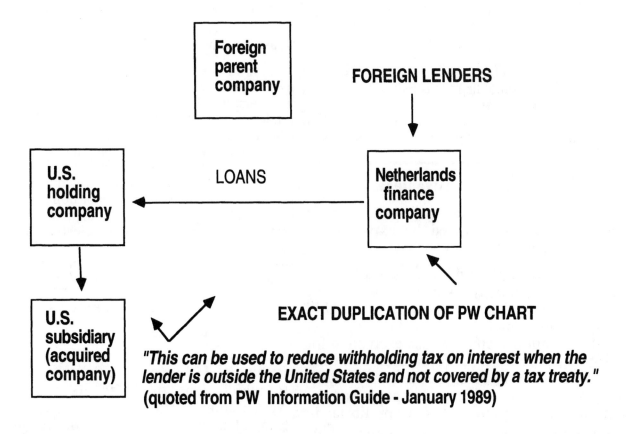

EXACT DUPLICATION OF PW CHART

"This can be used to reduce withholding tax on interest when the lender is outside the United States and not covered by a tax treaty."
(quoted from PW Information Guide - January 1989)

Method

1. The foreign parent company establishes a Netherlands corporation.
2. The capitalization must be adequate to meet the adequate capitalization concept and the foreign finance company must maintain "dominance and control".
3. The Netherlands company borrows the funds from foreign lenders and relends them in the same currency at .25% point profit.

Result

4. There are no US or Netherlands withholding taxes on any interest. However, with regard to similar (but not identical) structures, the Internal Revenue Service has taken the position that interest payments from US corporations to foreign finance company would not be "derived by" that company for purposes of qualifying for the reduced rate of (or exemption from) withholding tax under a treaty between the US and the jurisdiction in which the finance company is incorporated or resident.
5. The Netherlands Finance Company will be subject to Dutch tax at 42% rate on its "net" interest income.

In this statement Price Waterhouse is referring to Rev-Rul 84-152 & 84-153.

interest income. Since N pays $300,000 in interest to the offshore trusts, it can expense (and deduct) this amount from the $315,000 in interest income it receives from U.S. company X when computing its Netherlands corporate tax liability. N's net interest income of $15,000 will result in a Dutch corporate income tax of $6,200.

Under the **U.S.-Netherlands Income Tax Treaty** the 30% U.S. interest withholding tax is reduced to 0%. In addition, the Netherlands do not levy interest withholding taxes on Dutch companies even if paid to entities located in no-tax havens like the Bahamas, Bermuda or Cayman.

Other Benefits & Advantages

Aside from the tax relief detailed above, other benefits that can be secured by exploiting a Netherlands finance company include:

1. Under the U.S.-Netherlands income tax treaty if a Netherlands Company owns 10% or more of the *voting stock* of a U.S. subsidiary, the U.S. dividend withholding tax is reduced to 5%.
2. The Dutch allow a complete tax exemption for **dividend**s received from foreign or domestic subsidiary if *5% or more* of the subsidiary's stock is owned by the Dutch parent company, and the foreign subsidiary is subject to some profits tax in the country where it is incorporated. This exemption is called the **participation exemption**.

Article VII (Dividends) of the Netherlands-U.S. Tax Treaty

The following is **Article VII (Dividends)** of the old Netherlands-U.S. Tax Treaty, which was in force without amendments from January 1, 1947 to January 1992, when a newer Netherlands-U.S. Treaty came into effect. The **new** Netherlands-U.S. tax Treaty actually lowers the dividend withholding taxes (below) even further when certain criteria are met. See Chapter 13 for the lower new treaty rates.

(1) **Dividends** paid by a corporation of one of the Contracting States to a **resident or corporation** of the other Contracting State shall be taxed as follows in the former State:

(a) at a rate not exceeding 15% of the gross amount actually distributed; or

(b) at a rate not exceeding 5% of the gross amount actually distributed, if during the part of the paying corporation's taxable year which precedes the date of payment of the dividend and the whole of its prior year (if any), the **recipient corporation** owning at least 25% of the voting stock of the paying corporation, either alone or in combination with another (Netherlands) **corporation** of such other State (Netherlands), provided each recipient **corporation** owned at least 10% of such voting stock.

Editor's Point: Under "b" (above) the reduced 5% rate is available to **corporations** but not individuals or partnerships. The lowest rate available to individuals under the treaty is 15%. See "a" (above). Planners should further recognize that the Dutch **Participation Exemption** would be available on the U.S. dividends, making the U.S. dividends tax free in the hands of a Netherlands holding company. Dutch domestic tax law allows dividends from foreign or domestic companies to enjoy 100% tax exemption provided the Dutch recipient company owns a participation of at least **5%** of the other company's stock. Holland is positively a prominent tax haven for holding companies, though the Dutch corporate tax rate can reach **40%** for 1989.

Adverse IRS Revenue Rulings

In October, 1984 the IRS issued two rulings dealing with foreign finance companies. **Revenue Ruling 84-152** involved a Swiss parent company **P** which lent funds to its wholly owned Netherlands Antilles (NA) company, which in turn relent the funds to P's wholly owned U.S. corporation. In **Revenue Ruling 84-153** a wholly owned Netherlands Antilles subsidiary of the U.S. parent company **P** borrowed funds abroad from unrelated third parties and then relent the funds to P's wholly owned U.S. subsidiary. In each ruling the NA corporation charged interest on the funds at 1% point higher than its interest costs. While recognizing the validity of the separate NA corporations and their ability to demonstrate that the transactions may serve some business purpose, each ruling (by applying a corporate conduit theory) holds that the *"interest payments from the U.S. corporations to the NA companies are not 'derived by the Netherlands Antilles companies and are thus not exempt from U.S. tax under the applicable tax treaty."* - **PW**

Revenue Ruling 85-163

Both the legal theory and the policy behind Rev. Rulings 84-152 and 84-153 have been criticized, and the IRS, in **Revenue Ruling 85-163** announced that the 1984 rulings would **not** apply to interest payments on debt obligations issued before October 15, 1984. According to PW's international tax de*partment, "the extent to* *which the IRS may apply the theory of the 1984 rulings to similar transactions is unknown at this time."*

Editor's Note: It's a bit unfair (maybe even discriminatory) that U.S. tax laws should exempt all pre-October 15, 1984 transactions, then apply new restrictions to **post** October 15, 1984 transactions. Planners should note that Revenue Ruling 84-152 applies only when a foreign parent company owns stock in a U.S. subsidiary and the parent indirectly loans funds through an intermediary subsidiary.

Rev.Rul. 87-89 is the Latest IRS Attack on Back-to-Back Loans [4.]

Revenue Ruling 87-89 sets forth 3 factual situations in which the IRS may intervene and *"collapse"* **back-to-back loans** and tax the ultimate recipient if not treaty protected.

In the first situation a foreign parent company located in a nontreaty jurisdiction places $100X dollars on deposit at an unrelated bank located in a treaty country (like the Netherlands). The bank then lends $80X dollars to the parent's U.S. subsidiary under terms that allow the bank less than a 1% interest rate spread. The ruling states as fact that during the term of the loan the amount of the parent's deposits with the bank exceeds the outstanding loan balance, and further, that the interest rate charged by the bank would be different in the absence of the parent's deposit.

In the second example the situation is the same except the "deposit" and loan are made with a person that is not a bank.

In the third example, a **C F C** of a U.S. company makes the bank deposit, and the non-U.S. bank lends funds to a domestic U.S. parent company. However, both the bank and the CFC are located in the same treaty jurisdiction.

Rev.Rul. 87-89, which does not use the term *back-to-back loans,* scrutinizes whether the deposits and loans are *independent transactions;* that is whether the loan would have been made on the same terms irrespective of the deposit (LOC or guarantee). If so, the ruling says the transaction will be respected for U.S. tax purposes.

---

4. From an article by David Benson, Esquire (Practitioner's Viewpoint), <u>Tax Management International</u>, pg. 473.

In determining whether the transactions are "independent", if the IRS finds there is a contractual right on the part of the lender to offset the deposit against the liability on the loan, then the loan will be collapsed, because that would be presumptive evidence that the bank loan (or lender) would not have made the loan absent the deposit. Consequently, many collateralized loans would come under attack, whereas loans made without any parent company guarantee **deposit** would not be *collapsed* under Rev.Rul.87-89.

Situation #3 of Rev.Rul. 87-89 pertains to Controlled Foreign Corporations (CFC). In the case where the offshore company is a CFC, the loan would be treated as an equity investment under IRC §956 and no interest deduction would be permitted the U.S. subsidiary. Instead, repayments of interest would be treated as dividend distributions. It would be prudent to make certain the offshore lender is not a CFC.

Editor's Point: Rev.Ruling 87-89 would not apply to example #1 (above) because no collaterals or guarantees are involved in the transaction. In the case where the U.S. subsidiary pledges its own assets as collaterals with the Netherlands Finance company, Rev.Rul.87-89 would still not apply. Having the U.S. subsidiary pledge assets as collateral for the loan is good planning, as Rev.Rul.84-152 is only applicable where the foreign parent lender owns stock directly in the U.S. subsidiary and by-passes (treaty shops) using a third country tax treaty (i.e., Netherlands Antilles lending subsidiary). In the case where the Netherlands Finance Company owns all the stock in the U.S. subsidiary and maintains "control and dominance" over the outstanding loans, **Price Waterhouse's** guide (pg. #61) says Rev.Rul.84-152 does not apply.

Summary and Review

Recruiting offshore managers to run your finance company should be a high priority. Hurdling the *"substance over form"* rules will only succeed when adequate offshore staff is in place to run these operations. The aim of U.S. tax law is not only to raise revenue, but also to create jobs. Create a few jobs, and you reduce your risks. To summarize....

• Adequate capitalization of the U.S. subsidiary and Netherlands finance company is a must.

- Debt-to-equity ratios should be reasonable. No more than 4:1 is usually a safe harbor.
- If you must collateralize loans, have U.S. borrower pledge assets, not the foreign parent. Back-to-back guaranteed loans can be collapsed by the IRS.
- Netherlands finance company must retain *dominion and control* over U.S. borrowings. Holding shares (directly) in U.S. companies would be further evidence of dominion and control.
- The rate of interest charged U.S. borrower must be reasonable, within the guidelines provided under IRC §482.
- None of the offshore participants should be CFCs, as debt obligations could be treated as a direct investment in the U.S. company. i.e., if the Bahamian holding company is a CFC, then by the rules for **constructive ownership** the Netherlands Finance company would be a CFC too. See IRC §958(a) & (b). See IRC §957(a) & 956(a).

Tax planning for Foreign Investment in U.S. Real Property *by Richard M. Hammer*

Price Waterhouse's other guide, *Tax planning for Foreign Investment in U.S. Real Property* (December 1988) by Richard M. Hammer - Chairman of PW's International Tax Services Panel, offers other avenues offshore investors can exploit.

According to Price Waterhouse, the traditional tax planning aims for U.S. real property investments by foreign persons include: [5.]

- Avoidance of U.S. estate and gift taxes.
- minimization of annual U.S. tax liability.
- Repatriation of earnings as interest (or other deductible payments) while incurring the least amount of U.S., withholding tax possible.
- Repatriation of any remaining earnings in the form of dividends or tax free capital gains with the least amount of U.S. withholding tax or other taxes (this technique is oft called dividend stripping).
- minimization of worldwide tax liability.

Tax-favored financing after the TRA '86

1. *"Foreign corporations from certain favorable treaty countries such as the Netherlands, that would not be considered "treaty shopping" corporations, can take deductions for interest paid to shareholders while*

---

5. *Foreign Investment in US Real Property*, pg 3.

reducing or eliminating the 30% tax and, therefore, enjoy benefits formerly enjoyed by Antilles corporations.

2. If properly structured, even interest payments paid to investors in non treaty countries can be deducted and the U.S. withholding tax possibly avoided (or reduced) if it is paid by a U.S. corporation (which would hold U.S. real property) to a foreign finance company established by shareholders in a country that has a treaty with the U.S. that meets certain important criteria. Such a treaty should:

(a) Permit little or no U.S. withholding tax on interest flowing from the U.S. corporation to the foreign finance company; and

(b) Must not contain an article ("Limitation of Benefits" article) that prohibits treaty benefits to recipients whose stock is owned by residents of other treaty countries, or to corporations that pay out a large part of their income to Persons or entities from other countries.

A few of the older U.S. tax treaties, such as the Netherlands-U.S. treaty, meet this criteria." - Excerpt from **Price Waterhouse** Information Guide (pg 9).

New problems on the horizons

In conformity with the OECD Model, Dutch treaties are restricted in their personal scope to residents of one or both of the contracting states. Under Dutch tax law, a corporation is resident of *The Netherlands* if it is either effectively managed in *The Netherlands* or incorporated under Dutch law. Both types of resident companies qualify for application of Dutch tax treaties.

The U.S. and the Netherlands authorities are presently re-negotiating the U.S.-Netherlands tax treaty. While it may not be possible to predict with certainty what changes might be coming, recent U.S. Treasury treaty making policy has sought to interject **treaty shopping** provisions restricting the use of the treaty to **qualified residents:** Generally to meet the qualified resident requirement **(1)** more than 50% of the value of the corporation's stock must be owned by residents of such country and/or residents of the U.S., and less than 50% of the corporation's income is used to meet liabilities to persons who are not residents of such country and/or citizens or residents of the U.S. **Or (2)** The corporation's stock must be primarily and regularly traded on in an established exchange in its country of residency (This provision appears in the recently signed *Barbados-U.S. Income tax treaty*).

Companies that do not meet either of the above requirements will not be permitted the treaty benefits unless the treaty provides for an exemption under another article.

According to the *Wall Street Journal (6-27-89)*, the leading publisher in the Netherlands, **Verenigde Nederlandse Utgeversbedrijven,** purchased 3 small U.S. database companies with combined annual revenues US$76.6 million, employing 225 people. The companies were National Data Planning of Ithica, N.Y., Belden Associates of Dallas, and **Accounting Financial Services**, which was previously owned the Netherlands second largest publisher, **Wolters Kluwer, NV.**

Separately, **Wolters** said its **Aspen Systems Corp.** unit in the U.S. agreed in principle to acquire **Applied Management Services** of Silver Springs, Maryland.

Dividend Stripping

One strategy, called <u>dividend stripping,</u> is oft used to drive *after tax profits* offshore. **PW's** information guides suggest businessmen take advantage of this technique.

Barbados, with its low profits tax rates of 2-1/2% or less for IBCs and its tax treaty with the U.S., is a prime candidate. Under **Article 10 (Dividends)** of the treaty, if a Barbados company owns *at least 10%* of the *voting stock* of a U.S. subsidiary, the dividend withholding tax rate will be reduced to **5%**. See chart page # 78.

Example #2: Barbados company **Y** owns all the stock in U.S. real estate subsidiary **X**. **X** owns property (a hotel) valued at $5,000,000 with a tax basis of $1,000,000. If X sells the property it will incur a minimum of $1,200,000 in U.S. capital gains taxes. Instead, X borrows $4,000,000 from a U.S. bank, using the hotel as collateral. With the borrowings, X pays a $4,000,000 cash dividend to parent company **Y,** incurring a 5% U.S. withholding tax on the dividend (or $200,000). Barbados profits tax on the dividend will equal $95,000, making the total taxes paid on the dividend $295,000. This is a tax savings of almost $1,000,000, when considering the State taxes that **X** could incurred.

Anti-Treaty Shopping Provision, Article 22

Article 22 of the Barbados-U.S. treaty contains the model <u>anti-treaty shopping</u> provision being adopted in many re-negotiated U.S. income tax treaties. Paragraphs 1(a) and (b) reserve the treaty benefits for the most part to residents of the U.S. and Barbados. Paragraph 3(a) and (b) provides for **an "exception"** (opening the door for 3rd party players!) where the shares are regularly traded on a recognized NASDAQ type stock exchange. In such a case paragraph 1 of article 22 is not to apply.

[∬ 579Z] Article 22 Limitation on Benefits

1. A person which is a resident of a Contracting State and which derives income from sources within the other Contracting State shall not be entitled, in that other Contracting State, to the benefits of Article 6 (Income from Real Property (Immovable Property) through Article 23 (Relief from Double Taxation) if:

(a) 50% or less of the beneficial interest in such person (or in the case of a company, 50% or less of the number of shares of each class of the company's shares) is owned, directly or indirectly, by any combination of one or more individual residents of a Contracting State or citizens of the U.S.; or

(b) the income of such person is used in substantial part, directly or indirectly, to meet liabilities (including liabilities for interest or royalties) to persons who are residents of a State other than a Contracting State, or who are not citizens of the U.S.

3. The provisions of paragraph 1 shall not apply if the person deriving the income is a company which is a resident of a Contracting State in whose principal class of shares there is a substantial and regular trading on a recognized stock exchange. For purposes of the preceding sentence, the term "recognized stock exchange" means:

(a) The NASDAQ System owned by the National Association of Securities Dealers, Inc. and any stock exchange registered with the Securities and Exchange Commission as a national securities exchange for purposes of the Securities Act of 1934; and

(b) any other stock exchange agreed upon by the competent authorities of the Contracting States.

"Dividend Stripping" to offshore Netherlands & Barbados Companies
(Adapted from chart provided by Price Waterhouse**)

Comparison of a $1,000,000 U.S. source dividend paid to offshore parent companies.

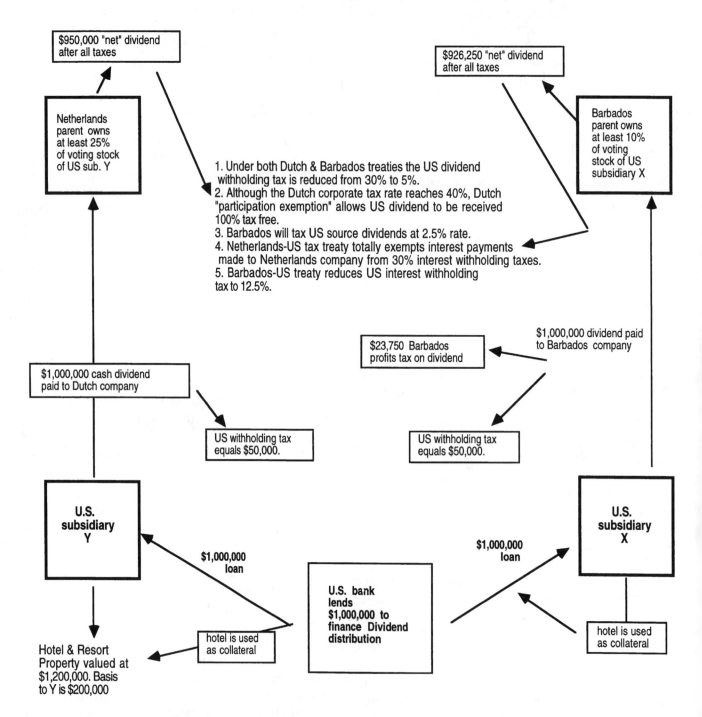

$950,000 "net" dividend after all taxes

Netherlands parent owns at least 25% of voting stock of US sub. Y

$926,250 "net" dividend after all taxes

Barbados parent owns at least 10% of voting stock of US subsidiary X

1. Under both Dutch & Barbados treaties the US dividend withholding tax is reduced from 30% to 5%.
2. Although the Dutch corporate tax rate reaches 40%, Dutch "participation exemption" allows US dividend to be received 100% tax free.
3. Barbados will tax US source dividends at 2.5% rate.
4. Netherlands-US tax treaty totally exempts interest payments made to Netherlands company from 30% interest withholding taxes.
5. Barbados-US treaty reduces US interest withholding tax to 12.5%.

$1,000,000 cash dividend paid to Dutch company

$23,750 Barbados profits tax on dividend

$1,000,000 dividend paid to Barbados company

US withholding tax equals $50,000.

US withholding tax equals $50,000.

U.S. subsidiary Y

U.S. subsidiary X

$1,000,000 loan

$1,000,000 loan

U.S. bank lends $1,000,000 to finance Dividend distribution

hotel is used as collateral

hotel is used as collateral

Hotel & Resort Property valued at $1,200,000. Basis to Y is $200,000

** See "Federal Taxation of Foreign Investment in US Real Estate" by R.F. Hudson, Jr., Esq. ((taxation degrees from U of Florida, U of Netherlands Antilles and U. of Barbados). Tax Management International. According to Hudson.."*The US company should borrow against or "mortgage out" the appreciated asset (hotel), while maintaining the corporation's investments until liquidation. Distributions in cash to foreign treaty beneficiaries will be taxed at the reduced treaty rates - normally less than the USA's 28% capital gains rate.*"

"Source of Income Rules"

Industrial countries that levy income taxes on their citizenry base their right to tax on several factors. These factors can be categorized as follows:

- **"Source of Income Rules"**: Where an item of income is generated is often a criteria for determining tax liability. For purposes of this discussion, source of income is broken down into *foreign source income* and *U.S. source income.*

- **Territorial Basis**: Countries that impose taxes based on the "territorial principle" first discern the source of the income. They generally tax income that is derived from activities carried on <u>within</u> their territorial borders, but allow "foreign source incomes" from activities carried on outside the country to go tax free. Panama, Costa Rica, Liberia, Singapore, Hong Kong and Venezuela tax corporations and citizens based on the territorial principle. Dividends, interests, and capital gains from U.S. sources, or any foreign source would be wholly tax exempt in these countries. Singapore is somewhat of an exception. If foreign source income is received or remitted back into Singapore it will be subject to tax.

- **Residency:** Some countries impose income taxes on the worldwide incomes of citizens and corporations <u>resident</u> in the country. Britain taxes residents on both foreign source income and domestic source income. Capital gains, interest incomes, dividends, and business profits from foreign or domestic sources are fully taxable to anyone "resident" and living in Britain. Canada, France and the Netherlands also use residency as a requirement to tax you, as do most other European countries. Generally, a stay of 183 days will qualify you as a resident, but each country has its own residency requirements. A citizen or resident of Britain can end his liability to pay UK income and estate taxes simply by leaving the country permanently and only "visiting home" occasionally.

- **Citizenship:** The United States is one of the few nations that taxes its people on their worldwide incomes based solely on their citizenship. Moreover, a U.S. citizen ordinarily cannot escape U.S. income taxes by moving abroad.

> "The Supreme Court held in 1924 that the United States has the power to tax its citizens on their worldwide income solely by reason of their citizenship.[6] The amount in controversy was less than $300 out of a total assessment of less than $1,200 under the Revenue Act of 1921, involving tax levied at rates between 4% and 8%. It is hard to believe a decision from another era could subject an estimated 1,000,000 United States citizens living abroad and earning billions of dollars of worldwide income to tax rates up to 70% (1981), since no major country taxes its nonresident citizens on their foreign-source incomes at all." - from <u>Practical International Tax Planning</u>, by **Marshall J. Langer - Professor of Law, Miami University**

"Source of income rules" can establish whether a tax liability exists

The United States tax system divides income into *foreign source income* and *United States source income.* When speaking of offshore foreign corporations, the differences between U.S. source income and foreign source income is meaningful. Foreign source income earned by a foreign corporation that does not have an office or permanent establishment within the U.S. is always free from U.S. Federal income taxes. U.S. source income earned by the same foreign corporation would ordinarily be subject to the 30% U.S. withholding tax, but some U.S. income tax treaties reduce the rate to 15% or 5%. Sometimes a section of the Internal Revenue Code will exempt U.S. source income from the withholding tax. [7,8]

Types of U.S. Source Incomes

- Dividends paid by a U.S. company are U.S. source income.
- Royalties and rents received from the USA are U.S. source income.

---

6. Cook v. Tait, 265 U.S. 47 (1924)
7. Interest income received from certain portfolio debt instruments issued after 7-18-84 are U.S. source, but exempt from withholding.
8. IRC 861(a)(1)(a) & (c) exempts from all tax interest paid to nonresidents by US banks or savings & loans or interest on monies held by a U.S. insurance company. Prior to the Tax Reform Act of 1986 these interests were even considered to be "foreign source income", but Congress decided to change the sourcing rule while allowing the interest to stay 100% free from the 30% withholding tax.

• Capital gains on sales of U.S. stocks are U.S. source income. [9.]

• Sales of personal property by a U.S. resident is U.S. source income under *new* Code-Section 865.

• Compensation for labor or personal services performed within the United States is U.S. source.

• All income from transportation that begins <u>and</u> ends in the U.S. is U.S. source income.

• for tax years beginning after 1986, the law treats 50% of all income from transportation that begins <u>or</u> ends in the U.S. (but not both) as U.S. source income.

• Income from sale of natural resources, U.S. farm, mine, timber track or well is U.S. source.

While all the above incomes are classified **U.S. source**, not all U.S. source incomes are subject to the 30% withholding tax. Capital gains on the sale of publicly traded stocks go tax free provided the shareholding does not amount to *more than* 5% of the U.S. company's "float". If the foreign corporation is "engaged in a trade or business within the U.S.", it will be held taxable on all its U.S. source income at the same rates that would apply to a domestic company. [10.]

Foreign Source Income

Foreign source incomes include foreign country dividends, interests, royalties, business profits, and foreign rents. Foreign source incomes can be received and accumulated by a tax haven holding company (or any foreign company for that matter) 100% free from U.S. taxes. What's important to grasp here is some incomes categorized as having a foreign source might actually involve the sale and transport of U.S. property manufactured and situated within the USA.

• IRC §865 provides that if a nonresident sells personal property the income is sourced outside the United States. If a U.S. resident sells the personal property the income is sourced in the United States. The source of income from the sale of property depends directly on the <u>residence</u> of the <u>seller</u>. It's immaterial where the product was manufactured or stored or transported from.

• Royalties from the use of intangibles such as copyrights, patents, and scientific know-how are sourced where the intangibles are put into use. If the intangibles are used to produce income in a foreign country the income is considered to be foreign source income.

• Personal service incomes (advisory fees, management fees, lawyer fees, commissions) for services performed solely outside the USA (even when performed in a tax haven) is foreign source income, regardless whether the U.S. payer of the fees resides within the USA.

Revenue Ruling 66-291 provides that, for purposes of the U.S. source rules, prize money won in puzzle contest by nonresident alien individual depends on where the puzzle solving was done. When contestant just mailed his entry to U.S. corporation giving prize, but solved the puzzle outside the U.S., income was *foreign source income*.

If entrant only fills in entry blank, source is country where contest is held. Nonresident alien individuals can avoid all U.S. income taxes on their prizes if they solve their puzzles from somewhere outside the United States.

Revenue Ruling 73-372 held that membership dues received from U.S. citizen members by sports club incorporated and operating in foreign country, which furnished equipment, staff assistance, meals and lodgings in connection with hunting safaris conducted in foreign country are income from sources without the USA. I'll bet the "new" Teddy Roosevelt Sports Club in the Bahamas loves this ruling!

Revenue Ruling 73-252 held that unemployment benefits paid by domestic employees association to citizen and resident of Canada, who at all times lived and worked in Canada, are *income from foreign sources,* not subject to 30% U.S. withholding taxes.

Hong Kong Estate Duties

Hong Kong (H.K.) does not apply its income tax to *foreign source income,* and capital gains go tax free in Hong Kong. However, estate duties are imposed by authority of the H.K. <u>Estate Duty Ordinance</u>, which levies an estate tax equal to 18% of the value of all property (valued at more than US$650,000) situated in Hong Kong that passes on the death of a person. Property includes bank deposits and other assets in H.K. owned by a resident <u>or</u> nonresident. Hong Kong estate duties apply to shares of a H.K. corporation regardless of the residence of the decedent.

Hong Kong estate duties do not apply to foreign assets held outside Hong Kong. Many Hong Kong companies are owned by foreign corporations to avoid H.K. estate duties. Often these are Panamanian corporations with Hong Kong directors. This is a legal tax planning device recognized by the Hong Kong courts.

---

9. But, capital gains are not subject to US withholding or income tax unless the gain is from the sale of a U.S. real property interest. See IRC 897.

10. See IRC §897(c)(3), IRC 881 & IRC 871.

Avoiding U.S. Capital Gains Taxes. Can it be done?

Foreign corporations, nonresident aliens and foreign trusts can effect Stock Market transactions through a U.S. stock broker, independent agent, or an employee, and not be liable to U.S. capital gains taxes. U.S. Treasury Regulation §864-2(c)(1) & (2) reproduced below provides an exception for what comprises "being engaged in a trade or business within the United States". Capital gains realized by a foreign corporation or nonresident alien individual are exempt from tax under IRC §871 and IRC §881 provided the foreigner is "not engaged in a trade or business within the United States". If the U.S. stock being traded is stock in a **U.S. Real Property Holding Corporation** as defined under IRC §897(a), Code-section 897(c)(3) limits the capital gains exemption to stock that is (1) regularly traded on one of the U.S. stock exchanges, and (2) where the amount of stock owned by the foreigner cannot exceed 5% of all the outstanding stock (float) of the U.S. company.

The United State Treasury Regulations are interesting in that they mention such speculative Stock Market transactions as *short selling, use of margin to buy stocks, options, and contracts*, i.e., the whole gambit of stock and bond investing. This T. Regulation is reproduced exactly as presented in the law books below.

T.Regs. §864-2(c)(1) & (2) *Trading in stocks or securities*.
For purposes of paragraph (a) of this section -

(1) *In general.* The term "engaged in trade or business within the United States does not include the effecting of transactions in the United States in stocks or securities through resident broker, commission agent, custodian, or other independent agent. This paragraph shall apply to any taxpayer, including a broker or dealer in stocks or securities, except that it shall not apply if at any time during the taxable year the taxpayer has an office or other fixed place of business in the United States through which, or by the direction of, the transactions in stocks or securities are effected. The volume of stock or security transactions effected shall not be taken into account in determining under this subparagraph whether the taxpayer is engaged in trade or business within the United States.

(2) Trading for taxpayer's own account. (i) In general. The term "engaged in trade or business within the United States" does not include the effecting of transactions in the United States in stocks or securities for the taxpayer's own account, irrespective of whether such transactions are effected by or through -

(a) The taxpayer himself while present in the United States,
(b) Employees of the taxpayer, whether or not such employees are present in the United States while effecting the transactions, or

(c) A broker, commission agent, custodian, or other agent of the taxpayer, whether or not such agent while effecting the transactions is (1) dependent or independent, or (2) resident, nonresident, or present in the United States, and irrespective of whether any such employee or agent has discretionary authority to make decisions in effecting such transactions. For purposes of this paragraph, the term "securities" means any note, bond, debenture, or other evidence of indebtedness, or any evidence of an interest in or a right to subscribe to or purchase any of the foregoing; and the effecting of transactions in stocks or securities including buying, selling (whether or not by entering into a short sales), or trading in stocks, securities, or contracts or options to buy or sell stocks or securities, on margin or otherwise, for the account and risk of the taxpayer, and any other activity closely related thereto (such as obtaining credit for the purpose of effectuating such buying, selling, or trading). The volume of stock or security transactions effected during the taxable year shall not be taken into account in determining under this subparagraph whether the taxpayer is engaged in trade or business within the United States. The application of this subdivision may be illustrated by the following example: [6.]

---

6. See the U.S. Treasury Regulations for their examples.

Selling U.S. real estate tax free.

Much has been written about the repeal of the General Utilities doctrine in the *Tax Reform Act of 1986* and the **FIRPTA** (Foreign Investment in U.S. Real Property Tax Act of 1980) provisions blocking tax free dispositions in United States Real Property. Together, these two Acts ended most tax free dispositions of U.S. Real property by the foreign investor. There are still situations where such tax free transactions can be executed within the confines of the tax Code.

Old IRC §337 Liquidations (Repealed in 1986)

Under old IRC §337 (repealed by the *Tax Reform Act of 1986)* a U.S. subsidiary could be liquidated into its parent and the U.S. subsidiary would not have to recognize any gain upon liquidation because the incidence of taxation was shifted to the parent shareholder. The parent company would usually be liable for any gain over its basis in the subsidiary's stock, but if the parent company was domiciled in a tax haven no U.S. capital gains taxes would be attached, and only the 30% U.S. dividend withholding taxes would apply. By locating the parent holding company in a low-tax haven that has a tax treaty with the U.S. that reduces the dividend withholding tax to 15% or 5% (i.e., the Netherlands, Barbados and old Netherlands Antilles Tax Treaties), it was possible to avoid the brunt of U.S. taxes.

IRC §897(c)(3) Exception for publicly traded stock

Prior to 1980, offshore holding companies, trusts and nonresident aliens could sell their U.S. holdings (whether raw land and buildings or company stock) free of capital gains taxes, because the U.S. did not tax the transaction unless the nonresident was doing business through an office or permanent establishment within the United States. FIRPTA stopped most of this by treating the gain or loss of a nonresident alien individual or foreign corporation as effectively connected with United States trade or business, regardless of whether the foreigner had a presence in the U.S.

A few exceptions (a.k.a. loopholes) were provided for in the FIRPTA law. IRC §897(c)(3) excepted shares of *publicly traded* U.S. companies, if the foreign shareholder did not own more than 5% of the entire outstanding stock available to all investors (float). Consequently, foreign companies and other nonresident alien entities domiciled in tax havens that do not levy any capital gains taxes were still permitted to trade U.S. stocks tax free if the company's stock was traded on one of the U.S. Stock Exchanges, and the total shareholding did not exceed the 5% limit.

Dispositions of shareholdings in privately held non-public U.S. companies, and holdings described under IRC §897(c) as *U.S. Real Property interests* (i.e., raw land, buildings), did become subject to U.S. capital gains taxes under FIRPTA. Dispositions of these assets are taxable at substantially the same tax rates that apply to dispositions by U.S. persons.

T.Regs. §897-2(e)(1) - Interests in Foreign Corporations

IRC §897 authorizes the Treasury Department to issue regulations providing guidelines for the attribution of stock of a USRPHC (**U.S. Real Property Holding Corporation**) or USRPI (**U.S. Real Property Interest**) through intervening foreign or domestic entities (trusts, corporations, partnerships). A foreign corporation can itself be classified as a USRPHC, but the sale or disposition of a foreign USRPHC is not treated as an effectively connected taxable sale if the seller is also a foreign corporation or nonresident alien.

If it was not for two examples provided in the U.S. Treasury Department's own regulations, few investors would realize or believe it legally possible to dispose of U.S. real estate free from U.S. capital gains taxes.

T.Regs. 897-2(e)(1) outlines how it is done:

(e) Special rules regarding assets held by a corporation - (1) Interests in foreign corporations. For purposes only of determining whether any corporation is a **U.S. real property holding corporation (USRPHC)**, an interest in a foreign corporation shall be treated as a **U.S. real property interest (USRPI)** unless it is established that the interest was not a U.S. real property interest under the rules of this section on the applicable determination date. However, regardless of whether an interest in a foreign

82.

corporation is treated as a U.S. real property interest for this purpose, gain or loss from the disposition of an interest in such corporation **will not** be treated as effectively connected with the conduct of a U.S. trade or business by reason of 897(a). The rules of this paragraph (e)(1) are illustrated by the following examples. In each example, the fair market value is determined as of the applicable determination dates under paragraph (d)(4)(i) of this section.

Example (1). Nonresident alien individual F holds all the stock of domestic corporation DC. DC's only assets are 40% of the stock of foreign corporation FC, with a fair market value of $500,000, and a parcel of country W real estate with a fair market value of $400,000. Foreign corporation FP, unrelated to DC, holds 60% of the stock of FC. FC's only asset is a parcel of U.S. real estate with a fair market value of $1,250,000. FC is a U.S. **Real Property Holding Corporation (USRPHC)** because the fair market value of its U.S. real property interests ($1,250,000) exceeds 50% ($625,000) of the sum of the fair market value of its U.S. Real Property interests ($1,250,000), its interests in real property located outside the United States (zero), plus its other assets used or held for use in a trade or business (zero). Consequently, DC's interest in FC is treated as a U.S. real property interest under the rules of this paragraph (e)(1). DC is a USRPHC because the fair market value ($500,000) of its U.S. real property interest (the stock of FC) exceeds 50% ($450,000) of the sum ($900,000) of the fair market value of its U.S. Real Property interests ($500,000), its interest in real property located outside the United States ($400,000), plus its other assets used or held for use in a trade or business (zero). If F disposes of her stock within five years of the current determination date, her gain or loss on the disposition of her stock in DC will be treated as effectively connected with a U.S. trade or business under section 897(a). **However, FP's gain on the disposition of its stock in FC would not be subject to the provisions of section 897(a) because the stock of FC is a USRPI only for purposes of determining whether DC is a USRPHC.**

Example (2). Nonresident alien individual B holds all the stock of domestic corporation US. US's only assets are 40% of the stock of foreign corporation FC1. Nonresident alien individual N, unrelated to US, holds the other 60% of FC1's stock. FC1's only assets are 40% of the stock in foreign corporation FC2. The remaining 60% of the stock of FC2 is owned by nonresident alien individual X, who is unrelated to FC1. FC2's only asset is a parcel of U.S. real estate with a fair market value of $1,000,000. FC2, therefore, is a USRPHC, and the stock of FC2 held by FC1 is a USRPI for purposes of determining whether FC1 is a USRPHC (but not for purposes of treating FC1's gain from the disposition of FC2 stock as effectively connected with a U.S. trade or business under section 897(a). As all of FC1's assets are USRPIs, the stock of FC1 held by US is a USRPI for purposes of determining whether US is a USRPHC **(but not for purposes of subjecting N's gain on the disposition of FC! to the provisions of section 897(a)).** As US is a domestic corporation and as all of its assets are USRPIs, US is a USRPHC, and the stock of US held by B is a USRPI for purposes of section 897(a). Therefore, B's gain or loss upon the disposition of the stock of US within 5 years of the most recent determination date is subject to the provisions of section 897(a).

The above U.S. Treasury Department examples were copied *word for word* from the Treasury's own Regulations. Because they are a bit difficult to follow, we'll provide our own examples, which we believe are much simpler to follow.

Our Example #3: On January 1, 1991, Bahamas company X purchases all 10,000 shares in Barbados Company Y for $100,000,000. Company Y then purchases all 10,000 shares in U.S. company Z. Z purchases a hotel in Miami for $100,000,000. Z is a USRPHC under IRC §897(a).

If Barbados company Y sells all its stock in U.S. company Z to foreign investor Q in 1995 for $200,000,000, Y will have to pay Federal capital gains taxes on the $100,000,000 profit under IRC §897(a) because Z is a USRPHC. However, if Bahamas company X sells all the shares it owns in Y to Q, no capital gains taxes are owed. See T.Regs. 897-2(e)(1) above. Effectively, Bahamas company X can trade $200,000,000 in U.S. real estate tax free.

Dividend and Interest stripping via Treaty Shopping

One widespread practice used by foreign investors investing in the U.S. involves the exploitation one of the U.S. Income Tax Treaties to strip dividends and interest income offshore where they can be reinvested tax free (often right back into the U.S. stock and bond markets).

Our Example #4: Under Article 11 of the current U.S.-Barbados Income Tax Treaty, interest income paid by a U.S. subsidiary to its Barbados parent is subject to a reduced interest withholding tax of 12-1/2% (reduced from 30%). Dividends paid to a Barbados parent company that owns at least 10% of the voting stock of the U.S. subsidiary are subject to a reduced U.S. withholding tax of 5% (normally 30%) under Article 10 of the Treaty. Capital gains go tax free in Barbados under the **Barbados Income Tax Act** and the **IBC Act**, whereas dividends and interest incomes are taxable at rates ranging from 1% to 2-1/2% if the company organizes under the Barbados IBC Act.

Suppose in January, 1991 Barbados IBC **Y** capitalizes U.S. subsidiary **Z** with $50,000,000 paid in capital in return for all the outstanding stock of Z. Suppose Y lends Z another $50,000,000 at an interest rate of 10% pa. U.S. subsidiary Z thereafter purchases a Miami hotel for $100,000,000.

Assuming the Miami hotel has a positive annual cash flow of $10,000,000 after expenses, U.S. subsidiary Z will need to pay Federal income taxes on net income of $5,000,000 ($10,000,000 minus $5,000,000 interest expense to Y). This would result in about $1,600,000 in federal taxes. U.S. withholding taxes on the $5,000,000 interest paid to the Barbados parent Y would amount to $625,000, putting Subsidiary Z in an overall U.S. tax bracket of approximately 22%.

If Z repatriates its profits back to Y as a dividend, a 5% dividend withholding tax on the $2,800,000 profits repatriated would add another $140,000 in U.S. taxes. The Barbados profits tax on the $2.66 million dollar dividend and the $5,000,000 interest payment would amount to another $90,000 in taxes, bringing the total taxes paid to approximately $2,455,000.

Example #5: Barbados company Y reinvests the interest and dividend remittances (≈ $7,545,000) from subsidiary Z in U.S. Treasury bonds paying 8% pa. No U.S. withholding tax is payable on the $603,600 annual interest income generated by the bonds. The *Tax Reform Act of 1984* repealed the interest withholding tax on bonds issued after July 18, 1984. The 2-1/2% Barbados profits tax on interest income would add an additional $15,000 in taxes.

Definitions:

United States Real Property Holding Corporation (USRPHC). Any U.S. corporation whose USRPI's equals or exceeds 50% or the combined total of (1) its interests in real property located outside the U.S. (2) its United States real property interests, and (3) any other of its assets held for the use of a trade or business.

Example 6: Occidental Petroleum's assets include $1,000,000,000 in U.S. real estate and oil wells + $2,000,000,000 in Peruvian oil fields and other minerals. Occidental is not a USRPHC because Occidental's USRPIs account for only 33% of its worldwide assets. Shares of Occidental can be sold by a nonresident alien free of capital gains taxes. Note, only a very few U.S. corporations can avoid the USRPHC classification.

United States Real Property Interest (USRPI). Under IRC §897(c) this term means an interest in real property (including a mine, well or other natural deposit) located in the U.S. or Virgin Islands, and any interest (other than an interest solely as creditor) in a domestic corporation, unless it can be shown that the corporation was at no time a USRPHC.

Real Property includes movable walls, furnishings, and other personal property associated with the real property.

Capital Gains Taxes Gone Berserk

In 1996, resident taxpayers of New York and California will face combined federal and state capital gains tax rates that approach 40%, and individuals of New York City could actually incur a combined capital gains tax rate of 41%. The chart below shows the combined capital gains tax rates for the 10 most populous states. Although State taxes are deductible on federal returns, the tax rates are nearly double what they were before the **Tax Reform Act of 1986.**

How States Compare			
Maximum capital gains taxes in 10 most populous states for a married couple filing joint return with taxable income between $71,000 and $171,090			
State	**Federal Tax**	**State Tax**	**Combined Rate**
California	33%	9.3%	39.2%
New York	33%	8.4%	38.2%
Texas	33%	0%	33%
Florida	33%	0%	33%
Pennsylvania	33%	2.1%	34.4%
Illinois	33%	2.5%	34.6%
Ohio	33%	6.9%	37.6%
Michigan	33%	4.6%	37.6%
New Jersey	33%	3.5%	36.5%
N. Carolina	33%	7.0%	37.7%
Sources: National Conference of State Legislatures: Smith Barney, Harris, Upham & Co. research division.			

CHAPTER 5 • The Cayman Islands & other Caribbean tax havens

"The Cayman Islands are an example for all in regard to the efforts made to introduce sensible and relevant procedures for regulation and supervision of the offshore financial sector. "

The Cayman Islands Government Information Services recently advertised that the total number of banks registered in the Caymans topped out at 594, with approximately US$500 billion dollars in deposits. Forty-six of the largest 50 banks in the world are represented in the Caymans, as well as all of the "Big Six" accounting firms.

To give you a comparison of how really gigantic the Cayman Banks as a group are, the banking deposits in all of California's Commercial banks stand at right around $220 billion. The banking deposits in the Bahamas have reached ≈ $300 billion dollars. According to the *Offshore Financial Review* (London), the $500 billion on deposit in the Cayman banks towers over the combined assets of all European offshore centers.

In addition, Cayman banks are said to have more dollars on deposits than the combined total foreign reserves of the Group of Seven industrial countries.

Ironically, banking deposits in the Caymans have dropped slightly since the end of 1991 when deposits reached $430 billion dollars. Yet the total number of banks registered in Cayman has actually grown.

The Cayman Islands are now the fifth largest financial center in the world, trailing New York, Tokyo and London.

Taxes

There are no personal income taxes, no corporate income taxes, no capital gains taxes, no withholding taxes, no estate, gift or inheritance taxes, no sales taxes, no employment taxes, no death duties, and no probate fees in the Cayman Islands. Guarantees against future taxes are available to exempted companies and trusts. Exempted companies can receive a guarantee from the government for a period not exceeding 30 years. Exempted trusts can receive a guarantee for 100 years. The Caymans have no tax treaties with any nation.

Caymanians have historically had a distaste for taxation, and this has provided a natural

setting for the system of laws and regulations, dating back to the 1960's, which have created and encouraged the growth of the Islands as an offshore financial center. Tax lawyers refer to the Caymans as a no-tax or zero tax haven. Taxes or all types simply do not exist in this country.

Like the other no-tax havens of the Bahamas, Bermuda, Anguilla, Vanuatu and Nauru (in the South Pacific), the Caymans have traditionally enjoyed a complete absence of direct taxation. The only form of direct taxation the Cayman Islands ever had was a $10 a year tax on adult males, but that was abolished in 1985.

MESSAGE FROM THE FINANCIAL SECRETARY

As Financial Secretary of the Cayman Islands, I am pleased to share with you the remarkable success story of our financial services industry.

In nearly every area—banking, trust companies, mutual funds, insurance, company formation—the marketplace has validated the professionalism, sophistication, and the value of services offered in the Cayman Islands.

However, it is my responsibility not just to encourage growth in Cayman's financial sector but, as importantly, to insist upon the right kind of growth. Cayman welcomes all legitimate deposits and investments but has no interest in, and, in fact, will not tolerate questionable transactions.

People, History, Accessibility, Currency

"The Cayman Islands... those that know us.., love us." So the song goes in the Cayman Island Tourist Bureau's television ads that appear on TV's across the America. Truer words were perhaps never spoken. The Caymans are a first-rate no-tax haven just 2 hours by plane from Miami. The Cayman Islands are an English speaking British Crown colony especially suitable for U.S. businessmen and Canadian businessmen owing to their close proximity to the U.S. and North America. There are more than 594 bank and trust companies, and over 300 insurance companies registered in this world famous tax haven. The Caymans receive over

500,000 tourists every year, most of them from the U.S.A.

The Cayman Islands are three small islands (Grand Cayman, Cayman Brac and Little Cayman) about 480 miles south of Miami, and just north of Jamaica in the Caribbean Sea. The population is now about 28,000, made up of about 20% Caucasian, 25% black and 55% mixed race. It is racially integrated, socially and otherwise, and color is not considered a real issue to these fun loving islanders. The capital and principal city is George Town, located on the largest of the three islands, i.e., Grand Cayman.

You don't have to travel for 24 hours or spend upwards of $1,500 to get to your tax haven in George Town, as you would if you had chosen Hong Kong, Vanuatu, Campione or Switzerland as an offshore base. The Caymans have daily flights from Miami year round, and weekly connections to 12 other cities in North America and Jamaica. There are several flights each week from Houston, Texas too. Travel time to Miami is just two hours, at a cost of about $200. You can catch a Concorde from Miami to London at Miami's International Airport if you're coming from Europe and you're in a hurry!

Columbus first sighted Little Cayman and Cayman Brac during his fourth and last trip to the West Indies in May, 1503. In 1655, Jamaica was captured from Spain by the British, and in 1670 was ceded along with the Caymans to the British Crown. The first Cayman settlers were buccaneers, shipwrecked sailors and debtors.

Today, the Governor is appointed by the British government, and there is no likelihood of independence being predicted for the Caymans for many years yet. The Cayman dollar floats against the pound sterling, and is roughly equivalent to US$1.20. There are no exchange controls in Cayman limiting what currency you can use.

Currently there are in excess of 35,000 companies registered in the Cayman Islands.

Type of entity	Number of entities		
	1975	1984	1990
Registered companies	6,618	17,639	22,260
Licensed banks & trust Co.	194	459	546
Licensed insurance companies*		299	360
* Not applicable.			

Who are the world's biggest tax avoiders?

According to statistics (through 1986) released by the Cayman Administrative Building in George Town, the **United States** leads the rest of the world in the amount of dollars it sends to Cayman Island banks - **$69.4 billion**. While the chart below does not reveal the origin of these funds (which would be a violation of Cayman's Bank Secrecy Code), it does tell an amazing tale of who's leading the way in the so-called art of legal (and perhaps illegal) tax avoidance scheming.

Country	Assets	% of Total	US$ millions	% of Total
Argentina	1,292	1%	1,815	1.4%
Bahamas	**3,071**	**2.3%**	6,681	**5.1%**
Belgium	1,450	1.1%	543	0.4%
Brazil	8,928	6.8%	5,185	4.0%
Canada	4,276	3.3%	1,675	1.3%
Denmark	1,312	1%	926	0.7%
France	4,126	2.5%	3,197	2.5%
Hong Kong	1,881	1.4%	1,535	1.2%
Italy	1,623	1.2%	445	0.3%
Japan	2,764	2.1%	359	0.3%
Luxembourg	1,259	1%	416	0.3%
Mexico	4,313	3.3%	1,745	1.3%
Netherlands	1,173	0.9%	1,655	1.3%
N. Antilles	386	0.3%	1,589	1.2%
Panama	5,387	4.1%	3,243	2.5%
South Africa	2,063	1.6%	1,865	1.4%
Saudi Arabia	254	0.2%	1,256	1.0%
Singapore	1,885	1.4%	874	0.7%
Switzerland	2,447	1.9%	1,746	1.3%
U.K.	17,340	13.2%	10,783	8.3%
USA	**50,357**	**38.4%**	69,420	**53.2%**
W. Germany	1,706	1.3%	1,741	1.3%
Other	11,988	9.1%	11,744	9.0%

Source: Offshore Adviser (November 1989)

Ordinary and Exempt Companies

There are principally two types of companies you can register in the Caymans; the exempted and the ordinary company. Foreign investors almost always choose the exempted company because its register of shareholders is not open to public inspection, and it may be kept inside or outside the Cayman Islands. The register of shareholders for ordinary companies are open to public inspection.

Exempted companies do not have to file annual returns with the Registrar, although an annual declaration must be filed. Typically, alternate directors or an assistant secretary are provided by the lawyer, trust company, bank or accountants that formed the company, so to meet this requirement, since the real beneficial owners and directors would not reside in the Cayman Islands.

No annual meeting of shareholders is necessary for an exempted company, and certain sections of the Companies Law do not apply.

Any proposed company the objects of which are to be carried out mainly outside the Cayman Islands may apply to be registered as an exempted company. A declaration signed by a director to the effect that the operation of the proposed exempted company will be conducted mainly outside the Islands must be submitted to the Registrar along with its memorandum and bylaws (a.k.a. the Articles of Association).

Every exempted company must maintain an office in the islands and the directors must hold at least one meeting in the Islands each calendar year, although it is common practice to appoint local alternate directors specifically for the purpose of fulfilling this requirement.

Shares without nominal or par value may be issued, as may bearer shares, provided they are fully paid, but any invitation to the public in the Islands to subscribe for shares or debentures is prohibited.

Other requirements:

1) The company name must be approved by the Registrar of Companies.
2) The company must have a registered office and agent in the Caymans.
3) Bank reference letters and a minimum US$500 initial deposit to open bank account with Cayman bank.
4) At least one director required.
5) Company secretary required before company can commence business.
6) Names of shareholders of non-resident and local companies must be disclosed. Bearer shares may be issued for exempted companies in which case no disclosure of shareholders is called for.
7) Exempted companies must hold a directors meeting in Cayman once a year.
8) No annual audits required.

An exempted company may be granted a guarantee by the Governor in Executive Council against future taxation for up to 20 years.

Costs to Incorporate

Government Registration and Annual Fees

Exempt Company
$500 registration and annual fee for Capital up to $50,000

$805 registration and annual fee for Capital of $50,000 to $1,000,000

$1,690 registration and annual fee for Capital of $1,000,000 to $2,000,000

$2,400 registration and annual fee for Capital over $2,000,000

Ordinary Company
$490 registration and annual fee for Capital up to $50,000

$690 registration and annual fee for Capital over $50,000

DISBURSEMENTS (for company seal, name strip and filing of directors)

$180 for an Exempt company
$125 for an Ordinary company

Penalties for Late Payment of Annual Fees

The Cayman Islands Registrar of Companies has introduced penalties for late payment of company annual fees effective January 1, 1999.

The penalties are as follows:
•   33.33% for payment after March 31.
•   67.67% for payment after June 30.
•   100% for payment after September 30.

•   The Registrar of Companies issued a further notice on March 31, 1999 that it would postpone implementation of the penalties due to take effect on April 1, 1999 and allow companies a further three months to pay fees and file the annual return before incurring the penalty.

Cayman companies can be used for a variety of purposes, including offshore captive insurance and reinsurance companies, bond issuing companies raising finance in the international markets, treasury and cash management companies with tax free accumulation of funds possible. Other uses include investment holding and property management companies and invoicing and trading companies.

Total start-up costs to form an exempted company range between $1,800 and $3,000. Annual maintenance costs and government fees thereafter run about $1,800. A Cayman accounting or law firm might charge US$900 per annum to provide you with a registered office.

The costs of incorporation includes the government fee and is for a company formed with a standard memorandum and articles of association. In situations where nonstandard companies are required or advice is required regarding the structuring, fees will be higher.

Exempt Companies

In addition to a 30 year guarantee against future taxes by the Governor in Council, there are other advantages to forming an exempted company.

1. The company name need not include the words "Limited" or "Ltd."
2. It is not required to maintain a register of shareholders, thus names (owners) are not a matter of public record.
3. No annual meetings of shareholders is necessary.
4. No annual return has to be filed with the Registrar, although an annual declaration must be made stating that the company continues to comply with the requirements of an exempt company.
5) Shares without par value (i.e., no-par value) or nominal value may be issued, as can **bearer shares.**

For many years the costs for registering an exempted company in the Caymans had remained fixed at US$1,025, but the annual fee the government now charges has fallen from US$700 to US$500. By comparison, the government start-up and annual renewal fees in the BVI is US$300, and in the Bahamas just US$250.

Directors and Shareholders

The day to day business of the company is carried on by the directors. Directors may be of any nationality and do not have to be Cayman residents. There are no restrictions as to how many directors a company must have. Directors are appointed by the casting of a majority vote by shareholders in a general meeting. Alternate or nominee directors can sub for the real directors. Use of nominee shareholders and directors is customary in the Caymans. Directors generally are responsible for the appointment of the President, the executive officers, the treasurer and the managing directors of a Cayman company. [1]

You can examine a copy of the Cayman **Companies Law** by writing the Registrar of Companies in George Town at:

---

1. Only shareholders that hold stock that carry voting privileges (voting stock) have the right to vote at shareholder meetings.

Registrar of Companies
Government Administration Building
George Town, Grand Cayman,
British West Indies
Telephone (809) 949-4844
Telex 4260

A Register of Companies

In your Cayman office it is required by **Companies Law** 25-(3) that a register of companies be kept in which the following particulars shall be annexed to the Memorandum of Association or Articles of Association (if any) in so far as they are not included therein:

(a) The **name** of the Company;
(b) The part of the islands in which the **registered office** is proposed to be situated;
(c) The amount of capital and the number of shares into which the company is divided and the fixed amount thereof;
(d) The names, addresses and occupations and subscribers to the **Memorandum**, and the number of shares taken by each subscriber (not required for **Exempted Companies**);
(e) The **date** of execution of the Memorandum of Association;
(f) The **date** of filing of the Memorandum;
(g) The **number** assigned to the company;
(h) In the case of a **limited company**, by guarantee or which no limit is placed on the liability of its members that the same is limited by guarantee or is unlimited.

"From the date of incorporation mentioned in the certificate of incorporation, the subscribers of the memorandum of association, together with such other persons as may from time to time become members of the company, shall be a body corporate by the name contained in the memorandum of association, capable forthwith of exercising all functions of an incorporated body, and have perpetual succession and a common seal with power to hold lands, but with such liability on the part of members to contribute to the assets of the company in the event of it being wound-up as in hereinafter provided in the Cayman Companies Law."

"Every copy of the Memorandum or Articles filed and registered in accordance with the above law, or any extract therefrom certified under the hand and seal of the Registrar of Companies as a true copy shall be received in evidence in any court of the Islands without further proof."

Copies of the Memorandum must be provided to Members

It is the law in the Caymans that you provide a copy of the memorandum having the articles annexed thereto to every member, at his request, on payment of one dollar for each copy as may be fixed by the rule of the company (rules are provided in the articles or *by-laws)*, and in the absence of any such rule, such copy shall be given gratuitously; and if any company makes default in forwarding a copy of the memorandum or articles (if any) to a member in pursuance of **Section 28**, the company so making default shall for each offense incur a penalty of **two dollars**.

Company name restrictions

In the Caymans (and in most other tax havens) a company cannot be registered in a name which is identical with that of another company in existence and already registered. No company may use the words "Chamber of Commerce", unless it is a company registered under license granted by the Governor. In addition, no company name may contain the words "Royal", "Imperial", or "Empire", as that would be calculated to mean that the patronage of Her Majesty or a member of the Royal Family or Her Majesty's government was being provided. You are also prevented from using the words "municipal" or "chartered" in your company name.

Articles of Association *(by-laws)*

The **Articles of Association** (referred to as *"Articles"*) contain the rules and regulations for your company. They are the equivalent to what U.S. lawyers call the *by-laws*. Every company should have a set of articles, but if you don't want to draft your own, you can adopt the set provided by the Cayman Government called **Table A**. You are permitted to modify **Table A**, or write up an entire set from **Table A**, and they will be acceptable by the Registrar. In the Caymans, if you don't provide articles when you file your memorandum, the government will assume you to have adopted their own Table A.

Books, Records and Annual Returns

Cayman law requires a company keep proper records of account with respect to receipts and payments, purchases and sales, and assets and liabilities. Proper books have been described as necessary to give a fair view of the state of the company's affairs, and to explain its transactions. An annual return is required by law, but it is not necessary that it be audited. [2.]

---

2. "Doing Business in the Cayman Islands" (Information Guide), Price Waterhouse, pg 34

Nominee Shareholders

The Caymans and other tax havens allow for the use of nominee shareholders when forming a company. Nominee shareholders help preserve your confidentiality, They are a tradition in places like the Caymans, the Bahamas, and Bermuda. The IRS will not recognize a nominee as the real owner of the shares, but as nominee shareholders make it doubly difficult for the IRS or any investigating agency to assemble information on a company or its owners, they are in widespread use anyway. Nominees help safeguard one of your "Constitutional Rights" - your right to privacy. Nominee shareholders should be used in combination with good tax planning and not exclusively as a means to evade disclosure to the home country tax authorities.

Nominees usually sign a declaration of trust in favor of the real beneficial owners of the company. Because it is the names of the nominees (generally lawyers or trust agents) that are printed or typed on the **Memorandum** and recorded in the Registrar of Companies, thus becoming a matter of public record, the true owner's identity is kept secret. Nominee shareholders costs about US$550 each. Nominee directors cost about $500. Businessmen seeking further anonymity in their affairs can also issue bearer shares.

Improving the Companies Law

Other changes that have recently been enacted to the Cayman's Companies Law include allowing companies to be formed with a single subscriber. Allowing companies to repurchase their own ordinary shares as well as redeemable preferred shares. A company's Memorandum of Association is now not required to stipulate its objects if its business is legal.

Exempted and Ordinary Trusts

Cayman trusts are governed by the Trust Law (Revised), 1976. A trust can be created by a resident of any country, and the settlor does not have to be physically present in the Islands. While the trustee should be located in the Caymans, it is not necessary to keep trust assets there. A stamp tax of US$50 is payable on a trust deed, but there is no requirement for public recording or registration.

No statutory restrictions exist in Cayman regarding accumulation of income, but the common law rule against perpetuities applies, except in the case of exempted trusts. The common law rule against perpetuities is that the duration may not exceed a period of 21 years after the death of the last named beneficiary living at the time the trust was created.

Cayman trusts are governed by the **Trust Law (Revised) of 1976**. The trustee of an offshore trust should be resident in the tax haven, but it is not necessary that trust assets be kept in Cayman. Foreign trustees are usually trust companies, banks, attorneys, but any person or company can be a trustee. A foreign trust in Cayman or elsewhere should always have as many foreign trustees as U.S. trustees, otherwise the IRS will probably not recognize the trust as "foreign".

An ordinary trust can be formed in Cayman upon payment of a stamp tax of CI$40. There is no requirement for public recording or registration of an ordinary trust. An ordinary trust usually assigns a bank or trust company to act as trustees, and it is customary to use local entities for this function. Neither the *settlor* (grantor) or the *beneficiaries* have to be physically present within Cayman, and the trust's assets may be kept outside the islands.

Upon special application by the trustees, the Registrar of Trusts may register a trust as an exempted trust, where the beneficiaries do not include and are not likely to include any persons resident in the Caymans. A registration fee of US$500 is payable to the Cayman Registrar for an exempted trust. An **exempted trust** must pay an annual fee of US$120 in March of each year, and the trustees must file with the Registrar such accounts, minutes and information as the Registrar may require.

Documents files with the Registrar are open to inspection by the trustees or any other person authorized by the trust and by the Registrar, but are not open to public inspection.

A trustee of an exempted trust may apply to the Governor in Executive Council for an undertaking that no future tax will apply to any property or income of the trust.

An exempted trust may provide for a perpetuity of up to 100 years, and during its subsistence the beneficiaries have no interest, vested or future; all rights of the beneficiaries are vested in the Registrar of Trusts, who is an official of the Cayman government.

A foreign trust amply drafted can (1) invest in U.S. stocks; (2) receive U.S. bank interest from U.S. commercial banks and S&Ls within or without the U.S.A.; [3.] (3) accumulate its income free of Federal Income Tax. Certain foreign "grantor" trusts can have U.S. beneficiaries who can receive "foreign source incomes" from the trust and not be taxable on such income distributions. [4.]

Investment Holding Companies

A Cayman company set-up (see page 47, supra) so it is not categorized as a **Controlled Foreign Corporation** (CFC) can trade U.S. stocks, options, commodity contracts, currencies, futures, Treasury and corporate bonds, free of **all** U.S. capital gains taxes. Exemptions are provided within the **Internal Revenue Code**. There are three exceptions:

1 - The foreigner is engaged in a U.S. trade or business inside the U.S.A. or has an office within the U.S.
2 - The gains are attributed to stock in a U.S. Real Property Holding Corporation or U.S. Real Property Interest as defined under IRC §897(c).
3 - Gains are ascribed to stocks that are not publicly traded on an established securities exchange. See IRC §897(c)(3).

Dividend and interest income received by a Cayman company would generally be subject to the U.S. 30% withholding tax under IRC §881(a). However, there are some exceptions. U.S. bank money markets and certificate of deposits as described under IRC §861(c) are excepted. Investments in U.S. Treasury Bills with maturities under 6 months will also be free of U.S. taxes. [5., 6.]

One change made by the **Tax Reform Act of 1986** was the modification of the bizarre **source rule** for U.S. bank interest. Under prior law, bank interest from U.S. banks was considered **"foreign source income"**, thus free of U.S. withholding tax. Under the **post** TRA '86 rules, bank interest was redefined as **"U.S. source income"**, but left exempt from the 30% interest withholding tax. Congress' decision to redefine its sourcing definition for bank interest is understandable. Puzzling is their reason for declaring that "U.S. source bank interest" should be exempt from the 30% interest withholding tax.

3. See IRC §861(a)(F)(I); IRC §861(a)(1)(A); IRC §861(c).
4. See Revenue Ruling 69-79, 1961-1 C.B. 182. See Chapter on "Foreign Trusts", supra.
5. See **Fundamentals of International Taxation**, by Bischel & Feinschreiber, pg 156, See IRC §881(a); IRC §882(a)(2); T.Regulation 1.864- 2(c)(1).
6. See IRC §871(a)(1)(C)(ii); See T.Regs. §871-7(a)(2).

Eurodollar Bonds & Other Interest Bearing Instruments

Eurodollar bonds are one of the safest offshore investments. More than $750 billion dollars of Eurodollars are now outstanding. Eurodollars are issued from either Delaware or the Netherlands Antilles by the international finance subsidiaries of giant multi-national corporations including Exxon, Mobil, RJR Nabisco, and Ford. Eurodollars are unconditionally guaranteed as to both principle and interest by the parent company. They are **free** from all U.S. withholding taxes.

Eurodollar bonds are often convertible into shares of common stock of the U.S. parent. This is an added incentive as the stock can then be sold tax free.

Banking in the Cayman Islands

You can form a bank in the Cayman Islands instead of a holding company, but a banking license must be obtained from the Cayman government. Banks are licensed under the **Bank & Trust Companies Regulation Law 1978**. There are two main classes of Bank licenses, Class A and Class B. Class A license holders are granted the right to operate inside or outside the Caymans. Class A licenses cost CI$30,000, and this fee is payable every January thereafter.

Class B licenses cost between CI$9,000 for an unrestricted, and CI$6,000 for a restricted license. Legal fees on formation of a bank vary from about CI$3,000 to CI$8,000.

Licenses are granted for banking business, trust business, or banking and trust services. The Governor may revoke a license if in his opinion the licensee is carrying on its business in a manner detrimental to public interest or to the interest of its depositors, or is contravening the law. [7.]

Banking & Financial Center unequaled

As of January 1, 1999 bank and trust companies licensed in the Cayman Islands passed the 594 mark, representing over 50 countries, and including 60 with their own local operations. The benefits of doing business in the Islands are reflected in the total of over 35,000 companies registered in the Government registrar, including more than 350 offshore insurance companies. Forty-three of the world's top 50 banks maintain subsidiaries or branches in Cayman. Many of the remaining 594 banks are said to be privately owned, established for a restricted clientele.

Banks are closely regulated by the Government's Inspector of Banks, and audited by such well-known international accounting firms as Price Waterhouse, Thorne Riddell and Peat Marwick. In the past 20 years there have been just three bank failures, none of which were of inter-banking significance. Downtown George Town has a myriad of gleaming new bank buildings a testament to her opulent and booming economy. [8.]

Bank Secrecy in the Caymans

Switzerland, Panama, the Bahamas and Caymans have well established bank secrecy laws designed to prevent unauthorized disclosure of a client's financial affairs to outside authorities. Nevertheless, occasional cracks in Cayman bank secrecy have occurred. In 1976, when the IRS initiated their **Operations Tradewinds** and **Project Havens** to penetrate Cayman and Bahamian bank secrecy, one Cayman bank director was requested by the IRS to cooperate. But the IRS ran into a hedgerow. Here's what happened.

In January of 1976 Anthony Field, then managing director of a Cayman Bank, was served with a subpoena right at the Miami International Airport directing him to appear before a federal grand jury. The grand jury was investigating possible criminal violations of U.S. tax laws.

Mr. Field refused to answer questions on the grounds that he would be in violation of the secrecy provisions of the Cayman Bank & Trust Companies Law of 1966. Charged with contempt of court the case went to the Supreme Court, but by this time Mr. Field, who had never broken his silence, was back in the Caymans. To try to force Mr. Field to testify the IRS would have to serve him with a new subpoena, should he ever step foot in the USA again. Needless to say, there was never another subpoena served Mr. Field.

In response to the Field case, the Caymans enacted a new secrecy law designed to strengthen the old law. Hon. Thomas C. Jefferson, Financial Secretary of the Cayman Islands said in July of 1986 while speaking about the new "Mutual Legal Assistance Treaty" with the U.S. designed to combat illegal money laundering...

---

7. "Doing Business in the Cayman Islands", Price Waterhouse (Information Guide), pg 24, 25.

8. From a Cayman Islands Government Information Services booklet - *Advantages of the Cayman Islands as an Offshore Financial Center (1989)*.

"Our government has always aimed for a clean operation of our financial center. This is not only good sense for the long term, but reflects the upstanding character of the Caymanian, whose Christian principles have led to the banning of casinos and all other forms of gambling.

At the same time, we have recognized the essential need of secrecy for the business transacted here, hence the "Confidential Relationships (Preservation) Law", enacted in 1976 and reinforced by heavier penalties in 1979. We remain convinced that the legitimate investor has a right to confidentiality when he does business in our islands..."

And it is important to note here that we in the Caymans do not recognize tax avoidance as a crime and the treaty (with the USA) specifically excludes tax offenses unless they involve the unlawful proceeds of a crime covered by the treaty. The treaty needs cause no fears to anyone who does not engage in crime." -

> Thomas C. Jefferson,
> Financial Secretary of the Cayman Islands,
> Government Administration Building,
> George Town, Grand Cayman, B.W.I.
> Telephone: 94844, Ext. 112

In 1976, secrecy of ownership was reinforced further when the Cayman government enacted its **Confidential Relationship Law** (Preservation Law of 1976).

As Andy McNab (deputy inspector of banking and trusts) points out, "The Caymans have an unparalleled infrastructure within the region and the islands' traditional use as a major transit point for inter-bank transfers, combined with political stability, have made the Caymans what they are today."

One final point about bank secrecy and legal tax avoidance. It was perhaps best expressed by international tax lawyer and professor Marshal J. Langer in his book, ***Practical International Tax Planning,*** what doctrine and code of conduct planners should stick to. In chapter 1, titled **"The Growth of Excessive Taxation"**, Langer writes...

"Tax evasion is illegal. This is not a book on how to evade taxes. Tax evasion is illegal. Tax avoidance is legal. This book will discuss foreign tax planning, including some ways in which tax havens and financial centers are used by taxpayers to avoid or reduce their tax liability in a legal manner." 9.

Cayman Islands Contacts

Cayman Islands Department of Tourism
420 Lexington Ave., Suite 2312
New York, N.Y. 10170
(212) 682-5582

---

9. Marshall J. Langer, Practical International Tax Planning, pg 5.

Cayman Islands Chamber of Commerce
The Secretary c/o
P.O. Box 1000
George Town, Grand Cayman, B.W.I.
Telephone: 94746

The Caymanian Compass
(newspaper, daily, Monday to Friday)
The Cayman Free Press LTD.
P.O. Box 1365
Grand Cayman, B.W.I.
Telephone: 95111

Mr. Richard Chalmers
Inspector of Banks & Trust Companies
Government Administration Bldg.
George Town, Grand Cayman, B.W.I.
Telephone: 94844, ext. 156

Advantages of using the Cayman Islands as an Offshore Financial Center

Apart from a nominal capitalization tax of CI$10 per adult male (which was abolished in 1985), the Cayman Islands never have had any form of direct taxation, so that "anyone doing business in the islands can be assured that his dollars will work for him free of such depredations as income tax, profits tax, or corporation tax."

Advantages to overseas investors, bankers or companies can be summarized as follows:

• The stability of a well and progressively governed colony of Britain.
• Low crime rate, social harmony, absence of racial tensions.
• Excellent telecommunications, the latest in technology, efficient air services provided by 4 international airlines, reliable shipping links, regular freight supply.
• Proximity to United States - about 2-1/2 hour to Miami, with good daily connections worldwide.
• Highly developed infrastructures, including ports, airfields, roads, utilities and medical and educational services.
• No exchange controls
• Fixed rate of exchange CI$1 = US$1.20
• Modern commercial legislation and legal judicial systems based on that in United Kingdom.
• Severe penalties ensure confidentiality between client and professionals under Confidentiality Relationship (Preservation) Law, qualified only by Government's accepted duty to assist U.S. Government in the investigation of drug-related and other serious crimes.

Offshore holding companies

According to Cayman Company Registrar, the number of companies registered in Cayman went over the 32,000 mark in 1993. This continues an upward spiral with a 200% increase in the last seven years. It is believed at this writing (May, 1999) that the number of companies is now in excess of 45,000 companies.

In 1993 there were 2,696 new exempted companies registered, making the total number of exempted companies 16,465. This is increasing - in the six months to June 30, 1994, there were 1,897 new registrations.

And the Cayman government has recently lowered the annual renewal fees for exempted companies to US$500. Most foreign investors choose the exempted company because names of shareholders and directors are not open to public inspection.

Editors note: Back in the 1970's author, attorney and professor Marshall J. Langer *(Practical International Tax Planning)* predicted that if the Cayman Islands continued to raise the costs of forming a company there, it would price itself out of the market. While professor Langer's prediction has not exactly come true, much of the offshore business is going elsewhere.

In 1984, the British Virgin Islands enacted its **International Business Companies Act.** Since then, approximately 240,000 IBC's have been registered in the BVI. The initial government fee for starting a BVI IBC is only $300. The annual business license fee is $300. These fees are still lower than for a similar company in Cayman.

In 1990, the Bahamas enacted its **International Business Companies Act.** Since then, approximately 90,000 IBC's have been registered. Start-up government fees in the Bahamas are near the lowest in the Caribbean, beginning at $250, with the annual fee being set at $250. If the company has an authorized capital of US $50,000 or issues no par value shares, the fees are $250. Far less than fees in the Cayman Islands.

New Mutual Fund Law

The Cayman government has been a leader in the introduction of new legislations specifically designed to attract new foreign investors. This is reflected in their new Mutual fund Law, designed primarily for institutions and wealthy individuals.

It was in June of 1993, that the Caymans passed its Mutual Fund Law. This legislation was designed to be self-regulating and flexible so to meet the needs of the 48 mutual fund administrators already licensed in the Caymans, including Goldman Sachs, State Street Bank, and BankAmerica. While the fund administrators need to be licensed, the fund itself need not be licensed.

The Section 4(3) Mutual Fund must stipulate the minimum investment per investor at $48,000 or have its equity interests listed on a recognized stock exchange. The Mutual Fund Law requires a simple registration with the CI Inspector.

Anthony Travers, senior partner of the law firm Maples & Calder, has argued that the new Mutual Fund Law wasn't really necessary. "There existed and continues to exist good argument that the introduction of mutual fund regulation was neither necessary nor essential."

"The Cayman's fund industry has always been privately placed or structured for specific institutions, and there was never any market-driven need to obtain Designated Territory or Ucits status for funds."

However, with the tremendous growth of Luxembourg's mutual fund industry, the Caymans thought it time and appropriate to jump on the bandwagon and create a Mutual Fund Law,

In the Bahamas and the BVI, mutual funds can be formed under the respective IBC Acts. Since this often requires the drafting of a special Memorandum and Articles of Association designed especially for an investment company, as well as Investment Advisory Agreements, Subscription Agreements, etc., the costs usually is run much higher.

Limited Duration Company

The Caymans was also the first to set up its Limited Duration Company, not primarily designed for funds but as a corporation which is treated as a partnership for U.S. tax purposes "enabling a flow-through" but without the complexity of the limited partnership structure.

LDCs have been used to establish mutual funds both for inward and outward investment in the U.S., and may be used to access double taxation treaty networks. [10]

---

10. Source: Offshore Financial Review, Greystroke Place & Fetter Lane, London, England EC4A 1ND • tele: 071-405-6969 • Fax: 071-831 2181 • subscription £50.00

Anguilla

Anguilla is a small British dependency located at the northern end of the Leeward Islands in the Caribbean Sea. It is a low-lying, semiarid coral island with an area of 91 sq. km (35 sq. mi) and a maximum elevation of 61 m (200 ft). Its dry climate and thin soil hamper commercial agricultural development. Anguilla has a population of 6,875 (1988 est.), which is predominantly black.

Anguilla has no taxes

Anguilla has no individual income tax, no corporate income tax, no capital gains tax, no withholding tax, no gift tax, no estate tax, no probate fee, and no value added tax. Anguilla has no taxes of any kind, except for small customs duties on selected items. Midway through 1980 there were at least 319 registered enterprises, including 46 banks. Today there are over 5,000 enterprises registered in Anguilla.

Current data on the growth of Anguilla as an offshore financial center show there are more than 75 registered banks, including some of the world's most prestigious names, i.e., Barclays Bank International and Bank of America. Anguilla is an excellent haven for the establishment of an offshore bank, as there are no exchange controls to hinder currency flow. Bank accounts can be maintained in any currency, and banking transactions may be conducted without restriction.

While the local economy is based on industrial fishing, boat building and live stock cultivation, the government has made it clear that it does not intend to impose taxes or disrupt Anguilla's growth as an offshore financial center.

History

Discovered by Christopher Columbus in 1493, Anguilla was made a British colony in 1650. It was governed as part of Saint Kitts-Nevis-Anguilla from the early 18th century. Rebellion and secession occurred in 1967; following British intervention in 1969, Anguilla became a separate dependency with internal self government. This status was formalized by the Anguilla Act of 1980.

Anguilla's is one of Britain's Dependent Territories in the Caribbean. Although essentially self governing, the British Governor is responsible for foreign affairs, defense, internal security and offshore financial services. The legal system is based upon English common law.

As early European explorers sailed past Anguilla for the first time, they must have marveled at the contrast between it and its mountainous neighbor St. Martin just a few miles to the south. The island is flat with only a few rolling hills rising to the highest elevation of 213 feet. However, they would have been equally enthralled by its most striking feature: the dozens of blinding white sand beaches which ring its coastline, some stretching for miles and others hidden away in tiny inlets. In a region renowned for pristine beaches, Anguilla's rank among the finest.

The island was first thrust upon the international stage in 1967 when it unilaterally opted out of a union with St. Kitts and Nevis. The tri-island Associated state was moving towards independence and the Anguillians decided that, rather than continue under the rule of St. Kitts, they would take their chances, seek to secede from the union and remain under British rule. The events which followed are well documented.

The island briefly became the subject to newspaper headlines worldwide. After much political and diplomatic maneuvering a political settlement was reached but not before British paratroopers had landed in Anguilla to restore order. Instead of the heavily armed rebel force which they expected, the British troops were met by islanders waving Union Jacks and singing "Rule Britannia"; this, after all, was precisely the objective which they were seeking to bring about.

In 1981 the island was formally separated from St. Kitts and Nevis. Today it remains a British territory with a similar constitutional status to Bermuda, the Cayman Islands and the British Virgin Islands.

The late '70's and early '80's saw a new and exciting development. Anguilla embarked on a major initiative to become a high quality, exclusive tourist destination. This saw immediate and remarkable success, and the '80's was a decade of rapid economic and social development for the island. The boom in construction as resorts were built, coupled with the creation of jobs in the new tourism sector combined to confirm Anguilla's position as one of the most affluent islands in the region. The secret of its success is undoubtedly the image which it has carefully built as a high end tourist destination and as a place where the discerning visitor can enjoy peace and privacy in some of the most luxurious resorts in the world.

Today, the British Dependent Territory of Anguilla is best known as an up market tourist destination, with intriguing-sounding names such as Prickly Pear Cays, Crocus Bay, Blowing Point Village and Sandy Hill Fort.

Financial Services

Anguilla has been involved in the provision of offshore financial services for many years. In 1991 the Government took the decision to develop the financial services sector as a means of strengthening and diversifying the overall economic base and to provide another employment source for Anguillians who were now obtaining university education in unprecedented numbers. The island already possessed most of the characteristics which are essential to an international financial services centre. These have assisted financial planners to put together structures requiring a zero tax jurisdiction.

Today, no financial services can hope to succeed unless it is well regulated. Anguilla is no exception.

The offshore financial services sector in Anguilla is the responsibility of the Governor, although day to day regulation is delegated to the Department of Financial Services. In carrying out its functions and in considering applications by organizations wishing to establish business within the sector, the Department aims to adopt a firm but flexible regulatory approach.

It is of paramount concern to the Government that Anguilla's reputation is not tainted by the use of the jurisdiction for money laundering or other illegal purposes. For this reason, all licensed institutions are expected to carry out proper due diligence and "know your customer" checks so that they are satisfied as to the identity of their clients and the legitimate origin of their clients' funds.

Although commercial confidentiality is ensured by legislation, the authorities in Anguilla will cooperate fully with law enforcement agencies and regulators in other jurisdictions in the case of illegalities. In common with other reputable jurisdictions the Department of Financial Services is, subject to safeguards to protect legitimate business, able to share regulatory information with overseas regulatory authorities.

Anguilla already has a well established professional infrastructure. The Government recognizes that, as a relatively new jurisdiction, an expansion of the sector would benefit the economy.

Applications from suitable professionals and organizations within the industry are, therefore, welcome. Any organization wishing to establish within the sector will be required to demonstrate that it is prepared to establish a real business on-island and a multi-year work permit program has been introduced to facilitate this. Alternatively, in the case of a licensed institution, an administered or managed basis for the issue of al license will be considered. This would entail the full management and administration of the licensee's business by an equivalent licensed institution on island.

When options for upgrading Anguilla's financial services legislation were being considered, the decision was taken to replace, rather than amend, the existing legislation with a wide range of specially developed Ordinances. Since 1995, Anguilla has had the benefit of a comprehensive, well integrated and cohesive package of financial services legislation.

The legislation is designed to afford flexibility to practitioners and contains many innovative provisions. The Trusts Ordinance, for example, abolishes the Rule against Perpetuities and permits accumulation of income throughout the entire term of the trust. In line with modern developments in trust law, purpose trusts are permitted and the concept of a protector has been introduced. Asset protection trust and forced heirship are also catered for in the new legislation.

The corporate Ordinances provide for international business companies, limited liability (or limited life) companies and ordinary companies which, due to Anguilla's true zero tax status, can be used as domestic or offshore vehicles. Companies limited by guarantee, hybrid companies and non profit companies are all permitted. Legislation covering limited partnerships, offshore banks and trust companies, insurance and company management has also been enacted.

The Mokoro Report

Anguilla once formed part of the Dependent Territories of St. Kitts, Nevis and Anguilla. Anguilla broke away from that union in 1967 but remained legally bound to it up to 1980. The British Crown Colony of Anguilla is a self governing dependency, and as such has adopted its own tax laws. Anguilla, on its own merit, has chosen to become a full-fledged **no-tax haven** like the Caymans and the Bahamas.

In February 1992, Anguilla passed new laws regulating offshore banks and trust companies that choose to do business there. As local lawyer Dan Mitchell puts it..., "Our hope is that it will now be difficult for persons who form banks for criminal proposes to form and use Anguilla offshore banks."

In December 1992 the British Government aid agency, the Overseas Development Administration, engaged the UK consultancy firm of Mokoro Limited to advise the Government of Anguilla on its economic strategy for the 21st century. The Mokoro Report was completed in April 1993 and identified the financial sector as the principal alternative way forward in the development of additional economic activity in Anguilla. The principal benefits identified were:

* Substantial additional government revenue.
  * Sizable increase in the contribution of professional services to the GDP (Gross Domestic Product).
  * Range of new employment opportunities for young people.
  * Increase in professional trading.
  * Inward migration of Anguillians living overseas.
  * Increase in the number of visitors and a decrease in their seasonability.

The Mokoro Report advised that the prerequisites for the development of the offshore financial industry were:

* Good Communications.
* Good modern legislation.
* A strong diverse professional community.
* Positive role by Anguillian Government in facilitating changes and adapting to marketing requirements.

The Anguillian Government has now accepted the Mokoro Report. Recognizing that the period of rapid growth in tourism has come to an end, the Government now acknowledges that the future economic development of Anguilla revolves around Anguilla becoming a competitive tax haven along the lines of some of its Caribbean neighbors, i.e., the Cayman Islands, the Bahamas, The British Virgin Islands, the Turks & Caicos Islands, and Panama.

The financial services section in Anguilla (banking and insurance) currently contribute about 10% of the GDP. In the Bahamas, the financial sector contribute about 30% of the GDP. In the British Virgin Islands, it is believed that the financial sector contributes to over 50% of that country's GDP.

The Anguillian government understands that the cornerstone of any offshore sector is the legislation regulating companies incorporated in that center. New legislation enacted on January 1, 1994 include:

1. An International Business Companies Act virtually identical to the IBC Acts enacted in the Bahamas (1989), Belize (1990) and the BVI (1984).
2. Insurance Act.
3. Trusts Act.
4. Fraudulent Dispositions Act.
5. Limited Liability Companies Act.
6. Limited Partnership Act.
7. Partnership Act.
   International Business Companies Act.

The new IBC Act which makes provisions for the incorporation and regulation of International Business companies. The IBC Act is in addition to the already existing Companies Act.

Companies Act, Cap 335 of Anguilla [11].

There are approximately 5,200 companies registered under the Companies Act (Cap 335 of Anguilla). In 1993, a total of 213 new companies were registered in Anguilla. No differentiation exists between a local or offshore company in the Company Registry.

---

11. From *Close up: Anguilla,* Offshore Investment (December/January 1993).

Such categories as ordinary or exempt company (Cayman Islands and Turks & Caicos Islands), IBC's (Bahamas, BVI and Antigua) are more or less irrelevant in Anguilla because there are no personal or corporate income taxes of any kind. Profits may be retained offshore or repatriated at will. Anguilla has no exchange controls.

Some features of Anguilla's Companies Act include:

1. Directors or Shareholders may be individuals (persons other than Anguillian citizens) or corporations. The Anguillian Register of Companies does not differentiate between a non-Anguillian shareholder or director in its records.

2. Companies other than banks, trust companies and insurance companies may operate legally in Anguillian using nominees as shareholders, rather than disclosing the names of the principals. Only a public company if authorized by its Articles can issue bearer shares.

3. No company may use or continue to use the words "bank", "trust", "trust company", "savings and loan" or any other similar derivatives in the company's name. To use such a title you would need to get a license from the Government under the offshore bank and trust companies ordinance. (see below).

4. In the Companies Act, companies are categorized as public or private. The number of shareholders in a private company is limited to a minimum of two to a maximum of fifty. A public company is limited to a minimum of five.

5. The name of the proposed company must have the word "Limited" as the last word of its name.

6. The place with which the registered office of the company is proposed to be situated.

7. The objectives for which the proposed company is to be established.

8. To incorporate a company, a Memorandum of Association stating the company's objectives must be signed by all the original subscribers. Nominees can be used to sign this document.

9. The Companies Act requires that the following statutory records be kept at the registered office.
- Register of Members.
- Register of Mortgages and charges.
- Register of Directors.
- Books of accounts.
- Register of transfer of shares.

10. An annual return containing the names and addresses of the shareholders and directors of the company must be files each year. The fact that Anguillians hold their shares in trust for a foreigner need not be declared.

11. Annual meetings are required, but need not be held in Anguilla.

12. Every Anguillian company must have a registered office in Anguilla.

Editors Note: No annual return of any kind needs to be filed in either the British Virgin Islands or the Bahamas.

Incorporation costs for IBCs

(a) For registration of a company where all the shares are par value and

(i) the authorised capital is $50,000 or less US$250
(ii) the authorised capital exceeds $50,000 US$1,000

(b) For registration of a company where:

(i) the authorised capital of the company does not exceed $50,000
and some or all of its shares are no par value, or
(ii) the company has no authorised capital and all of its shares are no par value US$250

(c) In the case of a notice of increase of authorised capital from $50,000 or less to more than $50,000 = US$750

(d) For registration of an amendment to the articles 100

(e) Subject to paragraph (f), for registration of articles of merger or consolidation = US$500

(f) In the case of articles of merger or consolidation that also constitute the articles of a company the authorised capital of which exceeds $50,000 or that amend the articles of a surviving company to increase the authorised capital from $50,000 or less to more than $50,000 = US$700

Annual fee (payable on or before every anniversary date of incorporation or continuation)

(i) where the authorised capital does not exceed $50,000; or where the authorised capital does not exceed $50,000 and some or all of its shares are no par value, = US$200
(ii) where authorised capital exceeds $50,000 US$700
(iii) where there is no authorised share capital and all its shares are no par value = US$250

(b) An international business company which fails to pay the annual fee under sub-paragraph (a) on or before the anniversary date shall, in addition to the annual fee, pay a penalty of an amount equal to 10% of the annual fee.

(c) An international business company which fails to pay the annual fee and the penalty due under sub-paragraph (b) shall, upon the expiration of three months from the anniversary date, be liable to pay in addition to the annual fee, a penalty of an amount equal to 50% of the annual fee.

Total additional costs to incorporate, excluding above government fee, range from US$800 to US$2,400 (depending on complexity). Fees for a corporate secretary or nominee director are US$100 to $400 annually.

Angullian Bank Secrecy Law

Anguilla has a bank secrecy ordinance similar to Montserrat's, called the **Confidential Relationships Ordinance, 1981.**

Offenses and penalties

(1) Subject to the provisions of subsection (2) of section 3, any person who -

(a) being in possession of confidential information, however obtained -
(i) divulges it to any person not entitled to possession thereof; or
(ii) attempts, offers or threatens to divulge it to any person not entitled to possession thereof;
(b) obtains or attempts to obtain confidential information to which he is not entitled,
shall be guilty of an offense:

Provided that it shall be a defense for a person charged with an offense under this subsection if he proves to the satisfaction of the court that, at the time when he divulged, attempted, offered or threatened to divulge or obtained or attempted to obtain (as the case may be), the confidential information in question, he did not know and did not have reasonable grounds to suspect that so doing would be a breach of an express or implied duty to preserve confidentiality or would be contrary to the provisions of this Ordinance.

(2) Any person who, being in possession of information which he knows or has reason to suppose is confidential information, makes use thereof, without the consent of the principal, for the benefit of himself or any other person, shall be guilty of an offense.

(3) Any person who commits an offense under this section shall be liable on summary conviction

(a) in the case of an individual to a fine of five thousand dollars or to imprisonment for 12 months or to both such fine and imprisonment; or
(b) in the case of a body corporate to a fine of twenty-five thousand dollars;

Provided that where an offense under this section is committed by a professional person, that person shall be liable on conviction -

(i) in the case of an individual to a fine of ten thousand dollars or to imprisonment for 12 months or to both such fine and imprisonment; or
(ii) in the case of a body corporate to a fine of fifty thousand dollars.

(4) Any person who is convicted of an offense under subsection (1) and is proved to have solicited, received or offered (as the case may be), on behalf of himself or any other person, any reward for doing the act which constituted the offense, shall be liable, in addition to any penalty imposed under subsection (3), to a further fine equivalent to the amount or value of the reward solicited, received or offered and to forfeit the amount or value of any reward actually received by him.
(5) Where an offense under this section is committed by a body corporate and is proved to the satisfaction of the court to have been committed with the consent or connivance of, or to have been attributed to any neglect on the part of, any director, manager, secretary or similar officer (by whatever name called) of that body corporate, or by any person purporting to act in any such capacity, he as well as the body corporate shall be guilty of an offense and be liable to be proceeded against and punished accordingly.
(6) For the avoidance of doubt, it is hereby declared that, subject to subsection (2) of section 3, a bank which gives credit reference in respect of a customer, without first obtaining the authority of that customer, shall be guilty of an offense under subsection (1).

New legislative changes

The Government aims to make some changes to the above Act. Some of these enhancements include:

• Private companies may have one director in addition to the company secretary, both of whom may be incorporated bodies.

• The company name may end in "Societe Anonyme" or "Sociedad Anonima" or the abbreviations "S.A." or "N.C.s".

• The authorized capital, if any, may be stated in any currency, or in more than one currency.

• Transfer of domicile is permitted. Any foreign corporation may transfer its domicile into Anguilla, so long as the laws of the foreign country do not expressly prohibit such transfer. Likewise, transfer of an Anguillian company to another jurisdiction will be permitted.

During 1994 and the early part of 1995, Anguilla introduced a modern package of financial legislation. It consisted of eight separate ordinances: Companies; Intentional Business Companies; Limited Liability Companies; Partnerships; Limited Partnerships; Trusts; Fraudulent Dispositions; and Company Managers. With the enactment of the new Companies Ordinance, International Business Companies Ordinance and Limited Liabilities Companies Ordinance, trust and tax practitioners now have a choice of corporate vehicles for their clients.

Offshore companies can continue to be formed under the domestic Companies Ordinance as Anguillan companies or as distinct offshore IBCs. There is also the option now of limited liability companies. The LLC, a US invention first enacted in the state of Wyoming in 1977, is a hybrid company/partnership with characteristics of a company (separate legal identity, capacity to sue and be sued, capacity to own and deal in property and limited liability of interest-holders) and a partnership (being considered 'pass through' entities for US income tax purposes). LLCs are commonly used in joint ventures, venture capital formation and real estate syndications.

Anguilla's new Companies Ordinance is based on the Caribbean Law Institute l)raft Bill, which in turn was largely taken from the modern Canadian model, and in particular- the Ontario legislation.

Some private companies, called specified private companies, are exempt from record-keeping and financial accounting on certain conditions. In addition, each company must have a registered office and agent resident in Anguilla. Directors and shareholders need not be Anguillans, nor is there any requirement for annual meetings to he held in the island. Annual returns listing directors, shareholders, registered office and agent must be filed annually. No financial statements need be filed unless the company is a public company. Nominee shareholders and directors can be used.

New Trusts Act

An important part of the new legislation for tax practitioners is Anguilla's new Trusts Ordinance. The Anguillan Ministry of Finance claims the law is a collection of the latest and most modern trust laws in the world.

Highlights of the new provisions arc:

• Abolition of the rule against perpetuities;
• Creation of commercial purpose trusts;
• Provision for the office of Protector of a Trust;
• Choice of governing law provisions to resolve the jurisdictional issues of international conflict of laws relating to trusts;
• Optional registration of trusts.
• Provision for recognition of variant forms of trusts and trusts to be written in foreign languages;
• Expanded definition of charitable trusts and authorized trustee investments;

Under the Fraudulent Dispositions Ordinance, an Anguillan trust is protected by imposing a three-year limitation period within which a creditor can attack a disposition of assets by proving a fraudulent transfer. The burden of proof is on the creditor to establish the fraudulent disposition.

Registration fees for trusts in Anguilla

The following fees shall be payable to the Registrar under the Trusts Ordinance for the following purposes:-

(a) For registration of trust under section 68(3) US$250

(b) For registration of a variation to a registered trust under section 68(5) = US$150

(c) For cancellation of registration of trust under section 68(6) = US$100

Editor's Note: The Bahamas, and a few other jurisdictions impose no government trust fee or requirement that a trust be registered.

The Offshore Bank and Trust Company Ordinance

The Offshore Bank and Trust Company Ordinance regulates Anguillan trust companies for the first time. A trust company must have a capitalization of at least Eastern Caribbean $1.2 million (US$447,760), of which at least EC$480,000 must be paid up in cash.

Under the new laws, the British Governor has wide powers to inspect and regulate and a license refusal is final with no court appeal possible.

Trust companies must have a principal place of business and authorized agents in Anguilla and accounts of trust companies will be audited.

A detailed questionnaire must be completed by each shareholder, director and officer. It is designed to enable agencies like Interpol, the FBI and Scotland Yard to check the background of applicants.

John Benjamin head of a local law firm says: "We like the idea of an inspector and a relationship with the Bank of England and the requirements for capitalization to make sure companies can do the job properly."

However, some practitioners fear that some of the stiff requirements on the application form are unnecessarily cumbersome, asking questions which people might find intrusive.

Offshore banks are supervised by the superintendent of offshore banks. According to superintendent Mr. Dowling: "It is a matter of improving the quality. The forms look a bit forbidding at first but they are not difficult to fill out and are only for approval when an institution is starting up."

Banks will incur fees of US$60,000 to start up, including a non-refundable application vetting fee of US$10,000. The bank license fee is US$20,000, with a stamp duty of US$2,000. Lawyers fees for incorporation run $15,000, and statutory agents cost US$10,000.

Offshore banks that engage in trust as well as banking business will have a higher capitalization requirement that a purely banking operation. Both a bank and a trust license is required.

Guidelines for Bank Licensing

The granting of a Banking License is discretionary; it is a privilege to be extended or withheld - it is not a right of any applicant. The key point of control in the regulation of the banking sector is when an application is being considered by the Licensing authority. Applicants should understand that the proper investigation of their application may take some time and they should plan accordingly.

The supervision of banks engaged in cross-border operations requires close ongoing cooperation between the respective national supervisory authorities. Dependent Territories have taken steps to ensure that legal gateways exist within their banking legislation to permit a free exchange of regulatory information with other recognized banking supervisory authorities where such information will assist those authorities in carrying out their responsibilities.

Licensing Policy

The policy with respect to bank licensing, and except where the bank is predominantly locally owned and primarily doing business in the territory and those banks in Anguilla and Montserrat which are the subject to supervision by the Eastern Caribbean Central Bank, is as follows:

a)   full banking activities will only be permitted by branches or subsidiaries of banks with a well established and proven track record and which are subject to effective consolidated supervision by their home supervisory authority.

b)   off-shore banking will only be permitted by:
(i)   branches or subsidiaries of banks with a well established and proven track record which are subject to effective consolidated supervision;
(ii) banks which, although not subsidiaries, are closely associated with an overseas bank, and which, by agreement, will be included within the consolidated supervision exercised by the overseas bank's home supervisory authority;
(iii)   wholly-owned subsidiaries of certain acceptable non-bank corporations whose shares are quoted on a recognized stock exchange, where the objective of the subsidiary is to undertake in-house treasury operations only, and where the operations are fully consolidated within the published financial statements of the parent company.

Banks will only be granted licenses if their place of incorporation, mind and management are within the same jurisdiction, or, in the case of a subsidiary, if the mind and management are located in the jurisdiction in which consolidated supervision is being exercised.

In line with internationally accepted good practice in relation to bank license applications, the Licensing Authority should expect as a minimum to be satisfied that:
(a)   the management has proven experience in a relevant field of banking
(b)   the controllers are fit and proper people to undertake the functions envisaged and that the ongoing management will be competent;
(c)   the institution will conduct its business in a prudent fashion;
(d)   the institution has devised an appropriate and sustainable business plan;
(e)   adequate capital and other resources will be provided in relation to that business plan;

(f) direct confirmation has been received from the supervisory authority in the country in which the institution or its proposed parent is incorporated, that the authority;

(i) consents to the establishment of the institution in the host territory;

(ii) will exercise consolidated supervision over the institution's overall activities, including within the host territory; and

(iii) will cooperate in the sharing of regulatory information with the Licensing Authority.

(g) the applicant will appoint approved auditors who will perform that work according to internationally accepted auditing standards.

(h) the applicant will disclose to the Licensing Authority all information that the latter legitimately needs to fulfill its overall supervisory responsibilities.

A prerequisite for the maintenance of sound banking standards is careful consideration of the financial standing, overall probity, skills and reputation of new banking applicants.

Any subsequent change of ownership one the license has been granted, will require the prior approval of the Licensing Authority and will be subject to independent verification and checking by the Authority, similar in scope to that required of the original applicant.

British and Anguilla Governments have jointly embarked

Anguilla has had a financial services industry for a number of years, but it is only recently that the British and Anguilla Governments have jointly embarked upon an aggressive program to launch Anguilla as an up-market, well regulated and exclusive financial services center.

The significant growth in Government revenues earned from the financial services sector over the last few years is a testament to the success of the policies to date. The Government has ambitious plans for the future and it is anticipated that by the turn of the century, Anguilla will be well positioned as a major player in the international arena.

When options for upgrading Anguilla's financial services legislation were being considered, the decision was taken to replace, rather than amend, the existing legislation with a wide range of specially developed Ordinances. Since 1995, Anguilla has had the benefit of a comprehensive, well integrated and cohesive package of financial services legislation.

Developments in 1997-98 led to new external and domestic insurance legislation, mutual funds legislation and amendments to the existing corporate and trust legislation.

Anguilla now has perhaps the most technologically advanced Companies Registry in the offshore world. Agents within and outside Anguilla will be able to access the fully computerized registry from their desktop either by direct modem link or via the Internet on a 24 hour, 365 day basis. The system, the development of which is being funded by the British Government, was designed by Companies House in the UK.

The facilities available will include on-line name checking and reservations, incorporation of companies (including International Business and Limited Liability Companies) and the electronic filing of standard company documents.

The system will be particularly attractive to overseas agents as they will be able to offer their clients the guaranteed incorporation of companies in real time. Law firms, accountants, trust companies and company formation and management companies will be eligible to be appointed as overseas agents. All companies will, of course, still be required to have a local registered office and registered agent.

The system will incorporate the highest standards of security to ensure that unauthorized access is not possible.

Exchange Controls

There are no foreign exchange controls in Anguilla. Although the official currency is the Eastern Caribbean Dollar, the United States Dollar is commonly used.

- British Dependent Territory
- Zero tax jurisdiction
- No foreign exchange restrictions
- Well regulated financial services industry
- Common law legal system based on English law
- Well developed professional infrastructure
- State of the art computerized companies registry
- Excellent telecommunications system
- Easy air access to North America & Europe
- Multi year work permits available for professionals within the financial services industry

Bermuda – captive insurance company tax haven

The islands of Bermuda have for decades been used as an offshore financial centre by international companies (and individuals) originating from the United States of America thanks to the island's close geographical proximity to North America.

Isolated archipelago

Bermuda is an isolated archipelago of 21 main islands and 160 islets located in the western Atlantic about 750 miles southeast of New York City and 3,445 miles from London. The Bermudas have a long history as a tax haven, and practitioners often refer to it as the *"Cadillac"* of the havens because it caters mainly to the rich and *carriage trade.* [12.]

Bermuda has the oldest parliamentary assembly in the western hemisphere (369 years) and the third oldest (behind Britain and the Isle of Man) in the world. Links with Royal England have been constitutionally preserved, and Bermuda today is the oldest self-governing British Crown Colony. With over 8,000 international exempted companies in her register, and the largest captive insurance market in the world, Bermuda is a celebrated tax haven. There is no form of corporate or personal income tax in Bermuda.

Bermuda is a British Crown Colony tax haven much like the Cayman Islands, the Turks & Caicos Islands, the Bahamas (now an independent member of the British Commonwealth) and Anguilla. Aside from being first-class tropical island tourist centers, what these five tax havens have most in common is that none of them impose taxes of any kind on companies and trusts organized under their laws.

Over the last few years Bermuda's financial service industry has pushed the Government to reexamine ways to attract new offshore business. Amendments to Bermuda's **Companies Act** have now been put into effect to ease the administration of mutual funds and investment companies - one of Bermuda's largest industries.

The new changes permit:

* Prospectuses for funds listed on an "appointed stock exchange" (like the NYSE or the Hong Kong exchange) no longer need to satisfy additional Bermudian requirements as to the contents.
* Companies listed on an appointed stock exchange are no longer required to have a quorum of Bermudian resident directors.
* Bermuda companies can pay dividends out of capital, not just out of profits.
* Companies can now be formed with just one member and the directors are no longer required to own qualifying shares.
* The holding of meetings be telephone and the passing of written resolutions has been adopted.
* Provisions have been made to allow "migration of companies to and from Bermuda.
* The use of limited partnerships in collective investment schemes has been facilitated.

In addition, Barclays Bank of Bermuda has recently sold its controlling interest in Bermuda's third largest bank - the Bermuda Commercial Bank. This has made banking in Bermuda more competitive, as the Bermuda government has granted banking licenses to only three banks.

Recently, Coutts & Co., Schroders, Royal Trust and Lombard Odier have organized trust companies in Bermuda.

Bermuda is home for many Fortune 100 subsidiaries

There are more than 12,000 Bermuda based international companies, 2241 locals, 300 overseas partnerships and 600 other non residents, many with a global business empire. They include subsidiaries of 75% of the Fortune 100 and their European equivalents. Only 235 or 3.4% of the internationals have local offices, yet account for 75% of internationals' spending. In insurance and reinsurance, Bermuda has an industry capital base exceeding US$ 35 billion and gross premiums of US$ 24 billion. It ranks with Lloyds of London and New York as a global leader.

Business Infrastructure

Much of Bermuda's success as an international financial and business centre has

---

12. Known also as the Bermudas or Somers Islands, collectively they are called the 'Island' of Bermuda. From *"Doing Business in Bermuda"*, by Price Waterhouse, pg. 1

been due to the high quality of its professional support services. Today, there are some 190 lawyers, 500 accountants and 50 chartered financial analysts on the Island. The world's major accounting firms are, in one form or another, represented in Bermuda.

Bermuda's legal system is based on English common law, the doctrines of equity, and Acts passed by the Bermuda Legislature. The resulting system is uncomplicated and free of the cumbersome restrictions imposed by excessive restraints - legal, supervisory and regulatory- sometimes found in other countries.

Equally important is the fact that Bermuda has a virtual absence of income taxes, withholding taxes, capital gains taxes, capital transfer taxes, estate duties or inheritance taxes. Moreover, a Bermuda exempted company can, under current policy, apply to the Bermuda Government for an exemption from paying any taxes until 2016 should taxes be imposed on corporate earnings after the company is incorporated. No stamp duty is payable in respect of any instrument executed by an exempted company or in respect of any instrument relating to an interest in an exempted company or on any transaction on the Bermuda Stock Exchange.

Banking Services

Although there is no "offshore banking" as such in Bermuda, some 90 international banks use the island, primarily through equity interests in Bermuda exempted companies, to carry on a wide range of financial activities, such as leasing, real estate ventures, group financing, collective investment schemes and the like. Any entity wishing to carry on "banking business" as defined by the Banks Act 1969 is required to obtain a license.

Presently there are three licensed banks in Bermuda, each listed on the Bermuda Stock Exchange: The Bank of Bermuda Limited, The Bank of N.T. Butterfield & Son Limited, and the Bermuda Commercial Bank Limited. The former two, and larger banks, have each been in existence for over 100 years. As at 31 December, 1994, the consolidated assets of the three banks were some $12.4 billion, while the assets under their administration were valued at several times that amount. Bermuda's licensed banks are supervised by the Bermuda Monetary Authority through its application of the Basle standards. Banks in Bermuda have voluntarily agreed with the Bermuda Monetary Authority to maintain capital adequacy risk ratios calculated on their world consolidated operations at 10 per cent. This ratio is comfortably in excess of the internationally recommended minimum standard of 8 per cent.

The three banks have, collectively, branch, subsidiaries and representative offices around the world including the Bahamas, the British Virgin Islands, the Cayman Islands, the Cook Islands, Guernsey, Hong Kong, Ireland, the Isle of Man, Jersey, London, Luxembourg, Mauritius, New York, New Zealand, Singapore and Western Samoa. As a consequence, Bermuda's banks have a global perspective which is enhanced by excellent telecommunications and computer systems, large networks of correspondent relationships and sophisticated money transfer systems. These attributes enable the Bermuda banks to compete successfully with the larger money centre banks worldwide for their services.

To bank in Bermuda write:

Donald P. Lines, OBE, CFA, JP
Bank of Bermuda, Ltd.
6 Front Street
Hamilton, 5-31, HM11 BERMUDA

Bank and Insurance Companies

There are only three banks authorized to do business in Bermuda, and if you want to form a private bank in Bermuda, don't bother. The Government will not issue you a license. As of 1987, Bermuda's three banks (Bank of Bermuda, Bank of NT Butterfield, and Bermuda Commercial Bank) held $7 billion in Bermuda dollars and $5.1 billion on deposit with foreign banks against foreign currency deposits.

There are about 1,600 insurance and reinsurance companies registered in Bermuda with assets in excess of US$30 billion, and capital and surplus in excess of US$12 billion. Annual premium volume is more than US$10 billion. In 1985, ACE Insurance established a presence in Bermuda with an initial capitalization of $250 million, but within 12 months had $1 billion in capital.

Bermuda has adopted a quality rather than a quantity approach to attracting client.

This strategy is clearly reflected in the country's high minimum annual government fee of US $1,680, which is based upon the minimum issued share capital requirement of US $12,000, and in the various regulations it imposes on companies.

Captive Re-insurance Business

One of Bermuda's greatest financial strengths is its insurance industry. As at 31 December, 1994, Bermuda's captive insurance and reinsurance markets comprised 1,343 companies. Today, Bermuda is the chosen home for more than half the world's captive insurers and has rapidly become a favorite location for catastrophe insurers. Bermuda's companies have total assets of almost US $70 billion, capital and surplus of almost US$29 billion and net premiums written in excess of US$13 billion. These figures include the significant growth that Bermuda experienced in 1993 with companies writing property catastrophe risks injecting over $4 billion dollars in capital and surplus into the Bermuda insurance market.

The local governments of most all the British Commonwealth tax havens, including Bermuda, the Cayman Islands, the Bahamas, the British Virgin Islands and Anguilla, have enacted special laws to provide foreign investors (i.e., foreign depositors) confidentiality in regards to their offshore financial affairs. It is particularly interesting to note that in all these tax havens the good blessings and seal of approval for these secrecy legislations are provided for by "The Queens Most Excellent Majesty" - Queen Elizabeth II of England.

Needless to say, there is nothing in the United States doctrine that offers investors any such protection. In Bermuda all the legislation (including The Banks Act, 1969, The Trust Companies Act 1991 and the Bermuda Stock Exchange Company Act 1992) come with the following preamble:

Be it enacted by the Queen's Most Excellent Majesty, by and with the advice and consent of the Senate and the house of Assembly of Bermuda, and by the authority of the same as follows:

The Bermuda Monetary Authority Act 1969, No. 57
1994 Unofficial Consolidation

Secrecy

31. (1) Except in so far as may be necessary for the due performance of his functions under the Act or other statutory provision, [and subject to subsections (1A), (1B) and (1C) any person who is a director of the Board or who is acting as, an officer, a servant, an agent or an advisor of the Authority shall preserve and aid in preserving secrecy with regard to all matters relating to the affairs of the Government or the Authority or of any person that may come to his knowledge in the course of his duties; and any director, officer, servant, agent or advisor who communicates any such matter to any person other than the Minister, Board or an officer of the Authority authorized in that behalf by the Chairman or suffers or permits any unauthorized person to have access to any books, papers or other records relating to the Government or the Authority, or to any person, shall be guilty or an offense and shall be liable on summary conviction to a fine not exceeding ten thousand dollars or to imprisonment for a term not exceeding six months or to both such fine and imprisonment and on conviction on indictment to a fine not exceeding twenty-five thousand dollars or to imprisonment for a term not exceeding two years or to both such fine and imprisonment.]

(1A) Subsection (1) does not preclude the disclosure of information -

(a) for the purpose of enabling or assisting the Minister to exercise any functions conferred on him by this Act or the Regulations made thereunder or in connection with the dealings between the Minister and the Authority when the Authority exercises its functions under section 21(1)(a);

(b) for the purpose of enabling or assisting the Board or the Authority to exercise any functions conferred on them by this Act or the Regulations made thereunder;

(c) if the information is or has been available to the public from other sources;

(d) in a summary or collection of information framed in such a way as not to enable the identity of any individual depositor, client or other customer of a financial institution or of any financial institution to which the information relates to be ascertained.

(1B) Subsection (1) does not preclude the disclosure of information for the purpose of enabling or assisting an authority in a country or territory outside Bermuda to exercise functions corresponding to those functions of supervision, regulation or inspection of the Authority.

(1C) Notwithstanding any provision in this Act, no information or document regarding the account or regarding any matter or thing relating to the business or other affairs of any individual depositor, client or other customer of a financial institution which has been obtained by the Authority in the exercise of its functions relating to the supervision, regulation or inspection of a financial institution shall be disclosed.

(2) [No director, officer, servant, agent or advisor of the Authority shall be] required to produce in any court any book or document or to divulge or communicate to any court any matter or thing coming under his notice in the performance of his duties under this Act or other statutory provision, except on the direction of the court or in so far as may be necessary for the purpose of carrying into effect the provisions of this Act or other statutory provision.

(3) Notwithstanding anything to the contrary in this section it shall be lawful for the Minister, where he is of the opinion that it is desirable so to do in the interests of internal security or for the detection of crime, to authorize any police officer of or above the rank of Inspector by warrant under his hand to inspect and take copies of any of the books or records of the Authority.

(4) The books of the Authority shall be deemed to be banker's books for the purposes of the Evidence Act 1905.

Banking and Exchange Controls

Under the Banks Act of 1969 no person, firm or body corporate can carry on the business of banking, or own a bank in Bermuda, unless it has been specially authorized by an act of the Legislature and obtains a license from the Minister of Finance. The government is not encouraging further application in the banking field.

Because of the strict regulations against the formation of new banks, only three now carry on regular banking business in Bermuda. The Bank of Bermuda Limited was established in 1889. The Bank of Butterfield, Ltd., which is the oldest bank in Bermuda, was established 30 years earlier in 1859. The Bermuda Provident Bank commenced business in 1969.

Exchange controls exist to protect the Bermuda dollar, but exempt companies can operate in any currency other than the Bermuda dollar.

Bermuda has no bank secrecy laws like the Bahamas or the Cayman Islands. It is virtually impossible for unauthorized persons of foreign governments to obtain information about Bermuda companies. The new tax treaty with the U.S. caused a ripple of concern among Bermuda's business community as the treaty allows for an exchange of certain information between Bermuda and U.S. authorities.

The Bermuda Stock Exchange

The Bermuda Stock Exchange is another plus for Bermuda. By the terms of the Bermuda Stock Exchange Company Act 1992 the Exchange is a self-regulatory body under the supervision of the Bermuda Monetary Authority. The Stock Exchange Act came into being as a result of Bermuda recognizing the need to transform the then existing informal local Exchange into a properly regulated modern, electronic exchange, on which international companies can be listed. To date the Exchange has attracted listings of some 35 international mutual funds and 12 international companies.

It is evident that as the Stock Exchange builds its infrastructure and standards, listings of an international nature will increase. Moreover, it is anticipated that the Exchange's tax-free dealing service will enhance Bermuda's attractiveness as an efficient, modern financial and business centre. In turn, this will provide additional incentives for international companies to move to the Island and seek a listing on the Exchange. In this connection it is worth noting that Bermuda has already become the preferred jurisdiction for companies re-locating from Hong Kong and, as at 30 September, 1994, 243 of the 511 companies listed on the Hong Kong Stock Exchange were incorporated in Bermuda.

Trust Business

Trust business continues to be an area of financial growth for Bermuda. With the passing of the Trust Companies Act in 1991, the Bermuda Government lifted the moratorium on the limit of companies providing trust services. Today there are more than 28 trust companies which have been licensed to carry on general trust business, including a number of notable international names. This represents a very significant shift in business opportunities for Bermuda and has broadened the range of the Island's international financial services. In this connection, there are a number of international names evident (for example , Coutts & Co., Barclays, Lombard Odier, Royal Trust of Canada and Schroders) which have a physical presence in Bermuda for trust business.

Bermuda trusts are governed by the island's 1975 Act, with a perpetuity period of 100 years.

Bermuda trusts draw their inspiration from English Common Law and precedent.

As a common-law jurisdiction, Bermuda is very suitable for the establishment of trusts. A resident of any country can form a Bermuda trust. The *settlor* (grantor) does not have to be resident or physically present in Bermuda, and the trust funds do not have to be remitted to Bermuda, but they must be under the trustees control. Trust corpus may consist of cash, land, securities, but not Bermuda currency or shares in a Bermuda local company.

Normally, no bank references or other identification needs be supplied to authorities to form a Bermuda trust. The **Trustee Act of 1975** sets out the general provisions relating to the powers and duties of trustees.

The Common Law Rule Against Perpetuities applies to a Bermuda trust, so the maximum duration of a trust is limited to the lives of the beneficiaries plus twenty-one years. Beneficiaries may include corporations, trustees, individuals, or other settlements.

A new Stamp Amendment Act of 1985 allows a trust to be moved into Bermuda at a cost of $250 regardless of the value of property transferred. If the trust was formed outside Bermuda less than two years before being moved, it will be subject to a stamp tax of 1/10th of 1% of the value of the non-Bermudian property.

For North Americans, Bermuda is probably the best bet, but many UK residents prefer Bermuda because it is further from the reach of both the *Inland Revenue* and influence of the UK government.

Bermuda's bank vaults are stuffed with several thousand family trust deeds but wealthy investors would probably do better to appoint trustees from one of the island's top law firms.

Banks the world over love bank charges and their fees are based on fixed percentages of moneys handled which works out to be a lot more than the administrative charges of an equally efficient legal trustee.

International Trust Company Bermuda, the local Barclay's offshoot, charges an annual administration fee of 0.25% on the first $1M in trust, 0.025% investment fee on all transactions, a withdrawal fee, and an income fee of 3% of the net income "where significant income is generated".

Tax Guarantees

Bermuda has no income or profits tax that applies to individuals or corporations. There are no capital gains taxes, no withholding taxes, no tax on accumulated earnings, no sales tax, no value added tax, no business tax, and no gift tax, estate or inheritance taxes. Bermuda has a small probate tax that covers real and personal property located in Bermuda. The rate is 2% on the first $100,000, and 3% on amounts over $100,000. Under the **Exemption Undertakings Tax Protection Act of 1966,** an exempt company formed by non-Bermudians can receive a written guarantee from the government providing a tax exemption from income taxes being imposed to the year 2006.

Exempt companies

Basically, three types of companies can be formed in Bermuda - local, exempt and overseas. If you plan to carry on business within Bermuda, it is required that at least 60% of the shareholders be Bermudians. Offshore investors usually form an **exempted company**, which is exempt from the 60% ownership requirement of "local" companies. Exempt companies make up the largest group of companies in Bermuda.

An exempted company is prohibited from doing business within Bermuda except for the furtherance of its offshore business. An exempt company can operate from an office or permanent establishment in Bermuda, but cannot trade with persons who are residents or companies resident in Bermuda, with one exception made for reinsurance companies. Exempt companies are further categorized as **"non-resident"**, in which case the companies are incorporated in another country but managed from Bermuda.

The primary attraction of Bermuda for international business purposes is the exempted company. An exempted company is one which is exempted from various provisions of Bermuda law applying to local companies which, among other things restrict the portion of share capital which may be held by non-Bermudians. Thus, exempted companies are predominantly owned by non-Bermudians. Although incorporated in

Bermuda, exempted companies may generally carry on business only in connection with transactions and activities external to Bermuda. As at 31 December, 1994, there were more than 8,000 exempted companies registered in Bermuda carrying out a full range of activities, including insurance, investment management, foreign sales corporations, private and corporate investment holding, shipping, oil trading and oil exploration, group financing etc.

Upon application to the Minister of Finance, an exempted company can receive statutory assurance against any legislation imposing tax on profits or income or a tax on capital asset, gain or appreciation, or any tax in the nature of estate duty or inheritance tax until the year 2016. Exempted companies are also free from exchange controls.

The Government is snobbish about who they permit to incorporate in Bermuda. Good bank references are essential. An advisory committee appointed by the **Minister of Finance** carefully screens applicants and passes on all applications. Incorporation usually takes longer in Bermuda then in other tax havens. Notwithstanding these drawbacks, Bermuda is a first-rate no-tax haven.

Apart from significant incorporation and maintenance fees - which average US$6000 to US$7000 a year assuming minimum capitalization - another distinguishing factor of the island's offshore business is that Bermudan exempt companies generally have a higher degree of bona fide local management and control than would exist in a traditional tax haven. Exempt companies are particularly popular for insurance, inter group financing, shipping and intellectual property activities. [13.]

Bermuda's Law Firms

Bermuda's law firms vary in size and degree of specialization. The largest are British style "barristers at law" and members of the Bermuda Bar Association. Some are also Notaries Public and have substantial corporate law departments engaged in specialty advisory services to tailor Bermuda's legal system to the needs of international clients. Many incorporate companies. In Bermuda, only lawyers may

---

13. From "A sparkling future ahead for the last jewel in Britain's Crown", by Barry Spencer-Higgins, *Offshore Review* (November, 1997)

undertake this process. Unlike in Britain, Canada, the USA and elsewhere, you cannot go directly to a state or national agency handling incorporation.

This makes the incorporation procedure more expensive. It may be why, in flight magazines, Bermuda is not mentioned for "off the shelf" fixed price companies. There is a two part fee for the incorporation process in Bermuda. The first is for the legal services, the second for the Bermuda Government incorporation fees. Both depend on the type of corporate entity desired. Typically, lawyers will draft and prepare the constitutive documents of companies and partnerships, the appropriate applications to the Bermuda Government authorities; and take all necessary action in connection with their registration.

Capitalization Costs & Other Fees

A minimum capitalization of $12,000 BD (about US$12,000) is required for every exempt company. If the company writes insurance, the minimum capitalization is BD$120,000, and the shares must be fully paid. A stamp duty of 1/4 of 1% of the authorized share capital is payable upon filing the **Memorandum of Association**. Lawyers' fees of about BD$2,000 to BD$6,000 (the higher figure is for insurance companies and open-ended mutual funds) should be expected.

Local Companies Tax

Every local company must pay an annual tax based upon issued capital as follows:

Issued Capital BD$	BD$
Less than 50,000	500
50,000 or more but less than 250,000	750
250,000 or more but less than 500,000	1,250
500,000 or more but less than 1,000,000	2,500
1,000,000 or more but less than 10,000,000	5,000

Company Registration

Registration under the new **Companies Act of 1991** commences with an advertisement in the Official Government *"Gazette"* setting out the proposed name, its principle objectives, and the fact that it is an *exempt company*. After making application to the Minister of Finance, the minister will check your bank references, unless you are well-known in the financial community. It can take as long as three months from the time you run your announcement in the government's *Official Gazette* before the company can commence business. The **Minister of Finance** has the final say-so, and can grant or refuse a permit without giving any reason for his decision.

Shares, shareholders and meetings

All shares must have a stated par value. Bearer shares are not permitted. The minimum number of shareholders needed to form a company is three. A company may issue stock with different privileges, and with or without voting rights or dividend preference. A company may raise capital by issuing bonds or debentures unless forbidden by its "by-laws". With the approval of the shareholders the *Memorandum* can be amended to increase or decrease the authorized capital. There must be at least one directors' meeting every year.

Investment Management

Over recent years, Bermuda has also become a leader in the offshore mutual funds industry. As at 31 October, 1994, there were some 557 collective investment schemes operating out of Bermuda (made up of 476 mutual funds and 64 unit trusts and 1 feeder trust, as well as 20 limited partnerships) with an aggregated net asset value of over US$12.3 billion. The granting of Designated Territory Status in 1988 under the United Kingdom Financial Services Act 1986 has also given international recognition of the quality of the Bermuda supervisory and regulatory process.

Shipping

Bermuda's shipping registry dates back to the early 1700's. As at 31 December, 1994 the register contained 93 commercial ships totaling 3,077,097 gross tons and 361 yachts totaling 42,605 gross tons. As part of the British registry, Bermuda registered ships fly the red ensign underfaced and are therefore entitled to the protection of the British Royal Navy. In this regard, Bermuda enjoys "Equivalent Exemption Status" under the U.S.A. Internal Revenue 1986 Code and, as a consequence, its registered vessels and shipping companies may apply to the Internal Revenue Service for exemption from the 4% freight tax levied on certain U.S. related income of foreign shipping corporations.

Aircraft Registration and Leasing

Bermuda's Aircraft register has existed since 1931. It operates substantially as an adjunct to the range of service provided by Bermuda to international company business. As at 1 March, 1995 there were some 109 aircraft on the register and 100 operators. Most of the aircraft are either privately owned or corporate jet aircraft used for the transport of their beneficial owners or company executives. More recently, a number of commercial aircraft have been added to the Register through the use of leasing structures. These factors demonstrate that Bermuda registration enjoys global acceptance and respect. Operations on the Register are therefore conducted with appropriate regulatory safeguards to ensure that this position continues.

People, Language, Political Stability

About 40% of the population of 65,000 is white and the rest is black. English is the official language. Christianity is the main religion. Kite flying is an island sport.

Bermuda is a British self-governing Crown colony. Representative government was introduced into the islands in 1620. Since 1684 the Governors have been appointed by the Crown. Queen Elizabeth maintains a palatial summer home here and is said to visit regularly. Hamilton is the capital city.

The government is biracial, but the white minority has always retained control over the economy of the islands. Bermuda could have gone the way of other Commonwealth colonies (like the Bahamas) and sought independence from Britain, but Bermuda chose to remain a crown colony. Unlike the Bahamas, where the black majority has gained political control, the black majority in Bermuda is still struggling. There has been political unrest in the past.

In 1973 Governor Sir Richard Sharpes and his aid were murdered by assassins. Six months before, the country's police chief was killed. The subsequent trial for murder and hanging of two black men touched off riots in December, 1977 causing millions of dollars in damage. British troops were sent in to keep order. Fortunately, these occasional disturbances have had little impact on the offshore companies operating here. Bermuda boasts complete racial integration.

Income Tax Treaties

Bermuda has signed an exchange-of-information agreement (treaty) with the United States which grants Bermuda complete exemption from U.S. excise tax on insurance and reinsurance premiums through December 31, 1989. The tax treaty took effect on December 2, 1988. Bermuda has no other tax treaties with other nations, including the United Kingdom.

The article that follows (abridged) by Rebecca Stephens appeared in the *Offshore Adviser (April, 1990)*, a subsidiary of the *London Financial Times*. It is interesting to note that the British media, unlike the American media, is not intimidated by political views that seek to tax the human being to the limit. The UK citizenry are very open in their dealings of the world's tax havens. To the English tax havens are a part of life deserving a spotlight.

Investing in Bermuda - by Rebecca Stephens

"For an island with virtually no natural resources, no manufacturing industry and a farming and fishing industry so small it is hardly worth noting on the books, Bermuda has a remarkably successful economy.

Based purely on two service industries - tourism and finance - it provides its people with an average per capita income of around $24,000, one of the highest in the world.

The island's greatest asset is it's location. Just 774 miles south-east of New York (not in the Caribbean as is so often thought), Bermuda is a 90 minute hop for city dwellers seeking recuperation in a semi-tropical paradise. Seen the other way around, it is also, of course, a 90 minute hop from the biggest business market in the world.

Bermuda's location, together with its well-proven infrastructure of accountants, lawyers and banking services, its political stability, and its legal system (based like that of the U.S. on English law) makes it one of the most attractive financial centers in the world.

At last count there were some 6,560 international companies registered on the island, including, since 1984, the giant Hong Kong based Jardine Matheson.

It is the international business that the three banks on the island - the Bank of Bermuda, the Bank of BT Butterfield & Sons, and the Bermuda Commercial Bank (formerly 1/3 owned by Barclays) depend for business. Indeed, these 3 banks maintain a banking monopoly, as the government does not grant banking licenses to any other world banks, so to register and open offices.

As well as serving the international companies on the island, they also manage substantial trust and executorship work (i.e., offshore estates), and act as custodians and administrators for offshore funds domiciled in Bermuda. The investment fund business, in particular, is expanding on the island with a growing number of funds on the register each year.

By law, each fund has one of three local banks appointed as custodian of its assets. No bank has been faster to capitalize on its position than the Bank of Bermuda - the biggest of the three with assets now exceeding B$5bn.

The bank provides legal and administrative services for over 200 funds, and worldwide has $12bn mutual funds under administration.

The oldest financial institution on the island, set up in 1858, the Bank of BT Butterfield, also has its own in-house managed group. Butterfield's Buttress Funds were launched by investment manager David Notman, who proudly claims they satisfy 99% of the clients wanting to invest in Bermuda. In 1988, the Buttress Income Fund ranked number one on the Lipper Overseas fund table."

Conclusion

All the above factors have contributed to Bermuda's status as a leading international financial and business centre. When combined with Bermuda's reputation as a first-class resort destination, they result in an offshore environment which is unequaled anywhere in the world.

Offshore Contacts

Bank of Bermuda, Ltd.
6 Front Street
Hamilton HM 11
P.O. Box HM 1020
Hamilton HM DX   Bermuda
Telephone: 809-295-4000
Tel: 299 5120
Donald P. Lines, OBE, CFA, JP

Bermuda Commercial Bank
Barclays International Building
44 Church Street
Hamilton HM 12
P.O. Box HM 1748
Hamilton HM GX Bermuda
Telephone: 809-295-5678

The Bank of N.T. Butterfield & Sons, Ltd.
65 Front Street
Hamilton HM 12
P.O. Box HM 195
Hamilton HM AX Bermuda
Tel: 295 1111

Government Offices

The Ministry of Finance
Government Administration Bldg.
30 Parliament St.
Hamilton, HM12 Bermuda

Nevis in the Leeward Islands

Saint Christopher ("St. Kitts") and Nevis form a twin island federation ("the Federation") located in the northern part of the Lesser Antilles chain of islands in the Eastern Caribbean. St. Kitts, with an area of 69 square miles (168 sq. km) has a population of 31,880. It is located at 17°15' North latitude and 62°45' West longitude. This places St. Kitts approximately 1,300 miles from Miami (3 hours flight time), 2,000 miles from New York (4 hours flight time), and 4,000 miles from London (8 hours flight time). Nevis, with an area of 36 square miles (93 sq. km) has a population of 10,080.

The two islands are separated by a channel which is about two miles wide. St. Kitts and Nevis are four hours behind Greenwich Mean Time (GMT-4). Average air temperature is 79°F (26°C) and humidity 71.5% with extremes in temperature and humidity tempered by breezes from the north-east trade winds. The average sea water temperature is 80°F (27°C). Average annual rainfall is 55 inches (1,397 mm).

Government

The Federation is a parliamentary democracy within the Commonwealth of Nations. Her Majesty, Queen Elizabeth II, is head of State and is represented on the islands by a Governor-General. Basseterre is the capital of St. Kitts and at the same time the administrative capital of the Federation. The capital of Nevis is Charlestown.

Legal System

The legal system is based upon English Common Law served by a High Court of Justice, a Court of Appeal, and Her Majesty's Privy Council in London. The official language of the Federation is English.

Currency

The currency used in the Federation is the East Caribbean Dollar ("XCD") which is fixed at XCD 2.70 per dollar of the United States of America ("USD").

Communications

The Robert L. Bradshaw International Airport on St. Kitts has a runway of 8,000 feet and is equipped to handle large passenger jets.

Newcastle Airport on Nevis can accommodate smaller twin-engine aircraft. There are at present no direct scheduled flights from North America or Europe. The islands are using Puerto Rico, St. Maarten and Antigua as their major gateways. Access from and to these gateways is by twin-engine turboprop aircraft operated by regional scheduled airlines on a daily basis and by smaller aircraft operated by local charter companies.

The deep water port in St. Kitts has modern facilities which include roll-on and roll-off docks and easily accommodates large cruise ships and freight carriers.

The telecommunication system is state of the art. Its modern network permitting smooth and prompt telephone, telex, facsimile and Internet connections throughout the world.

Political Stability

The Federation has a history of political stability based on the Westminster model of government and continuity of national policy. Since the Federation attained independence from Britain in 1983, it has consistently been adjudged to be among the world's freest nations by Freedom House, an independent and highly respected research organization in the United States of America.

The Government of the Federation wishes to promote St. Kitts and Nevis as a regional and international financial center. Accordingly it actively encourages financial activities and is making a deliberate effort to maintain the Federation's present attractiveness. Financial operations are viewed as a principal economic sector with the Government constantly reviewing new ideas and improving financial legislation.

Confidentiality • Secrecy

The Confidential Relationships Act of 1985 prohibits the disclosure of any information obtained in the course of business, and applies to banks and professionals as well as to Government officials.

Taxes & Tax Treaties

The Federation is party to double taxation treaties with Denmark, Norway, Sweden, the

United Kingdom and the United States of America (limited to social security benefits).
There are no Mutual Legal Assistance Treaties in effect.

Income Tax

There is no personal income tax in St. Kitts or Nevis. Ordinary companies are liable to a 38% tax on profits. This tax does not apply to trusts, limited partnerships and exempt companies or to enterprises which have been granted a tax concession.

Withholding Taxes

Individuals and ordinary companies remitting payments to persons outside of the Federation must deduct 10% withholding tax from profits, administration, management or head office expenses, technical service fees, accounting and audit expenses, royalties, non-life insurance premiums and rent.

This tax does not apply to trusts, limited partnerships and exempt companies or to enterprises which have been granted a tax concession.

No Capital Gains Tax

Essentially, the Federation does not impose capital gains taxes, with but a few exceptions. There is a capital gains tax of 20% on profits or gains derived from a transaction relating to assets located in the Federation which are disposed of within one year of the date of their acquisition.

This tax does not apply to trusts, limited partnerships and exempt companies or to enterprises which have been granted a tax concession.

Land and House Taxes

There is a tax on land located in the Federation, this tax is charged at various rates depending on the size and nature of the land concerned.

A house tax is charged at the rate of 5% of the annual gross rental value for residences in St. Kitts or Nevis with a 25% rebate for properties that are occupied by their owner solely as residence. The minimum annual rental value is XCD 600 (USD 222) in St. Kitts and XCD 48 (USD 18) in Nevis.

Other Taxes

There is no net worth tax, gift tax, sales tax, turnover tax, or estate duty.

Features of the Nevis Business Ordinance 1984

• No taxes are levied in Nevis upon income, dividends or distributions of a Nevis company which are not earned on the island. Corporate financial returns need not be filed in Nevis.

• No annual or other reports by shareholders or directors are required to be filed in the public records of Nevis; changes of shareholders, directors or officers need not be reported to the Registrar of Companies in Nevis.
• Shares may be in registered or bearer form.
• Shares with par value may be denominated in any currency.
• A Managing Director may be appointed to guide the corporation's activities.
• The corporate secretary may be a corporation or an individual.
• Companies may serve as directors. Alternate or substitute directors may be appointed.
• Shareholders and directors may act by unanimous consent, without a meeting. Shareholders and directors may issue proxies in writing or by telex.
• The company's records and its principal office may be located anywhere.
• Nevis companies may amend their Articles of Incorporation, merge or consolidate with foreign corporations or other Nevis corporations, or file Articles of Dissolution in accordance with liberal provisions contained in the Ordinance.
• Any corporation formed in another jurisdiction may redomicile on Nevis pursuant to certain easily followed provisions set forth in the Ordinance.

Advantages of Incorporating in Nevis

• Total confidentiality & anonymity. no requirement to disclose beneficial ownership; no requirement to file annual reports of financial nature or otherwise. Bearer shares permitted.
• Full exemption from all forms of Nevis taxation.
• Simple & Speedy Incorporation process. Facsimile filings permitted.
• No minimum capitalization requirement before commencing business. Complete freedom from currency regulations & exchange controls.

- Inexpensive incorporation charges and annual maintenance fees. Fixed annual fees for all corporations regardless of capital.

Banking in Nevis/St Kitts

The Eastern Caribbean Central Bank and The Eastern Caribbean Home Mortgage Bank have their headquarters in St. Kitts. Three international banks are represented in St. Kitts and two in Nevis. There is currently no investment banking services. Banks maintain deposits in XCD and USD only. Local foreign currency regulations regarding the conduct of USD current accounts stipulate that an account may not be opened with less than USD 1,000 and if at any time its credit balance falls below that amount such account shall forthwith be closed and shall not again be opened within one year at the same bank.

Professional Services

The legal profession is represented in the Federation by Barristers and Solicitors of the High Court. They alone have the right to practice before the Courts of the Federation, and alone may give advise on local law within the Federation. One of the five major international auditing firms is represented in the Federation.

Business Licences

Certain businesses need licenses, and applicants should seek advice locally on each occasion.

Foreign Companies

Foreign companies may be domiciled in the Federation under the Companies Act 1996 or the Nevis Business Corporation Ordinance 1984.

Citizenship & Passports by Investment

Foreign individuals can obtain citizenship under sub-section (5) of Section 3 of the Citizenship Act 1984 which stipulates that a person is entitled, upon making application to the Minister in the prescribed manner and upon payment of any fee that may be prescribed, to be registered as a citizen of the Federation without any rights of voting save under and in accordance with the provisions of any law governing the qualification of voters, if Cabinet is satisfied that such person has invested substantially in the Federation.

The minimum investment requirement may be satisfied in any of the following ways - a minimum of the equivalent in XCD of USD 200,000 in 10-year Treasury Bonds issued and guaranteed by the Federation; or
- a minimum of the equivalent in XCD of USD 250,000 in an investment project approved after March 1996; or
- a minimum of the equivalent in XCD of USD 150,000 in a real estate development approved before March 1996.

Treasury Bonds are issued at their nominal or par value and no interest is paid on them.

The registration fees currently in force are the XCD equivalents of -

USD 35,000 for head of household (male or female);
USD 15,000 for spouse;
USD 15,000 for each child under 18 years of age; and
USD 35,000 for each adult family member or other adult.

Each citizenship certificate of registration is USD 47 and the cost for each passport is USD 13. The appropriate citizenship registration fees must be paid to Government at the time of making the application. Funds for the payment of the required investment must be deposited by the applicant with a bank in St. Kitts. If the application is accepted, then the bank will be requested to release the funds to pay for the required investment. If the application is not accepted, the fees paid to the Government and the funds for the payment of the required investment will be returned to the unsuccessful applicant.

Every citizenship application must be made on the prescribed form which must be submitted together with various documents relating to the applicant's identity, civil status, criminal record, financial resources, and health. All documents must be in English or translated into English, and all photocopies of any document submitted must be notarized and properly certified.

A passport is valid for ten years, unless otherwise stated. It remains the property of the Government of the Federation and may be withdrawn at any time. Citizens of the Federation who are also citizens of foreign countries cannot avail themselves of the protection of the representative of the Federation, against the authorities of that foreign country, and are not exempt by reason of possessing the citizenship of the Federation from any obligation (such as military service) to which they may be liable under foreign law. A person having some connection with a Commonwealth or foreign country (e.g. by birth, by descent through either parent, by marriage or by residence) may be a national of that country, in addition to being a national of the Federation. Acquisition of the nationality of the Federation by a foreigner does not necessarily cause the loss of nationality of origin.

A citizen has the right to renew his passport upon its expiration. As at October 1994, no visas were required to travel to 56 countries and territories, but the United States was is included on this list.

Business Incentives

Under the Fiscal Incentives Act, four types of enterprises qualify for a tax holiday. The length of the tax holiday ranges from 10 to 15 years. The Federation provides companies with a further tax concession effective at the end of the tax holiday period.

Full exemption from import duties on parts, raw materials and production machinery is also available. Companies registered in the Federation can repatriate all profits, dividends and imported capital.

LEGAL ENTITIES

The usual entities available under British law, e.g. companies, partnerships and trusts are available in the Federation.

Companies

There are two laws governing companies in the Federation, namely:- The Companies Act 1996, which has effect in St. Kitts and Nevis; and The Nevis Business Corporation Ordinance 1984, which has effect only in Nevis.

Companies Act 1996
Formation and Registration

Any one or more persons associated for a lawful purpose may by subscribing their names to a memorandum of association form a company the liability of the members of which may, according to the memorandum, be limited either to the amount, if any, unpaid on the shares respectively held by them (i.e. a company limited by shares), or to such amount as the members may respectively undertake by the memorandum to contribute to the assets of the company in the event of it being wound up (i.e. a company limited by guarantee).

Any of the subscribers to the memorandum of association of a company, or a person acting on their behalf, may on delivering the memorandum to the Registrar of Companies and on payment of the prescribed registration fee apply for the registration of an incorporated company with limited liability. There must also be delivered to the Registrar of Companies articles of association if they differ from the model articles.

A company limited by shares must state in its memorandum of association the maximum number of shares that the company is authorized to issue and the minimum amount per share (which may be expressed in any currency or currencies) to be received by the company for shares issued by it (i.e. the stated value of a share). No subscriber to the memorandum of a company limited by shares may take less than one share.

A company limited by guarantee must state in its memorandum of association the number of members with which the company proposes to register and the amount of the guarantee (which may be expressed in any currency or currencies) that each member is required to contribute to cover the debts and liabilities of the company in the case of it being wound up. Companies may limit their period of existence.

Names of Companies

The name of a company must end with the word "Limited" (or the abbreviation "Ltd."), "Corporation" (or the abbreviation "Corp.") or "Incorporated" (or the abbreviation "Inc."). A company can use any name provided that the name chosen is not considered misleading or otherwise undesirable by the Registrar of Companies.

Private and Public Companies

A company which has 51 or more members is deemed to be a public company. A private company is a company which is not a public company but if it should make an invitation to the public to acquire or apply for any shares and debentures issued by it, or interest in any such shares or debenture, or rights to acquire any of the foregoing, it will become a public company even if it has fewer than 51 members unless such an invitation is addressed exclusively to a restricted circle of persons.

Corporate Capacity and Transactions

The doctrine of ultra vires in its application to companies is abolished and accordingly a company has the capacity and, subject to certain other provisions of the Companies Act, the same rights, powers and privileges as an individual.

Where a transaction purports to be entered into by a company, or by a person as agent for a company, at a time when the company has not been formed, then, unless otherwise agreed by the parties to the transaction, the transaction has effect as one entered into by the person purporting to act for the company or as agent for it, and he will be personally bound by the transaction and entitled to its benefits.

No person is deemed to have notice of any record by reason only that they are made available by the Registrar of Companies, or by a company, for inspection.

Register of Members and Share Certificates

Every company must keep a register of members but inspection of the register by persons who are not members or officers of the company is not permitted in the case of a private company which is an exempt company (i.e. a company which is exempt from all taxes under the Companies Act).

Subject as otherwise provided in the Companies Act, every company must issue share certificates in respect of shares allotted by it. A private company which is an exempt company may issue bearer certificates in respect of fully paid-up shares.

No share certificate issued by a company shall in any manner whatsoever bear any indication of the stated value of the shares comprised in it.

Administration

All companies must have a registered office in the Federation to which communications and notices may be addressed.

A private company must have at least one director and a public company must have at least three directors of whom at least two are not employed by the company or any of its related companies.

A body corporate may not be a director. Every company must have a secretary and may have one or more assistant secretaries who, or each of whom, may be an individual or a body corporate.

Meetings

Every company must hold an annual general meeting but if all the members of a private company agree in writing that an annual general meeting should be dispensed with, then so long as that agreement has effect, that company is dispensed from holding an annual general meeting.

In the case of an equality of votes the chairman of a meeting (whether it is a meeting of the members of the company or of its directors) has a second or casting vote in addition to any vote which he may have.

Where a company has only one member or, if all the shares of a particular class of shares are held by only one member, that member present in person or by proxy constitutes a meeting. If a private company has only one director, that director present in person constitutes a meeting.

Accounts

All companies must keep accounting records and prepare annual accounts. Where a company is a public company; or the articles of the company so require; or a resolution of the company in general meeting so directs, then that company must appoint auditors to audit its annual accounts.

A public company must deliver to the Registrar of Companies a copy of its audited annual accounts. A private company which is an ordinary company (i.e. a company which is not an exempt company) must deliver to the Registrar of Companies either a copy of its audited annual accounts or a certificate of solvency.

Winding-up and Dissolution of Companies

A company may be wound-up and dissolved either by a summary winding-up if the company is solvent, a winding up by the Court if the Court is of the opinion that it is just and equitable that the company should be wound up, or by a creditor's winding up if the company is insolvent.

A company will be dissolved without formal winding up if the Registrar of Companies strikes off the company's name from the register of companies, but the liability of every director and member of the company continues and may be enforced as if it had not been dissolved.

Tax and Other Exemptions

Companies are exempt from all taxes as long as they conduct their business exclusively with person who are not resident in the Federation. A company is called an exempt company if it qualifies for the tax exemption mentioned above. An ordinary company is a company which is not an exempt company.

Ordinary companies will not pay income tax on dividends, interest and royalties received from a qualifying participating interest in another body corporate.

No estate, inheritance, succession or gift tax, rate, duty, levy or other charge is payable by any person with regard to any property owned by, or securities issued or created by or in respect of, an exempt company.

No stamp duty or other tax is payable by any person with regard to any transaction in any securities issued or created by or in respect of an exempt company.

Government Fees

Registration and annual filing fees for companies are as follows:-
Ordinary private company USD 100
Exempt private company USD 200
Ordinary public company USD 400
Exempt public company USD 600

Limited Partnerships

Any two or more persons can form a limited partnership, but a limited partnership must consist of one or more persons who are general partners and one or more persons who are limited partners. A body corporate may be a general or a limited partner and a person may be a general partner as well as a limited partner at the same time in the same limited partnership.

Any of the general partners of a limited partnership or a person acting on their behalf may on delivering to the Registrar of Limited Partnerships a declaration of the formation of the limited partnership and on payment of the prescribed registration fee apply for the registration of the declaration.

An association of persons will not be a limited partnership until the Registrar of Limited Partnerships has issued a certificate in respect of the above mentioned declaration.

Names of Limited Partnerships

The name of a limited partnership must end with the words "Limited Partnership" or the abbreviation "L.P." A limited partnership may use any name provided that the name chosen is not considered misleading or otherwise undesirable by the Registrar of Limited Partnerships and does not contain the name of any limited partner who is not also a general partner.

Administration

Every limited partnership must have an office for service in the Federation. Except as otherwise provided in the Limited Partnerships Act, legal proceedings by or against a limited partnership may only be instituted by or against any one or more of the general partners and no limited partner may be a party to or named in such proceedings.

Accounts

The general partners of every limited partnership must keep accounting records which are sufficient to show and explain their transactions in respect of the limited partnership and are such as to disclose with reasonable accuracy at any time the financial position of the limited partnership.

Unless the partnership agreement otherwise provides, it is not necessary for the general partners of a limited partnership to appoint an auditor to audit their accounts in respect of the limited partnership.

Dissolution of Limited Partnerships

A limited partnership can not be dissolved by an act of the partners until a statement of dissolution signed by one of them has been delivered to the Registrar of Limited Partnerships. A limited partnership must be dissolved if there are no general partners, but if the limited partners elect one or more general partners, then its activities may be taken over and continued as provided for in the partnership agreement or a subsequent agreement.

The Court has the power to order the dissolution of a limited partnership if the Court is of the opinion that it is just and equitable that the limited partnership should be dissolved.

In the event of the dissolution of a limited partnership its affairs are wound up by the general partners or, if there are no general partners, in such manner as the Court may direct.

Tax and Other Exemptions

A limited partnership is not itself a subject for assessment to any tax in the Federation and the partners of a limited partnership are exempt from all income, capital gains and withholding taxes which may arise out of their interest in the limited partnership if the general partners of the limited partnership are in respect of it effecting transactions exclusively with persons who are not resident in the Federation.

A limited partnership is called an exempt limited partnership if its partners qualify for the tax exemption mentioned above. An ordinary limited partnership is a limited partnership which is not an exempt limited partnership.

No estate, inheritance, succession or gift tax, rate, duty, levy or other charge is payable by any person with regard to any property owned by, or securities issued or created in respect of, an exempt limited partnership.

No stamp duties are payable by any person with regard to any transaction in securities issued or created in respect of an exempt limited partnership.

Government Fees

Fees for the registration of the declaration of a limited partnership and for filing of its annual statement are as follows:-
Ordinary limited partnership USD 100
Exempt limited partnership USD 200

Nevis St. Kitts Trusts

There are two laws governing trusts in the Federation, namely:-

The Trusts Act 1996, which has effect in St. Kitts and Nevis; and The Nevis International Exempt Trust Ordinance 1994, which has effect only in Nevis.

Creation and Establishment of Trusts • Use of corporate settlors

Any person may create a trust, but a trust must have at least one trustee who ordinarily resides within the Federation or carries on business from an office or other fixed place within the Federation.

A body corporate may be the settlor or a trustee or a beneficiary of a trust and the settlor or a trustee of a trust may be a beneficiary at the same time of the same trust.

Any of the trustees of a trust or a person acting on their behalf may on delivering to the Registrar of Trusts an attestation of the existence of the trust and on payment of the prescribed registration fee apply for the registration of the attestation.

No trust will be recognized under the laws of the Federation as valid and enforceable until the Registrar of Trusts has issued a certificate in respect of the above mentioned attestation.

Types of Trusts

A trust under which the income or capital or the income and capital of the trust property is applied for a purpose regarded as charitable, is a charitable trust.

A trust under which the interest of a beneficiary is subject to restriction, diminution or termination, is a spendthrift or protective trust.

A trust established for the purpose, or having the effect, of providing, for persons having funds available for investment, facilities for the participation by them as beneficiaries under the trust, in any profits or income arising from the acquisition of any property whatsoever, is a unit trust.

A trust which is not a charitable trust; or a spendthrift or protective trust; or a unit trust, is a common trust. A common trust may be created for a purpose which is not a charitable purpose, provided that the trust must vest in natural persons within the perpetuity period applying or expressed to apply to the trust. Any trust so created must be enforceable by the settlor or his personal representative or by a person named in the terms of the trust as the person appointed to enforce the trust and the trust must be enforceable at the instance of the person so named notwithstanding that such person may not be a beneficiary under the trust

Proper Law

The proper law of a trust is the law of the jurisdiction expressed by the terms of the trust as the proper law; or failing that, implied from the terms of the trust; or failing either, with which the trust at the time it was created had the closest connection.

The term of a trust may provide for the proper law of the trust or the law governing a severable aspect of the trust to be changed from the law of one jurisdiction to the law of another jurisdiction.

Duration of Trusts

A trust which is not a charitable trust may continue until the one-hundredth anniversary of the date on which it came into existence.

Asset Protection Provisions

The asset protection provisions of the Act deal with the capacity of a settlor to transfer or dispose property to a trust, the retention of control and benefits by a settlor, the bankruptcy of a settlor and the prevention of fraud on a settlor's creditors.

Administration

Subject to the terms of the trust, the number of trustees must not be less than two, unless only one trustee was originally appointed or the sole trustee is a corporate trustee. Every trust must have an office for service in the Federation.

Except as otherwise provided in the Trusts Act, legal proceedings by or against a trust can only be instituted by or against any one or more of the trustees.

Accounts

The trustees of every trust must keep accounting records which are sufficient to show and explain their transactions in respect of the trust and are such as to disclose with reasonable accuracy at any time the financial position of the trust. Unless the terms of a trust otherwise provides, the trustees of a trust need not appoint an auditor to audit their accounts in respect of the trust.

Termination of Trust

A trust can not be terminated by an act of its trustees until a statement of termination signed by one of them is delivered to the Registrar of Trusts. Where all the beneficiaries of a trust are in agreement so to do, they may require the trustee to terminate the trust.

The Court has the power to order the termination of a trust if the Court is of the opinion that it is just and equitable that the trust should be terminated. On the termination of a trust the trust property will be distributed by the trustee in accordance with the terms of the trust to the persons entitled thereto.

Tax and Other Exemptions

A trust is not itself a subject for assessment to any tax in the Federation and the beneficiaries of a trust are exempt from all income, capital gains and withholding taxes which may arise out of their interest in the trust if the trustees of the trust are in respect of it effecting transactions exclusively with persons who are not resident in the Federation.

A trust is called an exempt trust if its beneficiaries qualify for the tax exemption mentioned above. An ordinary trust is a trust which is not an exempt trust.

No estate, inheritance, succession or gift tax, rate, duty, levy or other charge is payable by any person with regard to any property held in, or securities issued or created in respect of, an exempt trust.

No stamp duties are payable by any person with regard to any transaction in securities issued or created in respect of an exempt trust.

Government Fees

Fees for the registration of the attestation of a trust and for filing of its annual statement are as follows:-

Ordinary trusts USD 100
Exempt trusts USD 200

British Virgin Islands (B.V.I.)

The British Virgin Islands are a group of islands at the eastern end of the Greater Antilles, in the Caribbean Sea. There are 46 islands, of which only 11 are inhabited. The largest are: Tortola (21 square miles), Virgin Gorda (8.25 square miles), Anegada (15 square miles) and Jost Van Dyke (3.5 square miles). The topography of the islands ranges from coral reefs to mountainous.

Location : Approximately 60 miles east of Puerto Rico in the Caribbean

Size: 59 square miles

Population: 19,000

Currency: The US. dollar is legal tender

Capital: Road Town, on the Island of Tortola

Company formation and post -incorporation services

The British Virgin Islands is one of the world's premier corporate domiciles. Since adoption of the pioneering International Business Companies Act in 1984, more than 240,000 companies have been incorporated in the BVI. The Bahamas, which adopted its IBC Act in 1990, has slightly over 90,000 IBCs. [14.]

Other jurisdictions have introduced legislation similar to the BVI's in an effort to compete for company formation business. However, the BVI has maintained its leadership position thanks to the flexibility of its legislation, the quality of its financial services, its commitment to privacy, and its integrity and stability as a jurisdiction.

By incorporating in the BVI, a company gains a wide range of competitive advantages, including:

• Exemption from all local taxes and stamp duty

• Asset security -- Abilities to transfer domicile; protect assets from expropriation or confiscation orders from foreign governments; transfer assets to another company, trust foundation, association or partnership; merge or consolidate with any other BVI or foreign company in an accommodating jurisdiction

• Maximum confidentiality and anonymity -- availability of bearer shares; no requirements to file organizational or accounting information with the Registrar of Companies (except the Memorandum of Articles of Association); share registers available for inspection only by registered shareholders or by order of the BVI Court

• Statutory flexibility in filing Registers of Directors or Members at their own option and in their de-registering at any time. This facilitates an appropriate balance combining anonymity with the option to file such business information as determined by the business needs of the IBC

• Ease of operation, maintenance and control-- IBC's can:

- Re acquire and reissue their own shares;

- Issue shares for consideration other than cash, with or without par value, denominated in any currency;

- Have only one subscriber and thereafter only one shareholder;

- Have a single directorate;

- Have a corporate directors or shareholders;

- Hold shareholders' or directors' meetings, and maintain books of account, records and minutes outside the BVI

• No statutory requirement to hold annual general meetings
• Incorporation's within one or two days
• Excellent and flexible post incorporation follow up services
• Customized certificates and document verification geared to meet the unique business needs of individual IBC's

---

14. The Bahamas Government adopted the BVI International Business Companies Act legislation almost to the letter in an attempt to revitalize its own offshore industry.

- No disclosure or minimum capital requirements
- Highly competitive fees and costs.

TAX LOOPHOLE FOR NONRESIDENTS

A lot of Americans don't understand why offshore IBCs are so popular. So, here's a good example...

Under the U.S. Tax Code, if a foreign company (or IBC) based in the Bahamas purchased all the shares in a New York Corporation that owned the Empire State Building for $400,000,000 in 1990, and then in 1999, the foreign owners of the Bahamian IBC sell all the shares in the Bahamian IBC to a BVI IBC for $1 billion, there are no U.S. capital gains taxes legally owed on the transaction. Sounds impossible! Under U.S. tax law, capital gain taxes do not extend to the sale of shares of one foreign company by/to another foreign company, even if the downstream holding is a USRPI (U.S. Real Property Interest) or USRPHC (US Real Property Holding Corporation)(i.e., the New York Corporation which owns the Empire State Building). Reference T.Regs. §897-2(e)(1), Example (1) & (2). See page 82.

What Can An IBC Do?

IBC's can perform all corporate activities except:

- do business with BVI residents

- provide registered office or agent facilities for BVI incorporated companies

- own an interest in real property in BVI apart from office leases

An IBC may engage in all the following activities, which do not constitute doing business in the BVI:

- Make or maintain deposits with a person carrying on banking business within the BVI

- Make or maintain professional contact with solicitors, barristers, accountants, bookkeepers, trust companies, administration companies, investment advisers or other similar persons carrying on business within the BVI

- Prepare or maintain books and records within the BVI

- Hold meetings of its directors or members in the BVI

- Hold a lease of property for use as an office from which to communicate with members or where books and records of the company are prepared or maintained

- Hold shares, debt obligations or other securities in a company incorporated under this ordinance or under the company act; or

- Hold shares, debt obligations or other securities in the company owned by any person resident in the BVI or by any company incorporated under this ordinance or under the Companies Act

What can an IBC not do?

IBCs cannot perform the following activities requiring a license:

- Banking or trust business
- Business as an insurance or re-insurance company or insurance agent or insurance broker
- Business of company management

How to establish an IBC

The IBC registration process is quick and easy. For most companies, the documentation is simple and brief, and the official review and approval are completed in approximately 48 hours.

The process for banks, trust companies and insurers is governed by additional, specific laws, and requires more detailed documentation.

Step 1 is to engage a Registered Agent in the BVI.

Registered Agents are licensed by the BVI Government specifically to handle the affairs of offshore companies, including company formations. There are approximately 50

Registered Agents in the BVI. Further advice and information can be obtained from the Registrar of Companies.

Step 2 is to apply for incorporation.

Registered Agents are able to facilitate a quick and easy application.

If the applicant is registering a bank, trust company or insurer, local facilities may be needed: the application will require more detailed documentation including a business plan and approval of the appropriate supervisor within the Department of Finance. The approval time will depend on the quality of the information provided in the application.

Step 3 is the payment of statutory fees, which are based on the company's authorized share capital.

The fee to incorporate a company with capital up to $50,000 is $300; for an IBC with capital of more than $50,000, the fee is $1,000. The annual license fee is:

Authorized Capital	Fee
Up to $50,000	$300
No capital or par value	$350
Over $50,000	$1000

Post incorporation services

The following are the standard post incorporation services provided by the Company Registry:

- good standing certificates within 24 hours
- certified copies of all corporate documents on file
- customized certificates to meet specialized business needs
- continuation and/or redomiciliation into or out of BVI
- mergers of IBCs and foreign companies
- quick searches of all companies registered in the BVI
- voluntary dissolution and winding up of IBCs
- necessary follow up services in so far as they conform to existing BVI law.

A list of fees and service charges for procedures and services such as mergers, consolidations and dissolutions, and the documentation of such procedures, may conveniently be obtained from a Registered Agent.

Failure to pay the government's license fee on time (by July 31 of each year) will result in a 10% to 50% penalty assessment. BVI companies are stricken from they records if the do not pay the annual fee by the 31st of December of the year in which it is due.

While several offshore centers (including the Cayman Islands and Bermuda) offer similar advantages as the BVI, in most cases there are onerous administrative, legal and statutory costs to bear and these may have the effect of eroding the benefits of low taxes. Currently, only the Bahamas offer a less expensive cost regime for incorporating than the BVI.

The British Virgin Islands has succeeded in avoiding the necessity to involve the principal in hefty fees, duties and charges by virtue of its uncomplicated operating procedures and statutory requirements and has justly earned a reputation as one of the least costly offshore centers worldwide.

Change of Domicile

One advantage of an IBC is that it may change its domicile from the British Virgin Islands to another jurisdiction, i.e. it may, for whatever reason, de-register as a company in the British Virgin Islands but in order to continue as a corporate entity it will need to register in whatever other jurisdiction it goes to. [15.]

Non-British Virgin Islands incorporated companies may also change their domicile to the British Virgin Islands by lodging Articles of Continuation there, from which time they are recognized by the British Virgin Islands Government as having a legal corpus there. On seizure of assets or prejudice of interest of shareholders by a foreign government, an IBC may obtain a court order to disregard the actions of the foreign government.

---

15. From *International Operations* by Moore Stevens (Chartered Accountants).

Banking

The banks and Trust Companies Act of 1990 provides for three categories of bank licenses and two categories of trust company licenses:

Banks:
1. A General Banking License
2. A Class I Restricted Banking License
3. A Class II Restricted Banking License

Trusts:
1. A General Trust License
2. A Restricted Trust License

General Banking License

Holders of a General banking license must have a minimum paid up capital of $2 million and must deposit the sum of $500,000 in such a manner at the governor prescribes.
Annual fee: $10,000.

Class I Restricted Banking License

Holders may not take deposits from or make investments in or with any BVI resident except another licensee or an IBC. Minimum paid up capital: $1 million. Deposit of $500,000 required. Annual fee: $8,000.

Class II Restricted Banking License

A Class II Restricted banking license has the same restrictions as a Class I, but can only receive funds from undertakings named in the license. Minimum capital and deposit requirements: $1 million and $500,000 respectively.
Annual fee: $6,000.
General Trust License

Requires a minimum paid up capital of $250,000 and deposit of not less than $20,000 as the Governor prescribes.

Annual fee: $4,000.
Restricted Trust License

Under a Restricted trust license, business may be accepted only from undertakings specified in the license. No minimum paid up capital or deposit requirements. Annual fee: $100.

Amendments to the Banks and Trust Companies Act and the Company Management Act were passed in December 1995 to allow for the incorporation of statutory gateways into each act, following the precedent set by the Insurance Act. The gateways provide for the disclosure of information to regulatory authorities and law enforcement agencies in other countries and jurisdictions for the purpose of assisting them in the investigation of illegal or criminal activities.

> **"The BVI will not, however, allow the gateways to be used as a screen for so-called "fishing expeditions" by over zealous tax collectors for other jurisdictions." - the BVI government**

The BVI does not grant offshore banking licenses to individuals or unproved entities. Banks with established records are invited to consider the BVI. Their applications can be expedited through a local advocate or through a trust or service management company licensed in the BVI.

Tax Information
International Business Companies

International Business Companies (IBC's) are statutory exempt from all BVI taxes. Furthermore, all amounts paid by an IBC to persons not resident in the BVI are also statutorily exempt from all BVI taxes.

Trusts

Following the Trustee (Amendment) Act, 1993, all trust which:

• have no BVI resident beneficiaries;
• own no BVI land; and
• do not carry on business in the BVI

are exempt from all BVI taxes except for a "trust duty" of $50 which is payable by purchasing and affixing stamps to the trust instrument. Non-resident beneficiaries are exempted from all BVI taxes.

Other Companies

Resident companies are subject to tax on their worldwide income (less deductions). Non-resident companies are subject to tax only on income remitted to or derived from the BVI. The standard tax rate is 15 percent. Where a resident company obtains 90 percent or more of its profits from trading exclusively outside the BVI, the rate is reduced to 1 percent on those profits. There is also a 1 percent rate for companies on foreign investment income if the income is exempt from tax in the jurisdiction in which it arises.

A company is resident if it is effectively managed and controlled in the BVI, and this is deemed to be the case with respect to a CAP 285 company if a majority of its directors are BVI residents.

Capital Taxes

There are no capital or succession taxes (apart from stamp duty). Tax credit is allowed on foreign tax paid, and in many cases this includes tax paid in non-treaty countries.

British Virgin Island Trusts

The 1961 Trust Ordinance laid the foundation for the Trustee Acts that came later, and provides that BVI-based trusts are exempt from tax where all the assets (other than bank accounts) are outside the BVI. Stamp duty on the trust instrument is nominal if a small cash sum is settled originally and other assets added later.

In the British Virgin Islands, stamp duty is charged at a rate of US$1 on each US$500 or part thereof when a trust is set up unless an IBC (International Business Company) is the settlor (grantor) or trustee, in which case the transfer to the BVI trust is exempt from the stamp duty. Where neither the settlor nor the beneficiaries are resident of the BVI, no income tax is payable provided the trust receives no income in the BVI. The exemption from BVI income taxes applies even if the trustees are resident in the BVI.

Trust formation and operation

The British Virgin Islands is an ideal location for reputable, well-capitalized international trust operations. The BVI's trust operations include:

- flexibility

- protection of privacy, wealth, assets and inheritance wishes

- tax exemptions, competitive costs and swift, simple procedures

- strong network of experienced trust professionals in the BVI

- governmental commitment to a modern trust regime and effective partnership with the private sector

---

ESTATE TAX PLANNING TIP

Foreigners investing in U.S. property, including U.S. real estate, stocks and bonds should always use a tax haven holding company to hold those U.S. assets. If the nonresident alien invests $5,000,000 in a Texas oil lease directly under his own name, the entire $5,000,000 would be included in his estate for purposes of computing his U.S. estate tax liability. If the nonresident alien died in 1992, the $5,000,000 lease would be subject to U.S. estate taxes at rates to 55%, and the nonresident alien would be permitted only a $60,000 tax credit.

Using the estate tax table under **IRC §2001(c)** the nonresident alien would owe $1,290,800 on amounts up to $3,000,000, and 55% of everything above that. On his $5,000,000 estate, the nonresident alien's heirs would witness the payment of ≈ $2,390,800 in estate taxes to the U.S. Treasury.

HOWEVER, under U.S. estate tax law, shares of an offshore company **would not** be included in the nonresident alien's estate for purposes of calculating his **U.S. estate tax** liability, even if the only asset owned by the offshore company was the $5,000,000 U.S. oil lease. Offshore practitioners should never advise their non-U.S. clients to invest directly in the USA. A tax haven holding company should always be considered; unless the investment being planned is small - under $100,000.

Using a BVI trust to own the shares in the underlying IBC BVI?

BVI legislation provides a flexible vehicle for the establishment of trusts to hold shares in an IBC and in a variety of assets based outside the BVI. By utilizing a BVI trust in combination with an underlying company formed under the BVI's IBC legislation, a company gains a wide range of competitive advantages.[15.] These advantages are based on the two guiding principles of the BVI's legislation: namely, protection of the trust's interests and assets and facilitation of its management and operations.

They include:

• Protection of wealth benefits through the option of election of the BVI as the proper law of the trust

• Protection of inheritance wishes through anti-forced hiership provisions.

• Protection of trust interest through legal acknowledgment of the position and powers of the Trust Protector

• Protection of privacy: there is no public register of trusts

• Facilitation of more user-friendly trust deeds through extensive trust administration provisions

• Facilitation of comprehensive investment strategies through provision for broad investment powers for trustees

• Facilitation of a wide range of estate planning options through provision of a perpetuity period of up to 100 years and "wait and see" rules

• Facilitation of the formation of charitable and non-charitable trusts through recognition of purpose trusts

• Facilitation of swift, straight-forward and cost-competitive operation through:

• uncomplicated, user friendly procedures

• exemption from all BVI taxes provided that the beneficiaries are resident outside the BVI

• competitive, start up and operating costs

• specific facilitative provisions such as majority trustee decisions and short form trust deeds.

The legislation provides for the drafting of trusts to meet a wide range of client requirements, including:

• Revocable and non-revocable trusts
• Short-form and long-form trust deeds
• Full discretionary or fixed interest settlements
• Accumulation and maintenance settlements for minors
• Charities and protective trusts to remove future creditor risks

In addition to the specific advantages outlined above, companies can also derive a number of more generalized benefits form the BVI's IBC legislation relating to the protection of assets, preservation of wealth, commitment to privacy and anonymity, zero taxability, and ease and flexibility of operations.

Main Legislative Provisions

The BVI's trust legislation is based on the English Common Law system, and the BVI High Court follows English case law even when this is not technically binding, except where this specifically varies from local legislation or case law. It provides for three categories of trust (charitable,. personal and purpose) and two categories of trust license (general and restricted)

The relevant legislation is: the Trustee Act Cap. 303; the Trustee (Amendment) Act No.7 of 1993; and the Trustees Relief Act, Cap. 304.

The Trustee (Amendment) Act of 1993 has proved central to the BVI's development as a center for trust operations. Its adoption was motivated by the BVI's desire to;

• update BVI statue law by including certain provisions that had hitherto only been effective if specifically stated in trust instruments

• give greater flexibility in respect of perpetuities, provide for the establishment of purpose trusts and clarify the law relating to "forced heirship"

The main features of the 1993 legislation are:

• Perpetuity: updated provisions regarding the rules relating to perpetuities and the "wait and see" rule including:

---

15. This is a long standing planning devise favored by many of the Management and Trust Companies in most all of the British Commonwealth tax havens.

• an optional statutory perpetuity period of 100 years, instead of 21 years for suspension of the vesting of interests

• introduction of modern "wait and see" provisions to replace the common law rule holding a trust "void ab initio" if it is possible that an interest might vest outside the perpetuity period

• General Savings Provisions: reduction in the oppressive common law principles relating to the exercise of trustee powers

• Proper Law: statutory recognition to the practice of giving the trustee, or protector of the trust, power to change the proper law of the trust to the law of another jurisdiction, and provision for the automatic transfer of assets from one trustee to another trustee in another jurisdiction in certain pre-determined circumstances

• Jurisdiction of the Court: provision for the BVI court to have jurisdiction in cases where the trust's only real connection with the BVI is its proper law

• Inheritance: provision for a settlor of a trust to pass good title to trust assets notwithstanding the laws of his domicile relating to inheritance or succession once the settler is of full age and sound mind

• Purpose Trust: provision for the establishment of non-charitable trusts which neither require identifiable beneficiaries nor are subject to the rules against perpetuities and remoteness of investing

• Protectors, Managing and Custodian Trustees: establishment of a statutory basis for the appointment of protectors of trust, and provision for the appointment of a managing trustee and by implication a custodian trustee

• Privacy: exemption of all trust and settlement deeds from registration under the provisions of the Registration and Records Act, and exemption of trustees from requirements for the filing of annual returns or trust accounts, the audit of accounts and reporting requirements relating to the trust

• Income Tax Exemption: exemption from all taxation in the BVI provided that there is no BVI resident beneficiary or that the underlying assets do not consist of land, a business or a trade conducted in the BVI.

Limited Partnerships Legislation

Prior to 1996, the BVI operated under The Partnership Act, Cap. 295, a law that has been on the statue books since 1888. Realizing that this law is inadequate to deal with the demands of today's international financial world-- especially in the areas of securities and mutual funds-- the BVI has initiated a new Partnership Act.

A creative mix of "old and new" provisions, the new Partnership Act is a unique product designed to meet the needs of the international financial world and provide a workable investment vehicle.

The new Act is divided into seven parts. The first four parts deal with general partnerships and reproduce almost verbatim the provisions of the United Kingdom's Partnership Act of 1890. It deals mainly with the nature of a partnership, the relation of partners to persons dealing with them, and the relation between the partners themselves, dissolution of partnerships and its consequences.

Limited partnerships, the highlighted subject of the bill, are dealt with in Part VI. These provisions follow to a large extent the American pattern of modern limited partnership legislation adopted by the State of Delaware.

The style of drafting and procedural aspects of the new Partnership Act are closely patterned on the International Business Companies Act, which is the cornerstone of the BVI financial services industry. Two significant features of the new Act which should make the BVI a preferred site for the formation of limited partnership are:

a) the broad protection it affords limited partners from liability to third parties for the obligations of the limited partnership; and

b) the fact that the names of limited partners who are, in effect, sleeping partners do not have to appear in the name of a limited partnership-- thus preserving the privacy of such partners. Provisions are further made for the distribution of assets upon dissolution of a limited partnership and the priority of claims by partnership creditor and the limited partners with respect to their share of profits and the capital of their contributions. A limited partnership is required t

124.

maintain a registered office and have a registered agent in the BVI.

Provisions are made for striking the names of international limited partnerships off the register, the effect thereof, and the restoration of names to the register. Provisions are also made for the appointment of an official liquidator where the name of an international limited partnership is struck off the register. All of these provisions are similar to those contained in the International Business Companies Act.

Following the same pattern as the IBC, international limited partnerships are exempt from all income taxes. Payments made by such partnerships to non-residents are also exempt from BVI income tax. Similarly, there is an exemption from the provisions of the Stamp Act for all instruments relating to the business of international limited partnerships.

The Government in Council (Executive Council) is empowered to make regulations to improve administration of the legislation, as well as provisions giving power to the Minister of Finance to appoint inspector to investigate the affairs of a limited partnership. The new Partnership Act also provides for procedures on winding up and dissolution of a limited partnership, and lists the duties and powers of a liquidator.

Mutual Funds Legislation

The BVI's mutual funds industry has grown dramatically over the last few years. While hard data does not exist, it is estimated that there are several hundred mutual fund companies incorporated under the International Business Companies Act and that the assets under management are in the billions of dollars.

Prior to the Mutual Funds Act, no legislation existed in the BVI to deal with mutual funds. Realizing the increasing need for such legislation, the BVI recently designed a simple, flexible Mutual Funds Act designed to maintain its established reputation for integrity and responsibility and protect the interests of investors. The Act provides fund promoters and operators with a suitable location to manage their funds wherever they may be constituted or to establish new funds under available convenient

legal structures as international business companies, limited partnership or unit trusts.

The Act is relatively short and is divided into five parts and a schedule. The main thrust of the legislation is in parts two, three and four, which deal with public funds, private funds and administrators, respectively. The new legislations simply divides mutual funds into public funds which offer their shares or units to the general public, and private funds which offer their shares or units to a restricted number of investors.

Both public and private funds are allowed to operate in or from within the BVI, regardless of where they may be incorporated, formed or constituted. In the case of private funds, the only requirement is that they be recognized by the Minister of Finance upon proof that they are lawfully constituted under the laws of another country, and that they are not offering their shares or units to the general public. Private funds constituted under BVI laws are entitled to recognition, and cannot be denied recognition unless they fail to prove that they are private funds, within the meaning of the legislation.

Public funds must be registered in order to operate in or from within the BVI. Application for registration is made to the Government-in-Council on a prescribed form, accompanied by a statement of describing the nature of the applicant's business and proof of its lawful constitution. As public funds offer their shares or units to members of the general public, the proposed legislation seeks to strike the necessary careful balance between the principle of freedom of international enterprise on the one hand, and the need for a measure of regulatory accountability to assure investors of the safety of their investment, on the other. In striking the necessary balance, the proposed legislation requires that registered public funds maintain adequate records, prepare annual audited financial statements, file and publish a prospectus, and file an annual certificate of compliance if operating under the laws of another country.

These requirements are then made flexible by provisions which allow:

a) accounts and statements to be in accordance with generally accepted accounting principles applicable in any country or jurisdiction that the Minister may recognize and cause such recognition to be published in the Gazette;

b) accounting records and financial statements to be kept at any place as the fund's officers see fit provided the information therein is made available in investors and to the Registrar for examination:

c) any auditor acceptable to the Registrar to perform the audit of annual financial statement in accordance with generally accepted auditing standing applicable in any country or jurisdiction recognized by the Minister of Finance; and

d) flexibility, in that no mandatory form is required for a prospectus, as long as it provides full, true and plain disclosure to investors.

As a measure to protect mutual funds investors, the proposed legislation provides the right of action for rescission or for damages that may be exercised by investors relied on a prospectus containing misrepresentations of which they were not aware.

The Act provides a flexible definition of mutual funds managers and administrators, and requires that a person wishing to carry on business in or from within the BVI as a manager or administrator of mutual funds is required to apply for a license. The system of licensing is simple and flexible, the essential requirement being an application to the Minister of Finance. The application must be accompanied by a statement of the financial and human resources available to the applicant. Fund managers and administrators who are qualified and authorized under the law of a recognized jurisdiction, may be permitted to operate in or from the BVI without the need to be licensed. This particular facility is provided only where such fund managers and administrators are not ordinarily resident or domiciled in the BVI and receive the written permission of the Minister of Finance, which may be subject to conditions and for a limited period of time.

Insurance Companies

Companies wishing to carry on insurance business, either within or outside the British Virgin Islands, have to be licensed.

New Offshore Insurance Act

The Insurance Act 1994 "is the first in a series of major legislative measures, scheduled for adoption over the next six to nine months, that will deepen and expand our partnership with the intentional financial community," according to Lavity Stoutt. The Act is designed to provide an attractive vehicle for a wide range of high-quality insurance services such as: all types of captives; most types of reinsurance; protected life policies and annuities that are free of attachment; and credit life. Regulators in BVI are hoping that the new legislation will significantly enhance the territory's status and attractiveness as a center for legitimate international business activities.

One of the central features of the Act is the provision of an appropriate facility for exemptions. "This provision will enable the BVI to offer high-quality insurance operations, and an exceptionally flexible and attractive environment in which to operate and develop innovative insurance vehicles according to Robert Mathavious (head of the Financial Services Department).

An important feature of the Act is that it provides for the appointment of a commissioner of insurance whose powers will include general supervision of the insurance business being carried on in or from within the territory, ensuring that the laws and regulations relating to the conduct of insurance are enforced and obeyed, and examining all matters connected with insurance.

The BVI government says it is confident that the Act will provide a fillip to its efforts aimed at developing the offshore industry in an orderly and progressive manner and at keeping the BVI at the cutting edge of offshore financial centers. The objective is to develop the BVI as a full service international financial center.

The new legislation reflects a recognition by the BVI government and by the insurance industry that some measure of regulation is necessary for the proper conduct of insurance business. It is part of a continuing evolving process in which the BVI government participates and consults with the private sector.

The underlying philosophy and purpose of the legislation is to provide a regulatory environment that offers relative freedom to the insurance industry and is designed to minimize government interference in the day to-day operations of insurers which are financially sound and in a position to fulfill their commitments to their policyholders and creditors.

The insurance legislation is expected to play significant role in the economic growth of the BVI. Among the projected benefits are: new employment opportunities for islanders; additional expenditure in the local economy from new insurance companies, insurance management companies, insurance agencies and brokerage firms setting up offices in the territory and from their employees; more business for islanders providing support services and for professionals providing accounting, banking and legal services.

Legislation for other financial sectors is promised, but Robert Mathavious draws the line at asset protection trusts, at least for the time being. The jury is still out," he says. We won't lead, but maybe down the road.

Political Stability

A stable and established political structure is essential to the continued success of any offshore financial center. This is evident from the decline of many other offshore areas due to political uncertainty and turmoil. The strength and success of the British Virgin Islands as a low tax center is in no small measure attributable to its long-standing and stable democratic political system. Legal Structure and Expertise

Principals requiring the use of offshore facilities will want and need to understand the legal framework of the area within which they wish to operate. The legal system in the British Virgin Islands is based upon English law and is of Anglo-Saxon origin and therefore offers a tried and tested system with which many international operators will be comfortable and familiar. Furthermore, it is a system which is suited to company structures and which fully recognizes the Anglo-Saxon trust concept. This fact is most often crucial to the success of an international structure .

The British Virgin Islands can also boast a highly developed infrastructure of skilled professionals which is necessary to support an efficient offshore center.

Communications

The British Virgin Islands has frequent same day air communications with North America and Europe. Telephone, telex and facsimile facilities compare favorably with any international financial center and worldwide postal and courier services are available on Tortola.

Language

Certain offshore centers prove cumbersome when legal and other documents need to be translated into the official language of the territory. Apart from the obvious inconvenience caused, there are, as a result, additional costs to be borne with no benefit accruing therefrom. The official language of the British Virgin Islands is English and therefore these problems do not arise here. Communications are also, as a result, far easier.

Confidentiality

Unlike the majority of offshore centers, the British Virgin Islands offer the discretion of not having to disclose the beneficial ownership of companies to any authority or person in the British Virgin Islands. Furthermore, as seen earlier, British Virgin Islands IBCs have the power to issue bearer shares.

Montserrat - *"the Emerald Isle"*

An active Volcano in Montserrat has all but destroyed the country and its once promising offshore financial business. Plymouth, the capital, was the headquarters for registering companies and banks, but it is now under tons of volcanic ash. The government has moved its operations to another part of the island, but it's unclear as to whether much new business is going to Montserrat. But, because all of Montserrat's tax haven legislation is still in place, we will not totally discard Montserrat as a legitimate tax haven just yet.

Montserrat is a small ($\approx$ 40 square miles) mountainous, sparsely populated British crown colony located in the Eastern Caribbean southwest of Puerto Rico and about 27 miles west of Antigua. It's lush tropical beauty led writers to christen it the *"Emerald Isle"*. Celebrities such as Mick Jagger, Elton John, Beatles' producer George Martin, Britain's Princess Margaret (sister of Queen Elizabeth II) David Bowie, the Earl of Lichfield, and New York Restaurateurs Maguy & Gilbert La Coze have homes here cashing in on that precious intangible - peace and quiet.

In spite of its inaccessibility, Montserrat (prior to the current volcano problems) had excellent telephone, telex and fax communications and two international courier services. While Montserrat was a flourishing tax haven worth a second look, recently an active volcano spewing smoke and ash has been giving local residents much to worry about. [16.]

History and people geography

One of the Leeward Islands in the Lesser Antilles of the West Indies, it has an area of 106 sq. km (40 sq. mi) and a population of 12,504 (1991 est.). Plymouth is the capital and only port. The island is rugged and lush, with steep, thickly forested mountains, many of them active sulfurous volcanoes; deep valleys; and beaches of dark volcanic sands. The average annual temperature is 26 deg C (78 deg F), and rainfall averages from 1,015 to 2,030 mm (40 to 80 in) yearly. Montserrat is known for its sea-island cotton, limes, and tomatoes and other vegetables.

The great majority of the people are of African descent. Tourism and light industry are important to the economy.

Montserrat was discovered by Christopher Columbus in 1493, and it was named Montserrat for the mountain monastery in Spain. The island was colonized by Irish settlers in 1632, but the French took possession of it twice--in 1664-68 and in 1782-84. A British crown colony since 1871, Montserrat gave up attempts to federate with other islands in 1966.

Twenty-five year *guarantee* from income taxes

On December 4th, 1985 Montserrat's Governor A. C. Watson signed An Ordinance to make provisions for the incorporation and operation of *International Business Companies (IBCs)*. Under the new law, offshore IBCs that do not (1) carry on business with persons in Montserrat (2) own an interest in real property situated in Montserrat, other than leased office space (3) accept banking deposits from persons resident in Montserrat (4) accept contracts of insurance from persons resident in Montserrat, are totally exempted from Montserrat's regular income taxes, which top-out at about 40%.

Part XI (Income Taxes & Stamp Taxes)

111. (1) notwithstanding any provisions of the Income Tax Ordinance (1967),
   (a) a company incorporated under the (IBC) Ordinance, 1985;
   (b) all dividends, interest, rents, royalties, compensations and other amounts paid by the company to persons who are not persons resident in Montserrat;
   (c) capital gains realized with respect to any shares, debt obligations or other securities of a company incorporated under this Ordinance by persons who are not persons resident in Montserrat,

are exempt from all provisions of the Income Tax Ordinance, 1967 (as amended), the Exchange Control Ordinance, Cap. 115, the Foreign Currency Levy Ordinance 1980 and the Stamp Act, Cap 238, such exemption to continue for a period of not less than **25 years** from the date of incorporation under this Ordinance.

Managers of Montserrat IBCs can receive tax exemption for services rendered.

Under **111.(2)** when the Governor-in-Council is satisfied that a company registered under the IBC Ordinance requires the services of specially qualified persons in order to enable it to conduc

---

16. From *"On Tiny Isle of 300 Banks, Enter Scotland Yard"*, by Joseph B. Treaster, New York Times (July 27, 1989).

its business effectively from within Montserrat, and that it is neither able to acquire those services in Montserrat nor acquire them elsewhere without special benefits being made available to them, the Executive Council may, by order in a special case, provide that these persons:

(a) be exempted from specified taxes in Montserrat (individual tax rate ≈ 40%).

(b) be permitted to be paid in a foreign currency into a trust account without being liable to be taxed thereon or on the interest thereon, and

(c) be permitted to be paid in some prescribed manner in another currency or otherwise without being liable to taxes thereon in Montserrat.

Formation Costs

Part X (Fees & Penalties) of the **IBC Ordinance** outline what government fees the entrepreneur will encounter upon incorporating a company in Montserrat.

104. There shall be paid to the Registrar fees as follows;

(a) $300 upon the registration by the Registrar of a company incorporated under this Ordinance the authorized capital of which does not exceed $50,000.[17.]

(b) $1,000 upon the registration by the Registrar of a company incorporated under this Ordinance the authorized capital of which exceeds $50,000.

To keep a company in good standing annual license fee equal to the amounts prescribed above are payable to the Registrar's office on the 31st of December or before January 31 of the following year.

Option: Instead of paying the annual fees as prescribed above, a Montserrat IBC may opt to be taxed on its net profits at a rate of **1.75%**. This option is particularly beneficial for Dutch subsidiaries domiciled in Montserrat. Under the Dutch tax system the **participation exemption** (which permits dividends from foreign subsidiaries to be received 100% tax free by the Dutch parent company) is available only if the host country levies some form of tax on profits. The rate of the profits tax assessed is not a factor. Any tax rate (however small) will satisfy the Dutch tax authorities.

Provisions to thwart seizures by the IRS

Article 31.(1) states that where a governmental authority, whether it is legally constituted or not, in any jurisdiction outside Montserrat,

(a) by or in connection with any nationalization, expropriation, confiscation, coercion, force or duress, or similar action; or

(b) by or in connection with the imposition of any confiscatory tax, assessment or other governmental charge,

take or seize any shares or other interest in a company incorporated under this Ordinance, the company itself or a person holding shares or any other interest therein, including an interest as a creditor, may apply to the Montserrat Court for an order that the company disregard the taking and seizure and continue to treat the person who would have held the shares but for the taking or seizure of the shares as continuing to hold the shares or other interests.

Montserrat's Trustee Ordinance of 1961

Montserrat has a common law tax system styled after its British colonizer. The Trustee Ordinance of 1961 (Chapter 324 Trustee) refers *specifically to England, Canada and the Colony*, which leads one to think that the Ordinance was originally tailored to suite Englishmen and Canadians as well as those of the local residents. *The Trustee Ordinance* provides the legal framework by which lawyers and other professionals can establish a trust in Montserrat.[18.]

You are given much leeway in how you must draft a Monsterrat deed of trust. Under the title *"Interpretation"* on the cover of the Ordinance the term authorized investments is defined as "investments authorized by the instrument, if any, creating the trust for the investment of money subject to the trust, or by law." In Part II, Article #4 it states "A trustee may, unless otherwise prohibited by the instrument creating the trust, retain or invest in securities payable to bearer which, if not so payable, would have been authorized investments."

New offshore banking regulations

After being racked by several banking scandals in the 1980's, Montserrat's government is trying to get back into the offshore banking business. Nicknamed *Monster Rat* after Scotland Yard had to be called in to clean up Montserrat's

---

17. Under **Part I** (Short Title & Interpretation) of the IBC Ordinance, 1985 it states. *A reference to money in this Ordinance is a reference to the currency of the United States of America.*

18. Montserrat's new Ordinance for the formation of *International Business Companies (1985)* states in its text that the **U.S. dollar** is the currency which government fees shall be paid the Registrar's Office. The older *Trustee Ordinance* (1961) does not specify what currency is to predominate but uses the $ sign over the £ in its text. The fact that the US$ is the preferred currency leads one to conclude that this British Crown Colony is genuinely interested in attracting U.S. business concerns of all types and sizes.

banking mess, this Caribbean island paradise and UK dependent territory has just recently enacted new offshore banking regulations to woo respectable banks and bankers.

In the late 1980's, Montserrat flaunted itself as a "suitcase" banking center, offering banking licenses by the crateful for $10,000 apiece to bank charter wholesalers - the most notorious of which was Jerome Schnider of the Beverly Hills based WFI Corporation.

Hundreds of conmen sought and obtained banking licenses. Using names like "Chase Overseas", "Prudential Bank and Trust", and "Deutsche Bank (Suisse)", you would have thought Montserrat was a respectable banking center, but these brand name banks were nothing more than bastardly versions of their real-world namesakes.

What followed were a multitude of banking frauds as revealed in a report from Coopers and Lybrand commissioned by the UK Foreign Office in 1990. Overnight Montserrat revoked 311 banking licenses, representing fee income of $18 million.

Now, with slow, tentative steps, Montserrat wishes to refashion itself and get back into the offshore banking business. The government has issued new banking regulations and appointed a Washington D.C. firm called "Offshore Financial Services, Inc." to reform the island's battered image.

Today, Montserrat has about 23 banks, all but three of them from Latin America. Several years ago, Ms. Kathleen Tuitt, president of Offshore Financial Services, Inc. insisted the isle has "cleaned up its act". Her job is to introduce banks to Montserrat's chief minister, Mr. Ruben Meade, and banking supervisor, Mrs. Dulcie James, formerly with the Bank of England.

"So far we've visited banks in Miami and Latin America," said Tuitt, although James has visited banks in Ecuador.

The new Montserrat banking regulations expect bank applicants to meet the following criteria:

- pay an up-front, non refundable fee of $3,000;
- pay an annual license fee of $8,000 ($12,000 for bank insurers);
- submit a business plan to the Montserrat authorities;
- reveal directors' names;
- have a minimum capitalization of $500,000;
- file quarterly statements and audited annual accounts;

- agree to a three month inspection prior to receiving their licenses (to which the FBI, Scotland Yard, and Interpol would be privy).

Over the last several years, the Montserrat authorities have sweeping supervisory powers and have introduced new International Business Company (IBC) legislation, as well as legislation for APT (Asset Protection Trusts). Montserrat wants to attract wealthy retirees and expatriates, of which 2,000 presently inhabit the island.

Grenada's IBC Act of 1996

Grenada is located in the South Windward Islands. It is an independent member of the Commonwealth. With a population of 110,000 and 133 sq. miles of turf, Grenada has potential as an offshore base.

Discovered by Christopher Columbus in 1498, the ownership of Grenada was disputed between the French and the British until 1783, when the treaty of Versailles declared the island British. In 1974 Grenada gained its independence and became a member of The British Commonwealth.

Grenada has a strong democratic government, which is based on the British parliamentary system. Queen Elizabeth II is the head of state, represented by the Governor General of Grenada. The official language of the island is English. The international financial service industry plays a large role in Grenada's economy, and the government places high priority on the banking laws.

The local currency is East Caribbean Dollar but USD is widely accepted. The exchange rate is 2,70 ECD to USD1,00. As an ex-British colony, the official language and the legal system are both English.

Several years ago, the government of Grenada announced an overall development plan designed to make Grenada a tax haven along the same lines as Cayman, Bermuda and the Bahamas. Costs to start up an IBC in Grenada are about $1,200 US. The annual Government fee is $260.

The International Business Corporations Act of 1996 established laws for the formation of International Corporations. By incorporating in Grenada, a company gains a wide range of competitive advantages, including:

- Exemption from all local taxes and stamp duties.
- Maximum confidentiality and anonymity, no disclosure of Beneficial Ownership.
- Bearer Shares is permitted.
- No disclosure or minimum capital requirements.
- International Corporations do not have to file audited financial statement.
- Grenada has not entered into tax treaties with any other country.
- Annual meetings can be held anywhere in the world, telephone meetings are allowed.
- Incorporation's within two working days.

Registered Office Agent

Every offshore company must have both a registered office and registered agent in Grenada. The agent represents the offshore company to the local authorities and fulfills legal requirements on behalf of the company.

St. Vincent & The Grenadines

Located in the central Windward Islands, not far from Grenada, is St. Vincent and the Grenadines. St. Vincent and the Grenadines became independent in 1979. St. Vincent has enacted a International Business Corporation Act similar to that in Barbados. St. Vincent has also enacted legislation for the formation of trusts. Since January 1997 St. Vincent and the Grenadines has become an attractive and safe country for registration of offshore companies.

Message from J.F. Mitchell, Prime Minister of St. Vincent & The Grenadines

St. Vincent and the Grenadines welcomes all serious investors to our shores. Foreign investors in Industry are particularly welcome for it's Caribbean, North American and European markets to which we have preferential access through various agreements.

We have a responsible and easily trained work force. Our fiscal situation is stable, and our credit worthiness, established by sensible marco-economic policies over the last seven years, has assisted us in building up a sound infrastructure. Ours is a good country for relaxation. Top management employed in our country has easy access to pleasant environs for weekend relaxation.

We recognize that we are in the period of greatest technological change in production and are prepared to work to take advantage of change to keep ourselves competitive.

St. Barthelemy Death of a tax haven

The island of St. Barthelemy is located just to the south of Anguilla and some 120 miles north of Guadeloupe. St. Barthelemy was for some time a *"no-tax"* haven frequented by the French. When the French Decree of March 31, 1948 introduced income taxes to the rest of French possessions, it appeared to exempt St. Barthelemy by process of elimination. Someone it seems forgot to specifically mention St. Barts in the legislation.

French residents and islanders continued to enjoy their tax free status for almost 30 years, when in 1976 the French tax service abruptly started to levy income tax on the island's residents. Two residents who were bewildered to find an income tax bill in the mail one day decided to file action in Guadeloupe before the Administrative Court.

The Court decided (after five years) that income tax was illegal in St. Barthelemy, and so at the time it appeared a victory had been won, and St. Barthelemy became the only place in the world to become a tax haven by court decision. But the victory was short lived.

In March, 1985, the Consul d'Etat reversed the Administrative court's decision and reinstated income tax to St. Bart's residents. Lowering the hammer, residents were found not only liable for current income taxes on their worldwide incomes (this is how the U.S. taxes it's citizens and residents), but past income taxes as well. Residents were required to file tax returns for all years since 1981 and pay interest and penalties. Making matters worse, those who did not file returns were subject to direct assessments by the tax collector, and penalties in losing court cases could reach 400% of the tax due.

As if all this misfortune wasn't bad enough, the tax authorities were empowered to write mortgages on residential properties immediately after the assessments were made.

Is there a lesson to be gleaned from the problems of St. Barthelemy? Maybe so.

Montserrat's Confidential Information Ordinance, 1985

AN ORDINANCE TO REGULATE THE DIVULGENCE OF INFORMATION IMPARTED UNDER CONDITIONS OF PROFESSIONAL CONFIDENCE.

BE IT ENACTED by the **Queen's Most Excellent Majest**y, by and with the advice and consent of the Legislative Council of Montserrat and by the authority of the same as follows:

2. In this Ordinance, unless the context otherwise requires: "bank" and "financial institution" and "International Business Companies" have the meanings respectively ascribed to those terms by section 2 of the Banking Ordinance, 1978, and section 5 of the International Business Companies Ordinance, 1985, No. 19 of 1985;

"Confidential information" means information received by a professional person from or in respect of a principal concerning any property in which the principal has an interest and which the recipient of such information is not authorized by the principal to divulge;

"divulge" means without the authority of the principal express or implied, to disclose or communicate to any person not entitled to such disclosure or communication and includes unauthorized communications to persons at large;

"normal course of business" means the ordinary and necessary routine involved in the efficient carrying out of the instructions of a principal, including compliance with all relevant laws and legal procedures and the routine exchange of information between financial institutions and/or International Business Companies;

"principal" means a person who employs or instructs a professional person in the normal course of business matters relating to any property of the principal;

"professional person" means a bank or other financial institution, a barrister or solicitor, an accountant and **every person** subordinate or **in the employ or control of such person or institution for the purpose of his or its professional activities**;

"property" means every present, contingent and future interest or claim, direct or indirect, legal or equitable, positive or negative, in any money's worth, or any real or personal property (movable or immovable), and all rights and securities thereover and all documents and things evidencing the same or related thereto;

3. (1) Subject to subsection (2), this Ordinance shall apply to all confidential information as defined in this Ordinance which originates in or is brought into the Colony and to all persons coming into possession of such information, whether professional persons or not.

(2) This Ordinance shall not apply to the seeking, divulging or obtaining of confidential information -

(a) in compliance with directions of the High Court given in accordance with the provisions of section 4;

(b) by or to a professional person acting in the normal course of business or with the consent, express or implied of the relevant principal;

(c) by or to a police officer of the rank of Inspector or above investigating an offence committed or alleged to a have been committed within the Colony;

(d) by or to the Minister responsible for finance, the Financial Secretary, or the Attorney General;

(e) generally, in accordance with the provisions of this or any other Ordinance;

4. (1) Whenever a person intends or is required to give in evidence in, or in connection with any proceeding being tried, inquired into or determined by any court, tribunal or other authority, and confidential information within the meaning of this Ordinance, he shall before doing so apply for directions and any adjournment necessary for that purpose shall be granted.

(2) An application for directions under subsection (1) shall be made to and heard and determined by, a Judge of the High Court sitting alone and in camera. At least seven days' notice of such application shall be given to the Attorney General who is a party to the proceedings in question. The Attorney General may appear as *amicus curiae* at the hearing of the application and any party on whom notice has been served

as aforesaid shall be entitled to be heard thereon, either in person or by counsel.

3) Upon hearing an application under subsections (1) and (2) the Judge shall direct -
(a) that the evidence be given; or
(b) that the evidence not be given; or
(c) that the evidence be given subject to conditions to be specified by him whereby the confidentiality of the information will be safeguarded.

(4) In order to safeguard the confidentiality of evidence ordered to be given under subsection (3)(1) a Judge may order one or more of the following;
(a) that divulgence of evidence be restricted to certain named persons;
(b) that the evidence be taken in camera;
(c) that reference to names, addresses and descriptions of particular persons be by alphabetical letters, numbers or symbols representing such person, the key to which shall be restricted to persons named by the judge.

5. (1) Subject to the provisions of section 3 (2), and person who -
(a) being in possession of confidential information however obtained -
(i) divulges it; or
(ii) attempts, offers or threatens to divulge it;
(b) willfully obtains or seeks to obtain confidential information to which he is not entitled,

shall be guilty of an offence and liable on summary convictions to a fine not exceeding $50,000 or to imprisonment not exceeding 2 years or to both such fine and such imprisonment.

(2) Any person who commits an offence under subsection (1) and receives or solicits on behalf of himself or another person in the course of such offence any reward from any person shall be liable to a further fine not exceeding $50,000 or to imprisonment for a term not exceeding 2 years or to both such fine and such imprisonment and also to forfeiture of the reward if it was received by him.

(3) Any person in possession of confidential information who without the consent of the principal makes use thereof for the benefit of himself or another shall be guilty of an offence and liable on summary conviction to the penalty prescribed in subsection (2) and for that purpose any profit accruing to such person out of such transaction shall be deemed to be a reward.

(4) Any professional person, entrusted as such with confidential information, who commits an offence under subsection (1), (2) or (3) in respect of such information shall be liable to double the penalty prescribed in each of those subsections respectively.

(5) Subject to the provisions of section 3(2), any bank which gives a credit reference in respect of a customer without the express authority of such customer shall be guilty of an offence under subsections (1) and (4) hereof;

(6) Every person who receives confidential information by virtue of the provisions of subsection 4(2) shall be as fully bound by the other provisions of this Ordinance as if such information were entrusted to him in confidence by the principal.

6. The Governor-in-Council may make regulations for the administration of this Ordinance.

7. No prosecution may be instituted under this Ordinance without the express consent in writing of the Attorney General.
8. The Confidential Information Ordinance, 1980 is hereby repealed.

H.A. FERGUS *(Speaker)*

Passed the Legislative Council this 19th day of December, 1985.

E.R. Kirnon
Ag. Clerk of the Council

Turks & Caicos Islands

Back in the early 1980's when The Turks & Caicos Islands' government ran three full page ads in *Investor's Daily* promoting the TCI as an attractive no-tax haven for U.S. investors, you knew the TCI government was out to gain ground on the other Caribbean tax havens, and you knew the TCI was a tax haven on the move.

In July 1997, we received the official **TCI Financial News** letter, with comments from TCI's new Governor John P. Kelly (former Deputy Governor of Bermuda) who was recently appointed by HRH Queen Elizabeth II.

As the editor of the *Tax Haven Reporter* I've always been impressed by the smart, aggressive approach that the TCI government has taking to remind offshore investors that there are other tax havens besides the Bahamas and the Cayman Islands that want your business.

With excellent offshore legislation already in place for IBCs, insurance company formation, etc., the TCI will continue to grow in attractiveness. Below is Governor John P. Kelly invitation to visit and invest in the TCI.

HIS EXCELLENCY THE GOVERNOR
John P. Kelly

It gives me great pleasure to introduce myself as the new Governor of the Turks & Caicos Islands. I am no stranger to the Offshore Finance Sector, as my last two assignments as deputy Governor of Bermuda and as Deputy Head of the West Indian and Atlantic Department in the Foreign and Commonwealth Office enabled me to take a keen interest in the finance sector of the other British Dependent Territories as well as competitor countries.

It is an exciting time to be starting a tour of duty in the TCI. Development in the tourist sector during the past 15 years has been phenomenal - especially in Providenciales - but the other islands in the TCI group are beginning to benefit from investments in tourist projects also. One major project with an estimated investment of some US $300 million plus proposed for the uninhabited island of East Caicos will transform the economy of TCI by the millennium.

Such staggering development in the tourist sector shows a strong confidence in the long term economy of TCI and is important for the parallel growth in the finance sector. From a relatively slow start in the early 1985 TCI has emerged as a fast growing center for offshore finance and particularly the IBC.

The original Companies Ordinance of 1981 has undergone many improvements to ensure that it continues to meet the demands of the international business community. The financial services offered today cover banking, insurance, trusts, company formation, including limited life companies, partnerships and investment funds. There are-experienced professional practitioners to service the finance industry and while it is well regulated by the Financial Services Commission, company formation is made very easy. 1996 showed itself to be another record year for TCI company formations with an increase of 18% over 1995 and 30% over 1994.

I can see from my time here so far that TCI is a marvelous place to live. It is also a great place to do business. Accessibility to North America is through Miami which is just over one hour away. Communications are excellent and as good as you will find in any other offshore center. The future for the finance sector here is very bright. Why not try it for yourself !

His Excellency The Governor
John P. Kelly

The new Turks & Caicos Islands

One famous author wrote in the late 1970's that the Turks & Caicos Islands were a tax haven waiting to be discovered. Recent reports show there are about 12,000 exempted companies in this British crown colony a few hundred miles southeast of Nassau Bahamas. It appears the Turks & Caicos Islands have finally arrived.

Drafting legislation unmistakenly similar to that earlier enacted in the Cayman Islands, the Turks & Caicos Islands look to capture their share of the offshore tax haven business by offering lower incorporation fees than in Cayman. Both **exempted** and **ordinary** companies can be formed in the TCI for about 1/2 what you would spend for the same company in the Cayman Islands. Government registration fees are $275 for ordinary companies and $325 for exempted companies. Annual fees are $300.

Total costs (including lawyers, trust companies, agents and a registered office) are right about $1,200. Note, this is slightly higher than in the Bahamas. Further, none of the major airlines have direct flights to the Turks & Caicos Islands, and air fare is substantially higher than a flight to Nassau.

The Companies Ordinance 1981 was introduced to cater to the needs of the international financial community which comprise a diverse range of end-users, including attorneys, tax-advisers and private investment banking institutions. Some of the advantages under the new Ordinance include:

• Political stability, with a history of peace and a low crime rate.
• Geographically well positioned in the same time zone as New York City.
• The official currency is the U.S. dollar; there are no exchange controls.
• Registration fees are lower than in most • The Registry itself is extremely efficient. As a matter of course, a company is incorporated on the same day as the application is lodged, with incorporation documents usually being completed and available within twenty-four hours.
• A flexible and workable companies law giving rise to highly streamlined procedures of statutory administration.
• Official recognition of the importance of the Islands' economy for the development of a financial service industry and outgoing support at high levels of Government.

Type of Company In the Turks and Caicos Islands

Since the enactment of the Companies Amendment Act No.2 of 1992, the Exempt Company is the most commonly used body corporate for international trade and investment purposes. Exempt Companies are exempted from all forms of taxation for a period of twenty years from the date of incorporation.

Procedure to Incorporate

By submission to the Companies Registry of the Memorandum and Articles of Association

signed by the Subscribers. The Memorandum and Articles of Association should contain:

• the proposed name of the company
• the proposed registered office address
• the objects of the company
• a declaration that the liability of the members is limited
• a declaration confirming that the activities of the company will be undertaken outside the Turks and Caicos Islands

After incorporation the company should ensure that the location of the registered office is published in the Gazette.

Restrictions on Trading

Cannot trade within the Turks and Caicos Islands, and may not own real estate there. Cannot undertake the business of Banking, Insurance, Assurance, Re-Insurance, Fund Management, Collective Investments Schemes, the rendering of investment advice or any other activity which may suggest an association with the banking and insurance industries. Cannot solicit funds from the public, or offer its shares for sale to the public.

Powers of Company

A Company incorporated in the Turks & Caicos Islands has all the powers of a natural person.

Language of Legislation and Corporate Documents

The language of the Legislation is English. The corporate documents have to be in English, but may be accompanied by a foreign language translation, and which may be also filed at the Registry. The name of the company may also be translated into Chinese characters which can be printed on to the Certificate of Incorporation.

Registered Office Required

Yes, must be maintained in the Turks and Caicos Islands at the address of a licensed management company.

Shelf Companies Available

Yes.

Time Scale to Incorporate

Two days.

Name Restrictions

Any name that is similar or identical to. Any name that in the opinion of the Registrar is considered undesirable or obscene. Any name that suggests Royal or Government Patronage.

Language of Name

Can be in any language using the Latin alphabet, or Chinese with the language using the Latin alphabet.

Names Requiring Consent or a License

Bank, Building Society, Savings, Loans, Insurance, Assurance, Re-Insurance, Fund Management, Investment Funds, Friendly Society, Trust, Trustee, Guarantee, Indemnity, Underwriters, Co-operative, Commonwealth or their foreign language equivalents.

Limited Liability Companies

Limited, corporation, incorporated or their abbreviations. Can also be incorporated without a suffix denoting Limited Liability.

Disclosure of Beneficial Ownership to Authorities

No.

Authorized and Issued Share Capital

It is normal to incorporate an exempt company with an authorized share capital of $5,000; divided into 5,000 common voting shares of US$1 each, this being the maximum capital for the minimum duty payable at the time of incorporation. Thereafter if the authorized share capital exceeds $5,000, the capital duty is increased by 1% of any increase up to $50,000, by 0.5% of any increase over $50,000 and by 0.1% of any amount over and above $100,000. The minimum issued capital is one share of no par value or one share of par value.

Classes of Shares Permitted

• Registered shares.
• Bearer shares.
• Shares with or without a par value.
• Preference shares.
• Redeemable shares.
• Shares with or without voting rights.

Bearer Shares Permitted

Yes.

Taxation

The Turks and Caicos Islands has no direct taxation in the form of income tax, corporation tax, capital gains tax, inheritance tax or gift tax.

Double Taxation Agreements

The Turks & Caicos Islands are not party to any double taxation agreements.

License Fees

$300.00 payable annually in January.

Financial Statement Requirements

No requirement for filing, but financial records should be kept to reflect the financial position of the company.

Structure and Management

Directors

The minimum number of directors is one. The directors may be natural persons or bodies corporate, be of any nationality and need not resident in the Turks and Caicos Islands.

Company Secretary

All companies incorporated in the Turks and Caicos Islands are required to appoint a company secretary. The company secretary may be a natural person or body corporate, be of any nationality and need not resident in the Turks and Caicos Islands.

Shareholders

The minimum number of shareholders is one.

Ordinary and Exempted Companies

There are two main types of companies, the ordinary and the exempted company. There is also a third category of foreign company of which there are few in number.

The procedure for registering both ordinary and exempted companies are basically the same. Three copies of the Memorandum and Articles of Association are lodged together with the prescribed fee. Forms of Memorandum and Articles of Association are prescribed in schedules to the Companies Ordinance for both ordinary and exempted companies, and may be adopted in whole or in part. The subscriber(s) to the Memorandum of Association of an exempted company must file a declaration that the operations of the company will be carried on mainly outside the Islands. Agents lodging an application for registration must hold appropriate license issued pursuant to the Business Licensing Ordinance.

There is a legal requirement for a minimum of only one shareholder who may be an individual or a corporation. The liability of members may be limited to guarantee or to the amount unpaid on their shares. Shares may be of no par value, and the Articles of Association may include the power to issue shares in bearer form.

All companies must have a registered office within the Islands and exempted companies must also nominate a representative resident in the Islands for the purpose of service of process.

Special Privileges for Exempted Companies

• Confidentially. No requirement to file details of shareholders or directors.
• Authorized capital may be in any currency with no minimum paid-up capital requirement.
• Company name can be in any language with no requirement that the word "Limited" or "Ltd." be part of the name.
• Objects may be unrestricted.
• No requirement for annual general meeting of shareholders. Directors hold office until replaced.
• Availability of Governor's Undertaking conferring exoneration from future direct taxation and any increases in annual filing fees. (this is a real plus! - editor).

Confidentiality

As well as Part VIII of the Companies Ordinance, which applies specifically to business affairs of exempted companies, the Confidential Relationships Ordinance of 1979 imposes duty of confidentiality upon banks, professional advisers, and other persons holding positions of trust. Both these laws impose criminal sanctions for unauthorized disclosures. The Islands have no double taxation agreements with any nation, thus no exchange of tax information is provided by the Turk government.

Transfer to and from the jurisdiction is unrestricted, fast and easy.

Part IX of the Companies Ordinance makes provision for the transfer into the islands of companies incorporated in other jurisdictions. The law of the country of incorporation must not prohibit such transfers, and there are safeguards to protect the interests of creditors and shareholders. The company, on being transferred, becomes registered as if it was incorporated as an exempted company and registration fee is determined accordingly.

A company wishing to be in the position to transfer in the future at short notice may obtain a "standby" permit which can be activated without delay at a later date.

There are corresponding provisions in the Ordinance for transfers out of the jurisdiction by exempted companies registered in the Islands.

Turks & Caicos Trusts

An important example of an area of law as yet unaltered by statue is that of trusts. This allows for a great deal of flexibility in the creation of trust, but insofar as the applicable law is in some cases as it was in England prior to the Trustees Act of 1925, there are certain areas which could benefit from statutory interference. These is already in force a Trusts (Special Provision) Ordinance which gives persons using approved trustees the ability to invoke certain provisions of the U.K. Trustee Act and to abrogate certain rules of equity such as the rule against perpetuities and the rule requiring certainty of objects. However, this law was not widely utilized, and a New Jersey-style law of trusts was legislated as part of the overall package of legislation passed by Legislative Council in 1989.

Regulation of Funds in the Turks

Type of Funds Collective investment schemes may be created in TCI either by incorporating a mutual fund company or establishing a unit trust.

Laws Mutual funds/open ended investment companies are governed by the Companies Ordinance 1981, as amended. Unit trusts are governed by the general laws of equity and trusts. Unit trusts are governed by their trust deed rather than by company law. There are no minimum capital requirements. They are however subject to Financial Services Commission (FSC) supervision in the same way as mutual funds.

Managers and Trustees

There are no rules defining who may act as the manager of a fund in TCI. A company which acts as trustee must have a trust license under the Trustees (Licensing) Ordinance 1992. There are no legal restrictions on the fees which may be charged by managers or trustees.

Investment Restrictions

Generally restrictions are not imposed on the type of investment which a fund may make. Rather the emphasis is on demonstrating the managers expertise in the area of investment selected. Regulation is concentrated on the approval of promoters and their advisors on the establishment of the fund with subsequent monitoring of the activities of the fund.

Borrowing

There are no legal restrictions on the borrowing powers of funds in TCI although they may be contained in the memorandum and articles of association, or trust agreement.

Fund Ownership

There are no restrictions on the percentage of units which any person or group of persons may hold in the fund. However funds will frequently specify restrictions with regard to certain classes of persons (e.g. US persons because of the potential tax consequences of the fund of being considered a US corporation).

Accounts or prospectus A fund is not obliged to publish accounts in a manner that makes them available to the public but it is obliged to produce a prospectus which requires prior approval from the supervisory authority. Supervision The supervisory- authority in TCI is the Financial Services Commission (FSC).

Confidentiality/Bank secrecy

The Confidential relationships Ordinance of 1979 makes it an offense to make, use of confidential information for the benefit of anyone but the Principal. Fund Structure Funds of funds are permitted in TCI as are umbrella funds.

Overseas Marketing Designated territory status under the UK Financial Services Act 1976 has not been sought by TCI. The Turks & Caicos Islands do not have any double tax agreements with other jurisdictions. There is no direct taxation in TCI.

Island of Providenciales

The island of Providenciales has been the site of some major investment in recent years. This came about some twenty-five years ago, when a rich American named Fritz Ludington, en route by plane from the Bahamas to Haiti, was attracted by the pristine, white sandy beaches and the exceptional aqua blue, color of the oceans, and so landed on Providenciales to check it out. Further enthused by the friendliness of the inhabitants, Ludington returned home and was successful in engendering a group of friends from the old-moneyed Roosevelt and DuPont Nemours families. Together they established a development company named Provident Limited, which in turn negotiated the right to purchase 4,000 acres of Crown Land for 1¢ per acre. Work then began on the cutting of a road, the building of an airstrip, and the construction of the first hotel and marina. This was the beginning of the tourist industry and development of real estate on Providenciales.

More recent Providenciales developments include the site for a 700-bed Club Med Village, and an international airport financed by the British Government to the tune of $12,000,000. Club Med opened in December, 1984 and saw an additional $25,000,000 in new investment. As tourism increased, the island began to grow competitive with the other better known tax havens of Cayman, Bahamas and Bermuda. The surfacing of many roads and a modern telecommunications system have made the island even more attractive to visitors.

While land prices have doubled in the fifteen years since 1985, today's prices are still three to five times lower than those better known Caribbean islands such as the Caymans and St. Barthelemy. One has to wonder how much longer this will last. Already there is a Ramada Inn. And French builder Pierre Gely has completed at least one condominium and a marina for pleasure yachts in Leeward, on the eastern tip of Providenciales.

Further development is expected on the rest of the islands. The accessibility of the islands of North, Middle and East Caicos will be improved by a road system similar to that which serves the Florida Keys. Grand Turk, Salt Cay, Pine Cay and Parrot Cay are also expected to see new developments in the future.

Turks attract two giant U.S. firms

In August, 1995 the Turks & Caicos Islands (TCI) Government amended its exempt companies legislation to allow the registration of a "limited life company" (LLC). A limited life company can be incorporated without the usual corporate characteristics of perpetual life, free transferability of ownership interests and centralized management while retaining the principal liability for members. Entities such as LLCs will be treated as partnerships by the IRS, where expenses and incomes are passed through to the partners.

There has been a growing demand in the United States for the LLC following its recognition by the Inland Revenue Services as a "transparent" entity similar to a trust or partnership. This means that its profits and losses are regarded as attributable to the partners rather than to the company itself.

Texaco, Inc. and Enron Corp. have both taken advantage of the new legislation to set up TCI LLCs, and have used them to issue preferred shares with cumulative fixed rates of dividends. The whole of the proceeds raised by the issue are on loan to the parent companies, so that dividends paid on the preferred shares are deductible as if they were interest payments. Since the Turks & Caicos Islands have no taxes whatsoever, no withholding taxes will be made on the dividend pay-out. Had the same issue been offered out of New York or London, a 30% withholding tax would have applied to the dividend pay-out (absent a lower treaty rate).

Texaco Capital LLC announced the issue of US$350 million of Cumulative Guaranteed Monthly Income Preferred shares (MIPS) on 27 October, as US$25 per share, with an annual dividend rate of 6.9%, callable at par after 5 years. The payment of dividends and payment on liquidation or redemption of preferred shares are guaranteed by the parent company - Texaco Inc.

Enron Corp. a US company engaged in exploration, transportation, and marketing of natural gas, registered Enron Capital LLC in October and issued US$200 million of MIPS in a public offering through the new company in November at an annual dividend rate of 8%.

The public offerings were underwritten by international investment houses including Goldman Sachs & Co. which were responsible for the development of the MIPS. The MIPS of both Texaco and Enron will be listed on the New York Stock Exchange.

On September 1, 1996 Wittingham & Company, a local firm of Chartered Accountants that has been operating on Providenciales since August 1993, has joined with Deloitte Touche Bahamas to form Deloitte Touche T.C.I.

As one of the top six accountancy firms, Deloitte & Touche is a world leader in audit, accountancy and management- consulting. It is the third major firm to establish an office in TCI, roe others being - Coopers & Lybrand and KPMG. Deloitte Touche T.C.I. is committed to playing an active role in the long term development of the TCI financial services industry.

For more information on TCI contact at the address listed below.

Financial Services Commission
P.O. Box 173,
Front Street, Grand Turk,
Turks & Caicos Islands, B.W.I.
Tel: 809 946 2791
Fax ,809 946 -2821

Netherlands Antilles (Aruba & Curacao)

The fact that the six islands making up the Netherlands Antilles were one of the first offshore financial and tax planning centers offering a combination of low tax rates and a tax treaty network has proved an attractive feature to international investors, notwithstanding the unilateral termination of the U.S.-Antilles Income Tax Treaty in 1987.

Currently, the Netherlands Antilles is popular for the incorporation of the following Netherlands Antilles Companies: finance companies; mutual funds; ultimate holding and finance companies of multi-national operating corporations; shipping companies; trading companies; investment companies; Free Zone companies; royalty holding companies; offshore banks; insurance companies; foundations and limited partnerships. Netherlands Antilles Companies are known for being domiciled in a modern and stable jurisdiction.

Big Buyers of U.S. Securities - Tax Free

According to research from American investment bankers Goldman Sachs, the Netherlands Antilles accounted for the third highest net purchase of US shares in the second quarter of 1995, with deals worth $2.1bn, behind Singapore with $4bn and the UK with $2.8bn.[19]

With a population of just 170,000, the purchase of $2.1bn worth of US equities may seem astonishing, but as Ms Abbey Cohen analyst at Goldman Sachs suggests "many financial intermediaries are based in these locations, hence net purchases attributed to them may well be on behalf of individuals or institutions domiciled in other countries."

But why, even though the favorable U.S. tax treaty with the islands was repealed nearly ten years ago, are investors still accessing the US via Curacao'? Braham offers the following explanation: "Because companies incorporated here has been used so much in the past. The lawyers and everybody in the US are very familiar with a Netherlands Antilles company." And he adds there are "additional benefits such as confidentiality and some tax advantages."

Offshore companies incorporated in the Netherlands Antilles are taxed at between 2.4% and 3% on offshore income and are exempt of capital gains tax. Companies have to obtain authorization to be formed but it appears there are rarely any difficulties in obtaining permission. Apart from purchasing shares, companies formed in the Netherlands-Antilles are often used to buy real estate in the US.

US clients remain important, but the operation also draws on its origins in the Netherlands, to exploit an important client base of European nationals.

Dutch names such as ABN Amro, Meespierson and ING still dominate the Antilles business directories. The Dutch connection goes back a long way, with Curacao, the largest of the islands that make up the Netherlands Antilles, having been in Dutch possession since 1634, apart from a brief period during the Napoleonic Wars. And Dutch is also the official language.

The financial services industry was kick-started by the Dutch in the 1940s when Dutch corporates moved their assets to the region to escape seizure by the Nazis. After the war, many of the companies returned their headquarters to the Netherlands but left behind the infrastructure of an offshore center.

That infrastructure includes around 70 banks, more than 50 of them international, an established fund management industry with around $60bn of assets under administration, trusts and insurance companies.

All the major international audit firms are here doing both international and local work and there are numerous law firms. Most of these institutions are based in and around Willemstad, the capital of Curacao, about 30 miles off the coast of Venezuela.

Offshore Company Formation

Offshore Companies incorporated under the commercial code of the Netherlands Antilles that have received foreign exchange control permission.

---

19. From an article by Sandeep Deol (*Offshore Financial Review*)(*January 1996*)

Procedure to incorporate

Execution of Deed of Incorporation before Notary Public. Declaration of no objection to the draft articles of incorporation needs to be obtained from Ministry of Justice before incorporation. Once incorporated, an Offshore Company needs to obtain a Business Licence.

Restrictions on trading

Unless a special permit has been granted an offshore company cannot undertake banking or insurance activities,. Also cannot undertake investment business other than investment of a company's own assets. It can neither solicit funds from the public nor offer its shares to the public. It cannot trade within the Netherlands Antilles.

Powers of company

A Netherlands Antilles company has all the powers of a natural person.

Language of legislation and corporate documents
English.

Registered office required

Yes. Must be maintained in the Netherlands Antilles at the address of a licensed trust and management company, a law firm or accountancy firm.

Registered Agent Required
Yes.

Name approval required

Yes. By formal request to the Chamber of Commerce.

Shelf companies available
Yes.

Time to incorporate
Ten days.

Name Restrictions

A name that is similar to or identical to an existing company. A well known name that is known to exist elsewhere. A name that implies illegal activities. A name which in the opinion of the Registrar is considered undesirable, obscene or offensive. A name that implies royal or government patronage.

Language of name

The name of the company can be expressed in any language using the Latin alphabet. The Registrar may request a Dutch or English translation to ensure that the proposed name does not contravene name restrictions.

Names requiring consent or a licence

Bank, building society, savings, loans, insurance, assurance, reinsurance, fund management, investment fund, trust, trustees, Chamber of Commerce, co-operation, council, municipal or their foreign language equivalents or any name in English or a foreign language that may suggest association with the banking or Insurance industries.

All Netherlands Antilles companies must include the words Naamloze Vennootschap or the abbreviation NV. Where a company's activities are outside the Netherlands Antilles and the Articles permit, the suffixes Limited, Ltd, Inc or SA are allowable.

Disclosure of beneficial ownership to authorities
No requirement.

Share capital, taxation, licence fees and compliance matters

Authorised and issued share capital

The minimum authorised share capital is US$ 30,000, of which at least US$ 6,000 must be issued and fully paid up.

Classes of shares permitted

Registered shares, bearer shares, preference shares, redeemable shares and shares with or without voting rights. No par value shares are not permitted.

Bearer Shares Permitted
Yes, but must be fully paid up.

Taxation In Netherland Antilles

Netherlands Antilles Offshore Companies, i.e. those that derive all their income from outside the Netherlands Antilles, are liable to tax rates of between 2.4% and 6%, dependent upon activity. Investment holding companies pay 2.4% on first US$ 56,000 and 3% on balance. Trading Companies pay 4.8% on first US$ 56,000 and 6% on balance, subject to tax ruling.

Double Taxation Agreements

The Netherlands Antilles has double tax treaty agreements with Norway and The Netherlands.

Licence Fees

Every Netherlands Antilles company must pay an annual fee to the Chamber of Commerce, which is variable and dependent on authorised capital. The minimum is US$ 34.

Financial Statement Requirements

Whilst there is no requirement to file audited accounts with the Registry, a company is required to present a tax return and profit and loss statement and balance sheet to the Netherlands Antilles Tax Inspector.

Directors

The minimum number of directors is one. All Netherlands Antilles companies must appoint at least one resident managing director. Additional foreign resident directors may be appointed, who may be of any nationality. Corporate directors are permitted.

Company secretary

The Netherlands Antilles Companies Acts do not provide for the appointment of a company secretary.

Shareholders

The minimum number of shareholders is one.

Aruba (Tax) Exempt Corporations

The Caribbean island of Aruba, located 15 miles off the coast of Venezuela and some 78 miles square miles in area, was annexed by the Dutch in 1860. On January 1, 1986, Aruba assumed a separate status within the Kingdom of the Netherlands with full internal autonomy. The legal system is based on the law of the Kingdom of the Netherlands.

On January 1, 1988 the Government of Aruba introduced a new companies ordinance to attract foreign investors. The preamble to the legislation reads:

"...in connection with the further development of Aruba as a financial center it is desirable that there shall be in addition to the limited liability company a new form of legal entity, the Aruba (tax) exempt corporation, of which the structure compared to that of the limited liability company shall be simplified."

The National Ordinance for the registration of the **Aruba (Tax) Exempt Corporation** (or AVV) was promulgated on June 30, 1988. An AVV is a legal entity with limited liability and an authorized capital divided into shares. It is similar to the International Business Corporations (IBCs) in use in the Bahamas, the BVI and other offshore centers, but it is based on Dutch civil law, as opposed to English common law statutes.

Some of the more important features, aside from complete income tax exemption, of the AVV are:

(1) Freedom from exchange controls;
(2) A minimum authorized capital of US$5,600 and only one share is needed to start-up an AVV;
(3) Shares of an AVV can have full, limited, par or no par, voting or no voting rights, bearer or registered;
(4) Directors can be of any nationality;
(5) No requirement for annual financial statements or annual shareholder meetings, if "Articles" permit;
(6) Shareholders meetings can be held anywhere in the world and shareholders can be represented by proxy;
(7) An AVV cannot operate as a bank or insurance company, and does not qualify for any benefits under the tax regulations of the Kingdom of the Netherlands (i.e., the Participation Exemption).
(8) no withholding taxes on any payments by an AVV to its shareholders, and no estate, inheritance, gift or wealth taxes on the shares. [20]

Company formation in Aruba

An AVV is incorporated by notarial deed executed by at least one incorporator before a civil law notary in Aruba. Before the Deed of Incorporation can be passed, a draft must be submitted to the Ministry of Justice for a Declaration of No Objection.

---

20. From the *International Tax Report* (Sept., 1990), pg 8 to 10.

The Deed of Incorporation should be in the Dutch language, but it is standard practice that the Deed is accompanied by a certified translation.

Costs for Aruba Exempt Company (AVV)

- Notarial expenses and first year Government Registration fee = US710.
- Annual Government charges = US$285.
- Contribution to the Chamber of Commerce = US$35.
- Professional fee for incorporation = US$450
- Annual fee for registered office, registered agent = US$500.
- Managing Director's (optional) fee = US$350.

Naamloze Vennootschap or NV

Limited liability companies called NVs can still be incorporated in the "Antilles". Minimum annual maintenance costs of about US$1,500 can be expected. Such companies, if fully owned by non-resident shareholders, pay a profits tax of 2.4% to 3%. The advantages of paying a small tax (as opposed to none at all for AVVs) is important for purposes of obtaining the Netherlands "Participation Exemption". Dutch based holding companies that own shares in an NV can receive dividends and other distributions (including capital gains and liquidations) from an NV free of Netherlands income tax if it owns at least 5% of the NV's stock. AVVs are not eligible for this tax exemption.

Offshore companies are not allowed to carry on any business within the Netherlands Antilles unless they get approval from the Central Bank. The N.A. profits tax is 32-39% on incomes drawn from the local economy.

Netherlands Antilles Mutual Funds

Under the **Profits Tax Ordinance** (PTO), the tax payable by mutual funds is limited to US$10,000 per annum, irrespective of the funds (realized) gains or profits. The $10,000 profits tax is reached when the net asset value of the fund reaches approximately US$43,000,000. More than 45 mutual funds were registered in the Antilles through June, 1988. Famous Wall Street money managers George Soros and Michael Steinhardt run N. Antilles funds. Recently, these managers have run into a streak of poor stock picks after years of outperforming the markets.

Most Offshore Cities in tax havens impose **no** income or estate taxes on resident and non resident companies, trusts and individuals doing business or living there. Below is a list of cities in some of the top tax havens. Note, some havens will impose estate (£) and/or income taxes (√) on investors that take up permanent residence, or are doing business within the country deriving profits from the local economy.

City	Country/Island	Top Tax Rate
Nassau,	Bahamas	0%
GeorgeTown	Grand Cayman	0%
Freeport	Grand Bahama Island	0%
Douglas	Isle of Man	20% √ £
St. Helier	Jersey (Channel Islands)	20% √ £
St. Peter Port	Guernsey (Channel Is.)	20% √ £
British Virgin Islands	Road Town (Tortola Is.)	√ £
Hamilton	Bermuda	£
Avarua	Rarotonga Is (Cook Islands)	£ √
Panama City	Panama	√
Hong Kong	Hong Kong Island	√ £
Vaduz	Liechtenstein	√ £
Luxembourg	Luxembourg	√ £
Lugano	Switzerland	9.8% √ £
Campione	Italian enclave	0%
Bridgetown	Barbados	√ £
Zurich	Switzerland	9.8% √ £
Gibraltar	Gibraltar	√ £
Geneva	Switzerland	9.8% £
Vila	Vanuatu (Efate Is.)	0%
Apia	Western Samoa (Upolu Is.)	√ £
Willemstad	N. Antilles (Curacao Is.)	√ £

Source: *The Tax Haven Reporter* (1999)

Antigua & Barbuda • tax haven in Southeastern Caribbean

Since its independence in 1981, the twin-island state of Antigua and Barbuda in the Caribbean has continued to practice a tradition of English Common Law. Located less than 300 nautical miles Southeast of Puerto Rico, in the Leeward Islands. Its legal procedures are structured in accordance with strong democratic principles of good governance, patterned after the British parliamentary system. In 1982, legislation was enacted under the International Business Corporations Act, with subsequent amendments in 1984 and 1985, to make Antigua and Barbuda a choice jurisdiction for offshore banking. Operations under this Act are controlled by the Ministry of Finance in Antigua.

While Antigua and Barbuda is probably best known as an up-market destination for more discriminating tourists, its natural and developed assets have also allowed it to emerge as an attractive offshore business center. The country is in a convenient time zone, sharing the same time as New York, Toronto, Central and part of South America, and falling five hours behind the UK and Europe in the summer and four hours in the winter which allows international business to be transacted easily within an appropriate time frame. Antigua's international airport is a major gateway for the Caribbean, serving British Airways, Air France, Condor, American Airlines, Continental, Air Canada, BWIA and LIAT, with direct flights from New York, Miami, Toronto, London, Frankfurt and Paris. Its international telecommunications are excellent, with direct access into the global stream of financial and business data. Electronic funds transfer is readily accomplished, providing same day value, and securities can be placed and executed within 24 hours.

There is a prosperous English-speaking community, with a resident population just under 70,000. Its people are involved primarily in business related to the tourism industry and in commerce. The country enjoys the highest per-capita income in the Eastern Caribbean, and the absence of personal income tax results in a higher level of disposable income than most Caribbean countries.

International commercial banking has been conducted on Antigua for many years. Offshore banking is more recent, having started in 1983. Since that time the industry has grown rapidly. Working in co-operation with the private sector, the Government has improved Antigua's offshore company and banking environment through the introduction of new foreign residency, trust, and partnership legislation.

IBC Act of 1982

The prevailing offshore legislation provides for speedy formation of international business corporations (IBCs) at very competitive charges and with minimal compliance procedures. The formation can be carried out by a locally registered trust company or by an accountant or attorney. Formation can usually be completed within 24 hours and full corporate and trust services are available to both private and corporate investors including:
1. Registration and maintenance of corporate charters for offshore companies;
2. Reception, management, and disbursement of the assets of offshore companies;
3. Provision and maintenance of a registered office;
4. Maintenance of the company's records and statutory register;
5. Preparation of all necessary corporate returns and reports to the Director;
6. Provision of directors and officers on request;
7. Incorporation and management of offshore banks and captive insurance companies; and
8. A full range of traditional trust services.

Some of the benefits provided to offshore companies formed under the IBC Act include the full exemption of all direct taxes in respect of any international trading, investment or commercial activity including withholding taxes and stamp duties. No minimum capital is specified for an IBC and shares may have a nominal or no par value and may be issued in registered or bearer form. The transfer of the charter of an IBC to a foreign jurisdiction, or vice versa, is explicitly permitted. A trust company, lawyer or accountant for the corporation may serve as the sole member of the board of directors.

Confidentiality Provisions

The IBC Act provides criminal penalties for any disclosure of the business affairs of customers regarding banking or trust matters. The only exception for the disclosure of information relates to sound evidence regarding an alleged criminal offense that is triable in Antigua (or which would have been triable, if it has been committed in Antigua).

There are specific advantages for Canadian entities to form an IBC in Antigua that generates an active business income, because dividends paid out of income earned in Antigua are considered to be paid out of exempt surplus. Antigua is one of the countries listed in the Canadian Regulation 5907 (ii) which allows this arrangement. There are no tax treaties with European countries, except in the case of the UK and this is being updated through negotiations.

Incorporation Procedures

Every IBC must have a registered office and a resident agent in Antigua. This function is regularly performed by the trust company or by the professional who performed the incorporation process. The resident agent is responsible for paying the annual government fees and for keeping the company in good standing. The annual government license fee for an IBC is US$300; for an IBC licensed to carry on international banking it is US$15,000 and for an IBC licensed to carry on an international insurance business it is US$10,000.

Fees charged by trust companies or professionals for incorporation and annual maintenance will vary, but fees for the formation of an IBC without an international banking or insurance license start at about US$1,600, with an annual maintenance fee of US$950 to $1,200.

If the applicant for an IBC wishes to have a registered agent serve as its corporate director, an additional fee will be charged, between US$250 and US$1,000 for each director.

Incorporation and maintenance fees for an IBC with an international banking or insurance license are higher and may be related to the level of required management services. Fees for trust management services are also dependent on the nature and value of assets and the required level of service.

Ship Registry

In 1985, Antigua enacted the Merchant Shipping Act, which further expanded the facilities of its offshore center. The designated port of registry in St. John's, Antigua, is under the supervision of the Registrar of Ships, Department of Marine Services and Merchant Shipping. Registration can also be carried out in Germany by the Commissioner of Maritime Affairs, Department of Marine Services and Merchant Shipping, Hopfenweg 14, 26125 Oldenburg, Germany.

The procedures for ship registration or parallel (bareboat) registration are efficient and can be organized through several of the offshore operators. With the submission of required documentation, the Department of Marine Services provides quick response. The registration fees are competitive with other jurisdictions and are transparent, with no hidden costs. No age is set for the acceptance of ships for registration, but all ships over 499GRT must be in class. The Department of Marine Services does not duplicate safety inspections, but complements and controls the work of class societies. Unlike some other registers, Antigua has no nationality requirements for manning vessels.

Establishing a Financial Institution

An international banking license to an IBC is granted at the sole discretion of the Supervisor of Banks and Trust Corporations. The supervisor may revoke the license at any time if, in his opinion, the revocation is in the public's interest. The minimum capital requirement is currently five million US dollars or its equivalent in another major currency. However, it is exempt from any exchange control or foreign currency levy. IBC banks are required to appoint an auditor and to file unaudited quarterly returns and annual audited accounts with the Supervisor of Banks and Trust Corporations. The accounts are provided in a consolidated form.

Insurance License

An internal insurance license permits an IBC to engage in any insurance business other than domestic insurance. The Superintendent of International Insurance Corporations is empowered to revoke or suspend the license if its registration is deemed to be detrimental to public interest. A stated capital of at least US$100,000 must be maintained at all times. Annual audited accounts must be filed with the Superintendent of International Insurance Corporations.

145.

Trust Services

Trusts administered by Antigua and Barbuda trust companies are not subject to any legislation imposing taxes on inheritance, profits, income, or on any capital assets, gain or appreciation on any assets or dividends, and interest paid out by an IBC as a trustee on behalf of a non-resident of Antigua and Barbuda, for a period of 20 years from the date of incorporation of the IBC.

Although there is no requirement that a trust instrument be recorded, it may be recorded in the non-public records of the Director of International Business Corporations who will issue a Certificate of Recordation attached to the original of the trust instrument.

There is also no restrictions on accumulations by trusts and the rule of law known as the rule against perpetuities does not apply to any property vested in a trust corporation. The minimum capital requirement for a trust corporation is US$500,000. The IBC Act and domestic laws governing trusts, based on the British Common Law, which was adopted by Antigua as a colony and readopted after independence, still apply to all international trusts.

Offshore Banks and Companies

In 1982, the Government introduced the International Business Corporations Act permitting off shore banking, insurance and trust corporations. The benefits of the Act include:
• full tax exemption
• no control on exchange and freedom to operate bank accounts anywhere
• no minimum capital requirement (except for
(i) banking where US$1 million is required together with the filing of quarterly returns;
(ii) Trusts where a minimum capital requirement of US$500,000 and the filing of quarterly returns; and
(iii) Insurance companies which must file annual reports and have a reserve capital of US$100,000)
• 50 year guarantee of tax-free status
• no statutory audit required
• bearer shares permitted.

Permanent Residence

In June 1995, the government introduced a permanent residence scheme to encourage a limited number of high net worth individuals to establish tax residency tax in Antigua and Barbuda. As residents all their income would be free of local tax.
• To obtain a permanent residence certificate an applicant must:
• maintain a permanent place of abode in Antigua and Barbuda;
• obtain an alien landholding license costing 5% of the property value;
• pay a purchaser's stamp duty of 2.50%;
• pay an annual levy of US$20,000/annum;
• reside in Antigua and Barbuda for not less than 30 days a year.

Tax Incentives

Antigua and Barbuda has the benefit of comprehensive yet simple legislation to guide the international investor. It is important to note that legislation for international banking, trusts, insurance, manufacturing and other international commercial activities is contained in single statute known as The International Business Corporation Act, 1982. The major benefits to the international investor under this Act are as follows:
• Exemption from all corporate taxes on income or capital gains or any tax on the transfer of assets or securities to any person
• Exemption from withholding tax on any dividends, interest or other returns to shareholders
• No statutory audit requirement
• No minimum share capital requirements
• Availability of wide range of professional services
• Ability to issue bearer shares

Companies incorporated under the Act are given the following incentive:

• Exemption from Antiguan income tax, guaranteed by government for at least 50 years
• No estate, inheritance or other similar taxes
• No tax on the securities or assets of the corporation
• Exemption from all transfer taxes.

The income, profits, gains, funds and securities that are generated or acquired by a company registered under the Act in the course of its business are exempt from the provisions of the Exchange Control Act. A company can be incorporated with one director. The director of a company need not be a natural person. Neither is he required to hold shares in the company. There are no nationality restrictions for directors.

Barbados • low-tax haven in eastern Caribbean

Barbados has many of the prime tax haven attributes including low tax regimes and an expanding tax treaty network.

Barbados is a responsible, low-tax haven. Confidentially is respected, but secrecy is not permitted. Barbados has economic stability, quality infrastructures, accessibility from the United States, a wide range of offshore incentive legislations, and a liberal and flexible corporate law.

Taxes

All the offshore incentive legislation provides effective exemption from exchange controls. Income tax rates range from 1% to 2-1/2%. There are no capital gains taxes or estate duties, no withholding tax on dividends, interest or royalties, no taxes on share transfers, no stamp duties on capital for offshore corporations. Expatriate staff serving the offshore industry can readily get work permits and are exempt from tax on up to 35% of their remunerations. Offshore companies can import free of customs duty all machinery or materials they need for their business.

International Business Corporations

The International Business Companies (Exemption from Taxes) Act 1991 represented an upgrading and simplification of a financial services product which had been in existence in Barbados since 1966. The original legislation was a response in the 1966 era to complement the fiscal incentive legislation and the direct foreign investment which that latter legislation sought to encourage from metropolitan industrialized capitals. Since 1966, the international business companies legislation has undergone periodic amendment, which has itself been a reflection of the steadily increasing use of the Companies Act.

An IBC is a resident corporation (or branch of a foreign company that holds annual meetings in Barbados) which (1) does not carry on a trade in buying and selling goods in Barbados, nor selling services to resident CARICOM (Caribbean Community), (2) does not have more than 10% Barbados ownership, and (3) elects not to claim a foreign tax credit for income taxes paid outside Barbados.

International business companies pay taxes at the graduated rates of tax from 2.5 per cent to one per cent on profits. The old law had allowed only international business companies engaged exclusively in investment activities to qualify for the lower rates. International businesscompanies incorporated outside Barbados are only taxed in Barbados on profits earned from Barbados branch operations. Furthermore, such a company can take a credit for taxes paid to a foreign country, provided the credit does not reduce the tax payable in Barbados to less than one per cent of the profits and gains of the company in any income year.

However, an international business company whose shares form part of the assets of an Offshore Trust under the management of a licensed Barbadian offshore bank and whose activities are restricted to buying, selling, holding, or managing securities is completely exempt from tax. The exemption from tax is expanded to include all fees or other income paid or deemed to be paid (including those on dividends, royalties, interest, and management fees as enumerated in the prior Act) to non-residents of Barbados from any withholding tax.

Furthermore, international business companies which require the services of specially qualified individuals to carry out their business from within Barbados, and which are unable to acquire those services in Barbados, may obtain from the Minister specially provided tax concessions in respect of those specially qualified individuals. This is a provision present in the other financial services legislation related to banks, insurance companies, and foreign sales corporations.

International business companies receive benefits for an indefinite period and may request a guarantee of benefits for a period of fifteen years.

All international business companies whose assets or gross income do not exceed US $500,000 require a local audit.

The present legislation has simplified some planning opportunities. The United States originating real estate holding company for non United States persons and seeking to avoid the Branch Profits Tax will often generate no profits on which Barbados tax would be payable. Many of these companies are no longer required to suffer the expense of an audit which often represents a nil return to the Barbados Commissioner of Inland Revenue; for many such entities will have assets under US $500,000.

Planning is further enhanced by the introduction into the legislation of the provision whereby the Minister may allow an international business company to pay tax at any rate not less than one per cent, thereby granting to planners the option and facility to pay taxes in different baskets, depending on the particular treaty framework which is being used.

A special planning opportunity is provided by the ability afforded to an individual not to be deemed resident in Barbados if such an individual is living in Barbados by virtue of an employer-employee relationship with an international business company licensed under the Companies Act. This provision facilitates a larger number of persons in seeking residence in Barbados so as to actively manage their own international business companies.

International Trust Act

The International Trusts Act 1995 was introduced with specific recognition of features related to purpose trusts, the legal effect of foreign laws, asset protection, and other important legislative provisions. An international trust may be set up in Barbados, provided that the settlor is resident outside of Barbados when the trust is created and on every occasion that new property is added to the trust. At least one of the trustees must be resident in Barbados, and the trust property cannot include any immovable property in Barbados or any interest in such property. Beneficiaries may not be residents of Barbados at the time of the creation of the trust or when new property is added, except in the case of exempt insurance companies, offshore banks, international business companies, charities, or persons specified by the Minister.

One of the useful provisions within the legislation relates to the area referred to as the proper law of the trust. The position is that the proper law is the law of the jurisdiction which is stated as the proper law in the trust instrument; in the absence of any statement to that effect, it is the jurisdiction with which the trust had its closest connection at the time of its creation.

The advantage of this provision is the ability to set up a Barbados international trust which is governed by the laws of another jurisdiction if so stated or inferred. The proper law is central to any trust since it will apply to the administration of the trust, as well as its construction and its validity. Provision also is made for the proper law to be changed, provided the other jurisdiction recognizes the feature of such a change.

The provision also has special benefits in cases where individuals of Civil Law jurisdictions wish to avoid harsh 'forced heirship' rules. These rules essentially restrict the free disposition by an individual of property on death. As long as the Barbados trust is established in accordance with the requirements in the Companies Act, any matters which arise as to whether the trust will be governed by the laws of Barbados, or any question which falls to be decided in respect of any disposition of trust property, will be determined solely under the laws of Barbados without reference to the laws of any other jurisdiction with which the disposition or the trust itself may have a connection.

The international trust legislation also makes provision for asset protection trusts. A disposition of property made with the intention of defrauding or which is transferred at an undervalue may become ineffectual if an action is pursued by a creditor who has been affected. The creditor, however, has a legal requirement to prove his case, and that case may only be brought within three years after the disposition of the property.

In recent years, there has been an increasing use of trust protectors. This concept is not one of Common Law, but may be introduced by way of stating in the trust deed the desired powers to be given to such a protector. The protector is much in the nature of a safety valve or a lender of last resort; hence, the power to appoint and remove trustees, to change the proper law, and to receive information on the accounts are all specifically mentioned in the legislation. More protector powers may, however, be inserted in the trust deed and, not surprisingly, the power to approve the adding and excluding of beneficiaries as well as the approval of trust distributions are powers which are not infrequently given.

There are certain formalities which are required with the setting up of a Barbados international trust. In this regard, there must be an instrument in writing, and there must be a declaration within the trust instrument that it is an international trust. This trust also has a useful life potentially of 100 years because of an extended 'perpetuity period'.

One interesting innovation within the international trust legislation is the ability to set up a purpose trust, which is a trust with no named or ascertainable beneficiaries, or which may be for the benefit of a group of persons bearing an identity by reference to some personal relationship. One of the attractions of the purpose trust is that it need not be set up for charitable purposes and, thus, may be established for a group that does not otherwise meet the criteria of a charity. The purpose trust allows for creative use in a variety of business transactions.

Taxation of trusts

There are a variety of taxation options in the use of the various types of Barbados trusts, be it the pure domestic trust, the trust under the Offshore Banking Act (with its variant of the interposed International Business Company), or the international trust under the International Trusts Act. This is a useful feature in a low-tax jurisdiction such as Barbados where some planning structures require the use of a trust vehicle which is prima facie taxable.

In the case where a resident Barbados trust is taxable, it is subject to income tax at the same rates as applicable to an individual; in determining taxable income, allowance is made for expenses which have been incurred, as well as any amounts payable to beneficiaries. In determining the amounts which are deductible for distributions to beneficiaries, any amounts paid in respect of that year, as well as amounts that were enforceable by the beneficiary may be included. Non-resident beneficiaries will only be taxable on income derived from Barbados.

In the case of trusts established under the Offshore Banking Act, no tax is payable either by the trust or the beneficiaries, and there is no tax payable by an international business company owned as part of the trust assets, provided that the company is only engaged in dealing securities or holding of such securities. Under the Act, no tax is payable by the trust or beneficiaries. In the case of trusts under the International Trust Act, there is no taxation since such a trust is deemed not to be domiciled in Barbados. Non-resident beneficiaries are not subject to income tax in Barbados on distributions.

The Barbados trust legislation has appeal to a variety of jurisdictions, and particular interest to Canada where there is the benefit of a double-taxation treaty with Barbados. In the case of Canadian residents who expect a large inheritance from family members who are living abroad, there is scope for the drafting of their wills such as to provide for the creation of an offshore testamentary trust for the benefit of the Canadian resident.

In the case of wealthy persons who are in the process of immigrating to Canada and who have not previously lived in Canada for a total of five years throughout their entire lives, there also is scope for the creation of an international trust in Barbados. For wealthy persons who are in the process of emigrating from Canada, there also is an opportunity to set up a tax-efficient Barbados international trust and for appropriate accumulation and periodic distribution to Canadian resident beneficiaries as trust capital.

Taxation

The principle taxes in Barbados are:

- Corporation tax;
- Income Tax (individual);
- National insurance contributions;
- Customs and excise duties;
- Consumption tax;
- Stamp duties;
- Hotel and restaurant sales tax;
- Land tax;
- Property transfer tax;
- Tax on insurance premiums;
- Tax on life insurance company investment income;
- Tax on bank assets;
- Travel tax; and
- Residential property rental surcharge.

Residents of Barbados, individuals or corporations, are subject to tax on their worldwide income; individuals resident in

Barbados, but domiciled elsewhere, are not liable to tax in Barbados on income earned outside of Barbados from which no benefit is received in Barbados providing that such income is not from an office or employment exercised in Barbados. Non-residents are subject to Barbadian tax only on income derived from Barbados. There are no capital gains or inheritance taxes.

Taxation of Companies

Companies, including all bodies corporate and unincorporated associates which are resident in Barbados, are subject to corporation tax. This does not apply to partnerships. Resident companies are taxed on their worldwide income, whether remitted or not. Non-resident companies are only taxable to the extent that they conduct a business in Barbados through a branch or agency and the income directly or indirectly attributable to that branch or agency is subject to corporation tax.

Income will be regarded as having a Barbados source if the property that constitutes the source is located in Barbados. There is no statutory definition of residence, but a company will be deemed to be resident in Barbados if its management and control rest in Barbados.

Tax Rates

The corporate tax rates below are applicable to the domestic sector (i.e., not IBCs and foreign owned trusts) are as follows:

- Basic rate for local corporations, 40 per cent;
- Unit trusts, 40 per cent;
- Building societies, 20 per cent;
- Income derived from the construction of two or more wall houses in any year, 20 per cent;
- Branch of non-resident corporation, 40 per cent (A branch - adjusted gross income - pays an additional 10 per cent on its net profits if those profits are remitted or deemed to have been remitted. This tax does not apply if the profits are re-invested in Barbados for other than the replacement of fixed assets. For this purpose, re-investment does not include merely replacing fixed assets. The branch profits tax is a withholding tax that must be paid to the Commissioner of Inland Revenue by June 30 of the year following the income year);

- Income from Barbados government securities, 12.5 per cent (Residents of Barbados pay at 12.5 per cent, and this represents the full tax liability on this source of income. Non-residents pay no tax.);
- Income paid to non residents, nil;
- Management, administrative, or technical aid fees, 15 per cent;
- Services other than management, 25 per cent;
- Interest, 15 per cent;
- Royalties, 15 per cent;
- Dividends from taxed profits, 15 per cent; and
- Gross earnings of entertainers, 25 per cent.

The corporate tax rates applicable to the offshore sector are as follows:

- International business companies, 2.5 per cent (reducing to one per cent);
- Offshore banks, 2.5 per cent (reducing to one per cent);
- Foreign sales corporations, nil;
- Exempt insurance companies, nil; and
- Exempt insurance management companies, nil.

A Barbados-resident company must withholding tax at 12.5 per cent on the distribution of dividends on ordinary shares to a resident individual. The distributing company must pay the tax withheld to the Commissioner within 15 days of the end of the month of withholding as payment in full of the recipients' liability to tax in respect of the dividends.

Exempt Insurance Companies

The introduction into Barbados in 1983 of captive insurance was a logical progression in the development of its financial services legislation. There were already in existence various other statutes to meet the special needs of the legitimate offshore investor, ie, the International Business Companies Act 1966, the Shipping Incentives Act 1982, the Shipping Act 1981, the Fiscal Incentives Act 1974, and the Offshore Banking Act 1981.

Barbados Captive Legislation

The Barbados legislation embodies the basic features of a flat rate minimum capitalization of US $125,000; no tax or duties on profits, investments, premium and stamp duty on capital;

a license fee and annual government fee of US $2,500; and no annual or other taxation.

The legislation has been enhanced by two series of amendments. The first set of amendments related to the establishment of mutual insurance companies and required amendment to the existing Companies Act. The second set, promulgated in June 1988, related to:

• The ability to incorporate holding companies and related provisions;
• The need for the appointment by each licensee of a resident representative with responsibility for knowledge of ongoing solvency of the company; and
• The extension of the period for the filing of financial statements from three to six months and in compliance with generally accepted accounting principles.

The legislation avoids the committee screening process required in other jurisdictions. It also requires the appointment of only one local director. Furthermore, in the Barbados case, there are no limits on investments so long as authorities are satisfied that the liquidity of assets is sufficient to meet liabilities.

There are presently more than 300 active captive insurance companies and more than 20 active insurance management companies registered in Barbados.

Although not specifically provided for in the legislation, the Minister of Finance will provide for United States-originated companies a Certificate of Residence which is written to comply with the Ruling Request requirements of the United States Internal Revenue Service.

Provision is made in the Companies Act, at section 32(1), for the Minister to give assurances or guarantees to a company that the benefits and exemptions as set out in the Companies Act will continue for a period of 15 years immediately following the company becoming a licensee or a holding company. The approved form of guarantee is now given on a routine and regular basis to companies as applications are made on their behalf. Naturally, a guarantee is essentially of a symbolic nature since, under English and Barbados law, one Parliament may not bind a successor. Nevertheless, a licensee could instigate an action based on breach of contract, in the unlikely situation of a breach of the provisions in the Companies Act related to taxes and embodied in the form of guarantee.

Barbados-United States Tax Treaty

The Convention between the United States and Barbados for the Avoidance of Double Taxation and Prevention of Fiscal Evasion, otherwise known as the double-taxation treaty, presented special benefits to the Barbados captive insurance industry. The treaty, signed on 31 December 1984, took effect on 28 February 1986 and served as the catalyst for a steady flow of United States companies establishing exempt insurance companies in Barbados. This was a result of essentially two features within the treaty, namely:

• The waiver by the United States of the collection of the excise tax on premiums paid to foreign insurers and re-insurers; and
• The limiting of the United States to taxing business profits attributable to a permanent establishment or a fixed base.

Barbados-Canada Tax Treaty

The Barbados resident captive insurance company is in a unique position vis-à-vis companies in the other traditional offshore domiciles. As a result of the Canada-Barbados Tax Treaty, Barbados is a listed jurisdiction under section 5907(11) of the Canada Income Tax Regulations and, accordingly, dividends paid from the active business income of a Barbados captive insurance company are treated as paid out of the exempt surplus of the payer and are tax exempt in the hands of the Canadian recipient.

Barbados also is appealing to Canadian companies seeking to avoid paying Federal Excise Tax, which is not payable under a reinsurance contract. Hence, fronting by a Barbados licensed exempt insurance company, where possible, has proved to be useful.

Recent changes to the taxation of Canadian-owned foreign affiliates affect some of the Canadian companies presently licensed in Barbados, but some of the changes also clarify the rules and enable decision-making with greater certainty. Additionally, recent indications are that some income which would originally have qualified as exempt surplus and been capable of being remitted to Canada tax free might no longer be interpreted as such; however, it will only be taxable on remittance and remain capable of being redeployed into non-Canadian investment via a non-Canadian holding company.

The most recent change was in respect of the 1996 Revenue Canada technical interpretation which essentially indicated that, since exempt insurance companies were not paying tax in Barbados, their tax-free dividend status would not apply to income earned after 1995.

The response of Barbados policy makers has been amendment to the Exempt Insurance Act to allow for the taxation of exempt insurance companies by way of converting of the US $2,500 annual license fee into a tax. It was clearly a change without effective transparency and Revenue Canada did not delay in reaching this conclusion.

In 1997, the Barbados policy makers took new legislative steps to remedy the amendment and recapture the lost Canadian insurance business. The draft legislation is far reaching in that it seeks to create with the necessary licensing arrangements a new category of international insurance business under the Barbados Insurance Act. It also provides that companies licensed under the legislation will pay an effective tax of 2.5 per cent on their taxable incomes and, where applicable, companies will be able to make use of the tax credit system under the relevant double-tax treaty.

The purpose and scope of these amendments is to return to Canadian owned captives the ability to enjoy tax-free repatriation of dividends to Canada. The legislation was expected to be enacted by the end of 1998.

Foreign Sales Corporations

The Foreign Sales Corporation Act 1984 provides incentives for corporations to establish foreign sales corporations in Barbados. There are approximately 2,200 foreign sales corporations licensed to operate in Barbados.

Under the Foreign Sales Corporations Act, foreign sales corporation operations are called 'foreign trade transactions'. A foreign trade transaction is any transaction made by a foreign sales corporation or a former foreign sales corporation with persons not resident in the CARICOM and which, under foreign sales corporation legislation in certain countries outside of Barbados, is the source of foreign trade income. The Barbados legislation defines eligible foreign sales corporation countries broadly since it is expected that the foreign sales corporation legislation will be applied to future foreign sales corporation legislation from countries such as Canada. To qualify as an foreign sales corporation, a company must:

• Be incorporated under the Companies Act;
• Have as its principal object and activity engaging in foreign trade transactions;
• Be owned by shareholders none of whom are residents of the CARICOM; and
• Establish that it is designated (or qualifies to be designated) as a foreign sales corporation.

A company applying for a foreign sales corporation license from the Ministry of International Trade and Business first pays an application fee of US $100. An application, on the prescribed form, is then submitted to the Ministry, along with a copy of the company's Certificate of Incorporation, a copy of the attorney's declaration filed on incorporation, the receipt for the application fee, and the license fee of US $500 for small foreign sales corporations and US $1,000 for other foreign sales corporations. The license is then issued by the Minister. Application for renewal of the annual license, along with the license fee of US $500 for small foreign sales corporations and US $1,000 for the other foreign sales corporations, must be submitted before 1 January of every year thereafter.

Foreign sales corporations are not required to file annual income tax returns with the Department of Inland Revenue but the audit provisions of the Income Tax Act apply. Hence, although foreign sales corporations are exempt from the filing of returns, the Barbados government retains the power to audit in the event of a problem, such as a request for information from a United States competent authority. Furthermore, a foreign sales corporation is exempt from the Companies Act requirement of filing financial statements.

Customs duties exemptions apply to foreign sales corporations. A foreign sales corporation in Barbados may import, free of customs duties, and consumption tax, articles that it certifies to the satisfaction of the Comptroller of Customs as necessary to conduct its foreign trade transactions from within Barbados. Once an article is imported under the exemption, the foreign sales corporation must not dispose of it for five years unless it pays, or provides security for, the exempted duties.

In substitution for the percentage rates of the Stamp Duty Act, a substitute stamp duty of no more than B$10 is due on documents executed in Barbados during the operation of the foreign sales corporation.

Special concessions apply to attract uniquely qualified persons. Special salary concessions can be obtained for specially qualified persons, if a foreign sales corporation requires a service to conduct its business effectively, and if such services are not available in Barbados and cannot be obtained elsewhere without special tax benefits. In such a case, the Minister may exempt a prescribed percentage of the salary or fees of a director, employee, or contractor from Barbados.

In March 1994, Barbados enacted legislation amending the Barbados Foreign Sales Corporation Act. The definition of foreign sales corporation is amended such that a Barbados foreign sales corporation can now qualify under the Companies Act if it does business within CARICOM. Furthermore, the definition of 'foreign trade transactions' is amended, such that transactions may qualify even outside of Barbados, but within CARICOM.

Another change in the licensing requirements allows a foreign sales corporation to qualify for a license in Barbados if it is incorporated under the Companies Act, its principal object and activity is engaging in foreign trade transactions, and none of its shareholders is a resident of Barbados. To previously qualify, the applicant had to show that its shareholders were not residents of CARICOM. A further amendment allows the Minister of Finance to, by order, grant benefits under the foreign sales corporation Act to a licensee for a period not exceeding 30 years.

Offshore Banking in Barbados

Offshore banking in Barbados was introduced in 1979 by virtue of the Offshore Banking Act. The Central Bank of Barbados is responsible for the general administration of the Offshore Banking Act, and the Minister of Finance is responsible for the issuing of licenses.

Offshore banking is recognized and limited to foreign-sourced banking and trust activities. The Act stipulates that a license may only be issued to an eligible company or a qualified foreign bank, full definitions of which are contained in the statute. However, an eligible company must be locally incorporated, its activities restricted to offshore banking, and at least one of its directors a resident and citizen of Barbados. For a non-resident-controlled company, the authorized capital is B$2 million, of which B$1 million must be paid up in cash. The license fee payable is B$25,000 on the issue of the license and B$25,000 on 1 January of each year thereafter. Offshore banking is defined as the business of:

• Accepting foreign money deposits payable on demand, after a fixed period, or after notice;
• Selling or placing foreign bonds, certificates, notes, or other debt obligations, or other foreign securities; or
• Any similar activity involving foreign money or foreign securities.

The foreign funds must be used for:

• Loans, advances, and investments; or
• Activities of the person carrying on the business.

Offshore banking also includes the acceptance in trust of:
• Amounts of money in foreign currencies, foreign securities, or both;
• Foreign personal or movable properties; and/or

Real or immovable property outside Barbados from persons resident outside Barbados to be administered, managed, invested, or otherwise dealt with for the benefit of persons resident outside Barbados, including any activities related, incidental, or ancillary thereto.
The Act makes provision for qualified foreign banks to become an offshore banks. A qualified foreign bank is:

• A foreign bank licensed under the Offshore Banking Act 1979 at the time it took effect;
• A foreign bank with the prescribed minimum capital and assets that was not licensed under the Offshore Banking Act 1979 at the time it took effect; or

• A financial institution, approved by the Central Bank that is directly or indirectly a wholly owned foreign subsidiary of a foreign bank.

An eligible company must meet the capital requirements. If the controlling persons are not Barbados residents, the paid up capital must be at least B$2 million, at least BS$1-million of which is subscribed and paid up in cash. If the controlling persons are Barbados residents, the paid up capital is only B$500,000, with at least B$250,000 being subscribed and paid up in cash. There are plans to increase the paid-up capital obligations.

There also are reserve requirements. The company must keep a reserve fund to which it must transfer, annually, at least 25 per cent of the profits (before dividends) if the reserve fund is less than the issued and paid-up capital. However, the Central Bank may waive these requirements if it is of the view that the aggregate reserves are sufficient to conduct business.

The pre-clearance procedure is greatly encouraged for use by prospective licensees. Under this procedure, the interested party submits a proposal to the Minister by way of the Central Bank of Barbados. After thorough investigations by the Central Bank, an indication will be given by letter to the effect that an application based on the proposal will be favorably considered. This pre-clearance procedure, or tentative application, requires applicants to provide sufficient information to clearly establish that they are either an eligible company or a qualified foreign bank. Important details on the personal and business history of the directors is requested and a very detailed exposition on the various particulars of the applicant's intended business also is required. Various documents must be submitted, including a current financial statement of anyone who will directly or indirectly possess or control five per cent or more of the voting power of the bank or 10 per cent or more of the non-voting shares of the bank.

Similarly, it also is necessary to supply particulars of any proposed or existing agreement dealing with the voting of shares or the management of the bank's affairs, as well as any agreements which allow for the issue of options to acquire shares for a consideration other than cash. There are other requirements, such as the projected financial statements of the bank's first three years of operation. After the tentative application has been approved, it is possible to incorporate and capitalize the company, and then provide an auditor's certificate in respect of the capitalization, along with a formal application and license fee for licensing. Such an application is then automatically accepted and the license issued. Offshore banks are being used in a variety of ways ranging form deposit taking, brokerage transactions, asset management, trusts, and issuance of letters of credit.

Ship Registration

The Shipping Act, which came into effect in 1994, provides a comprehensive scheme for the registration of ships under the Barbados flag and regulation of ships so registered. The Act generally covers all Barbados registered ships whomever the owners may be but, in certain matters, it distinguishes between Barbados-owned ships and foreign-owned ships, also governing activities of ships registered elsewhere, even they are operating within Barbados territorial waters. Barbados also has enacted the Shipping (Oil Pollution) Act, which establishes a code or regulations, enforcement procedures and liabilities for the discharge of oil by any ships in Barbados waters and for the discharge of oil anywhere in the world by Barbados registered ships.

The Barbados government joined the International Maritime Organization (IMO) in 1969 and became party to the principal conventions agreed to by IMO and which are included by reference in the shipping legislation. These include the current International Convention on Safety of Life at Sea, the Convention and the International Regulations for Preventing Collisions at Sea, the International Convention on Load Lines, the International Convention on Tonnage Measurement, and the International Convention for the Prevention of Pollution of the Seal by Oil, among others.

The Shipping Act and the Shipping (Oil Pollution) Act are modeled on United Kingdom legislation and are supplemented by Schedules of Applied Regulations that, in most cases, consist of regulations adopted by the United Kingdom authorities and incorporated by such reference in the Schedules.

Belize • Western Caribbean low-tax haven

Belize is an English speaking Central American country of 8,867 square miles and 194,000 people. Previously known as British Honduras, this former colony of Great Britain gained its independence on September 21, 1981. The government is considered responsible, but there is some doubt that political stability really exists in Belize.

Located on the eastern Caribbean coast south of Mexico and east of Guatemala, Belizean countryside is replete with beautifully undulating rivers, a terrain of mountains and a lush tropical rain forest.

Belize is probably best known as one of the deep sea diving and fishing capitals of the Caribbean. The largest barrier reef in the western hemisphere is found just off the Belizean coast. Fisherman and divers will tell you the reef is one of the most prolific in the world. [21]

Bananas, sugar cane and citrus fruit alone are not enough to sustain the Belizean economy. Like many small countries dependent on basic commodities, Belize's government realized the need for tax-reforms to boost foreign investment. Shortly after independence, Belize' leaders began to introduce legislation to make Belize attractive to foreign investors. The new legislation followed much the same format as found in the other British style tax havens of Cayman, the British Virgin Islands, the Bahamas and Bermuda.

Belize has been trying to become an offshore financial center for some time. According to Jose Alpuche, second secretary to the High Commission of Belize in London, many foreign businesses may qualify for tax holidays under the Belize Development Incentives Ordinance.

International Business Companies (IBC's)

Belize introduced its own International Business Companies Act in 1990. IBCs registered in Belize are granted freedom from all local Belizean taxation. Because Belize' corporate income tax rates are relatively high - reaching 35% - registering under the new IBC Act is the only way to go. [22]

The Belizean IBC Act was modeled after the 1984 IBC Act of the British Virgin Islands and the 1989 IBC Act of the Bahamas. The Belize IBC Act has some cost advantages over the BVI IBC Act, but annual government registration costs are slightly higher than under the Bahamas IBC Act.

The Belizean registrars office is computerized and modern. An IBC can be listed in the government's Registrar with only a one hour turn-around. This compares with 24 hours in the BVI and the Bahamas, and a week or longer in Bermuda. Practically speaking, the turnaround advantage over the BVI and Bahamas is of little real significance. [23]

As is called for under the BVI and Bahamian IBC Acts, Belizean companies must maintain a registered office and registered agent within Belize. Start up costs, which include a registered office, registered agent and local directors start out at $900 but go higher, and these costs are comparable with fees in both the Bahamas and BVI.

The International Business Companies Act, 1990 provides that any person may singly, or jointly with others, form an IBC by subscribing to a Memorandum and Articles of Association. IBCs are granted freedom from all local taxation.

An IBC need have only one shareholder which may be an individual or corporation. Only one director is required and it too may be a corporation.

Meetings of shareholders and/or directors may be held in any country, at any time, and may be attended by proxy.

---

21. From *Belize offers new product, old pitch* by Paul Ham (**Offshore Financial Review**)(August 1992)

22. Individuals living in Belize are subject to a similarly high tax rate. By comparison, the top corporate and individual income tax rate in the British Virgin Islands is only 15%, whilst there are no corporate or individual taxes of any kind in the totally tax free Bahamas.

23. From *Belize - a rapid increase in offshore developements*, by Larry Turner, **Offshore Investment Magazine** (pg. 47-48).

Registered or bearer shares may be issued with or without par value. Shares must be fully paid but capitalization is minimal.

No accounts or information concerning the identity of shareholders or directors is required to be filed or made a matter of the public record. The company's shareholder register may be inspected only by a shareholder or by order of a Belizean court at the request of a shareholder.

The IBC's company name may be in any language but must include the words "Limited", "Corporation", "Incorporated". "Society Anonyme" or "Society Anonima" or their usual abbreviations. There are no accounting or audit requirements.

As in the Bahamas and the BVI, an IBC registered in Belize cannot (1) do business inside Belize with persons resident in Belize; (2) own an interest in real property situated in Belize, other than a lease of property for use as an office from which to communicate with members or where books and records of the company are prepared or maintained; (3) carry on a banking business; (4) carry on a business of insurance or reinsurance company; (5) carry on the business of providing a registered office for companies.

Marine Registry in Belize

Ships can be registered under Section 3 of the Merchant Ships Act of 1989 and then become listed on the International Merchant Marine Registry of Belize (IMMARBE). The registry was established to offer ship owners and operators a modern ship's registry based on fast and efficient service, reasonable fees and a high standard of safety.

IMMARBE's head office is located in Belize City with designated satellite offices located in main ports and shipping centers of the world. These offices are empowered to process applications and issue all necessary documents related to the registration of vessels under the Belizean flag.

The Registry of Belize is open to any type, class or size of vessel used for navigation that is engaged in any lawful trade, service or international maritime activity including but not limited to dry cargo, tankers, passenger ships, oil rigs, supply boats, barges, stationary storage vessels, non-self-propelled vessels, fishing vessels, submarines, yachts or pleasure boats. Vessels may be registered at the head office or at the designated office via FAX or telex communication.

Vessels registered under IMMARBE may, in order to comply with the terms of the charter contract, obtain a second registration in another country without affecting their status with IMMARBE.

Belize Trust Act of 1992

In March of 1992, Belize introduced the **Belize Trust Act, 1992.** Trusts formed in Belize can have a life of 120 years. There is an option to convert trusts of finite duration to charitable trusts with indefinite duration. Provisions relating the appointment of protector of the trust and the payment of trustees are included in Act.

Trusts need not be registered with the Belize government, but trusts may be registered when necessary. A trust can be switched from another foreign jurisdiction into Belize. The local rules that apply to the settlor's community can be adapted when such trust transfers are implemented.

Belize already has a professional body of attorneys, accountants and administrators who will undertake the task of establishing and administering the new system. The Belizean legal system provides for the right of appeal to the Privy Council in London, which will be regarded as an important safeguard by some settlors.

Offshore Belizean trusts are exempt from all taxes and duties, including income tax, estate tax and exchange controls.

The Belize legislation also offers advanced asset protection facilities against creditor and foreign revenue services similar to those already in existence in the Cook Islands, Bahamas, Cayman and British Virgin Islands.

The new Belize Trust Act of 1992 was passed by the National Assembly of Belize in March. While the *Belize Times* declares the new legislation would establish Belize as a "major offshore financial center in the world" and "blazes a new trail and uniquely stands as a model of trust law', this is probably a premature overstatement. New Trusts and Trustee Acts exist in most all the major tax havens, and competition remains fierce.

Only a handful of trust companies have set-up operations in Belize - the most prominent being the Baron Bliss Trust Fund.

Political Stability

Belize' political stability is in question. In a letter to the investor publication *Moneyworld* one person writes:

Dear Editor: *"After reading the article about Belize by Gary Scott in the September issue, I had to explain that I have just returned from that country and would not consider going back. Scott acknowledged, Belize City is not a pretty place nor does it smell good. I stayed at the Bellevue Hotel; though $79 per night, it would be considered a poor third-rate hotel in this country. And when I would return to the hotel by cab at night, the driver would tell me to go straight in and not walk around, as I would be robbed. On the flight home I sat next to a young man born in Belize who had just visited home for the first time in seven years. His parents live in constant fear of being robbed; the local newspapers were filled with stories of shootings & hold-ups. He explained that the previous government had granted amnesty to aliens from surrounding countries, and drug dealers took advantage of that to establish bases in Belize, which was not equipped to handle the resulting crime wave.*

Be informed of the other side of the coin - there are real dangers in Belize." - C.A.Diegel,

Combined **State** and **City** income tax rates can boost the overall tax rate of upper and upper-middle-class Americans to 50% or better. Below are the top combined state and local income tax rates for the 48 largest U.S. cities.

City	Top Tax Rate	City	Top Tax Rate
New York	11.275%	Los Angeles	9.3%
Chicago	3.%	Houston	none
Philadelphia	7.06%	Detroit	7.6%
San Diego	9.3%	Dallas	none
San Antonio	none	Phoenix	8%
Baltimore	7.5%	San Francisco	9.3%
Indianapolis	3.4%	San Jose	9.3%
Memphis	6%	Washington	9.5%
Jacksonville	none	Milwaukee	6.93%
Boston	5% to 10%	Columbus	8.9%
New Orleans	6%	Cleveland	8.9%
Denver	5%	El Paso	none
Seattle	none	Nashville	6%
Austin	none	Oklahoma City	6%
Kansas City	7%	Fort Worth	none
St. Louis	7%	Atlanta	6%
Portland	9.6%	Pittsburgh	6.1%
Miami	none	Tulsa	6%
Honolulu	10%	Cincinnati	8.9%
Albuquerque	8.5%	Tucson	8%
Oakland	9.3%	Minneapolis	8%
Charlotte	7%	Omaha	5.9%
Toledo	9.15%	Virginia Beach	5.75%
Buffalo	7.9%	Sacramento	9.3%

Source: *The Wall Street Journal (1998)*

Panama compared with other well known tax havens

	Panama	British Virgin Islands	Cayman Islands	Switzerland
Accessibility from New York	5.5 hours	6-1/2 hours	5 hours	7 hours
Size	30,000 sq. miles	59 sq. miles	118 sq. miles	15,940 sq. miles
Population	2,000,000	12,000	18,000	6,366,000
Language	Spanish	English	English	Swiss/Italian/German
Political Stability	questionable	excellent	excellent	excellent
Corporate tax rate	0% - 30% [1.]	0% [3.]	0%	3.63% to 9.8%
Resident Individual's tax rate	30%	0%	0%	0% to 20%+
Yearly company maintenance costs	US$1,000	US$800	US$1,400	Fr.2,000 - 4,000
Initial Costs to	US$700	US$800 to $1,000	US$2,000	Fr.3,000 - 5,000 Incorporate
Annual Government tax	US$150	US$300 to $1,000	US$580 (exempt companies)	Tax return
Tax on bank deposits	none	none	none	no
Bearer Shares	Yes	Yes	Yes	Yes
Trusts laws	Yes [2.]	Yes	Yes	Recognized
Resident Agent Req.	Yes ($250/Yr.)	Yes	No	No
Time to Incorporate	up to 2 weeks	48 hours	24 - 48 hours	Several days
Location of Shareholder meetings	Anywhere	Anywhere in World	Anywhere	Anywhere
Location of Board Meetings	Anywhere	Anywhere in World	Anywhere	Switzerland
Exchange Controls	None	None	No	None
Financial Statements for Shareholders	Required	Yes	Yes	Yes
Filing annual return with Government	for Companies - Yes	No	No	Yes - tax return
Minimum number of shareholders to form company	3 directors	One	One	Three
Tax Treaties	None	None with US	None	Many
Capital gains taxes	No	No	No	Yes
Estate/Inheritance taxes.	Yes	Yes	No	Yes [4.]

1. Panama does not tax foreign source income but the individual tax rate on local economy is as high as 30% (corporate = 30%)(1999).
2. Panama is a civil law country but recognizes common law trusts and has enacted legislation governing their use.
3. The BVI impose personal and corporate income taxes up to 17% on business profits drawn from the local economy.
4. Nonresidents are not subject to Swiss estate taxes.

CHAPTER 6 • Panama & other Shipping Havens

Panama is a Republic located between Costa Rica and Columbia. It is approximately 30,000 square miles in area and has a very muggy, tropical climate. Panama's population is about 2,000,000. The largest concentrations are found inside the cities of Panama City, Colon and David. Spanish is the official language, but business is conducted in English and Spanish. Panama has a long tradition as tax haven. Panama has never taxed income from **sources** originating outside Panama.

The Panama Canal has been the dominant factor in the life of this former Spanish colony since it became independent from Colombia in 1903. Treaties negotiated between the United States and Panama in 1977 came into effect in 1979. They provided for eventual Panamanian control of the canal and for the virtual abolition of the Panama Canal Zone. Concerns for the security of the canal contributed to a December 1989 invasion of Panama by U.S. forces that ousted Panamanian strongman Manuel Noriega.

Panama was once the unchallenged leader in the Caribbean (if not the world) in the number of *offshore companies* it had on its corporate register. In the early 1970's Panama could probably boast more companies than all the Caribbean tax havens combined. Some estimates ran as high as half a million companies.

But, Panama has had a history of political unrest. And while political instability had not been a cause of great concern to the offshore business community in the past, the General Manuel Noriega crisis sent many offshore companies scurrying to other tax havens. Under Panamanian law, a company can be set-up for removal from Panama on short notice.

One of the biggest beneficiaries of the General Manuel Noriega crisis of 1986-89 was the Crown colony of the British Virgin Islands. Since the enactment of the BVI *International Business Companies Act of 1984* there have been a total of 280,000 IBC's registered in the BVI. Many of these companies emigrated from Panama.

The Bahamas enacted their own version of the BVI *International Business Companies Act* in 1990. Since then, over 90,000 IBC's have been registered in the Bahamas. Start-up fees and annual fees for an IBC formed in the Bahamas are less than in any of the other Caribbean tax havens, and about a third less than the costs for a similar company in the Caymans.

The Caymans, like the BVI, received a large number of migrate companies from Panama, although not nearly as many as the BVI, owing to the fact that the cost of forming a company in the Caymans is higher than in either the Bahamas or BVI. The Caymans however remain the Caribbean's biggest banking tax haven in terms of depositor dollars. It is estimated that more than $500 billion dollars are on deposit in the Caymans more than 590 banks.

While it is correct to speculate that before the Noreiga crisis there were more offshore holding companies registered in Panama than in any tax haven in the world, there were nearly 300,000 active companies on the Panamanian Register at the end of 1993. In 1994, there were 1,300 new companies formed each month, keeping Panama one of the largest tax haven in the world.[1]

Territorial Concept of Taxation

Panama became a tax exempt offshore jurisdiction in 1916 upon approval of its first Fiscal Code which exempted all natural or judicial persons carrying out commercial transactions abroad from payment of taxes.

Panama only assesses taxes on income from activities performed within the Republic of Panama, regardless where such income is received. Operating a mine, manufacturing consumer goods, or construction of buildings are taxable events in Panama. The tax rates are high, ranging up to 50%. Special tax incentives for businesses operating in Panama's Colin Free Zones, plus the fact that Panama will not tax **foreign source profits**, make Panama one of the world's most celebrated havens in the world.

---

1. The number of companies in Panama is still estimated at over 350,000 thru 1999.

No tax on "foreign source incomes"

Panama is not a zero-tax haven like the Bahamas or the Caymans. Panama is a tax haven because it refuses to tax companies on their **foreign source incomes**. The exemption for foreign source incomes is unlikely to be changed in the foreseeable future. The Panama economy derives substantial benefit from its tax haven business. The following lists items of income considered **foreign source under** the Panamanian tax system, thus **exempt** from all tax.

1. Income from subsidiaries incorporated and doing business in other countries.
2. Dividends received on foreign investments from anywhere in the world.
3. Capital gains on the sale of shares in foreign companies.
4. Interest and royalties received from foreign sources.
5. Income earned by branch operations located in other countries.
6. Income from international maritime commerce earned by ships registered in Panama.
7. Interest on savings accounts and time deposits in Panama banks are not taxable to non-residents.
8. Profits on liquidation proceeds of a foreign branch or subsidiary.

Currency and Exchange Controls

The Panama currency is the U.S. dollar and Panama has not issued its own paper money. The balboa is the official unit of currency. It is at par and equivalent to the U.S. dollar. Panama coins do exist (along with U.S. coins) and are circulated freely at face value. The public is allowed to have gold, and there are no exchange controls of any kind. Panama has used the U.S. dollar as its currency since 1904.

The "new" Panama has not scrapped its Bank Secrecy Codes

Panama's bankers are not planning to abandon the country's strict bank secrecy codes now that the U.S. government has ousted strong man General Noriega and solved Panama's biggest political problem.

According to Joseph Salteiro, an international banker who sits on Panama's new banking commission..

"In many ways, Noriega was a product of Panama's bank secrecy. Noriega could control hidden accounts and wire-transfer drug cash anywhere in the world without anybody knowing. We don't want another Noriega ever to happen. We plan to police the financial services system better and provide more legitimate investment."

The U.S. Commerce Department is already providing grants and consultants to rebuild the shattered offshore banking infrastructure - offshore deposits slipped from $38 Billion to $12 Billion during the December (1989) crisis. U.S. taxpayer's tax dollars are unwittingly helping a celebrated tax haven get back on its feet.

While beholden to the U.S. for its help, the Panamanian government has made it clear it doesn't plan to scrap all aspects of its banking confidentiality which helped make Panama the richest nation per capita in Latin America.

"We gain nothing if we become another New York or Miami." says Salteiro. We'll probably strike some middle ground, something closer to Switzerland than the Caymans or Hong Kong.

Robert Alfaro, a sub-secretary in the Panamanian Commerce Department, said the government will leave most bank code regulations untouched, but will close loopholes used by large scale money-launderers.

Meanwhile, the U.S. has filed requests with the governments of Britain, France, Switzerland, Luxembourg and West Germany to freeze accounts thought to contain more than $10 million in Noriega drug proceeds.

Herr Henning Horstmann, spokesman for the West German government in Washington, said the U.S. must know the specific bank and account numbers and provide a reason the funds should be frozen. Otherwise, they should remain secret, he said.

Despite its tarnished image, Panama has a lot going for it. Its long history as a tax haven and offshore finance center has meant that representatives of most of the big US Banks can be found there. Over 100 offshore banks hold assets of around US$28.5 billion in the republic.

Legal Entities in Use

Corporations, branches or agencies, partnerships (not including law firms), inheritance estates, and trusts are all recognized by the Panamanian authorities. Panama has a trust law based on civil law principles, so common law precedents concerning trusts do not apply. Some advisors counsel against using Panama or any civil law country for the establishment of a trust, if the client is from a common law country like the United States or the UK. There's no guarantee a common-law court will recognize a trust drafted in a civil-law jurisdiction.

Incorporation is Quick and Easy

Incorporation is quick and easy. Panama's Corporation Law is an adaptation of the Delaware Law as it existed in 1927 in its original form. When a company is registered it is subject to a one time share tax that ranges from $20 upward. In addition, there is an annual "franchise" tax of $150 per year payable to the Registrar.

A Panamanian company may issue bearer shares. Furthermore, it isn't required that you provide the Panamanian Government with the names of the shareholders, and there is no requirement to file an annual report if you don't do business in Panama (i.e., your income is all "foreign source income").

Share capital may be issued in any currency, nominative shares may be subscribed even without full payment, and there is no limit for the payment of the Authorized Share Capital.

At least three directors, in addition to a President, secretary and treasurer, are required for every company. Directors can be of any nationality, but you cannot appoint anyone other than a natural person to be a director.

Shareholder meetings and director meetings may be held anywhere in the world. Minutes must be kept for some meetings, and a stock registration book must be registered at the Public Registry Office. Every company must have a registered agent in Panama who is either a lawyer or law firm. Cost of the registered agent is about $250 to $500 per year.

A company can still be formed here for about $1,000. Some companies advertise start-up incorporation costs significantly below even this moderate amount.

Other important features

Panamanian law firms and attorneys offer services of "nominee directors" and "nominee shareholders" on par with other jurisdictions.

Lawyers are required to maintain full secrecy and anonymity in connection with the beneficiaries of the company.

Banks in Panama still offer uncomplicated openings of personal, corporate and numbered accounts, with full banking secrecy.

Ship Registration Capital of the World

Panama probably still has the world's largest merchant fleet. Through July 1, 1984 Panama had more freighters, bulk carriers and tankers registered than any other country including the USSR, Japan, the United States, Greece and the UK. Liberia, another shipping haven refusing to tax **foreign source income**, runs a distant 2nd. One of the reasons Panama is such a dominant shipping haven is the presence of the Panama Canal Zone. Ships flying the Panamanian flag are exempt from all Panamanian taxes even when the shipping contracts are negotiated and signed in the country.

By October 1994, Panama's fleet registry contained 12,830 vessels and 83,806,185 tons.

Panama has an **exchange-of-note-agreement** with the United States that allows Panamanian registered ships to enter U.S. ports, even open a representative office in New York or LA, yet stay free from U.S. Federal income tax. Many American and foreign shippers register their ships in Panama. Documenting a ship in havens like Panama and Liberia can also reduce a ship owner's labor costs. [2.]

In return for the favorable tax treatment under the **exchange-of note-agreement**, Panama makes her entire merchant fleet available to the United States in the event of war.

---

2. IRC 883(a) & (c).

Colon Free Zone

The Colon Free Zone is located on the Caribbean side of the Isthmus right by the entrance to the Panama Canal. It is a separate area where merchandise may be landed without customs duties. Especially low income tax rates are provided for corporations operating here. Income gotten from re-export sales to foreign countries are taxed at rates beginning at 2-1/2% on the first B/15,000 to 8-1/2% on the net income over B/100,000. In addition to reduced tax rates, tax credits are granted to those companies employing Panamanians. Reduced rates are as follows:

Number of employees • Percent of net taxable income

from	To	Over	
30	100		0.5%
101	200		1.0%
	200		1.5%

The Free Zone law regulates what activities can be carried on. Permissible activities include, "bring in, store, exhibit, unpack, manufacture, put in containers, mount, assemble, refine, purify, blend, alter, and in general perform operations with and handle all kinds of merchandise, products, raw materials, containers, and other articles of commerce."

Retail trade is forbidden within the Free Zone. [3.]

McDermott International & others operating in Panama

Many drug manufacturers are doing business in Panama's Free Zone. These include Siemens, Miles Laboratories, Singer, and Sieberling. Forbes Magazine reported in their March 11, 1985 issue that McDermott International, the world's largest drilling and exploration company, had moved its headquarters out of the United States into Panama. According to McDermott's Chairman, over $1,000,000,000 in U.S. Treasury bonds paying 12% interest *pa* were being held offshore as a hedge against a down-turn in the oil drilling and exploration business. If the issue date on these T. bonds was July 18, 1984 or later, there would be no 30% U.S. interest withholding tax. The **Tax Reform Act of 1984** repealed the U.S.

3. From *"Doing Business in Panama"* by Price Waterhouse **Information Guide**, pg. 46. See also *"Taxation in Panama"*, Deloitte Haskins + Sells (International Tax & Business Service).

30% interest withholding tax on corporate and treasury bonds issued after 7-18-84.

Transportation Facilities

Panama's high speed highways and modern airports make her easily accessible both from within and without. More than 25 airlines provide passenger and cargo service for the Free Zone companies. Some 60 steamship lines also service the region. A 49 mile long transcontinental railroad operates between Panama City and Colon, and there are port facilities and linking railroads along both coastlines.

Secrecy and Confidentiality

Panama has always been known as a safe place to hide assets. It's tough bank secrecy laws make it nearly impossible to trace money once it enters the country. Bank secrecy laws impose fines and jail terms to violators who disclose information concerning Panama's ciphered and coded bank accounts. Panama like Switzerland does not view tax evasion as a crime. One Panamanian lawyer who set up several shell companies for the disposed Philippine President Marcos summed up the attitude of many of his colleagues when he said... "It's none of my business where the money comes from."

Secret numbered & ciphered bank accounts

Panama's secret numbered or ciphered bank accounts may be necessary for residents of some South American troubled spots, where governments are toppled one after the other and fortunes are always at risk and subject to confiscation, but the U.S. person might be wiser to decipher the Internal Revenue Code first, rather than risk a tax evasion case in U.S. tax court. The IRS has the power to **lien** on you bank accounts and home mortgage. I'm not convinced that secret numbered bank accounts are for everyone. U.S. citizens should operate within the confines of U.S. tax laws and file the necessary disclosure forms when called for.

Nestle' Panamanian subsidiary beats $119,515,542 IRS tax deficiency claim

Tax havens like the Cayman Islands, Panama and the Bahamas are often used in re-invoicing schemes and the like to avoid billions of dollars in taxes. The offshore governments openly support and promote this type of income tax evasion.

Westreco, Inc. v. Comm. [T.C.M.]

Westreco, Inc., is a Panamanian corporation with a principal office in the United States. Westreco conducted research that was indirectly controlled by its ultimate parent, Nestle, S.A., a publicly held multinational corporation headquartered in Switzerland. The Nestle group engages in worldwide research, development, manufacturing, and marketing of processed food products, and technological development is vital to the success and growth of Nestle's business. Among its product lines are instant milk, coffee, tea, and cocoa products. During the years 1978 through 1982, Nestle operated through at least 25 subsidiaries.

Nestec was a Swiss subsidiary of Nestle engaged in food-related research and development and technical assistance in the manufacture and marketing of Nestle products around the world. Nestec's research and development expenditures were equal to approximately 1 percent of Nestle's sales. Westreco was a subsidiary of Nestec. Nestle Holdings, Inc. (NHI), was and is a subsidiary of Nestle and is the holding company for the Nestle operating subsidiaries located in the United States. The Nestle Company, Inc. (TNCo) was a subsidiary of NHI engaged in the manufacture and sale of processed food products, primarily in the United States.

Westreco was incorporated in 1957 and contracted to provide research and development services to Nestec and, ultimately, Nestle. Westreco had operations at Marysville, Ohio, and New Milford, Connecticut. The operations at the Marysville location concentrated on instant coffee and tea and the manufacturing processes associated with those products. The New Milford facility performed technological development and technical assistance services principally in the area of culinary products.

The IRS issued a statutory notice of deficiency to Westreco for the years 1979 through 1982, reallocating under section 482 additional fees of $119,515,542 from Nestec to Westreco. Although the statutory notice did not explain the method used by the IRS to allocate additional income to Westreco, the method was a multiplier applied to salaries paid by Westreco to its employees. At trial, the IRS offered no evidence or explanation to support the multiplier method, but rather relied upon fees paid to purportedly comparable businesses to support its reallocation of income to Westreco.

Tax Court Senior Judge Goffe has held that the IRS' determinations were an abuse of discretion because the fees Westreco charged Nestec were reasonable and clearly reflected income within the meaning of section 482. The court first noted that the purpose of section 482 is to prevent the artificial shifting of the true net income of controlled taxpayers by placing them on a parity with uncontrolled, unrelated taxpayers. Citing regulation section 1.482-2(b)(7)(ii)(a), the court wrote that all the particular facts and circumstances of Westreco's arrangement with Nestec must be considered to determine whether the amount Westreco received for services performed was equal to an arm's-length amount.

The court concluded that the IRS' use of the salary multiplier method was flawed because the multiplier was applied to 100 percent of Westreco's salary expenditures, which included sick leave, vacation, holiday pay, and similar items. Furthermore, the court pointed out, the IRS allocated 100 percent of Westreco's salary expenditures to salary paid by Westreco with respect to services performed for Nestec, when in fact Westreco performed services for TNCo. The income from TNCo assistance was not at issue in the section 482 determination, yet no allocation of salary between services performed for Nestec and services performed for TNCo was made.

The court also concluded that the IRS' comparison of Westreco to other corporations providing similar services was defective, noting in particular that one of the IRS' expert witnesses admitted under cross-examination that Westreco's rate of return was in the range of "observed arm's-length dealings." The court agreed with the admission, and accordingly held that no reallocation of income to Westreco was warranted.

Liberia – "flag of convenience" tax haven

Liberia has been a popular tax haven for registering ships for over 40 years. Found on the western coast of Africa, Liberia boasts a merchant shipping fleet more than three times the size of the United States. Liberia was founded in 1847 by freed American slaves with much help from the USA. Monrovia, its capital, was named in honor of President James Monroe, the 5th President of the United States. Liberia's Constitution and government are patterned after that of the United States, but Liberia has only one political party. Recent civil war has made Liberia a poor choice to domicile a shipping company, and one would do best to wait until the current political conflict is over.

Political stability

Liberia has recently been experiencing a civil war, so its political stability is in question. Liberia's population consists of 16 indigenous ethnic groups, each with its own language, as well as the English-speaking Americo-Liberians.

Liberia is officially Christian, but a majority practice traditional religions, and there is a significant Muslim minority.

Of the country's urban population, almost half live in the area of Monrovia, the capital and largest city, which was badly damaged during the civil war.

Currency

The Liberian Dollar is on par with the U.S. Dollar, and both currencies are accepted as legal tender in Liberia. There are no exchange controls.

Taxation

Provided that no more than 25% of the voting powers of the company is resident in Liberia, and all income derives from outside Liberia, the company will not be subjected to any income tax. There is, however, an annual fee of US $150 payable to the Liberian authorities. Liberia has negotiated Double Tax Treaties with Germany and Sweden.

Shareholders

Only one shareholder is required. Bearer shares are permitted. Details of shareholders do not appear on public file.

Disclosure of The Beneficial Owner

There is no requirement to disclose details of the Beneficial Owner to any Government Authority.

Directors

A Liberian company requires three directors, who will be named in the Articles. However, there is no need to register changes in directors. There is no residential qualification imposed in respect of directors.

Annual Reporting

There is no requirement to file accounts, or a requirement for the company to appoint Auditors. No returns are required to be filed.

Times to incorporate

Incorporation can be effected within 48 hours of the receipt of the full information by the Liberian authorities, but the authorities take some time to release the incorporation papers.

Liberia is often called a **"flag of convenience"** haven for the registration of ships. Ship owners from around the globe register their ships here because Liberia does not tax foreign source shipping income of non-resident Liberian registered corporations. Exemption of shipping income is authorized in the **Liberian Business Corporation Act of 1977.** [4]

Like Panama, Costa Rica, Hong Kong, and Gibraltar, Liberia's tax system is said to be territorial. Only domestic source incomes earned within the country is taxable. While there are no guarantees in the Liberian Code against the future imposition of income taxes (as in the Cayman Islands), the exemption for foreigners of non-resident Liberian companies will likely remain indefinitely.

---

4. Liberian Internal Revenue Code 140.

Reciprocal Tax Exemption Agreements

IRC §883(a) exempts from taxation U.S. source earnings of a foreign ship or aircraft when the earnings are derived from the operation of a ship documented or aircraft registered under the laws of a foreign country, and if the foreign country grants an **equivalent exemption** to U.S. citizens and U.S. domestic corporations. The exemption only applies to international shipping operations that begin or end in the United States. Profits arising from a route that begins in, say New York and ends in Miami are not entitled to the exemption. Today, **Reciprocal Tax Exemption Agreements** exist with Panama, Liberia, Cyprus, and the Bahamas. In addition, the IRS has recently ruled that the corporate laws of the Cayman Islands meet their criterion for the Reciprocal Tax Exemption. [5.]

About 35% of the world's merchant fleet is registered with flag of convenience nations, up from about 26% ten years ago. Flag of convenience registries have competitive licensing and registration fees and offer additional incentives through tax exemptions and amiable employment and corporate regulations. Vessels so registered are subject primarily to the rules and regulations of the maritime authority under which they are registered. Most countries restrict foreign vessels from domestic shipping, and restrict international business through cargo sharing agreements. [6.]

Ship Registration

Liberia has operated a flag registration since 1948. Registering a ship in Liberia is easy and straight forward. You don't have to fly to Liberia to form a corporation or register a ship. A Liberian Trust Company with correspondents in New York and Zurich can handle all the formalities. Because Liberia's corporate law is modeled after Delaware Law, they are easily understood by most Americans.

The procedure generally followed goes like this. The instructions for incorporation are given by the client to a New York service company which relays the information by cable to Liberia.

Model articles of association (by-laws) are generally supplied at a modest price, and a company can be formed in as little time as 48 hours. A cable from Liberia notifies the client that the company has been registered on such and such a date, and you are officially in business.

Some people believe Liberia's ship registration service is now the largest in the world in terms of gross tonnage, and its lead will likely increase over its arch rival Panama. There are no restrictions on crew nationality or routes, or on charter, mortgage, or transfer of vessels.

The Liberian maritime regulations require Liberian ownership of Liberian registered vessels. This is complied with by forming a Liberian corporation which then becomes the registered owner of the vessel. There are no restrictions on the nationality of shareholders, directors, or officers, and complete anonymity is available. There are no statutory annual corporate filing requirements. Income from the operation of vessels is exempt from local Liberian income taxes, unless the vessel engages exclusively in domestic Liberian traffic. There are no exchange controls on shipping income.

Costs

It costs about $700 to register a company in Liberia, with an annual license fee of $250 (up from $100) payable to the government after that. It is required that you maintain a registered business agent in Liberia, and the **Liberian Trust Company** (in NYC or Zurich) that handled your incorporation can provide you with an agent for a nominal sum.

There is no requirement that you or any company director be physically present in Liberia at any time. If you need a nominee director (the company ordinarily has three), the Liberian Trust Company will provide them at no extra charge.

There are no minimum capital investment requirements to start a Liberian company, but to maintain **"non-resident domestic corporation"** status at least 75% (previously 50%) of the company shares must be owned and controlled by non-residents.

---

5. International shipping profits are also exempted under the U.S. tax treaties. Treaties with Barbados, Bermuda, Greece, and Jamaica provide essentially the same exemption as under the **Reciprocal Tax Exemption Agreements.**
6. From an essay by Freddie Ashiabor - senior tax manager in the Price Waterhouse office in Monrovia. International Tax Review (Jan./Feb. 1990), pg. 9.

Liberia uses the U.S. dollar for its currency, with Liberian coins. There are two income tax treaties with Sweden and West Germany in force.

No Bank Secrecy Laws

Liberia has no special bank secrecy laws like other tax havens, but this is not a deterrent as few Liberian offshore corporations actually handle their banking transactions within Liberia's territory borders. Moreover, there is no requirement that they must bank in Liberia.

Corporate records are available for public inspection but there is no requirement that the real beneficial owners of the company be publicly disclosed.

Liberia has a vested interest in keeping its status as a haven for shippers upright. Liberia derives substantial revenues from annual fees. The annual fee required of every ship registered in Liberia to help finance Liberia's marine safety program was $725 in 1980, plus an additional one cent per net registered ton.

Great American Shippers

Daniel K. Ludwig (a.k.a. the *"Tanker Man"*). Thirty years ago, **Daniel K. Ludwig** was thought to be the wealthiest American with an estimated net-worth of over $2,000,000,000. Little is known about this titan of industry, as Ludwig always kept a low profile, never granted press interviews, and avoiding photographers like the plague - going about his business much like the reclusive Howard Hughes had done.

Daniel Ludwig's company, **National Bulk Carriers**, was once thought to run the largest independent tanker fleet in the world, bigger than even Aristotle Onassis. Ludwig began his career buying repossessed tankers that bankers had put up for auction, and tankers that were ready for the scrap yard but still had a lot of life left in them. In time, his shipping empire grew to mammoth proportions.

Keeping his offices up on Avenue of the Americas in Manhattan for years, D.K. Ludwig has just recently passed away. He was over 90 years of age at the time of death. His death, as was his life, may forever be masked in mystery. It is believed a son or daughter has taken over the business.

Ted Arison is the principal owner of Carnival Cruise Lines, with headquarters in Panama and Biscayne Boulevard in Miami, Florida. Carnival Cruise Lines, Inc. was incorporated under the laws of Panama in November 1974, and today is the world's largest cruise line based on number of passengers. Carnival operates seven ships servicing the Caribbean, Mexican Riviera, and the Crystal Palace Hotel & Casino in Nassau, Bahamas. Carnival recently acquired a luxurious Cable Beach Hotel in Nassau and HAL Antillen in the Netherlands Antilles.

Ted Arison owns about 75% of Carnival's Class "A" stock. His son Micky Arison is Chief Executive Officer. Carnival's revenues reached $1,375,000,000 in 1990. Three new Superliners are currently under construction and should begin twice weekly service in 1990 and 1991.

A Controlled Foreign Corporation (CFC) is entitled to the benefits of a Reciprocal Tax Exemption Agreement under new IRC §883(c)(2), but this is not a usable loophole U.S. shippers exploit because The Tax Reform Act of 1986 repealed Code §954(b)(2), and now foreign base shipping income earned by a CFC is classified as FPHCI (Subpart F), and taxable under new IRC §954(b)(2) & (g). U.S. shareholders in a CFC must input the offshore shipping profits and include them on their tax returns.

United States Exchange-of-Note-Agreements

Aside from the 36 or so bilateral income tax treaties with other nations which provide tax exemptions for shipping and aircraft operations to residents of both countries, the United States has entered 20+ **Exchange-of-Note-Agreements** with various other foreign countries. These **E-O-N Agreements** do not require Senate ratification to become operative because Section §872(b) and §883(a) of the Internal Revenue **Code** provides for the exemptions simply on the basis that the foreign country provide a **"reciprocal exemption"** to U.S. corporations and citizens.

The framework for the exclusion of shipping income from U.S. taxes has its roots in the **Revenue Act of 1921** some 68 years ago. The exclusion has stood unscathed since the Revenue Act of '21. According to the Senate Finance Committee of the 67th Congress, in an effort to avoid mass confusion which would result if all countries were to levy their own tax rates on port-of-call shippers, and in view of the fact there was no accurate way to compute accurately a foreign shipper's U.S. source profits, Congress thought it best to exempt shipping profits entirely.

IRC §883(a)

Under IRC §883(a) U.S. source earnings of a foreign ship or aircraft are exempt from federal taxation when the earnings are derived from the operation of a ship documented or aircraft registered under the laws of a foreign country, and the foreign country grants an **equivalent exemption** to U.S. citizens and U.S. domestic corporations. Today, exchange of note agreements exist with at least three tax havens, i.e., Panama, Liberia and the Bahamas.

Tax Reform Act of 1986 adds "new" Section §883(c)

The Tax Reform Act of '86 added new Section §883(c) to the Code. IRC §883(c) states that the exemption will not apply to any foreign corporation if 50% or more of the value of the stock of such company is owned by individuals who are not **residents** of such foreign country or another foreign country meeting the E-O-N requirements. Also excluded from the E-O-N benefits are **Controlled Foreign Corporations** as defined under IRC §957(a). One way to explain how these provisions operate is with an example:

Example #1: Fifty-one percent of Bahamian cruise line company **X** shares are owned by Bahamian **resident Y**. Shipping company **X** has an office in N.Y.C. and Miami. It's cruise liners regularly enter U.S. ports to pick-up customers for round trip voyages to foreign ports. The income from U.S. customer receipts are excluded from Bahamian company **X**'s gross income for purposes of **federal income taxes** under IRC §883(a) because the Bahamas have a **reciprocal E-O-N agreement** with the U.S. It makes no difference that the Bahamian company has an office in N.Y., or is "carrying on a trade or business in the United States". It's shipping profits will not be subject to federal income tax. Neither will it be subject to the new **"4% gross basis tax"** explained in **example #3** below.

Conversely, a U.S. shipper flying the U.S. flag (i.e., a U.S. registered ship) would owe U.S. taxes on its shipping income, the same as any U.S. corporation doing business within the United States. IRC §883 and IRC §872(b) (for individuals) exempts foreign corporations and non-resident aliens from U.S. taxes. IRC §883 does not ascribe to exempt U.S. corporations from federal income taxes. [7]

> **Residency** is a prerequisite to get the exemption under IRC §883. The **new** Technical & Miscellaneous Revenue Act of 1988 states that only **resident individuals** who own 50% or more of the Bahamian ship company will be permitted the exemption. Moreover, a citizen of a foreign country that is **resident** in the country with a E-O-N agreement will qualify for the exemption, even if his home country does not have an E-O-N agreement with the U.S.

The new tax law, denies the **Reciprocal Tax Exemption** if 50% or more of the value of stock in the corporation is owned by individuals who are not residents of such foreign country or another foreign country having a **Reciprocal Tax Exemption Agreement**. This **residency** requirement, leaves little room for Americans to qualify for the same tax benefits offered the foreigner. Is it possible for American shippers to obtain the same tax relief offered foreigners operating in a tax haven?

The only logical solution appears to be to form a non-controlled foreign company with no U.S. shareholders (i.e., no 10% voting stockholders) and avoid CFC status, and either take the company public to qualify for the **Reciprocal Tax Exemption**, or satisfy the foreign owner residency requirement under IRC §883(c)(1).

According to Tax Management, the foreign residents must be "individual owners" for the reciprocal exemption to apply. But, IRC §883(c)(B) says **any stock owned in another corporation which is owned directly or indirectly by a corporation meeting the requirements of subparagraph "A" (i.e., the publicly traded company) shall be treated as owned by individuals who are resident of a foreign country in which the corporation meeting the requirements of subparagraph "A" is organized.** Using two holding companies organized in the same tax haven should be considered, but one of the offshore companies must be brought public.

---

7. The U.S. merchant fleet cannot compete with foreign registered shippers that operate out of the world's tax havens, and Congress now subsidizes many companies to keep them from going out of business.

Exception for publicly traded stock (boom or bust?)

Prentice-Hall (November, 1988) writes:

"The new ('88) law modifies the publicly traded exception to the residence-based requirement under IRC §883(c). The change provides that a foreign corporation qualifies for the reciprocal exemption if it's organized in a country that exempts U.S. corporations from tax and the foreign corporation's stock is primarily and regularly traded on an established securities market in that country, another foreign country that grants U.S. corporations the appropriate exemption, or the United States.

In addition, if stock of one foreign corporation (organized in a country that exempts U.S. corporations from that country's tax) is owned by a second publicly traded corporation (organized in either the same foreign country, a second foreign country that exempts U.S. corporations from that country's tax, or the United States), and the second corporation's stock is primarily and regularly traded on an established securities market in its country of organization, another foreign country that grants U.S. corporations the appropriate exemption, or the United States, then the new law treats the stock of the first corporation as owned by individuals who are resident in the country in which the second corporation (that is the shareholder) is organized." - (word for word from the nation's top publishers of U.S. tax laws).

Example 2: Four foreign corporations own all the stock of another foreign corporation. All five corporations are organized in countries that exempt U.S. corporations from tax. The stock of the first four corporations is primarily and regularly traded on established securities markets in their respective countries. **Result**: Each of the four corporations' stock will be treated as owned by individuals resident in the four corporations' respective countries of organization. (The same conclusion would follow if the stock of one or more of the first four corporations were primarily and regularly traded on an established U.S. securities market, or a foreign securities market that exempts U.S. corporations from tax). Because more than 50% of the value of the fifth corporation's stock is considered owned by residents of countries that exempt U.S. persons from their tax, the fifth corporation is eligible for the reciprocal exemption. [8]

The **publicly traded stock exception** allows any publicly traded Bahamian holding company (trading on the NASDAQ or other exchange) to avail itself of the exemption under IRC §883. Thus, Americans (and foreigners) can operate an **international** shipping company free from U.S. federal income taxes, and free from the new 4% gross basis tax. [9]

New 4% Gross Basis Tax

The TRA '86 enacted a gross basis 4% tax on certain transportation income of foreign persons. This tax was intended to apply to shipping income treated as 50% U.S. source, i.e., income where the shipment (or trip) ends or begins in the U.S. Shipping income to which the 4% tax applies is the same income eligible for the **reciprocal exemption** of IRC §883(a), thus the 4% tax does not apply when a company satisfies the **Reciprocal Tax Exemption** requirements.

Example #3: All the stock in Bahamian cruise line company **X** is owned by publicly traded Bahamian company **Y**, which trades on the NASDAQ. Bahamian company **Y** is a closely-held non-controlled foreign public corporation owned by Americans T & S. In the month of January, 1990 Bahamian cruise line company X picks up 5,000 U.S. cruise customers in Miami and sails to ports in the Caribbean, returning only to drop off and pick up new customers. Each customer pays $800 for his ticket. The total revenues for the month of January, 1990 amount to $4,000,000. This $4,000,000 is **not** subject to the USA's **federal income tax** (**28%** rate in 1990), and is also **not** subject to the new **4%** gross basis tax (which would amount to a tax of $160,000). Both Bahamian company Y and company **X** are entitled to the exemption under IRC §883. Bahamian company **X** is entitled to the exemption because its parent company is publicly traded on a U.S. stock exchange.

It isn't necessary to use **2** Bahamian holding companies to procure the "reciprocal exemption". One publicly traded Bahamian company **X** would be enough. However, to avoid the CFC provisions under IRC §951, it might be prudent to use two foreign companies (or one company and a trust).

---

8. Example #2 was taken word for word from an example published in Prentice-Hall's **Tax Law**. See paragraph [¶ 1213].

9. The transportation exemption under IRC §883 does not apply to shipments between points within the United States. For example, between NY and LA.

Cyprus • Eastern Mediterranean tax haven

Cyprus is situated in the strategic north-eastern corner of the Mediterranean Sea. Greeks represent the majority of the population with Turkish Cypriots accounting for 18 percent. After obtaining independence from the UK in 1960, the country established a presidential system of government.

The Cypriot legal system is based on English common law, and most lawyers are graduates of British Universities or members of the UK Inns of Court. The majority of auditors in Cyprus are members of the UK's accountancy regulatory bodies. [10.]

In contrast to tax havens, Cyprus is a tax incentive country which offers benefits aimed at foreign individuals and enterprises, attracting those who wish to conduct their international affairs from the island. The Government, in recognition of direct and indirect benefits accruing to the island, considers the continuing development of Cyprus into a centre for international business among its top priorities.

Cyprus may be used as an offshore base simply by establishing a "brass plate" company, with registered offices usually supplied by lawyers and accountants or by establishing a company which will have its management and control in Cyprus. The latter option many enable an investor to take advantage of various tax advantages, provided under the 26 Double Taxation Agreements which Cyprus has concluded with a respective number of countries.

Foreign residents wishing to establish an offshore enterprise should apply to the Central Bank through an advocate or an accountant practicing in Cyprus. The application must contain the necessary information and must be accompanied by bank references for the beneficial owners.

If confidentiality is desired, it is possible to use nominee shareholders with the permission of the Central Bank. Only the names of nominee shareholders appear on the public records kept by the Department of the Official Receiver and Registrar of Companies. The Central Bank knows the identity of the beneficial owners, but it is prevented by legislation from acting as a source of information either on individuals or corporations. The Central Bank, however, is also concerned that the island's reputation should not be tainted in any way by the proceeds of crime and there are, therefore, obvious exceptions to confidentiality that other respectable offshore jurisdictions also have in order to prevent money laundering. Legitimate business, however, can be assured that it has the protection of complete confidentiality.

Tax Benefits

Offshore enterprises, their beneficial owners and expatriate employees, are entitled to a wide range of tax and tax related benefits, which include a complete exemption from exchange control, favorable treatment with regard to customs duties and considerable concessions on income tax.

The major fiscal incentives offered to offshore enterprises are as follows:

• Offshore branches of companies which are managed and controlled from abroad as well as offshore partnerships are totally exempt from income tax.

• Offshore companies, irrespective of their place of management and control, as well as offshore branches of companies which are managed and controlled from Cyprus, are taxed at only 4.25 per cent of their net taxable profit.

• The beneficial owners of offshore enterprises are not liable to an additional tax on dividends or profits over and above the amount payable by the respective legal entities.

• Foreign employees of offshore enterprises living and working in Cyprus are taxed at half the standard rates applicable to personal income i.e. from 0 per cent to 20 per cent.

---

10. From an article by Peter Economides (P.G. Economides & Co., Limassol, Cyprus), *"An attractive business haven"*, - **Offshore Advisor** (May 1988)[updated 1999 by Tax Haven Reporter from information provided by Cyprus government]

• Foreign employees of offshore enterprises living and working outside the island are exempt from income tax if they get paid through any bank in Cyprus or taxed at 10 per cent of the standard rates if they get paid directly abroad.

No capital gains tax is payable on the sale or transfer of shares in an offshore company. No estate duty is payable on the inheritance of shares in such a company.

Offshore enterprises maintaining fully fledged offices, and their expatriate employees in Cyprus, may purchase motor cars, office and household equipment (except furniture) duty free.

The attractions of Cyprus as a financial centre can be summed up as follows:
• Double taxation treaties with more than 25 countries
• Low tax (4.25%) paid by qualifying offshore enterprises
• Solid reputation as a well regulated financial centre
• Modern and efficient accounting, legal and banking sectors
• Exemption of offshore branches and partnerships from income tax
• No withholding tax on dividends by offshore companies
• No capital gains tax payable on the sale of shares in an offshore company
• Exemption from exchange controls for offshore entities and their expatriate employees
• Strong confidentiality rules supervised by the Central Bank
• Excellent infrastructure with modern transport and telecommunication facilities
• Advantageous maritime and shipping legislation
• Low company formation and operating costs
• Wide use of English in commerce and government

Offshore Banking Units/Administered Banking Units

The Central Bank of Cyprus vets very carefully all foreign banks looking to take advantage of the island's various benefits. Offshore banking business licenses for the establishment of Offshore Banking Units ('OBUs')

are only granted to established overseas banks which are subject to adequate banking supervision in their country of incorporation or to banking subsidiaries whose parent banks are established in countries which apply adequate banking supervision. Foreign banks are required to establish a real presence in Cyprus and are actually expected to operate as fully staffed units and not merely as "brass plate" entities.

An exception to the above is a new category of offshore banking units known as Administered Banking Units ("ABU's). This enables foreign banks which do not wish to establish fully fledged offices in Cyprus, to create a set up where their day to day administration is carried out, on their behalf, by another bank, which is already licensed by the Central Bank of Cyprus to operate in or from within Cyprus. An ABU may take the form of either a branch of a foreign bank or of a locally incorporated subsidiary of such a bank. It must, however, be emphasized that ABUs are also subject to the same supervision and regulation as OBUs.

The Central Bank of Cyprus supervises all OBUs/ABUs, whether in the form of a branch or a locally incorporated company, by both on-site inspection and monitoring of the various periodic returns which are submitted to it by OBUs/ABUs. The main purpose of the supervisory framework is to ascertain that all OBU/ABUs abide by the conditions attached to their banking licenses, to assess the quality of their lending and to verify that they follow prudent policies in regard to the various risks which they assume in their daily operations.

In general OBUs/ABUs may only transact business with non-residents and in foreign currencies. They offer services such as private banking, credit related services, treasury services, investment services financial advice etc.

There are thirty two OBUs/ABUs and 6 bank representative offices currently in operation. These come form a variety of countries: Belgium, Bulgaria, Cayman Islands, France, Greece, Jordan, Lebanon, Romania, Russia, Switzerland, United Kingdom, United States and Yugoslavia.

Shipping haven

All non-Cypriot owners who wish to register their ships under the Cyprus flag must incorporate a Company in Cyprus which will either acquire the ship in its name, or bareboat charter the ship. Practice and custom have created a special type of Cyprus ship owning company which is limited by shares and has a nominal capital, usually C£1000.00 divided into 1000 shares of C£1.00 each. The Cyprus merchant shipping legislation allows for the provisional registration of a vessel (in case the vessel concerned has not been previously a Cyprus ship) and most Owners usually opt to have their ship provisionally registered. This will allow them time (up to nine months) during which they will be able to complete the administrative formalities for the permanent registration.

Offshore Trusts

Cyprus is an attractive center for Offshore Trusts due to the significant tax planning possibilities available.

There are two statutes that govern trusts in Cyprus, one being the Trustee Law of 1955 which is almost identical to the English Trustee Act of 1925 and the International Trusts Law of 1992.

The new Law which complements and builds on the Trustee Law, applies only to "international trusts" which are broadly defined as trusts made by, non-residents of Cyprus and of which no resident of Cyprus is a beneficiary. The international Trusts Law offers considerable advantages to non-residents wishing to set up a trust in Cyprus.

The International Trusts Law, 1992 governs all trusts established in Cyprus. All income of a Cyprus offshore trust derived from outside Cyprus is exempt from local tax. Dividends, interest or other income received by a trust from a Cyprus offshore company are not taxable or subject to withholding tax. Capital gains realized on the sale of assets by the trust are not subject to tax in Cyprus. The trust and beneficiaries are exempted from local taxation. Offshore trusts and non-resident bank deposits with Cyprus banks are exempt from exchange control. There are no registration reporting requirements for trusts established in Cyprus. The Central Bank must be informed of the creation of an offshore trust if the trust owns shares in a Cyprus offshore company.

Key factors in growth of investments from within Cyprus

• The tax regime, relating to offshore enterprises is extremely, favorable and the existence of a wide network of treaties for the avoidance of double taxation creates many tax, planning opportunities.
• Cyprus has been characterized, by independent observers, as a "financial oasis" situated in a geographic area which very often suffers from political and economic upheavals. The track record of the offshore sector of Cyprus of the last 10 years has clearly indicated the opportunities which Cyprus can offer to businessmen and investors.
• Cyprus's legal framework is based on Anglo-Saxon common law. With internationally understood, legislation in place, there are no 'gray" legal areas which may create uncertainties and risks in business relationships.
• Cyprus has diplomatic relations with all countries in the Middle East and entry as well as re-entry formalities into the country are relatively simple.
• Cyprus does not face any overcrowding problems.
• Cyprus is offshore to the vast European Union market and yet very near the Middle East and Africa. It lies midway between the Far East and America. If offers a time niche fro which financial markets can be accessed 24 hours a day.
• Cyprus is a sovereign country with a multi-party liberal democratic political system which has full respect for human rights.
• Availability of educated and skilled professional and clerical staff as well as expert legal, accounting, management and other services.

Offshore enterprises are not required to employ a minimum number of persons whether local or expatriate.

• Offshore enterprises and OBUs/ABUs/OFCs in particular are not subject to costly over-regulation. Although the Central Bank does supervise their operations, it is recognized that for small and medium size firms the cost of compliance with a multitude of rules and regulations, as is the case in some EU countries, can be prohibitive for the development of their business.

• Banking confidentiality, as determined by English Common and Case Law, governs the relationship of banks with their customers, while banking secrecy governs the relationship between the Central Bank and OBUs/ABUs.

Moreover, expatriates who already live and work in Cyprus have discovered that the country's excellent communications and telecommunications, the country's low crime rate, its excellent climate and European lifestyle, the availability of high standard foreign language schools, its professional infrastructure and the fact the English is widely spoken are just a few of the additional advantages which contribute towards making their living in Cyprus very pleasant.

Offshore Exempted Companies

Cyprus taxes domestic companies at the regular corporate tax rate of 42.5%. In the case of offshore companies that derive their income from outside Cyprus the applicable tax rate is 4.25%. A company that is **registered overseas**, and whose management and control are outside Cyprus, is exempt from tax. This includes the profits from any **profession** carried on outside Cyprus. If the management and control are in Cyprus, such overseas company will be taxed at the 4.5% rate.

Since 1975, when the Republic of Cyprus introduced the first incentives, more than 4,500 offshore companies have been registered by non-residents. The island has exchange control regulations for its domestic companies, but offshore companies are exempted. Bank accounts may be kept anywhere in the world, and after tax profits may be transferred anywhere in the world.

Foreign employees of Cyprus' offshore companies pay tax from 0 to 6% on their salaries if working out of Cyprus, and 0 to 30% for work in Cyprus. Personal allowances are deductible from income and there is earned income relief of 14% on salaries and pensions. Business consulting and services is the second biggest activity of Cyprus offshore businesses, after trade.

The latest figures estimate that 50% of the total registered offshore companies originated from Western Europe, North America and Australia. The Middle East accounts for 25% more. Offshore companies employ more than 1,200 expatriates with 2,400 dependents and 1,100 locals.

Formation Costs

Offshore company formation is done through the central Bank of Cyprus with the aid of a professional adviser, accountant or lawyer. Processing is swift and easy. Including the professional adviser's fees, the cost is roughly US$1,500. It is estimated that gross revenues from offshore companies amounted to over $80 million in 1987. The Cyprus government openly supports the development of these offshore companies on their island.

Income Tax Treaties

Cyprus has tax treaties with 19 nations, including the U.S., UK, Canada, Germany, France. Sweden and Norway.

Shipping Companies

Shipping companies whose ships fly the Cyprus flag enjoy a full income tax exemption. Cyprus has signed an income tax treaty with the United States which exempts Cyprus shippers from U.S. federal income tax.

Other Incentives

Ninety percent of the profits or dividends imported into Cyprus is exempt from income tax. This is applicable to any business carried on outside Cyprus by a Cypriot residing in Cyprus or by a company controlled by Cypriots having not less than 15% interest. When the 90% exemption applies, the foreign tax credit is not available.

172.

Gibraltar – Rock Solid European Tax Haven

Gibraltar, like Panama and Liberia, is known as a haven for the registration of ships. Gibraltar is 3/4 of a mile wide and 3 miles long, give or take a few hundred yards here or there. It is located on the southern tip of Spain, jutting out into the Mediterranean Sea (most people think it juts into the Atlantic Ocean). It's population of about 30,000 are mainly English speaking citizens, and Gibraltar is a British Crown Colony. Gibraltar's tax laws are based on British common-law principles.

After nearly 400 years of Spanish rule, Gibraltar fell into British hands during the great European wars of Louis XIV and has remained a Crown Colony since the Treaty of Utrecht (1704). Today, a British army garrison is everywhere in evidence, and soldiers stand outside the British governor's residence where a military band makes regular appearances.

While Gibraltar has been a British colony since 1704, there has been outside political and military pressure from Spain in an attempt to regain sovereignty. In a referendum vote in 1967 Gibraltar residents expressed an almost unanimous desire to remain attached to Britain. Two years later in 1969 Spain passed sanctions against Gibraltar in an act of reprisal. Spain, to win control, closed her frontier to Gibraltar and prevented land traffic to or from the territory. In the face of this indignation, Gibraltar's residents nevertheless remained staunchly pro British openly defying the Spanish.

The political problems with Spain has made Gibraltar less accessible and less attractive as a tax haven, but its excellent air and sea transportation links allowed Gibraltar residents to cope with the Spanish embargo. Recently, Spain reopened its borders to Gibraltar and political frictions have ceased to be a problem.

Shipping Haven Since 1864

Gibraltar has been a British port of registration since 1864. As of January 1988, the total tonnage of merchant vessels registered in Gibraltar stood at 2.5 million tons. Gibraltar shipping companies are exempt from tax.

Gibraltar registered ships do not fly the Gibraltar flag, but fly the British Red Ensign.

In order to apply for registration the ship must be a 'British ship'. A 'British ship' is one owned wholly by (a) Natural born or naturalized British subject, or (b) Companies established under the laws of some part of Her Majesty's Dominions. Usually a British ship registered in Gibraltar will be owned by a company resident in Gibraltar.

Some types of vessels have been refused registration by the Port of Gibraltar. These include fishing vessels, nuclear powered vessels, gas or chemical tankers and large passenger ships. A large number of pleasure yachts are registered in Gibraltar.

Ships owned by a Gibraltar Tax Exempt Company can keep the beneficial owners of such companies confidential by law. Directors and shareholders usually are nominees. The beneficial owner may appear on the shareholder's Register if he wishes.

Non-Gibraltarians and non-residents owners of Gibraltar ship companies can apply for a 25 year **Tax Exemption Certificate**. An annual fee of £225 will thereafter keep you free from all Gibraltar taxes from trading operations. A Gibraltar exempt shipper can trade with other exempt Gibraltar companies, but may not carry on other trade or business in Gibraltar.

Accessibility

Non stop flights to London take about 2-1/2 hours. Flights leave and arrive daily. There are regular flights between Morocco and Gibraltar.

Language and Currency

The unit of currency in Gibraltar is the Pound Sterling although there is a local note and coinage issue which is at par with Sterling. In addition, in 1991 Gibraltar was the first EC state to issue ECU based coinage which is legal tender. There are no exchange control restrictions in force, there being complete freedom to remit funds into and out of Gibraltar and to convert funds into other currencies.

Gibraltar's official language is English, although French and Spanish are also spoken.

The Gibraltar pound is equal to 100 pence British.

Gibraltar's Companies Ordinance, 1974 provides Concessions for "Exempt Companies"

Gibraltar's legal system understandably is styled after English law, and lawyers are English trained. There are currently 50,000 companies, of which 8,000 are exempted (from tax) companies. Foreigners usually choose the exempted company for their international operations.

The Gibraltar Companies (Taxation and Concession) Ordinance of 1974 are based on the English 1929 Companies Act. Companies registered in Gibraltar can be limited by shares, by guarantee or unlimited. By filing a Memorandum of Association with the Registrar and stating the company's name and objects, its limited or unlimited liability, and how the shares are divided, a Gibraltar company becomes a legal entity. Articles of Association may be drafted by the members or a statutory model (Table A) may be adopted.

For purposes of Gibraltar income taxes, a company is treated as resident in Gibraltar if it is managed and controlled there. The same will apply if it carries on business in Gibraltar but its management and control are exercised outside Gibraltar by persons resident in Gibraltar. The rate of taxation applicable to both resident and non-resident companies is 35%, but non-resident companies are so taxed only on Gibraltar source income.

The Gibraltar *Companies (Taxation and Concessions) Ordinance* permits exempted companies, whether incorporated in Gibraltar or elsewhere, to be granted total tax exemption from income tax, stamp duty on documents, dividend, interest, director's fees and other annual sums and remunerations payable to non-residents. Debentures and shares of an exempt company are also free from Gibraltar estate taxes.

Exempt companies are further broken down into overseas companies (i.e., incorporated under the laws of a foreign country), ordinary resident companies (Gibraltar registered - managed in Gibraltar) and ordinary non-resident companies (management outside Gibraltar).

Company management services in Gibraltar can be hired to provide resident directors and officers including the company's registered address. A company which is managed in Gibraltar pays an annual tax of £225, whilst the tax for a company management outside Gibraltar is £200.

Where a company is incorporated outside Gibraltar the annual tax is £300 regardless of profit. The minimum paid up capital requirement for an exempt or overseas company is £100 or its equivalent in a foreign currency. An exempted company receives a tax exemption certificate from the government which continues in force for a period of 25 years. Registry of an exempted company is fast - taking 24/48 hours.

Gibraltar does not have a capital gains tax, a surtax, a tax on capital or a wealth tax. It does have estate taxes, but exempt companies are relieved of any estate tax liability. The exemption from estate tax and income tax is guaranteed by the government for 25 years.

To acquire exempt company status the company must apply to the registrar and await approval. For approval to be granted the company must have.

1. Paid-in capital of at least £100 at all times.
2. May not engage in business inside Gibraltar, except for managing the affairs of enterprises outside Gibraltar.
3. A company must keep its register of shares inside Gibraltar **exclusively**.
4. An **overseas company** must keep a true copy of its register of members in Gibraltar.
5. The company cannot have shareholders that are residents of Gibraltar.

Costs: Incorporation and Maintenance

An ordinary resident exempt company managed and controlled in Gibraltar pays an annual tax of £225 (US$425), while the tax for a company managed outside Gibraltar is £200 (US$380). Overseas companies pay an annual tax of £300 (US$570) regardless of the size of its profits. The tax for an overseas company is paid in two installments on the first day of April and the first day of October in each year. A company that fails to pay the tax 30 days after the due date automatically ceases to be an exempt company and will only be reinstated on payment of a penalty of £25, if the Financial and

174.

Development Secretary is satisfied the default was excusable and made or allowed without intent to defeat the provisions. [11]

Yearly fees for company secretarial services, maintaining a registered office and director's services (which include annual filing fee) cost an addition £445 (US$845). An additional fee for the application for tax exemption costs £95 (US$180). In addition, an £75 exempt company audit fee is payable to external auditors.

An exempt company's exemption certificate continues in force for a period of 25 years from the time when issued provided its conditions are not breached.

Banking in Gibraltar

Banks operating in Gibraltar now stand at about 28. An application for a banking license must be submitted to the Commissioner of Banking who then receives an assessment from the Banking supervisor.

There are four distinct types of licenses, divided into Class A or Class B, which may be either full or limited. Class B licensed Banks have offshore status and so deal with non-residents. They are restricted to taking deposits only from non-residents of Gibraltar, holders of Class A licenses, and certain types of locally registered offshore companies. The holder of a Class B license, on meeting the requirements of the Companies (Concessions and Taxation) Ordinance, is eligible for exemption from Gibraltar Income Tax, and will pay only a flat annual fee of £225. The minimum paid up capital for a full license is £1,000,000 and £250,000 for a limited license.

One of the principal areas of Gibraltar's success is banking. Gibraltar has a total of 28 banks with aggregate deposits of £2.6 billion. British and Scandinavian banks like Barclays, Lloyds and Jyske Bank are well placed to offer services to the thousands of retired and semi-retired sun seekers on the Costa del Sol. Interestingly also, branches of Spanish banks jostle for space with their British competitors in Main Street as if to demonstrate that business does not recognize the petty boundaries of politics.

Banks in Gibraltar come from a wide range of countries. National Bank of New York, Banque IndoSuez and Credit Suisse are just some of the famous names here.

Several of Gibraltar's banks offer a full service to high net worth individuals where, apart from the usual banking functions of deposit-taking, money transfer and foreign exchange, they will trade in securities on behalf of clients, often on a discretionary basis.

Gibraltar, which does not distinguish between 'onshore' and 'offshore' banking institutions, has managed to attract some 28 of the world's major deposit taking names. These operations now hold over £2.6 billion on the rock for savers based throughout the world, but particularly those resident on the Iberian peninsula.

To some degree or another, the mix of international banks are all attracted by the ability to offer interest from Gibraltar to depositors free of taxes deducted at source.

The most recent to join these banks on the rock is an offshore offshoot of the Newcastle building society. The Newcastle already had two building society branches in Gibraltar, but the new operation is a banking arrangement located right opposite rival Abbey National and not far from the Norwich & Peterborough's shopfront.

Dean Witter Reynolds' Discover Card Bank

American brokerage firm Dean Witter Reynolds set up its first European offshore subsidiary, Discover Card Bank, in Gibraltar's Europort. The company offers the Discover Card, a credit and charge card, deposit accounts in dollars and other major currencies, and foreign exchange transactions. There is a minimum balance of US$5,000 on call deposits, with interest paid quarterly. Fixed deposits with a fixed term of investment and a fixed interest rate have a minimum balance of $25,000. As yet Discover Card Bank in Gibraltar is a small operation, but plans include expansion into private banking.

Gibraltar was chosen as the site of the Discover Card Bank, says manager James Gordon, after Dean Witter Discover & Co looked

---

11. **"Close-up Gibraltar"** (with interview of Mr. Joe Bossano, chief Minister of Gibraltar), from <u>Offshore Investment Magazine</u>.

at several offshore centers outside the Americas. The company stresses Gibraltar's freedom from exchange controls, multiple tax advantages, political and economic stability, and the anonymity and discretion afforded by its disclosure laws.

Gibraltar's location, between Europe and north western Africa, is also important to Discover Card, as American institutions with offshore subsidiaries in Europe tend to use them to service clients throughout Europe and the Middle East. James Gordon says he is interested in attracting not just an American clientele to the Gibraltar operation, but a wider market of intentional investors. [12.]

Gibraltar's Banking Ordinance has recently been rewritten and now meets all the requirements of the banking Directives in its licensing and control requirements. It incorporates some of the related Directives which together are designed to produce the fully integrated European banking system of which Gibraltar is a part. The principal amendments which have been implemented are those setting out conditions on which a bank authorized in one member State has a right to establish a branch in, or provide a wide range of banking services on the strength of its home country authorization. The services covered by this "single passport" would include deposit taking, lending, money transmission services, leasing, participation in securities issues, securities trading and portfolio management and advice. Provision is made for a minimum capital base of 5m ECU and limitations on bank's holdings in non-financial companies.

Gibraltar's Foreign Trusts

Gibraltar has common-law trust principles based on English law. **The Trustee Ordinance** stipulates that trustees can be either corporations or individuals, but they must be residents of Gibraltar. The perpetuity period for a Gibraltar trust is one hundred years, and the accumulation period has recently been increased to 100 years also.

The fact that a Gibraltar trust must have resident trustees is not a deterrent to the U.S. tax planner, because the IRS will not recognize a

foreign trust as being *"foreign"*, if the majority of the trustees are U.S. citizens or entities.

The income of a trust created by a non-resident of Gibraltar is exempt from Gibraltar tax provided that the trust deed specifies that no Gibraltarian or resident of Gibraltar is or may be a beneficiary. Further, trust income must be derived from sources outside Gibraltar to be exempt. Recent tax exemptions have been provided from estate taxes in respect to interests held by non-residents in Gibraltar trusts. Gibraltar's trust legislation is based on the UK *Trustee Act of 1893*.

As a common law jurisdiction, Gibraltar is an attractive location for offshore trusts. Gibraltar also has specific legislation permitting the establishment of asset protection trusts.

Tax Treaties

Gibraltar has no double taxation agreements with any nation, thus a Gibraltar based company or trust will enjoy no treaty tax relief on its U.S. source interests, dividends and royalties, and will be subject to a flat 30% withholding tax on these passive incomes.

Open relations with Spain

The reopening of the border with Spain in 1985 has enabled Gibraltar, a British possession since 1713, to expand its role as a major offshore finance center, against a background of political stability and administrative and legal systems derived from the English models. The absence of any exchange control restrictions together with exemptions and concessions from domestic taxes to certain categories of companies, non-resident individuals who do not work in Gibraltar itself, and trusts administered for non-residents has created many opportunities for offshore investors and led to substantial growth in financial sector services. This has been augmented by strong investor protection legislation passed in 1990 and 1991 leading to the creation of the Financial Services Commission and the appointment of a Financial Services Commissioner.

Taxes

Gibraltar taxes are generally modeled on those in the United Kingdom, but there are a number of major differences. In particular, Gibraltar does not have any Capital Gains Tax or Inheritance Tax (although Estate Duty applies).

---

12. From *Offshore 95* by Ian Yule (Charterhouse Publications • London • UK).

In addition there is specific tax legislation which is designed to favor the development of the territory's commercial and tourist infrastructure and to make it an attractive offshore finance center.

Though Gibraltar is a member of the European Economic Community under the provisions relating to dependent territories, it is specifically excluded from the regulations concerning the Common Agricultural Policy and Value Added Tax.

Income Tax

The taxation of income of both companies and individuals is governed by the Income Tax Ordinance (1984 reprint) as amended by the various Income Tax (Amendment) Ordinances.

Income tax is charged on most classes of income "accruing in, derived from, or received in Gibraltar'. The year of assessment runs from 1st July in any year to 30th June of the next year. Taxation in any year of assessment is normally levied on income derived from the preceding year except in the case of income from employment which is subject to deduction on an actual basis via a Pay-As-You-Earn system.

There are no double-tax treaties in force between Gibraltar and any other country. However, tax relief is available in respect of UK income tax paid on income which is similarly chargeable to Gibraltar tax up to the lower of Gibraltar tax or UK tax. In respect of Commonwealth income tax, the relief is the lower of one half of the Gibraltar tax or the Commonwealth tax on the income. In certain cases, income earned, taxed and retained overseas is not taxable in Gibraltar.

Non-resident Controlled Companies

Non-Resident owned and controlled companies incorporated in Gibraltar which do not trade, earn or remit income to Gibraltar are not liable to company taxation.

Exempt Companies

A Gibraltar incorporated company or a registered branch of an overseas incorporated company may apply for registration under the Companies (Taxation and Concessions) Ordinance. Such registration entitles the company and/or beneficial owner to exemption from all income tax and estate duty in Gibraltar. The main requirements for exemption status are that no Gibraltarian or Gibraltar resident has a beneficial interest in the shares of the company and that the company does not trade or carry on business in Gibraltar.

The Company can maintain office premises in Gibraltar for the purposes of transacting business with non-residents or with other exempt or qualifying companies. There are no restrictions on the appointment of directors or officers of an exempt company (but either the company secretary or a director must be a Gibraltar resident) and meetings may be held inside or outside Gibraltar thus allowing the company to be managed and controlled locally. A secrecy provision in the Ordinance prevents the disclosure of details concerning the beneficial owners of the company.

A fixed annual tax is payable by the company of £225 if ordinarily resident and £200 if not so resident. A registered branch of an overseas company pays £300 per annum.

Qualifying Companies

A Gibraltar incorporated company or a registered branch of an overseas incorporated company may apply for registration under the Income Tax (Qualifying Companies) Rules 1983. Qualifying companies are chargeable to tax on their profits at such rates as may be prescribed but not less than 2% and not more than 18%. The requirements for obtaining and retaining qualifying status are similar to those covering exempt companies. Additionally, however, the share capital must not be less than £1,000 and a further sum of £1,000 must be deposited with the Gibraltar Government as security for future taxes. A fee of £250 is payable for obtaining a qualifying certificate.

A separate piece of tax legislation issued in December 1991 created the concept of the **Gibraltar 1992 Company** which has the following characteristics:

1) it is incorporated or registered in Gibraltar under the provisions of the Companies Ordinance on or after 1st January 1992;
2) it is ordinarily resident in Gibraltar; the principal object of the company is to hold

interests amounting to relevant participations (defined as interests of at least 5% in the voting share capital of other body corporates); in any year of assessment at least 51% of its income is derived from relevant participations;

3) it has a proper physical presence in Gibraltar (i.e.. business premises of at least 400 sq. ft. and a minimum of two employees);

4) no resident of Gibraltar has a beneficial interest in its share capital; a reasonable debt to equity ratio is maintained.

Once the above criteria are satisfied, the Financial and Development Secretary will issue a certificate to this effect.

Although a Gibraltar 1992 Company is assessable to Gibraltar income tax in the normal way (the current company rate is 35%) its significant attraction is in the area of withholding tax where tax at the rate of 1% shall apply to dividends paid by such companies. Furthermore, interest payments are totally exempt from withholding tax.

There is no further liability to Gibraltar tax by the recipient of any dividends or interest paid by a Gibraltar 1992 Company.

Legal System

The legal system in Gibraltar is based on English Common and Statute Law with variations introduced by local Statute Law or "Ordinances". The administration of justice in Gibraltar is undertaken by a Chief Justice; there are three courts, a Magistrates Court, a Court of First Instance and a Supreme Court. The ultimate Court of Appeal is the Privy Council in the United Kingdom.

The Economy

The economy is primarily dependent upon service industries and port facilities with income being derived from tourism, trans-shipment and, perhaps most importantly in terms of growth, the provision of financial services. Boosted by the re-opening of the border, the rapidly expanding economy has however also benefited the construction industry with multinational companies linking with local firms to build hotels, office blocks and other commercial and residential accommodation. A wide range of Internal banks provide both domestic and offshore banking facilities on the Rock. Banking confidentiality is guaranteed by Statute. Bank accounts may be maintained in any generally recognized currency and are exempt from Gibraltar taxes when held by non-residents. Gibraltar enjoys virtually full employment and also provides jobs for blue and white collar workers commuting from Spain.

Transport and Communications

Gibraltar's strategic location at the entrance to the Mediterranean places it at the center of a network of communications. Gibraltar has both an international airport and a harbor which continues to be a prime port of call for many of the world's shipping lines as a result of both its location and its free port status. In Spain the airports at Seville, Jerez and Malaga are all within two hours' drive of the Rock and allow access to a wide variety of Spanish domestic and international flights.

Following the recent installation of a fully digital network, Gibraltar has excellent telecommunications with the rest of the World. 13.

The early development of a Finance Center in Gibraltar was based on supplying a relatively narrow range of services to a well defined group of customers largely in the UK and on the Costa. With a combination of (somewhat dated) company related laws and the addition of provision for a few specialist investment vehicles such as the tax exempt Company, the legal infrastructure was perfectly adequate for this original limited ambition.

Development depends on Gibraltar being able to offer the increasingly complex and sophisticated range of services which businessmen and investors alike expect to be able to call on as an integrated package. It is well understood in Gibraltar that the financial sector legislation must come to reflect this requirement for well rounded and fully integrated legislation which is such an essential entry requirement into the genuinely international market place where the future lies. It is, therefore, no accident that legislative development has been at the forefront of the strategy that Government is developing in conjunction with the private sector for achieving the growth of the Finance Center.

---

13. Information was supplied by Coopers & Lybrand, Chartered Accountants.

High Net Worth Individuals

In 1992, Gibraltar joined the select band or jurisdictions which actively seek to attract new, wealthy residents by designing special residence and tax laws for them. As well as a beneficial tax treatment, these high net worth individuals (HNWls) can qualify for a British passport (though not the right of abode in the UK). In a briefing prepared by Gibraltar solicitors Marrache & Co, under the terms of the legislation, a high net worth individual is classified as such where he or she: has available to him or her for exclusive use, for a period of not less than seven months, residential accommodation in Gibraltar -
• resides in Gibraltar, in the properly, for a minimum of 30 days in each year; and has not otherwise been resident in Gibraltar during the last five years (although in certain circumstances this requirement may be waived).

In return for meeting these criteria, HNWls qualify for a special annual tax charge which is currently capped at £20,000.

The Financial Services Commission Ordinance

The Financial Services Commission Ordinance provides for the appointment of an independent Commissioner and a Commission of six voluntary members appointed as individuals having the necessary experience to contribute. The role of the Commission is to advise the Commissioner on matters of policy. At an executive level the Commissioner is supported by the office of the Commissioner which he is free to recruit as his needs change.

The financial services covered by the Commissioner/Commission include:
• Banking,
• Insurance,
• Investment Business including the operation of Collective investment schemes,
• Company management,
• Professional trusteeships,
• Insurance brokering,
• Investment exchanges and clearing houses.

Good progress has been made in implementing the detailed licensing arrangements that are the cornerstone of the investor protection envisaged under the Financial Services Ordinance. The approach of the Commission has been very much one of a very careful scrutiny of those who are able to do business using Gibraltar as a base and only to require approval of individual products or product ranges where there is a particular sensitivity or vulnerability.

Under the Ordinance provision is made for the Commission to be self-financing from charges raised and the initial scale of the main annual charges is as follows:

investment dealer	£,3000
Investment broker	£3,000
Life assurance and collective investment scheme	£2,000
intermediary	£3,000
Investment manager	£3,000
Investment advisor	£1,500
Collective investment scheme operator	£3,000
Collective investment scheme trustee	£3,000
Insurance broker	£3,000
Insurance agent	£1,500
Professional trustee	£3,000 to £4,500
Company manager	£2,000 to £4,000

The next group of Ordinances that require consideration are those which to a greater or lesser extent are affected by the requirements of EEC Directives. A major element in marketing of the Finance Center is the ability to provide gateway access to the single European Market. But to maintain this advantage, it is necessary to ensure that Gibraltar institutions are fully European in construction and in their obligations.

In respect of Company legislation, EEC requirements are both more fundamental and more complex. The Gibraltar Companies Ordinance has as its root in the UK Companies Act of 1929. Clearly much water has passed under the bridge since then. Proposals have now been

In a world in which the attitude of Caveat Emptor has given way to expectation of independent investor protection as a sign of international responsibility, the statutory basis for such protection is perhaps a logical place to start. It is worth noting that this has probably been one of the most difficult areas for legislators worldwide over the last decade as they seek to tread a path between the unscrupulous or incompetent on the one hand and over regulation incapable of practical application on the other. It is as much due to ability to learn from the mistakes of others that Gibraltar's Financial Services and Financial Services Commission Ordinances of 1989 reflect a practical and effective solution. In particular, the legislation is probably the best shot yet in

Europe in terms of providing a fully integrated approach to Supervision rather than the considerable fragmentation that still exists elsewhere.

Background To Gibraltar's Company Law

Promulgated to implement amendments to the Ordinance to give practical implementation to the requirements of the 2nd Company Directive dealing with public limited companies and the 4th Company Directive which introduces minimum accounting requirements with regard to all Companies. In this latter case, full use has been made of flexibilities with regards to "small" companies in adopting a practical and realistic basis for compliance. Other areas are receiving attention, including the authorization and regulation of Auditors.

Finally under this grouping of EEC requirements, there is the anti money laundering legislation. The Drug Trafficking Offenses Ordinance of 1988 is second to none in Europe in its rigorous approach to deterring the money laundering of drug related money. However, a new EEC Directive introduced in 1991 will require more extensive anti-money laundering legislation extending not just to the proceeds of drug related crime. These requirements are under review.

The final group of financial sector legislation is concerned with legislation designed specifically with new financial services in mind. In this case we are using our legislative capacity as the cutting edge in forming new markets.

A good example in this respect is the Collective Investment Scheme Regulations which were introduced in April 1991 under powers contained in the Financial Services Ordinance. By drawing pooled investment within the ambit of supervision of the Financial Services Commission on terms which meet minimum EEC requirement, the groundwork has been created for the establishment of funds capable of pan-European marketing from a base in Gibraltar. (To further enhance marketability in this area Gibraltar is also associated to the OECD, which makes funds based in Gibraltar much more marketable in countries such as Japan).

Other areas of opportunity currently under consideration include offshore pension arrangements and captive insurance management. Both services are capable of being provided within existing legislative provision, but consideration is being given to whether they would benefit from a dedicated body of law in their own right. In these and in any other areas that come to light, Government is very willing to consider promoting legislation to ensure that the framework of legislation that Gibraltar has in place, really does meet modern requirements.

And this really is the message of this article. The financial services market is now truly global and constantly changing with market demands. There are no senses in which a body of financial sector legislation can ever be under anything than constant review whether it be to respond to a developing understanding of supervisory needs, a change in market products or simply to ensure that the integrity of the whole is maintained. The Government of Gibraltar, in consultation with practitioners, is committed to this process of constant renewal. [14.]

Gibraltar is within the EC by virtue of its status under Article 227(4) of the Treaty of Rome, it being a territory for whose external relations a Member State (i.e.. the United Kingdom) is responsible.

In all other respects EC Directives are considered to apply to Gibraltar and Gibraltar, in its turn, has been demonstrating a strong commitment to implementing these Directives, most particularly in areas such as banking, fund management and more recently, company law. One of the most interesting Directives, from a fiscal planning point of view to have emerged from Brussels in recent years has been directive 90/435 which requires most Member States to exempt from withholding tax dividends paid by subsidiary companies to parent companies when both such companies are located within EC Member States. Furthermore, it requires Member States to exempt from further taxation those dividends in the hands of the parent company. Clearly the two principal objectives of the Directive were to ensure that profits earned with the EC were subject to corporate taxation only once, and to remove fiscal barriers to cross-border investment.

---

14. Contributed by Peter J. Brooke, Financial Secretary, Gibraltar Govemment).

CHAPTER 7 • Switzerland & the European tax havens

No discussion of tax havens would be complete without mention of Switzerland. Switzerland is a financial center and money haven more than it is a tax haven. The Swiss tax resident companies on three levels - federal, canton and municipal. Federal tax rates range from 3.63% to a maximum of 9.8%, and that's in the ball park with other low tax havens, but Swiss cantonal and municipal taxes can effectively raise the tax rate on a resident Swiss company to as high as 20% or 30%. That's more in-line with industrial nations' tax rates. Switzerland is very much an industrial country. It's banking system is world renowned. It has negotiated many tax treaties with other industrial nations, including the USA.

What makes Switzerland more in-line with the low-tax and no-tax havens and boldly different from the industrial nations is the way the Swiss look upon income tax evasion and income tax avoidance. Income *tax evasion* is not a crime in Switzerland as it is in the industrial nations. *Tax evasion* is a misdemeanor. The Swiss do not consider tax evasion (or tax avoidance) a crime unless the taxpayer has falsified records. Swiss Courts will not lift the elaborate veil of secrecy that Swiss institutions offer unless a violation of a Swiss criminal statutes has occurred.

Opening a secret Swiss bank account (either a numbered or ciphered bank account) is perfectly legal in Switzerland. Hiding information from outsiders has always been a tradition here. In this respect Switzerland is very much a tax haven like the Caymans, Panama, Vanuatu, the Bahamas or Hong Kong. Author Midas Malone sums up the Swiss attitude when he writes....

"In the U.S., tax evasion - failure to declare all income - is a criminal offense. In Switzerland (and several other countries) it is not. For that reason, if the U.S. Internal Revenue Service asks Switzerland for information on an American suspected of not paying all his taxes, the Swiss Government politely refuses on the grounds that no Swiss law has been broken. A Swiss citizen might be asked by his government to provide documents or other information supporting his tax claims, but Swiss law bars the government from fishing expeditions to dig up hidden information on its taxpayers.

It is interesting to note that the Swiss meet all their tax needs without resorting to strong-arm methods. The Swiss attitude is that people will voluntarily support reasonable government spending and fair taxation... Obviously, their policy works, and they simply will not participate with other governments in activities they feel are unnecessary, nonproductive, and which they basically disagree. They will cooperate in prosecuting tax fraud, however, which is different from tax evasion." [1].

Swiss bank secrecy law

In Switzerland, it is not a crime for you (or a Swiss citizen) to evade U.S. taxes, but it is a criminal offense if your Swiss banker or one of your Swiss corporate directors violates Switzerland's official secrecy laws. *Violations of trust,* as they are called by the Swiss, are prosecuted ex-officio by law. A person who is subject to the Swiss banking secrecy law is bound from giving up such secrets for the rest of his life. Anyone, including yourself as a director of a Swiss company, who willfully divulges a secret entrusted to him can be punished by a prison term of up to 6 months in jail and a fine of up to $50,000 Swiss francs.

In addition to protection offered by Swiss civil and penal law, customers of banks in Switzerland are afforded additional protection by the provisions of Article 47 of the Banking Law.

Although the law does not define what constitutes secret information, legal precedent supports the assumption that nothing should be disclosed which might in any way harm the interest of a customer of a bank or impinge on his or her rights to confidentiality.

In practical terms this means that absolutely no information about customers can be given by a bank to third parties- public or private - without the customer's specific approval. An important exception to this rule applies in criminal cases, bankruptcy or debt collection

---

1. From *How to do Business Tax Free,* by Midas Malone, pg. 65.

procedures, where relevant disclosures are mandatory.

The disclosure of secret information to foreign authorities or government agencies is also not permitted unless an international treaty (tax treaty on mutual assistance in criminal matters) specifically provides for such disclosure. In these situations the foreign authority could in principle only obtain information that would be available to the Swiss authorities under similar circumstances.

Article 4 quinquies of the Banking Law specifically addresses situations where the parent companies of Swiss banks are supervised by banking or financial market supervisory authorities. In these cases the Banking Law specifically permits banks to transmit information or documents not publicly available to their parent companies which are necessary for the purpose of consolidated supervision, provided that:

- the information is used exclusively for internal control or direct supervision of banks or other financial intermediaries subject to license;
- the parent company and the supervisory authorities responsible for consolidated supervision are bound by official or professional secrecy; and
- the information may not be transmitted to third parties without the prior permission of the bank or on the basis of a blanket permission in a state treaty.

In cases of doubt, banks may request a decision from the Federal Banking Commission allowing or forbidding the transmission of information.

There is currently a general trend towards increased co-operation between national regulatory authorities, especially in the fight against organized crime. In more recent times this has resulted in an increased readiness to exchange information.

The Richie Rich case

Fifteen years ago American entrepreneur Marc Rich (now a resident in Switzerland) was indicted in New York for racketeering, fraud and tax evasion. The U.S. asked the Swiss to extradite Rich to the U.S., but the Swiss government refused. Later Rich made good the U.S. government's tax claims against his companies, paying $200,000,000 in taxes and penalties in one of the largest tax claims ever collected. But, the U.S. still refused to drop charges against Rich. While Rich's companies were allowed to resume their U.S. operations, Rich remains a fugitive in the eyes of the U.S. tax authorities to this day, although he is a popular hero in his home canton of Zug.

Numbered Accounts

Numbered accounts are available for individuals as well as for corporations. A code word combined with the account number can also be utilized. Numbered accounts help to better maintain and protect the financial privacy of the client. Account statements and advices only show the number of the account (and code word, if applicable). Names are not shown anywhere on statements. A copy of a valid identification is also required for each signer on the account. Numbered accounts are treated just like name accounts under Swiss banking rules.

Many firms have a US $250,000 minimum amount to establish a Swiss bank account. Accounts can be opened in any major currency. Switzerland has a multi-currency banking system unlike the United states where one can only open an account in US-Dollars.

Numbered accounts are customer accounts identified only by a code number instead of by a client name. The identity of the owner of the account must be known to management of the bank.

The purpose of a numbered account is to assure additional discretion as to the number of people with knowledge of the details of an account. Banking Law auditors are required to inspect these accounts in undertaking their responsibilities under the Banking Law. They are, however, bound by the general obligation to observe bank secrecy, and this inspection role does not, therefore, violate the principle of the banker-client professional relationship. [2.]

Swiss Banking System

Switzerland has a highly developed banking system encompassing approximately 400 banks, of which more than 150 are subsidiaries or branches of foreign banks. The number of banks

---

2. From *Banking and Finance in Switzerland* (1996)(KPMG)

in the market has been consistently shrinking since 1990 as a result of competition and rationalization. Mergers and acquisitions have streamlined and strengthened the position of the remaining participants. There has also been a growing trend towards specialization and away from traditional full service ("universal") banking.

At 31 December 1995 the following categories of banks made up the banking community:

	Number	Total Assets (SFR billions)
Big banks	4	730.6
Cantonal banks	25	261.5
Regional & savings banks	127	72.3
Loan associations	1	49.9
Private banks	17	7.1
Foreign banks (including branches)	155	11.6
Other banks	84	90.4
Total @ 31 DEC 95	413	1,323.4
Comparative total	625	1,059.1

These figures only show part of the picture. Swiss banks are heavily engaged in private banking, and total funds under management are commonly estimated to be between SFR 2.0 and SFR 2.5 thousand billion. Because such figures are not publicly reported, the exact size of the market remains a well kept secret.

Big Banks

The three largest banks in Switzerland - Swiss Bank Corporation, Union Bank of Switzerland and Credit Suisse Group (formerly Swiss Credit Bank) - dominate the banking community. Their activities are universal, spanning acceptance of deposits, extension of credit, dealing in foreign exchange and precious metals, portfolio management, trust activity, underwriting, and many others. They operate not only throughout Switzerland but in virtually all the major financial centers of the world.

The fourth bank in this category - Swiss Volksbank- has been a wholly owned subsidiary of Credit Suisse since 1992. The total assets of these banks at 31 December 1995 were as follows:

	Total Assets(SFR billions)
Union Bank of Switzerland	287.5
Swiss Bank Corporation	242.1
Credit Suisse Group	163.7
Swiss Volksbank	37.3
	730.6

Cantonal Banks

At the end of 1995 there were 25 cantonal banks operating in Switzerland, mainly in the areas of acceptance of savings and the issue of mortgages and debentures. Their funds are primarily used to finance local commercial and private needs and to extend loans to public authorities. Since the late 1980's their operations have become more diversified, now including services such as asset management, consumer credit and export financing and leasing.

Cantonal banks vary substantially in size, with balance sheet totals ranging from SFR 1 billion to over SFR 54 billion.

Private Banks

Private banks represent the oldest members of the Swiss banking system and still occupy an important position in the banking community, even though they represent a fraction of the credit market.

Private bankers still operate as partnerships, and are therefore fully liable to their creditors to the extent of their entire private assets.

These institutions have traditionally dealt with private customers in the areas of asset and portfolio management, although more recently they have engaged in other commercial banking activities.

Foreign Banks

A large number of foreign banks operate in the Swiss market either through closely held, locally incorporated entities (the majority) or through branches of an offshore group entity.

The main reasons for foreign banks to operate in the Swiss market, apart from image and prestige, are:

- to provide foreign banking services to their domestic customers (including foreign subsidiaries of those customers)
- to maintain a presence in one of the most important and stable financial centers in the world
- to solicit business from Swiss companies operating in their own country (for example, loans to foreign subsidiaries of Swiss companies operating in their home country)
- to participate in the capital markets

- to provide portfolio management services to non-resident nationals of their own countries and other nationalities where possible
- to take advantage of the comparatively low interest and tax rates prevailing in Switzerland, by borrowing funds in the country for re-lending abroad.

Foreign control is deemed to exist where "foreigners" hold more than half of the voting rights of capital stock or otherwise have a controlling interest. Foreigners are legal entities or partnerships with their registered offices abroad or who are controlled by non-resident individuals even if their registered office is in Switzerland. In terms of individuals, a person who possesses neither Swiss nationality nor a permanent residence permit for Switzerland is deemed to be a foreigner. It is possible under these definitions for Swiss banks to be controlled by foreign nationals who are permanent residents of Switzerland.

Company Formations

Swiss Companies Law is embodied in the **Swiss Code of Obligations**, which is issued in Swiss, German and Italian. An unofficial English translation of the part of the Code dealing with companies incorporated with legal liability was published by the Swiss-American Chamber of Commerce in 1980, and copies are available on request.

At least three founders (individuals, or entities) are needed to form a Swiss (**AG/SA**) company. To form a private company (**GMbH/Sarl**) two shareholders are required.

The minimum paid-up capital required to start a Swiss company is 20,000 Sfr (about $12,400). Upon formation, a one time Federal Stamp duty of 3% is due on the total share capital. The total expenses incurred to form a Swiss corporation starts out about Sfr.5,000, but may be considerably higher if the authorized capital is sizable.

The Pure Holding Company, The Participating Company, and The Domicile Company

In Switzerland there are three types of companies that you can choose to use. The first is called **Pure Holding Company**. A pure holding company normally acquires and permanently holds *"substantial participations"*

in the equity capital of other corporations. Its income consists of dividends, interests on bank accounts and capital gains. Pure holding companies generally pay no canton or municipal taxes. They do pay taxes on their capital gains and other ordinary incomes.

A pure holding company that holds **20%** or more of the shares in another **Swiss** or **foreign** corporation is **exempt** from Federal tax with respect to dividends and liquidating dividends from the *substantial participation*. If the shares in the other company are worth at least Sfr.2 million (about US$1.3 million) the *substantial participation* exemption still applies.

Another category of Swiss holding company, called a **Participating Company**, is an everyday commercial or industrial company which holds equity investments in other companies. It is a mixture of *holding company* and *industrial company*. It is permitted the same tax relief that a pure holding company can get with regards to *substantial participations* in other Swiss or foreign corporations.

The third type of Swiss holding company is the **Domicile Company**, which can engage in any type of business, but not from its *registered* Swiss office (which is merely an address for official communications). Its transactions must originate from places other than its registered office, and management board and directors must supervise operations essential from outside Switzerland.

Taxation

Swiss resident companies are taxed on their worldwide income from all sources, and on capital and reserves at 0.825% rate pa. The tax rate on accessible income (including capital gains) for federal income tax purposes ranges from 3.63% to 9.8%. Nonetheless, certain items of income are exempt from Swiss income taxes. Aside from the *substantial participation* privilege described above, the following items of income are not subject to corporate tax;

- Income from a foreign branch or permanent establishment.
- Foreign source real estate income.

Income Tax Treaties

What makes Switzerland a powerhouse in the financial community is her ability to negotiate important income tax treaties with the other industrial nations while persevering her own perspectives in regards to confidentiality and bank secrecy.

New U.S. Swiss tax treaty

After seventeen years of negotiations, the Switzerland-U.S. Income Tax Treaty, which was signed October 2, 1996, came into force on December 19, 1997. A new Retroactive Ordinance passed on June 15, 1998 brings the Treaty into effect for withholding taxes on dividends, interest and royalties, for amounts paid or credited on or after February 1, 1998. For all other taxes, the Treaty is effective for taxable periods beginning on or after January 1, 1998. This treaty replaces the 1951 treaty.

The 1996 Treaty follows recent U.S. income tax treaties and the OECD model. Real property capital gains are taxable in the country where the real estate is located. The new Treaty includes a comprehensive limitation on benefits under Article 22 and provides for exchange of information under Article 26 between the two countries. Double taxation may be avoided by adjusting the timing of the taxation of certain classes.

New dividend withholding tax rate

In regard to withholding rates, Article 10 provides for a withholding tax at 5% on dividends where the beneficial owner owns at least 10% of the voting stock of the corporation paying the dividend. In all other cases, the withholding tax is 15%.

Article 11(1) provides that interest derived from beneficial ownership by a resident of one country is taxable only in the country of residence. However, if the beneficial owner is a resident in one country and conducts business in the other country through a permanent establishment, or performs, in the other country, independent personal services from a fixed base, the interest is attributable to such permanent establishment or fixed base, subject to Article 7 (Business Profits) or Article 14 (Independent Personal Services).

Dividends paid by a Swiss company are subject to a 35% Swiss withholding tax, but resident Swiss individuals and companies get a full refund, so the 35% Swiss dividend withholding tax really doesn't apply to Swiss entities. Foreign companies and individuals are subject to the 35% Swiss withholding tax,

however. Here again, some Swiss tax treaties reduce the rate and allow for a refund. Under the U.S. treaty, the Swiss will refund **30%** of the tax if the U.S. company owns 10% of the voting stock of the Swiss company paying the dividend. Under the Netherlands-Swiss treaty the entire **35%** withholding is refunded if a Dutch company owns at least 25% of the Swiss company.

Combining the Swiss *substantial participation* privilege, the dividend refund provisions (above), and the tax treaty benefits can lead to a very low effect tax rate, even though the Swiss federal and canton taxes can approach 30% on other types of incomes.

EXAMPLE: Swiss Holding **Company X**, owned by Swiss brothers **A & B**, purchases **all** the shares of U.S. company **Intermedics.** In 1999, Intermedics pays a $50,000,000 dividend to Swiss parent company X. Under the new Swiss-U.S. treaty, the U.S. dividend withholding tax rate is reduced to 5%, so only $2,500,000 of the $50,000,000 dividend is withheld. Absent the Swiss-U.S. treaty $15,000,000 would have to be withheld by the payor of the dividend.

Swiss holding **company X** pays a $40,000,000 dividend to Swiss brothers A & B in 1999. This dividend is subject to a 35% Swiss withholding tax, but is fully refundable under the Swiss tax system. Had the shares in Swiss company **X** been owned by a nonresident of the Cayman Islands, the withholding tax would have equaled $14,000,000 and would not have been refundable. On the other hand, had 25% of Swiss company X been owned by a **Netherlands** holding company, the Swiss withholding tax would have been reduced to zero under the *Swiss-Netherlands Tax Treaty*. The Dutch **Participation Exemption** (5% or more of Swiss Company X) would exempt the Swiss source dividend from Dutch income taxes.

The transaction above actually occurred in 1990 under the old Swiss US tax treaty.

Campione – tiny tax haven in Swiss Alps

Campione is a tiny Italian enclave surrounded by Switzerland. Located on just 1.6 km of sloping land, residents enjoy an almost unrestricted, panoramic view of Lake Lugano and the surrounding Swiss Alps. In size, Campione ranks as one of smallest tax havens in the world, about 1/4 the size of tiny Gibraltar in the Mediterranean sea, and equal in size with Monaco.

Campione owes its tax haven status to a more or less *laissez-faire* attitude by the two neighboring countries (Switzerland and Italy) that rightfully, it would seem, have the jurisdiction to impose taxes on this tiny ink-spot on the map. Although properly the property of Italy, the Italians have never enjoined to levy taxes in Campione, partly because Italian tax agents would have to leave Italy and pass through Switzerland to impose Italian law in Campione, and partly because of a mutual understanding with the Swiss that has traditionally kept Campione safe from tax collectors. Switzerland, on the other hand, doesn't impose its tax laws in Campione, because Switzerland has no jurisdiction to tax. The Italians are the legitimate landlords. Being small and self-governing, Campione has no income taxes and no local taxes.

The sole source of revenue for the economy is Campione's famous gambling Casino, which is owned by the Italian government. Because enough revenue is generated by the Casino operations alone to keep the enclave economically self-sufficient and satisfy the Italian government's own revenue objectives, no effort to levy taxes on residents (foreigners or locals) is likely to occur. Campione would probably disappear as a tourist and business attraction if taxes were levied. As far as the Italians are concerned, why ruin a good thing? Yes?

Language, Population & Accessibility

Campione's official language is Italian and its people are predominantly Italian. In Italy "Campione d'Italia" means "sample of Italy". English speaking schools can be found in nearby Switzerland, and educational facilities are said to be excellent. A European school in nearby Varese, Italy is also available.

Geographically, Campione lies within the Swiss canton of Ticino making Campione economically more allied with Switzerland. The Swiss franc is the currency in use, and Swiss telephone and telegraph services handle all the communications for Campione's 2,500 residents. The Swiss postal system delivers the mail, and if you write anyone in Campione, you always use the Swiss postal code CH-6911.

Campione resident permits are easy to get, something that cannot be said for Swiss permanent resident permits. Consequently, foreigners often reside in Campione, and make the short trip to Lugano to do their banking and take care of other business. Lugano is only minutes away, across the lake, and some 40+ banks there will welcome your business. Ironically, Campione has no banks or banking system of its own and for this relies on the Swiss.

Aside from no revenue agents to contend with, there are no border patrols to restrict your crossing Campione's borders.

Campione is about an hour by car or express train from Milan, two hours from Zurich, and six hours from Geneva. While there are no direct flights from the USA to Campione, frequent direct flights to the major Swiss cities make Campione only slightly less accessible than the major Caribbean tax havens.

Company Formation

Most lawyers and accountants live in Lugano, the center for local banking. It can be said there are two corporate forms a Campione company can take. In addition, the Swiss Aktiengesellsschaft (joint stock company) and the Liechtenstein Anstalt (establishment - a sort of "foundation") are commonly used when doing business in or from Campione. [3]

• **S.R.L.** (*Societa Responsibilita Limitada*) is a private limited liability company. The formation time is about <u>two</u> months. During the waiting period it is permitted to operate "under foundation". Advantages are:

- minimum paid-up capital of about $1,000.
- names of shareholders (anonymity) of the company can be kept secret.
- foreigners can start-up and own all the shares of a company, without the need for nominees or resident shareholders.

---

3. <u>Campione d'Italia</u> (the Swiss Back Door), by J.W. Windisch, Esq., pg 18, 19.

S.R.L.'s must keep proper books, and audited accounts must be presented to the Italian authorities each year. If the company does not carry on business with Italy, there is no tax liability to speak of. If it is essential that you carry on business with an Italian firm, it is best to form a Swiss or Liechtenstein intermediary company.

• **S.A.S**. (*Societa Accomandeta Semplice*): is a private unlimited liability company. Formation time is about <u>one</u> month. Note, however, this corporation is subject to Italian taxation and anonymity (keeping the real identity of the shareholders a secret) is not allowed. The main advantages include:

- minimum paid-up capital of about $1,300.
- bookkeeping is "closed" to Italian review.
- business with Italy creates no special tax problems.

• **Swiss Aktiengesellschaft** (joint stock company) or "A.G." will obtain the Swiss "domiciliary" status under Swiss law if it does not conduct business in Switzerland (including the canton of Ticino) and is managed from Campione. Swiss Federal taxes at the regular Swiss rates of up to 9.8% apply, with a further reduction if the "A.G." is merely a "holding company". Dividends from "substantial holdings" (20% or more) in foreign companies can be received by a "pure holding company" in Switzerland free from the Swiss Federal Tax. 4.

• **Liechtenstein Anstalt** (establishment) is a special type of company that is commonly used by Campione business persons. Formation is quick, anonymity of ownership is allowed, but some taxes in Liechtenstein are incurred, although they are low.

No tax treaties & no unauthorized disclosure

Campione has signed no income tax treaties with any nation, including the USA and Switzerland. Unauthorized disclosure of ones financial affairs would be a violation of local law.

Interestingly enough, the Swiss-U.S. Income Tax Treaty which allows the exchange of information between the IRS and Swiss tax authorities in specific but limited instances, does not make Switzerland a less attractive tax haven to be domiciled in. The Swiss and U.S. views on tax evasion have always been quite different, and the Swiss refuse to look upon tax evasion as a crime, unless records were falsified. Furthermore, Swiss bank secrecy laws have rarely been successfully penetrated by the IRS or other U.S. investigating bodies when no Swiss laws were broken.

Case in Point

Take for example the Iran-Contra arms-for-hostages scandal. It wasn't a breach of Swiss bank secrecy law that led to the problems Oliver North and General Richard Secord encountered. Why did these bandit-entrepreneurs choose to use Switzerland as a base to export arms to the Iranians in the first place? The answer to this question is simple. TAXES.

Under the old Swiss-U.S. income tax treaty (& before the *Tax Reform Act of 1986),* a Swiss employee (in this case General Secord or Hakim - both U.S. citizens) of a Swiss company could arrange for the sale of U.S. products (arms) from within the USA, and based on these facts alone, no U.S. income tax would be incurred because the income was considered "foreign source income" so long as the title of ownership was passed outside the USA. The Swiss-U.S. treaty excepted from taxation the Swiss company's "foreign source income". It would even have been permissible if Secord & Hakim opened a Swiss branch office within the USA to help set up the sales. Such income would still be considered from "foreign sources". The newer Swiss treaty closes this loophole.

Post Tax Reform Act '86 law made a few material changes to the "sourcing rules". While the "title passage rule" is still an important factor, it is also important that a foreign office *plays a material role* in the actual sale or transaction if the income is to be categorized as having a "foreign source". "New" Section 865(e)(2)(A) states when a **U.S. office** is involved in the transaction, income is treated as having a "U.S. source" regardless where title passes. This change in the "sourcing rules" could make Swiss exporters that operate through a U.S. **branch** office liable to federal income tax because the U.S. is allowed to tax "U.S. source income" of a Swiss branch (the treaty uses the term "permanent establishment"), but cannot tax "foreign source incomes". Luckily, Section §865(e)(2)(B) provides an "exception" from the sourcing rule for inventory, so the Section §865(e)(2)(A) *office sourcing rule* is overridden. 5.

---

4. Although Swiss canton and federal taxes can be substantial, there are some genuine loopholes in the Swiss tax system that make Switzerland a super-power of a financial center. For one, the Swiss do not tax foreign <u>branch</u> profits of a Swiss company, until remitted back to Switzerland. this is so even though, Swiss corporations are taxed on all their other worldwide incomes as it accrues. Furthermore, Switzerland levies its corporate tax every other year, not every year as in the US.

---

5. IRS published Notice 87-56 provides that 28 countries with tax treaties with the U.S. are not subject to the "new" branch level tax, Switzerland being one of the 28 excepted. See IRC §884.

Luxembourg

Little Luxembourg, located on the southeastern border of Belgium, is just 51 miles long and 34 miles wide. The country has existed since the 10th century when the counts owed their allegiance to the German Emperor. Although tiny in size, Luxembourg is a giant of a financial center (and tax haven), rivaling its neighbor Switzerland as the premier international banking center in Europe.

Luxembourg is generally considered to be a high tax jurisdiction with a corporate tax rate that ranges up to 33.3% to 39% in (1998). However, Luxembourg is a popular base for *Holding Companies* and *Investment Funds* which under Luxembourg's law of July 31, 1929 enjoy a complete exemption from income taxes. These *special* holding companies and mutual funds pay a small registration tax of 1% on capital subscribed upon incorporation or upon capital increases, and an annual *tax d'abonnement* which is computed roughly as 0.2% of the actual value of the shares issued (in the case of holding companies), and 0.06% in the case of *Investment Funds* (another name for mutual fund).

A Luxembourg holding company typically will hold the shares and bonds in domestic and foreign corporations, but it cannot engage in other types of business activities. A holding company or investment fund is not liable to tax on any of the following:

• dividends and interest and royalties collected.
• interest paid on bonds issued.
• profits arising from the sale or purchase of securities.
• participation in the profits of affiliated companies.
• capital gains from the sale of shares or other intangibles or fixed assets.

As of 1996 there were more than 5,000 registered holding companies in Luxembourg. More recently, the Investment Fund (UCIs) has become the prevalent investment vehicle. Through 1995 there were over 1,300 tax exempt funds with US$300 billion dollars under management. Today, practically every foreign bank in Luxembourg has a fund or plan to establish one soon.

As of 1996 there were 222 quality banks of international standing, and most of these came from Western Europe, the United States and Japan. Luxembourg's banks have been involved in the investment fund business for more than 25 years and are well equipped to meet two requirements of the **Law** on **collective investment**: (1) the assets of UCIs must be entrusted for safe-keeping to a custodian bank situated in the Grand-Duchy, and (2) the capital administration of UCIs established in Luxembourg must be located in the same country. today, Luxembourg's banks have over $400 billion in total deposits. [6.]

Bank Secrecy & Prevention of Fraud

To prevent fraud and create a respectable atmosphere in which to do business, Luxembourg requires that all companies file annual financial statements and publish these statements in the official gazette. However, numbered bank accounts are very common here, and bank secrecy is respected. In addition, Luxembourg corporations almost always issue *bearer shares.* A striking dissimilarity between U.S. law and Luxembourg's **Code Penal** is that bank officers here are not required to inform authorities of criminal acts by its clients.

Secrecy for Lux Banks Reaffirmed

Luxembourg reaffirmed its commitment to secrecy several years ago by giving legal backing to local banks that refuse to disclose account information to foreign tax authorities. The new laws were presented by special decree, signed on March 24, 1994 - bypassing normal parliamentary procedures. **Source: Financial Adviser**

Type of Company for International Trade and Investment

• 1929 Société Anonyme Holding Company
• 1929 Société à Responsabilité Limitee Holding Company
• 1990 Société de Participation Financière (SOPARFI) Trading and Holding Company

Procedure to Incorporate

The Acte de Constitution (Articles of Incorporation) have to be prepared in the form of a deed. This deed should include:

---

6. From *Investment Funds in Luxembourg - Booming Busines* by the <u>Association des Banques et Banquiers Luxembourg</u> (14, b Fr. Roosevelt L-2450 Luxembourg)(revised data from statistics i *Offshore 95* • Charterhouse Communications • London England).

- the name of the person(s) wishing to form the corporate entity
- the address of the Registered Office
- the amount and currency of the authorized capital
- type of shares and classes
- amount of capital paid up
- voting rights of shares
- names addresses and nationalities of the proposed directors.

In addition to the aforementioned a Certificate of name acceptability issued by the Trade Registry is required, together with a Certificate of Blockage produced by the proposed company's Luxembourg Bankers confirming that the paid up capital is deposited with them.

The aforementioned documents and information then have to be presented before a Notary Public by the proposed company's appointed representative. After notarization the Notary Public lodges the Articles of Incorporation and Bye-Laws with the Department of Registration and Trade Registry. The Articles of Incorporation are then published in the Official Gazette.

The Luxembourg Holding Company

A Luxembourg holding company is exempt from all forms of Luxembourg taxation but its activities are restricted to the holding of shares and certain other investments. In particular the company may not advance funds to its shareholders, invest in commodities or futures or carry out any sort of commercial or industrial activity.

The company may only hold property in so far as it is necessary for its own use but could, for example, own the shares of a property investment company. This type of company is specifically excluded from the tax treaties signed by Luxembourg except the treaty signed by China.
A 1929 Holding Company may:

- acquire, hold and dispose of shares and bonds in Luxembourg or foreign companies
- hold cash and foreign currencies and negotiate securities
- finance subsidiaries or companies where it has a direct shareholding

- hold and license patents and receive income from the granting of licenses
- issue bonds by private or public subscription of up to ten times the amount of its paid up capital
- borrow up to three times its issued capital.

Restrictions on Trading
A 1929 Holding Company may not:

- be an active member of a general partnership or partnerships limited by shares
- carry on any commercial or industrial activity
- carry on brokerage or banking activities
- carry on insurance, assurance or re-insurance activities
- own real estate other than its own premises
- grant loans to companies which are not subsidiaries
- render any type of advice or management services.

Taxation

A 1929 Holding Company is exempt from local taxation, but pays 0.2% per annum on its share capital, which is payable quarterly.

The Luxembourg Societé De Participation Financiere (Soparfi)

Luxembourg has recently extended its participation exemption regime and SOPARFI's are now subject to the normal rate of national and municipal Luxembourg tax except that, subject to the fulfillment of certain conditions, dividends and capital gains are not taxed.

Such companies are therefore able to take advantage of the EU parent/subsidiary directive 90/435 A SOPARFI is not excluded from the scope of the tax treaties concluded by Luxembourg and this may make this type of company extremely attractive for certain tax planning exercises.

Double Taxation Agreements

Luxembourg has entered into many double taxation agreements. As 1929 Holding Companies are exempted from local taxation, they are excluded from benefit of the Agreements.

Luxembourg companies with SOPARFI provisions may access Luxembourg's extensive treaty network. The centers include:

Austria, Italy, Belgium, Japan, Brazil, Morocco, Bulgaria, Netherlands, The Czech and Slovak Republics, Russia, Denmark, South Korea, Finland, Spain, France, Sweden, Germany, Switzerland, Greece, CIS (air traffic treaty only), Hungary, United Kingdom, Iceland (air traffic only), United States of America and Ireland.

Taxation of the SOPARFI Company

A SOPARFI company pay duty of 1% on the issue of new share capital. The minimum share capital is FLUX1,250,000 and at least 25% of the authorized capital must be paid up.

Shareholders

A minimum of two shareholders are required. Details of the shareholders appear on the public file but bearer shares are allowed. However, if bearer shares are to be issued then the full amount of the authorized capital must be paid up on incorporation so if anonymity is required it is often preferable to use nominee shareholders.

A minimum of three directors are required who may be corporate or individual. Details of the directors appear on the public file so anonymity may only be retained by appointing third party professionals to the Board.

As a matter of Luxembourg law the company MUST maintain a registered office address with in Luxembourg and must also appoint a Luxembourg based statutory auditor. We would generally provide these services as part of the domiciliary service fee.

All Luxembourg companies must file full audited accounts and books of accounts must be maintained at the registered office and updated on a regular basis.

Incorporation time is approximately 48 hours from receipt of capital and fees. Ready made companies are not generally available.

Restrictions On Name And Activity

Names must end with the word "Limited". The following words and their associated activities can not be used: Assurance, Bank, Building Society or any other words deemed sensitive or offensive, any name that is similar or identical to an existing name and any name of a major international corporation, where written consent to incorporate is not available. There are no other specific rules regarding name restrictions.

The 1990 normal Luxembourg Trading and Investment Company with SOPARFI provisions has no trading restrictions other than without the appropriate licenses it may not undertake the business of Banking, Insurance, Assurance, Re-Insurance, Fund Management, Collective Investment Schemes and any other activity that may suggest an association with the banking and insurance industries.

The real advantages of a 1990 normal Luxembourg Trading and Investment Company with SOPARFI provisions can be summarized as follows:

Companies investing in shares can benefit from the affiliation privilege; which means that these companies are fully subject to corporation tax, but exemptions are granted by law for dividends received from shareholdings; capital gains made on the sale of shareholdings; liquidation gains on liquidation of companies in which shares are held. This corporate tax exemption is granted with the following conditions:

• Dividend and liquidation gains exemption on shareholdings of at least 10% or a cost of at least LFR 50 million held at the start of the financial year of receipt, and at least 12 months prior to the end of the financial year of receipt.
• Capital gains exemption of shareholdings of at least 25% or costs of at least LFR 250 million held at least 12 months prior to the start of the financial year of sale.
• Under certain conditions financing costs, value adjustments and administration expenses are tax deductible.
• Zero withholding tax applies to dividends paid to an EC parent company (EC Directive 27 of 1990)
• Withholding tax on dividend payments to non EC countries, but may be reduced through tax treaty relief.

Holding companies in Belgium, Netherlands or Luxembourg

A holding company is a corporation that for the most part owns only shares (stock) in other related (i.e., subsidiaries) and unrelated companies. When international tax planners talk of offshore holding companies they most often mean companies incorporated in a no or low tax jurisdiction like Panama, Gibraltar, Barbados, Bermuda, the Bahamas or the Cayman Islands where stock holdings in other companies can be sold free of capital gains taxes, and dividends and interests received are free from local corporate taxation.

Be what it may, a number of high tax countries in western Europe have adopted corporate tax laws that offer significant tax advantages to holding companies that register within their territorial borders. The Netherlands, Luxembourg and Belgium make excellent domiciles for offshore finance and investment holding companies that invest in other companies domiciled in other high tax jurisdictions such as the U.S., UK, Canada and Germany. In addition to significant tax breaks for dividends and capital gains received on such stock participations, the Netherlands, Luxembourg and Belgium have important bilateral tax treaties with the other industrial countries (including the U.S., Canada, the UK, Germany and Australia) that reduce or eliminate withholding taxes on interest, dividends and royalties received by these holding companies.

Dutch "Participation Exemption"

Under the Netherlands tax code, a Dutch **"holding company"** that owns "at least 5%" of the par value of the paid-in capital in another **foreign** or **domestic company** from the beginning of the fiscal year can receive dividend distributions from this "subsidiary" 100% tax free. To qualify for the so called "participation exemption", the "downstream subsidiary" must meet the following conditions: [7.]

1) In the case of a foreign subsidiary the company must be subject to a corporate income tax comparable to the Netherlands corporate tax, but the rate and amount of corporate tax paid is immaterial.

2) the "participation" in the foreign subsidiary must be held for a business-related purpose, not as a mere "portfolio" investment. In this respect, if the Dutch parent company has a director on the board, or is actively engaged in the supervision of the subsidiary, than the company will qualify for the participation exemption provided the foreign subsidiary is not directly or indirectly merely an investment company.

Treaty Benefits for Dutch Finance Companies

Combining the Dutch Participation Exemption with the treaty benefits can and does lead to substantial tax savings for Dutch based holding companies. Under the U.S.-Netherlands tax treaty the 30% U.S. interest withholding tax is reduced to 0%. Moreover, under the Dutch tax system no interest withholding taxes on payments made to any nation (even to tax haven companies) are imposed on any Netherlands company because interest withholding taxes are unknown in the Netherlands. Because Holland maintains a net-work of tax treaties with many industrial nations that reduce significantly interest withholding taxes, the Netherlands make a first-rate base for the formation of an international bank, holding company or finance company. Other benefits of the participation exemption include:

1) the willingness of the Netherlands corporate tax inspector to grant special tax rulings in favor of Netherlands based finance companies.

2) interest payments made to foreigners are fully deductible when computing Dutch corporate income taxes so long as the payment is made at "arms length". Usually the Dutch corporate income tax inspector will "fix" the net taxable income of the company at a certain percentage of the total outstanding debt, or require that a certain "interest spread" between interest received and interest paid-out be used to

---

7. Not just dividends paid by the foreign subsidiary to the Dutch holding company qualify for the participation exemption, but cash distributions, dividends in kind, constructive dividends, shares issued from the share premium reserve, and capital gains realized on the liquidation proceeds from the disposal of the subsidiary's shares qualify as well. A capital "loss" is not deductible.

calculate the tax. A "spread ruling" from the tax inspector of 1/8% or 1/4% can usually be **"negotiated"** by the tax advisor. [8.]

3) so called "back-to-back loan arrangements" between a Dutch company and a tax haven entity are common and not looked on unfavorably by the Dutch tax authorities.

It's not surprising that by years-end 1987 the Netherlands with some $48 billion in U.S. investments could claim the second highest <u>direct</u> investments in the U.S., surpassing Japan's $32 billion, Canada's $22 billion, West Germany's $19 billion, and Switzerland $14 billion, and trailing only the United Kingdom's $76 billion investments in the USA.

Belgium's new "Participation Exemption"

Belgian holding companies that hold a participation in other companies can exempt 95% of any dividend received from such companies provided the other company is not located in a country that (1) does not tax corporate income or (2) which has a tax regime which is substantially more favorable than that in Belgium.

In addition, capital gains from the disposition of participation shares are 100% tax free from the 1992 tax year onward.

> **Editor's Note:** Unlike the participation exemption in the Netherlands, there is no minimum holding period and no minimum participation to qualify for the Belgian participation exemption.

The Belgian participation exemption does not apply if;

1) The dividends are distributed by companies which are not subject to taxation similar to Belgian corporate income tax. This includes no-tax jurisdictions:

Andorra
Anguilla
Bahamas
Bahrain
Bermuda

Campione
Cayman Islands
Ciskei
Grenada
Nauru
Saint-Pierre-et-Miquelon
Sark
Tonga
Turks & Caicos
Vanuatu

Also excluded from the participation exemption are IBCs in Jamaica, Barbados, Antigua and the British Virgin Islands and exempt companies in Gibraltar, and the Isle of Man. Also included are holding companies in Liechtenstein, Luxembourg and shipping companies based in Cyprus and Malta. In addition, countries that do not tax **foreign source income** - Panama, Singapore, Hong Kong, Costa Rica the Cook Islands, Djibouti, Malaysia, Nevis, and Oman.

2) Dividends distributed by a mere investment company.

Interest expenses are fully deductible

The Belgian corporate tax rate is 39%, and companies are taxed on their worldwide income. Since finance charges on loans (mainly interest) incurred to purchase the participation are deductible by the Belgium parent company, tax planning revolves around incurring the least amount of taxable income possible.

Tax treaties & withholding taxes

No Belgian withholding tax is due on (1) interest on commercial debts (including debts evidenced by commercial documents) and (2) interest paid by banks established in Belgium to foreign banks.

Dividends paid by a Belgian company to a nonresident individual or corporation is subject to a 25% withholding tax unless reduced by a tax treaty. Under the treaty with the U.S. dividend withholding is reduced to 5% or 15%.

Withholding taxes on dividends paid by U.S. company to a Belgian company that owns substantial holding in the U.S. company is reduced to 5%. Royalties are 100% free from U.S.

---

8. *"Non-Resident Owned Dutch Holding, Finance & Royalty Companies"*, published by the ABN Bank (Box 1469, 1000 BL Amsterdam), pg. 33.

withholding tax unless they are film and television royalties in which case the full 30% U.S. withholding tax applies. U.S. interest withholding tax is reduced to 15% under the Belgium-U.S. tax treaty.

Luxembourg's Participation Exemption

Luxembourg has been famous as a domicile for holding companies since 1929 when the Grand Duchy of Luxembourg abolished all income taxes and applied only a 0.2% annual subscription tax on share capital and a capital duty of 1% payable on this issue of new shares.

However, Luxembourg holding companies that qualify for the above tax exemption do not qualify for any treaty benefits that Luxembourg concluded with other nations.

Recently, to increase Luxembourg's attractiveness as a business and financial center, the Luxembourg government passed a law extending Luxembourg's participation exemption, which already existed for dividends, to capital gains if the company would be subject to Luxembourg's normal corporate tax regime (i.e., companies not exempt from tax under the 1929 Law). For 1991,

The participation exemption exempts cash dividends, dividends-in-kind, hidden profit distributions, capital gains on liquidation distributions, and capital gains on the sale of the qualifying subsidiary.

To qualify for the participation exemption and the tax treaty benefits the following conditions must be met.

(1) The parent company must be a resident and fully taxable in Luxembourg;

(2) For dividends to be exempted, the participation in the foreign subsidiary must equal at least 10% of the subsidiary's share capital or have an acquisition cost of at least LF 50 million;

(3) The participation must be held for an uninterrupted period of 12 months prior to the end of the taxable year in which the dividend is received;

(4)   For capital gains to be exempted, the shareholding in the foreign subsidiary must equal at least 25% of the subsidiary's share capital or have an acquisition cost of at least LF 250 million.

(5) To qualify for the participation exemption on dividends and capital gains, the nonresident subsidiary must be subject to corporate tax in its home country at a rate of at least 15%.

The exemption covers corporate income and wealth tax as well as municipal and local taxes.

Interest expenses are deductible

Interest paid on a loan to purchase a qualifying participation is deductible to the extent it exceeds the tax free dividends and gains. Luxembourg does not levy an interest withholding tax on interest paid to a foreign person, and there are no debt/equity ratio rules. Ratios as high as 33:1 are acceptable by the tax authorities.

A Luxembourg company may be collapsed without any tax consequences, and there is no capital gains tax on the disposal of shares in a Luxembourg corporation by a foreign person.

Tax Treaties & withholding taxes

Luxembourg has tax treaties with Austria, Belgium the U.S., France, Germany, the Netherlands, Spain, Sweden, Norway and the UK. Under the treaty with the U.S., Luxembourg' dividend withholding tax on portfolio investments paid to a U.S. resident is 7.5%, and reduced to 5% on substantial holdings where the recipient corporation owns at least 25% of the Luxembourg company's voting stock.

The U.S. dividend withholding rate is reduced from 30% to 15% on portfolio investments, and to 5% on substantial holdings. U.S. interest withholding tax is reduced to 0% if the Luxembourg company is subject to Luxembourg's regular corporate income tax.

Principality of Liechtenstein (an alpine refuge)

Tucked away neatly in the mountain valley between the Swiss canton of St. Gaul on the south and west and Austria on the east and north is tiny Liechtenstein, one of the smallest countries in the world. While small in size (just 65 square miles), Liechtenstein is a giant as far as offshore financial centers and tax havens are concerned, and is reputed to be the third richest country in the world. Liechtenstein's fame doesn't stem from the mere selling of postage stamps, although a sheet of pre-war agricultural designed stamps with a face value of SFr 5 is now worth some SFr 3,000. It's Liechtenstein's celebrated tax and political systems, renowned for its minimal taxation of foreigners, its strict bank secrecy (more impregnable than Switzerland's), and its long history of political stability that make her a powerhouse among the financial centers.

Crown Prince Hans Adam succeeded to the throne in 1989, on the death of his father, Prince Franz Josef II. Hans Adam's Gutenberg castle overlooks the capital of Vaduz. Inside the castle is a vast fortune in paintings, sculptures and tapestries, many bought directly from the great masters themselves. The royal family is also the principal owner of one of only three banks doing business in Liechtenstein, i.e., the **Bank In Liechtenstein**, or **BIL**. According to the 1921 constitution, Liechtenstein is a constitutional monarchy, hereditary in the male line.

> The top two U.S. debt rating agencies, Standard & Poor's and Moody's currently provide Liechtenstein with a triple A rating, primarily based on Liechtenstein's very favorable financial position and institutional political stability

Historically the **Principality of Liechtenstein** comprises the former territories of the County of Vaduz and the Lordship of Schellenberg. These were first united by inheritance in 1434 with the status of fiefs of the Holy Roman Empire. As you would expect, Liechtenstein today is predominantly Roman Catholic. At the beginning of the eighteenth century the two territories were purchased separately by Prince John Adam Andrew of Liechtenstein, whose name was taken from Liechtenstein's Castle, a former family possession south of Vienna. In 1719, the two territories were formerly reunited as the "Principality of Liechtenstein".

As a sovereign state since 1806, Liechtenstein has developed strong ties with both Austria and Switzerland. The official currency is the Swiss Franc, which is freely convertible into any other currency at prevailing market rates. Because Liechtenstein maintains no standing army (the frontier defence is furnished by the Swiss), there is no military budget to appropriate. This little haven boasts inflation of only 1.4%, a budget surplus, and no national debt. As if all this wasn't enough to be shout about, Liechtenstein levies no income taxes against any company that is domiciled there, provided the company does not receive Liechtenstein source income.

Today, a 5-member government is appointed by the prince on the recommendation of the Landtag (parliament), whose 15 members are elected every 4 years by direct universal suffrage; women won the right to vote in 1984. Liechtenstein's foreign affairs are handled by Switzerland. On Sept. 18, 1990, Liechtenstein became a member of the United Nations.

Anstalts, Stiftungs, Holding and Domiciliary Companies

For a country of just 28,000 people, pint sized Liechtenstein boasts more nonresident business entities than population. It is said there are between 30,000 and 70,000 trusts (called **Anstalts**), although the exact number appears to be a well-kept state secret. In Vaduz the lawyers outnumber the bankers. Moreover, with some 330 firms specializing in consulting, management and insurance, employing over 1,600 people, you don't have to look long for advice.

A nonresident can form an **anstalt** (English translation is *establishment),* which must have a minimum paid-in capital of **SFr 30,000** (about US$ 18,000), or a joint stock company (or **AG**) with a minimum capital of **SFr 50,000** divided into either registered or bearer shares. There are two types of joint stock companies permitted, i.e., **holding** and **domiciliary**. Another unique entity called a **Stiftung** *(foundation)* is also popular in Liechtenstein.

An **anstalt** is a separate entity much like a corporation. Like a corporation, it can have a business purpose. The original founder of an anstalt is generally a Liechtenstein lawyer of trust company, but he commonly resigns after the registration and transfers all rights on a *"declaration of cession"* to an unnamed successor (the real investor). This document is often held in a Swiss or Austrian bank vault, keeping the identity of the client doubly obscured.

An anstalt may elect to divide its capital into shares like a holding company, but if it so elects it will be subject to Liechtenstein's 4% **coupon tax** (a type of dividend withholding tax), as are all holding and domiciliary companies. Other than this **coupon tax**, an anstalt would not be subject to any income taxes in Liechtenstein. Its tax liability would be limited to Liechtenstein's annual **capital tax,** calculated as 0.1% of all capital and reserves.

> Aristotle Onassis is said to have kept over half his wealth in a Liechtenstein "public wealth foundation", the purpose and activity of which was, and still is, a well-kept secret.

There is some doubt among professionals whether the IRS will recognize an anstalt as a legal entity, and some European courts (namely the Belgium and Italian) have held that they are not. U.S. Professor Marshall J. Langer believes the IRS might categorize an anstalt as either a trust or an *alter ego* of the current holder of the founder's rights. Revenue Ruling 77-214 and several letter rulings published in 1977 (and later revoked) requires every company to have associates if it is to be classed as a company for tax purposes. Since an anstalt has no associates, Langer believes Americans and other nonresidents might do best to steer clear of exploiting the anstalt, and opt instead for a **domiciliary or holding company**. According to Professor Langer.....

"A nonresident alien should avoid using an anstalt to invest in U.S. property or securities, otherwise he runs the risk that he will be taxed personally on its income and, even worse that the Anstalt's U.S. stock and real estate will be taxable U.S. property for estate tax purposes upon his death." [9.]

Holding and Domiciliary Companies

A **holding company** is a corporate body having its registered seat in Liechtenstein with a purpose of entirely or mainly administering or managing assets and investments. The **domiciliary company** is a legal entity incorporated in any of the forms governed by the **Persons and Companies Code** that has its registered seat in Liechtenstein, but carries out **no** commercial activities within the country. The status for the qualification as domiciliary or holding company is therefore merely a question of the company's purpose.

Business entities having the status of domiciliary or holding companies are: 1) exempt from any income tax, property tax (with exception for real estate in Liechtenstein) and capital gains tax, 2) not required to file a tax return, but merely furnish audited financial statements to the tax authorities, 3) must maintain

an office in Liechtenstein, but the registered seat need be nothing more than a mailing address, 4) afforded absolute secrecy regarding tax matters.

> A holding company is an AG that primarily holds shares in other companies. A domiciliary company is an AG that has its corporate seat or domicile in Liechtenstein but carries on its commercial activities *outside* the country. Neither pays any income tax, but instead pay an annual capital tax of 1/10th of 1% on their capital and reserves, with a minimum tax of SFr 1,000 (about US$620) payable annually.

Stamp taxes & 4% Coupon tax

Liechtenstein has a thriving industrial base in addition to its tax haven styled economy. Normal tax rates range from 7.5% to 15% for companies manufacturing within the country, with an innocuous 4% **coupon tax** (another name for dividend withholding tax) on cash (or in kind) distributions to shareholders. The **withholding tax** applies to holding and domiciliary companies and anstalts limited by shares. It is also applicable to certain loans with durations over two years. [10.]

Other *hidden* Liechtenstein taxes to consider are a stamp duty due on the transfer of shares or bonds in foreign (0.3%) or domestic issuers (0.15%), and a 3% formation stamp tax due on the creation of shares or participation rights in a company.

To understand better how a typical anstalt **domiciliary** or **holding** company might be *started-up* and taxed under the Liechtenstein tax system, let's look at an unpretentious example.

> **EXAMPLE #1**: Nonresident international businessman **X** claims Campione in the nearby Swiss Alps his tax home. **X** invests $50,000 as paid-in capital in his Liechtenstein holding company **Y,** and lends an additional $950,000 short-term for two years to **company Y**. In 1989, holding company **Y** re-invests the entire proceeds in U.S. Treasury bonds issued after July 18, 1984 paying 10% interest pa.
>
> The annual interest earned on the T. bonds would amount to $100,000 pa. No U.S. withholding tax will be withheld by the U.S. Treasury on payments of interest to Y, because the **Tax Reform Act of 1984** repeals all interest withholding taxes on "portfolio" type bond interest. Since company **Y** does not carry-on any business within Liechtenstein, no income taxes will be levied on **Y**. However, a **capital tax** equal to 1/10th of 1% of the **paid-up capital and reserves** of **Y** (but excluding the 1st year profits of Y) will be payable annually to the Liechtenstein tax administration. This

---

9. From <u>Practical International Tax Planning,</u> pg 276.

10. A withholding (coupon) tax of 4% is levied on interest from bonds and similar loans and on time deposits with domestic banks with a term in excess of 12 months and loans in excess of SFr 50,000 with a minimum term in excess of two years, but not on interest of normal intercompany loans.

computes to a capital tax of $50. However, a **minimum** capital tax of SFr 1,000 (about US$620) is payable by every company, so the actual first year **capital tax** paid will equal $620. This equates into a 0.62% profits tax rate, so far.

Assuming no dividends are paid to non-resident shareholder X, the 4% **coupon tax** could be avoided, leaving no further taxes to be levied against company Y. To secure a tax free capital gain, X might sell the shares in Liechtenstein holding company Y to a friend in Campione.

It should be pointed-out that when holding company Y purchases or sells the $1,000,000 in U.S. treasury bonds a stamp transfer tax equal to 0.3% (or $3,000) will be payable to the tax administration. In addition, a 0.15% stamp tax on the face value of the $950,000 Liechtenstein corporate loan (or $1,425) will be payable upon its culmination with X. A one time formation stamp tax of 3% (or $1,500) of the $50,000 paid-up share capital of Y would also be payable. Effectively, the overall tax rate of nonresident X's holding company would equal about 7% in start-up year 1989. In 1990 the taxes payable would drop to only $620, for an effective tax rate of only 0.62%, assuming no additional stamp transfer taxes were incurred.

Bank in Liechtenstein (BIL)

Liechtenstein's banks are smallish by international standards, and tend to be overshadowed by the Principality's specialized business in trusts and domiciliary companies. More than 25,000 foreign businesses and banks have established nominal headquarters in Liechtenstein because of favorable tax policies.

Outside the small National Bank there are just three banks in Liechtenstein you can contact. The oldest is Liechtensteinische Landesbank founded in 1861. Landesbank, however, was recently acquired by the Bank in Liechtenstein - or BIL for short. BIL was founded in 1920.

BIL has approximately US$3.8 billion dollars on its balance sheet. Top management is cosmopolitan, consisting of board members from First Austrian Bank and Bank Leu in Zurich. Chairman of the Board Christian Norgren is from the Walenberg empire in Sweden. BIL's Paris branch boasts Prince Philip of Liechtenstein as the vice-chairman. Prince Phillip's presence highlights the fact that BIL has one voting shareholder - a Foundation for the Royal Family's assets.

According to Reinhard Schmolz, chief executive officer of BIL (UK), there is a grand total of SFr 340 billion (or **US $210 billion dollars**) in funds being managed by BIL. The true figure has never been made public. BIL has offices in Hong Kong, Cayman, New York, Rio de Janeiro, Frankfurt, Lugano, Zurich, Geneva and London. It's overseas staff has increased by about 320 in the past three years.

BIL is a subsidiary of the **Prince Franz Joseph II Von und zu Liechtenstein Foundation**. Guided by a formidable board of trustees, including Dr. Alfred Herrhausen of Deutsche Bank (Germany's largest), BIL has convinced many of Europe's millionaires to invest their money with them, making BIL's private client portfolio management department one of the largest in the world.

Accessibility

For Americans, landlocked Liechtenstein is only slightly less accessible than the Bahamas, Bermuda and Cayman Islands. The northern border touches the international railway between Basel, and Innsbruck while the highway from Switzerland to Austria leads right through Vaduz. Zurich's airport is only one hour away by highway.

If you travel by train you should depart at the Swiss border town of Buchs and take one of the frequent yellow PYY coaches to Vaduz. The journey takes about 20 minutes less than if you go through the other Swiss station at Sargans, or Feldkirch in Austria.

Vaduz has no taxicabs and no major hotels, but there are about 200 first-class beds available, including 30 at the grand old *Vaduzer Hof*. If you're looking for a place to put your money where taxes are low, you should take a trip to pint sized Liechtenstein and explore the possibilities.

For more information on starting a business in Vaduz, Liechtenstein write:

Bank IN Liechtenstein AG
P.O. Box 85
FL-9490 Vaduz, Liechtenstein
Tele: 51122 Telex 889222 BIL FL
or
Private Trust Bank Corporation
Postfach 885
FL-9490 Vaduz, Liechtenstein
Tele:56655 Telex 889200 VPB FL

Bank secrecy and confidentiality of one's financial affairs are so guarded in this community that Professor Naylor publisher of *"Hot Money"* has alleged that various foreign secret services and criminal groups are using the tiny territory for their money laundering. While screening out spies and undesirables may be a difficult task for Liechtenstein's little government, legitimate tax planners and financiers can rest assured that Liechtenstein's landlords aim to keep a respectable image. According to Crown Prince Hans Adam, Liechtenstein's **Regent**, a 1980 revised company law now requires that "any commercial enterprise administering trusts or investment funds, to have qualified managers and auditors which requires a government license to operate." [11]

11.*"Discretion rules (and money talks) in pint sized Principality"* by John Burke, **Offshore Adviser**, March 1989, pgs. 20 to 24.

Monaco • Eden on the French Riviera

If it was not for its size (2 square kilometers), Monaco might someday evolve into a Goliath of a tax haven like Luxembourg or the Bahamas. Extending only four blocks from the sea, Monaco's three casinos, the old fortress like Palace of Prince Rainier ("the Rock"), and the high-rise apartments for the rich and famous along "Avenue Princess Grace", leave little room for construction of 20th century style bank and office buildings. Monaco's attraction is her magnificent medieval buildings, interspersed among splendid restaurants, gardens and small stores, and a harbor chock full of luxury yachts from all corners of the Mediterranean. Very simply, there just isn't much room left for high-rise office buildings in pint size Monaco.

World famous city of Monte Carlo

The *Principality of Monaco* is the official name for the country. *Monte Carlo* (the city) is the name most people associate with the area around Monaco's famous gambling **"Casino"**, a Gothic structure architecturally similar to the Paris Opera House. Across the street at the Loew's Hotel is yet another casino where high-rollers from Las Vegas, Atlantic City, Beverly Hills, and Palm Beach meet to gamble and socialize. The streets and parking lots outside are replete with Rolls Royces, Maseratis, Ferraris, Cadillacs, Lamborghinies, Porsches, antique Deusenbergs, and Mercedes.

Aside from the very rich and famous, the aristocrats and multi-millionaires, Monaco's 35,000 permanent residents are just middle and upper-middle-class folks sharing in the good life. While French is the official language, English, Italian and German are spoken by almost everyone. About 1,000,000 tourists pass through Monaco each year, with approximately 25,000 Americans and Englishmen among them in any given month. A friendlier more lovable place you will never find.

No Personal Income Taxes

The Grimaldi family has presided over Monaco's constitutional monarchy for over 500 years even while France was being torn by war and revolution. For a brief period between 1793 and 1813 Monaco did become part of France, but independence was later reinstated. In 1918 France and Monaco signed a treaty providing that should the Grimaldi dynasty die out Monaco would revert to the French.

After **WWII** Monaco developed into a favorite tax haven for French industrialists looking to escape France's rising tax rates. This loss of tax revenue from French coffers prompted former President Charles de Gaulle to declare Monaco's tax haven status dangerous to France, and a new treaty was forced upon Monaco's rulers and signed in 1963.

Under the new treaty French citizens who take up residence in Monaco after 1957 would have to pay income taxes. Luckily, the treaty provides that Monegasques and foreigners could stay exempt from French income taxes.

Setting up business in Monaco

Monaco's economy, with more than 3000 businesses, continues to be robust and diverse. More than 3000 businesses work in the sectors of vitality, and a diversity which is confirmed year after year. Traditional sectors such as Tourism and Construction remain steady, while new sectors such as telecommunications, computing and shipping continue to develop. Monaco thus remains a favorable business climate.

A preliminary authorization from the Sovereign Government is a prerequisite to any business, craft, or industrial activity or provision of service.

In order to apply for an authorization, one must: 1) Address a completed dossier to:

Department of Economic Expansion
Director : M. Jean-Pierre Campana
9, rue de Gabian
Corporations: Tel. +377 93 15 84 93
Individuals: Tel. +377 93 15 84 14

Legal forms of companies sanctioned in Monaco Individual enterprises and collective commercial bodies other than companies :
• Individual Enterprise
• Guild for mutual economic assistance (GIE)

Commercial companies :
• General Partnership (SNC)
• Limited Partnership (SCS)
• Partnership Limited by Shares (SCA)
• Monegasque Limited Company (SAM) Minimum capital 1,000,000 F.
Administrative offices and sub-offices :
• Administrative Office, acting purely on behalf of the group(s) it represents.
• Agency, Sub-office to a foreign concern. Once these formalities are satisfied, commercial

and industrial companies must enroll on the Trade and Industry Register (Répertoire du Commerce et de l'Industrie), which will provide them with a registration number.

Today, companies doing more than 25% of their business outside Monaco are subject to tax. Monaco's corporate tax rate is a flat 35%, but this can be circumvented with a little planning. Typically, to avoid taxation on one's foreign profits, a Monaco **base company** will keep only its administrative offices in Monaco while organizing subsidiaries in other tax havens. Under such a set-up the base company would pay a 35% Monegasques tax on 8% of its office expenses. If office expenses amount to US$50,000 a year the tax would amount to US$1,400.

Residency for foreigners in Monaco

Persons of foreign nationality (non-Monegasque Citizens) wishing to stay for a period of more than 3 months in the Principality must apply for a visa from the French Consular Authority nearest their most recent domicile, in accordance with the mutual assistance agreement ("Convention de Voisinage") signed by France and Monaco in 1963.

Anyone of foreign nationality residing in France with a valid "carte de séjour" (residence permit), and wishing to transfer to Monegasque residence is exempt from these visa formalities.

Application for a visa should include proof of means of existence (work contract or membership of a foreign company, bank references, lease), and documents relative to housing conditions in the Principality (ownership agreement, lease agreement, lodging certificate). The visa may be granted about three months after request. The visa entitles the holder to a "carte de séjour", a renewable residence permit issued by the Monegasque Authorities and valid for a period of one year.

Artists, consultants, authors, script writers and others *without* permanent staff can do business from one's own apartment provided the business is neither labor intensive nor a nuisance. The Government encourages such enterprises, not even calling for such operations to be registered.

The rock-bottom cheapest room available in Monaco would cost you about $100/month, but unless you're hiding from the IRS or KGB you probably wouldn't want to live there. A pleasant studio with a decent view, marble floors and good appliances can be rented for as little as $750. Those with means seeking the best accommodations should check-out the apartments on *"Avenue Princess Grace Boulevard"*. Here rents begin at $2,000 per month and move upwards. Almost all the apartments buildings in this area of town are owned by the wealthiest family in Monaco - the Pastores.

Estate, Gift & Inheritance Taxes

Assets situated within Monaco are subject to estate taxes. For those in direct-line (wife, parents, or children) to the deceased the tax is zero regardless of the amount.

Gifts or inheritances to brothers and sisters are taxed at 8%; uncles, aunts, nephews, nieces at 10%; other blood relatives at 13%; unrelated parties and foreign charities at 16%. Securities held by a Monaco bank are subject to inheritance taxes. To avoid Monaco's estate, inheritance and gift taxes, an offshore trust or holding company located in a no-tax haven is recommended.

Real estate transfer taxes

Real estate taxes in Monaco, France, Italy and Spain are more or less nonexistent. This, however, is not a windfall or loophole the investor can exploit because **transfer taxes** on the sale of a real estate property situated in Monaco can amount to 16% or more.

Monaco requires all transfers of real estate to be registered, with a 7.5% fee going to the State. More fees of 3% to a Notaire, and 3% to 6% to the real estate agencies can be expected. Turning-over a real estate property for a quick profit is not possible with expenses these high, but there are some steps you can take to duck these **transfer taxes**.

Acquiring your Monaco apartment or condominium with an *offshore holding company* will allow you to avoid the transfer taxes. Use of *bearer shares* is sometimes recommended. Later, when you want to sell the Monaco property, you simply sell the shares in the company to the buyer in the offshore tax haven. The State of Monaco recognizes that such transactions happen frequently, but there is no change of ownership as far as the Monaco tax authorities are concerned.

Malta – *New* tax haven in the Mediterranean

Situated almost exactly in the center of the Mediterranean Sea between southern Europe and North Africa is an archipelago known as **The Republic of Malta.** Total land area of this archipelago is 122 square miles (about the same as the Cayman Islands), with the island of Malta (95 sq. miles) and Gazo (25 sq. miles) being, for all practical purposes, the only isles with human inhabitants.

History & People, Language, Religion

Malta has a long and varied history, as is evidenced by the many megalithic temples and other sites among the finest in the region. The **Phoenicians** appear to be the first foreign people to occupy the islands, followed by the **Carthaginians.** After the destruction of Carthage, Malta was absorbed into the **Roman Empire**. St. Paul the Apostle was shipwrecked on the islands in AD 60, and the country has been Christian ever since. The Feast of St. Paul's Shipwreck is a statutory holiday celebrated on February, 10 - every year. There are 13 other national holidays, and business comes to a halt on each one of them.

Approximately 320,000 people live in the Maltese islands. Malta is one of the most densely populated countries in the world. As a people, the Maltese are considered Southern Europeans.

The *Maltese* language is Semitic in structure, with 50% of the words being of European origin (mostly Sicilian, Italian and English). Nearly all of Malta's people are bilingual. **English** is the second official language of the country, and spoken by almost everyone.

Publications, including laws, are issued in both *English* and *Maltese.* Banking and legal documents, including official correspondence, are drawn up in English. In most secondary schools, instruction is carried out in English. [12.]

Malta's new tax incentives are for the "small fry as well as the big fry"

Efforts have been under way since the 1980s to transform Malta into a prime international industrial, financial and maritime center. Around that time, John Borg Bartolo, chief executive of the Malta International Business Authority (MIBA), announced Malta plans to become the Switzerland or the Luxembourg of the Mediterranean. *"We believe we have the edge over other centers. Switzerland has become far too expensive even for the big fry, and the Swiss are rude and arrogant people towards the small fry. Yes. I do believe we will replace Switzerland and Luxembourg in 10 to 15 years. I do not mean we will drive them out of business, but with a little tact and diplomacy we should get much of the new investment. We believe there is a huge private market from the Middle East and the south of Malta, and a huge corporate market from the developed countries."*

Malta's **Industrial Development Act** (enacted in June 1988) provides attractive incentives to export-oriented industrial concerns, including a 10 year tax holiday. This together with Malta's Association Agreement with the European Community (EC) allows total accessibility to the EC for all industrial products of Maltese origin. In addition, legislation passed in late 1988 to attract foreign investment elevates Malta into a competitive position with other offshore centers.

- Malta International Business Activities Act, 1988 (MIBA).
- Offshore Trusts Act, 1988
- Merchant Shipping (Amendment), 1988
- Industrial Development Act, 1988

- Companies Act 1995; Malta Financial Services Act Centre 1994; Investment Services Act 1994; Banking Act 1994; Financial Institutions Act 1994.

Malta's Tax System

The sole taxing authority is the Government of Malta. There are no municipal or local taxes to worry about.

Unless a company qualifies for one of the incentives mentioned above, Malta generally levies a flat rate of tax (35% for 1998) on companies resident or managed and controlled in Malta. Maltese companies are taxed on their worldwide income irrespective of whether this has been derived in Malta or elsewhere. Foreign source income is taxed exactly as Malta source income. **Capital gains are not taxed** unless it can be shown that the relative transaction was itself an act of trade or business.

Individuals are taxed on their worldwide incomes if they are either domiciled or ordinary

---

12. Thanks to Price Waterhouse for their Information Guide - *"Doing Business in Malta"* (May 1983 - update January 1, 1998)

resident in Malta. A person is considered domiciled in a country where he has his permanent home. A person is considered resident in Malta when he is so resident in the ordinary course of his life.

Persons who are not ordinary resident or domiciled in Malta are taxable only on their Malta source income and on foreign source income that is remitted back to Malta. Whether foreign source income is actually remitted is a question of fact. Malta does not tax capital gains unless they are of speculative nature. Speculative capital gains from outside Malta received by persons not ordinarily resident in Malta are usually not taxed even if remitted back to Malta.

Expatriate employees and directors of offshore companies pay a top income tax rate of 30% (only on Malta generated wages, and income) while ordinary residents pay a top rate of 55%.

International Business Activities Act, 1988

The **MIBA Act** provides for the setting up of an Authority which will act as a channel for prospective applicants and the government departments to make contact, and transmit requests and exchange information. The MIBA Authority was officially constituted on January 24, 1989.

The incentives and exemptions in the Act are available only to offshore companies that register with the Authority, and they are not allowed or granted uniformly. They depend on the type of offshore company, and the type of activities it proposes to carry on. In this respect, offshore companies are divided into trading and non-trading companies.

Offshore banking, insurance or general trading companies

Trading companies, including banking and captive insurance companies, receive the following incentives:

1. A low **5% rate of income tax** and the right to self-assessment. "It's up to the tax people to prove your returns are not correct", according to Borg Bartolo.
2. **Exemption** from all exchange controls, stamp duties, death and donation duties and withholding tax, as well as **no capital gains tax.**
3. **Exemption** from custom duties on the importation of the company's requirements and of the personal belongings of nonresident officers or employees of the company.

4. **Guarantee of the rights,** exemptions and other privileges under the Act by creating a contractual obligation between the government and the registered offshore company.

Banking and Insurance companies are exempt from several requirements imposed on onshore banks and insurance companies. These include, liquidity ratios and solvency margins in the case of banks, inadmissible assets and reserve funds in the case of insurance companies.

Offshore Investment holding (nontrading) companies.

Nontrading companies are those founded for the management of any kind of personal property, such as investment portfolios - stocks, bonds, etc. Nontrading companies under the Act include a company which, in respect to ships, has as its object not only the ownership and management thereof, but also their operation, provided the ship is registered in Malta. The concept of nontrading company is new to Malta, as the law speaks about companies as **"commercial partnerships"**.

Investment (i.e., nontrading) Companies are given complete exemption from income tax. Directors, shareholders and assets of nontrading companies are guaranteed total anonymity and confidentiality. A nominee company, will, when necessary, appear as the only registered director of such company. The Malta government promotes this form of secrecy of one's financial affairs openly.

Other advantages of **Offshore Companies** include:

1. Provisions for transmission of shares and debentures on death as set out in the Articles of Association, including quasi-testamentary provisions which will take effect notwithstanding **any** law, including the home-country laws of the share or debenture holders otherwise applicable.
2. Removal, in the case of nontrading offshore companies, of the normal accounting and audit requirements.
3. Provisions for the continuance, without liquidation and reconstituting under the local law of the companies originally constituted under the law of any other country, and the continuance under the law of foreign countries of companies constituted under the said local law.

Offshore Nontrading Companies are required by law to be formed through local nominee companies run by Maltese residents. These nominee companies service the offshore company to insure local accountability and compliance. Nonresidents can participate up to 40% in the nominee companies.

Offshore Trusts Act, 1988

Up until just a few years ago, Malta did not provide legislations for the formation of offshore trusts. With the creation of the **new companies** law for offshore companies the government felt it would enhance their competitiveness if they also provided laws for the creation of offshore trusts.

The Offshore Trusts Act is limited to the creation of trusts by nonresidents, where the property held in trust does not include immovable property in Malta, and where the beneficiaries, at least initially, are nonresidents. The Offshore Trusts Act follows closely the U.K. law for trusts as found in Jersey in the Channel Islands.

The trustees must be Maltese nominee companies in possession of a valid warrant issued by the Authority.

Merchant Shipping (Amendment) Act, 1988

This Act revises the arrangements for the registration of ships under the Malta flag, the issue of certificates of registry, and the cancellation of registry. The new fee structure is very competitive with initial registration fees transferred from Panama set at US$2,400.

The Maltese government issued the following statement on December 11, 1988 saying.

"The free flow of international shipping and world trade are an essential lifeline for Malta, an island State located in the centre of the Mediterranean. A number of measures intended to minimize the inconvenience and expense of shipowners wishing to re-flag their vessels following the ban on Panamanian ships are being put into immediate effect.

"The introduction of round-the-clock service at the Registry of Shipping in Malta, and the appointment of Registrars in London, New York, Hong Kong and in Bonn, together with the service given through Consulates, particularly the one in Piraeus, will ensure a quick and efficient service".

"Not only are Maltese ships not hindered by trading restrictions, but in certain ports they even enjoy a special treatment. This, together with a tax system favorable to shipowners, charters and financiers of Maltese ships, and the introduction of the new measures just announced, make the Malta register an even more attractive and competitive alternative ensuring minimal inconvenience to shipowners."[13.]

All types of vessels from pleasure yachts to oil rigs to ships under construction, irrespective of their age, may be registered in Malta as follows:

1. The maximum size of Maltese ship that need not be registered will be limited to 24 meters, rather than to tonnage.
2. Two (or more) persons or companies may constitute a body corporate;
3. All shareholders and directors may be non-Maltese;
4. A local representative may be authorized to form the company;
5. Minimum amount of paid-up capital is £M400; and
6. Minimum company registration fee (paid once only) is £M100, with an annual registration fee of £M25 thereafter.

Dividend distributions of profits earned from the operation of exempted ships are tax free to shareholders.

Further information on registering a ship in Malta can be obtained by writing:

The Registrar of Partnerships,
Department of Trade,
Valletta, Malta
telephone: 224411, 605399
telex: 1106 or 1107 TRADMINMT

Industrial Development Act, 1988

Ordinarily, profits derived from the conduct of a trade or business within Malta are taxable. In an effort to create a better investment climate for foreign investment, Malta's government enacted its Industrial Development Act, which provides tax holidays of up to ten years for qualifying enterprises. Briefly, some incentives under this Act are:

1. **Tax Holiday:** Ten year tax holiday to new industries which are export oriented (95% of turnover).
2. Export incentive scheme: For existing industries and for new industries which do not meet the 95% test of "1" (above), exemption is given from tax on additional export profits.
3. **Reduced tax rate:** A substantial reduction of tax rates on profits earned from projects approved by the Malta Development Corporation.

---

13. From *Malta eases registry for transfers of ships,* by Clemens Kochinke (Berliner & Maloney), **International Tax Report**, pgs 8-10 (March, 1990)

Principality of Andorra

Tucked away high in the Pyrenees mountains on the borders of France and Spain lie tiny Andorra, Europe's most remote tax haven. It takes three and a half hours by car to reach Andorra from the nearest airports in Barcelona in Spain and Toulouse in France. Talk in Andorra is than an airport is scheduled to be completed within two years, but currently access is limited to ground transportations.

Andorra is a tiny state of 453 sq km (175 sq mi), located on the border of France and Spain and surrounded by them. It has a population of 54,428 (1992 est.), with the capital city of Andorra-la-Vella accounting for 15,698.

The land and people

Set in the eastern Pyrenees, Andorra is a contrast of high mountains and deep valleys. The Valira River drains the area. Temperatures in the valleys can reach 32 deg C (90 deg F) in the summer, but the winters are cold (average January temperature is about 0 deg C/32 deg F), with an abundance of snow. One major highway connects Andorra with France and Spain, and other roads make the whole area accessible by automobile. The country has no railroad and no airline.

Approximately 60% of Andorra's citizens are of Spanish origin; 6% are French. One-third are descendants of an ancient tribe known in Roman times as Andosians, from whom the country got its name.

Legend has it that Charlemagne granted the mountaineers of Andorra independence in gratitude for them guiding his army through the Pyrenees in his battle to expel the Arabs from southern France and Spain.

The main language is Catalan, and Spanish and French are spoken widely. Roman Catholicism is the official religion.

Economy

Only 4% of Andorra's land is arable, so that the country must import food from France and Spain. Tobacco, potatoes, rye, and buckwheat are grown in the lower valleys, where a few vineyards and olive groves are also located. Large flocks of sheep are brought from France and Spain each summer to graze on the abundant mountain pastures. Small quantities of iron, lead, silver, and alum are mined. Three major hydroelectric plants enable Andorra to export electricity to Spain.

For many centuries Andorra's most profitable, although unofficial, industry was smuggling between Spain and France. This remains a profitable sideline for some, but in recent years tourism has become by far the nation's largest industry. Tourism and rapid growth were spurred in the 1960s when Andorra established itself as a duty-free area. Excellent skiing in the winter, hunting and fishing, and the many folk festivals in the summer, as well as the mineral baths at Les Escaldes, have generated a tourist flow of more than 6 million visitors a year.

Currency

Andorra has no sales tax, and both French and Spanish currency are recognized as legal tender (it has none of its own). Its postal system is free, being totally supported by the sale of Andorran stamps to collectors around the world.

No taxes & no political parties

Andorra advertises itself as having no political parties, no race problems, no unions, no serious crime, and, no income taxes of any kind. Andorra also claims to have no immigration difficulties, no restriction on the movement of money and no obstacles to purchases or resales of real estate properties. Cisa, the main Andorran developer, can guarantee 60% mortgages in any currency and offers rental programs.

Until recently, Andorrans were governed jointly by two 'suzerains' - the Spanish bishop of Urgel and the French president. But, in a referendum, a modem constitution was voted in which restricts the powers of the 'co-princes' and puts decisions on the future of Andorra and its 50,000 foreign inhabitants firmly in the hands of the people.

Since the arrival of the first non-feudal government, with the centre-right Agrupament Nacional Democratic party leading a reform-minded coalition government, Andorra has moved to relax its strict foreign-owned financial services operators rules. It has been thought that one way of raising revenue would be to attract the international financial services community and apply small stamp and customs duties. But the French fiscal authorities, who keep a close eye on their citizens' dealings with Andorra, have strong objections to Andorra's politicians turning Andorra into a British style tax haven like Gibraltar.

Foreigners have no problem living in Andorra. To obtain residency foreigners must prove that they are self-supporting with income sources from outside of the country and must make a minimum deposit in a local bank that is to be permanently available. Retirees are almost always given preference. The low cost of living is yet another reason why retirees find Andorra attractive. Real estate, however, can be somewhat expensive due to demand.

Already there are some 1,200 UK expatriates and tax refuges, *"too rich to die and too poor to live"* in the words of one resident, who have settled in Andorra. According to Sr. Candid Noudi Mora, whose family owns Cisa, Andorra is presently negotiating with the EC with a view to having the advantages of EC membership but none of the disadvantages. *"We will make no concessions regarding taxation matters."*

> Several years ago, a group of suspected share traders calling themselves **"Medatlantic"** who had previously worked out of Holland, lasted two weeks in **Andorra** before being expelled. *"We have no agreement with INTERPOL, but we exchange information and if we don't like somebody we politely tell them we don't want them in Andorra tomorrow."* says Sr Noudi.

Government and History

In 1278 the feudal state of Andorra was placed under the joint rule of the Spanish bishop of Urgel and the French count of Foix. The system remained technically the same until 1993, when Andorra's citizens voted to adopt a constitution establishing a parliamentary co-principality, with separate executive, legislative, and judicial branches. The country, which is governed by a general council of 24 elected representatives, is independent and pays token homage to Spain and France. Women obtained the right to vote in 1970. Andorra, like Switzerland, maintains a policy of strict neutrality in international affairs.

The tiny principality set in a Pyrenean valley wedged between France and Spain is still, according to local property agents Roc Proprietas, "one of the few remaining tax havens. Its prosperity is based upon free trade, freedom from taxes and an absence of bureaucratic excesses". Roc Proprietas also highlight the safe crime-free environment for the resident, a moderate cost of living, excellent communications, a highly-efficient and totally confidential banking system and generally excellent weather. In addition, they promise the investor sustained growth of property values, total absence of taxes and guaranteed security.

It is debatable whether Andorra qualifies for the title of international finance centre. Though there is neither value added tax nor income tax, most of Andorra's very high income per capita of over US$16,000 is derived from skiers and shoppers. The signs of financial life are in Andorra La Vella's three miles of duty-free shops where banks jostle for attention, conducting offshore business in freely-interchangeable francs and pesetas and without the hindrance of exchange controls.

Andorra's politicians will he careful of trying to raise revenue by taxing the citizens, however indirectly. On previous occasions when the government attempted to impose a bank deposit tax and a hotel guest tax, it has been forced to resign, such was the strength of the opposition to anything resembling taxation.

Andorra's peculiar status seems set to continue - not a complete international financial services centre, but a place where business can be conducted tax-free; not a part of the European Community, nor a specially recognized external area like Gibraltar, Madeira, nor completely separate, like the Channel Islands or the Isle of Man. It is likely to remain a place for skiing and shopping rather than international financial services until legal changes allow the Pyrenean state to be promoted as an offshore centre with tax incentives for international business.

Maderia (island paradise and tax haven)

The Madeira Islands, a volcanic archipelago in the Atlantic Ocean 645 km (400 mi) west of Morocco, constitute the Madeira Autonomous Region of Portugal. They comprise the inhabited islands of Madeira and Porto Santo and the uninhabited Desertas and Selvagens, having a total land area of 798 sq km (308 sq mi) and a population of 273,200 (1989 est.). FUNCHAL, the capital and largest town, is on Madeira.

Madeira, the largest and most important island, is mountainous with a subtropical climate. Sugarcane and tropical fruits are grown. The island is famous for its wine and for the embroidery and wickerwork produced; it is also a popular resort. On Porto Santo Island, northeast of Madeira, wheat, barley, and grapes are cultivated. When you ask people what comes to mind when you mention Madeira, most will say fortified wine and Reid's Hotel, but there is much more to this pleasant and rugged island which lies 625 miles south west of Lisbon and more than 500 miles off the coast of Africa.

Explored by Phoenicians and Genoese, the islands were colonized in 1420 by Portuguese sponsored by Prince Henry the Navigator.

Today, Madeira is a picturesque self-governing island province on the Atlantic coast off Portugal. Madeira has a stable political and economic environment, offering complete tax exemptions for International companies. To obtain the tax exemptions companies must be organized within the new Trade & Industrial Free Zones now being developed near the capital, Funchal.

Intentional Business Center (IBC)

Madeira offers a zero-rate corporate tax until 2011 for all companies licensed to operate within the legal framework of the IBC. This dispensation was granted by the EU as a means of stimulating new alternatives and opportunities for the economy of Madeira. Exemption from capital gains tax, withholding taxes, stamp duty and value added tax are also on offer. Offshore financial center institutions are also exempt from exchange controls.

International Companies

Application fee to start a Madeira international company costs US$750, and a month should be allowed for a decision on your application. If you are interested in incorporating in Madeira's new Trade & Industrial Free Zone, you should write the Madeira Development Corporation, Rua Imperatriz Dona Amelia, P.O. Box 4164, Funchal, Madeira for more information.

International companies are exempt from corporate income taxes until 2011, a guarantee of some 17 years. The exemption covers all local taxes, value-added-tax, withholding taxes on dividends and interest, exchange control and stamp duty.

Also exempt are gift and inheritance tax for all transfer of shares or other participations in the capital of companies operating in the Zone.

Banking

There are 32 banks, most of which are Portuguese. Foreign banks include Manufacturers Hannover, Credit Lyonnais, Deutsche Bank and Lloyds Bank Fund Management (Channel Islands).

Typically these offshore banks, which display the sign 'Sucursal Financeira Exterior', market deposit accounts with interest paid without deduction of tax. Other services include investment in securities, foreign exchange and money market transactions, as well as short to long-term loans. Deposits come from both Portuguese expatriates and foreigners.

Insurance companies

Companhia de Seguros Bonanca SA was the first Portuguese insurance company to have been granted a license to operate an insurance branch in Madeira's offshore financial center It has now been joined by Axa Reassurance SA.

Offshore International Services

Madeira's offshore business is called its international services. Activities under this heading, include international trading, management services, property companies and consultancies, can be established anywhere in Madeira, including Funchal, the capital.

International services includes the setting up of trusts. Although Madeira is a non-common law jurisdictions it recognizes the trust concept. Under Madeira law the settler may select the trust law of the country under which the trust is to be administered, and the confidentiality of the names of the settler and beneficiary of the trust is assured. The main provisions for the tax-exempt status of trusts are that trust income must not arise from local investments and trust property cannot be located in Portugal.

Free Trade Zone

Madeira's free trade zone comprises activities which the Madeira authorities have identified as ones which should provide employment for Maderia's people. One quarter of the island's population of approximately 270,000 is aged under 14 and, while unemployment is not yet a major problem, it is necessary to plan now for the employment projects to help meet the challenge of young people looking for jobs.

The site of the free trade zone area is a large fenced-off location at Canical, on the east coast of Madeira. It is about one hour's drive from Funchal and eight kilometers from the airport. The location was chosen because it is one of the few parts of the island where the land is relatively flat and because its proximity to the sea provides it with natural port facilities. Among the companies which have been licensed so far are ones engaged in activities as diverse as manufacturing plastics, optics, electronics, textiles and marble.

Shipping registry

Madeira has an international shipping register, which offers the global shipping industry some of the most favorable and competitive conditions available today. All vessels registered fly the Portuguese flag.

INCOME TAXES HAVE OFTEN BEEN OPPOSED with the argument that by taxing high incomes they reduce people's incentive to work hard. Here, a U.S. cartoon of the 1930's protests particularly against the corporation tax.

CHAPTER 8 • The Channel Islands & Isle of Man

Situated in the southern part of the English Channel closer to France than to Britain lie an archipelago of plateau like islands called the Channel Islands. There are five main islands that comprise the group, namely Jersey, Guernsey, Alderney, Sark and little Herm, but only Jersey and Guernsey are adequately equipped with an infrastructure of banks and trust companies to handle tax haven, a.k.a., financial center, activities. Sark has a population of just 600, and Alderney only 1690. Tiny Herm is not even half the size of Sark, and neither Sark or Herm have codified laws for offshore companies. Alderney, Sark and Herm economies are based for the most part on agriculture and tourism, and are dependencies of Jersey and Guernsey.

Jersey (and the rest of the Channel Islands) is a dependent Territory of the British Crown, but the island retains a unique constitutional position. Jersey has its own independent government and enjoys complete autonomy in its domestic and fiscal affairs. It's legal jurisdiction is known as a Bailiwick and the Crown.

Each island has its own Bailiff who is nominated by the Queen of England, and is the effective head of each government. His other titles of Chief Magistrate of the court and President of the States or Parliament give him far reaching powers. Members of the States are generally elected, but there is no real political activity to speak of.

Represented by the Lieutenant Governor (or Bailiff), the Bailiwick maintains an independent legal stance and its elected members of the Island's parliament legislates on all domestic matters including the raising of taxes.

The Channel Islands take full responsibility for its own tax system, its own court system, its own domestic laws and its own administration policy, relying on the protection of the United Kingdom for its defense from foreign aggression. With the protection of the Royal Navy you might think these isolated islands would stay free from foreign domination, but during most of World War II Hitler's Nazi's occupied the islands.

Recently, HRH the Prince of Wales unveiled a sculpture titled Liberation Square to mark the fiftieth anniversary of the island's liberation.

The period of occupation by the Nazi's was the only time since the Norman conquest that part of the British Isles were occupied by enemy forces.

The "Sark lark" & The Dame of Sark

Several years ago the island of Sark burst into the newspaper headlines when its hereditary Seigneur, The Dame of Sark, miffed over the use of agriculture tractors despite her ban on the use of autos, threatened to sell the island to Guernsey. Her threats were opposed by most of Sark residents, as such a sale would have subjected residents to Guernsey's "local income tax" (20% rate). As it turned out, the Dame eventually dropped the proposal to the relief of many. Since the demise of the Dame her successor Seigneur Mr. Michael Beaumont has officially pledged to keep Sark free from taxes.

During the era of the Corporation Tax Companies, Sark played an important role in how business affairs were carried on in the Channel Islands even though Sark has only two banks (the Bank of Westminister and Midland Bank) with but one bank employee each. Under the old CTC law, the annual director's meetings had to be held outside of Guernsey and Jersey. [1]

To comply with the management restriction under the old CTC law, thousands of Jersey and Guernsey CTCs appointed Sark directors and held board meetings in Sark or in nearby French towns. It was estimated that 20% to 40% of Sark's population of 600 had been acting as CTC directors for fees of between £100 to £200 a year per company. Husband and wife teams were earning £10,000 a year, and a few families were pulling in over £100,000 a year.

The use of a **"Sark lark"** (director) came under increased criticism by the administrative authorities because Sark has no company law or financial services regulatory body. To end the

---

1. *"Only people domiciled on Sark may hold accounts in Sark banks. Statements and correspondence are not mailed off the island by the banks."* from **The Sark Report**, by W.G. Hill, pg 14.

criticism, the Channel Island authorities decided to abolish the CTC (see Corporation Tax Companies below) legislation altogether and replace it with a brand-new law.

Jersey & Guernsey abolish Corporation Tax Company legislation

Corporation Tax Companies (CTCs) have existed in the Channel Islands of Guernsey, Jersey and Alderney since the 1930's. Through September 1988 there were nearly 6,000 CTCs on Guernsey, 10,000 on Jersey, and another 195 on Alderney. CTCs could escape the Channel Island's local 20% income tax in return for a fixed annual fee of £500. Such nonresident companies had to promise not to conduct business within the island of registration and were required to be managed and controlled outside the jurisdiction.

By the end of 1994, Jersey could boast no less than 26,000 incorporated companies. In addition, there were a total of 78 banks registered on the island, nearly all of which are wholly owned or partly owned by the world's foremost banking institutions.

During 1994 there were 3,370 new company formations - an increase of 10% over 1993. Approximately 60% of these new companies were formed for residents outside of Britain.

As a safeguard against unlawful activities by boiler-room operators, Jersey's Financial services Department (FSD) require the identity of the real beneficial owner, but this information is kept confidential by the FSD and does not become a matter of public record.

According to Richard Syvret, director of the FSD, Jersey is considering even more controls to screen out undesirables. One proposal is to regulate fiduciaries who form and administer companies and trusts, but this proposal is proving controversial in both Jersey, Guernsey and the other Channel Islands.

Jersey companies are governed by the new Company Law of 1991 (as amended). Under the 1991 law both private and public companies are recognized. For tax purposes, there are two types of companies.

The **Income Tax Company** will either trade or be managed and controlled in Jersey and pays a flat tax at a 20% rate.

Exempt Companies

The **Exempt company**, which pays a flat rate of £600 (about US$900) per annum, cannot have its beneficial owner living or trading on the island.

Exempt companies have many uses, including employment or constancy operations to avoid tax for salaried individuals, a money box company to act for other companies in a group, to protect assets from exchange control or repatriation of profits, or a holding company for international trading. [2]

Every exempt company must hold an annual general meeting of its members which need not be held in Guernsey. An annual return must be filed with the authorities as at 31st January each year showing its authorized and issued share capital and the names and addresses of its directors and registered shareholders.

The annual registration fee is £100. The return is open to inspection by members of the public. The identities of the beneficial owners are not required to be disclosed in the public record and no accounts have to be filed. The Companies (Exemption from Audit) Ordinance, 1991, exempts from audit companies which have less than ten members which are either dormant or asset holding companies. A company name must end with the words "Limited", with "Limited Liability" or "avec responsabilité limitee".

> "Jersey trusts are used in a variety of tax and estate planning procedures for private clients, and are often formed with an underlying Jersey company." "Set up fees and annual management costs for a Jersey trust amount to about £750 minimum."

The annual Exempt Company fee is £600 and is reduced pro rata to the number of months remaining to the end of the year of incorporation in the case of companies formed during a calendar year.

International Companies

The Income Tax (International Bodies) (Guernsey) Law, 1993 introduced the International Company. An International Company is resident in Guernsey for all purposes of the Income Tax Law but will not pay tax at

---

2. From **A new crop of companies set for harvest,** by Sue Stewart *Offshore Financial Review)* (May/1995) page #9.

the 20% standard rate. Instead the company pays at a rate of above zero but not more than 30%. The actual rate of tax is determined on a case by case basis with the Income Tax Authorities, taking into account the business plan and international circumstances of the applicant. Once set, the rate is fixed for a five year term.

Protected Cell Companies

Guernsey is one of the first offshore jurisdictions to provide, through its corporate laws, the ability for companies to create protected cells within the capital of the company to segregate the assets within that cell from unrelated claims. Creditors who have contracted with a Protected Cell Company in respect of one particular cell will only be able to make claims against the assets of that cell and against the general non-cellular assets of the company but not against the assets in other protected cells.

Guernsey Trusts

Guernsey Trusts are established under The Trusts (Guernsey) Law, 1989 which in particular codifies the duties and obligations of the Trustees and gives the Court certain powers which it will exercise on application from a Settlor, Trustee, Beneficiary or Protector. The Law and its subsequent amendments contain the following provisions of note:

• Trusts are not registrable on any public or private register in Guernsey and are not subject to any stamp or other duty in Guernsey.
• There is no requirement for details of Trusts or accounts to be made available to any authority.
• Neither the Settlor not the Beneficiaries under a Guernsey Trust need be residents of Guernsey.
• The creation of the Trust and the transfer or disposition of assets to that Trust are not invalidated by any foreign rule of forced heirship or by reason of the fact that the concept of trusts is unknown to or not admitted by the law of a jurisdiction other than Guernsey.
• A Guernsey trust can continue for up 100 years.

Disclosure of Beneficial Ownership

The ultimate beneficial ownership of all Jersey and Guernsey companies are disclosed to the Financial Services Department at the time of incorporation. If the owner is a trust, details of settlors, trustees and beneficiaries must be disclosed. If the ultimate beneficial owner is a public company, a copy of the most recent annual report has to be submitted. If the beneficial owner is resident outside Jersey and the U.K., the Registrar will not disclose such information to any other department, individual or foreign government agency. In other cases information will be given to the Jersey Income Tax Office and available to the U.K. Inland Revenue under the exchange of information agreement with the U.K.

All changes in beneficial ownership must be advised to the Registrar.

Jersey's 78 International Banks & Guernsey's 300 captive insurance companies

In terms of statistics, Jersey can boast approximately £25 billion pounds in collective investment funds, and £64 billion pounds in bank deposits. About £40 billion pounds are non-sterling bank accounts. While the figures for banking deposits alone don't come close to the estimated $590 billion dollars in Cayman Islands banks, the numbers do represent a substantial amount when you include Guernsey's bank deposits and investment funds.

Guernsey has 72 licensed banks with total deposits of £43 billion. More than 3/4 of this total is in non-sterling currencies. Guernsey also celebrated the licensing of its 300th captive insurance company in 1994.

Eight new banks were approved by Jersey's Financial Services Department in 1994, bringing the total number of registered institutions to 78. The national origin of the banks setting up new operations in Jersey reflect the global spectrum, defying the view that Jersey is an offshore tax haven for UK institutions only.

Among the newcomers taking deposits were the head office of the British Bank of the Middle East (part of the Hong Kong and Shanghai Banking Group), the Union Bancaire Privee and the Banque Transatlantique (Jersey) Limited. These banks join blue chip banking institutions such as Barclays and Royal Bank of Canada.

Innovation in the banking world is growing in Jersey. Recently, the Royal Bank of Scotland announced that it was launching a 24 hour telephone banking service for offshore customers.

The fiscal services industry account for 52% of all of Jersey's revenues.

Income Tax (Exempted Companies and Trusts)(Guernsey) Ordinance of 1984

Guernsey law provides that a company resident in Guernsey can be classified as exempt if it complies with certain other conditions, basically that it be a public investment company managed in Guernsey by nonresidents. Such companies pay an annual fee of £1,000 plus a separate annual fee of £300 (total £1,300) in lieu of income tax. Unit trusts and investment companies registered outside the C.I. and UK pay only a £1,000 annual fee. The Income Tax (Exempted Companies and Trusts)(Guernsey) Ordinance of 1984 sets out the conditions and procedural matters which permit these resident companies and trusts to pay a fixed fee in place of local income tax at the 20% rate. As a restriction, these public Unit Trusts or investment companies may not have Guernsey participants.

Individual Tax Rates in Channel Islands

Jersey (pop. 81,000), Guernsey (pop. 60,000) and Guernsey's sister isle of Alderney impose a 20% income tax on resident individuals. Sark has no income taxes at either the corporate or individual level.

Allowances in Jersey permit a family with two children to pay no tax if their income is below £13,900 (about US$24,000). In Guernsey a married couple with two children and income of £12,000 a year will pay a net £512 in tax. This represents a 31.7% improvement on their 1988 tax situation.

In 1989 Jersey's government expected gross revenues of £181 million, of which £160 million will come from income taxes and the corporation tax. In Guernsey gross revenue for 1989 was estimated at some £113 million, about 70% of which will come from income tax receipt. At these levels, each island's government expects to produce annual surpluses to fund capital spending programs and to build large revenues.[3]

Offshore Funds & Unit Trusts

Jersey is said to have about £22 billion under management in collective investments. But an additional £25 billion is thought to be held by Jersey's COBO (Control of Borrowing) schemes, according to John Pallot, deputy director, investments and securities, of Jersey;s FSD.

COBO's are investment schemes offered to less than 50 people. They are virtually like *joint ventures,* says Pallot.

The minimum subscription for such schemes is in the region of £2m to £5m.

There are about 450 funds holding assets of around £3.5 billion with Guernsey connections according to Nigel Taylor, Guernsey's superintendent of investment business. Jersey has some 350 funds with assets of around £4 billion. Over 100 new offshore funds are expected to apply to the Guernsey Financial Services Commission and the SIB for authorization to market in the UK. This follows the granting of designated territory status by the UK to Jersey and the Isle of Man in 1986.

Business in the offshore tax haven of Guernsey has been booming for years. At the end of 1989, there were 123 funds authorized on the island of Guernsey - worth £2.56 billion - and 60,000 investors. Funds based in Guernsey and Jersey are free from attacks by the Inland Revenue. Profits accumulated and reinvested go untaxed to foreign investors, until remitted as a dividend or redemption - when they become taxable if the investor lives in a country that taxes foreign source income.

> • Channel Island mutual funds and unit trusts can trade the stocks of both UK, U.S. and Japanese issuers free from capital gains taxes. •

Meanwhile, Jersey's **Article 131C of the Income Tax (Jersey) Law of 1961** came into effect on January 1, 1990. This new law is particularly attractive to U.K. expatriates employees and all individuals non-resident in the U.K. and Channel Islands. Under Article 131C individuals can effect personal pension plans with the following advantages:

1. Contributions need not be related to earnings. Any amount may be paid regardless of income.
2. The whole of the pension fund may be taken as a tax free cash sum at any time.

---

3. *Offshore Adviser*, pg 4 (January 1989)

3. Retirement can be at any age, as low as 20 and as high as 75.

4. The plan holder may return to the UK and retain the benefits accrued to date, and later take all benefits as a tax free lump sum at any time.

Non-Resident C. I. Trusts

The concept of trusts is based on English common law and has been fully recognized by the local courts, although the islands are not Anglo-Saxon common law jurisdictions. Non-resident trusts are the most common type chosen, even though for some time there was no codification of trust laws to guide the local courts. Jersey enacted a **Trust (Jersey) Law 1984** giving jurisdiction over foreign and domestic trusts administered from Jersey to the Royal Court of Jersey. A Jersey trust may now be formed for 100 years. The new law permits a trust or its terms to be revoked or varied. 4.

The **Trust (Jersey) Law 1984** was amended by the Trust (Amendment)(Jersey) Law 1989 and the Trust (Amendment #2)(Jersey) Law of 1991.

Non-resident trusts, where the grantor and the beneficiary are not residents of the Channel Islands, are not taxed. Neither is a tax levied on the distributions from the trust to the nonresident beneficiaries.

Nonresident trusts are a particularly attractive way for foreigners to hold assets in the Channel Islands, and they are in extensive use here. There are no tax consequences for the foreigner who settles an estate in trust, as there are no gift or estate taxes in the islands. Nonresidents are also not liable for local taxes, and the trust deed can be kept private, and drawn to protect against overseas expropriation, high taxation and exchange controls.

Discretionary trusts & fixed interest trusts

The offshore discretionary trust has been the vehicle of choice for private client planning for over 25 years. The trust industry in Jersey is said to be custodian to some £50 billion in assets, and the earnings from these funds provide significant revenues to the island's financial industry.

There are about 200 trust companies on the island, ranging from small independent firms to major banks or professional institutions. The client base for trusts has shifted from mainly UK to a truly international spread.

The confidentiality between trustee and settlor is guaranteed in Jersey. While many jurisdictions require the registration of trusts, Jersey has turned its face against this and, therefore, a regulatory framework which would impede trustee/settlor relationships and breach confidentially has been deliberately left out of Jersey's trust law. In the Caribbean, the Bahamas are one lone example of a domicile where trusts do not have to be registered with the local government.

Company & trust tandem - i.e., the most commonly used offshore tax plan

According to David Boleat (President of JATCO - Jersey Association of Trust Companies), Jersey's deputy director for the FSD, "Jersey trusts are used in a variety of tax and estate planning procedures for private clients and are often formed with an underlying Jersey company."

The most popular types of trusts in Jersey are the **fixed interest** and the **discretionary trusts**.

In a discretionary trust, the trustee has wide latitude as to whom to pay income and capital out of a predetermined list of beneficiaries.

The person putting the assets into the trust(i.e. the settlor), normally also gives the trustee a letter of wishes regarding how trust assets are to be distributed.

In a fixed interest trust, the settlor predetermines disposal of the assets, including the entitlement of each beneficiary.

The settlor can be named in the trust deed or he can remain anonymous.

Set up fees and annual management costs amount to about £600 minimum.

The costs of administering a trust depends on a number of variables, including the complexity of the trust deed and the amount of work involved.

Corporate use of trusts in Jersey is becoming very popular for pension funds and off-balance sheet transactions.

"Purpose trusts are used in corporate structures as part of a larger arrangement.",

---

4. From *"Doing Business in the Channel Islands"*, by Price Waterhouse, pg. 44.

according to David Boleat (President of JATCO - Jersey Association of Trust Companies).

Local tax on resident C. I. Companies

Companies that carry on business within their island of registration are required to pay a "local" income tax of 20% on their worldwide incomes.

Jersey's Exempt Companies

All Jersey companies will be subject to Jersey tax unless they make a claim for Exempt Company status or apply to be incorporated as an International Business Company (IBC).

An Exempt Company is one which has:

• made an Exempt Company election within a prescribed time limit;
• paid the £500 exemption fee for the current year; and
• has no Jersey resident beneficial owners during the year.

Under the Exempt Company regime the place of management and control of a Jersey Company is not relevant in determining its tax status in the Island. A company incorporated outside Jersey but controlled from Jersey will be considered resident for tax purposes but can also apply for exempt status.

Companies must file an Exempt Company election within 3 months of the date of formation with the Comptroller of Income Tax. In subsequent years the election must be filed by 31st March of each year. Failure to file an annual exemption claim may result in the Comptroller raising an estimated assessment to income tax.
Change in Status

An Exempt Company may become an Income Tax company and vice versa. However, further changes will not normally be allowed, and the second such change in status will only be approved in certain special circumstances. An example would be where a beneficial owner takes up residence in the Island and then leaves. Even in such cases, specific prior approval will have to be sought.

International Business Company

An International Business Company is one which has:

* made an IBC election within a prescribed time limit;
• paid advance tax of £1,200 for the current year; and
• subject to certain exceptions, has no Jersey resident beneficial owners during the year.
• not been anything other than an IBC for any prior year of assessment.
• provided the Comptroller of Income Tax with sufficient information to assure him that the proposal is not a transaction, the main purpose (or one of the main purposes) of which is the reduction of Jersey Income Tax liability of any person.

Jersey Trusts

The Trusts (Jersey) Law, 1984 is widely regarded as having established the standard for offshore trust legislation. The Act is a codification of common law trust principles and is held in high regard by international advisors.
The Act contains the following provisions of note:

• The Royal Court of Jersey will have jurisdiction where the proper law of a trust is Jersey, where the trustee of a foreign trust is resident in Jersey, trust property of a foreign trust is situate in Jersey, or the administration of any trust property of a foreign trust is carried out in Jersey.
• Neither the settlor nor the beneficiaries under a Jersey trust need be residents of Jersey.
• The beneficiaries must be identifiable by name or ascertainable by reference to a class.
• The maximum duration of a Jersey proper law trust is one hundred years.
• The proper law of a Jersey trust may be changed to the law of another jurisdiction.
• No trust may be created over immovable property situate in Jersey.
• Income of the trust may be accumulated.
• There is no restriction on who may or may not be appointed as trustees of a Jersey trust.
• Directors of a corporate trustee which commits a breach of trust are each personally liable for any damages and costs which might be awarded against the corporate trustee.

No government duties or fees are payable with respect to the execution of a Jersey trust. Trusts are not required to be registered.

Isle of Man (Manx)

The Isle of Man, sometimes called **Manx**, is one of the world's most famous tax havens. Located in the Irish Sea, just a few hours by plane from London (including a change in Liverpool), the Isle of Man, like the Channel Islands, does not tax *"foreign source income"* of Manx companies managed and controlled outside the island.

The Isle of Man is geographically part of the British Isles, but is not part of the United Kingdom. It is a self governing territory within the British Commonwealth. Like the Channel Islands, the Isle of Man is a Crown possession with its Chief of State being Queen Elizabeth II. The Queen's official title here is *"Lord of Man"*, and she appears on Manx postage stamps as such.

The Court of Tynwald is the legislative body on Man. It claims to be the oldest representative legislature in the world. Tax laws passed in England have no effect on Manx business or residents unless consultation with the Court of Tynwald is held beforehand and written legislation passed.

Population

The population of the Isle of Man is approximately 70,000 resulting in a population density of roughly 300 people per square mile.

Language

The official and spoken language is English. However, owning to the islands Celtic origins it also has its own Gaelic language, which is spoken by local enthusiast and it's shortly to become part of the curriculum in state schools.

Taxes

In the Isle of Man there are no capital gains taxes, no inheritance taxes, no wealth taxes and no gift taxes. And there are only two forms of direct taxation. A small social security contribution payable by employers and employees and a low 20 per cent income tax on companies and associations. Apart from a limited treaty with the United Kingdom the Isle of Man is not party to any double taxation treaties. In addition, most international financial transactions and business can be carried out tax-free!

When management and control is based on the Isle of Man, a company's profits are taxable at a rate of 20 per cent.

Non-Resident Companies

When management and control is established outside the Isle of Man (by persons who reside outside of the Isle of Man) companies are liable to non-resident duty of £750. The non-resident duty is payable on presentation of the non-resident declaration and thereafter annually when the company files its annual return, irrespective of magnitude of profits. Profits are not subject to any other Isle of Man taxes unless profits arise on trading in the Isle of Man.

Exempt Companies

These may be resident, managed and controlled in the Isle of Man and exempt from taxation in the Isle of Man when owned by non-residents. There are certain conditions which must be adhered to. These Exempt Companies are liable to Annual Duty of £400.

The Isle of Man does not impose taxes on
i. Capital Gains
ii. Wealth
iii. Property
iv. Death
v. Capital Transfers

An exempt company must be owned by non-residents and must have at least one Manx resident director and a professionally qualified company secretary. Exempt status can be obtained provided that the company's business and trading is carried on outside of the Isle of Man. Banking activities may be controlled from within the Island and any income and profit derived from the account will not be subject to Isle of Man taxation.

Whilst resident companies are subject to income tax at the rate of twenty per cent certain types of businesses may be eligible for tax exemption or a reduced rate, namely

i. The film industry
ii. Ship management
iii. Banking
iv. Insurance

Such companies do have to meet various Government criteria with respect to their share capital and licenses.

Taxation of Companies

Isle of Man exempt and non resident companies are not subject to any form of tax on profit in the Isle of Man but do pay a flat rate annual fee to the Isle of Man Government which is £750 for the non resident company or £400 for the exempt company.

Shareholders

A minimum of 1 shareholder is required which may be an individual or a corporate body. Details of the shareholders must be filed on the public file but anonymity can be preserved by the use of nominee shareholders

Directors

Each Isle of Man company requires a minimum of two directors and corporate directors are not permitted. Details of the directors must be filed on the public file but anonymity can be preserved through the use of third party professional directors. It is important to note that an exempt company must have at least one Isle of Man resident director and would usually have all its directors resident to clearly demonstrate that the control and management of the company takes place on the Isle of Man. This is not a requirement for a non resident company which may have non resident directors.

Annual Reporting

An annual return must be filed each year showing details of shareholders and directors. There is no requirement to file accounts with the registrar, but please note that resident companies do need to produce accounts for the tax authorities.

There are currently over 12,000 Manx registered nonresident companies, almost a third of the companies registered as Isle of Man companies and the rest foreign registered. Granting of the nonresident status to a company is done by the Manx Assessor of Income Tax under the Non Resident Duty Act 1986. [5]

Bank deposits & bank references

Interest arising on bank deposits in the Isle of Man is payable gross to non-residents. The Isle of Man Government has introduced a Depositors' Protection Scheme similar to that in the United Kingdom. However, there is one major advantage to the Isle of Man arrangement compared to the United Kingdom in that the cover offered by the Isle of Man Government extends to non-residents. Clients who are introduced to banks located in the Isle of Man will be required, by the banks, to agree to a status inquiry report. This will involve the Manx bank contacting your present bankers to establish how long you have held that account and confirm that the account has been managed in a proper manner. A certified photocopy of a client's passport is also requested. In addition to sterling, funds may be held on deposit in a number of currencies including :-

- U S Dollars
- Irish Pounds
- Deutsch Marks
- French Francs
- Canadian Dollars

Manx LLC

On the 17th October 1996 it became possible to form LLCs in the Isle of Man under the Limited Liability Company Act 1996. This is based on the simple Wyoming model but has the advantage of being in a reputable offshore financial center.

Key features of a Manx LLC are:

- it has a separate legal existence (legal personality and capacity);
- it must be dissolved within 30 years of being formed;
- liability of members is limited to their contributions;
- unanimous consent is required for the full transfer of an interest;
- it is managed by its members (but they can appoint a manager);

---

5. From *"Manx clamps down on its black sheep'*, **Offshore Adviser**, pg. 6.

- it is wound up on a change of membership, unless members elect to continue;
- its profits are treated as the income of its members for tax purposes.

Isle of Man Banking Act of 1975

Under the Isle of Man Banking Act of 1975 (as amended) all banks have to be licensed by the government. Interest on deposits paid to nonresidents is free from all withholding tax.

Manx Trusts

The Isle of Man has extensive common law trust legislation to guide the local courts and help planners draft and execute a trust instrument. Formal registration of a trust deed is not required, and there are no stamp duties. It is common for a nonresident grantor to create a Manx trust for nonresident beneficiaries. Trust profits can accumulate 100% tax free as long as the income of the trust is from *foreign sources*.

"Peripheral (bogus) tax havens" The Pitcairn Islands – British colony with 65 to 75 inhabitants!

"From time to time we hear about tax havens. Some are real countries, often remote and impossible to reach, while others may not exist except as a figment of someone's imagination. The Pitcairn Islands in the far off South Pacific are tax free, but with a total population of only about 70 persons, and no bank and trust facilities to speak of, it's not at all suitable as a tax haven." [6.]

Pitcairn is a mountainous, volcanic island in the South Pacific Ocean about 2,170 km (1,350 mi) southeast of Tahiti. Since 1970 it has been administered - along with its three neighboring islands of Ducie, Henderson, and Oeno - by the British High Commissioner in New Zealand.

---

6. From *Practical International Tax Planning* (formerly **"How to Use Tax Havens"**), pg. 321, by Marshall Langer. Marshall Langer is the adjunct professor of law at Miami University and has practiced law for over 40 years.

Adamstown on the north coast is the administrative center and principal settlement. The island has an area of 5 sq km (2 sq. mi) and a population of 65 (1985 est.). The wooded island rises to 335 m (1,100 ft), and sheer cliffs along all its coast make it almost inaccessible except by local longboats. The natives, almost all descendants of mutineers from the *Bounty,* support themselves by fishing, farming, and the sale of postage stamps.

Once probably inhabited by Polynesians, The Pitcairn Islands were discovered by Robert Pitcairn, sailing with Philip Carteret in 1767. In 1790 it was chosen by Fletcher Christian and 8 other mutineers from the *Bounty* as their refuge. Along with 6 men and 12 women from Tahiti, they remained isolated; by 1800 only one male was alive. Pitcairn was made a British colony in 1838.

North Korea and **Albania** abolished income taxes in 1974 and 1969 respectively. Unfortunately, North Korea is still a communist State, whereas Albania has only recently begun the difficult process of moving from a one-party Communist regime to a multiparty democracy, and from a centrally controlled economy to a free-market system. It may be easier getting your money (and yourself) into these Communist places, than out of them.

Svalbard off the coast of Norway has its own income tax laws, and rates are much lower than in Norway. Corporations pay a flat rate tax of 10%.

Svalbard, which is actually a Norwegian dependency, consists of a cluster of glaciated islands in the Arctic Ocean, lying about 645 km (400 mi) north of Norway. The dependency's population is 3,646 (1989 est.). The Spitsbergen group within Svalbard is composed of five major, as well as many smaller, islands. West Spitsbergen, the largest island, has more than 60% of the dependency's total land area of 62,049 sq. km (23,957 sq. mi). Longyearbyen on West Spitsbergen is the administrative center.

According to Professor Langer, there's a major obstacle should you choose Svalbard. Svalbard experiences total darkness from the end of October until the beginning of March. The annual mean temperature is well below freezing. There's no regular air service, and boats arrive on a limited schedule every two weeks, weather permitting. There are also no lawyers or accountants practicing in Svalbard. Svalbard seems more fitting a place for polar bear and sea lion, than for people and financial planners.

Minerva is a series of reefs in the South Pacific which were classified as the "Free and Independent Republic of Minerva". The King of Tonga objected to this attempted creation of a new country and took steps to annex the Minerva reefs - some 250 miles away - to Tonga, rather than have neighbors he doesn't know. While the Minerva reefs may have no taxes (or tax laws), they may not be above sea level at high tide!

The Sealand fantasy

According to an article by Tony Heatherington which appeared in the *Offshore Financial Review* (London), Sealand is administered from a post office box in Villach, in Austria - "for technical reasons", Baier says. But its real location is about seven miles off the east coast of England, near the port of Harwich. As anyone with a passing knowledge of this bit of coast line will know, there are in fact no islands in the area. What there is, though, it Rough's Tower, a metal and concrete anti-aircraft gun platform left over from World War II and abandoned by the British government in 1947.

In 1967, the disused tower, which resembles an oil rig, was seized by a former army major named Roy Bates, who promptly issued a declaration of independence from the United Kingdom, labeled himself as Prince Roy of Sealand, and his wife as Princess Joan.

Their venture could have been laughed off, but for the fact that a year or so later, their son, Prince Michael opened fire with a riffle on a ship which he decided was sailing too close to

Sealand. Hauled before a court in Essex on firearms charges, Prince Michael demanded to be released immediately as the UK- courts had no jurisdiction over Rough's Tower. To the surprise of everyone probably including the Prince himself - the judge agreed.

With this legal ruling behind him, Prince Roy and his Royal family have exploited their independence ever since. There have been plans for a casino and private radio station , but neither has materialized.

During the Falklands War, a group of Argentineans negotiated to buy Sealand, to set up a piece of Argentine territory just off the coast of England. Prince Roy turned them down. But the venture which attracted most official attention came in the 1980s, when Prince Roy took on board as a partner an American banker named Wallace Kemper. Together, they unveiled Sealand Television, with a 1,000 foot mast and a potential audience of 200 million. Kemper announced plans to broadcast daily from 5 PM to 2 am, with 20 new films each month, plus sports events, music videos and variety shows. Advertising slots were offered at £10,000 for 30 seconds of prime time, and topless Page 3 girl Suzanne Mizzi was recruited as the station's presenter. "I'm talking to Roy Bates about making her Sealand's first countess", Kemper boasted.

The scheme came to nothing, though. Sealand Television collapsed amid claims Kemper had ripped off his partners. All of which should not exactly have come as a surprise to anyone. For in 1983, Kemper was in hot water over allegations that his Arab Overseas Trust & Bank - registered in Anguilla - had been charging fees of op to $2,500 for business loans which then failed to materialize. And in 1986, he and three other men were charged with conspiracy to defraud, involving a $3 million bank draft. At the same time, Kemper described himself as head of the European Overseas Bank. In 1988, Kemper, who was born in New Orleans in 1932, was jailed for three and a half years for fraud.

Sealand's state affairs then seem to have gone quiet for a while, until in 1990 they burst into life again. Suddenly, Sealand passports began to crop up. Advertisements offering Sealand citizenship appeared in newspapers in the Gulf And the government of Qatar warned that Sealand's claims to offer a back door into the European Community were false. Close on the heels of phony passports came phony banks. The Sterling Bank of Sealand was chartered, headed by well known flim-flam Teddy Hunsaker.

And now, with Sealand already issuing stamps, currency, passports and banking licenses, as well as "trade missions", almost the only thing missing is Sealand's bible! But Sealand has yet to name its first spiritual leader, so we must give it time. [7.]

Norderfriedrichskoog - A cow-shed tax haven inside Germany

According to the *Offshore Financial Review,* the world's most provincial tax haven has loomed from the depths of nowhere. It is Norderfriedrichskoog on the North Sea coast. Norderfriedrichskoog consists of 13 thatched homesteads, 50 inhabitants and er...70 offshore companies. There is no pub, no shop, no hotel in this hamlet along the coast of the German state of Schleswig Holstein.

But a number of companies have come rushing in to the hamlet spurred by the huge tax incentives of the village. Indeed there is no taxes whatsoever.

A thoroughly disgruntled tax office has apparently accepted the tax incentives of the village, but ruled that a company's records, communications and core business activities must be based in Nordfriedrichskoog to benefit.

First came the name plates, then farmers began renting out attics, barns and cow sheds. Wives were hired out as office managers and Deutsche Telekom came in to lay extra telephone cables among the cabbage patches to cope with the explosion of faxes. It's all abuzz in Nordfriedrichskoog amidst the pigs and the chickens

For example, Margaret Dirks has 19 firms based in her farm house, Another farmer has three in his. Business, by all accounts, is booming.

The Schleswig Holstein audit office is not exactly happy with the situation. One company made DM220m in the hamlet and because of the zero trade tax the federal government missed out on DM1.5m in tax.

There is nothing the government can do as German communities can set their own taxes. The hamlet was founded on a tax exemption. Around 300 years ago a local duke issued a decree freeing locals from "tithes and other tributes" in return for building a dike to keep the sea out.

No-one knows the wealth of the locals, although it is said that the boom has created up to 20 new jobs in a community of just 50 people. The number of firms has been estimated at around 70 and office rents, for prospective businesses, are said to be around £1,000. Luxembourg eat your heart out.

For other interesting articles on the "offshore" subscribe to:

Offshore Financial Review
Maple House
149 Tottenham Court Rd.
London, England   WIP 9LL
44 171-896-2608/2609
fax: 44 171-896-2587
annual subscription £75
email: stuart.fieldhouse@ft.com

---

7. From an article by Tony Heatherington appeared in the *Offshore Financial Review* (London)

Comparing the Pacific and Far East offshore financial centers

	Hong Kong	Cook Islands	Nauru	Singapore	Vanuatu	Seychelles
CORPORATE COSTS						
Incorporation	HK$5,500	US$1,500	US$1,000	US$2,700	US$2,000	US$1700
Annual - Registered Office	HK$1,500	US$1,500	US$650	US$1,500	US$1,250	US$100-$1000
- Directors Fees	HK$3,500	included	US$850	US$2,000	(included)	US$300
- Registration	HK$1,000	included	included	US$1,000	(included)	-
CORPORATE TAXES						
Resident	-	-	None	31%	None	-
Resident Exempt	0.5%	None	None	NA	None	None
Non Resident			None	None	None	
LAWS						
Exchange Control	No	No	No	No	No	No
Bank Secrecy	Yes	Yes	No	Yes	Yes	Yes
Forced Inheritance	Yes	No	No	No	No	Yes
Protection for Trusts	Yes	Yes	No	Yes	Yes	Yes
Trust Perpetuity Law	Yes	Yes	No	No	Yes	No
Company Mobility	Yes	Yes	No	No	Yes	Yes
Ownership disclosure	Yes	No	No	Yes	Yes	No
Annual Return required	Yes	Yes	Yes	Yes	Yes	Yes
Share Register available for public inspection	Yes	No	Yes	Yes	No	No
COMMUNICATIONS						
Air	Good	Good	Poor	Good	Fair	Good
Mail	Good	Good	Fair	Good	Good	Good
Telephone/Fax	Good	Good	Fair	Good	Good	Good
SERVICES						
Accounting	Good	Fair	Poor	Good	Good	Good
Banking	Good	Good	Poor	Good	Good	Good
Legal	Good	Fair	Poor	Good	Good	Good
Trust	Good	Good	Good	Good	Good	Good
Corporate	Good	Good	Good	Good	Good	Good
Insurance	Good	Poor	Poor	Good	Poor	Good
Investor Protection	Good	None	None	None	None	Good
POLITICAL STATUS	BCC	Independent	Independent	Independent	Independent	Independent

Source: International Money Marketing   BCC = British Crown Colony

CHAPTER 9 • Tax Havens of the Far East

Singapore consists of the island of Singapore and about 57 islets located at the very tip of the Malay peninsular. The city of Singapore, where most of the financial business is carried on, is found on the southern tip of the island. Modern Singapore was founded in 1819 by Sir Stamford Raffles as a trading post of the East India Company. In 1867 the Straits settlement of Singapore, Penand and Malacca became British colonies. Later, in 1956 Singapore became a separate crown colony of the UK, and shortly after that an independent state with a president as its head. Today, Singapore is a member of the British Commonwealth. Its judicial system relies on the Judicial committee of the Privy Council in the UK as the final court of appeals. [1]

Territorial System of Taxation

Singapore taxes its residents on a *territorial* basis. Unless offshore profits are remitted back to Singapore, the income will not be included with the company's assessable income.

The corporate tax is 26%, and this rate also applies to Singapore branches of foreign corporations.

A concessionary corporate tax rate of 10% is granted in respect of -

• income generated from offshore business of banks, insurance companies, operational headquarters and members of Singapore International Monetary Exchange (SIMEX)
• international oil trading companies granted the status of approved oil traders
• companies which set up special finance and treasury centres in Singapore.
• Approved international trading companies trading in approved commodities including rubber, timber, edible oils, coffee, cocoa, metals, minerals and bulk chemicals.

Resident and non-resident companies

For tax purposes, a company is considered to be resident in Singapore if the management and control is exercised in Singapore. A non-resident company incorporated outside Singapore is exempt from Singapore tax on income remitted to Singapore, if the company does not have a permanent establishment in Singapore.

Capital allowances

Generally, accelerated capital allowances of 33.33% are granted for all plant and equipment used for business purposes. A 100% allowance is granted for expenditure incurred on any computer or prescribed office and industrial automation equipment, in the year of purchase. Undeducted capital allowances may be carried forward for deduction against future income of all kinds. Capital allowances cease to be eligible for carry forward in the event of substantial change in shareholders (i.e., more than 50%). But companies whose shareholders change substantially for reasons beyond their control can continue to carry forward.

Losses

Losses arising from the carrying on of a trade or profession are deductible against future income and may be carried forward indefinitely. No carry back is allowed. The ability to carry forward losses is also subject to rules on substantial change in shareholders, as with capital allowances.

Taxation of dividends

Singapore applies the full imputation system, so that tax paid by a company resident in Singapore is imputed to its shareholders, who receive a tax credit when they receive dividend payments.
Dividends paid out of foreign income for which there is insufficient franking credit due to the foreign tax credit given are exempt from imputation.

Credit for foreign taxes

A unilateral tax credit can be claimed by a Singapore-resident company for foreign tax paid on dividend income derived from investments in countries with which Singapore has no double taxation agreement. The unilateral tax credit also covers the underlying foreign corporate tax, provided the Singapore company owns at least 25% of the capital of the foreign company paying the dividend.

---

1. From *"Doing Business in Singapore"* by Price Waterhouse Information Guide, pg. 1.

Withholding tax

Certain kinds of payments made by Singapore resident companies or permanent establishments to non-residents are subject to withholding tax. The rates of withholding tax vary from 0% to 26%, depending on the recipient's country of residence and the double taxation agreement provisions with that country. Where there is no double taxation agreement, the rate is 26%, except for interest, royalties and rental paid for moveable properties, for which the rate is 15%.

Payments are deemed to have been made, and therefore to be subject to withholding, if they are reinvested, accumulated, capitalized, carried to any reserve or credited to any account however designated.

The following payments to non-residents are subject to withholding tax:-

1. Interest, commission and fees in connection with any loan or indebtedness
2. Royalty and rental payments for the use of any movable property
3. Payments for the use of or the right to use scientific, technical and industrial knowledge or information
4. Management fees
5. Remuneration paid to non-resident directors.

Non-residents are taxed only on income derived from or accrued in Singapore. They do not have to pay taxes on foreign income received in Singapore. Also, they are exempted from income tax if they work in Singapore for 60 days or less in a calendar year.

Besides income taxes, Singapore has a property tax, stamp and customs duties, a payroll tax, and estate taxes. Foreign source income not remitted back to Singapore is not taxed.

The personal income tax rate for individuals is ranges from 5% to 28%. Individuals that have passive investments held offshore are not taxed on the income from those investments provided it is not remitted back to Singapore. There are no withholding taxes on dividends paid to foreign or domestic shareholders of a Singapore company.

Capital Gains

Singapore does not tax capital gains of either foreigner or resident shareholders. A foreign company can dispose of its shares in a Singapore company free from Singapore income taxes.

However, where a series of transactions takes place which the authorities view as a "business transaction" **within** Singapore, then capital gains are **sometimes** taxed as ordinary income. What constitutes a capital gain has led to taxpayer disputes in the past. Notwithstanding, in this regard gains derived from the sale of stock held over 18 months are not subject to tax.

Singapore banks and insurance companies, by the nature of their business, are taxable on any gain from the sale of shares unless they can substantiate that the gain did not arise from the sale of trading stock. Similarly, stock-brokering and securities companies are taxed on their profits from the sale of shares. Approved investment holding companies can elect to be taxed at a special low graduated rate on shares they hold for less than 18 months.

Banks & Insurance Companies

To develop Singapore as an international financial center, offshore income derived by Asian Currency Units (ACU) of banks is taxed at **10%**.

Singapore does not tax interest on deposit earned by nonresidents who open so called "external accounts" in an "approved bank" in Singapore.

Special rules are used to determine the taxable income of insurance companies carrying on general insurance business within Singapore. To encourage offshore insurance and reinsurance operations, the income from the insurance or reinsurance of offshore risks (excluding life insurance) is taxed at a reduced rate of 10%, instead of the normal rate of 32%. Life insurance companies are not taxed on their premiums income, but only pay tax on the investment income and profit on sale of investments.

Nonresident Investment Companies & Unit Trusts

The government recently announced that unit trusts beneficially owned by nonresidents will enjoy complete tax exemption on their income. This new policy of **exempting** foreign owned investment companies is designed to make Singapore an attractive and competitive base for its rivals Hong Kong and Tokyo.

"I take this step because there is good potential for the offshore unit trust industry in Singapore to flourish, and to provide additional impetus for the development of unit trusts here." - Singapore Finance Minister Richard Hu

Singapore based Unit Trusts have some definite advantages over Hong Kong and Tokyo based funds, which currently are the leading centers for fund management in the Far East. [2.] Rents in Hong Kong are the highest in the world, after London and Tokyo. Hong Kong workers, although skilled, are in short supply, and finding even low-grade office help can be expensive. Moreover, Hong Kong's future is in doubt in view of the transfer of control to the Chinese Communist in 1997. While the Chinese have pledged to maintain Hong Kong's capitalist system for another 50 years, the idea of a Communist run offshore haven for free capital stretches the credulity of even the most optimistic. [3.]

The exemption from tax for Unit Trusts will only apply when **all** the unit holders are **nonresidents**. In the case where shareholders are residents of Singapore, an election can be made by the fund's management to be taxed on the gain realized upon the sale of investments held for less than 18 months at rates from 3.3% to 32%.

Operational Headquarters Company

To invite companies to establish regional offices in Singapore, an approved operational headquarters company which provides management, technical or other support services to its affiliates outside Singapore is granted tax exemption on dividends received from foreign affiliates. Other incentives allow offshore income, such as management fees, interest and royalties to be taxed at a reduced rate of 10%.

To qualify for these incentives the holding company must have a paid-up capital of $500,000, and it cannot act merely as a passive

holding company, but must provide services from Singapore.

Dividends paid out of exempt income are also tax free to the shareholder. This incentive is granted for a period of up to 10 years with provisions for extensions. "Non qualifying income" of an operational headquarters company is taxed at the 32% rate.

Public & Private Companies

Singapore's corporate tax laws are modeled after those of its colonizer, the British. Companies can be incorporated as either private or public, limited by shares, by guarantee or unlimited. The fact that a company is limited and/or private is indicated in its name, either in English (i.e., Limited, Private Limited, Pte Ltd.) or in Malay (i.e., Berhad, Sendirian Berhad, Sdn Bhd.). Companies, and branches of foreign companies are incorporated under the Companies Act.

A private company cannot have more than 50 shareholders, excluding employees and former employees. If it has no more than 20 shareholders and no beneficial interest is held by any corporation it will qualify as an exempt private company. An exempt private company is relieved from filing copies of its accounts with the Registrar of Companies, which would then be available for public inspection.

Rights to transfer shares in a private company are restricted. Private companies may not invite the public to subscribe to their shares or debentures or deposit money with the company.

A public company must file a prospectus with the Registrar of Companies before shares or debentures can be made available to the public. All public companies must file financial statements annually with the Registrar of Companies.

Formation costs

Only public accountants and lawyers are permitted to engage in the formation of companies. Professional fees and other costs of forming a company range from $2,000 to $3,500. In addition, a registration fee is payable at the time of filing of the Memorandum. This fee is determined on a sliding scale depending on the amount of authorized capital. For a company with a capitalization not exceeding $25,000 the fee is S$1,000, plus S$20 for every additional S$5,000 up to S$500,000. For capitalizations

---

2. Hong Kong based funds benefit from no capital gains taxes, no taxes on inter-company dividends, and no tax on foreign source incomes (interest, dividends, royalties), as well as light regulation by HK administrative bodies. HK has state of the art communication systems and a skilled labor force.

3. From *"Hu's exemptions in Singapore"*, by Harvey Warren, pg 10, **Offshore Advisor**

above S$50,000,000 there is a $3 fee for every additional S$20,000 or part thereof.

Investment Incentives

Singapore offers a number of outstanding tax incentives worth mentioning. Pioneer industries involving large expenditures or sophisticated technology ventures may be granted exemption from income tax for 5 to 10 years. To be eligible for the incentive a company must be in business of manufacturing a product which the government considers to have favorable prospects for development. There is no restriction on foreign ownership of such companies.

An approved **pioneer company** is granted a five to ten year tax holiday. There is no tax on dividends paid out of profits earned during the tax holiday. Other income such as interest and dividends are not covered by the tax exemption, and are subject to tax at the 32% corporate rate. The exemption apples to the manufacture and sale of the pioneer product.

A **post-pioneer incentive** is available after the pioneer tax holiday expires. Effectively, an extension is provided the pioneer company which incurs a tax rate of 10% for a period of up to five years. After the expiration of this **extension** the regular corporate tax rate of 32% becomes applicable.

Pioneer Service Companies

The pioneer incentive is also available to service companies which carry on the following activities.

- Engineering or technical services including laboratory, consultancy and research development.
- Computer based information and other related services.
- Development or production of any industrial design.

Investment Allowances (IA)

An alternative to the pioneer incentive programs is the investment allowance (IA) incentives.

The **IA** tax exemption is granted on an amount of income based on a specified percentage (not exceeding 50%) of fixed capital expenditure incurred for any of the following activities.

1. Manufacturing or increased manufacture of any product.
2. Provision of specialized engineering or technical services.
3. Research and development.

4. Promotion of the Tourist Industry.
5. Any Engineering or technical service, including laboratory, consultancy, and research and development services.
6. Computer-based information and other computer related services.
7. Other prescribed services or activities.

The allowance is granted over a five-year period. Any balance of IA that has not been used up can be carried forward to reduce future tax liabilities.

In addition to the **IA exemption**, there is an **export profits exemption** available for any **approved product** or **approved service**. This exemption is equal to 90% of the increased export profits over a fixed base.

Exchange Controls & Tax Treaties

Singapore has no exchange controls. No government approval is required to transfer any currency or make any payments anywhere in the world.

Singapore has 25 bilateral tax treaty agreements with various nations, but none as yet with the United States.

Singapore is a Shipping Tax Haven

Complete exemption from Singapore income tax is granted on income derived by a shipping enterprise from the operation or chartering of seagoing Singapore-registered ships. Nonresident shipping or airline companies operating ships registered outside Singapore are taxed at a rate of 5% on gross freight receivable, unless reduced or exempted under one the tax treaties.

Trusts

Trusts are not in common use in Singapore. Trust income is assessable to either the grantor, the beneficiary or the trustee, depending on the circumstances. [4.]

---

4. From *"Doing Business in Singapore"*, Price Waterhouse

Hong Kong
(largest tax haven in far east)

Hong Kong (HK) is the third largest financial center in the world behind Tokyo and New York. Its gross national produce is surpassed in the Pacific basin only by Japan, New Zealand and Australia, and is about equal to its financial rival Singapore.

Hong Kong is known for its political stability despite the fact that Communist China is right at its doorstep. Peking, it is said, has far more to gain be leaving its *window to the west* open. Others are not so sure.

Hong Kong is one of the world's premiere financial centres strategically located in the most economically dynamic area of the world. Hong Kong's open economy, freedom of capital movements, a well understood legal system, modern infrastructure and the wide use of English in business have contributed to its unique status. On 1 July 1997, Hong Kong became the Special Administrative Region ("Hong Kong SAR") of the People's Republic of China (PRC). According to the Basic Law, which serves as its constitutional legislation, the Hong Kong SAR will exercise a high degree of autonomy from the PRC and enjoy executive, legislative and judicial power, including that of final adjudication of legal disputes.

The laws in Hong Kong remain basically unchanged as a result of its change of status. The Basic Law safeguards the capitalist system and way of life until 2047 with protections against the application of a socialist economic system.

Hong Kong will continue to play its role as a free port and international financial, trading and shipping centre and to serve as an important bridge for economic, scientific, technological and cultural exchanges between the PRC and the rest of the world.

International trade and finance through Hong Kong has been a key factor in Hong Kong's growth. An equally important factor in Hong Kong's success is that it is a semi-tax haven with all foreign source income exempt from local taxation. In addition, tax rates on local source income are substantially lower than in almost all recognized financial centres.

Territorial System of Taxation

Hong Kong is really not a tax haven in the conventional sense, as HK does tax local business corporations at a rate of 16.5% and individuals at 15.5%. HK does not tax *foreign source income* even if repatriated back to Hong Kong. This is unlike Singapore's tax system which will tax *foreign source income* when repatriated back into Singapore. HK is said to have a territorial system of taxation.

Hong Kong Companies

Companies incorporated or registered in Hong Kong are governed by the Companies Ordinance (Chapter 32 of the Laws of Hong Kong).

The name of a company should be stated in its memorandum of association. The name can be in English, in Chinese or in both English and Chinese. The company name must end with the word "Limited" or its equivalent in Chinese characters. A company name may not be identical with that of an existing company. Prior to incorporation a company name search must be conducted as to the availability of a proposed name. Ready made companies are available.
Memorandum and Articles of Association

Every company must have a constitution consisting of a "Memorandum of Association" and "Articles of Association". The Memorandum states the company's name, that its registered office will be in Hong Kong, its initial authorized share capital and that the liability of its shareholders is limited. The Articles set out the regulations governing the administration of the company including the procedures for shareholders and directors meetings and any restrictions on the issue and transfer of shares.
Subscribers to the Memorandum and Articles of Association

At least two subscribers are required and each of the subscribers must subscribe to at least one share in the Company.
Share Capital

There is no limitation on the amount of authorized or issued share capital. Capital duty at the rate of 0.3% of the authorized capital is payable to the Government on incorporation and subsequent increase of any amount of the authorized capital. Shares must be expressed in a fixed amount; "no par value" shares are not permitted. While it is usual for the share capital to be expressed in Hong Kong dollars, shares may be expressed in other currencies. A multiple currency share capital is also permissible.

A private company must have at least two registered shareholders but either or both shareholders may be nominees for a third party whose name need not appear on official documents. There are no restrictions on the nationality or residence of shareholders and shareholders meetings may be held in or outside Hong Kong. Bearer shares are not permitted.
Directors

A minimum of two directors must be appointed. They may be either individuals or companies. Listed companies and their subsidiaries must have individuals as directors.
There are no restrictions on the nationality or residence of directors and meetings may be held in or outside Hong Kong.
Secretary

A company secretary must be appointed. An individual secretary must be ordinarily resident in Hong Kong. A corporate secretary must have its registered office or a place of business in Hong Kong.

Registered Office

A company must maintain a registered office in Hong Kong. A P.O. Box address is not permissible. Notice of the company's registered office must be given to the Registrar within 14 days of incorporation.
Time

A company is incorporated by sending to the Registrar of Companies the Memorandum and Articles of Association signed by the two initial subscribers. The actual incorporation takes place when the Registrar issues the certificate of incorporation and this normally takes approximately seven days after filing the papers.
Business Registration

Every company is required to register with the Commissioner of Inland Revenue under the Business Registration Ordinance. The application for a business registration certificate must specify the type of business to be carried on and all places of business maintained in Hong Kong. The certificate is valid for a twelve month period and must be renewed annually.

Annual Meetings

The Companies Ordinance requires that a general meeting of members be held at least once every calendar year. At that time the Profit and Loss Account and Balance Sheet of the Company is laid before the members together with the directors' and auditors' reports.

Public Filings

Upon incorporation, the names and personal particulars of the directors and secretary must be filed with the Companies Registry. If shares other than subscriber shares are issued, a Return of Allotment must be filed with the Registrar, disclosing the identities of the members and their shareholdings. However, where nominee shareholders and directors are used, the beneficial shareholders need not be disclosed. A register of the company's members, directors and secretaries, mortgages and charges (if any) together with its minutes and accounts must also be kept by the company but may only be inspected by shareholders.

A company is required to file an annual return each year within forty-two days of the company's anniversary date of incorporation.

Accounts and Auditors

Directors are required under the Companies Ordinance to cause proper books of accounts of the company to be kept at its registered office or at such other place as the directors may think fit. Every company is required by law to appoint an auditor or firm of auditors each year at its annual general meeting. The first auditor may be appointed by the directors and he may hold office until the following annual general meeting. An auditor must be qualified by virtue of the

Hong Kong Professional Accountants Ordinance and completely independent of the company. A directors' report and auditors' report must be attached to the company's annual accounts before the same are presented at the company's annual general meeting for consideration by its members. In case of a private company (other than a member of a group of companies which contains a public company), its audited accounts must be laid before its annual general meeting not more than nine months from its financial year-end.

Taxes

A Hong Kong company is only taxed on its profits arising in or derived from a trade or business carried on in Hong Kong. There is no tax on dividends paid by a company otherwise chargeable to profits tax. Local tax law does not discourage the accumulation of profits in a Hong Kong company. Accordingly, there is no tax on accumulated earnings and profits and no requirement that a dividend must be paid.

Apart from profits tax, there is also a personal income tax and a property tax in Hong Kong, both of which must be taken into account when establishing a local Company.
Foreign Companies

Any company incorporated outside Hong Kong that establishes a place of business in Hong Kong is subject to Part XI of the Companies Ordinance. Within one month of establishing a place of business, the Company must deliver for registration the following documents and information to the Registrar of Companies:

• A copy, certified in specified manner, of its Memorandum and Articles of Association or equivalent document defining the construction of the Company, and its certificate of incorporation.
• A list of the directors and secretary showing the full name (including former names or aliases), residential address, nationality, number and issuing country of passport of each.
• The address of the principle place of business in the place of incorporation (if any); the address of the registered office in the place of incorporation; and details of the intended address of the principal place of business in Hong Kong.
• A Memorandum of Appointment of one or more persons (who must be Hong Kong residents) who are known as the authorized representative and authorized to accept service of process ad any notices on behalf of the Company in Hong Kong.
• Unless an exemption has been granted, a copy, certified in specified manner, of the company's latest audited accounts which must be in the form required by the law of the place of its incorporation or, if no such form is specified by law, in the form in which they are submitted to the shareholders of the Company.

> Panama, Costa Rica, Venezuela and Singapore have a **territorial** system of taxation - only taxing income derived from activities carried on within the country.

No capital gains taxes, no taxes on dividends

Capital gains go tax free in Hong Kong. Dividends, whether from HK sources or from abroad are excluded from the taxpayer's gross income and are entirely exempt from tax. There

are no withholding taxes on dividends paid to nonresident shareholders of HK companies. There are no payroll, sales, value-added, or gift taxes imposed in Hong Kong.

Banking and other nontaxables in Hong Kong

There are more than 160 licensed banks with 128 foreign banks having representative offices in Hong Kong and a further 225 licensed deposit-taking finance companies.

1. Interest on HK or foreign currency deposits placed with licensed banks and deposit taking companies carrying on business in HK are not taxed.
2. There are no withholding taxes on royalties, bank interest (described in #1 above), or dividends.
3. There is no accumulate earnings tax in HK. A company does not have to distribute its profits to its shareholders.
4. The part of an annuity payable in HK that is computed and deemed to be the capital element under provisions of the HK Inland Revenue rules is exempt from tax.
5. Alimony payments for maintenance from a husband or former husband are excluded from the computation of taxable income.

Other Incentives

Royalties and professional fees paid to nonresidents are not subject to withholding taxes, and are deductible by the HK payer as long as the expenses are commercially realistic. Only 10% of the gross royalties received for the use of a trademark, copyright, secret process, cinematographic or television film or tape, etc. are subject to HK tax. A foreign company with HK subsidiary would pay tax at an effective rate of just 1.7% for the *lending* of its trademark, etc. The expense incurred by the HK subsidiary permitted to be deducted when computing taxable income. Also deductible as a business expense is interest paid.

Company Formations & Costs

The principal forms of business enterprises used by foreign investors in Hong Kong are the public and private company, and the branch of a foreign company. The **Companies Ordinance** governs the formation of all HK companies. Companies may be limited or limited by guarantee.

A **private** company can have no more than 50 shareholders, and cannot invite the general public to subscribe to its shares. A private company restricts the rights to transfer shares. Unlike a public company, a private company is not required to file a copy of its annual accounts with the **Registrar of Companies**.

Typically the costs for forming a HK company, excluding capital registration fees, is HK$7,000 to HK$8,000 (about US$1,200). This represents costs for lawyers, printing, and other incidental expenses. Capital fees payable to the Registrar of Companies are HK$600 plus HK$6 (about US$ 80¢) per HK$1,000 (about US$141) of authorized capital.

Companies are formed by lodging a **Memorandum** and articles of association with the Registrar, upon which a certificate of incorporation will be issued you in about 6 weeks. A public company must also file a prospectus. A company can commence business immediately after receiving its certificate of incorporation. In the case of a public company, a statutory meeting of shareholders is required no sooner than 1 month, and not later than 3 months, after the date it is allowed to commence business.

Every company is required to keep proper books at the company's registered office, which must be in Hong Kong. An independent auditor must be appointed by the company to report to the shareholders on the accounts examined by him.

Estate Taxes

There is an estate duty on resident and nonresident estates over HK$2,000,000. The estate tax rate begins at 6% and tops-out at 18% on estates over HK$5,000,000. Shares held in HK companies are subject to estate duty upon the demise of either a resident or nonresident stockholder. Shares and other assets in HK companies held by another offshore company are not subject to HK estate taxes. HK businessmen often use a Panamanian or Vanuatu holding company to hold their HK and other assets to avoid the HK estate taxes. This is a legitimate and recognized tax planning techniques.

Hong Kong Trusts

Hong Kong is a common-law jurisdiction. The HK **Trust Ordinance** was modeled after the English **Trustee Act of 1925**.

Because HK does not tax capital gains, dividends or foreign source incomes, passive investments of many types can be held in a HK trust. For example, interest on U.S. Treasuries paying 11% pa could be received 100% tax free by a HK trust. Note, the issue date of the U.S. Treasuries would have to be after 7-18-84, as the Tax Reform Act of 1984 repealed interest withholding taxes on bonds issued after (but not before) that date.

Beneficiaries, whether resident or nonresident, are not subject to any form of tax on the distributions made by the trust. There is no requirement that a trust be registered, and a HK trust does not have to file annual returns.

Mauritius
(low tax haven in the Indian Ocean)

Mauritius, in the Indian Ocean 500 miles east of Madagascar, is a little island democracy about 2/3rds the size of Rhode Island. Mauritius has a topography and subtropical climate much like the Hawaiian Islands. Oval shaped, only 38 miles long and 28 miles wide, Mauritius is almost completely surrounded by a coral reef. Average temperatures of 74° on the coast and 67° on the misty central plateau make Mauritius a land of enchantment.

The first Westerners to visit Mauritius were the Portuguese in the 16th century, and they found the island totally uninhabited. Since then much of the original plant and animal life has been displaced, including the flightless dodo bird. After the Portuguese came the Dutch, who gave up establishing a settlement there in 1710. The French took possession next, introducing sugar, spices, coffee, tea and other crops to the island.

During the Anglo-French wars of the 1700s the French made the mistake of attacking British shipping from their *I'le de France* (Mauritius' French name). In 1810 the British captured the island and renamed it Mauritius. Today, Mauritius an independent nation and member of the British Commonwealth of Nations. A governor general is appointed by Great Britain representing the Crown.

Political Stability

Mauritius is politically stable, although the government is run by former leftists who balked at carrying out radical socialistic policies in 1983 to redistribute the sugar cane fields owned mainly by French-Mauritian families. As Minister of Finance V. Seethanah Lutchmeenariaidoo said. "Either we had to nationalize the land and distribute it to co-operatives in a Mexican style agrarian revolution, or we had to use consensus and dialog. We chose the second route."

Ministry official Emmanuel Arouff insists that the *"spirit of democracy and free enterprise are deeply ingrained in Mauritius. We are only too happy that our socialist experiment lasted only 9 months. We value our little bit of prosperity and independence."*

Mauritius maintains ties with the government of South Africa yet openly opposing apartheid. The Mauritian government believes there should be a negotiated settlement. Tourist that visit Mauritius are struck by the island's lack of racial friction and a 94% literacy rate.

Currently, trade (mainly food and machinery) with South Africa account for 10% of Mauritius imports. With its one economy crop Mauritius must import food stuffs heavily.

Territorial System of Taxation

Mauritius is not a no-tax haven like the Bahamas. It's tax system can best be described as territorial, somewhat like Singapore's but with lower rates. All companies in Mauritius, whether resident or nonresident, are taxed only on their net profits earned in Mauritius. There are no capital gains taxes, and stocks and bonds in publicly traded companies and private companies can be sold tax free. There is a land development tax, called *Capital Gains Morcellement Tax,* which is levied on real estate developers who parcel out land for development (resale) purposes. Mauritius tax system is designed to make it a regional warehouse and re-export center to Africa.

Four corporate tax brackets

There are four tax brackets for the corporate taxpayer. Special Certificate Companies pay a flat rate of 15%. Companies listed on the Mauritius stock exchange pay a 25% income tax. Non-Certificate Companies pay at a 35% rate. Generous allowances can often reduce the effective tax rate to a much lower level. For example, investment tax credits for industrial, manufacturing, shipping or tourist activities permit a deduction from income tax equal to 30% of the *cash* actually paid up as share capital. The credit is spread out over three years, but limited to R$30,000 for individuals and R$100,000 for companies. There ia also a fourth type of company - called **International Company** - which can pay no taxes.

International Aspects of Taxation

Residents of Mauritius are eligible to foreign tax credit in respect of foreign source income. The foreign tax credit includes tax sparing credit and in case of dividends credit for underlying tax charged on profits out of which the dividends are paid.

Companies operating in the offshore sector

A special tax regime offering interesting tax incentives exists for companies in the offshore sector.

Although many financial centres have flourished without any tax treaties, Mauritius being a tax planning jurisdiction, has focused the development of its offshore centre on the use of its growing network of Double Taxation Agreements. The expanding network of Double Taxation Treaties reinforces the seriousness of Mauritius as a tax efficient offshore jurisdiction for structuring investment abroad.

Many multinational corporations have used Mauritius to route their investments into emerging regions such as India, China and Pakistan. The various tax treaty benefits have appealed to investors aiming to minimize their costs when repatriating income from their investment in the treaty country where they have invested. Substantial foreign investments have been channeled through Mauritian offshore vehicles and this is expected to increase as the Mauritius treaty expands and as investment prospects in the region flourish.

So far Mauritius has concluded 23 tax treaties and is party to a series of treaties under negotiation. The treaties currently in force are with:
Belgium,   Botswana Luxembourg
South Africa Democratic Republic
Socialist Republic of Sri Lanka
Madagascar   Swaziland Kuwait
France Malaysia   Sweden   Singapore
Germany   Namibia   Thailand
India   Oman United Kingdom
Indonesia   Pakistan   Zimbabwe
Italy   People's Republic of China

Most of the treaties in force have been in existence as from the period when Mauritius launched its offshore sector in 1992.

7 treaties await ratification with:

Bangladesh   Malawi   Russia   Nepal
Mozambique   Vietnam
Lesotho
7 treaties are being negotiated with : Canada, Czech, Greece, Portugal, Tunisia, Uganda and Zambia..

An Offshore Company or Offshore Trust wishing to avail of the benefits of a tax treaty must obtain a Tax Residence Certificate issued by the Commissioner of Income Tax in Mauritius.

International companies pay no taxes

The International Company provides for greater confidentiality and is suited for holding and managing private assets. It es exempt from all Mauritius income taxes. It is however not allowed to raise capital from the public. An International Company is not required to submit audited accounts and confidentiality is ensured by structuring shareholding as bearer shares or through nominee shareholders. However the International Company is debarred from benefitting from double taxation relief under the tax treaties and is not allowed to operate in the freeport. The International Company may either be limited by shares or by guarantee or limited by shares and guarantee or simply unlimited. An International Company may also be registered as a Limited Life Company.

Individual Tax Rates

Resident individuals are taxed on their gross personal income on a sliding scale from 5% to 30%. Personal income consists of earned income (salary, wages, bonus, commissions, fees, pensions and benefits in kind) and unearned income (dividends, trade profits, rents, interests partnership profits). Capital gains are not taxed. Dividends paid on shares of Special Certificate Companies are exempt from tax during the first 10 years starting from the company's production date. Dividends that accrue to foreign investors who get approved status may be repatriated without tax being levied.

For more information on doing business in Mauritius write:

Minister/Finance,
Government House,
Port Louis, Mauritius
Indian Ocean

Pacific Basin tax havens – Western Samoa, Vanuatu, Cook Islands, and Nauru

As we head into the 2,000's, the Pacific basin tax havens are clearly in a position to rival the European and Caribbean havens in both size and importance. With communication and satellite systems improving to the point where businessmen can now reach anyone, anywhere at any hour, and with air travel to all points on the globe becoming faster and more reliable, countries offering tax concessions to outsiders, or imposing little or no taxes on them, are bound to become popular dwellings for the incorporation of foreign subsidiaries and housing of private estates. Following the lead of Nauru, Vanuatu, New Caledonia, Hong Kong, Singapore, Malaysia, The Philippines, The Seychelles and the Cook Islands, is the newest entrant to the Pacific basin tax haven scene - the South Pacific islands of Western Samoa.

Western Samoa - new Pacific Basin haven

Western Samoa is a cluster of Pacific Polynesian islands about halfway between Hawaii and New Zealand. Most know Samoa as the home of legendary author Robert Louis Stevenson, who spent the last 5 years of his life on the main island of Upolo. With towering mountain peaks piercing the great cloud masses above the lava formations from centuries past, with pristine ocean waters meeting beaches of unspoiled tropical beauty, it's no wonder the mainly Polynesian people making up a total population of 160,000 think of their islands as a land of enchantment delivered to them by some ancient God.

Today, Western Samoa is an independent nation with a parliamentary government. The Constitution provides for a Head of State, Prime Minister and Cabinet of Ministers who comprise the Executive Council and the Legislative Assembly. There are two major political parties, and **both** strongly support the new Offshore Banking, Insurance and International Companies legislations allowing for tax free operations by foreigners.

Western Samoan tax law has its foundation in English and Commonwealth statutory common law. The five Acts which are the basis for the Offshore Finance, Banking and Insurance Center are based upon English law, with an intermingling of the laws of the various financial centers. English remains the authentic text, and documents and records are required to be kept in the English language.

Accessibility & Communications

Apia on the island of Upolo is the commercial capital and administrative center of Western Samoa. Accessibility is good. There is a modern international airport which can accommodate 747 type aircraft. The country's national airline, Polynesian Airlines, is managed by Ansett Airlines of Australia. Other carriers that service Western Samoa include Air New Zealand, Air Pacific, Samoa Air and Hawaiian Air. Direct flights to New Zealand, Tonga, Australia, Fiji, Cook Islands, American Samoa and Hawaii operate daily.

The international telephone system is first-class, and direct dialing under the country code (685) can be made 24 hours a day. Cable, telex, facsimile services, DHL and Skypack express courier services are available at a moments notice.

Taxation & exchange controls

Only companies organized under one of the *special* Offshore tax regimes are exempt from Western Samoa's domestic corporate income taxes which top out at 39%. Individual residents are taxed on their worldwide incomes at rates as high as 50%. However, Western Samoa **does not** tax capital gains, and dividend income of residents is taxed at a top rate of 10%.

International Companies, **Offshore Banks, Insurance Companies,** and **International Trusts** are exempt from income tax or other duties, including direct or indirect tax or stamp duty on any transaction or profits of or on dividends and interest paid by or to any company registered or licensed under the various Off-shore Acts.

In addition, there are no currency or exchange controls, restrictions or regulations, and no foreign exchange levies payable on the taking or sending of any foreign currency out of Western Samoa by an international or registered foreign company or trustee company, nor in respect of the transactions of an off-shore bank or registered trust or the business of a registered insurer.

Strict privacy provisions

Western Samoa has signed no tax treaties with any nation. It is against the law for anyone having information pertaining to the business profits of any bank, company, insurer or trust to divulge that information to outside tax collectors or other investigators. Each of the various Acts have built-in provisions within their texts vigorously forbidding the divulgence of confidential information. Fines to $50,000 and jail terms to 5 years are provided for under Samoan law for anyone who contravenes Samoa's secrecy provisions.

Files kept by the Registrar and documents lodged with them are confidential and are not available for inspection by the public.

Section 26. of the Offshore Banking Act 1987

26. **Breaches of professional secrecy** - (1) Every person commits an offense against this Act who -
(a) Divulges any information in Western Samoa or elsewhere in relation to -
   (i) Any off-shore banking business in Western Samoa;
   (ii) The transfer of money or property into or out of Western Samoa in the course of any off-shore banking business; or
   (iii) The account of any person with a licensee or any item of such account or the fact of any person having had such account, which he has become aware of in his capacity as an officer, employee, or authorized agent of a licensee or as an officer or employee of an approved auditor; or
(b) Tries to induce others to breach professional secrecy in relation to such matters.

International Companies Act (1987)

The procedures for incorporating an International Company are simple and rarely take more than one or two days. No prior Government approval is needed, and except for the incorporation fee, no other government charges will be incurred.

Application is made to the Registrar of International & Foreign Companies through a trustee company, accompanied by a Memorandum and Articles of Association. The government provides a standard Memorandum and set of Articles which can be adopted with or without variation. There need be only one subscriber and normally this would be a trustee company or a nominee company acting on behalf of the beneficial owner, whose name need not be disclosed.

Taxation

Companies incorporated under the International Companies Act of 1987 are not liable to pay any income or corporation tax.

An International Company pays an annual license fee of US$ 300, unless at the time of incorporation, it elects to pay a license fee to cover the following periods:

5 years US$ 1,000
10 years US$ 1,500
20 years US$ 2,000.

No requirement under the International Companies Act of 1987 to file accounts. A company is required to keep financial records, which reflect the financial position of the company.

Shareholders: The minimum number of shareholders is one unless a specific type of debenture is outstanding in which case it is permitted to have no shareholders. Details do not appear on the public register.
Capital: There is no minimum capital requirement and shares may have par value or no-par value.
Currency and share warrants issued to bearer may be issued or exchanged for fully paid up shares.
Directors: There need be only one director. A trustee company, if requested, will make available an officer for appointment as a resident director, but it is not a requirement that a director be a resident of Western Samoa. A director may be a company. Director's meetings need not be held in Western Samoa and written resolutions signed by all directors may be minuted instead of meetings.
Secretary: A company must have a residential secretary who is an officer of a registered trustee

company. A company's legal obligations are fulfilled by the resident secretary. Additional non-resident secretaries may be appointed.

Registered Office: The registered office is required to be at the office of a trustee company.

Certificate of Incorporation are valid for 12 months and is renewable on payment of the annual renewal fee and lodging of the company's annual return.

Accounts: A company must keep proper accounts and records which must be presented at any meeting with a profit and loss account and a balance sheet. These do not require filing with the Registrar. Audited accounts are not required if the company does not invite the public to subscribe to its shares.

Names requiring consent or a License: Bank, building society, savings, loans, trust, trustees, insurance, assurance, reinsurance, co-operative, council, Chamber of Commerce, university or their foreign language equivalents.

Suffixes to denote limited liability: Limited, Corporation, Incorporated, Sociètè Anonyme, Sociedad Berhad Anonima or the relevant abbreviations.

No Disclosure of beneficial ownership to authorities required

Language of legislation and corporate documents: The corporate documents of an International Company may be in any language.

Procedure To Incorporate

By submission of the company's Memorandum and Articles of Association and registration fee to the Registrar of International and Foreign Companies.

Restrictions On Trading

An International Company cannot trade with Samoans nor own local real estate. An International Company cannot undertake the business of banking, insurance, assurance, reinsurance, fund management, the management of collective investment schemes, trust management, trusteeship or any other activity that may suggest an association with the bank or insurance industries without obtaining the appropriate license.

Banking licenses

Western Samoa is one of the better offshore jurisdictions which currently offer restricted offshore banking licenses. Unrestricted licenses are not obtainable by anybody other than existing banks and require a minimum paid up capital of USD 10 million. This will probably be unattractive to most applicants. Restricted licenses require a minimum paid up capital of USD 250,000 but the operations of the bank must be run through a local trust company. This does mean that an element of third party control and involvement in the affairs of the bank is required but this has the advantage that local expertise is readily available.

Costs for a restricted license would be USD 22,500 and application time would be approximately one to three months.

Offshore Management & Trustee Companies

Trustee companies in Western Samoa must be licensed under the *Trustees Companies Act of 1987* before they can carry on the business of servicing non-residents. Before the government will issue a license a trustee company must have a paid-up cash or unimpaired reserves of not less than US$210,000.

Accounts of trustee companies must be audited at least once a year in every year, and a copy of the auditors report submitted to the Registrar within 6 months of the end of the company's financial year, with an annual report.

No shares of a Western Samoan trustee company may be transferred without the prior written approval of the Minister of Finance.

A trustee company's license may be canceled if it has contravened or failed to comply with any condition of registration, is in breach of any provisions of the *Trustees Companies Act 1987,* or if the Minister considers that it is undesirable that it should continue to be registered. A trustee company that commits a criminal offense anywhere in the world can have its license revoked.

All monies paid to a trustee company under a trust must be held separate from its own monies and in trust for the purpose for which it was paid.

Asset Protection

Western Samoa is a very good jurisdiction in which to open a company. The International Companies Act of Western Samoa was passed in 1987, so they have been in the business for many years and have experience. Western Samoa is still a relatively unknown offshore jurisdiction, and is might not be viewed with as much suspicion as some of the more well known tax havens such as the Cayman Islands.

Total exemption from taxes is granted to "International Companies" incorporated under the 1987 Act as well as to "International Trusts" registered under the International Trusts Act, 1987. The International Companies Act stipulates that entities operating under the offshore legislation are exempted from all taxes, any direct or indirect levy and exchange or currency controls as long as the company is in business i.e. into perpetuity.

Western Samoa is not party to any mutual assistance, gateway, or information exchange agreements unlike some of the British Dependent Territories. While taking a hard line on money laundering and fraud, Samoa has legislated to protect the confidentiality of its International Companies. In addition to common law protection, it is a legislated criminal offense to divulge any information regarding the shareholders, officers or operations of a Samoan International Company.

The International Companies Act expressly denies any right to disclose information that "will, or is likely to, result in the payment of any tax, other penalty or any fine by the company" (section 227 (4) (c) of the Act). Western Samoan legislation also gives far reaching powers to an International Company. Of particular interest to prospective clients is Article 4, Schedule 1 of the International Companies Act, 1987 (Section 20). It states that under The Powers of an International Company "it may acquire, hold, dispose of or deal with the whole or any part of the undertaking of any other company, association or business".

A court order is only possible in cases of improper conduct of directors during winding up, fraud or dishonesty, or money laundering. Also, in Western Samoa the definition of "debt" specifically excludes any "taxation, fines or penalties imposed by any government". A foreign taxation authority is therefore unable to petition the court for the winding up of an International Company in Western Samoa for the recovery of tax related debts, because the court cannot recognize any taxation payable as debt.

The uniqueness of the Samoan legislation is also demonstrated by an asset protection section

of the Act (Section 228 (B)) whereby a member can elect that his shares in the company can be automatically vested in a specified person on the occurrence of a specified event. The definition of "specified event" is flexible but it typically includes the occurrence of a foreign expropriation or court order. This can also be used by the original beneficial owner to pass a company on to his or her beneficiary upon presentation of the death certificate of the original owner. There are no similar statutory provisions protecting member interests in BVI or other traditional jurisdictions.

In addition, in Western Samoa, the statutory limitation for a creditor to petition the court for the reinstatement of a corporation previously struck off is only two years (Section 197 (6) of the Act). The comparable limitation period in some other countries is ten years, giving rise to a period of contingent liability five times greater than that of Western Samoa.

OFFSHORE LEGISLATION

The following legislation was introduced in 1988-1989:
- Trustee Companies Act 1987
- Offshore Banking Act 1987
- International Trusts Act 1987
- International Insurance Act 1988

Amendments to the offshore legislation have been enacted regularly in response to recommendations from the offshore industry.

The legislation now incorporates some of the most up to date features of offshore legislation. It is designed to attract a high quality international clientele whilst providing for maximum flexibility, an efficient service and a minimum of formality, all at an acceptable cost. Further legislation to cover other aspects of offshore business and to improve the facilities offered by the Western Samoa offshore finance centre will be introduced as required.

Much of the information presented here was furnished *Registrar of the International and Foreign Companies*. **Central Bank of Western Samoa** • Office of Registrar of International & Foreign Companies • P.O. Box **Private Bag** • Apia, Western Samoa • Tele: (685) 24-071 • Telex: 200 SX
Cable:CENBANK

Niue Island seeks to become tax haven

Back in 1994, when I began reading about Niue on the front page of the *Offshore Financial Review*, I thought the article was a fabricated spoof. But the bureaucracy on the tiny coral island just halfway between Western Samoa and the Cook Islands are serious in their aspirations.

Niue, once called Savage Island, is a self-governing territory of New Zealand in the southwestern Pacific, about 2,300 km (1,400 mi) northwest of New Zealand. A coral island 23 km (14 mi) long and 16 km (10 mi) wide, Niue's area is 259 sq. km (100 sq mi).

Alofi is its administrative center and only port. Niue has a population of 2,531 (1986), composed of mostly mixed Polynesians and Melanesians. Its population has been declining because of emigration to New Zealand. Agriculture is hampered by a heavily wooded interior, rocky soil, and a lack of surface water, but the island exports copra, sweet potatoes, and bananas as well as woven goods. Niue is linked by air to Tonga and Western Samoa.

Settled for at least 1,000 years, Niue was visited by James Cook in 1774. He was received by the natives with hostility--hence the name Savage Island. Niue was annexed by New Zealand in 1901 and was made a self-governing territory in 1974.

According to the country's Finance Minister, Mr. Coni Lakatani, Niue recently enacted 10 pieces of legislation modeled after laws in the British Virgin Islands and the Cook Islands.

The 20-member Legislative Assembly has passed laws which permit offshore banking, and international companies register, and the issue of Niue bonds and commercial banking.

Minister, Mr. Coni Lakatani stresses that Niue's new laws were designed to keep out money launderers and drug traffickers. Minister, Mr. Coni Lakatani, also said the reason Niue wants to enter the tax haven business along with the Cook Islands, Vanuatu, the Bahamas and Cayman was to reduce the country's dependence on New Zealand aid.

Niue's population is only 2,500. Niue's land area of 258 sq km makes Niue is about the same size as the Cayman Islands.

Niue is a self governing member of the Commonwealth with New Zealand. New Zealand responsible for its defense and foreign affairs as well as providing most of the money to run the island. The major Niuean export is vegetables.

According to MOSSACK FONSECA & CO., Niue's now has 4,432 IBCs on the public registry, but only one banking institution - Westpac Banking Corporation (Niue) - which operates as a domestic retail bank, only for the residents in Niue.

Niue's International Business Companies Act 1994 offers:

• Total secrecy and anonymity;
• Incorporation documents may be drafted in English or any other language, together with a translation into English. The Company's books may be kept anywhere in the world. It is not mandatory to send a copy of the Register of Directors or Shareholders to the Registered Office. The Corporate Seal is optional.
• Bearer shares/shares of no par value are permitted. One shareholder and one director is all that is required.
• No exchange controls; no annual return required; meetings can be held anywhere in the world.

First Year Incorporation cost ≈ $1400
Minimum Annual Fee $675
Government Tax / Filing Fee $150
TOTAL $825

Niue's main problem is it currently has little infrastructure in place to support a sophisticated tax haven business. In addition, Niue is relatively isolated. There are only a very few flights per week which operate out of Western Samoa via the Cook Islands. On April 26, 1999, Hon Premier Sani Lakatani announced that flights from Rarotonga Cook Islands will commence in two weeks time.

Most foreign investors would probably prefer to operate out of the more established tax havens of Western Samoa and the Cook Islands, rather than spend the extra time and money to get to underdeveloped Niue. For Niue to break into the tax haven business and become a serious player, more major bank like Westpac would need to establish a banking presence.

Vanuatu – South Pacific no-tax haven

Since time began, Vanuatu has levied no income or capital gains taxes on profits. Some businessman before 1971 had made good profits in Vanuatu, formerly jointly administered by a French/British Condominium government, taking advantage of what was then a fiscal paradise with no formal structure. [5.]

The British Government created corporate and other legislation in 1971, which developed into a legal framework for a tax haven with the elements of secrecy for "exempted" private companies (those that did not do business in Vanuatu), possibly because the British saw this as a means by which the heavily aid-funded country could become more self-sufficient economically.

Background

Vanuatu, formerly known as the New Hebrides, is an independent nation and member of the Commonwealth. Prior to independence in 1980, the English and French legal system governed the foreign inhabitants that resided in Vanuatu while native New Hebrideans were governed by a code of native law interpreted by "native courts".

This condominium form of government was made even more bizarre when in 1914 the Anglo-French protocol provided that the joint court of the island would be made up of one British, one French and a third judge to be appointed by the King of Spain. As fate would have it, from 1931 to 1975 there was no King of Spain, so the British and French judges took turns as presiding judges. The also decided to share the salary of the vacant judge's office.

There were rumors that Vanuatu would relinquish its no-tax haven status after independence (there were never any laws offering guarantees against future imposition of taxes), but Vanuatu's new *Constitution* states that until otherwise provided by Parliament, pre-independence British and French laws shall continue to prevail. **The Companies Act, Bank Regulation** and the **Trust Companies Regulation** form the statutory framework for which common-law decisions are based.

Geography

Vanuatu is an archipelago of 80 tropical islands lying 1,100 miles east of Australia and 500 miles west of Fiji. The topography is varied, with heavily forested, rugged mountains and high plateaus inland, and rolling hills and terraces on the coast. The 250,000 square miles of territorial waters surrounding the 80 islands are regarded as an important resource for future development. The arable soil and climate is ideal for the development of livestock husbandry. There are several active volcanoes on the islands.

Port-Vila - the capital

The port city of Vila (population 25,000) is the capital of Vanuatu. It is both charming and primitive. Ninety percent of the people of Vanuatu are dark skinned Melanesians. Asians, Polynesians, and Europeans make up the rest of the population. French, English and Bislama (the national language - a Pidgin English) are the official languages. Christianity is the major religion. Vanuatu's national anthem is *"Yumi, Yumi, Yumi"* (we, we, we).

Transportation and Communications

From the capital city of Port Vila a businessman can fly direct to Australia, New Zealand, Fiji, New Caledonia, **Nauru** (another no-tax haven) and the Solomon Islands. There, connecting flights to other parts of the world can be arranged with no trouble.

Twenty-four hour telecommunications in the form of telephone, facsimile, telex, and telegraph via satellite keep Vanuatu in touch with the rest of the world. Domestic and international postal services are reliable and courier services are available.

Over 1,000 Corporations in Vanuatu

Vanuatu's growth has not been as dramatic as that of the British Virgin Islands where today

---

5. From *Close-up Vanuatu* by Lindsay D. Barrett and Adrian Sinclair (Coopers & Lybrand) **(Offshore Investment)** (November 1992) pgs 11 thru 20

over 60,000 IBCs have been registered. By mid-1988, only three major banks were servicing the island, but these were all major prime banks. Accounting firms now number seven, and include KPMG Peat Marwick, Coopers & Lybrand and Price Waterhouse.

Today there are well over 1,000 companies doing business in Vanuatu. The British administration there has always nurtured Vanuatu's tax haven status. Laws continue to be drafted and enacted to attract offshore banks, captive insurance companies and exempt corporations.

Vanuatu's corporate laws were extracted from the British type, as enacted in the **New Hebrides Companies Regulation of 1971** and changed by the **Queen's Regulation**. Companies can be exempt or ordinary, but most offshore investors choose the exempt type company.

International Business Companies Act

Vanuatu recently enacted its own International Business Companies (IBC) Act. The new laws complement existing legislation controlling formation of exempted companies, banks, insurance companies and trust companies.

Exempted company names can now be reserved by telephone, and the Registrar provides for same day incorporation service for private exempted companies.

Vanuatu's new IBC Act has been modeled after the International Business Companies Acts already in place in the Bahamas and the BVI. One copy of the Memorandum and Articles of Association are lodged with the government and kept on file.

Exempt companies no longer have to file audited annual reports and provide the full name and home address of each beneficial owner as a pre-clearance to incorporation. Instead, an annual certification is lodged with the annual $300 registration fee.

Any improper disclosure of any financial information to outsiders is subject to criminal prosecution. Like other no-tax havens, Vanuatu relies on strict bank secrecy to attract business.

Some advantages of incorporating a company in Vanuatu include:

• A professional infrastructure that is experienced.
• During Vanuatu's working day, you can communicate using the latest communication systems and technologies with Europe and across the Pacific to Los Angeles and New York.
• Vanuatu's business law is published in French and English.
• Exempted (offshore) companies can be incorporated within a day.
• Vanuatu has not had a drug trafficking or money laundering problem.
• Vanuatu was the first tax haven to introduce legislation for the reconciliation of companies into or from Vanuatu.
• Bearer shares or warrants are available.
• The shipping registry is based on the Liberian model and charges, thus costs are modest.
• Exempted banks can be formed with a limited amount of costs. It is estimated that there are over 200 private banks officially registered in Vanuatu.
• There are no death or succession duties.
• There are no tax treaties for the exchange of financial information with other nations.
• New legislation is being planned that will provide for
(A) increased confidentiality.
(b) Delimit the perpetuity period of trusts;
(c) introduce asset protection trust legislation;
(d) Reduce annual registration costs for exempt companies to US$300.
(e) create a new category of company (the IBC) to replace the existing exempt company legislation.

Costs to Incorporate

The costs of forming an exempt company in Vanuatu is about US$1,600. Annual maintenance costs, including government fees, director's meetings, and office space might run $1,500 per year additional.

Vanuatu's Trust and Trustee fees

Trusts can be formed in this common-law jurisdiction. Trust statutes are styled after UK legislation as in force January 1, 1961, and modified by the **New Hebrides Perpetuities and**

Accumulations Regulation, 1974. Trusts can be formed for up to 80 years.

Trusts can be established quickly and are normally completed on the day the settlement is received. Special purpose irrevocable and revocable (grantor) trusts may be set up in Vanuatu.

At present there is no requirement to register the trust deeds with the Vanuatu government. A stamp duty is assessable on each instrument of settlement at a rate of 0.5%, with a minimum duty being equivalent to US$75. It is normal for the initial settlement to be under US$15,000 so the minimum stamp duty applies.

Further transfers, if made without an instrument (i.e., cash), to a Vanuatu trust require no further duty. Additional settlements made be instrument where the instrument itself does not come under the jurisdiction of Vanuatu are not subject to stamp duty, but such instruments may not be admissible in court if it were needed as evidence, unless it was brought into the jurisdiction and the stamp duty paid at that time.

Normally, the minimum annual trustee fee charged in Vanuatu is between US$400 and US$500, but if the trust holds as its sole asset the shares of a limited liability company administered by the trustee, than that fee is reduced to an even lower level. Typically, the annual trustee charges are on a sliding scale such as:

0.4% on the first US$250,000
0.2% on the next US$250,000
0.15% on the next US$500,000
0.1% on the next US$1,000,000

In addition, the trustees may, depending on the value of the trust, charge for the time spent in carrying out their trusteeship and for the accounting work in keeping the books of the trust.

Exempt Insurance Companies

Exempt insurance companies or Captive Insurance companies can be formed under New Hebrides Insurance Regulation, 1973. Exempt Insurers can sell securities, unit trusts or mutual funds under the **New Hebrides Prevention of Fraud (Investment) Regulation 1971**, but cannot solicit insurance business with the general public in Vanuatu.

Application for insurance licenses are processed by the Registrar of Companies and are usually available within two weeks, depending upon the satisfactory submission of details of the beneficial owners or principals behind the proposed company.

Independent written references that provide evidence of good character and standing of the principals are required.

Incorporation and licensing costs are competitive and first year costs may be as little as US$2,000. Annual fees thereafter can be kept as low as US$1,200 if only a minimal amount of services are required.

Exempted Offshore Banks

Exempted banking licenses cost about US$5,500, with an annual fee of US$4,500 due each year thereafter. An exempt bank cannot do business within Vanuatu, other than with other exempted companies. Exempted banks do not have to meet any reserve requirements, and need not submit detailed statistical returns.

Generally, the requirements of the government in making an application for an exempted bank or insurance company require a paid up capital of at least $150,000.

There are only a limited number of reputable, full service bank and trust companies that can help you with an incorporation in Vanuatu. At least five Australian banks are open for business in Vanuatu, even though the Australian government has made it increasingly demanding for Australians to use the tax haven entities. Barclays Bank (P.O. Box 123, Port Vila, Vanuatu) and representatives of banks in Hong Kong, Switzerland and France are also open for business. Peat Marwick, the U.S. accounting firm, can be contacted about its trust services by writing:

Peat Marwick
P.O. Box 212
Port Vila, Vanuatu
The South Pacific

Currency, Bank Secrecy, Exchange Controls and Tax Treaties

Vanuatu has no tax treaties with any nation. This means the government will not exchange tax information with any outside jurisdiction. Secrecy is protected by the **Government Act**. In addition, management companies often require all officers and staff to sign a **Declaration of Secrecy** at commencement of employment to further protect client confidentiality and privacy.

Vanuatu's local currency is the VATU (**VT**) which is tied to the International Monetary Fund's **S.D.R.** (Special Drawing Rights). The VATU, the Australian dollar (once the legal tender) and other currencies can be used within Vanuatu, as there are no exchange controls. Government approval is not required to transfer or withdraw funds to anywhere in the world.

For more information on Vanuatu write:

Finance Centre Association
P.O. Box 1128
Port Vila
Vanuatu, South Pacific

Fraud scandal rocks Vanuatu in 1994

The island archipelago of Vanuatu in the South Pacific has been rocked by a fraud scandal, but the local government acted quickly to break up the ring of international share fraudsters, jailing three of its members for 18 months.

Mr. Brian Luftspring, Mr. Michael Rhodes and Mr. Narendra Singh - all Canadians - arrived in Vanuatu early in 1994 to work for two phony stock brokerage companies called Buchannan Weir Limited and McCullen & Suarez Limited. [6.]

According to the Offshore Financial Review (London), the two bogus companies rand advertisements in the Australian newspapers and also hired New Zealand salesmen to cold call potential investors in Australia.

Investors who showed interest were sent professionally produced newsletters which promoted Mexico as an investment area with good potential. The Vanuatu sales team then followed up with high pressure telephone call aimed at selling shares in two companies, Mexigulf Sealand, Inc. and BW Mexican Real state Fund, Inc.

Investors were told these companies controlled undeveloped land in Mexico, but in fact these companies were just Turks & Caicos shell companies with no assets.

Following inquiries from Australian investors, Vanuatu's Financial Services Commissioner - Richard Carpenter - aided by former Gibraltar FSC boss William Penman Brown, who was helping to set up Vanuatu regulator - obtained a search warrant and raided the offices used by the defendants.

Simultaneously, orders were obtained from the Vanuatu Supreme Court, freezing a number of bank accounts which were known to have been used by fraudsters. A mass of documents and computer evidence was seized, and this enabled the Commission to identify the organizers of the fraud, who were not on the island. Details have been passed on to other countries' police forces and financial regulators.

During the trial of the three salesman, three investors from Australia told how they had been duped. One had invested almost A$200,000. Before it was closed down, the scam is believed to have netted the fraudsters a total of A$1.2 million.

---

6. From *Vanuatu fraud web uncovered,* by Tony Hetherington **(Offshore Financial Review)** (page #1).

Cook Islands – Wonderland in the South Pacific

It is said roughly one-half of Australia's top 200 companies have subsidiaries in tax havens. Australia, like the United States, is a high tax jurisdiction with a corporate tax rate in 1998 of 20%. Moreover, the 33% corporate rate is a _flat rate_ (no separate income brackets apply) levied on all assessable income from within or without Australia.

The underlying legal system is based on English Common Law as applied to the islands by the Cook Islands Act of 1915. The Cook Islands owe their affiliation to Captain James Cook (1728-1779), English navigator and explorer.

But, the Australian government was not always so incredulous in its tax collecting manner. Up until a few years ago Australia did not tax most capital gains, nor did it tax _foreign source income_ (even if derived from a low-tax haven), provided the income was not totally exempt in the source country, and provided the income did not originate in the UK, New Zealand, Japan, the Netherlands, West Germany, France or Belgium. While tax rules have changed for the worse; even as I write Australia's top executives are finding lucrative loopholes in the Australian tax code to exploit.

A little over ten years ago, the flagship company of Australian entrepreneur Alan Bond - the Bond Corporation - (which had just sold its stake in Mr. "Tiny" Rowland's Lonrho) declared a tax free profit of A$152,800,000. Most of the profit appears to have been generated in the tiny Cook Islands, a Pacific tax haven, formerly a New Zealand dependency but now independent. With a revamped _Companies Code_ allowing for total tax free operations, the Cook Islands are fast becoming an attraction for tycoons and tax haven Robinson Crusoes like Alan Bond. [7]

Accessibility, Communications

The Cook Islands consist of 15 South Sea islands south of Hawaii and due west of Polynesia. Formerly, part of New Zealand, the country became a self-governing democracy in 1965, with Queen Elizabeth II as head of state. Growth as an offshore financial center was spurred on by flexible legislation, coupled with a responsible approach by the Government which created and administer such legislation. The CI Government is very much committed to

developing the islands as a tax haven base for foreigners, and imposes high standards on the Licensed Trust Companies which do much to administer the offshore statutes. [8]

Rarotonga International Airport is shared by Cook Islands International Airlines and Hawaiian Airlines. These airlines provide links to New Zealand, Auckland and Sydney, Australia, Fiji, Honolulu, Tahiti and Samoa.

Excellent international telecommunications (telephones, facsimile, telex and direct dialing system) have been introduced. Postal and courier services are said to be reliable.

Tax System

Company tax (for domestic, not international, companies) is levied at 20 percent. A turnover tax of 10 percent is imposed on all transactions, except for wholesale and export sales where the rate is one percent. New ventures may be taxed at a rate of five percent for five years.

Withholding tax of 15 percent is imposed on payments of interest and dividends for overseas investors (payments to local residents attract a tax of five percent). Withholding tax may be rescinded for companies which are contributing to national development.

Individual taxation commences at a rate of seven percent when income reaches US$2,3 10 per annum and increases incrementally to 37 percent at approximately US$2 1,000 per annum.

An altogether separate tax regime exists for offshore entities. Such regimes run parallel to the domestic onshore legislation, but it is the offshore jurisdiction which provides the generous tax free environment within which international companies, partnerships and trusts may operate freely, and in which many offshore banks and insurance companies are registered. There are no taxes, exchange controls, stamp or other duties imposed on offshore entities. There are no reporting requirements.

International Companies (ICs)

Offshore companies, similar to the International Business Corporations (**IBC**) used by the Caribbean tax havens, can be formed

---

7. From _"The Tax Haven Weltanschauung"_ by Bill Harcourt, **Offshore Adviser** (April, 1989), pg. 9.

8. From _"Perfect Hosts who never tax foreign companies"_, by Robert Miller (Cook Islands), pg 50 to 52, **Offshore Investment Magazine**, June, 1988,

under the **International Companies Act 1981-82** (ICA). Also authorized to register under this act are foreign companies incorporated outside the Cook Islands.

The IC Act contains provisions which permit the company to repurchase their own shares, issue bearer debentures, make gifts, issue bearer shares, distribute profits to non-shareholders and effect redomiciliation in and out of the Cook Islands. Only one shareholder is needed to form a CI company. [9]

The ICA grants that no Act of the Cook Islands Parliament shall impose "any (i) liability, duty, responsibility, obligation or restriction; (ii) any fee, impost, tax, levy, dues, duty or excise; or (iii) any fine or penalty on an international or foreign company."

Shares in a Cook Island International Companies need not have a par value and may be designated in one or more world currencies. Redemption of shares may be effected from capital, and fully paid shares may be canceled and bearer obligations issued in their place. A company needs only one director, and it is not a requirement that he be a resident. A resident secretary is required who must be an officer of a licensed trust company.

Foreign companies seeking to register as a foreign company must lodge certain basic information with the Registrar and provide a registered office, which must be the principal office of a trustee company in the Cook Islands.

Trust Law in the Cook Islands

The trust law of the Cook Islands is derived from the English Common Law. That law has been amended in the offshore jurisdiction by specific statutory enactment of the Cook Islands Parliament.

The relevant legislation to Cook Islands offshore asset protection trusts ("offshore trusts") is the International Trusts Act 1984 ("the Act")(as amended 1985, 1989, 1991 and 1995-96). The object of the Act is to statutorily simplify many of the difficult aspects of trust law while at the same time not losing the familiar fundamentals of the trust relationship and the trust concept. Foreign legal and financial advisors therefore find Cook Islands trust law familiar, but without some of the

pit-falls that can exist in the law of trusts that has evolved over the centuries.

The Act provides a registration system whereby a registered offshore trust is sheltered from both the general Common Law and Cook Islands general statute law insofar as those laws are inconsistent with the Act. Application for registration is made by a licensed trustee company. The application must certify that no resident of the Cook Islands is a beneficiary of the offshore trust, advise the date of the trust instrument, the name of the trustee and the name of the offshore trust. There is no requirement to file the trust instrument with the Registrar nor is there any requirement to disclose the beneficiaries, settlor or any other parties to the offshore trust. There are no accounting disclosure requirements.

The Act has removed some of the difficult aspects of the Common Law relating to trusts thereby creating a flexible tax effective environment in which the familiar English trust concept can be used both as a tax planning and an asset protection vehicle. Specific technical features of offshore trusts are:-

Trust taxes

The trust, the trustee and all the parties to the trust are not subject to any form of taxation whatsoever in the Cook Islands.

Perpetuity Period

The Common Law perpetuities rule applicable to trusts has been abolished. A settlor can provide in the trust instrument for an offshore trust to continue indefinitely, terminate on a specified date or terminate on the happening of a specified event.

Other Common Law Rules

The rule against accumulations and double possibilities does not apply.

Bankruptcy

Notwithstanding any law of the settlors home jurisdiction, an offshore trust is neither void nor voidable in the event of the settlor's bankruptcy.

Foreign Judgements

No foreign judgement affecting an offshore trust, the parties to or property thereof shall be

---

9. ***"Bearer shares"*** do not carry (identify) the name of the owner on the shares on the stock certificate, and are payable to anyone who has them in his possession. U.S. companies are prevented by law from issuing bearer shares.

entertained in a Court in the Cook Islands if that judgement is based on the application of any law inconsistent with the Act or if the judgment relates to a matter governed by the law of the Cook Islands.

Retention of Control and Benefits by the Settlor

An offshore trust shall not be invalid nor shall a disposition be declared invalid or affected in any way if a settlor either retains or acquires:

- a power of revocation of the trust
- a power of disposition over trust property
- a power to amend the trust instrument
- power to remove, appoint or direct parties to the trust
- any interest in the trust property

Spendthrift Beneficiary

An offshore trust may provide that a life or lesser interest given to a beneficiary shall not be alienated or pass by bankruptcy or be taken in execution by process of law.

Heirship Rights

No offshore trust or disposition of property to an offshore trust shall be void, voidable or defective by reason that such trust may avoid an heirship right held by a person in relation to the Settlor.

Purpose Trusts

The Act provides for purpose trusts and has relaxed the application of Common Law rules in relation to such trusts. The Act makes it clear the purpose of such a trust does not have to be charitable and provides guidelines as to how the trust can be enforced.

Fraud

The Act provides specific rules as to when an offshore trust may be challenged for fraud. Where a creditor proves beyond reasonable doubt that an offshore trust was settled with the principal intent of defrauding that creditor and that the Settlor was thereby rendered insolvent or without property by which the creditors claim could be satisfied, the trust shall not be void or voidable BUT shall be liable to satisfy the creditors claim out of the property which would have been available had the settlement not taken place.

An offshore trust shall not be fraudulent as against a creditor of a Settlor:
- if the settlement or disposition takes place either prior to a creditor's cause of action arising or more than two years after a creditor's cause of action arose; or
- where the settlement or disposition takes place within two years of the date of the cause of action accruing and the creditor fails to bring that action within one year of the settlement or disposition.

A cause of action is deemed to accrue as from the date upon which the act or omission relied upon first occurred.

Community Property

The Act provides that subject to contrary provision in the trust instrument, where "community property" is transferred to an offshore trust by a husband and wife, then the property shall continue to be community property after the transfer.

Delegation

Where permitted by the trust instrument, trustees can delegate all functions, except dispositive powers. The delegation must be made in good faith. Trustees are also able to act by majority decision.

Custodian Trustee

A custodian trustee can be appointed for the sole purpose of holding trust property, whilst the day to day decisions relating to the administration of the trust, or dispositive decisions, are made by a managing trustee.

Protector

A protector of a trust can be appointed in the trust instrument. The protector will have the powers and functions provided in the Act, subject to the terms of the trust instrument.

Trustees Duties

The Act codifies the Common Law principles relating to trustee's duties to beneficiaries. The standard of care imposed on a trustee towards a beneficiary is that standard which a prudent person of business would exercise in managing the affairs of others.

Procedural Matters

The Act also provides certain procedural protections. Any action to set aside a settlement or disposition, or any claim against property of the trust must be commenced in the High Court of the Cook Islands. Furthermore the action must be commenced within two years from the date of the subject settlement or disposition.

International Trusts are created pursuant to the *International Trusts Act* 1984 (ITA). At least one of the trustees, donors or holders of a power of appointment must be an international or foreign company or a trustee company. CI trust laws are based on UK common law trust principles, but are more streamlined and less cumbersome to work with.

Confidentiality • Acts of Parliament

Confidentiality is provided in the form of a special penal code. Inspection and search of registers is restricted to company officers, members, debenture holders, and others with written consent of a director, liquidator or **Registrar**. Government officials are not immune to these restrictions.

Acts of Parliament provide the legislative parameters for the offshore jurisdiction. These include the **Trustee Companies Act of 1981-82, International Companies Act, 1981-82, Offshore Banking Act 1981, Offshore Insurance Act, 1981-82, International Trusts Acts 1984, Cook Islands Monetary Board Act 1981, International Partnerships Act 1984, and the Development Investment Act 1977.**

Cook Islands player in Internet casino

The Cook Islands is trying to revive its economically troubled tax haven by licensing a casino operation on the Internet. Casinos of the South Pacific is running the electronic gaming, with 80 per cent of net revenues going to a company called Torrey Pines, located in the US state of Nevada.

Players use their credit cards to place bets on electronic versions of popular casino games. Alternatively, the company will accept money wired to the Cook Islands branch of an unnamed international bank registered in Rarotonga before any bets are made.

Cook Island residents are not allowed to play and New Zealand press reports have quoted a casino spokesman as saying the casino would accept bets only from countries where such gambling is legal.

Meanwhile, the New Zealand government is mounting a publicity campaign against such betting, telling the public that Internet gambling will cost hundreds of millions of dollars a year in lost duties and taxes.

Solution to BVI Competition

Hong Kong's security regulators have been told that the simplification of company rules could lure firms back from registering in tax havens such as the British Virgin Islands.

A former law professor from Canada's McGill University, Ms. Cally Jordan, was commissioned by the government to look at the Companies Ordnance and its effect on the privately controlled companies. She said as many as 100,000 Hong Kong owned companies were registered in BVI because it imposed fewer demands on private companies.

Hong Kong law requires even family firms to undertake mandatory audits, have more than one shareholder and director, hold board meetings and meet other procedural rules. Ms. Jordan recommended the ordinance be changed to make firms easier to set up and run.

Contact for Further Information:
Secretary
Department of Trade, Labour and Transport
Rarotonga
COOK ISLANDS
Tel: (682)28810
Fax: (682)23880

Editorial: In a hearing in June 1987, on the then proposed taxpayer's bill of rights, a Senate finance subcommittee produced a memo from an IRS branch office chief that suggested he would promote employees according to the number of seizures they had made. A Pennsylvania businessman then testified that the IRS seized his girlfriend's farm and bank accounts because it claimed he owed $247,000. Later the IRS said he owed nothing. So sorry to have ruined your friend... By contrast the *Crown Guarantee* against appropriation of Cook Island company property is, in effect, an unofficial blessing and endorsement of tax havenry from her *Highness The Queen of England.* What we see here is a real divergence in tax policy (political freedom) by America's best ally and trade partner. Perhaps the Senate Finance Committees should seriously consider restoring some of our Constitutional rights and freedoms. After all, we're only human beings like the British.

241.

Seychelles • tax haven in the Indian Ocean

The Seychelles are a string of 92 small islands that lie about 1,000 miles off the east coast of Africa in the middle of the Indian Ocean. The Seychelles islands have historically been a tourist destination. Devoid of human inhabitants until the early part of the 17th Century, when it was ruled by France, the Seychelles' multi-lingual population today is made up of Indian, African, Chinese and Europeans, with English the official language. The Seychelles population numbers about 73,000, with most living on the main island of Malle.

The U.S. Air Force pays the Seychelles government $2.8 million a year l to maintain a tracking station there, I and Americans also send $200,000 a year in aid.

Heading in a new direction

Seychelles gained its independence in 1976. Since then a number of major economic, social and political developments have taken place. In the early 1990s a major shift in policy was announced. In 1993, a new constitution was drafted and approved by national referendum based on multi-party democracy.

Following the new constitution, the new Government undertook a total reform of the economy and material policy decisions were announced, with a number of steps taken to promote inward bound investment by the private sector. In 1994, the Seychelles announced its intention to turn the country into a full fledged international business centre (a.k.a. a tax haven), following a study which had been commissioned and implemented by foreign consultants.

Many of the Acts, which comprise the legal basis of the offshore activities, have been enacted in the last few years. The corner stones of the jurisdiction's new economic expansion was the setting up of a collection of modern business legislations modeled after other successful havens, including the British Virgin Islands, the Bahamas, the Cook Islands, Panama, and the Caymans. The new legislation include:

The principal acts are:

- Business Tax Act 1987, and Regulations.
- Social Security Act 1987, and Regulations.
- Trade Taxes Act 1992.
- Investment Promotion Act 1994, and Regulations.
- Seychelles International Business Authority Act 1994.
- International Business Companies Act 1994.
- International Trusts Act, 1994 and Regulations.
- International Trade Zone Act 1995 and Regulations.
- Financial Institutions Act 1984 as amended 1995 and Regulations.
- Central Bank of Seychelles Act 1982 as amended 1986.
- Insurance Act 1994 as amended 1995 and Regulations 1995 and 1996.
- The Anti-Money Laundering Act 1996.
- The Mutual Fund Act 1997.

Aside from these legislations there was a necessity for a regulatory body. In early 1995, the Seychelles International Business Authority (SIBA) was set up to act as regulator for the new of business legislation being introduced. Made up of both private sector members and Government Statutory members, the SIBA's main role is to advance the jurisdiction as a center for International business activity, safeguard that international business transactions are conducted in a proper fashion, and carry out the function of an Authority or Registrar under the law. [10]

Building the international business center

Another pillar in the establishing of the nation as an offshore center has been the development within four main areas of the International Business Center. These include: the incorporation of international businesses in the jurisdiction: the development of Seychelles as an International Trade Zone; the development of financial services (i.e., banking) to support international trading and international businesses; the promotion of the registration and licensing of certain activities in the jurisdiction including those under the Merchant Shipping Act and the Air Navigation Act.

---

10. From *Mature and ready to do business,* by Conrad Benoiton, Managing Director (Seychelles International Business Authority(SIBA) (published in Offshore Investment Magazine (September, 1995).

Low and no taxes - guaranteed

If new legislation and the creation of International trade centers were to be the keys to converting the jurisdiction into a successful tax haven like the Cook Islands or BVI, then the need for a steady tax regime has been another. Recognizing this need, the Government has recently enacted the Investment Promotion Act 1994, which enables businesses to operate under a guaranteed taxation climate with special incentives laid.

Employers receive an automatic entitlement to employ up to 25% of employees from overseas, at a confessional fee of SR. 500 per month per employee out in the legislation. In order to assist investors a 'one stop shop' IDEAS (Investment Development Advisory Service) has been set up in the Ministry of Finance and Communications.

The IBC Act 1994

IBCs must pay an application fee and an annual license fee of US$ 100 for a company with an authorized capital of US$ 5,000 and are not subject to stamp duty, capital gains, corporate or any other local taxes. Application and license fees for companies with an authorized capital of up to US$ 50,000 are US$ 300 and for companies with over US$ 50,000 authorized capital are US$ 1,000. Unusually, the Seychelles government guarantees that these license fees will not be increased once companies are on the register.

International Business Companies Act

The 1994 International Business Companies Act (IBC Act) is a modern and progressive piece of legislation incorporating many of the best features of the acts of the Caribbean offshore financial centres. The IBC Act has been a distinguished success. Over 3,500 companies have been set up in the last four years.

An IBC is exempt from tax on international activities and has various fiscal advantages. It is also very useful to combine formation of an IBC with activities within the Seychelles International Trade Zone and in conjunction with an international trust. Overall, the Seychelles has gained the reputation for being a hospitable country. The same applies to its reception to potential international investors.

The Seychelles IBC is an extremely flexible vehicle and has been incorporated in several forms such as a registered company and as a limited life company. Formation of an IBC is through a registered agent who applies to SIBA. Features of an IBC are ease and speed of formation where and name approval and company formation can take place often on the same day.

IBC companies may open foreign currency accounts and are not subject to exchange controls.

Common law trust legislation

The jurisdiction's legal system has been influenced by the principles of the Napoleonic civil code and common law. As such the trust concept, which is familiar to all English speaking jurisdictions, is not recognized by the Seychelles civil code. Nevertheless, in order to provide a strong legislative environment for international trusts, the International Trusts Act 1994 has been introduced recently by the Government.

International Trust Act 1994

For the most part, there are few restrictions as to what a trust can and cannot do in Seychelles. Revocable and irrevocable Trusts are permitted. Trusts cannot involve any land in Seychelles, but trusts may own and trade-in other shares, open bank accounts or even deal in Government securities in the country.

Neither the trust, nor the transfer or disposition by a person creating an international trust can be nullified by any foreign rule or forced heir ship. An international trust may be charitable or non-charitable. An international trust may be created by an oral declaration or by an instrument in writing, a will or codicil. There are no limitations on the accumulation of income.

No requirement to specify the name of the grantor or the name of the beneficiary, unless the latter is a Seychelles national or a body corporate resident in Seychelles. Confidentiality is maintained, and it is illegal to divulge or produce any information or certificate relating to an international trust, except under an injunction of the Seychelles. An international trust is valid and executable in Seychelles.

An international trust may be set up to trade (commercial trust), to deal with life insurance (life insurance trust), to manage provident and pension funds or cash deposits etc. The grantors (i.e., trust creator or settlor) or the trustees can be named as beneficiaries under the trust. The grantor does not at any time during the duration of the trust have to be a resident of Seychelles, but at least one trustee must be so resident. The law governing an international trust is the law chosen by the grantor to be the proper law, expressed or implied, in the terms of the trust.

Setting-up an international trust

How can you form an International Trust in Seychelles, and what about taxation? It is required that you apply through a licensed trustee incorporated in the jurisdiction. The licensed trustee would prepare the necessary documentation on your behalf and submit it to the SIBA, which would then register the cost. The standard fee for government registration is US$100. There are no taxes on international trusts and there is no demand for stamp duty or capital gains tax.

Insurance Act of 1994 & The Financial Institutions Act of 1984

The rules governing insurance, the Insurance Act in 1994 as amended in 1995, require that no person can carry on any class of insurance business without a license.

The licensing procedure for establishing a bank is governed by the Financial Institutions Act 1984 as amended. The Central Bank must license any person wishing to operate as a bank. In considering any applications, the Central Bank may conduct any investigation, which it considers necessary to determine the validity of any documents submitted.

The banks in the Seychelles include several top world class banks, such as Barclays.

The Financial Institutions Act is a comprehensive Act aimed at maintaining the financial proprietary of the banking operations in Seychelles. Expansion of Seychelles' banking activities can be expected by the development of offshore banking by the established banks and overseas banks. Applications for banking licenses whether for domestic or offshore licenses are particularly closely scrutinized.

International Trade Zone

The current legislation proposes that most of the earnings of a Seychelles International Trade Zone (SITZ) company would have to originate from the re-export of goods through the jurisdiction. All companies who operate within the SITZ will enjoy the following: Exemption from all trades tax and duties on imports and exports Exemption from Business Tax and all

1 - Income and Corporate Taxes
2 - Exemption from the payment of Social Security Contribution and Pension Scheme
3 - Exemption from payment of work permits for expatriate workers.

The success of the International Business Center revolves around maximizing the use or the strategic location of the Seychelles, and in particular the development of an International Trade Zone. A number of elements favor the jurisdiction in this regard, not least its geographical location, centrally placed and surrounded by Africa, India and Australia in an area with perfect climatic conditions. A modern airport and port are operational, prime area land is available for development, and there are 6 licensed banks, in addition to 8 licensed management companies, operating in the country.

The Seychelles is a signatory to the Lome TV convention benefiting from the provisions of the convention, a member state of the African Caribbean Pacific countries, and a signatory to the Multilateral Investment Guarantee Agency, which protects all investors from expropriation. With extensive co-operation of neighboring countries, the region is coming to be known as the 'Indian Pacific Rim.'

Mutual Funds Act 1997

The Mutual Funds Act of 1997 regulates mutual funds, unit trusts, and fund administrators. The Act requires that the mutual funds and mutual fund managers may not operate in Seychelles unless they are approved under the Act and a license to operate issued and any conditions attached to the license fulfilled. The Act also governs mutual fund administrators. A licensed administrator requires a license and must operate from an office or principle place of business in Seychelles.

Nauru – tiny South Seas tax haven

Nauru (pronounced nah-oo'-roo) in the South Pacific Basin is one of the world's tiniest nations with a total land area of just over 8 square miles. This South Sea island was first visited by Captain John Fearn of the whaler "Hunter" in 1798, who called it "Pleasant Island". To find Nauru on the map look for an ink spot approximately 2,500 miles northeast of Sydney, Australia.

British law is the foundation for Nauru law

Nauru is a member of the British Commonwealth of Nations, but not the U.N. The language of Nauru is English and Nauruan, but only English is written. Nauru is administered by a president chosen by the popularly elected 18-member legislative council.

Nauru's government has never made much of an effort to promote Nauru's no tax haven status. Press enquiries are never answered, visas are virtually unobtainable, and foreigners can't purchase land. As of 1997, Transportation services were horrible. Approximately 18 banks, one hotel and one insurance company do service the island.

Nauru enacted corporation and trust laws in 1972 to make itself attractive as a modern financial center. Incorporation costs about $900 with an equal amount due annually to keep a company in good standing. Nauru trusts and companies can be used to hold land overseas, manage stock portfolios, and avoid inheritance and estate duties. There are probably only a few hundred companies registered in Nauru at this writing.

Nauru was one of the first tax havens to allow corporations to move in or out without dissolution. A corporation organized anywhere can change its domicile to Nauru by notifying the Nauru Registrar of Corporations that the original jurisdiction permits the transfer.

Nauru is a relatively stable democracy with an independent judiciary. Nauru has no capital city. Nauru has no currency of its own and uses the Australian dollar as a legal tender. Australian tax authorities have blacklisted the country because of its tax haven status. Nauru does not impose any taxes. Nauru has not signed any income tax treaties with any nation.

Banking Licenses

The Banking Act 1975 governs banking business in Nauru and provides for two types of licenses, namely - resident and non-resident. Licenses are renewable annually. A resident license permits the bank to carry on a banking business within Nauru, whereas a non-resident license allows the bank to carry on a banking business outside Nauru. Non-resident banks are restricted from advertising or soliciting funds from the general public, and their activities need to be confined to those of an in-house nature.

Nauru offers the possibility of setting up a bank with no requirement for local directors or any local presence apart from a registered office and company secretary in Nauru. These services would normally be provided by a management organization.

Nauru will accept applications for unrestricted licenses or for non-resident type banks but in practice the authorities are unwilling to grant unrestricted licenses to anybody other than an existing bank and would also impose a requirement that the applicant set up an office and associated infrastructure in Nauru. The capital requirements for an in-house (non-resident) bank are low - USD 100,000 - and the time scale is in the order of one to three months. It is said that a banking license (charter) can also be expanded to include an insurance license. We recommend you proceed with caution, and contact the Nauru Central Bank before you proceed.

A non-resident Nauru bank is prohibited from dealing with anybody other than associated companies and individuals but it might be possible to set up an affiliated finance company which conducts a broader range of activities.

People

Citizenship is limited to native Nauruans, who number about 9,000 and are chiefly of Polynesian, Micronesian, and Melanesian descent. They speak Nauruan, a language unrelated to the Polynesian or Micronesian linguistic families. Nauruans pay no taxes and enjoy free education, health care, and other social services. Many jobs, especially in the phosphate industry, are held by foreign contract laborers. Nauru is a tropical island, where the weather is

245.

perfect and nobody has to work. "The government takes care of every need and even gives $35,000 a year to spend freely."

Economy

Nauru's prosperous economy is based on the export of phosphate rock, which is expected to cease in the mid-1990s. To provide for a secure economic future, the government has invested much of the phosphate revenue overseas in projects ranging from a skyscraper in Melbourne to phosphate plants in the Philippines and India. The country imports most foodstuffs and virtually all manufactured goods. Phosphate mining has rendered most of the island barren and unsuitable for agriculture without massive imports of topsoil. Nauruan attempts to purchase another Pacific island have floundered on the question of sovereignty.

History

First visited by British navigators in 1798, Nauru was annexed by Germany in 1888. Following World War I the island was mandated to Britain, New Zealand, and Australia by the League of Nations. Occupied by the Japanese during World War II, the island later became a UN trusteeship administered by Australia. Phosphate mining made Nauru increasingly uninhabitable, so it was long thought that the people would have to be resettled elsewhere. They insisted on independence, granted in 1968. The government then took control of the phosphate industry and increased its profits.

Nauruans are said to be looking for a new island to move to because their own tiny isle has been devastated by over mining of phosphate ore. It is said Australia may decide to relinquish sovereignty of Curtis Island, and if this happens Nauru may become the first tax haven to transfer itself to another island.

South Seas investment scam

Recently, the Fiji-based *Pacific Island Monthly* has linked Nauru to an investment scam originating out of another South Seas tax haven - Vanuatu. One of the alleged participants, a "Dr. Gopal", has apparently managed to lose money belonging to Nauru's own Phosphate Trust.

According to another newspaper source, $A21m ($13.9m) was lost by investing in a dubious scheme sold to Nauru's representatives in London. The scheme involved the purchase of $21.5m worth of prime bank notes through a company registered in the BVI.

It seems that Nauru Phosphate Trust commissioned $60.4m to Adrian Powles, the London partner of Australian law firm Allen, Allen & Hemsley. Of the original $60.4m, it is believed $8.5m of these funds got lost. Exactly what happened to these funds is still not publicly known, and several paths of the money trail remain obscure. The money was supposed to be invested in a secret interbank trading scheme. Millions of the missing money apparently went to pay fees and commissions as the money moved around.

The money trail included a brass plate company based in Antigua, a trust account in Switzerland, an apartment in the Bahamas, a British Virgin Island company, and finally to Luxembourg.

Dr. Gopal's real name is Gopalan Nair, and the *good* doctor is really a Melbourne based Fijian-Indian who once worked for Wespac bank in Suva. Gopalan Nair co-owned a Vanuatu registered company called Linpar, which operated out of an apartment in Lausanne, Switzerland, before reportedly moving to a new address in Nassau in the Bahamas. Nair and Powles had met through other business connections.

Some of the Nauruan money went through the Commonwealth National Bank of Antigua - a brass plate operation owned by two New York businessman.

Money transfers of the Nauruan funds were allegedly made through accounts in Swiss Volksbank and Bank Albis in Zurich, Wespac in London, Bank of Austria in Vienna, Unibank in Copenhagen and Bank of America in Los Angeles.

The newspaper - *Australian Financial Review* - has linked Powles and the Nauruan money with First Boston Moody Co. in the BVI and Canadian Imperial Bank of Commerce in Nassau, Bahamas. Police don't believe Powles was the "mastermind" behind the scheme, but the day after resigning from the firm Powles was found in an overflowing bathtub with slashed wrists. Powles survived the suicide try and later discharged himself from a psychiatric hospital. He has since resigned from Allen, Allen & Hemsley Some of the cash has been found and frozen in Luxembourg in late 1992 - thus ending a nine-month long financial juggling act.

[From *Tortuous trail to Nauru's Millions*, pg #4 (Offshore Financial Review, London)]

Labuan and other Pacific Basin tax havens

Labuan is a Federal Territory of Malaysia with a population of 35,000. It consists of 7 small islands located just off the coast of Sabah, just north of the Island of Borneo.

Currently, the main economic activities in Labuan include offshore oil and gas operations, shipbuilding and repairing, manufacturing and re exporting. The Island enjoys a free port status with the exception of petroleum products. All other products are free from customs duties and service taxes. The Minister of Finance, Malaysia is committed to the development of Labuan as a functioning offshore center - but not a money laundering haven.

There is no bank secrecy code, but confidentiality is provided for in the *Offshore Companies Act 1990, the Offshore Banking Act 1990, and the Offshore Insurance Act 1990.* Trust companies and its officers are prohibited from making any disclosure as to the existence of any trust or estate or the identity of any settlor, appointee or beneficiary, unless required to do so under the local law.

Malaysia

Malaysia can now be considered a tax haven along side of Singapore. Foreign-source branch profits are not taxed unless remitted back to Malaysia. Apart from land and buildings, gains on capital assets are not taxed. Capital gains on the disposal of real property (including shares in a real property company) situated in Malaysia are subject to gains taxes ranging from a maximum of 20% for assets held less than two years to 5% for assets held for more than 5 years. Interest on deposit with approved financial institution (banks and insurance companies) are subject to tax at a flat rate of 5% on the gross amount. Interest paid to nonresident individuals or foreign corporations by a commercial or merchant bank operating inside Malaysia are exempt from all taxes.

The **Philippines** tax *resident foreign corporations* only on their Philippine source-income. Multinational companies can set-up regional headquarters in Manila and be exempt from tax on their foreign source incomes. International carriers are subject to income tax at a 2.5% rate.

New Caledonia is a South Pacific island belonging to the French. Supposedly, New Caledonia does not yet have income taxes.

New Zealand has no capital gains taxes as such. The NZ government is deliberating whether to pass capital gains tax legislation like its neighbor Australia. While not considered to be much of a tax haven, NZ residents can and have exploited the tax systems of neighboring tax havens, and can continue to do so if the tax plan is carefully thought-out and executed.

In new Zealand, a foreign trust is one whose settlor was not a New Zealand resident at any time from 17 December 1987 to the date of distribution, or from the date the trust was first settled to the date of distribution, whichever period is shorter. As with a qualifying trust, trustee income is taxed to the trustee at the rate of 33%. Only New Zealand-sourced trustee income is taxed. There is no New Zealand tax on distributions to a non-New Zealand resident. However, taxable distributions from a foreign trust to a New Zealand beneficiary are taxed to the beneficiary at the beneficiary's ordinary tax rate. Taxable distributions do not include realised capital profits or gains or the corpus of the trust.

A foreign trust may elect to become liable to New Zealand income tax (i.e. to become a qualifying trust). In this case, the trustee will be liable for income tax on all of the trust's trustee income regardless of its source.

There is currently no inheritance tax or estate duty in New Zealand.

Kiribati and Kanton Island – new tax havens offer passports for $15,000.

The Republic of Kiribati, formerly the Gilbert Islands, straddles both the equator and the international date line in the Pacific Ocean. The national territory extends over 5 million square kilometers (2 million square miles), but the land area is less than that of New York City. Kiribati's 33 islands are grouped into the Gilbert Islands (including Tarawa, the capital, and Banaba, or Ocean Island), the Line Islands, and the Phoenix Islands. Kiribati was part of the Gilbert and Ellice Islands colony until 1975, when the Ellice Islands gained independence as Tuvalu. When the

247.

Gilbert Islands became independent in 1979, they took the name Kiribati, based on the pronunciation of "Gilberts" in the indigenous language, which has only 13 letters in its alphabet.

According to one source (*Offshore Financial Review, London*) there is an offshore offer from this Pacific island which the Hong Kong business community should find to hard to refuse. The tiny Pacific island nation of Kiribati (pronounced Kiribati) is offering wealthy Hong Kong Chinese a special passport and the chance to do business on a remote island with a population of just 45 people (Kanton Island).

Numerous South-pacific nations (including the Cook Islands and Vanuatu) have been keen to get their hands on Hong Kong money, with schemes varying from the respectable (in New Zealand case) to what might be called irregular in the case of Tonga selling its passports to Chinese business figures.

But there have also been burned fingers: the Fijians have gone quiet about a plan to allow Hong Kong Chinese investors to migrate there after a public uproar, while New Zealand has recently introduced a stiff migrant English language test following a number of racial incidents involving Asians

The real offshore finance centers of Vanuatu, Western Samoa and the Cook Islands have been more successful in simply offering tax havens and asset protection to Asian clients. Kiribati, which itself has only 75,000 people and was part of the old British colony of the Gilbert and Ellice Islands, will issue foreign investor passports for US$15,000.

However, the deal does have its disadvantages. One, holders of these passports cannot actually live in Kiribati - which given the rather slow pace of life there, may not actually be a disadvantage.

Two, the holders have to operate their business from **Kanton Island**, a coral sand bank about 14 km long and barely 600 metres wide. It does have a large airstrip, used first in the Pacific War and then as a refueling stop for Pan Am and Qantas in the days before long range jets. Disadvantage number three is that Kanton is 1,700 km from the Kiribati capital of Tarawa, which itself is a long way from everywhere and not included on many airline schedules - you cannot get to Tarawa via Fiji on Marshall Islands Airlines or jump on charter flights which run out of Honolulu. Kanton can be reached on the domestic airline, Air Tungaru. Nevertheless, the Kiribati Government is bullish; President Teburoro Tito says he wants it operating next year and the passport revenue will be handy. [11.]

Climate, topography, economy

All off the islands except volcanic Banaba are low coralline structures with few elevations above 4 m (13 ft). Kiribati is thus one of the nations whose very existence is threatened by a possible rise in sea level due to global warming. The soil is poor, composed of coral sand and rocks. Vegetation is limited to coconut palms and pandanus trees. Temperatures in Kiribati vary more during a 24-hour period than during the year, with minima of 26 deg C (79 deg F) and maxima of 32 deg C (89 deg F).

Phosphate, mined on Banaba, was once the leading source of income. The economy suffered severely when phosphate mining ceased in 1979 due to a dispute with Banaban landowners, although Kiribati continues to receive interest income from a phosphate reserve fund established in 1956. Copra is now the leading export.

People And Economy

The Kiribati people are overwhelmingly Micronesian, with some Polynesians and Europeans. Many inhabitants migrate to other Pacific island nations in search of jobs; others have been resettled on outlying atolls to relieve overcrowding on Tarawa.

History and Government

Kiribati's earliest inhabitants are thought to have been Samoans, who sailed there in the 13th century. Great Britain established the High Commission for the Western Pacific in 1877 to oversee the islands and their European inhabitants. Gradually all of the present islands were brought under the commission's jurisdiction. Soon after Kiribati gained independence in 1979, the United States renounced its claims to the Line and Phoenix islands.

_____

11. From an article by staff writer Robin Bromby (*Offshore Financial Review*).

248.

CHAPTER 10 • U. S. Virgin Islands • Puerto Rico

The U.S. Virgin Islands comprise 68 islands and cays located in the Caribbean Sea, 1,075 miles southeast of Miami and 40 miles east of Puerto Rico. Three miles separate the two smaller inhabited islands of St. Thomas (32 sq. miles) and St. John (20 sq. miles). Both islands are distinguished by a rugged mountainous topography with numerous sandy beaches and inlets along the shore line. St. Croix (84 sq. miles), lying 40 miles south of St. Thomas, has rolling hills and a broad central plain. All the islands enjoy a mild, tropical climate.

Christopher Columbus landed in St. Croix on his second voyage to the new world in 1493. He named the islands after the legend of St. Ursula and her 11,000 virgin martyrs. Claims to all or part of the U.S. Virgin Islands were made by Spain, England, Holland, France and the Knights of Malta. In 1670 Denmark took control of St. Thomas, expanding its control to St. John, and later bought St. Croix from the French in 1733. Under Denmark, the islands developed as sugar growing, slave holding estates.

Around the turn of the twentieth century, the U.S. became interested in purchasing the islands, and finally bought the Virgin Islands in 1917 from Denmark to build a naval base against the German threat to the Panama Canal.

Today, St. Croix (54,300), St. Thomas (52,300) and St. John is a premier tourist resort center with the highest standard of living in the Caribbean.

"Mirror" System of Taxation

The U.S. Virgin Islands, Guam, the Northern Mariana Islands and American Samoa currently use the mirror system of taxation. Each possession transforms the Internal Revenue Code, as amended, into a local code by substituting its name for the name of the "United States" when appropriate. According to the VI Naval Appropriations Act of July 12, 1921 "...the income tax laws now in force in the United States and those which may hereafter be enacted shall be held likewise in force in the Virgin Islands of the United States, except proceeds of such taxes shall be paid into the treasuries of the Virgin Islands. " Additionally, all U.S. Treasury Regulations, Revenue Rulings, procedures and policies with certain exceptions are applicable.

Those exceptions involve definitions of income, residency and taxing jurisdiction between the U.S. and the USVI.

The USVI offers incentives and tax breaks for many types of businesses that serve and supply the local population, as well as opportunities that service the tourist trade in such areas as retail stores and gift shops, hotels, restaurants, and attractions such as dive operations and the like. If you establish a qualifying business and hire local employees, your business will be eligible for generous government tax incentives, which will eliminate almost all income taxes, and local taxes for ten years or more. [1]

American and foreign individuals living in the USVI would not find much tax relief from U.S. taxes on their portfolio stock, bond and other passive income investments, but the nonresident alien (i.e., a foreign individual not resident in the USVI) who uses a USVI exempt company could obtain much the same benefits as they would if they used a no-tax haven like the Cayman Islands or the Bahamas, and could legally avoid Federal income taxes.

The mirror system applies differently to corporations than to individuals. One of the differences is that in addition to the regular corporate tax rate, corporations are also subject to a 10% corporate tax surcharge which brings the maximum corporate graduated rate to 38.5%. There are no local income taxes or surcharges imposed on individuals over and above the mirror system rates so that the overall rate of income tax for individuals is equivalent to the rate that a resident of a state without a state income tax would pay.

One of the results of the mirror system is that a corporation incorporated in the United States, along with a corporation incorporated elsewhere outside of the USVI, is considered foreign for USVI tax purposes. See footnote 2 on page 251.

U.S. citizens and permanent residents with income from the USVI, but who are not resident there, pay the same total amount of tax as they would if all their income were from U.S. sources,

---

1. Information provided by William L. Blum, Esq. (USVI)

but the tax is apportioned between the United States and the USVI. This is done on IRS form 8689. These individuals file their form 1040 returns, along with the form 8689, with the IRS and they file a copy with the Virgin Islands Bureau of Internal Revenue.

Virgin Islands Industrial Development Program Investment Incentives

The USVI Industrial Development Program provides exemptions from nearly all local taxes and a 90% income tax exemption. In order to qualify, a business must invest $50,000 or more in a USVI business and employ ten persons. Initial tax benefits are granted by the USVI Industrial Development Commission for either ten or fifteen years and may be renewed for five year periods. The Industrial Development Program is typically used by hotels, light manufacturing enterprises, and service businesses. Benefits are usually not granted for businesses which primarily serve the local market. USVI resident shareholders of companies which have benefits are also entitled to 90% income tax exemptions.

Manufacturers which plan to import products into the United States can combine the benefits of the Industrial Development Program with those of a federal law to eliminate U.S. customs duties if there is a sufficient amount of value added to the product in the USVI.

It's the tax incentives offered by the VI Industrial Development Commission (IDC) that make the USVI an attractive place to do business. The IDC is the investment development agency of the VI government. Applications for tax benefits are made through the Director in St. Croix. A seven-member commission reviews an application, and forwards its recommended applications to the Governor of the VI for approval. There is nothing comparable in the U.S. domestic tax system to the incentive programs offered by the governments of our U.S. "territories & possessions". Eligible types of activities include:

• Tourism Related: Hotels and Guest Houses; Transportation Services; Selected Recreation Facilities.
• Goods Producing: Agriculture, Mariculture (Marine farming); Manufacturing-processing raw materials; assembly operations; utilities.

• Service Businesses: (providing service to customers located outside the Virgin Islands) International Commercial Distribution & Trading Services; International Public Relations, Economic, Management, Scientific Consulting Services, Public Auditing, Mail Order Firms (postal rates & service is the same as in the States), news syndicates, Dental, optical and medical laboratories, Prefabricated Houses of any type of material, Exempt insurance management companies (captive insurance), maritime vessels & aircraft services, and many more.

In addition, the IDC may grant benefits to other industries or businesses if it is determined that such activity will be beneficial to the Virgin Islands.

Qualifying for tax incentives

• invest $50,000 exclusive of inventory in eligible business.
• employ 10 U.S. Virgin Island residents full time. • meet the requirements of IRC §934 or IRC §936 of the U.S. Internal Revenue Code.

Editor's Note: Congress repealed most of IRC §936 (above) in late 1997.

Maximum IDC tax exemptions and subsidies are offered for 10 to 15 years depending on the location. These tax incentives include:
• A 90% exemption of local corporate income tax payments.
• A 90% exemption of income taxes paid by resident stockholders on dividends received from the enterprise.

Tax Free Entities in the USVI

There are three types of entities that can be established in the USVI which are either fully or partially exempt from USVI taxes and U.S. federal income taxes. One type of entity is a USVI corporation which obtains the benefits of the Virgin Islands Industrial Development Program for its business activities in the USVI. These companies are fully exempt from most local taxes and receive a 90% exemption from USVI income taxes. They also enjoy a special customs duty rate of one percent. These companies are generally not subject to U.S. federal income taxes on their USVI operations.

Another tax free entity is a USVI foreign sales corporation (FSC) which pays no local taxes except for a nominal annual fee. Thousands of USVI FSCs have been set up by U.S. exporters as a means to reduce U.S. federal income taxes on their export sales by about 15%.

USVI Exempt Companies Act of 1986

The USVI Exempt Companies Act of 1986 is authorized under new provision IRC §934(b)(3) of the U.S. Internal Revenue Code (added by the Tax Reform Act of 1986). It became operative on February 24, 1987 with the signing of the Tax Implementation Agreement (TIA) between the U.S. and the Virgin Islands. Under this law, qualified foreign owned companies can elect for a 20 year local exemption from all taxes except for a $1,000 annual franchise tax. To qualify the company must pass certain tests:

• No U.S. person (or VI person) can own (within the meaning of Code Sec. 958") 10% or more of the total voting power or value of its stock. The company must not have U.S. source income, nor income effectively connected with the conduct of a trade or business within the U.S. [2.]

• cannot carry on a USVI trade or business.

• must disclose certain information to the IRS about its activities (but pays no taxes).

For foreign persons, even more generous exemptions are available through the use of the USVI exempt company. The USVI is the only jurisdiction in the world where a non-U.S. person can establish a tax-free entity under the U.S. flag. USVI exempt companies are often used as holding companies for portfolio investments, for the ownership of aircraft that are registered with the U.S. Federal Aviation Administration, or as captive insurance companies. There are a number of other offshore tax planning structures that can take advantage of USVI exempt companies.

Except in the case of certain captive insurance companies, U.S. and USVI citizens, residents, and companies are prohibited from owning, directly or indirectly, ten percent or more

---

2. The U.S. sourcing rules appear to permit an exempt VI foreign company to export U.S. products tax free, as such income would be "foreign source income" for purposes of the U.S. tax Code. It's less clear whether the exporting activity would be considered as "doing business within" the USVI however. It would be prudent therefore to seek a ruling from the USVI authorities over the scope and extent of the exemption.

of the stock of a USVI exempt company. With respect to income from all sources except those in the United States or the USVI, an exempt company is entirely free of all U.S. and USVI income taxes. Furthermore, except for a nominal annual franchise fee ($1,000), an exempt company is free from all local taxes as well. These tax benefits are guaranteed for 20 years by contract with the USVI government. The identity of the owner of a USVI exempt companies is not public information but it is subject to disclosure to the Virgin Islands Bureau of Internal Revenue or the IRS upon proper request.

U.S. Export Incentives for USVI Foreign Sales Corporations

The U.S. Internal Revenue Code authorizes the establishment of foreign sales corporations (FSCs) in the U.S. Virgin Islands. FSCs are established by U.S. exporters in order to reduce their income tax on profits from export sales by approximately 15%.

Since the FSC program was established by Congress in 1984, more FSCs have been established in the U.S. Virgin Islands than in any other jurisdiction in the world. They have come to take advantage of the professional infrastructure and the excellent communications and transportation links between the USVI and the U.S. mainland, as well as for the tax benefits. Local benefits for FSCs include complete exemption from all local taxes and Virgin Islands income taxes, except for a nominal annual franchise tax and license fee. Benefits are guaranteed by a contract with the government for up to thirty years.

FSCs are usually established with the assistance of a licensed USVI FSC management company, many of which have offices in the United States mainland as well.

A regular FSC (one with export sales in excess of $5 million annually) is required to hold its annual meetings in the U.S. Virgin Islands, although this can be handled by a management company if desired. A small FSC (one with export sales of $5 million or less annually) does not have to hold such meetings. Small FSCs must pay a flat annual franchise tax to the USVI government of either $400 or $900 depending on the volume of sales. The annual franchise tax for regular FSCs starts at $1,000.

Foreign investors who do not seek residence or citizenship in the U.S. Virgin Islands or the United States can establish a tax free U.S. Virgin Islands exempt company for their worldwide investments (other than investments in the United States or the U.S. Virgin Islands). Not surprisingly, the U.S. Virgin Islands have seen a rapid increase in the establishment of exempt companies.

A foreign investor can use a U.S. Virgin Islands exempt company to hold his or her worldwide assets because such entity pays no taxes in the U.S. Virgin Islands, except for an annual US$1,000 franchise tax on its non-U.S., non-virgin Islands income.

The irony in all this, is that the U.S. government offers tax haven status to non-U.S. citizens while denying the same tax breaks to its own citizenry. This is political hypocrisy at its worst! Why should a foreigner be offered freedom from current and future taxes, while citizens of the U.S. living on the mainland are excluded from the same policy?

In addition, a U.S. Virgin Islands exempt company is covered by the United States extensive network of treaties of Friendship, Commerce and Navigation and bilateral investment treaties that offer protection against expropriation of assets and other benefits. A Frenchmen from Paris could form a U.S. Virgin Islands exempt company, have it purchase bonds in a Canadian utility paying a 12% interest, and not pay any Canadian withholding taxes (normally 25% on the interest paid to countries without an income tax treaty with Canada). Under the U.S.-Canadian income tax treaty, dividends and interest withholding taxes are reduced to 15% and 0%.

An investor from a country without extensive treaty networks (like Bermuda the Caymans or the Bahamas) could structure an investment into one of the 60 plus countries with which the U.S. has an investment treaty through a U.S. Virgin Islands exempt company to obtain the benefits of the treaty. It's all perfectly legal, and the U.S. government is backing the idea!

Moreover, a U.S. Virgin Islands exempt company has access to the Federal court system, and stock in a U.S. Virgin Islands exempt company is not subject to U.S. Virgin Islands inheritance tax, nor to U.S. estate tax, nor are the underlying assets held by the U.S. Virgin Islands exempt company.

Exempt International Banking

Legislation for exempt companies provides for a complete tax exemption (except for a $1,000 annual franchise fee and a $4,000 annual license fee) for exempt international banking facilities. USVI International Banks may operate the same as any V.I. bank except it may not serve local USVI persons. Section 9934(b)(3) of the U.S. Internal Revenue Code restricts the U.S, ownership in such banks to 10% or less. International USVI banks may obtain a 20-year contract exempting them from taxes through the Lieutenant Governor's Office.

Captive Insurance Companies

Title 22, Chapter 55 provides for USVI exempt insurance companies or "captives" as they are commonly called. Firms that underwrite insurance or conduct reinsurance business with respect to risks situated exclusively outside the USVI are exempt from USVI insurance laws, and are eligible for a complete tax exemption, except for a $1,000 franchise tax and a $6,000 or $3,000 license fee depending on the class of the insurer. Exempt Insurance Management companies, which are equivalent to the management company of a mutual fund, are eligible for the Industrial Development Commission tax incentives.

The USVI insurance companies are exempt from most local regulation so long as coverages do not involve USVI risks. The exempt insurers statute permits the licensing of "International Insurance Companies" also known as captive insurers. An International Insurance Company may also qualify as a USVI exempt company and thus be eligible for exemption from income and other local taxes. Unlike other types of exempt companies, an International Insurance Company may be owned by U.S. persons and still be eligible for these benefits so long as its income is effectively connected to a USVI trade or business.

The USVI is unique among offshore insurance domiciles in that it is considered a state for the purposes of the Employee Retirement Income Security Act of 1974 ("ERISA"). As a result, it is possible to establish a captive insurance company, or branch, in the U.S. Virgin Islands which may write employee health and retirement plan coverage in the United States. Captives established in foreign jurisdictions are not allowed to write this type of coverage in the United States.

FAA aircraft registration by foreign owners using USVI exempt companies

According to Marjorie Rawls Roberts (chief council and technical advisor to the U.S. Virgin Islands Bureau of Internal Revenue), a foreign investor can use a U.S. Virgin Islands exempt company with a U.S. Virgin Islands voting trust to own an aircraft used overseas in order to qualify for the 'N' registration number from the U.S. Federal Aviation Administration. This is an interesting suggestion, as the exploitation of a voting trust by a U.S. government official in a foreign tax structure is quite revolutionary.

In order to meet the FAA requirements, the stock of the exempt company must be owned by a voting trustee who is a U.S. citizen. Using a USVI exempt company for this purpose is preferable to using a Delaware company (which is the traditional corporate vehicle) because, unlike a Delaware company, a USVI exempt company is free of federal income taxes.

Editor's comments: If the chief council and technical advisor to the U.S. Virgin Islands Internal Revenue Service recommends the exploitation of a *voting trust* for foreign investors, what would be so wrong in using a *voting trust* for American taxpayers in tax havens like the Bahamas and Cayman Islands?

Obtaining U.S. Citizenship in the USVI while avoiding U.S. Estate and gift taxes

In many cases the U.S. federal estate and gift tax apply in the USVI to U.S. citizens and permanent residents domiciled there at death or at the time of the gift. There is an important exception, however: the federal estate tax does not apply to property located outside the United States which would otherwise be part of the estate of an individual who acquired his or her U.S. citizenship as a result of birth or naturalization in the U.S. Virgin Islands or another U.S. possession, so long as the individual resides in the USVI at the date of death. There is a similar exception for the gift tax. For persons considering becoming naturalized U.S. citizens, this provides an attractive planning opportunity.

Property located in the USVI, or stock of a USVI corporation (including a USVI exempt company) is not considered U.S.-situs property under the U.S. federal estate tax. Therefore it is not included in the estate of a non-resident alien of the United States.

A foreign investor seeking U.S. citizenship can qualify by investing a minimum of US$500,000 on the island of St. Croix in the U.S. Virgin Islands which offers available flat land and a highly educated work force. The business should employ at least 10 persons.

The investor will qualify for an immigrant employment creation visa for such investment from the Immigration and Naturalization Service, leading to U.S. citizenship.

An investor can also qualify for the U.S. Virgin Islands\industrial development benefits by making the investment.

The U.S. sourcing rules appear to permit an exempt VI foreign company to export U.S. products tax free, as such income would be "foreign source income" for purposes of the U.S. tax Code. It's less clear whether the exporting activity would be considered as "doing business within" the USVI however. It would be prudent therefore to seek a ruling from the USVI authorities over the scope and extent of the exemption.

The investor will thus be exempt from any property taxes and gross receipts taxes on the investment, receive substantial reductions in excise taxes and customs duties, and as a resident of the U.S. Virgin Islands pay income tax at less than a 4% rate on his income from the investment.

Once the investor obtains U.S. citizenship in the U.S. Virgin Islands, the investor will be exempt from Federal estate and gift taxes on all his/her non-U.S. situs assets (including the investment in the U.S. Virgin Islands) and will be similarly exempt from all U.S. Virgin Islands inheritance and gift taxes.

Other Taxes

There are no sales taxes in the USVI. There are several other taxes that do apply, however, including the following:

- Real Property Taxes
- Gross Receipts Taxes
- Excise Taxes and Customs Duties

Exempt companies and foreign sales corporations are exempt from the above taxes. In addition, beneficiaries of the Industrial Development Program are exempt from all of these taxes except for customs duties, where a special one percent rate applies.

Real Property Taxes

USVI real property is subject to an annual tax at a rate of 1.25% of assessed value. Assessed value is defined by statute to be 60% of actual value.

Gross Receipts Taxes

The USVI imposes a tax of 4% on the gross receipts of USVI businesses. Businesses with annual gross receipts of less than $150,000 are exempt from tax on their first $5,000 per month of gross receipts.

Excise Taxes and Customs Duties

Articles imported into the U.S. Virgin Islands for use or resale in a trade or business are subject to an excise tax. Because the USVI is outside the U.S. customs zone, foreign (non-U.S.) made goods are also subject to a customs duty which is separate from the U.S. customs duty. The rate of excise tax on most goods is 4%, while the rate on certain products, such as cigarettes, is higher. Alcoholic beverages are subject to a flat rate based on volume. Certain other goods are subject to a lower rate of excise tax, and most tourist items, such as jewelry, watches, crystal, artwork, electronic goods, and leather goods, are exempt entirely. Tourist items are also exempt from the 6% U.S. Virgin Islands customs duty.

U.S. Virgin Island's old inhabitant rule - one extraordinary U.S. tax loophole has ended

Residents of the British Empire, upon which it is said the sun never sets, have a choice of 10 to 20 tax havens in which they can move to escape the jurisdiction of the Inland Revenue (Britain's IRS). Citizens of the United States are generally held taxable on all their worldwide income, no matter where they move. The United States has no network of low and no-tax havens comparable with the British, but certain territories of the United States have in the past been blessed (by a combination of Congressional legislation and local law) with tax breaks that effectively make them suitable tax havens in certain situations. Unfortunately for the USVIs and the American taxpayer, one extraordinary loophole - the old "inhabitant rule" - was repealed by Congress several years ago.

Under the old inhabitant rule, a U.S. citizen or foreigner who qualified as a bone fide U.S.V.I. resident by December 31st of that year was not required to file a U.S. federal income tax return with the IRS for any tax year he/she was resident of the V.I., and more important had no U.S. tax liability. This rule is repealed for tax years starting in 1987.

Additional information on the USVI Industrial Development Program can also be obtained directly from the USVI government as follows:

Industrial Development Commission
36C Strand Street - 2nd Floor Suite 2AB
P.O. Box 3499, Christiansted
St. Croix, V.I. 00822

Phone: (809) 773-6499
Fax: (809) 773-7701

Puerto Rico declines in importance as U.S. tax haven

Prior to the changes made by the Small Business Job Protection Act, signed into law by President Clinton in October 1996, Puerto Rico was a U.S. controlled tax haven, having all the benefits of any State in the Union, but with an internal tax system all its own.

The United States Congress actually prompted the unique relationship with PR when it enacted special legislation exempting PR based U.S. subsidiaries from the Controlled Foreign Corporation provisions, even if they are 100% owned (Controlled) by the U.S. parent. The regulations governing the use of a Puerto Rican subsidiary are found under IRC §957(c) (Corporations organized in United States Possessions), IRC §931 (Income from Sources within Possessions of the U.S.). It is the combination of these laws, plus newer legislation under IRC §936, plus Puerto Rico's own tax incentive legislation under the **Industrial Incentives Act (IIA)** that made for the tax breaks.

In 1963, PR enacted its **Industrial Incentive Acts (IIA)** (revising earlier Acts of 1954 and 1948) providing 100% exemption from PR's income tax, property tax and municipal tax for up to 30 years if the company was a qualifying manufacturer or hotel operator. Later, in 1978, a New Act, the Industrial Incentive Act of 1978 amended the previous Act by cutting back on the degree of the tax exemption. Up until then, U.S. companies could get a partial exemption of 90% for the first five years on income and property taxes. Qualified U.S. subsidiaries are allotted a 100% exemption from PR municipal taxes. Puerto Rico's regular corporate income tax rate for 1988 was 45%, but under the tax holiday the effective tax rate is only 4.5%.

> **The changes made by Clinton's Small Business Job Protection Act are ending the above unique relationship. How can Clinton politicians call an Act that undermines thousands of jobs in Puerto Rico a Small Business Job Protection Act? It sounds crazy.**

Small Business Job Protection Act of 1996

Two years after Congress voted to phase out tax incentives for companies investing in Puerto Rico, some of the island's top manufacturing employers have pulled out, laying off thousands of factory workers, and few new companies are coming in to replace them.

A few years ago, Motorola announced it would shut its beeper factory in Vega Baja, just west of San Juan. The plant's 1,500 workers will lose their jobs or be transferred by the end of this month. The company will shift most of its production to Boynton Beach, said Motorola official Miguel Pereira. Other expected major plant closures this year include: Next Level Systems, a telecommunications company, which will closed its factory in Barcelonetta, leaving 900 jobless. Brassiere manufacturer Maidenform, which plans to dismiss 800. Pharmaceutical companies Hoesch Marion Roussel, which will leave 230 jobless by year's end, and Roche Products, which is laying off 190 workers.

Politicians and business executives are blaming this disturbing trend on the loss of Section 936, a federal tax program that has helped create hundreds of thousands of jobs on this Caribbean island.

Under a provision of the Small Business Job Protection Act, signed into law by President Clinton in October 1996, corporate tax breaks for all existing factories operating under 936 will disappear within a decade, with no federal incentives for new investments. As such, Section 936, which was sacrificed to offset anticipated federal revenue losses from tax breaks given to small businesses - and to help Congress pay for the minimum wage hike - was eliminated for any business not already claiming it.

For all other companies, the law continues a phase out process begun in 1993, providing a new cap on the credit beginning in 2002, and abolishing it altogether for active business income by Jan. 1, 2006, meaning that existing 936 companies are grandfathered in for the next 7 1/2 years.

Clinton himself has never been happy about eliminating the program. Recognizing the damage it could do to Puerto Rico, the president asked Congress immediately after signing the bill to "act to ensure that the incentive for economic activity remains in effect" to prevent multinationals from fleeing Puerto Rico once the tax credit is history.

New firms staying away

Yet it may be difficult to stop them from leaving - as well as attract new companies to the island. Countries such as the Dominican Republic, Mexico and Ireland can offer similar benefits at much lower labor costs.

"Since 936 was modified in 1993, there's been a significant drop-off in the number of new companies investing in Puerto Rico," said Peter Holmes, spokesman for the Puerto Rico -USA Foundation in Washington.

Over the years, Section 936 has been crucial to the economy of Puerto Rico, an island of 3.8 million people captured by U.S. forces in the 1898 Spanish - American War and made into a US Commonwealth in 1952.

An outgrowth of President Truman's postwar Operation Bootstrap, Section 936 since the mid 1970's had exempted manufacturers from paying federal income tax on profits earned by their subsidiaries in Puerto Rico. That drew some 2,000 factories to the island, when in the peak year of 1989 they employed 161,000 people in the production and export of everything from Hanes underwear to Microsoft software - all for a hungry American market.

Since then, manufacturing employment has fallen to around 148,000, through U.S. subsidies and direct factory investment have given the island a per-capita income of about $7,500. Though this is far less than the poorest U.S. state, Mississippi, it tops most other Caribbean islands and ranks Puerto Rico the highest in Latin America.

Manufacturing decline cited

According to a recent Price Waterhouse study commissioned by the Puerto Rico Federal Affairs Administration in Washington, the island's current manufacturing decline is "a logical consequence" of the repeal of 936.

Between 1980 and 1993, says the study, employment commitments averaged nearly 8,500 jobs per year. Between 1994 and 1997, these commitments suffered a 40 percent reduction to only 4,765 jobs per year.

U.S. executives rarely consider the island these days when thinking about where to put their next factory, said Colorado, a former secretary of state for the island who lobbied hard to save 936 in the mid-'90s.

"Nobody is looking at Puerto Rico as a place to invest. People looking from outside see no stability, so it's no longer an incentive," he said, noting that in 1989, 1990 and 1991, Puerto Rico ranked first in the world in terms of safety from political risk- even higher than the United States. In 1997, the island ranked No. 22, according to The PRS Group of Syracuse, NY. Holmes said he's seeing a similar trend.

"In the days when 936 was whole, Puerto Rico was such an attractive site for investment that when multinational corporations had problems requiring a company-wide reorganization, their Puerto Rican factories were never in the equation. It was sort of held separately because it was a great moneymaker thanks to the tax benefits," said Holmes, whose organization represents 50 or 60 large U.S. multinationals that represent 60 percent of the Section 936 investment in Puerto Rico. "Now, with the loss of 936," he says, "there's no uniqueness attached to the Puerto Rican operation. So when there's a market change, the Puerto Rican subsidiary is factored into the decision making process."

Some are staying

To be sure, not everyone is pulling out, and some companies such as Intel are even adding jobs to take advantage of 936 as long as they can. Pharmaceutical giant G.D. Searle recently announced plans to invest $200 million in a factory expansion that will create 700 jobs.

But in order to remain competitive, some U.S. firms, including Searle , have given up their 936 status and have reorganized as Controlled Foreign Corporations (CFCs), which puts them outside the U.S. tax code until they remit profits back to stateside headquarters. CFCs, says Holmes, "provide a deferred tax benefit that can be put off for many years if the company is global and it can invest its Puerto Rican profits in properties around the globe."

It's still too early to gauge the full impact of the repeal. "Companies are certainly going to try to stay in Puerto Rico if they possibly can, because many of them have substantial capital investments there," Holmes said. "The question is whether those companies will grow or contract."

Qualified companies with approved products and services benefited

Under Puerto Rico's **Industrial Incentives Act (IIA),** any foreign or domestic manufacturer, hotel operator, and service industry is eligible for the partial exemption. For example, drug manufacturers and manufacturers of woman's, men's and children's apparel, hosiery and gloves, rugs, leather goods can obtain the effective low 4.5% profits tax rate. Service industries, including but limited to, investment banking, international commercial distribution facilities, public relations services, economic, scientific or management consulting services, processing, editing and dubbing cinematographic films, commercial and graphic arts, insurance firms, mail order firms, computer service centers, maritime vessel and aircraft repair, and international banking operations can also obtain the tax exemptions. [3.]

Predecessor - successor businesses: Persons owning at least 25% of an exempt business (the *"Predecessor"* business), may request a new exemption for a single product (the *"Successor"* business). In addition, any integrated expansion requiring common facilities can obtain a separate exemption with approval from the Governor.

Exemption Rate Schedule

Zones	Years of exemption	tax exemption	tax rate
All	1 - 5	90%	4.5%
All	6 - 10	75%	11.25%
II, III, IV	11 - 15	65%	15.75%
III, IV	16 - 20	55%	20.25%
IV	21 - 25	50%	22.5%

In addition, an **IIA** exempt business may apply for a 10 year **extension** of its grant within 12 months before the expiration date of its tax-exemption decree. Depending on the zone in which the business is located, the grantee will receive a partial exemption, which varies from 50% for the first 5 years to a low of 35% for the remaining 5 years.

Dividends from Exempt Entity

Dividends paid by a corporation operating under the IIA grant are exempt from income tax in the hands of a PR domestic company or an individual resident in PR.

Dividends from an exempt corporation paid to nonresident individuals are partially exempt from Puerto Rico's withholding tax (called a tollgate - normally 29%), if the individual can show he is either not taxable on the dividend elsewhere or that he is not allowed a tax credit in his home country.

Dividends paid by a PR subsidiary to its U.S. parent are generally subject to a PR withholding tax of 10%, but this is reduced to 7% if a specified percentage of the earnings are retained and reinvested in PR property. The PR tollgate (withholding tax) can be further reduced to 5% in some cases. In addition, the U.S. parent will not have to pay **any** U.S. income tax on the **dividend** it receives from its PR subsidiary under U.S. tax statutes. The **Tax Reform Act of 1976** made it possible for U.S. **possession corporations** to return profits to the U.S. parent at any time 100% tax free. [4.]

Other Advantages

Puerto Rico lies within the customs territory of the United States. Goods, equipment and supplies can be transferred from the States duty free. PR based manufacturers can use the U.S. postal system, and pay the same postal rates as U.S. companies. In addition, PR and the U.S. observe identical immigration laws. U.S. citizens can travel to and from PR without passports, the same as they can within the States.

Puerto Rico's Inhabitant rule

U.S. citizens that pick up and take up permanent residence in PR are permitted tax privileges unfounded in any territory or state of the United States.

Puerto Rican residents (including relocated U.S. citizens) can receive dividends from their tax exempt corporations without paying any taxes - U.S. or Puerto Rican. This is nothing more than the same old inhabitant rule that was repealed in the USVI.

---

3. Other approved items including balls for sports, bed springs and mattresses, bodies and chassis for motor vehicles and trailers, distilled spirits, many canned food products, cosmetics, cigars and cigarettes, paper products, shoes & slippers, metal containers, publishing of books, slaughtering of animals, animal feed, and many others have been qualified for manufacture.

---

4. See IRC §931 and IRC §936.

257.

679. Foreign trusts having one or more United States beneficiaries

679. Foreign trusts having one or more United States beneficiaries:

(a) Transferor treated as owner ....

(1) In general   A United States person who directly or indirectly transfers property to a foreign trust (other than a trust described in section 404(a)(4) Or section 404A) shall be treated as the owner for his taxable year of the portion of such trust attributable to such property if for such year there is a United States beneficiary of any portion of such trust.

(2) **Exceptions.....**

Paragraph (1) shall not apply--

(A) Transfers by reason of death ......

To any transfer by reason of the death of the transferor.

(B) Transfers where gain is recognized to transferor

To any sale or exchange of the property at its fair market value in a transaction in which all of the gain to the transferor is realized at the time of the transfer and is recognized either at such time or is returned as provided in section 453.

(b) Trusts acquiring United States beneficiaries
   If--
      (1) subsection (a) applies to a trust for the transferor's taxable year, and (2) subsection (a) would have applied to the trust for his immediately preceding taxable year but for the fact that for such preceding taxable year there was no United States beneficiary for any portion of the trust, then, for purposes of this subtitle, the transferor shall be treated as having income for the taxable year (in addition to his other income for such year) equal to the undistributed net income (at the close of such immediately preceding taxable year) attributable to the portion of the trust referred to in subsection (a).

(c) Trusts treated as having a United States beneficiary
   (1) In general

      For purposes of this section, a trust shall be treated as having a United States beneficiary for the taxable year unless--

(A) under the terms of the trust, no part of the income or corpus of the trust may be paid or accumulated during the taxable year to or for the benefit of a United States person, and

(B) if the trust were terminated at any time during the taxable year, no part of the income or corpus of such trust could be paid to or for the benefit of a United States person.

(2) Attribution of ownership
      For purposes of paragraph (1), an amount shall be treated as paid or accumulated to or for the benefit of a United States person if such amount is paid to or accumulated for a foreign corporation, foreign partnership, or foreign trust or estate, and--

(A) in the case of a foreign corporation, **more than 50 percent** of the total combined voting power of all classes of stock entitled to vote of such corporation is owned (within the meaning of section 958(a)) or is considered to be owned (within the meaning of section 958(b)) by United States shareholders (as defined in section 951(b)),

(B) in the case of a foreign partnership, a United States person is a partner of such partnership, or

(C) in the case of a foreign trust or estate, such trust or estate has a United States beneficiary (within the meaning of paragraph (1)).

Reg. Sec. 1.367(a)-1T;   26 U.S.C. 367 (ii) Grantor trusts.

A transfer of a portion or all of the assets of a foreign or domestic trust to a foreign corporation in an exchange described in section 367(a)(1) is considered a transfer by any U.S. person who is treated as the owner of any such portion or all of the assets of the trust under sections 671 through 679.

CHAPTER 11 • Foreign Trusts

Trusts, one of the most ancient and legally complex tax planning devices, are an English invention originating in early medieval courts of equity. As such they have been exported to most former UK colonies and protectorates (including the United States), though never taking root in France, Italy, Germany and Continental countries whose legal system has derived from Roman law, usually via that splendid product of Enlightenment - the Napoleonic Code. [1]

Even on mainland Europe there are exceptions. Liechtenstein felt the need to develop its own trust legislation to meet the needs of the *international investment company.* As is well-known, the ownership of a large part of assets managed by publisher Mr. Robert Maxwell are safely stored away in a Liechtenstein foundation established for the benefit of members of his family.

And other tax havens such as the Channel Islands and Monaco - where the trust is an alien concept - make provisions for trusts in one form or another. Guernsey, whose jurisprudence never developed courts of equity, has recognized the concept of trust for many years. In 1988, Guernsey passed the *Trusts (Guernsey) Law,* providing a "perpetuity period" of 100 years from the date a trust is formed.

Jersey's (adjacent isle to Guernsey) recent statute, the *Trustee Act,* dates back to 1984, and is closely modeled on the *UK Act of 1925.*

Bermuda trusts are governed by the island's 1975 Act, also with a perpetuity period of 100 years. But in all these jurisdictions trusts have a much longer history, drawing their inspiration from English Common Law and precedent.

Trusts are three legged animals. The person with the money or assets - called the *"settlor"* (or *"grantor"* if a U.S. trust) - passes them onto *trustees,* who administer the settlement on behalf of specified *beneficiaries.* The tax advantages of trusts seem to have stemmed the difficulty of deciding who to tax.

It would obviously not be fair to tax the settlor or the trustees since they would not normally have the power to enjoy the assets or income of the trust. It is therefore possible for income to be accumulated in a trust for many years without actually belonging to anyone. [2]

Many of the tax havens covered in this book are members of the British Commonwealth of nations and use common-law principles in their commercial codes modeled after those in Britain. The United States, which was once a part of the British Empire itself, logically applies common-law tax principles to its own commercial code, based on many of the same legal precedents and court decisions of its former colonizer. Common-law jurisdictions all recognize both the foreign and domestic trust.

New trust legislation is continually being promulgated by their legislative bodies, then codified into a commercial Code to guide the courts and the taxpayers. The Bahamas, the Cayman Islands, Hong Kong, Bermuda, Gibraltar, Australia, Canada and Vanuatu are all common-law tax jurisdictions. Trusts are recognized and in extensive use in these countries.

Civil-law countries, such as Germany, Panama, Costa Rica, the Netherlands and the Netherlands Antilles, customarily do not provide for the use of trusts in their commercial codes. Germany might not recognize the trust as a legal entity, so trusts should not be formed inside Germany as that would be a violation of German public policy. Likewise, Germany might not recognize the foreign laws governing the establishment of foreign trusts, thus it would be bad advice for a Bermuda management company to suggest to a German expatriate that he should use a trust in his tax planning. Trusts should generally not be used in a civil-law country because civil-law courts are often left without guidelines to solve differences involving the enumerated powers in the trust deed, such as administrative policy powers; questions of

---

[1] From an essay *"Trusts: ancient tools in good working order"* by Paul Cooper. Reprinted compliments of the *Offshore Adviser* Greystroke Place & Fetter Lane, London, England EC4A 1ND) (October 1989)(page 16).

[2] The *Tax Reform Act of 1976* curbed the use of foreign trusts with U.S. grantors when the trust has a U.S. beneficiary. Most direct or indirect transfers by a U.S. person to a foreign trust will call for the US transferor to include the trust's income with his other taxable U.S. income. See IRC §679(a). In this respect, U.S. statutes differ greatly from their UK counterpart.

ownership of property placed in the trust; trustee discretionary powers; a trust's rightful beneficiaries; and so on, and so on.

Some civil-law jurisdictions have adopted *skeleton rules* to make up for the lack of codified trust and estate legislation, but many planners have found them to be inadequate. Most international tax practitioners and lawyers still counsel against using a civil-law jurisdiction for drafting a deed of trust. Panama is a civil-law country that accepts the use of trusts, and many Panamanian law firms offer trust services to Americans. Still, U.S. citizens should probably forgo using a civil-law country for a common law trust, because there is some doubt U.S. courts will honor a common law deed of trust prepared in a civil-law jurisdiction.

U.S. Grantor and non-grantor trusts legislation

Within the United States Tax Code, for purposes of determining the taxability of trusts, trustees, beneficiaries and grantors there are, for the most part, just two sections of trust law that must be consulted. The grantor trust provisions *(Subpart E Grantors and others Treated as Substantial Owners)* under IRC §671 to 679, and the non-grantor trust provisions *(Sub-part A - General rules for taxation of Estates and Trusts)* under IRC §641 through 668. Although various other names, such as "simple trust", "testamentary trust", "discretionary trust", "living trust", "accumulation trust" and "grantor trust" are in everyday use by lawyers and accountants, when speaking about trusts for purposes of determining the taxability of a trust (foreign or domestic, whatever the case may be), the statutes found within the Internal Revenue Code and the U.S. Treasury regulations are what's binding.

Under the non-grantor trust rules (IRC §641 - 668), when property or money is transferred to a trust for the benefit of the beneficiaries, and all rights to the property transferred are given up by the transferor (called the grantor), then either the trust or the beneficiaries are held taxable on the earnings or distributions from the trust.

Under the grantor trust provisions, when money or property is transferred to a trust, and the transferor (grantor) retains a grantor trust power (such as the power to revoke the assets in favor of himself, or a power to control the beneficial enjoyment of the trust), then the

taxability of the trust reverts to the grantor. For income tax purposes the IRS does not try to tax the trust or the beneficiaries of the trust. Instead, the grantor is held accountable for all taxes due on the profits and the distributions of the trust. The grantor trust provisions are bunched together between IRC §671 and 679 *("Grantors and others treated as substantial Owners").*

Foreign Trusts (U.S. definition)

When the U.S. person moves offshore the same policy that applied to domestic type trusts can generally be relied on to determine the tax liability of a U.S. person's interest in a foreign trust. I say generally, because the **Tax Reform Act of 1976** added a special Code-Section 679 aimed squarely at foreign trusts with U.S. grantors. See page 258 for this very important, revolutionary addition.

Under current U.S. tax law, an entity is subject to U.S. income tax as a *foreign trust* if it (1) is classified as a trust, and (2) if its contacts with a foreign situs are sufficient, and its contacts with the U.S. so insubstantial, as to render it a foreign entity. **IRC §7701(a)(31)** says that a foreign trust is one *"the income of which from sources without the U.S. which is not effectively connected with the conduct of a trade or business within the U.S., is not incredible in gross income under Sub-part A."* In effect, to avoid U.S. income tax liability, the trust must take the appearance of a *nonresident alien.* [3.]

The IRS uses **6 factors** to determine the situs and nationality of a trust.

1. The country under whose laws the trust was created.
2. The situs of the trust's corpus.
3. The nationality and residence of the trustee(s). You should not use any U.S. trustees..
4. The situs of the trust's administration.
5. The nationality and residence of the grantor.

When all these factors are foreign, the character of the trust as being foreign are clear. If the trust has a U.S. trustee, U.S. beneficiaries, and the situs of the trust's assets are in the U.S., the likelihood that the trust, even though registered in a foreign country, will be treated as a domestic U.S. entity is almost certain.

---

3. <u>Tax Management, Inc.</u> (1981) pg B-3.

Judicial, administrative and legislative precedents clearly show that no single factor or group of factors is determinative of nonresident status, but all relevant factors must be examined. In 1976 the tax writing committees in Congress met to discuss what major revisions of the tax laws on foreign trusts were in order. The Senate Finance committee stated this:

"The Internal Revenue Code does not specify what characteristics must exist before a trust is treated as being foreign as compared to a nonresident alien individual. However, the IRS rulings and court cases indicate that the situs depends on various factors, including residence of the trustees, the location of the trust assets, the country whose laws the trust was created, the nationality of the grantor. If after examination of those factors the trust has enough foreign contacts, it is thought comparable to a nonresident alien individual, and thus a foreign trust."

The Trust Deed

What is a trust? A trust is an equitable obligation binding a person *(trustee)* to watch over the property *(the trust's corpus or assets)* and administer to it for the benefit of certain designated persons *(the beneficiaries)*. Almost always the trust is created by a written document which sets forth the manner, and limits the powers, the trustee(s) will have with respect to the trust's property.

Common-law trusts allow any one of the beneficiaries to enforce the obligation (also called a trust instrument), but this is not to imply that a beneficiary has unlimited powers over the trust, or powers superior to the trustee or the grantor. Although a common-law trust is not a contract under the eyes of the law, the beneficiaries of a common-law trust can sue to enforce the obligation. Strangely enough, the grantor cannot sue to enforce the trust obligation unless he is also a beneficiary, or unless he has the power to revoke the assets of the trust.

Powers of Appointments

When lawyers and other practitioners draft a deed of trust for a client they invariably convey rights and duties to different administrators. These rights are called **powers of appointments**. There are two kinds of powers of appointments. One is called a general power of appointment, and the other a special power of appointment.

If a trustee (or beneficiary) has the right under the trust instrument to appoint the trust income to himself, then he has what is called a general power of appointment, and he will be held taxable on the trust's income. If the trustee or beneficiary has the power to appoint the trust's income to someone else, other than himself, he has a special power of appointment, and he will not be held taxable on the trust income. The Internal Revenue Code and the Treasury regulations under IRC §641 to 679 contain all the guidelines necessary to draft a foreign or domestic trust document. How you draft your deed of trust, and how you deal out powers of appointments, ultimately determine what (and where) U.S. income tax liability exists, if any.

Business Trusts vrs. Private Trusts

If a foreign trust is used for a business purpose, and carries on a general profit making enterprise, then the IRS will view it as an association, and taxable as a corporation. Thus, beneficiaries of a trust taxable as an association would be treated as shareholders of a corporation, not beneficiaries of a trust. Income distributions would be taxable the same as dividend distributions from a company. For this reason, the foreign trusts I speak of in this chapter should fit the genre of trust the IRS calls a **fixed investment trust**, as defined in Reg. §301.7701-4(c), so as not to be treated as a business trust or association.

In a fixed investment trust the powers of the trustee and the depositor (who is similar to an agent or manager) must be considered together. If the trustee's powers consist of conserving the property and distributing income, and the depositor can sell the securities of the trust to eliminate unsound investments, the trust will not be considered taxable as a corporation. But, if the trust depositor can vary the investment of the certificate holders (i.e., the beneficiaries), the trust may be taxed as a corporation (Section 301.7701-2).

261

Foreign Grantor Trusts & Revenue Ruling 69-70

If it was not for one peculiarity in our federal estate and trust laws, foreign profits might somehow be accumulated tax free in the offshore tax havens, but eventually a tax would be owed upon the repatriation of profits (i.e., as dividends or capital gains) back into the United States. Using a foreign corporation to accumulate profits might solve some tax avoidance problems.

In any case, there is one way to bring *foreign source incomes* into the United States without anyone incurring a tax. For the most part, only international tax attorneys and other tax specialists are familiar with this technique which was made clear to the taxpayer through **Rev.Rul. 69-70,** issued by none other than our own IRS.

In 1970 the IRS issued a statement (Rev. Rul. 69-70) which describes a case whereby *foreign source income* can be received by a U.S. person (a beneficiary of a foreign trust), without any tax liability resulting to the U.S. recipient, the foreign trust, or the foreign grantor of the trust. Think about it. There's not a domestic entity, trust, corporation or partnership that is afforded such immunity from federal income tax under federal tax law. Not even your tax free religious organizations are afforded such leeway. Moreover, Revenue Ruling 69-70 is about the best legal advice that can be gotten anywhere. Not even your top law professor, tax advisor or big 8 accounting firm could provide you with better advice than Rev.Rul.69-70. The IRS' own advice, certainly! The entire ruling appears below:

Revenue Ruling 69-70 states: **"An individual beneficiary who is resident of the United States is not taxable on a distribution from a foreign trust considered to be owned by a nonresident alien grantor under subpart E of subchapter J of the Code":**

Rev-Rul 69-70: "Advice has been requested whether the income of a foreign trust, under the circumstances described below, is taxable to the beneficiary, an individual who is resident of the United States.

X, a nonresident alien individual, created a foreign trust for the benefit of a resident of the United States. Under the terms of the instrument, X reserves the absolute power to dispose of the beneficial enjoyment of both the income and the corpus of the trust. The trustees are nonresident aliens, and all the trust property had a situs outside the United States.

When income-producing property is placed in trust, the Federal income tax liability generally shifts from the grantor to the trust and beneficiaries in accordance with subparts A through D of part I, subchapter J, Chapter 1, subtitle A of the Internal Revenue Code of 1954 (sections 641 through 669).

However, where the grantor retains dominion and control over the income and corpus of the trust, subpart E of subchapter J (sections 671 through 678) rather than subparts A through D of subchapter J, is applicable. Since X, a nonresident alien grantor retained the absolute power to dispose of the beneficial enjoyment of both the income and corpus of the trust, he is treated as the owner of the trust under IRC §674(a) of the Code. Accordingly, an individual beneficiary who is a resident of the U.S. is not taxable on that portion of the income distributed to him from the foreign trust which is considered to be owned by the nonresident alien grantor under subpart E of subchapter J of the Code.

It should be noted that United States source income of a foreign trust considered to be controlled by a nonresident alien grantor is taxed to the grantor. If the grantor is a resident of a non-treaty country, the provisions of section 871 of the Code apply concerning the tax. However, if the grantor is a resident of a treaty country, the provisions of the treaty may determine the tax." **[Author of this ruling is our own IRS].**

Applying Rev-Rul 69-70 to an example is one practical way to show off its significance.

EXAMPLE: Number 1 son **Y** of successful Bahamas businessman **X** marries American debutante **Z** in June of 1999. Both Y and Z plan to live in the United States permanently. Instead of giving them a lump sum of money as part of their wedding gift, Mr. **X** (a nonresident alien for purposes of U.S. tax law) asks his Bahamas lawyer to place $1,000,000 in trust for Z and Y. The Bahamian trust is revocable by the non-resident alien grantor X. meaning he can call back the assets any time.

The trust designates **Y** and **Z** (both residents of the United States) as the sole beneficiaries, and stipulates that Y and Z have the power to add new names to the list of beneficiaries, should there be any little Zs or Ys in the future. The corpus of the trust consists of Dutch Antilles issued Eurodollar bonds of Exxon Corporation paying 10% interest pa. Income of the trust is to be distributed to the beneficiaries, as it accrues.

Under the U.S. grantor trust rules neither **Y** nor **Z** is viewed as the owner of the trust corpus ($1,000,000), because neither has the power to vest the trust assets in favor of his or herself. Having the power to name "new" income beneficiaries is not a grantor trust power under U.S. tax law, and will not shift the incidence of taxation away from the grantor to the U.S. beneficiaries. In addition, it is clear that income distributions paid by the foreign trust to **Y** and **Z** can be received free of all Federal Income taxes via Rev-Rul. 69-70, so long as there is a non-resident grantor for the trust (i.e., as long as Mr. **X** lives).

If the foreign trustee takes care not to purchase investments that incur a U.S. tax liability (such as dividends from U.S. stocks which incur a 30% withholding tax), the trust will have no tax liability to discuss with the IRS.

As for the U.S. beneficiaries, they should answer item 11(a) (YES) and item 12 (NO) on **Schedule B, Part III** which appears on the back of every U.S. taxpayer's IRS **Form 1040.** But this disclosure is frivolous.

One ending statement needs to be made here. While nonresident alien individual **X** was chosen to be the grantor for our Bahamas trust, it is not a prerequisite under U.S. tax law that the grantor be an individual. Any nonresident alien can act as a grantor, including a Bahamas corporation, partnership or trust. Indeed, a foreign corporation might make a more suitable grantor for the trust because the grantor trust relationship would continue long after the demise of Mr. **X**. Keep in mind, if a resident of the UK is chosen as the grantor he might be taxable on the trust's income under Inland Revenue procedures, regardless of the fact the U.S. beneficiaries receive most or all of the income distributions. [4.]

What is a Revenue Ruling

A revenue ruling is not a law passed by Congress; it is a proclamation by the **Internal Revenue Service** explaining the facts as they relate to a particular set of laws. Several years ago I ordered Internal Revenue Service publication 1140-Rev.4-87 ("Special Enrollment Examination for Tax Preparers"). According to Pub. 1140.... *IRS employees must follow the rulings. While taxpayers can rely on the rulings, they can also appeal adverse return examination decisions based on the rulings to the Tax court or other Federal courts.*

Caveat: Checking YES to item 11 means the U.S. beneficiaries may have to file Form TD F 90-22.1 with the Department of the Treasury (this is not attached to your 1040 that goes to the IRS). If the beneficiaries have a "signature authority" (which they can have) over the trust, but no "financial interest" (defined on the back of TD F 90-22.1 as (d) a trust in which the U.S. person either has a present beneficial interest in more than 50% of the assets **or receives more than 50% of current income**), then they will merely be required to tell the Treasury their U.S. address and social security number, and sign the form. No disclosure regarding the amount of income received is mandatory.

To avoid having a "financial interest", the trust creator should limit **Y** and **Z**'s beneficial enjoyment to **50%** or less. If necessary, this can be done by naming a third income beneficiary to receive **2%** or so of the trust's income distributions, leaving **Y** and **Z** with 49% each. See (d) in the previous paragraph.

Revenue Rulings and Revenue Procedures
(from Pub 1140-Rev. 4-87, pg. 3.).

Revenue Rulings are the published conclusions of the IRS concerning the application of tax law to an entire set of facts.

Revenue procedures are official statements of procedures that either affect the rights or duties of taxpayers or other members of the public, or should be a matter of public knowledge.

The purpose of these rulings is to promote a uniform application of the tax laws, and therefore IRS employees must follow the rulings. While taxpayers can rely on the rulings, they can also appeal adverse return examination decisions based on those rulings to the Tax Court or other Federal courts.

Revenue rulings and revenue procedures are published by the IRS in the Internal Revenue Bulletin (I.R.B.) and issued weekly to the public. The contents of the I.R.B. are consolidated at least semiannually into a permanent, indexed Cumulative Bulletin (C.B.).

---

4. *See* Regs. §1.671-2(e); also Rev-Rul 66-72, 1966-1 C.B. 58

Do we dare test the U.S.A.'s own Foreign Grantor Trust laws?

Non-Resident Alien Grantor
Mr. X

ADVICE FOR OFFSHORE TRUSTEES

Let trust income accrue in a Bahamas bank account. Keep this information confidential even from beneficiaries. IRS has no authority to ask questions in the Bahamas. Use of Rev-Rul 69-70 is authorized by the IRS. Have a copy on hand if you're ever asked to explain. Direct the IRS agent to your lawyers and trustees in Bahamas.

See pgs 262 & 263

Bahamas Grantor Trust

The penalty for not filing TD F 90-22.1 with the Department of the Treasury include a fine of not more than $500,000, and imprisonment of not more than 5 years.

Questions 7a & b & 8 on the back of 10,000,000+ IRS Form 1040s remains an enigma to most tax planners and U.S.taxpayers alike. Schedule B, Part III appears below.

U.S. income beneficiaries Y and Z are not liable to Federal Income Taxes on distributions they receive from a Bahamas Grantor Trust thanks to IRS Rev-Rul 69-70.

See pgs 262 & 263

Part III Foreign Accounts and Trusts (See page B-2.)	You must complete this part if you **(a)** had over $400 of interest or ordinary dividends; **(b)** had a foreign account; or **(c)** received a distribution from, or were a grantor of, or a transferor to, a foreign trust.	Yes	No
	7a At any time during 1998, did you have an interest in or a signature or other authority over a financial account in a foreign country, such as a bank account, securities account, or other financial account? See page B-2 for exceptions and filing requirements for Form TD F 90-22.1		
	b If "Yes," enter the name of the foreign country ▶ --		
	8 During 1998, did you receive a distribution from, or were you the grantor of, or transferor to, a foreign trust? If "Yes," you may have to file Form 3520. See page B-2		

For Paperwork Reduction Act Notice, see Form 1040 instructions.   ✲   Schedule B (Form 1040) 1998

Foreign trusts under attack

Successive United Kingdom governments have introduced legislation to discourage the use of trusts in tax planning starting with the *Statute of Uses* in 1535, designed to inhibit the use of trusts to avoid feudal dues, and continuing to this day. But trusts with their infinite flexibility remain one of the most efficient tax planning tools.

As Blackstone Franks, the London based international accountants, expressed it in their publication:

"Since a trust is a separate legal entity, it can be used in estate planning to hold assets in suspense, in capital gains tax planning to avoid time apportionment, in income tax planning to reduce the effective rate of tax, and by changing the residence to defer income tax and capital gains tax, often for long periods of time."

To anyone familiar with adolescents, it must seem strange that for every one parent who disinherits his progeny, there are approximately 156,389 whose only wish is give share certificates, second homes, hard-earned savings, land and valuables to their children in such a way that the taxman cannot touch any part of them.

Be that as it may, for this majority of parents trusts are an ideal vehicle. While some virtuous citizens set aside assets in trusts for charities, the overwhelming majority are **family trusts** designed to preserve as much as possible of the settlor's wealth for his children, grandchildren and associated relatives.

The re-introduction of capital gains tax on gifts of non-business assets in the UK's *1989 Finance Act* gives just one example of the way in which tax liabilities can be reduced through the use of *discretionary trusts.*

Mr. Lance Blackstone, senior partner of Blackstone Franks, points out that by making gifts of non-business assets into a trust, holdover relief on taxable capital gains is obtained. And if the donor is made beneficiary of the trust he can have use of the relevant assets.

If the asset is to be sold in the near future, Mr. Blackstone suggests it might be better to transfer it into a discretionary trust, and then convert it into a *life interest trust,* since life interests trusts pay capital gains tax at only a 25% rate.

One of the commonest uses of a family trust is as a depository for shares in a family business or a management buy-out. When a new company is formed the shares have little or no value. Ten years down the track they might be valued in seven figures, and liable to huge amounts of capital gains or inheritance tax.

When the founder of the business or the directors want to pass on their shares to their children, nearly half the value might have to go to the *Inland Revenue* (the British IRS).

In these cases directors and shareholders have to choose between UK and an **offshore trust.** A non-UK resident trust is significantly more expensive to run than a UK one. But as the law stands, it is still possible to put assets into a UK trust and emigrate them at a later date by appointing offshore trustees.

Trusts are also an essential for parents wishing to leave assets worth more than the nil-rate band of inheritance tax (currently £118,000 per parent). The advantage of the trust is that it enables the settlor to give early, thus beating the seven-year rule, but prevent children getting control of the gift until they are thought to be sufficiently mature to make good use of it.

And, a children's trust can be an attractive vehicle for such activities as property dealing where substantial profits can be generated. By accumulating funds within the trust until the child is 18, valuable tax savings can be gained.

Trusts are particularly important tax planning devices for immigrants to the UK. Hong Kong residents, accustomed to much lower rates of taxation and planning to take up residence in the UK, are particularly advised to set-up offshore trusts for any overseas assets they wish to retain intact from capital gains and inheritance tax.

For the UK resident an Isle of Man or Channel Islands trust residence is normally the most convenient offshore location.

For North American tax planners, Bermuda, the Bahamas and the Caymans are probably the best bet. Indeed, some UK residents prefer

Bermuda as being further from the reach of the *Inland Revenue* and influence of the UK government, in the event of exchange controls returning to shore up a sliding pound.

Bermuda's bank vaults are stuffed with several thousand family trust deeds, but wealthy investors would probably do better to appoint trustees from one of the island's top law firms.

Banks the world over love bank charges, and their fees are based on fixed percentages of monies handled, which works out at a lot more than the administrative charges of the equally efficient legal trustees.

Thus, **International Trust Company Bermuda,** the local Barclay's offshoot, has an annual administration fee of 0.25% on the first $1M in trust, 0.025% investment fee on all

transactions, a withdrawal fee, and an income fee of 3% of the net income "where significant income is generated".

By contrast, Appleby, Spurling & Kempe, one of the island's top three law firms, would charge about $1,200 for setting up a trust, and a minimum of $750 a year as an administration fee, subject to the time spent.

The fee for large settlements involving greater responsibilities would be subject to negotiation.

It has its own trust company, **Harrington,** running some 700+ trusts, an administrative convenience ensuring that the settlor and beneficiaries are not inconvenienced by the death or absence on holiday of a trustee, as other partners of the firm can take up the reins.

United States laws for *Foreign Trusts* – clouded, muddled and intentionally ambiguous.

If the UK statutes regulating the formation of domestic and foreign trusts can be described as concise and for the most part easy to apply, the United States statutes for **foreign trusts** are anything but straightforward and easily applied. Indeed, our Congressional lawmakers appear to have deliberately muddled and grayed the laws as they apply to the offshore trust - probably seeking to discourage their use, but also to remind the end-user that U.S. citizens need to be cautious when venturing offshore to shelter assets. [5.]

Before the enactments brought on by the **Tax Reform Act of 1976**, a U.S. citizen might simply find an attorney in the Bahamas, Bermuda or Cayman to draft him a non-grantor type discretionary or accumulation trust, fund the trust with lots of cash, and thereafter let the money grow unimpeded by tax collectors. As long as the income was not distributed currently to the U.S. beneficiaries (his children, wife, mother), no immediate U.S. income tax liability would ensue.

The foreign trust would not incur Federal Income taxes provided it did not maintain an office within the United States, and provided its investments were free from the U.S.A.'s 30% withholding tax. In this respect, all *foreign source income* (dividends, interests, etc.) would go entirely untaxed. The U.S. beneficiaries of the trust were not taxed on trust income until it was actually distributed to them. The grantor generally incurred no tax liability if he surrendered all rights to the trust's corpus and income.

Section 679 added by the **TRA 1976** ended the aforementioned tax scheming by rendering the U.S. grantor currently taxable on the income earned by the foreign trust, but only when **all four** of the following requirements are met:

1) The transferor of property to the foreign trust must be a U.S. person;
2) The transferor must make either a direct or indirect transfer to the trust;
3) The trust must be a foreign trust; and
4) The trust must have a U.S. beneficiary.

The statute speaks in terms of transfers made by a "U.S. person". The term "United States

---

5. U.S. income tax regulations for **domestic trusts** and **estates** are lengthy but easier to fathom and apply than those for foreign trusts. See IRC §641 (non-grantor trusts) through §671 (grantor trusts); See IRC §679 (foreign trusts).

person" is not specifically defined in IRC §679, but H. Report No 658 makes it clear that the definition of that term found in §7701(a)(30) is intended to apply without further expansion, and without the use of any other attribution rules. A **"U.S. person"** is defined as:

1) a citizen or resident of the United States,
2) a domestic partnership or corporation,
3) any estate or trust [other than a foreign estate or trust within the meaning of §7701(a)(31)]. [6.]

It would seem safe to presume that a transfer by a foreign trust, estate or a foreign corporation would not be a transfer by a U.S. person, but this is not always the case.

The legislative history goes on to explain what may be construed as an *indirect transfer to a foreign trust,* stating:

"A transfer by a domestic or foreign entity in which a U.S. person has an interest may be regarded as an indirect transfer to the foreign trust by the U.S. person if the entity merely serves as a conduit for the transfer by the U.S. person or if the U.S. person has sufficient control over the entity to direct the transfer by the entity rather than himself." [Senate Rep. No 948, at 219]

Seemingly, a transfer by a foreign corporation in which the U.S. person is a controlling shareholder would be an **indirect** transfer to a foreign trust if that trust has a U.S. beneficiary. The committee reports go on to illustrate one situation in which an indirect transfer is found to be made by a U.S. person:

*"For example, if a U.S. person transfers property to a foreign person or entity and if that person transfers that property (or its equivalent) to a foreign trust that has U.S. beneficiaries, the U.S. person transferring the property to the foreign person or entity is treated as having made a transfer of property to the foreign trust **unless** it can be **shown** that the transfer of property to the trust was unrelated to the U.S. person's transfer of property to the foreign person or entity."*

Example #1: Suppose in January 1990 U.S. person **A** purchases 20% of the 1,000,000 shares of **non-voting stock** in Cayman company **X.** Seventy-seven percent of the nonvoting stock is owned by foreign trust **Y.** Assume also that all 100 shares of company X's **voting stock** is owned <u>equally</u> by Cayman Bank **Q** and foreign

trust **Y.** Under the terms of the trust instrument all income is to be accumulated solely for the benefit of Cayman company X - trust Y's only beneficiary. Remaining shareholders of X's non-voting stock are as follows:

1% - Cayman tax attorney John Henry
1% - Cayman banker Jay Quincy
1% - Cayman company director Bill Bloch

Suppose in January 1991 Cayman company X moves $1,000,000 in profits (rent receipts from condominiums, hotel, and office building) into trust Y. Is trust Y considered to have a U.S. beneficiary due to U.S. person A's 20% non-voting stockholding? Is Y an IRC §679 trust?

Answer: The answer to both questions is no. Trust Y has no U.S. beneficiary. Under the attribution of ownership rules for section §679(c)(2)(A), trust Y will not be considered to have a United States beneficiary unless the U.S. Shareholders of X own "more than 50%" of the voting stock of company X. See section §679(c)(2)(A) on page #258. Moreover, IRC §679 is only applicable when all four conditions outlined on page #266 are present.

Removing assets from your gross estate

Under U.S. rules, to keep the assets of trust "Y" out of A's gross estate, the settlor of trust Y (in the example above this is Company X) cannot also be a beneficiary except in one particular case. The exception is provided under IRC §678(a). **IRC §678(a) says a person other than the grantor shall be treated as the owner of any portion of a trust, if he has the power exercisable solely by himself to vest the corpus or the income therefrom in himself.**

Possible Solution: Allow another foreign company Z or foreign trust Z the power to revoke the corpus of trust Y. This will guarantee trust Y status as a non-grantor trust for income tax (& estate tax) purposes. By allowing trust Z or company Z to annex assets of trust Y, the Treasury resolves the "transfer by a U.S. person to a foreign trust" problem for you. In no way can foreign trust Z or foreign company Z be construed to be a U.S. person.

Sec. 678(b) says Sec. 678(a) will not apply with respect to a power over the *income* as originally granted. **Commerce Clearing House**

---

6. From *Foreign Grantor Trusts* by <u>Tax Management Inc.</u> (a subsidiary of the Bureau of National Affairs, Inc.), pg A-10.

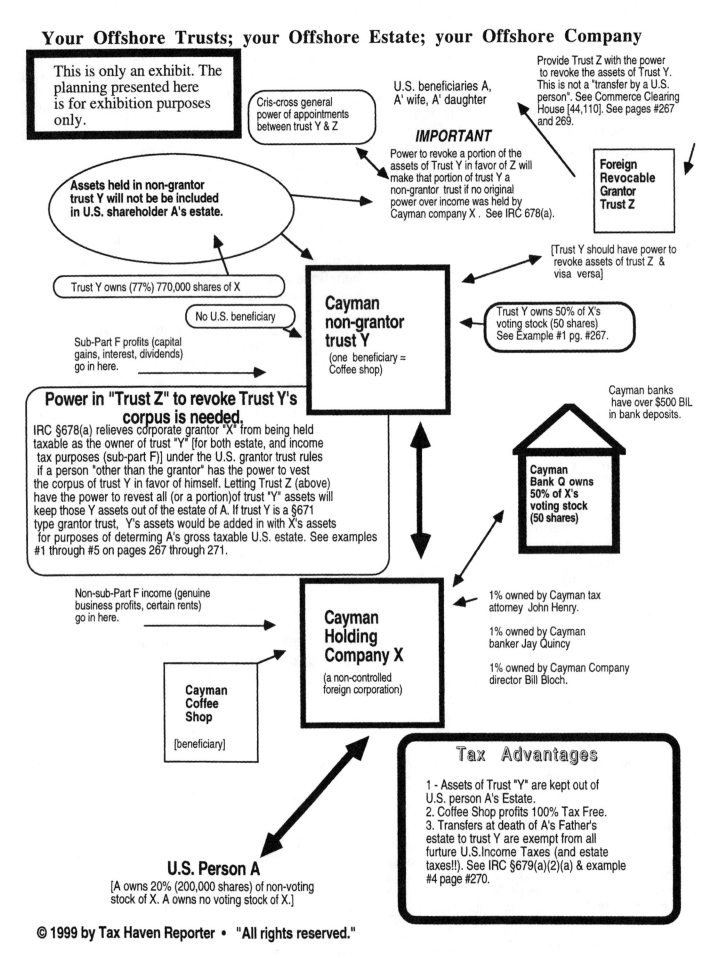

This is only an exhibit. The planning presented here is for exhibition purposes only.

Cris-cross general power of appointments between trust Y & Z

U.S. beneficiaries A, A' wife, A' daughter

Provide Trust Z with the power to revoke the assets of Trust Y. This is not a "transfer by a U.S. person". See Commerce Clearing House [44,110]. See pages #267 and 269.

IMPORTANT

Power to revoke a portion of the assets of Trust Y in favor of Z will make that portion of trust Y a non-grantor trust if no original power over income was held by Cayman company X . See IRC 678(a).

Foreign Revocable Grantor Trust Z

Assets held in non-grantor trust Y will not be be included in U.S. shareholder A's estate.

[Trust Y should have power to revoke assets of trust Z & visa versa]

Trust Y owns (77%) 770,000 shares of X

No U.S. beneficiary

Trust Y owns 50% of X's voting stock (50 shares) See Example #1 pg. #267.

Sub-Part F profits (capital gains, interest, dividends) go in here.

Cayman non-grantor trust Y

(one beneficiary = Coffee shop)

Cayman banks have over $500 BIL in bank deposits.

Power in "Trust Z" to revoke Trust Y's corpus is needed.

IRC §678(a) relieves corporate grantor "X" from being held taxable as the owner of trust "Y" [for both estate, and income tax purposes (sub-part F)] under the U.S. grantor trust rules if a person "other than the grantor" has the power to vest the corpus of trust Y in favor of himself. Letting Trust Z (above) have the power to revest all (or a portion)of trust "Y" assets will keep those Y assets out of the estate of A. If trust Y is a §671 type grantor trust, Y's assets would be added in with X's assets for purposes of determing A's gross taxable U.S. estate. See examples #1 through #5 on pages 267 through 271.

Cayman Bank Q owns 50% of X's voting stock (50 shares)

Non-sub-Part F income (genuine business profits, certain rents) go in here.

Cayman Holding Company X

(a non-controlled foreign corporation)

1% owned by Cayman tax attorney John Henry.

1% owned by Cayman banker Jay Quincy

1% owned by Cayman Company director Bill Bloch.

Cayman Coffee Shop

[beneficiary]

Tax Advantages

1 - Assets of Trust "Y" are kept out of U.S. person A's Estate.
2. Coffee Shop profits 100% Tax Free.
3. Transfers at death of A's Father's estate to trust Y are exempt from all furture U.S.Income Taxes (and estate taxes!!). See IRC §679(a)(2)(a) & example #4 page #270.

U.S. Person A
[A owns 20% (200,000 shares) of non-voting stock of X. A owns no voting stock of X.]

tax writers state [44,110] **"present law provides that a person** *other than the grantor* **can be considered the owner (Code Sec. 678), such as one with a power of appointment, but these others (i.e., foreign trust Z in example Z or even a foreign corporate grantor) will not be subject to the new rules of IRC §679."** Thus, Trust Z in the chart on page 268 would not be subject to IRC §679 rules if it had power over a *portion* of the CORPUS of Y, and no power over income (or portion thereof) as originally granted was held by the original grantor (i.e., Cayman Company X). Apparently, the U.S. lawmakers are providing at least one avenue for planners to transfer to a foreign trust without running amuck of the "direct or indirect transfer by a U.S. person" problem.

Estate Tax Planning Device

A foreign trust can sometimes be used to shelter assets from U.S. estate taxes, but it depends on which type trust you choose i.e., **non-grantor** trusts under IRC§661 through §668 **or** grantor trusts, IRC §671 through 678. When assets are properly placed in a **non-grantor trust,** they are excluded from the grantor's estate upon his demise. To obtain the exclusion the grantor usually must relinquish future claims to both income and assets.

Example #2: U.S. citizen A in our example owns 20% of the non-voting stock of Cayman company X (which runs a Cayman coffee shop with a Fair Market Value of $1,000,000). Suppose foreign trust **Y** (a non-grantor type trust – i.e., Company X has no power to revoke the assets of trust Y) holds $3,000,000 in foreign securities and bank deposits. Assuming the shares in company X are A's only foreign asset, A's U.S. estate will be valued by his 20% stockholding in company X. For purposes of computing A's U.S. gross estate, assets held in non-grantor trust Y would not be considered owned by company X. A's estate would have a value of $200,000 (20% of the FMV of X stock). The $3,000,000 held in the trust would not be included in A's U.S. gross estate.

Query: If Cayman company X owned a Cayman coffee shop with annual profits of $50,000, would it or U.S. citizen A owe any taxes to anyone? What about estate or gift taxes?

Answer: No-tax havens like the Caymans, the Bahamas, Bermuda, Vanuatu, Anguilla and Nauru, do not levy <u>any</u> corporate or personal income taxes. In addition, estate, inheritance, gift, sales, and withholding taxes are nonexistent in these countries. Because the U.S. government only imputes offshore profits (that are sub-part F

incomes; and coffee shop profits are not considered subpart F income) to U.S. Shareholders (a U.S. Shareholder is defined as a US person who owns 10% or more of the voting stock in a foreign company) of Controlled Foreign Corporations, U.S. citizen A (not a U.S. shareholder) would not need to include any of the $50,000 in coffee shop profits to the IRS on his income tax Form 1040. [7]

Gift Taxes: Transfers of assets between foreign entities in no-tax havens like Cayman and the Bahamas are entirely free from gift taxes. Moreover, the U.S. Tax Code does not impose gift taxes on a foreign giver unless the property is tangible property situated within the United States. See IRC §2511(a)(1) & (2).

More riddles for us to decipher

The tax planning possibilities are further complicated by the presumptions contained in some of the legislative history of §679. The U.S. Senate Committee Reports state: "whenever a U.S. person transfers property to a foreign entity (**other than a trust**), and that entity thereafter transfers similar property to a foreign trust, the U.S. person is presumed to have made an indirect transfer, unless it can be shown that the transfer of property to the trust was unrelated to the U.S. person's transfer of property".

Are the Congressional tax committees being sportsmanlike with us here, or is the above statement more muddled prose than sensible legislation? Why have the lawmakers suddenly decided to give immunity to **foreign trusts**? I have yet to meet a U.S. tax professional that truly understands what they mean. Couldn't foreign trust Y transfer property into a second foreign trust (Z) without making the U.S. person guilty of having made an indirect transfer to a foreign entity?

Example #3: Cayman citizen John Henry, Esq. (see Example#1, supra) is the managing director of Cayman company X. On July 1, 1990 Henry drafts a deed of trust for his American friend, U.S. person A,

---

7. Many foreign countries offer tax concessions where the investor can obtain a 5 to 20 year tax holiday from local taxes. Singapore, Western Samoa, Mauritius, Australia (total exemption for gold mining through January 1, 1991 only), Cyprus (professional, manufacturing and public corporations), Luxembourg, Netherlands Antilles (tax holidays for hotels and insurance and patent holding companies), Panama (Colon Free Zone exemptions), Puerto Rico (tax holidays for manufacturers), Taiwan.

contributing $100 to the trust's corpus to kick things off. Under the trust instrument, **trust Y** is given absolute power to dispose of all income and corpus of **trust Z**.

Trust Z has 3 U.S. beneficiaries, A, A's wife, and A's daughter. Trust Z is an IRC §671-68 type trust.

In 1991 Trust Z revokes some assets of trust Y and starts paying premiums on a pension-life-annuity policy purchased from one of the 300+ insurance companies registered in the Cayman Islands (we'll say Lloyds of London). The beneficiary of this pension-annuity policy is foreign trust Z. Consequently, as beneficiaries of trust Z, A, A's wife and A's daughter are entitled to receive their share of the insurance policy income flowing through trust Z. [8]

Using Corporate Grantors

According to Howard Zaritsky, Esq. (Zaritsky & Zaritsky, Fairfax, Virginia)..."When the trust's grantor trust status makes the beneficiary's income tax free, retaining that status for as long as possible becomes important. To solve the problem of the grantor predeceasing the beneficiaries, thus inconsiderately ending the trust's favorable tax status, use of a corporate grantor is recommended.

It is clear that a corporation may be the grantor and owner of a trust. Thus, a foreign grantor (or grantor with highly tax sheltered income) could create a corporation which in turn would create a grantor trust. The death of the creating shareholder would terminate neither the corporation's separate existence nor the trust's grantor trust status." [9]

Continuing Uses of Foreign Trusts

A U.S. individual can create a testamentary foreign trust which will come into existence upon his death. IRC §679 (2) (A) EXCEPTIONS - says "any transfer by reason of death of the transferor" will be excluded from provisions of Section §679.

The exception for transfers at death is a gift from the IRS, although it seems only logical and fair that the Code should not continue to tax the deceased assets (or transfer) after he is dead.

Nevertheless, this IRS "gimme" can be a useful loophole if applied properly.

Example #4: Suppose U.S. citizen **AA** (the father of U.S. citizen **A** dies in 1992 leaving an estate with a value of $1,000,000 after probate fees and U.S. estate taxes. Suppose AA's son lives in a State that has high inheritance taxes as well as income taxes. If the $1,000,000 is paid to A directly, he would have a continuous tax problem, as interest and other profits earned on the $1,000,000 would be taxable in the United States. Inheritance tax could be levied in the year of his father's death.

Should AA's **Will** instructs his attorney to pay the entire $1,000,000 to foreign trust Y, instead of to A directly, no additional U.S. or State income taxes would be incurred in the future. Any State inheritance taxes would also be avoided. [IRC §679 (2) (A) - Exceptions]

Transitory Trusts for Resident Alien Individuals

Non-U.S. individuals only become taxable in the United States when they take up residence here. Non-resident alien individuals planning on taking-up *temporary* residence in the U.S. should consider creating a non-grantor *transitory* trust (but with no named U.S. beneficiary) before coming to the United States.

Taxation under IRC §679 would not follow because the trust's grantor is a not a U.S. person. One of the requirements that must be present before IRC §679 can apply is the trust must have a U.S. transferor. [See page # 266. All "4" requirements must be present for §IRC 679 to apply].

Income earned by the foreign trust will not be taxable by the U.S., and the value of purely foreign assets, as well as the value inherent in U.S. assets (such as stocks in U.S. corporations owned by a foreign holding company whose stock is held by the trust - which has no U.S. beneficiary), will not be subject to U.S. estate tax, should the settlor die while a U.S. person. [10]

When the non-U.S. citizen later leaves the U.S. and establishes residence elsewhere, the trust can be collapsed or the income stripped out via payment from a corporation owned by the trust to the settlor. In the event funds are needed while

---

8. Since a foreign grantor trust would have superior tax advantages over a straight lace offshore employee pension plan, management should seriously considered the trust as a viable tax planning device. Planners might even allow the foreign corporation to pay the insurance/pension plan premiums for key personal.

9. Regs. §671-2(e); also Rev-Rul 66-72 (corporate grantor could receive dividend-received exclusion for dividends received by wholly owned grantor trust).

10. From "*U.S. taxation of Foreign Trusts: Post-1976 Act Changes and Continued Uses*", by Charles M. Bruce, Esq. & S. Gray, Esq. (Oppenheimer, Wolf & Donnelly, Washington, D.C.), pg 202.

in the U.S., salaries can be paid to the grantor as compensation for services rendered to the trust's underlying corporations.

Protection-of-Assets trusts

U.S. persons can create grantor trusts taxed as U.S. trusts. Such trusts are tax neutral, but the presence of a foreign trustee and assets held outside the USA can be used to divest the grantor-owner of assets potentially subject to creditors, and also place such assets outside the reach of a creditor's claims. [11.]

Non-Grantor Accumulation Trusts

Section 1014 of the *Tax Reform Act of 1976* added Section §668 to the Code, which invokes a penalty "interest charge" to the accumulated distributions of foreign non-grantor trusts received by its U.S. beneficiaries. The *interest charge* is 6% of the partial tax on the accumulated distribution times the number of years the tax has been deferred. The tax is to be paid by the U.S. beneficiary receiving the accumulated distribution, not the foreign trust making the distribution. The aim of the **6% interest charge** was to end the tax-free accumulation of income in foreign trusts. Effectively, the 6% interest charge can wipe out the entire accumulation if the period of accumulation runs 10 or more years.

The penalty interest charge applies to **non-grantor** type foreign trusts (IRC §662 through §668) with U.S. beneficiaries. Foreign grantor trusts described under IRC§671 to §678 are relieved from paying the 6% interest charge even if income has been accumulating tax free in the trust for 10 years or longer.

Professor Marshall J. Langer, in his book *Practical International Tax Planning ($225),* warns against using a non-grantor foreign accumulation trust (i.e., trusts covered by IRC §662 through §668) after 1976 when the trust has U.S. beneficiaries. [12.]

---

11. See Bruce & Gray, *Offshore Protection of Assets Trusts* (Prentice-Hall *U.S. Taxation of International Transactions,* para. 13,510.1)

12. Marshall J. Langer has received many awards for his books on tax havens and international taxation. Most good law libraries carry his *Practical International Tax Planning* (formerly titled *"How to use tax havens"),* and his 4 volume hard-bound set on the *Taxation of International Transactions.* Langer is a graduate of the Wharton School of Finance; and the U. of Miami Law

If the big "5" accounting firm Delete Haskins + Sells exploits Rev-Rul 69-70, why shouldn't you?

On a visit to Honolulu, Hawaii in 1989, I spent three hours in the downtown offices of the big 5 accounting firm Delete, Haskins + Sells discussing tax havens with two of the firm's partners - both international tax specialists. One of my queries concerned the use of Rev. Rul. 69-70 in practice. "Do any of Delete Haskins + Sells clients exploit the loophole in this ruling," I asked? I was more than a bit surprised when they assured me.. "Yes. We do have clients living in the United States who receive "foreign source income" from foreign grantor trusts via IRS Rev. Rul 69-70."

Example #5: Australian rancher/actor Mick Dundee (**MD**) moves to the U.S. in 1977, taking up permanent residence. In 1980 Mick gets married and purchases a cattle ranch outside San Antonio and becomes a U.S. citizen.

Mick's father (**MF**) is an 88 year old cattle baron living in Queensland, Australia. In 1978 MF **cau**ses a grantor trust to be formed in Vanuatu (one of the Pacific no-tax havens) for the benefit of son MD. $10,000,000 in foreign securities makes up the trust's corpus.

Beginning in 1979 and through 1989 the trust distributions totaled $7,000,000. This amounts to $700,000 per annum. By virtue of the exemption under Rev.-Rul 69-70, none of this income is taxable to son **MD,** even though he lives in the U.S. and is a U.S. citizen. Further, under current filing guidelines, **MD** need not report this income to the IRS on his annual income tax Form 1040.

The fact that the foreign trust pays no income taxes in the host country where it is established prior to distributing its income to the U.S. beneficiary is not a factor in deciding if taxes should be paid on the receipt of such income. The IRS's premise is that the trust's grantor has already paid the taxes. Whether any taxes have been paid in the host nation is irrelevant under current U.S. tax law. See pg. #262 for Rev.Rul 69-70.

Alternative Minimum Tax (AMT): Distributions of *foreign source income* from a

---

School (summa cum laude) where he is the Adjunct Professor of Law. Langer keeps his offices in Switzerland.

foreign grantor trust like the ones outlined here are not subject to the **AMT**. IRC §55(b)((2) says the starting point for figuring one's AMT is one's "taxable income". Foreign source income from a foreign trust taxable to a foreign grantor is not "taxable income" for purposes of the AMT.

To determine if the foreign trust has a U.S. beneficiary, Code-Section 679(c) states:

(1) In GENERAL - For purposes of this section, a trust shall be treated as having a U.S. beneficiary for taxable years unless -

(A) under the terms of the trust, no part of the income or corpus of the trust may be paid or accumulated during the taxable year to or for the benefit of a U.S. person, and

(B) if the trust was terminated at any time during the taxable year, no part of the income or corpus of such trust could be paid to or for the benefit of a U.S. person.

(2) **ATTRIBUTION of OWNERSHIP** - For purposes of paragraph (1) an amount shall be treated as paid or accumulated to or for the benefit of a U.S. person if such amount is paid to or accumulated for a foreign corporation, partnership, or foreign trust or estate, and -

(A) in the case of a **foreign corporatio**n, more than 50% of the total combined voting power of all classes of stock entitled to vote of such corporation is owned [within the meaning of Section 958(a) or is considered to be owned (within the meaning of section 958(b)] by U.S. shareholders (as defined in Section 951(b),

(B) in the case of a foreign partnership, a U.S. person is a partner of such partnership, or

(C) in the case of a foreign trust or estate, such trust or estate has a U.S. beneficiary (within the meaning of paragraph (1).

Example: Robert Rho owns 25% of the single class of stock (which carries voting privileges) of Rho Pacific Bahamas (RPB). The remaining 75% of RPB stock is owned by foreign trust **T** (located in the Cayman Islands). Applying the constructive ownership rules of IRC §958 (b), R. Rho owns 25% of RPB's voting stock **directly** and an additional 25% indirectly (25% of the 100% owned by the foreign trust). His total ownership of voting stock is 50%, which is under the "more than 50%" threshold of IRC §679(c)(2)(A) thus, foreign trust T is not considered to have a U.S. beneficiary. More important, Robert Rho will not be taxable under IRC §679(a) on any annual profits that are distributed by the trust.

Note foreign trust T is deemed to own 100% of RPB's voting stock (25% more than it actually owns) under constructive ownership rule 958-12(c)(2), making the total amount of voting stock owned to be 125%, or 25% more then the actual amount of voting stock outstanding. See constructive ownership rules below.

Under **Constructive Ownership rule** Reg.§1.958-2(c)(**2**) **Rules of Application**: If a partnership, **trust**, estate of corporation owns directly or indirectly more than 50% of the total combined voting power of all classes of stock entitled to vote in a corporation, it shall be considered as owning **all** the stock entitled to vote.

Constructive ownership rule Reg.§1.958-(c)(1)(i)(a): *To beneficiaries*. Stock owned, directly or indirectly, by or for a trust shall be considered as owned by its beneficiaries (Rho Pacific Bahamas - the sole beneficiary of trust T) in proportion to the actuarial interest of such beneficiary in such trust.

Note by application of these two Constructive Ownership rules **foreign trust T** is made out to own **100%** (actually more than the 75% it really owns) of Rho Pacific's voting stock. Thus, Robert Rho directly and indirectly owns 50% of Rho Pacific's voting stock (25% directly + 25% of 100% indirectly owned by the trust). For purposes of IRC §679(c) the trust has no U.S. beneficiary because no U.S. Shareholder owns "more than 50%" of the voting stock through the attribution of ownership rules.

Advice from Professor Marshall J. Langer and Rufus von Thulen Rhoades

"In calculating value for purposes of determining whether the corporation is a CFC, only the value held by U.S. Shareholders is counted. As a result, if a U.S. person who is not a U.S. Shareholder holds 60% to 70% of the value of the corporation's outstanding stock that person will not make the corporation a CFC. "

- Marshall J. Langer/Rufus von Thulen Rhoades, *Income Taxation of Foreign Related Transactions* (Matthew Bender) (Times Mirror Books). 1987

Transfers of non-U.S. property to a foreign trust by a foreign corporation triggers no U.S. income or gift tax liability. Because tax havens like the Bahamas and the Caymans have no gift or income taxes, such transfers can be made routinely, without an income or gift tax liability. The U.S. Internal Revenue Code does not cover the "taxability" of such transfers, other than to say they are outside the scope of U.S. tax rules.

Tax Planning with Foreign Trusts

The use of foreign trusts in the offshore tax havens is widespread. It can probably be said there are as many foreign trusts established by taxpayers in the nearby Cayman Islands and Bahamas as there are holding companies, and there are at least 30,000 of them. The foreign trust has always been a viable and popular vehicle to invest through offshore because: (1) trusts are relatively inexpensive to form. The Government stamp tax on a Cayman deed of trust is only about US$50, whereas a company could incur government registration fees of $1,000 or more; (2) foreign trusts ordinarily do not have to be registered with the tax haven government, thus names of beneficiaries, trustees, and grantor are not a matter of public record; (3) a properly arranged foreign trust(s) does not require any U.S. registration, including the disclosure filings of Forms 3520-A or 3520.

The following article appeared several years ago in the *London Financial Advisor* - a wholly owned and widely read newspaper publication of the *London Financial Times*.

OFFSHORE TRUSTS for UK Residents

"United Kingdom residents often opt for the foreign trust in their tax planning because under UK law a foreign trust is still a legal and suitable vehicle to use to preserve one's assets and avoid high UK taxations. UK Inland Revenue procedures will allow a foreign trust registered in a tax haven to invest and trade in stocks free from capital gains taxes, and this is one of their main benefits to UK residents.

The basic tax advantages of offshore trusts is that they enable an individual to defer and possibly avoid capital gains tax on sale of an asset.

The advantage stems from one of the fundamental rules of the CGT (Capital Gains Tax). A person is only liable to CGT on the disposal of assets if he/she is a UK resident or ordinary resident. Offshore trustees will not satisfy either of these conditions so no CGT arises when they sell or otherwise dispose of assets.

This means the payment of tax can be indefinitely deferred until cash is brought back into the UK for the beneficiary's benefit. And tax can be avoided altogether if it is ultimately applied for the benefit of a beneficiary who is not a UK resident.

Although offshore trusts can provide other tax benefits - inheritance tax benefits for the settlor who is non domiciled - in most cases the settlor will be UK resident and will want to retain an interest in the trust so that he can benefit from the capital growth one day.

Clearly, the most suitable assets to place into an offshore trust will be those whose value is likely to increase substantially in the future - that is on a later sale. One category of asset that has been successfully used is shares in private limited companies. Generally, a reasonable valuation can be agreed with the Inland Revenue when such shares are owned by proprietors of a company run as a going concern.

There can be a tax price to pay when setting up an offshore trust. This is because when assets are placed directly into an offshore trust a CGT charge (aka excise tax) will be triggered at that time based on the latent capital gain within the asset."

Much like the UK excise tax mentioned in the article above, was the United States **excise tax** under IRC §1491, which imposed a 35% excise tax on the transfer of appreciated assets (including appreciated shares in U.S. companies, bonds, etc.) to any offshore entity, including corporate capitalizations, or into a foreign trust or foreign partnership. fortunately for the American taxpayer, IRC §1491 was recently repealed.

The following is an example of how Revenue Ruling 69-70 can be applied in the 1990s.

Example: Suppose B.T. Butterfield, Sr. of the Butterfield Banks in Bermuda, the Cayman Islands and the Bahamas (and throughout the world) decided to send his son, B.T. Jr. to Harvard School of Business to learn all about U.S. tax laws as they relate to tax havens and offshore financial centers. We'll assume B.T. Sr. is a resident of London and resides their part of each fiscal year. If Mr. Butterfield Sr. gave his son $300,000 out of his own pocket for tuition and living expenses he might incur a UK gift tax liability, whereas his son B.T. Jr. conceivably could be liable to U.S. income taxes.

Instead, B.T. Sr. has one of his offshore holding companies move $3,000,000 in Eurodollars into a revocable foreign grantor trust based in Bermuda, appointing the Butterfield Banks & Sons in Bermuda as trustee. Interest income from the Eurodollars (we'll assume the rate of return is 10% pa for a yield of $300,000 pa) could be passed along to B.T. Jr. (legal residence living in the U.S.) pursuant to Rev.Rul. 69-70 tax-free.

In many college libraries across the United States there are a series of books published by *Tax Management Inc.* These books are in this author's opinion the absolute authority on U.S. international tax matters. In the series titled "Foreign Grantor Trusts" you can find a complete and detailed disclosure concerning direct and indirect transfers to a foreign trust. Covered are such gambits as loans between offshore entities when the guarantor is not a U.S. person. Also covered are transfers by foreign entities not deemed to be indirect transfers because no interest in the entity making the transfer is owned by any U.S. person(s). But heed this warning, nominee transfers by foreign attorneys or agents are considered to be shams by the IRS. Giving money to a foreigner to place in a trust for you is not recognized as legitimate tax planning by the U.S. tax authorities.

IRS Disclosure Forms for Foreign Trusts

Form 3520 (*Creation or Transfer to certain Foreign Trusts*) is required to be filed (1) upon the creation of a trust by a "United States person", or (2) the transfer of any money or property to a foreign trust by a U.S. person. The definition of "United States person" is identical to the "definition" found in form 3520-A.

Form 3520 also requires the *transferor* of property to the foreign trust file if the *transferor* is a U.S. person. IRS instructions for the "new" form 3520-A (1998) (Annual Return of Foreign Trust with U.S. Beneficiaries) appears in back of this book in Appendix A.

Schedule B, Part III of your IRS Form 1040

If you need proof that foreign grantor trusts with U.S. beneficiaries are in use today, just pick up your IRS income tax return from 1040 and turn it over on its back. Schedule B, Part III, Questions 10 and 11 ask for very general information about an offshore foreign grantor trust. See the chart on page # 264. *"Were you the grantor or transferor to a foreign trust during the current taxable year, whether or not you have any beneficial interest?"* asks question #11.

ESTATE TAX PLANNING TIP

Foreigners investing in U.S. property, including U.S. real estate, stocks and bonds should always use a tax haven holding company to hold those U.S. assets. If the nonresident alien invests $5,000,000 in a Texas oil lease directly under his own name, the entire $5,000,000 would be included in his estate for purposes of computing his U.S. estate tax liability. If the nonresident alien died in 1992, the $5,000,000 lease would be subject to U.S. estate taxes at rates to 55%, and the nonresident alien would be permitted only a $60,000 tax credit.

Using the estate tax table under **IRC §2001(c)** the nonresident alien would owe $1,290,800 on amounts up to $3,000,000, and 55% of everything above that. On his $5,000,000 estate, the nonresident alien's heirs would witness the payment of ≈ $2,390,800 in estate taxes to the U.S. Treasury.

HOWEVER, under U.S. estate tax law shares of an offshore company would not be included in the nonresident alien's estate for purposes of calculating his **U.S. estate tax** liability, even if the only asset owned by the offshore company was the $5,000,000 U.S. oil lease. Offshore practitioners should never advise their non-U.S. clients to invest directly in the USA. A tax haven holding company should always be considered; unless the investment being planned is small - under $100,000.

U.S. foreign trust tax law in the 1990's

Under current law, income from a foreign trust taxable to a legitimate foreign grantor is not subject to any U.S. income as long as the trust corpus it is revocable by the grantor.[13.] Nor, is the income subject to the Alternative Minimum Tax (AMT), because only taxable incomes are subject to the **AMT**. Incomes from municipal bonds issued before August 7, 1986, and foreign grantor trust income are currently not considered taxable income when computing your regular tax liability. Such incomes would not be taxable income for purposes of computing the AMT. Although the U.S. lawmakers continue to discourage the use of foreign trusts by its citizenry, there are still some situations where a revocable foreign grantor trust with a nonresident grantor should be considered.

1. Transfers at death by a U.S. transferor (grandfather, grandmother, father,) are still permitted. See pg. 258.
2. Transfers by nonresident aliens with children living inside the United States.
3. A genuine loan is not a transfer to a foreign trust. Lending money to a foreign trust will not violate IRC §679 transfer rules.
4. Selling property at it's fair market value to a foreign trust. See pg. 258 (exceptions).

If you are going to transfer to a foreign trust it is recommended that you:

1. Keep transfers to the foreign trust as **unrelated** as possible.
2. Never transfer U.S. property or money directly to a foreign trust as that triggers IRC §679 automatically.
3. Always use a combination of trusts and foreign corporations. A single trust or two trusts (back-to-back), will not insulate you from IRC §679.
4. Find or create a legitimate foreign grantor.

Comments from a Pro

Marshall J. Langer, author of <u>Practical International Tax Planning</u>, has practiced law for more than 35 years. He's also the adjunct professor of law at the University of Miami. He has given lectures on international tax planning in the Cayman Islands, the USA, Europe and Japan. He writes in his book...

"Certainly foreign trusts are still viable tax planning tools. ... Therefore, despite the new United States rules (i.e., IRC 679) the foreign tax planner should know what a foreign trust is and how it works. Even after the 1976 Tax Reform Act there are still circumstances in which a foreign trust should be considered.. For example, when a foreign trust is created by a bona-fide foreign grantor (not an accommodation grantor) for U.S. beneficiaries. Here it may be best to use a grantor trust that is currently taxable to the foreign grantor rather than an accumulation trust." This statement by Professor Langer is followed with a footnote that reads. **See Rev.Rul.69-70, 1969-1C.B.** See pg. 262.

Avoid distributions from non-grantor foreign trusts

Foreign accumulation non-grantor trusts, which are not revocable grantor trusts, are no longer viable tax planning devises when the trust has a U.S. beneficiary. U.S. beneficiaries who receive distributions from a foreign trust whose income is not taxable to a foreign grantor (i.e., a revocable grantor trust) are fully liable to pay income taxes on such distributions. Moreover, the Tax Reform Act of 1976 added a nondeductible 6% per year interest charge, which has been increased beyond 6% for years beginning after January 1, 1996. The income tax plus the new penalty can wipe out the entire accumulated distribution if there is a long period of accumulation. [15.]

IRC 679 governs the use of Foreign Trusts

On page 258 is Code-Section §679, the U.S. Treasury Department's guidelines for foreign trusts that have U.S. grantors. As yet no Treasury regulations for this section of the Code have been issued.

At first brush IRC §679 seems a real obstacle. But, some lawyers and tax practitioners have suggested Code §679 creates as many loopholes for tax planners as it closes.

Query: What about the creation of a foreign trust by a foreign company that has U.S. shareholders?

---

13. The term "current law" means through and up until the publishing date of this book – September of 1999.

15. Under current law, a foreign trust not revocable under the grantor trust provisions of IRC § 674 would be taxable under the non-grantor trust rules of IRC §641 through 668. These non-grantor trusts have various names and are sometimes called accumulation trusts. The liability to pay federal income tax is shifted to the beneficiaries of an accumulation trust or the trust itself. The 1996 Clinton "Jobs Act" raised the interest penalty on accumulated distributions by these nongrantor trusts even higher than the 6% per year level imposed by the Tax Reform Act of 1976.

If a U.S. person cannot be the grantor for a foreign trust, can a foreign company somehow be implanted as a substitute? Answer: The irony is that IRC §679(c)(2) provides for just such a situation, if the U.S. shareholders do not own "more than 50% of the total combined voting power". Foreign trusts found not to have U.S. beneficiaries are not subject to IRC §679 rules by virtue of this built-in loophole.

Revenue Reconciliation Act of 1990 adds new rule for foreign grantor trusts

Under this law (effective for any trust created after 11-5-90), foreign grantors that transfer (their) funds to a foreign trust using third party relatives or friends as intermediaries will continue to be taxable on the trust's distributions (i.e., Rev.Rul. 69-70 will not apply). In effect, the trust will not be treated as a bona fide foreign grantor trust the income of which can be passed along to U.S. beneficiaries tax free. Instead, the immigrating grantor will stay taxable on the foreign trust's distributions.

Example #1: Bob Smith, a wealthy foreigner, expects to reside in the U.S. Before moving to the U.S., he transfers a substantial amount of his assets to his brother, Jim Smith. Jim then sets up a trust (i.e., in a tax haven like the Bahamas or Cayman), naming Bob as the income beneficiary. But, Jim retains an interest or power that causes him to be treated as the owner of the trust under the grantor trust rules. Bob then moves to the U.S. The IRS tries to tax Bob as beneficiary on the trust's income. Bob argues that he can't be taxed on the trust income because Jim is the owner of the trust under the grantor trust rules. Jim is outside the reach of the U.S. tax authorities.

The **Revenue Reconciliation Act of 1990** closes off this avenue of tax avoidance. It does so by treating any U.S. person as the grantor of a trust if that U.S. person:

(1) is a beneficiary of the trust.
(2) makes a direct or indirect gift to a foreign person of property that was contributed to the trust, and
(3) that foreign person would otherwise be treated as the grantor of the trust without the application of the new Act's rules.

Example #2: Andrew and Bill are foreign persons. Andrew transfers property to Bill's spouse, Cathy. Cathy places the property in a trust in which Andrew is a discretionary income beneficiary. Andrew becomes a U.S. person. Under the new provision, Andrew is treated as the owner of the portion of the trust in which he has an income interest. [17]

Editor's Comments and Advice

Note that the new law was added onto Code-Sec. 672 (f) (*Special Rule Where Grantor is Foreign Person*, not Code-Sec. 679 (*Foreign Trusts having one or more U.S. Beneficiaries*). Yet, Congressional intent was clearly meant to cover any transfer, direct or indirect, to any trust (whether foreign or domestic) when the trust has U.S. beneficiaries.

But tax planners can take heart. The new 1990 law covers only one particular situation, and does not override or amend any of IRC §679. In addition, Rev.-Rul. 69-70, which permits *foreign source income* from a foreign grantor trust to be passed along to U.S. beneficiaries tax free, is left unscathed by the **Act**. Rev.-Rul. 69-70 is still a viable and exploitable tax planning devise if:

(1) There is a legitimate foreign grantor who transfers his assets to a **revocable** foreign trust that has U.S. beneficiaries. [18]
(2) For transfers by reason of death of the U.S. transferor as excepted under IRC §679(a)(2)(A).
3) If the U.S. transferor can somehow successfully (i.e., legally) maneuver past the direct and indirect transfer to a foreign trust rules prescribed under IRC §679. This is not necessarily impossible to do. Both the *Internal Revenue Code* and *Tax Management's* portfolios (*i.e., 427-2nd T.M. - Foreign Trusts, Estates and Beneficiaries*) (found in any good college law library) can give you good guidance (tips) on how to exploit foreign trusts.

---

[17] This example was extracted from **Commerce Clearing House**'s *Explanation of the Tax Law of 1990*. The House Bill contains an almost identical example substituting the letters "A" and "B" for Andrew and Bill.

[18] The new Clinton Jobs Act of 1996 tightened the grantor trust rules even further. Under the Jobs Act, the foreign trust must now be revocable by a foreign grantor. Interestingly, all these minor trust law changes seem to revolve around Revenue Ruling 69-70, which was issued by the IRS in 1970. Revenue Ruling 69-70 has never been repealed and can still be applied today in some cases. The entire ruling appears on page 262 of this book. The new rules for foreign grantors added by the *Revenue Reconciliation Act of 1990* were added to commingle (exist in harmony) with Rev.Rul.69-70. It was not Congress' intent to close off Rev.Rul.69-70 entirely to foreign or U.S. investors (persons). If it was, IRC §679(c) (transfers to a foreign trust through a related foreign holding company or the transfers at death of a U.S. person - §679(a)(2)) would have been amended or repealed. Rev.Rul.69-70 has never been overridden or repealed.

U.S. trust law discriminates against U.S. taxpayers

As a tax planner, I am forever being hammered with questions from clients and subscribers about the use of Rev.Rul. 69-70 in their own tax plan. Rev.Rul. 69-70 has always been easier for the nonresident alien grantor to apply than for the American citizen. Elsewhere in the tax code you can find other unfair discriminatory rules.

For example, offshore banks, nonresident alien individuals, foreign trusts and offshore companies are not subject to U.S. capital gains taxes on their publicly traded Wall Street type stock, bond, and commodity trades. The United States has never taxed the capital gains of the non-resident alien, unless the foreigner was "doing business within the U.S." "Doing business within the United States", generally means operating through a U.S. office or permanent establishment from within the U.S. However, the U.S. tax code even exempts a non-resident company from U.S. capital gains taxes even when it does have an office and staff inside the U.S., if all the company's business amounts to merely trading in the Stock Market. From his home or office on Fifth Avenue in New York, or the Sears Tower in Chicago, or from Beverly Hills, any person working for an offshore company could call his broker at Merrill Lynch or Payne Webber and day trade NYSE, NASDAQ or AMEX listed securities 1,000 times a week, and no tax on the profits would be owed the U.S. Treasury.

Unfortunately, the American taxpayer cannot qualify for the aforementioned tax exemptions allowed nonresidents, unless he can avoid both the Controlled Foreign Corporation provisions enacted during the Kennedy Administration and the Passive Foreign Investment Company provisions enacted in 1986. Most tax attorneys and big 10 accounting firms will probably tell you that is not possible. This is not to imply that U.S. taxpayers don't attempt to secure the above tax breaks afforded the foreign investor.

The investment-banking firm of Warburg, Dillion Read (on Park Ave. N.Y.) has offices in 39 foreign countries - including the Bahamas, the tiny Cayman Islands, Hong Kong and the Channel Islands. Makes you wonder why, doesn't it?

Several years ago, an international tax lawyer who graduated from NYU School of Law (one of the most respected U.S. University for training International tax lawyers), with offices in Geneva, Switzerland as well as London writes:

I would like to repeat that I find your analysis of *the Tax Code to be excellent. I enjoy each and every issue of the* **Tax Haven Reporter**. *You might be interested to know that while you indicate the use of foreign non-grantor corporate settlors may be construed as an aggressive use of the U.S. Tax Code, such* **entities** *as settlors are specifically referred to in Marshall Langer's chapter on Taxation of Trusts and Estates at Section 2B 04 (2) - (5), pages 2B - 22, 2B - 26 - 26, and are widely used even in non-U.S. estate planning. Of course, the use of foreign grantor corporate settlors is equally widespread outside the United States.*[19]

Grandfather clauses in TRA of '76

Foreign trusts with U.S. beneficiaries created before the Tax Reform Act of 1976 were given some immunity from those new trust laws with a grandfather clause.

Before Congress enacted IRC §679 in 1976, there were literally tens of thousands of foreign trusts existent in the Cayman Islands, the Bahamas and Bermuda (to name just a few tax havens where foreign trusts are popular investment vehicles). Yet, as far as we know not one of these foreign trust with U.S. beneficiaries has ever come under attack by the IRS or the U.S. courts, and we know of not a single instance where the IRS has collected any taxes from the U.S. beneficiary or these foreign trust. One possible reason why these trusts remained immune to 679 is because there was a "grandfather clause" clearly stating that transfers before 1974 were not to be covered.

As for how much tax revenue the IRS has been able to garnish from the hundreds of thousands of offshore trusts existent right now, I haven't a guess. Surely, it would help if our lawmakers or the IRS would make such information known to the U.S. public.

---

19. The use of a corporate grantor for an offshore (tax haven) trust is recommended by other reputable sources (i.e., U.S. tax lawyers), including (1) Tax Management Portfolio 427-2nd (2) Howard Zaritsky, Esq. (Zaritsky & Zaritsky, Fairfax, Virginia) and (3) Richard Graham-Taylor, partner Ernst & Young, Grand Cayman (January 1990) in his recent article published in the *International Tax Report* (London).

Example #3: It is clear under current 1999 U.S. tax law if Crown Prince Fahd (*the* papa) of Saudi Arabia formed a foreign grantor trust in the Bahamas, funding the trust with a partnership interest in 10 Saudi wells that produce annual partnership revenues (after expenses) of $50,000,000, while retaining the power to revoke all the assets of the Bahamian trust for himself, the income beneficiaries of the trust (i.e., Crown Prince Abdul Al-Fahd, Jr., his wife and two sons - all living permanently in Houston, Texas on their $10,000,000 U.S. estate) could receive the trust's income distributions (we'll say $25,000,000 annually), then put it in any U.S. bank, and not owe any Federal Income Taxes on the $25,000,000 so received.

On the other hand, if Ted Turner (the *papa*) forms a Bahamian trust, funding it with $5,000,000, and names his son and daughter as U.S. income beneficiaries, then Ted Turner will have to pay the Federal Income Taxes on any of the trust's earnings attributed to the $5,000,000. Note the differences. IRC §679 makes a transfer to a foreign trust with U.S. beneficiaries taxable to the U.S. person (Ted Turner) making the transfer. For more information, see Form 3520-A in the appendix of *Tax Havens of the World*, or write the IRS and have them forward you a copy.

Question: Is the use of an offshore company in combination with a foreign trust a common planning technique? What advantages does such a combination have over other planning techniques?

Answer: Many offshore trust companies, banks, lawyers, and other practitioners advocate the use of an offshore company in combination with a foreign trust. In fact, most all the offshore tax haven government Act not mention the use of a trust-company combination somewhere in their legislation.

The U.S. Internal Revenue Code under IRC §679(c)(1) even outlines what limits such a company/trust combination can have if it to be an effective offshore tool. The offshore company/trust combination has been exploited by British tax practitioners for many years in the Isle of Man and the Channel Islands to avoid British tax rules.

Tim Bennett is legal counsel at Trident Trust Company (UK) Limited, based in London. Bennett writes: "A discretionary trust is usually the "engine room" of the structure, and most offshore structures will also involve one or more underlying offshore companies."

Richard Graham-Taylor, partner Ernst & Young (Grand Cayman) writing for the International Tax Report (London) counsels: "One of the most effective applications of offshore trusts is in an ownership combination with a limited company." - (January 1990).

Charles M. Bruce Esq. & S. Gray (Oppenheimer, Wolf & Donnelly, Washington, D.C.) in their article - "U.S. taxation of Foreign Trusts: Post-1976 Act Changes and Continued Uses" (pg 202) - state. Income earned by certain foreign transitory trusts will not be taxable by the U.S., and the value of purely foreign assets, as well as the value inherent in U.S. assets (such as stocks in U.S. corporations owned by a foreign holding company whose stock is held by the trust - which has no U.S. beneficiary), will not be subject to U.S. estate tax, should the settlor die while a U.S. person.

According to Howard Zaritsky, Esq. (Zaritsky & Zaritsky, Fairfax, Virginia)..."When the trust's grantor trust status makes the beneficiary's income tax free, retaining that status for as long as possible becomes important. To solve the problem of the grantor predeceasing the beneficiaries, thus inconsiderately ending the trust's favorable tax status, use of a corporate grantor is recommended.

It is clear that a corporation may be the grantor and owner of a trust. Thus, a foreign grantor (or grantor with highly tax sheltered income) could create a corporation which in turn would create a grantor trust. The death of the creating shareholder would terminate neither the corporation's separate existence nor the trust's grantor trust status."

According to Lindsay D. Barrett and Adrian Sinclair of Coopers & Lybrand (Vanuatu)... "Trusts in Vanuatu can be established quickly and are normally completed on the day the settlement is received. Special purpose irrevocable and revocable (grantor) trusts may be set up in Vanuatu.

Normally, the minimum annual trustee fee charged in Vanuatu is between US$400 and US$500, but if the trust holds as its sole asset the shares of a limited liability company administered by the trustee, than that fee is reduced to an even lower level. (from Close-up Vanuatu (November 1992).

Small Business Job Protection Act of 1996 (the Act) • Public Law 104–188

Background • Section 1904 of the Small Business Job Protection Act of 1996 (the Act), Public Law 104–188, 110 Stat. 1755 (August 20, 1996), amended section 672(f) and certain other sections of the Internal Revenue Code (Code). The amendments affect the application of sections 671 through 679 of the Code (the grantor trust rules) to certain trusts created by foreign persons.

Important note from editor: The regulations presented below are the "proposed regulations". The "final regulations" for 672(f) have not yet been issued by the Treasury, and until they are issued taxpayers can only wait and standby. "Proposed regulations" are often changed along the way. Sometimes parts are deleted, and sometimes the proposed changes never make it to become "final regulations" at all. For example, strange as it may sound, the Treasury Department has had its tax lawyers writing final regulations for Section §679 (see page 258), since *the Tax Reform Act of 1976* was enacted, but no final regulations of any kind have ever been published, and Code §679 remains basically unchanged over the last 24 years. Even if/when the proposed regulations become final regulations, it will still be possible to exploit Rev-Rul 69-70 (see page 262) so long as the foreign trust settlor has the power to "REVOKE".

Background & Prior Law

Under the prior rules, if a foreign person created a trust with one or more U.S. beneficiaries that was treated as a grantor trust with the foreign person as the grantor, a distribution of income from the trust to a U.S. beneficiary was treated as a gift and was not subject to U.S. income tax in the hands of the beneficiary. See Rev. Rul. 69–70 (1969– 1 C.B. 182). If the income of the trust was not taxable to the foreign grantor under section 871 and also not taxable to either the grantor or the trust by either the grantor's country of residence or another foreign country, the income of the trust was, thus, not subject to tax by any jurisdiction.

A special rule contained in section 665(c) provided generally that intermediaries or nominees interposed between certain foreign trusts and their U.S. beneficiaries could be disregarded. However, that rule applied only to trusts created by U.S. persons.

Overview of Changes

The Act's changes are of particular significance to-

• Trusts classified as domestic trusts under prior law with foreign trustees or subject to foreign court supervision which now risk reclassification as foreign trusts and attendant imposition of a 35 percent excise tax on the unrealized gain inherent in the trust's assets,

• Trusts designed to avoid U.S. taxation of U.S. beneficiaries through the use of foreign grantors and the prior grantor trust rules,

• U.S. taxpaying beneficiaries who face a substantially increased tax burden on foreign trust distributions,

• U.S. beneficiaries of foreign trust having outstanding loans to such beneficiaries or to related persons,

• U.S. transferors to foreign trusts structured to avoid the U.S. grantor trust rules through the sale of property to the trust for installment obligations,

• Nonresident grantors and beneficiaries engaged in trust tax planning prior to immigration to the United States and

• U.S. recipients of gifts from foreign sources.

In addition, foreign trusts with U.S. grantors or beneficiaries, as well as those grantors and beneficiaries, are now subject to more burdensome U.S. information reporting requirements and increased penalties for noncompliance.

Foreign trusts with foreign grantors

Prior to the Small Business Job Protection Act of 1996, U.S. beneficiaries of foreign trusts were not subject to U.S. federal income tax on trust distributions where a foreign person was treated under the so-called "grantor trust" rules as the owner of the trust property, irrespective of whether income tax was imposed by any jurisdiction on the income of the trust. As an exception to this general rule, a U.S. beneficiary of a foreign grantor trust who made a gift to the foreign grantor was treated as the owner of trust property to the extent of the gift. Another special rule provided that intermediaries or nominees interposed between foreign trusts created by U.S. persons and their U.S. beneficiaries could be disregarded.

Legislative changes come with built in loopholes (i.e., the exceptions)

If it were not for a few exceptions in the new legislation, which I have bolded below to make it easier to review, foreign grantor trusts distributing income to US beneficiaries tax free via Revenue Ruling 69-70 would not be possible.

The Act amends the grantor trust rules so that they apply only to the extent their application results in an amount being currently taken in account (directly or through one or more intermediate entities) in computing the income of a citizen or resident of the United States or a domestic corporation. **This new rule does not apply to, and a foreign grantor continues to be treated as the owner of, any portion of trust property if either (i) the power to revest in the grantor title to the property comprising such portion of the trust is exercisable solely by the grantor without the approval or consent of any other person or with the consent of a related or subordinate party who is subservient to the grantor or (ii) the only amounts distributable from such portion of the trust during the grantor's lifetime are distributable to the grantor or the grantor's spouse.**

EDITOR'S NOTE: The key word is "REVEST" – which has the same meaning as "revoke". If the foreign grantor cannot revoke the trust assets, Revenue Ruling 69-70 would be made obsolete. The general powers of appointment that make some one the taxable grantor of a trust are found in sections 671 through 679. Only, section 674 contains the "power" to revoke, and foreign grantors after 1997 must have this power to revoke or the beneficiaries will be held taxable on the trust's distributions.

In addition, except as provided in implementing U.S. Treasury Department regulations, the new rule does not apply (i) to so-called "compensatory trusts" where distributions are taxable as compensation for services rendered, (ii) where the foreign grantor is a "controlled foreign corporation" (a "CFC") and (iii) for purposes of determining whether a foreign corporation is a "passive foreign investment company" (a "PFIC").

The proposed regulations include similar rules for trusts created by passive foreign investment companies (PFICs) or foreign personal holding companies. Section 672(f)(3) also provides that the general rule of section 672(f)(1) shall not apply for purposes of section 1296. The proposed regulations implement this rule by providing that, for purposes of determining whether a foreign corporation is a PFIC, the grantor trust rules shall be applied as if section 672(f) not come into effect. Consequently, a foreign corporation cannot avoid PFIC status by transferring passive assets to a trust that would be treated as a nongrantor trust if section 672(f) were applied.

The Act retains but modifies prior law relating to gifts by a U.S. beneficiary of a foreign grantor trust to the foreign grantor. If the foreign grantor would be treated as the owner of trust property but for application of the new rule then the U.S. beneficiary in turn is treated as the owner of trust property to the extent of any transfer of property by the U.S. beneficiary to the foreign grantor, **except transfers for full and adequate consideration and gifts qualifying for the annual gift tax exclusion of Internal Revenue Code section 2503(b).** The Act also grants the IRS authority to recharacterize certain purported gifts from a partnership or foreign corporation. Act § 1904(a) amending IRC § 672(f).

The Act also provides that, under regulations to be adopted by the U.S. Treasury Department, where a foreign person that would be treated as the owner of a trust but for the new rules actually pays tax on the income of the trust to a foreign country, U.S. beneficiaries that are subject to U.S. federal income tax on the same income will be treated, for foreign tax credit purposes, as having paid the foreign taxes. Act § 1904(b) amending IRC §§ 665(d)(2), 901(b)(5).

The Act also expands the rule treating certain payments to U.S. beneficiaries derived from foreign trusts but made through intermediaries as made by the trusts directly so that it applies to any foreign trust of which the payor is not the grantor and not just to trusts created by U.S. persons. Act § 1904(c) adding IRC § 643(h) and repealing IRC § 665(c).

The new rules took effect on August 20, 1996, the date of enactment of the Act, but do not apply to any trust the property of which is treated as owned by the grantor under Internal Revenue Code section 676 (power to revoke) or 677(a)(1) or (a)(2) (income for the benefit of the grantor) and which was in existence on September 19, 1995. This exception does not apply to the portion of any such trust attributable to any transfer after September 19, 1995. Act § 1904(d). Under a special transition rule the 35 percent excise tax of Internal Revenue Code section 1491 is not to be imposed if as a result of the new rules any person other than a U.S. person ceases to be treated as the owner of a portion of a domestic trust and before January 1, 1997 such trust becomes a foreign trust or the assets of such trust are transferred to a foreign trust. Act § 1904(e).

Foreign Corporate Grantors

The proposed regulations also exercise the regulatory authority conferred by the Act with respect to exclusion from the new foreign grantor trust rules for trusts created by certain foreign corporations. For purposes of the new rules, a controlled foreign corporation is treated as a domestic corporation to the extent that income earned by the trust for the taxable year would be currently taken into account under the subpart F rules in computing the gross income of a citizen or resident of the United States or a domestic corporation if the basic grantor trust rules were applied.

Similarly a passive foreign investment company is also treated as a domestic corporation to the extent that application of the basic grantor trust rules results in income earned by the trust for the taxable year being currently being taken into account under the passive foreign investment company rules in computing the gross income of a citizen or resident of the United States or a domestic corporation.

In addition, for purposes of determining whether a foreign corporation is a passive foreign investment company the new rules of Internal Revenue Code section 672(f) are disregarded. Finally, a foreign personal holding company is treated as a domestic corporation to the extent that the basic grantor trust rules result in income earned by the trust for the taxable year being currently being taken into account under the foreign personal holding company rules in computing the gross income of a citizen or resident of the United States or a domestic corporation. Prop.Income Tax Regs. § 1.672(f)-2.

> **Editor's note: This new rule for foreign corporate grantors (above) does not apply to, and a foreign grantor continues to be treated as the owner of, any portion of trust property if either (i) the power to revest in the grantor title to the property comprising such portion of the trust is exercisable solely by the grantor without the approval or consent of any other person or with the consent of a related or subordinate party who is subservient to the grantor**

Purported Gifts

In exercising the regulatory authority granted by the Act with regard to purported gifts, the *proposed regulations* define a purported gift to mean any transfer by a partnership or foreign corporation (other than a transfer for fair market value) to a person who is not a partner in the partnership or shareholder of the foreign corporation. If any U.S. person directly or indirectly receives a purported gift from a partnership, the purported gift is included in the U.S. person's gross income as ordinary income. If a U.S. person directly or indirectly receives a purported gift from a foreign corporation, the purported gift is included in the U.S. person's gross income as if it were a distribution from the foreign corporation. For this purpose, the U.S. person is treated as having no basis in stock of the foreign corporation and as having a holding period for such stock on the date of the deemed distribution equal to the weighted average of the holding periods of the actual interest holders.

> **These new rules do not apply if the U.S. person receiving the purported gift can establish that a U.S. citizen or resident alien who directly or indirectly holds an interest in the partnership or foreign corporation treated the purported gift as a distribution to the U.S. partner or shareholder and a subsequent gift to the U.S. person.**
>
> **The new rules also do not apply to transfers to charitable organizations described in Internal Revenue Code section 170(c) nor during the taxable year of a U.S. person if the aggregate amount of purported gifts to such U.S. person does not exceed $10,000. These rules are applicable for any transfer by a partnership or foreign corporation on or after August 20, 1996. Prop.Income Tax Regs. § 1.672(f)-4.**

Existing Trusts

The *proposed regulations* implement the grandfather rule of the Act for trusts in existence on September 19, 1995 but require separate accounting with respect to transfers made to such trusts after September 19, 1995. Prop.Income Tax Regs. §§ 1.672(f)-3(a)(2) and (b)(4).

The changes made by section 1904 of the Act are designed to ensure that U.S. persons who benefit from offshore trusts created by foreign persons (inbound trusts) pay an appropriate amount of U.S. tax. Generally, the grantor trust rules now cause a person to be treated as the owner of a trust only to the extent such application results, directly or indirectly, in an amount being currently taken into account in computing the income of a U.S. citizen or resident or a domestic corporation. **Exceptions are provided for certain revocable trusts and for trusts from which the only amounts distributable during the lifetime of the grantor are to the grantor or the grantor's spouse, and for certain compensatory trusts. There also are grandfather rules for certain trusts that were in existence on September 19, 1995.**

As a result of the changes, many inbound trusts that were grantor trusts under prior law are now nongrantor trusts. Distributions of trust income to the U.S. beneficiaries of such trusts are now taxable to U.S. beneficiaries and may be subject to an interest charge on accumulation distributions. Section 1904 of the Act also includes some special rules. Section 643(h), which replaces former section 665(c), treats any amount paid to a U.S. person that is derived directly or indirectly from a foreign trust of which the payor is not the grantor as if the amount is paid by the foreign trust directly to the U.S. person. Section 672(f)(4) allows the IRS to recharacterize a purported gift or bequest from a partnership or foreign corporation when necessary to prevent the avoidance of the purpose of section 672(f). Section 672(f)(5), which is an expansion of prior section 672(f), generally provides that if a U.S. beneficiary of a trust created by a foreign person transfers property to the foreign person, the U.S. beneficiary is treated as the grantor of the trust to the extent of the transfer.

The regulations provide a de minimis rule for distributions that do not exceed in the aggregate $10,000.

Author's note: Some of the less important proposed regulations relating to foreign trusts sited by the Small Business Jobs Protection Act of 1996 have been left out here because of their importance and space requirements.

Section 1.671–2(e): Definition of Grantor

The proposed regulations provide a definition of grantor that applies for purposes of the grantor trust rules generally. A grantor is any individual, corporation, or other person to the extent such person (i) creates a trust or (ii) directly or indirectly makes a gratuitous transfer to a trust. For purposes of the proposed regulations, a gratuitous transfer is any transfer other than a transfer for fair market value, or a corporate or partnership distribution.

IRS won't accept accommodation grantors

If a person creates or funds any portion of a trust primarily as an accommodation for another person, the other person will be treated as a grantor with respect to such portion of the trust.
See, e.g., Stern v. Commissioner, 77 T.C. 614 (1981), rev'd on other grounds, 747 F.2d 555 (9th Cir. 1984).

Foreign grantor cannot be a CFC

A grantor of a trust may or may not be treated as an owner of the trust under sections 671 through 677 and 679. A person other than a grantor of a trust may be treated as an owner of the trust under section 678.

4. Section 1.672(f)–2: Trusts Created by Certain Foreign Corporations Section 672(f)(3) provides in part that, except as otherwise provided in regulations, a controlled foreign corporation (CFC) shall be treated as a domestic corporation for purposes of section 672(f)(1). Under the **proposed regulations**, a CFC

that creates and funds a trust will be treated as a domestic corporation to the extent that, if the basic grantor trust rules were applied, income earned by the trust for taxable year would be subpart F income to the CFC that would be currently taken into account in computing the gross income of a U.S. citizen or resident or a domestic corporation. However, the CFC will not be treated as a domestic corporation to the extent the income of the trust would not be subpart F income or to the extent it would be subpart F income but would not be taken into account in computing gross income of a U.S. citizen or resident or a domestic corporation (e.g., the CFC had no overall earnings and profits). The proposed regulations include similar rules for trusts created by passive foreign investment companies (PFICs) or foreign personal holding companies. Section 672(f)(3) also provides that the general rule of section 672(f)(1) shall not apply for purposes of section 1296.

The proposed regulations implement this rule by providing that, for purposes of determining whether a foreign corporation is a PFIC, the grantor trust rules shall be applied as if section 672(f) had not come into effect. Consequently, a foreign corporation cannot avoid PFIC status by transferring passive assets to a trust that would be treated as a nongrantor trust if section 672(f) were applied

---

Editor's Note: If the above proposed regulation is included in the final regulations, avoiding the PFIC status as outlined in Chapter 3 (pg. 64) will most likely not be possible.

Proposed Regulations

The June 5, 1997 edition of the Federal Register also contains another IRS Notice of Proposed Rulemaking with respect to regulations implementing the foreign grantor trust provisions of the Act. A hearing on these proposed regulations is scheduled for August 27, 1997.

Some confusing legislative history and definitions

Under Section 679, when the statute speaks of transfers made by a "U.S. person", the term "United States person" is not specifically defined in IRC §679. H. Report No 658 makes it clear that the definition of that term found in §7701(a)(30) is intended to apply without further expansion and without the use of any other attribution rules. A **"U.S. person"** is defined as:

1) a citizen or resident of the United States,
2) a domestic partnership or corporation,

3) any estate or trust [other than a foreign estate or trust within the meaning of §7701(a)(31)]. [21.]

It would seem safe to presume that a transfer by a foreign trust, estate or a foreign corporation would not be a transfer by a U.S. person, but this is not necessarily the case.

The legislative history for section 679 explains what may be construed as an *indirect transfer to a foreign trust,* stating:

"A transfer by a domestic or foreign entity in which a U.S. person has an interest may be regarded as an indirect transfer to the foreign trust by the U.S. person if the entity merely serves as a conduit for the transfer by the U.S. person or if the U.S. person has sufficient control over the entity to direct the transfer by the entity rather than himself." [Senate Rep. No 948, at 219]

Seemingly, a transfer by a foreign corporation in which the U.S. person is a controlling shareholder would be an **indirect** transfer to a foreign trust if that trust has a U.S. beneficiary. The committee reports go on to illustrate one situation in which an indirect transfer is deemed to be made by a U.S. person:

*"For example, if a U.S. person transfers property to a foreign person or entity and if that person transfers that property (or its equivalent) to a foreign trust that has U.S. beneficiaries, the U.S. person transferring the property to the foreign person or entity is treated as having made a transfer of property to the foreign trust **unless** it can be **shown** that the transfer of property to the trust was unrelated to the U.S. person's transfer of property to the foreign person or entity."*

"Transfer of property to a foreign entity (other than a trust)." What on earth do they mean?

Forthcoming Treasury regulations might explain another ambiguous committee report statement that has kept tax planners puzzled for years. Here's what one old Committee Report says. Can you figure it out!

*"Whenever a U.S. person transfers property to a foreign entity (**other than a trust**), and that entity thereafter transfers similar property to a foreign trust, the U.S. person is presumed to*

have made an indirect transfer, unless it can be shown that the transfer of property to the trust was unrelated to the U.S. person's transfer of property."

What the Congressional tax committees mean by a transfer to a foreign entity (other than a trust) is a total mystery to even the most astute legal mind. Apparently there is an exception from the transfer rules for an entity that is a foreign trust, but other committee reports contradict this conclusion. Treasury regulations would certainly be helpful in clearing this up.

Transfers at death are an exception to the rule. Let's hope no new changes are forthcoming.

At first blush, IRC §679(a) appears to severely restrict U.S. taxpayers from using foreign trusts that possess U.S. beneficiaries. Yet, some international tax lawyers believe IRC §679 might have created as many loopholes as it tried to close. Through June, 1999, no new changes to IRC §679(a)(2) for transfers at death have been enacted.

IRC §679(a)(2) **EXCEPTIONS** - *excepts any transfer by reason of death of the transferor* from the provisions of IRC§679(a). Thus, a U.S. transferor (hereafter called Mr. T) who transfers $10,000,000 at death by will would not be subject to IRC §679(a) rules.

To understand how this exception can be put to good use, let's provide a little example.

Example #1: Assume the following conditions. Bahamian trust W is set-up before the death of Mr. T to receive $10,000,000 from his U.S. estate. The trust's grantor is Bahamian corporation X, and under the trust indenture the Bahamian corporation has the power to revoke all the assets and income earned by the trust. The foreign trustee for trust W invests the $10,000,000 in British gilts paying 10% interest pa.

The shareholders in Bahamian company X are Mr. T's sons A, B and C, and trust W. No voting stock is owned by the U.S. shareholders and company X is not a controlled foreign corporation under IRC §957. The only assets transferred to the foreign revocable trust W is the $10,000,000 left by Mr. T's estate (in his will). All the beneficiaries of foreign trust W are U.S. citizens (Mr. T's sons and grandchildren).

Based on these facts, foreign trust W is a foreign trust with a foreign corporate grantor that has the power to revoke the assets. Because the trust's grantor has the power to revoke the assets of the, the trust is taxable under IRC §676 - Power to Revoke. IRC §679 is not

21. From *Foreign Grantor Trusts* by <u>Tax Management Inc.</u> (a subsidiary of the Bureau of National Affairs, Inc.), pg A-10.

applicable because IRC §679(a)(2) excepts transfers at death.

E-mail message from the IRS dated 7-27-99 appears below.

From: null@irs.gov
Subject: IRS Email Tax Law Assistance

NOTE: Our response to your tax law question appears below. If you have additional questions on this or any other general tax law topic, you must post it to our web site at:

(http://www.irs.ustreas.gov/prod/help/newmail/user.html

    We are not able to receive E-mail messages directly from our customers because of current limitations to our system.

    After researching your question, we find that there has been no final regulation issued on 1.672(f)-1, only a proposed regulation. A proposed regulation is what the IRS will go by until a final regulation is issued. Sometimes final regulations are not issued for years. I do not have any insight as to when the permanent regulation will be issued.

Thank you for your question,
 J. McAlister, 75-14069
Customer Service Representative-24

For more information write:

Internal Revenue Service
International Tax Compliance (Foreign Trusts)
Philadelphia, Pennsylvania 19225

Associate Chief Counsel IRS
Technical & International CC: IND:D:C
P.O. Box 7604
Ben Franklin Station,
Washington, D.C. 20044

> • *"One of the most effective applications of offshore trusts is in an ownership combination with a limited company."* - Richard Graham-Taylor, partner Ernst & Young, **Grand Cayman (January 1990)** •

> • *"The absence of income or significant corporate income taxes, along with political stability, is the bedrock on which foreign investment in The Bahamas has been built."* - Embassy of the United States (Nassau, Bahamas)(April, 1990)

Other essays worth reviewing:

U.S. Taxation of Foreign Trusts: Post 1976 Act Changes and Continued Uses, by Charles M. Bruce, Esq., Stephen Gray, Esq. (publisher Tax Management International)

Foreign Trusts: Still an Effective Tool for Tax Planning and Foreign Transactions, by LeMaster (pub Tax Management, Estate, Gift & Trust Journal (August/July 1982)

Offshore Protection-of-Assets Trusts, by Bruce & Gray (P-H *U.S. Taxation of International Operations* para. 13,510.1).

Foreign Trusts, Estates & Beneficiaries, by Zaristky (publisher, Tax Management, Inc.)

Some reasons for Use of Irrevocable Common law Trusts in Common Law & Civil Law Countries, by Kanter, in Foreign Trusts in International Planning [publisher, Practicing Law Institute (Manhattan)]

Tax aspects of Protective Devices Against Expropriation, by Klein, publisher - **TAX LAW** (1977)

"Selecting and Changing the Situs of a Foreign Trust", by H. Zaritsky, Esq. (Fairfax, Virginia), Tax Management International (1988), pg 431-443.

"The Use of Foreign Grantor Trusts in Income and Estate Planning" Chopin (U. of Miami Est. Plan.) Institute, ch. 10 (1987), and Zaritsky, *"The Hollow Crown - What's left of Grantor Trusts",* 21, U. of Miami Est. Plan, Inst. ch. 15 (1987).

Federal Income Tax Regulations (4 volumes set @ $30), and **Internal Revenue Code of 1986** (2 book set costs about $19.95). [22]

Commerce Clearing House or Prentice-Hall,
4025 W. Peterson Ave.   Englewood Cliffs, NJ
Chicago, Illinois 60646   07632

"A Complete Guide to the Omnibus Budget Reconciliation Act of 1990"
Commerce Clearing House
4025 W. Peterson Ave.
Chicago, Illinois 60646

Foreign Trusts, Estates and Beneficiaries (Portfolio 427-2nd)
Tax Management, Inc.
1231 25th Street, N.W.
Washington, D.C. 20037

"Foreign Trusts: Still an Effective Tool for Tax Planning and Foreign Transactions" by LeMaster (Est. Gifts & Trusts Journal. 4 (1982).

---

[22] **Commerce Clearing House**, and **Prentice-Hall** both publish the Code of 1986 and Treasury Regulations in an inexpensive soft-bound version. You can order them by writing the company direct, or buy them at a bookstore that stocks them for students, tax lawyers, and federal tax judges.

CHAPTER 12 • Estate Tax Planning – *the art of giving*

The real world of offshore Wills

In practice, offshore estate planning often relies on the host country's bank secrecy laws to circumvent the U.S. estate laws. Recently, this has caused problems for many offshore banks and their U.S. clients, and today many of the larger Bahamian banks will no longer form a trust for a U.S. client. Under U.S. laws, the penalty for merely not reporting the transfer of money or property to an offshore trust can amount to 35% of the value of the transferred asset. This is a fine, not a tax.

But since the IRS cannot freeze, seize or investigate banks, trust companies, and other non-U.S. fiduciaries here in the Bahamas (and the other tax havens, as well), a secret offshore **will** to hold only the client's offshore assets is a planning technique that should be over looked, even though it's in violation of U.S. tax laws. In the past, such planning (hiding) has been successful in shielding offshore assets from the IRS. Most often these separate offshore **wills** are just for offshore assets (home, stock, offshore bank accounts, etc.), to keep them free of U.S. estate taxes. This has been successful, but it's important that your U.S. probate lawyer know nothing at all of this offshore will, as he will call it into your estate when you die – causing bigger tax problems and bigger probate fees.

Federal estate taxes when you die

The **Federal Estate Tax** was incorporated into U.S. tax law with the **Revenue Act of 1916.** The introduction of the estate tax was not so much to generate large revenues for the government, as it was to prevent large concentrations of wealth being kept within the family for many generations. The Federal Gift Tax was enacted in 1936 to complement the estate tax. Without any tax applicable to lifetime transfers by gift, it would be possible to completely avoid the estate tax by simply gifting (giving) away assets to younger family members.

In 1942, with the introduction of the Economic Recovery Act, Congress decided to provide an annual exclusion of $3,000 per year per donee on transfers by gift. The original intent was to fix the amount of the annual exclusion sufficiently large to cover weddings, birthdays and Christmas gifts, which Congress felt should not be taxed unless the gift was greater than $3,000. Over the years, inflation substantially reduced the real value of the exclusion, and in 1981, with ERTA, the gift tax exclusion was increased to $10,000 per year per donee.

Married couples can split their annual donee exclusion and transfer a total of $20,000 per year to each son, daughter, grandchild, relative, or person completely free from gift tax liability.

In this chapter we will explore the methods most favored by shrewd U.S. tax lawyers and accountants to reduce and eliminate estate taxes from their client's estates. We will show how it's possible to integrate tax havens into your estate tax plan, to further free family assets from future income, estate and gift taxes, legally as provided under the Code. Tax havens like the Bahamas, the Cayman Islands, Bermuda, the British Virgin Islands, Gibraltar, the Channel Islands, the Isle of Man, Anguilla, the Turks & Caicos Islands, Vanuatu, and the Cook Islands (to name a few) allow foreigners to transfer their assets into local trusts and holding companies free from all future or present income, estate, gift or inheritance taxes.[1]

Estate and gift tax aspects of the 1997 Budget Act

Modest size U.S. estates of under $650,000 don't have to worry much about federal estate taxes because the **Unified Estate Tax Credit** allowed the first $650,000 of the estate to be passed onto heirs 100% tax free through 1997. For years beginning in 1998, the Unified Estate Tax Credit is increased by $25,000 per year, accelerating all the way to $1,000,000 by the year 2,006 and beyond.

1997:	**$600,000**
1998:	**$625,000**
1999:	**$650,000**
2000-01:	**$675,000**
2002-03:	**$700,000**

[1] Before October 16, 1962 real property situated outside the United States (i.e., homes, cars, real estate) was excluded from the gross estate of the U.S. taxpayer. The Revenue Act of 1962 ended this exclusion.

2004:	$850,000
2005:	$950,000
2006 +	$1,000,000

In addition, spouses may bequest any part of their estate (no matter how large) to the surviving spouse, and claim the marital deduction under IRC §2056. Thus, a husband could bequest that his share of their $10,000,000 estate go solely to his wife, and no federal estate taxes would be incurred.

While the unlimited marital deduction looks attractive, the transferring of one's entire estate to one's spouse only solves the estate tax problem until the death of the surviving spouse. Since each spouse is allowed to exclude the first $650,000 (1999) of his/her share of the gross estate under IRC §2010 (Unified Credit Against Estate Tax), it is usually recommended that each spouse use their allotted credit, and pass some estate assets onto other family members (sons, daughters, grandchildren).

> It's also important to recognize that although the increase in the "unified credit" will substantially reduce the number of estates subject to federal estate taxes, the bulk of federal estate taxes are collected on the largest 1% of estates, and in the largest estates (above $21 to $25 million), the entire "unified credit" and all of the under-55% estate tax brackets are rescinded, so that the estate tax is unchanged for large estates, even under the new law.

$10,000 Annual Donee Exclusion

The $10,000 annual donee exclusion ($20,000 for married couples) allows wealthy families to transfer their estates to their heirs while they are still alive. If the gift giving is begun early enough in the lives of the family patriarchs, substantial savings in estate taxes can be secured. Let's look at an example:

Example #1: Mary and Philip Blackacre are 65 years old, with a gross estate of $3,200,000. They own all 300 shares of a family corporation that owns 2 hotels in Los Angeles valued at $3,000,000. Mary and Phil have two sons (Conrad and Bob) and a daughter Barbara. Conrad has 2 sons, Bob has 2 daughters, and Barbara has just gotten married.

Beginning in 1990 Mary and Philip Blackacre make gifts to their heirs as follows:

Conrad	$20,000
Conrad's wife	$20,000
Conrad's Son #1	$20,000
Conrad's Son #2	$20,000
Bob	$20,000
Bob's wife	$20,000
Bob's daughter #1	$20,000
Bob's daughter #2	$20,000
Barbara	$20,000
Barbara's husband	$20,000

Total gifts for 1990 = $200,000

Mary and Philip Blackacre continue their gift giving in 1991, 1992, 1993, 1994, 1995, 1996, 1997, 1998 and 1999. At the end of 1999 they have given $2,000,000 of their assets to close family members. They are 75 years old, and there is only $1,200,000 left to their gross U.S. estate.

Suppose Mary Blackacre dies in the year 2,000. Instead of leaving her share ($675,000) of the Blackacre estate to her husband, Mary's **Will** leaves $600,000 (60 shares of the family corporation - valued at $10,000/share) to her eldest son Conrad (25 shares); Bob (20 shares) and Barbara (15 shares). There will be no federal estate taxes payable on Mary's estate because the $675,000 Unified Estate Tax Credit under IRC§ 2010 allows Mary to transfer $675,000 tax free. When Philip Blackacre dies, the remaining $600,000 in assets left in the estate can be passed onto heirs and others free from federal estate taxes. He can use up to $675,000 of his unified estate tax credit, just as his wife had.

Under U.S. gift tax law, the **donor** of the gift is responsible for the payment of any gift tax, but only when the gift is in excess of the $10,000 per year per donee exclusion. The recipients of the gifts (Conrad, Bob, Barbara, etc.) owe no federal income taxes on the receipt of their gifts.

Cost-of-Living Increases for Annual Gift Tax Exclusion Amount (and GSTs)

The first $10,000 of gifts are excluded from gift taxes under current law; but starting in 1999, that amount will be increased based on the cost of living. However, the increases will only be made in $1,000 increments, so that no increase is likely until the year 2001.

Transfers at death to an offshore trust

The *Tax Reform Act of 1976* (i.e., IRC §679) curbed the use of offshore trusts by U.S. person, but did not out-law their exploitation by any means. IRC §679(a) says if a U.S. person makes a direct or indirect transfer to a foreign trust that has U.S. beneficiaries, then the U.S. person will stay taxable on the trust's income regardless whether he (the grantor) surrenders all future rights to the income of the trust.

There are two exceptions to IRC §679(a). Most important for our purposes here is the **Exception** found under IRC §679(a)(2)(A). IRC §679(a)(2)(A) excepts *"Any transfer by reason of death of the transferor."*

Example #2: Mary Blackacre (in example #1 above) upon her death in 2,000 transfers $675,000 cash into foreign trust Y. This transfer is permitted under IRC §679(a)(2)(A) even if the offshore trust has a U.S. beneficiary. With a little careful planning, the $675,000 can be reinvested in offshore bank and security accounts by the foreign trustee free from all future U.S. income, estate, and inheritance taxes, and even pass the income onto the U.S. beneficiaries (her children) via Revenue Ruling 69-70 (see page #262) TAX FREE, so long as the trust is revocable by a foreign grantor.

If a foreign corporation is chosen as the grantor for the trust, Mary's children cannot own more than 50% of the stock in the foreign company.

IRC §679(c) provides special rules for determining whether a foreign trust has U.S. beneficiaries. Under these rules, if U.S. persons own more than 50% of the voting stock in a foreign corporation which is the beneficiary of the foreign trust, than IRC §679(a) is to apply, and the 51% shareholder will be considered a U.S. beneficiaries of the trust. In addition, if the foreign trust has as a beneficiary another foreign trust that has U.S. beneficiaries, than the first trust is considered to have U.S. beneficiaries too. [2]

There are several ways to avoid the *more than 50%* voting stock requirement of IRC §679(c). Allowing a reputable offshore management trustee company or offshore banker to own 50% or more of the voting stock is one legitimate way to satisfy this requirement. A better way, but perhaps a bit riskier, is to allow a foreign trust to own all the voting stock of the foreign company should avoid any adverse tax consequences too. U.S. persons (also, non-voting shareholders in Bahamian company X) should never be designated trustees of a foreign trust.

Type of assets ceded offshore by U.S. Will

Now that we are assured by the Internal Revenue Code that transfers at death to a foreign trust are unequivocally permitted, the next question is what type of assets can be transferred.

It is our opinion, that real property assets should be liquidated by the decease' estate before the transfer, and cash wired into the offshore trust account.

Corporate and U.S. Treasury bills, notes and bonds, where the date of issue is after July 18, 1984, can be transferred to the trust. Interest income on these investments are not subject to U.S. withholding or income taxes.

Partnership interests and income producing U.S. property (real estate, immovable, depreciable assets such as buildings), should not be transferred into a foreign trust. Income paid to a nonresident trust will be taxed annually on a grossed-up basis at the U.S. 30% withholding tax rate, with no allowance for business deductions (i.e., interest expense, depreciation, and maintenance expenses).

Non-income producing real estate, such as raw land, timberland, oil leases, can be transferred to the foreign trust. These assets should be placed in a domestic corporation before the transfer by the estate, and a foreign company should be set-up to accept and hold the shares. If the non-income producing property is held directly by the foreign trust, a sale would be subject to U.S. capital gains taxes under IRC §897(a). However, sale of shares in the foreign company that holds shares in the U.S. company can be sold in the tax haven to another foreign investor free from all U.S. capital gains taxes. [3]

While title to the deceased home could be transferred to a foreign trust, it is probably not good policy to transfer the deceased U.S. home, as the tax law is always being amended, and risk

---

[2] IRC §679(c) adopts the same attribution of ownership rules found under the Controlled Foreign Corporation provisions of IRC §958(a) & 958(b). However, these rules are far more liberal as no reference is made to IRC §957(a), which can make a foreign corporation a CFC, if say, the foreign owner of the voting stock does not vote the stock independently, or votes in favor of a U.S. shareholder all the time. See also Rev. Rul. 80-74 where foreign double trusts were rules a sham by the IRS.

[3] See T. Reg.§ 897-2(e)(1).

of an IRS enquiry or lien are always possible. While a foreign trustee in the Turks & Caicos Islands, the Caymans or the Bahamas would never surrender assets to the IRS or other unfit creditors (unless ordered by a local tax haven court - a rare occurrence) the offshore trustee should not be put into a position where he has to deal with the IRS or the U.S. courts in an estate tax controversy. Liquid, intangible assets that can be kept offshore, out of the reach of the IRS, are the ideal holdings for the foreign trustee.

Best assets for domestic giving

Mary and Philip Blackacre can transfer any property, as long as there are *no strings* attached. Transfers to minors who have not attained the age of 21 can be made to pass onto them when they attain 21 years of age (called a future interest). If the minor dies before 21 years of age, the gift will be included in the youngster's estate, not the donor's.

Publicly traded stocks and securities make for excellent gifts. Mary & Phil could transfer $20,000 worth of Wal-Mart stock in 1990 to each child and grandchild. If the Wal-Mart stock triples in price by 2,002, so much the better. The donees will pay a capital gains tax only when they sell for a gain.

Closely held stock in the family corporation can be given away. In Example #1, each share of Blackacre's company had a value of $10,000, so 2 shares of stock could be gifted each year to each son, daughter, and grandchild tax free.

Note: Recipients of gifts under the annual donee exclusion are not liable to federal income taxes. Furthermore, under IRC §6019, no gift tax return has to be filed with the IRS by the donor. Annual gifts of $10,000 per person do not reduce the donor's Unified Estate Tax Credit. The deceased estate can still claim the full amount (i.e., the first $600,000 in assets go tax free).

If Mary and Philip Blackacre do not take advantage of the annual $20,000 donee exclusions during their lifetimes, the estate tax liability for the surviving spouse on their $3,200,000 estate would equal $1,025,000 on the first $2,500,000 in taxable estate + 50% of the excess over $2,500,000. With only $600,000 of their U.S. estate protected by the unified estate tax credit, the Blackacre estate could pay about $1,125,000 in estate taxes (gross estate $3,200,000 - $600,000 = taxable estate $2,600,000).

State Gift, Inheritance & Estate Taxes

The Federal government levies an estate tax on all your assets worldwide when you die. The Federal government does not levy an inheritance tax. Inheritance taxes are a tax levied on the recipient of your estate (i.e., your children or wife), after your federal estate taxes have been paid.

Through 1983, all states except Nevada levied some sort of death tax. California has since abandoned its estate tax. About 60% of the states levy an inheritance tax. About 40% of the states impose a death tax on the estate, instead of the heir. In addition, about a dozen states impose a gift tax. [4]

The newest trend in state estate taxes is referred to as a "sponge tax". Under this version, the estate remits to the state whatever amount qualifies for the maximum state death tax credit allowed by the Federal government under IRC §2011(b).

For example, if the Blackacre's taxable estate was $2,040,000, the federal government would allow a state estate tax credit of $146,800. Since this is the maximum amount the Federal government will allow, the states, to collect the most they can, usually require the estate to pay $146,800 in State estate taxes.

Only a few of the tax havens impose estate, gift, inheritance or income taxes on foreigners. A few apply both estate and income taxes if the foreigner takes up residence in the tax haven (*). Virtually all the tax havens levy small stamp taxes on real property transfers of local property. Havens that do not tax the estates of foreigners include:

Cayman Islands	Bahamas	Vanuatu
Bermuda	Nauru	Anguilla
British Virgin Islands *	Gibraltar *	Nevis *
Isle of Man *	Turks & Caicos Islands	
Panama *	Cook Islands *	
Western Samoa *	Channel Islands *	
Luxembourg *	Netherlands Antilles *	
Antigua *	Barbados *	
Liechtenstein *	Monaco*	

Non-Resident Aliens Investing in the United States

Foreigners or *non-resident aliens,* have long held an edge over U.S. citizens when exploiting tax havens and investing in the United States. The Controlled Foreign Corporation provisions (IRC§951 through §958), the PFIC provisions under IRC§ 1291-98), the Foreign Personal Holding Company provisions (IRC §552 through §557), and the Foreign Trusts with U.S. beneficiaries provisions (IRC §679) do not apply to them. [4.]

These international tax laws have practically no impact on non-resident aliens, thus a non-resident alien's tax planning strategy when investing in the United States is less complicated. In this respect, the U.S. Tax Code is highly discriminatory against it's own citizenry.

One very popular tax haven of the 1970's and 1980's was the **Netherlands Antilles.** It was a well-known fact that more U.S. real estate was owned by N.A. companies than any other nation in the world, except Great Britain. Several Princes of the Saudi Royal family had established holding companies here to invest inside the United States, not to mention all the Dutch, W. German, British and Swiss businessmen that the Antilles catered to. [5.]

Why you may need an offshore company?

Astute non-resident aliens almost always elect to use offshore holding companies for investing in the United States. If a non-resident alien individual invests directly, holding U.S. assets in his/her name, his investment will be subject to U.S. estate taxes at rates as high as 55% when he dies, and often subject to estate taxes in his home country. On the other hand, shares in his offshore holding company will not be subject to any U.S. estate taxes regardless as to the size or asset mix of the offshore company. Because, nearly all the tax havens exempt the transfer of offshore company shares owned by non-residents from local estate taxes, estate tax planning for the foreigner is limited to the tax laws of his home country.

[4.] It is possible that both federal and state gift, estate and income taxes could apply to the deceased estate.

[5.] Under the now repealed U.S.-N.A. Income tax treaties, mortgage interest could be received by the offshore Antilles company subject to reduced U.S. withholding tax rates of 15% or 0%, and the interest itself was tax free in the Antilles

The Federal Tax Rate for American families whose net-worths are over $3,000,000 is more than 70.9% per year.

So you think the taxes you pay to the Federal Government doesn't exceed 28% to 33% of your annual income? My fellow Americans, you should redo your thinking! The marginal Federal Tax Rate is really much higher than 28% or 33%.

For upper middle-class American families filing joint tax returns, whose combined net-worth is $3.0 million or more, and whose annual income is $200,000, the federal tax rate is really closer to **70.9%**, not 28% to 33% as the government would have you believe. Let me explain.

Example: John and Sally Goodcitizen are a married couple with combined incomes of $200,000 per year from the operation of a family business. They are both 55 years old, and their combined net worth is already $3,000,000.

A married couple filing a joint tax return showing $200,000 in taxable income will pay Federal Income Taxes (29.1%) of $58,234 in 1989, and every year after that, assuming Congress doesn't increase the Federal Income Tax Rate any further. Being self-employed individuals, Sally and John each has to pay $6,249.60 in social security-self employment taxes in 1989. That's another $12,499.20 that goes to the Treasury department, bringing their 1989 tax bill to a grand total of $70,733.20, or 35.4% of their earnings. After paying their income taxes, Sally and John Goodcitizen will have $129,266.40 left for their bank savings account.

Federal Estate Taxes

The Federal Estate tax rate on the part of the surviving spouses taxable estate that exceeds $3,000,000 is 55%. Suppose John and Sally's income stays the same ($200,000 per year) for 10 years, and suppose they bank the entire $129,266.40 every year. After 10 years they would have saved $1,292,664. These savings are subject to U.S. estate taxes, the same as all John and Sally's other assets.

If John Goodcitizen dies in January, 1999 and Sally dies in December, 1999, the $1,292,664 in bank savings in the surviving spouses' bank account will be subject to Federal Estate taxes at a rate of 55%. Thus, $710,965 in Federal Estate taxes will be paid by Sally Goodcitizen - the surviving spouse.

Adding up all the taxes paid over the ten years (income + estate), Sally & John have given the IRS $1,418,297. While they earned $2,000,000 over the 10 year period, they got to **keep** less than half of it. Effectively, 70.9% of everything Sally and John earned and saved over the previous 10 years went to pay Federal Taxes. Sally and John Goodcitizen were really in a 70.9% Federal Tax bracket, not a 28% to 33% tax bracket.

The $650,000 estate tax exclusion for 1999

A U.S. citizen's estate that is not larger than $600,000 will not have to pay federal estate taxes, because the Federal Unified Estate Tax Credit allows the first $600,000 to be passed onto family heirs 100% tax free. On a $610,000 estate, the Federal estate tax would equal $1,800. On a $710,000 estate, the tax would equal $26,800. On Sally and John's $4,292,664 estate, the federal estate taxes would equal about $1,998,765.

When the decease' estate is larger than $650,000, estate taxes can be deferred until the surviving spouse dies. SEC. §2056 allows a spouse to pass his/her half of their estate to the surviving spouse free from all estate taxes. This is called the unlimited marital deduction. Tax lawyers usually recommend (in the WILL) that each spouse pass the first $650,000 to their children and grandchildren, and the remainder to the surviving spouse. In this way, each spouse can use up their Unified Estate Tax Credit, (i.e., the first $650,000 of one's estate). The rest of the estate can then be passed onto the surviving spouse, and all federal estate taxes are deferred until the next death in the family. [8.]

Other taxes we pay

Most states impose a sales tax on merchandise and services. In Texas the sales tax

---

[8.] A married couple can reduce the size of their gross U.S. estate by giving $20,000 per year to each son, daughter, grandchild or any person. This annual donee exclusion is not subject to a gift tax or income taxes. For unmarried persons, the annual donee exclusion is reduced to $10,000. With 5 sons and daughters and 10 grandchildren, a married couple could give up to $300,000 per year - every year ($20,000 to each person), thus reducing the size of their U.S. estate by $300,000 every year.

equals 8%. The tax on gasoline is a hidden federal tax most of us hardly ever think about, but we pay it every time we go to the pump to fill up. Aside from sales and gasoline taxes, U.S. citizens pay:

1) State income taxes (as high as 12% in some states). State Inheritance or Estate taxes.
2) Real Estate taxes.
3) City & Municipal taxes (as high as 9% in NYC).
4) Probate fees.
5) Social Security or Self Employment taxes.

Who's sheltering it offshore?

Many of America's elite have been using the offshore tax havens for years.

- The daughter of Lyndon Baines Johnson married a Cayman Island Banker.

- Brown Brothers & Harriman is a well respected NY City Investment banking firm with offices in Cayman and other tax havens;

- The Rockefellers have at least one venture capital firm in Bermuda.

- Merv Griffin, the Hollywood star former owner of Resorts International - Bahamas Gambling Casinos and Hotels.

- Coniston Partners are N.Y. City arbitraguers with Panama, Cayman and Luxembourg companies.

- McDermott International is the world's largest offshore drilling company now headquartered in Panama. McDermott recently won a tax case with the IRS over its reorganization from the USA to Panama. Shareholders were saved from paying millions of dollars in taxes by virtue of the courts decision in favor of McDermott.

- Larry Gatlin and Loretta Lynn (Country Western singing stars - owners of the Treasure Island Hotel - Cayman).

- George Soros, John Templeton and Michael Steinhardt run billion dollar offshore mutual funds based in the Antilles, the Caymans and the Bahamas.

- Sylvester (Sly) Stallone produced one of his Rocky movies through a Netherlands Antilles company. Royalties paid by the U.S. theater owner on the rented movie reels to the

Antilles company was exempt from the 30% royalty withholding tax under the old US-N.A. Income tax treaty (canceled in 1987). Royalties were taxed in the Antilles at rates as low as 2.4% to 3%. The U.S. theater owners were even allowed a deduction for the royalties they paid.

- Even former Secretary of the U.S. Treasury Department – Nicholas Brady – has a home in exclusive Lyford Cay, in Nassau, in the Bahamas. Lyford Cay is a very wealthy community like Hollywood - with celebrity owned homes worth. Thousands of the very rich and famous live there.

Properly set-up offshore holding companies and trusts that do not carry on a trade or business within the United States are not required to file income tax returns or information returns with the IRS. U.S. taxpayers can still shelter income in offshore tax havens using:

(1) **Holding companies** that generate primarily non-subpart F incomes from the carrying-on of a business in a tax haven incur no U.S. income taxes.

2) **Foreign trusts:** If properly set-up and managed by the offshore management trustee company, a trust can be used to hold sub-part F type assets (stocks, bonds, bank accounts, royalties). The U.S.A.'s Controlled Foreign Corporation provisions (IRC §951 to 958) do not apply to foreign trusts. Capital gains, interest and dividend incomes can be accumulated in foreign trusts (and non-controlled foreign holding companies) tax free.

3) Under IRC §911(a), U.S. citizens that live in a tax haven for 11 of 12 months can obtain a yearly $72,000 exemption from U.S. taxes on their foreign source earned income (salary, wages from consulting, doctoring, legal fees, writing, most any self-employment income). No deductions are allowed when using the $72,000 foreign earned income exclusion. In addition, a housing cost allowance under IRC §911(c) can increase the amount they can exclude to over $100,000.

Independently wealth Americans that reside in the European tax havens of Campione or Monaco for at least 330 days of the year could qualify for the $72,000 *foreign earned income exclusion* mentioned above.

Letter Rulings and Revenue Rulings

From time to time the IRS issues letter rulings and revenue rulings designed to help the taxpayer determine what tax consequences he can expect under certain situations. Below are a few Rulings that should be considered by the U.S. settlor (transferor) of a foreign trust.

LTR 9332006 ™ Full Text

ISSUE (3). IS THE TRUST A TRUST DESCRIBED IN SECTION 679? Section 679 provides (with exceptions not here relevant) that a United States person who directly or indirectly transfers property to a foreign trust shall be treated as the owner for his taxable year of the portion of such trust attributable to such property if for such year there is a United States beneficiary of any portion of such trust. Section 7701(a)(30)(A) provides in part that the term "United States person" includes a citizen of the United States. Under section 679, the term "United States beneficiary" includes a trust beneficiary who is a United States person.

Each Settlor, a United States person, is considered to have transferred property to the Trust. Further, each Settlor and Beneficiary A is a "United States beneficiary" within the meaning of section 679. Accordingly, whether the Trust will be treated as a grantor trust under section 679 depends upon whether it is a foreign trust.

It has been represented that the Trust is a foreign trust. If that is so, the Trust will be treated as a grantor trust under section 679, and each Settlor will, for the taxable year in which the Trust is funded and in each succeeding taxable year during his or her life in which the Trust continues to have a United States beneficiary, be treated as the owner of a portion of the Trust income and corpus. That portion shall be determined in accordance with the principles of Treas. Reg. section 1.671-3, and each Settlor shall be required to take into account, in computing his or her federal income tax liability that Settlor's appropriate portion of the Trust's items of income, deductions, and credits.

IRS LTR 9332006 ™ Full Text

The use of an offshore **testamentary trust** to receive a U.S. persons assets only upon his death might afford some definite tax advantages, especially if the trusts assets are revocable by a nonresident alien individual or corporation. IRS LT. 9332006 confirms that upon his death, assets held in a foreign trust will no longer be subject to U.S. taxes, and not considered part of the U.S. person's U.S. estate, even if there are U.S. beneficiaries for the foreign trust.

LTR 9332006 -- ISSUE (4). UPON A SETTLOR'S DEATH, WILL THE PORTION OF THE TRUST TREATED AS OWNED BY THAT SETTLOR CEASE TO BE SO TREATED EVEN IF THEN TRUST BENEFICIARIES INCLUDE UNITED STATES PERSONS? Section 679(a)(2) (A) provides that the rules of section 679(a)(1) do not apply to "a transfer by reason of death of the transferor." While section 679(a)(2)(A) does not expressly address the tax consequences of the termination of foreign grantor trust status by reason of the grantor's death, the legislative history of the enactment of section 679 (H.R. Rep. No. 658, 94th Cong., 1st Sess. at 209 (1975); S. Rep. No. 938, 94th Cong., 2d Sess. at 218 (1976)) provides that "an inter vivos trust which is treated as owned by a U.S. person under [section 679] is not treated as owned by the estate of that person upon his death." Accordingly, any portion of the Trust that is treated as owned by a Settlor under the rules of section 679 shall cease to be so treated upon that Settlor's death.

Campione - tax haven for fabulously rich

Campione, a tiny island of 1.6 sq. km on Lake Lugano, is one of the few tax havens established exclusively for the fabulously rich. Like Monaco on the French Rivera, everything about the place has a whiff of idle, prepossessing luxury, from its man-made beach and alpine-air-resistant palm trees, and central casino - the main source of the island's revenue.

According to Michael Maskall, a tax partner at Price Waterhouse, Campione's residents are generally extremely wealthy, and live there part time. The cost of living is very high - at least as expensive as living in Switzerland.

A villa starts between $300,000 and $500,000, and residents are expected to have a private income.

The cost of living is explained by Campione's peculiar relationship with Switzerland. The island is, in fact, an Italian enclave. Yet, it is completely surrounded by the Swiss canton of Ticino.

Campione uses the Swiss franc for its currency, the Swiss telephone grid, Swiss electricity and other Swiss public utilities. Most residents shop and bank in Switzerland. Campione has no banks of its own.

Being Italian owned, Campione is subject to Italian fiscal law. Italian nationals living in Campione are obliged to pay Italian taxes. The tax office in Como is, in fact, responsible for assessing and collecting taxes. Foreign residents living in Campione do not have to pay taxes however.

Maskall says Campione is not suitable for offshore companies because it lacks the necessary legislation. Nevertheless, branches of foreign companies operating in Campione incur no tax liabilities on their operations.

There are tax advantages for Campione registered companies operating elsewhere - i.e., out of Switzerland or Liechtenstein. The shareholders of a Campione company operating out of Switzerland or Liechtenstein have complete anonymity. In addition, a Campione company need not employ personnel so that taxes may be kept to a minimum in Liechtenstein or Switzerland.

Obtaining residence is reasonably simple if you have the money. You simply buy or rent or timeshare a property in Campione. Most of the lawyers and bankers in Lugano specialize in estate planning for Campione residents. A residence permit can be obtained from the local police station in Como. The process takes about ten days, and once obtained the resident can then purchase a Swiss drivers licence, Swiss licence plates and a Swiss car registration number. [9]

---

9. From *Campione: a slice of Switzerland*, by Paul Ham (**Offshore Financial Review**)(August 1992)

CHAPTER 13 • United States Income Tax Treaties

The United States is currently a party to more than 60 *bilateral* income tax treaties, with more certain to be ratified in the future. The principle purpose of these bilateral treaties is to eliminate double taxation of income by two different taxing jurisdictions. If two governments have the power to levy their full rate of tax on the same entity under their own laws, then it's theoretically possible that a person or corporation could incur a tax liability in excess of 100% of his earned income. Double taxation can effectively prohibit operations in a particular country, taking away the profit motive. For this reason, governments draft and then ratify tax treaties between one another.

Elimination of Double Taxation

The foreign tax credit system authorized by the Internal Revenue Code alleviates "double taxation" problems by providing U.S. taxpayers with a tax credit for foreign taxes paid. The tax treaties go much further than this, actually exempting (or lowering the rates on) certain kinds of income (such as **passive** interests, dividends and royalties) from the U.S. withholding taxes altogether. In other cases, the treaties might allow a particular item of income to be taxed only in the host country where it is earned.

In theory, the provisions of the "Code" and the various tax treaties are equally weighted, but where specific provisions of a treaty apply they generally take precedence over the "Code". IRC §894 states... *"Income of any kind, to the extent required by any tax treaty obligation of the United States shall not be included in gross income, and shall be exempt from taxation under this subtitle."* Where the treaty is silent in its description and treatment of certain items of income the normal rules of the Internal Revenue Code are to be applied.

To illustrate, under **Article 10 (Dividends)** of the Barbados-U.S. Income Tax Treaty (same article appeared in the canceled Netherlands Antilles-U.S. Income Tax Treaty) dividends paid to a Barbados company not having a permanent establishment (office) within the U.S. are subject to reduced rates of withholding of 5% or 15%.

Absent the tax treaty, the normal withholding tax rate of 30% would apply. Other items of income such as royalties (0%), interest income (0%), and so-called "non-commercial industrial profits" are exempt from all U.S. withholding taxes under the other treaty articles.

The following is the actual "language" from the U.S. Treasury department's model treaty which the Treasury uses when negotiating and drafting the **articles** pertaining to dividends in its tax treaties with other nations. Most tax treaties being signed with the U.S. contain this provision.

Dividends

1. Dividends paid by a company which is resident of a Contracting State to a resident of the other Contracting State may be taxed in the other State.
2. However, such dividends may also be taxed in the Contracting State of which the company paying the dividends is a resident, and according to the laws of that State, but if the beneficial owner of the dividend is a resident of the other Contracting State, the tax charged shall not exceed:
   (a) 5 percent of the gross amount of the dividends, if the beneficial owner is a company which owns at least 10% of the voting stock of the company paying the dividend.
   (b) 15 percent of the gross amount of the dividends in all other cases. This paragraph shall not affect the taxation of the company in respect of the profits out of which the dividends are paid.
3. The term **"dividends"** as used in this convention (tax treaty) means income from shares or other rights not being debt claims, participating in profits, as well as income from other corporate rights which is subject to the same taxation treatment as income from shares by the laws of the State of which the company making the distribution is a resident."

What the U.S. Treasury is saying in paragraph #2(a) is a Barbados investment holding company can receive U.S. dividends from an U.S. corporation at a reduced treaty rate of 5%, if it owns "at least 10%" of the U.S. company's voting stock. Otherwise the U.S. withholding rate is 15% under #2(b). Absent the tax treaty, the Internal Revenue Code provides for a flat statutory withholding rate of 30% on dividends paid to non-residents.

Planners should note that **Article 10** of the Barbados tax treaty not only reduces the U.S. dividend withholding tax rate, but also allows the recipient offshore company to pay only a small profits tax in Barbados (2.5%) on the U.S. dividends received. When the U.S. Treasury department enters into a tax treaty agreement with a tax haven country like Barbados it is veritably fostering the growth and use of tax havens.

Price Waterhouse, one of the largest international accounting firms, says this about the new Barbados-U.S. income tax treaty.... *"Barbados' exchange of information agreement with the U.S. is part of a conscious (and successful) effort to fill a tax haven niche."* [1]

Termination of the U.S-Antilles tax treaty

Up to the date of termination on June 30, 1987, the "Antilles-US treaty" was the most prolific and famous income tax treaty in the world. Indeed, the termination of the **40 year old** U.S.-Netherlands Antilles tax treaty on June 30, 1987 would have been even more calamitous than it was if there had been no signing of a "new" Barbados-U.S. income tax treaty in February, 1986, which effectively left at least one avenue of hope open to offshore financial planners (the tax treaty with the Netherlands (Holland) offers planners yet another avenue).

U.S. Treasury retreats

Only weeks after sending a letter of termination to the Antilles authorities, the Treasury announced it would seek legislation from Congress that would protect pre-July 18, 1984 Eurodollars from the standard 30% U.S. interest withholding tax (which would apply to Antilles issued bonds absent the tax treaty). *"We didn't anticipate the full reaction of the market,"* said Roger Mentz, assistant Treasury secretary for tax policy. Another Treasury official put it more bluntly.. *"We screwed up!"*

While the termination of the treaty had no impact until after December 31, 1987, the treaty loss had serious implications for tax planners. The reason is simple. The Antilles tax treaty covered many other tax exemptions, including relief for real estate companies, portfolio dividends, royalties and shipping and air transport profits. Without the treaty these benefits would be wiped-out. Netherlands Antilles companies would be forced to look elsewhere. Many will have to liquidate their U.S. holdings and reorganize in other havens.

The following is a short list of some major U.S. companies that have been using the Netherlands Antilles as a tax haven. Many of these companies will remain because bond interest paid by their U.S. parent remains exempt from the 30% interest withholding tax under the **Tax Reform Act of 1984**, and because the Antilles have important income tax treaties with other industrial countries, including the UK, the Netherlands, Denmark and Norway. [2]

Caterpillar NV $400 million yielding 14% pa.
RJR Nabisco $400 million in zero-coupon Eurobonds.
Bank of Boston $100 million in 14.5% notes due in 1989.
General Electric   zero coupons due in 1992
Beneficial Corporation 14.75% 1992 Eurodollar bonds.
Northwest Natural Gas 15.375% 1992 Eurodollar bonds.
GMAC $200 million in Eurodollar bonds.
J.C. Penny   large Eurodollars issued and outstanding.
Citicorp   large Eurodollars issued and outstanding.

Many of these companies operated under the *interest spread* concept, whereby the interest paid by the U.S. parent to its Antilles subsidiary would be repaid to foreign lenders at a differential rate of 1/4% of 1%. Typically, an Antilles finance subsidiary would pay a tax equal to 24% to 30% of 1% of the *face value* of the loan, with no withholding tax applicable on interest paid to the Eurodollar bond holders, as the Antilles impose no withholding taxes on interest, dividends or royalties. [3] On the $100 million dollar Bank of Boston Eurodollar issue (above), the Bank of Boston's Antilles finance subsidiary might incur a tax of $300,000 annually. The parent company in the United States could deduct the interest expense (about $14.5 million) annually, and reduce its U.S. tax liability. Moreover, the offshore profits of the finance subsidiary usually could be reinvested tax free. [4]

The U.S.-Netherlands (Holland) Income Tax Treaty.

Most of the bilateral income tax treaties that the United States has entered are not with tax

---

[1] From *"Barbados: Offshore Financial Center"*, Price Waterhouse's **International Tax Review**, pg 2 May/June 1986.

[2] ABN Trust N.V., *"Netherlands Antilles Companies"*, pg. 34, 47.
[3] ABN Trust N.V., *"Netherlands Antilles Companies"*, pg. 23.
[4] IRC 954(c)(4)(A) & (B). See IRC 954(c)(3).

haven countries. In fact, very few tax havens have double taxation agreements with the U.S. Most U.S. tax treaties are with industrial nations like the UK and the Netherlands. Nevertheless, the tax planner should not pass over these high tax jurisdictions when drafting a business plan. The Dutch tax system is famed for the benefits offered the "holding company". The Netherlands **Participation Exemption** can lead to substantial tax savings when combined with the tax benefits offered under the U.S.-Netherlands tax treaty.

• Tax Treaties are **"reciprocal agreements"**. Under the U.S-Netherlands tax treaty the U.S. dividend withholding tax rate is **reduc**ed from 30% to 15%, and to 5% when a Dutch company has a "substantial holding" in the U.S. company paying the dividend. A "substantial holding" is 10% of the U.S. company's stock.
• To compensate for the USA's reduction in rates, the regular Dutch dividend withholding rate of 25% is reduced to 15%, with a further reduction to 5% if the U.S. recipient corporation owns at least 25% of the voting stock of the paying company, or if the U.S. recipient and another U.S. company together own at least 25%, and each owns at least 10% of the voting stock of the Dutch company.

Dutch "Participation Exemption"

In 1998, the top Dutch corporate income tax rate of about 35%, but Dutch tax reform goes much further than U.S. tax reform in providing tax relief for its corporations. A Dutch "holding company" that owns "at least 5%" of the par value of the paid-in capital in another foreign or domestic company from the beginning of the fiscal year can receive dividend distributions from the "subsidiary" 100% tax free. To qualify for this "participation exemption" the "downstream subsidiary" must meet the following conditions: [5.]

• In the case of a foreign subsidiary, the company must be subject to a corporate income tax comparable to the Netherlands corporate tax, but the rate and amount of corporate tax paid is immaterial.

• The "participation" in the foreign subsidiary must be held for a business-related purpose, not

as a mere "portfolio" investment. In this respect, if the Dutch parent company has a director on the board, or is actively engaged in the supervision of the subsidiary, then the company will qualify for the Participation Exemption, provided the foreign subsidiary is not directly or indirectly merely an investment company.

Combining the Dutch **Participation Exemption** with the treaty benefits can and does lead to substantial tax savings for Dutch based holding companies. It's not surprising than that by years-end 1987 the Netherlands with some $48 billion in U.S. investments could claim the second highest direct investments in the U.S., surpassing Japan's $32 billion, Canada's $22 billion, West Germany's $19 billion, and Switzerland's $14 billion, and trailing only the United Kingdom's $76 billion investments in the USA. [6.]

Treaty Benefits for Dutch Finance Companies

Under the U.S.-Netherlands tax treaty the 30% U.S. interest withholding tax is reduced to 0%. Moreover, under the Dutch tax system no interest withholding taxes on payments made to any nation (even to tax haven companies) are imposed on any Dutch company, as interest withholding taxes are unknown in the Netherlands. Because the Dutch maintain a network of tax treaties with many industrial nations reducing those nation's interest withholding tax rates, the Netherlands make a first-rate base for the formation of an international bank or finance company. Other reasons for basing in Holland include:
• The willingness of the **Netherlands corporate tax inspector** to grant special tax rulings in favor of Netherlands based finance companies.
• Interest payments made to foreigners are fully deductible when computing Dutch corporate income taxes so long as the payment is made at "arms length". Usually the Dutch corporate **income tax inspector** will "fix" the net taxable income of the company at a certain percentage of the total outstanding debt, or require that a certain "interest spread" between interest received and interest paid-out be used to calculate the tax. A **"spread ruling"** from the tax inspector of 1/8% or 1/4% can usually be **"negotiated"** by the tax advisor. [7.]

[5.] Not just dividends paid by the foreign subsidiary to the Dutch holding company qualify for the participation exemption, but cash distributions, dividends in kind, constructive dividends, shares issued from the share premium reserve, and capital gains realized on the liquidation proceeds from the disposal of the subsidiary's shares qualify as well (with the exception that a capital "loss" is not deductible).

[6.] From the Plain Truth, pg 29 (January 1989).

[7.] "Non-Resident Owned Dutch Holding, Finance & Royalty Companies", published by the ABN Bank (Box 1469, 1000 BL Amsterdam), pg. 33.

• Recent changes in the Dutch tax administration's attitude to finance companies shows a slightly different approach. In the future, where there is a relationship between the debtors and the Dutch finance company, i.e. the company is used solely as a conduit company, the acceptable spread is maintained at 1/8%, or, if the relevant loan exceeds NLG 3,000 million, the spread may be as low as 1/16%.

• So called "back-to-back loan arrangements" between a Dutch company and a tax haven entity is common, and not looked on unfavorably by the Dutch tax authorities.

New U.S. - Dutch tax treaty

A *new* U.S./Netherlands income tax treaty was signed in Washington D.C. on December 18, 1992 after more than 10 years of negotiations. The *new* treaty replaces the *old* treaty which had been in force since 1947, a period of 45 years.

Anti-treaty shopping provisions aimed at limiting who can benefit from the *new* treaty are of great concern to international taxplanners. Under the *old* U.S./Netherlands tax treaty, any company that could meet the Dutch or U.S. residency requirements would qualify for treaty benefits. Not so under the newly signed treaty.

The negotiations for the *new* treaty took some ten years to iron out because the Dutch resisted the U.S. efforts to insert its treaty-shopping provisions. Generally speaking, the *new* treaty denies benefits to corporations owned by third-country shareholders, unless they can pass one of four special tests.

The anti-treaty shopping provisions [Limitation of Benefits Article (Article 28)] of the *new* treaty were based on the 1981 U.S. Treasury Department's Model Treaty which stated that a corporation is not resident of a country for treaty purposes unless (1) at least 75% of its shares are owned - directly or indirectly - by individuals who are residents of that country, and (2) is not a conduit company to pass on deductible interest and royalties to residents of a third country. The *new* U.S.-Netherlands treaty reduces the stock ownership test to *more than 50%*.

One loophole under the 1981 U.S. Treasury Model Treaty was that the 70% stock ownership requirement could be met if the shares of the company were listed and its stock regularly traded on a recognized stock exchange in either country. Tax practitioners should note the *new*

U.S.-Netherlands income tax treaty contains this valuable loophole.

The *new* treaty applies in general to residents of either the Netherlands or the U.S. The term "resident" also includes exempt pension trusts and other exempt organizations (i.e., charitable, scientific, religious and educational type organizations). Generally, interest and dividends paid by unrelated U.S. companies to a Netherlands pension trust would be 100% free of U.S. withholding tax, normally 30%.

Four main tests for treaty benefits

The Limitation of Benefits Article (Article 28) provides that a resident corporation is a resident for treaty purposes if it passes any one of the following tests:

* The Stock Exchange Test
* The Shareholder test
* The Active Trade or Business test
* The Headquarters test

Stock Exchange Test

The Stock Exchange test is somewhat discriminatory in that it favors large, well capitalized companies that can afford the time and expense to get its shares listed (or are already listed) on one of the recognized Stock Exchanges. Nevertheless, the Stock Exchange test is probably the single most important test to consider, because once a corporation goes to the trouble of being listed on the NYSE, NASDAQ, AMEX, Dutch, London, Paris or Frankfurt Stock Exchanges it will qualify for all the treaty benefits, even if it is a mere conduit company channeling interest into an offshore affiliate based in a tax haven.

Conduit companies - bank & finance companies

A conduit company typically borrows money from an offshore company domiciled in a tax haven country and relends the money to an U.S. company. Under both the *new* and the *current* U.S.-Netherlands tax treaty, the 30% U.S. interest withholding tax is reduced to 0%. Additionally, under the Dutch tax system no interest withholding taxes on payments made to any nation (even to companies domiciled in tax havens) are imposed on any Dutch company. Interest withholding taxes are unknown in the Netherlands.

The *new* tax treaty restricts the use of third party conduits, unless the conduit's stock is regularly traded on one of the recognized stock exchanges, or unless the conduit meets other rather stringent tests described below.

Stock Exchange Test for Subsidiaries

Non-publicly traded companies also qualify for treaty benefits if (1) more than 50% of the aggregate vote and value of their shares are owned by five or fewer companies, each of which meets the stock listing and trading standards, and (2) they are not conduit companies (or if they are conduits, they pass either the "conduit test", "the base reduction test", or the "conduit base reduction test").

"Conduit test"

Under the *new* U.S.-Netherlands treaty, a conduit company is one that, in any year, makes deductible payments of interest and royalties equal to 90% or more of its aggregate receipts of interest and royalties.

A conduit traffics in treaty withholding rates, and may be unrelated to either the payor or the payee of interest and royalties in back-to-back loan and royalty arrangements.

The conduit is compensated by a thin spread between the payment it receives and the payments it makes. In Rev-Rul 84-153 and 84-154, the U.S. unilaterally attacked conduit arrangements be denying treaty benefits on the basis that the conduit did not have dominion and control over the payments that quickly pass through its hands.

Under the *new* U.S.-Netherlands treaty, a conduit passes the base reduction test if its payments of deductible interest and royalties to companies that are not entitled to benefits of the treaty (i.e., third-country residents) are less than 50% of its gross income.

"Base reduction test"

The treaty provides that a conduit gets treaty benefits if it passes the "base reduction test". A company passes the test if its payments of tax deductible interest and royalties to companies not entitled to the benefits of the treaty (i.e., third-country residents) are less than 50% of its gross income. This means that companies of substance can have offsetting interest income and interest expense (or royalty income and royalty expense) without losing their treaty benefits.

"Conduit base reduction test"

This test is easier than the conduit test and can be used as an alternative for the Stock Exchange test for subsidiaries of publicly listed companies (more than 50% ownership by 5 or fewer public companies). The test is the same as the base reduction test except that deductible interest and royalties are taken into account only if they are made to associated enterprises in whose hands they will be taxed at a rate less than 50% of the Dutch rate (the Dutch corporate rate is 40% on profits up to Dfl 250,000 and 35% thereafter). Consequently, payments made to most tax haven companies are the only ones that will be considered.

Non-publicly traded companies

A non-publicly traded company qualifies for treaty benefits if (1) more than 50% of its shares are owned, directly or indirectly, by "qualified persons" (i.e., U.S. citizens and residents of the Netherlands and U.S., and (2) it meets the "base reduction test".

Active Trade or Business Test

A Company not qualifying for treaty benefits under one of the above tests, can still qualify if it is engaged in a trade or business in the residence country that is complementary to its (or a related party's) activities in the treaty partner.

A trade or business in the residence country is "substantial" if the average of the following three ratios exceeds 10% and each exceeds 7.5% for the preceding year.

- The value of the assets in the residence country to the value of assets in the source country;
- The gross income in the residence country to the gross income in the source country; and
- The payroll expense in the residence country to the payroll expense in the source country.

Since the activity in the source country qualifies if it is carried on by a commonly controlled company (i.e., member of the same multinational group), an example of the benefit would be manufacturing subsidiary of a Japanese multinational in The Netherlands (i.e., Toyota Netherlands) licensing know-how to a related manufacturing company in the U.S. (i.e., Toyota USA) that is in the same business. Withholding on royalties would be zero instead of 30% (the U.S. statutory rate).

Headquarters test

"Headquarters" status gives a company full treaty benefits, but most small and medium size enterprises won't be able to meet the treaty's strict requirements to qualify as a "headquarters company".

A "headquarters company" must provide a substantial portion of the supervision and administration of the group, which can include group financing (although financing cannot be its principal function).

A "headquarters company" consists of at least five companies operating in at least five different countries, each of which generates 10% of the gross income of the group.

The gross income generated in any one of the countries (other than the residence country) cannot exceed 50% of the gross income of the group, and not more than 25% of its gross income can be from the source country.

Dividends

Both the *new* and the *old* U.S.-Netherlands tax treaty lowered the U.S. 30% dividend withholding rate to 15% and 5% respectively. But the *new* treaty is actually superior to the *old* treaty in that to qualify for the lowest 5% dividend withholding rate, the recipient company needs only own 10% of the payors voting stock. Under the *old* treaty, the recipient company had to own 25% of the payors voting stock.

Dividend withholding is 15% for all other shareholders (including individual shareholders and corporations owning less than 10% interest in the payor).

Interest and royalty withholding taxes are reduced to 0% under both the *old* and the *new* treaty.

Demise of the Swiss branch of a Dutch company

A long-standing tax planning device takes advantage of the fact that the interest and royalty income of a Swiss branch of a Dutch company is lightly taxed in Switzerland and not taxed at all in the Netherlands. The "Basis of Taxation" article of the new treaty takes dead aim at this technique

by disallowing treaty benefits for interest and royalties paid by the finance branches or intangible property ownership branches of Dutch companies operating in tax havens. Switzerland is the main target, but other low-tax countries also will be affected.

IRS Rev. Ruling 87-89 attacks some back-to-back loan schemes

Back-to-Back loan schemes have been attacked by the IRS in the past under RevRul 84-152 & RevRul 84-153, which purport to "look through" conduit type loan arrangements involving Netherlands Antilles finance companies and U.S. companies in certain limited cases where the Service believed the tax planning was overly abusive of the U.S. tax rules. Following the **Tax Reform Act of 1986**, Congress again felt that *back-to-back* loans needed to be policed, and stated that *back-to-back loan schemes* should be *collapsed* by the IRS, and the ultimate recipient, if not treaty protected, should be subject to U.S. tax." [8.]

The IRS responded to Congress's concern by issuing **RevRul 87-89** which defined three types of arrangements that will be *collapsed*. In the first, a foreign parent company located in a nontreaty jurisdiction places $100x dollars as a demand deposit at an unrelated bank located in a treaty country. The bank then lends $80x dollars to the foreign parent company's U.S. subsidiary under terms allowing for a 1% interest rate spread. The ruling states as facts that during the term of the loan the amount of the parent deposits with the bank exceeded the outstanding loan balance, and further, that the interest rate charged by the bank would have differed in the absence of the parent's deposit.

The IRS asserts through this ruling that under these conditions the loan arrangement is to be collapsed based on the fact that the "collateral monies left on deposit" by the U.S. subsidiary's foreign parent was not an "independent transaction". Rev-Rul 87-89 is not meant to imply that a back-to-back loan made through an independent Netherlands bank or Dutch Finance Company (even through a Cayman or Bahamian affiliate which provides the money) to an unrelated U.S. company will be collapsed by the

---

8. See "Rev.Rul 87-89 latest IRS attack on back-to-back loans", by David Benson, Esq., pg 473, Tax Management International, Inc. (1987)

IRS, as the ruling is not to apply to "independent transactions" such as these. Consequently, a Dutch finance company that is unrelated to the U.S. borrower has nothing to fear from RevRul 87-89. [9]

IRS **Example #3** reinforces this hypothesis as it directs its attack to the CFC of an U.S. company which makes the bank deposit with a non-US bank, which in turn lends the money to the domestic U.S. parent. In example #3, both the bank and the CFC are in the same treaty jurisdiction. In case **#1** the IRS will collapse the loan and apply the 30% U.S. withholding tax to the non-treaty protected recipient, but in case #3 the IRS will consider the loan by the offshore CFC to be a **direct investment** by the CFC in its U.S. parent, thus an investment in U.S. property under IRC §956. In case #3 the U.S. parent will be held taxable on the CFC profits.

The "new" Barbados–U.S. Income Tax Treaty

Just a few hundred miles east of the Antilles lie Barbados, another Caribbean low tax haven. The tax rate here tops out at just 2.5% for International Business Corporations (called **IBC**'s). Barbados' recent signing on December 31, 1984 of a tax treaty with the United States, followed by the U.S. Senate's ratification on February 28, 1986, makes Barbados one of the few tax havens in the world to have a tax reducing treaty with the U.S. Without question, the Barbados treaty offers many of the same benefits found under the canceled Antilles treaty, though admittedly the Antilles treaty contained bigger and better exemptions. Still, Barbados will benefit from the loss of business to the Antilles. Operators such as Prince Talal Bin Abdul-Aziz el Saud's (P.O. Box 930, Riyadh, Saudi Arabia) Vanguard N.V. (Handelskada 8, Curacao,

Netherlands Antilles) and many other foreigners hold billions of dollars worth of U.S. real estate through Antilles holding companies, where once favorable treaty benefits provided extensive tax relief.

A tactic utilized prior to the Tax Reform Act of 1986 called **dividend stripping** was often practiced by Antilles real estate holding companies. Dividend stripping entailed incorporating a wholly owned U.S. subsidiary which would channel its U.S. profits to its Antilles parent disguised as a dividend subject only to a 5% U.S. withholding tax. Often the U.S. real estate company would take on a large debt to pay out the dividend. Since the interest it paid would be deductible against Federal Income taxes, the tax liability of the U.S. real estate company was sometimes reduced to nothing.

Under **Article 10(2)(a)** of the current Barbados-U.S. income tax treaty the U.S. dividend withholding rate is reduced to 5% if the Barbados parent company owns at least 10% of the voting stock of the U.S. company paying the dividend.

Article 11(Interest) of the Barbados-U.S. Income Tax Treaty

While the Tax Reform Act of 1984 eliminated the 30% interest withholding on corporate and government bonds issued after July 18, 1984, bonds issued before that date are subject to the full 30% rate of withholding unless a tax treaty provides for a lower rate. Article 11 (Interest) of the Barbados treaty, which appears below, provides for a reduced withholding rate of 12.5% on U.S. corporate and government bonds. Thus, pre 7-18-84 issued bonds will be subject to a 12.5% U.S. withholding tax. [10]

[§§ 579N] Article 11 (Interest)

1. Where interest is derived from sources within a Contracting State and beneficially owned by a resident of the other Contracting State, the rate of tax imposed thereon in the first-mentioned State shall not exceed 12.5% of the gross amount of the interest. Notwithstanding the preceding sentence, interest derived from sources within a Contracting State, beneficially owned by a

---

[9]. David Benson, Esq. further states that the "collapse" authorized under Rev.Rul.87-89 is to be applied outside the branch tax context. This appears to imply that a Dutch Bank or finance company operating within the USA through a branch office could borrow directly from one of its tax haven affiliates (Cayman, Bahamas, B.V.I.), if it wanted to (not a good idea, as the Dutch will tax the offshore branch profits, but will not tax profits of an offshore Cayman subsidiary), and not fit any of the examples attacked by Rev.Rul 87-89; and thus, no US interest withholding tax or BLT should be applied to a direct loan from say a Cayman or Bahamian lender, as Article XII of the Netherlands-US treaty (eliminating the US interest withholding tax) would still apply even to the tax haven affiliate.

---

[10]. Under the Antilles tax treaty the U.S. withholding tax on interest was reduced to 0 in most cases. Furthermore, since **Article VIII** of the terminated Antilles tax treaty was "grandfathered" by the U.S. Treasury, there may still be cases where a NA company could be useful.

resident of the other Contracting State, and paid in respect of a bond, debenture or other similar obligation issued, guaranteed or insured by the government of that Contracting State or by a political subdivision, local authority or instrumentality thereof shall be taxable in that other State.

```
┌─────────────────────────────────────────┐
│         The First U.S. Income Tax Treaty │
│                                           │
│  The first U.S. tax treaty was signed on │
│  April 27, 1932 with France, and promptly │
│  ratified by the U.S. Senate. France,    │
│  however, did not ratify the treaty until │
│  after 1934 when Congress enacted        │
│  legislation authorizing the President to │
│  double the rate of tax on any country   │
│  who was imposing an unfair,             │
│  discriminatory or extraterritorial tax  │
│  on U.S. citizens or corporations (which │
│  France was doing at the time). France,  │
│  seeing that President Roosevelt could   │
│  thereby tax French citizens and         │
│  corporations at rates as high as 80%,   │
│  quickly ratified the treaty. The treaty │
│  became effective shortly thereafter on  │
│  January 1, 1936.                        │
└─────────────────────────────────────────┘
```

Model Income Tax Treaties

Bilateral Tax treaties drafted today with the United States follow the scheme set-down by the Organization for Economic Cooperation and Development (OECD) and the U.S. Treasury's Model Income Tax Treaty. The U.S. treasury's model prescribes how a treaty shall be negotiated from a U.S. point of view, so the other side knows what they are bargaining with beforehand.

The Treaty itself includes a **preamble**, a **title**, and a set of **articles**. The **title** tells you the names of the two countries to which the treaty applies, and the type of assets covered (i.e., income, estate or gift taxes). The preamble states the purpose of the treaty, the names of the governmental representatives that were present, and the fact that an agreement was made. The articles of a typical treaty deal specifically with tax questions and are organized into paragraph form.

One of the most important concepts found in the articles of every treaty is the definition for Permanent Establishment. If a foreign corporation doesn't meet the treaty's definition for having a permanent establishment, its commercial and industrial profits from dealings with the United States will often escape all taxation.

What entails a permanent establishment is not found in the Internal Revenue Code and is peculiar to the tax treaties. While treaty definitions vary, Article 5 of the 1986 Barbados definition is typical...

[∫∫ 579G] Article 5 (Permanent Establishment)

1. for the purposes of this Convention, except as otherwise specified in this Article, the term "permanent establishment" means a regular place of business through which the business of an enterprise is wholly or partly carried on.

2. The term "permanent establishment" shall include especially;

    (a) a place of management;
    (b) a branch;
    (c) an office;
    (d) a factory;
    (e) a workshop;
    (f) a store or premises used as a sales outlet;
    (g) a warehouse, in relation to a person providing storage facilities for others;
    (h) a mine, an oil or gas well, a quarry, or any other place of extraction of natural resources; development of natural resources within a Contracting State.....
    (i) the furnishing of services, including consultancy, management, technical and supervisory services within a Contracting State by an enterprise or employees or other persons, but only if:
    (j) activities of that nature continue within the State for a period or periods aggregating more than 90 days in a 12 month period, provided that a permanent establishment shall not exist in any taxable year in which such services are rendered in that State for a period or periods aggregating less than 30 days in the taxable year; or

3. Notwithstanding the preceding provisions of this Article, the term permanent establishment shall be deemed not to include any one or more of the following:

    (a) the use of facilities solely for the purpose of storage, display or delivery of goods or merchandise belonging to the enterprise, other than goods or merchandise held for the sale by such enterprise in a store or premises used as a sales outlet; .... *abridged due to the length of Article 5...*

5. Notwithstanding the provisions of paragraphs 1 & 2, a person acting in a Contracting State on behalf of an enterprise of the other Contracting State shall be deemed a permanent establishment of that enterprise in the first mentioned State, if:

    (a) he has and habitually exercises in the first-mentioned State an authority to conclude contracts on behalf of the enterprise, unless his activities are limited to those mentioned in paragraph 3 which, if exercised through a regular place of business, would not make a permanent establishment, or
    (b) he habitually maintains in the first-mentioned State a stock of goods or merchandise from which he regularly delivers goods or merchandise on behalf of the enterprise.... *abridged due to length.*

6. An enterprise shall not be deemed to have a permanent establishment in a Contracting State merely because it carries on business in that state through a broker, general commission agent, or any other agent of an **independent status**, provided such person are acting in the ordinary course of business. However, when the activities of such person are devoted substantially on behalf of that enterprise, he shall not be considered an agent of independent status, if the enterprise and agent do not deal under "arms length" conditions.

"In **Revenue Ruling 80-222** a foreign company reinsuring U.S. risks was held ***not*** to be doing business in the U.S. In the ruling's facts, the reinsurance policies were neither signed nor countersigned in the U.S. by an agent of the foreign company, and no personal services were performed on a regular basis in the U.S. on behalf of the foreign company. As a rule, to avoid being considered engaged in a U.S. trade or business, a company must not have an agent or employee actively carrying on business in the U.S."

The treaty with Barbados permits a greater degree of U.S. activity than this before "permanent establishment" status is reached. And the activity threshold is clear-cut. In general, if a Barbados insurance company does not have an office in the U.S., it will not have a permanent establishment unless it has an employee (or agent who is not an "independent" agent) in the U.S. who "habitually exercises an authority to conclude contracts on behalf of the enterprise..."

Thus, under the treaty, a Barbados insurance company with no U.S. office can solicit business in the U.S. through employees or dependent agents without being taxed in the U.S., unless the employees have and habitually exercise the authority to conclude contracts. Absent a treaty, such solicitation could be deemed to be doing business in the U.S." - **Alan S. Woodberry, partner Price Waterhouse** [11.]

Brokers and Independent Agents

Use of a bona-fide commission agent, broker or independent agent can result in unlimited volume of sales without U.S. tax liability. Moreover, according to IRS Revenue Ruling 55-617, an absolute exemption from U.S. taxes is conferred when an independent agent is engaged

---

[11.] *"Barbados: Offshore Financial Center"*, PW's International Tax Review, May/June 1986.

though a substantial amount of trade or business is carried on within the U.S.

Rev-Rul 55-617: *"The corporation does extensive business through the medium of a commission agent and is engaged in trade or business through the medium of a commission agent and is engaged in a trade or business within the U.S. as defined by Section 871(c) of the Internal Revenue Code of 1954. However, the corporation has no permanent establishment in the United States."*

Tax planners should not overlook the **independent agent** exemption provided under all the U.S. tax treaties as it opens the door to a whole host of activities and trade with little worry of IRS scrutiny, providing the agent is truly an **independent.** The following lists the functions an independent agent must adhere to secure the exempt status:

1. An independent agent is a broker, commission agent or public warehousemen, but also includes processor, real estate management agents and other independent agents and intermediaries.
2. His rates are published, standard, customary and openly offered to the trade.
3. His services are provided openly to all in the trade.
4. Authority to negotiate and sign contracts in the name of the foreign principal must be obtained from, or contracts approved by, the foreign principal (a commission agent must take title in his name) -- alternatively, agent has general authority to conclude specific class of contract, but only at preset terms determined by foreign principal.

Treaty Shopping

Treaty shopping is the act of relocating your corporate entity (or assets) or operation to a U.S. treaty partner's jurisdiction to take advantage of the tax relief offered under one of the U.S. income tax treaty. **Treaty** shopping provisions are aimed at third party users of a tax treaty, i.e., entities not normally resident of either of the countries a party to the tax treaty.

How the IRS views treaty shopping has been the subject of many discussions and articles. While no provisions under the Internal Revenue Code directly seek to prevent treaty shopping, the IRS has addressed **treaty shopping** through its **letter rulings**.

Oddly enough, some letter rulings issued by the IRS have been favorable to the taxpayer, sometimes even condoning treaty shopping. A few rulings denied the exemption from interest withholding tax, but this was not meant to apply to portfolio investment interest, which has never been challenged by the IRS.

Revenue Ruling 75-73 permitted persons who were not residents of the Netherlands Antilles to form N.A. corporations to invest in U.S. real estate through a U.S. partnership. Ironically, the IRS recognized the arrangement even though the participants (who could have invested directly in the U.S. partnership) supplanted the N.A. corporation to avoid having to file income tax returns.

Two rulings in 1984 (Rev-Rul 84-152 & 84-153) went against the taxpayer in a blatant "back-to-back" loan scheme. On closer inspection these rulings applied to deny the U.S. interest withholding exemption only for a specific type of abuses involving Netherlands Antilles Finance Companies. It wasn't meant to apply to portfolio interest received by offshore holding companies.

Barbados' Anti-Treaty Shopping Provision, Article 22

Article 22 of the Barbados-U.S. treaty contains an anti-treaty shopping provision that is innocuous. While paragraphs 1(a) and (b) reserve the treaty benefits for the most part to residents of the U.S. and Barbados, paragraph 3(a) and (b) provides **for an "exception"** where the shares are substantially traded on a recognized NASDAQ type stock exchange. In such a case paragraph 1 of article 22 is not to apply.

[∫∫ 579Z] Article 22 Limitation on Benefits

1. A person which is a resident of a Contracting State and which derives income from sources within the other Contracting State shall not be entitled, in that other Contracting State, to the benefits of Article 6 (Income from Real Property (Immovable Property) through Article 23 (Relief from Double Taxation) if:

(a) 50% or less of the beneficial interest in such person (or in case of a company, 50% or less of the number of shares of each class of the company's shares) is owned, directly or indirectly, by any combination of one or more individual residents of a Contracting State or citizens of the U.S.; or

(b) the income of such person is used in substantial part, directly or indirectly, to meet liabilities (including liabilities for interest or royalties) to persons who are residents of a State other than a Contracting State, or who are not citizens of the U.S.

2. The provisions of paragraph 1 shall not apply if the income derived from the other Contracting State is derived in connection with, or incidental to, the active conduct by such person of a trade or business in the first-mentioned Contracting State (other than the business of making or managing investments). The preceding sentence shall not apply with respect to a person engaged in the business of banking or insurance in a Contracting state, if the income of such person is subject to tax in the Contracting State in which it is resident at a rate of tax which is substantially below the rate generally applicable to business income in that State. Notwithstanding the preceding sentence, the income of such a bank which is not derived from the conduct of a banking business (including but not limited to income attributed to the taking of deposits and making of loans, managing of investments and performance of trust or other services as fiduciary) shall be subject to the provisions of the first sentence of this paragraph.

3. The provisions of paragraph 1 shall not apply if the person deriving the income is a company which is a resident of a Contracting State in whose principal class of shares there is a substantial and regular trading on a recognized stock exchange. For purposes of the preceding sentence, the term "recognized stock exchange" means:

(a) The NASDAQ System owned by the National Association of Securities Dealers, Inc. and any stock exchange registered with the Securities and Exchange Commission as a national securities exchange for purposes of the Securities Act of 1934; and (b) any other stock exchange agreed upon by the competent authorities of the Contracting States.

> Paragraph 3 above is part of the treaty shopping provision of Article 22. It permits any company that registers its stock on a stock exchange to qualify for the other treaty benefits by causing paragraph 1 of Article 22 not to apply.

"Portfolio Interest" - defined

Portfolio interest is interest paid on two kinds of obligations. One is called *Bearer Shares* as described in IRC §163(f)(2)(B), and the other is called *Registered Obligations* with respect to which the U.S. withholding agent (a securities clearing house, bank or other financial institution) has been presented a statement saying in effect that the beneficial owner is not a U.S. person.

Bearer Shares under IRC §163(f)(2)(B)

An instrument will qualify for the "portfolio interest exemption" if the interest is paid on a **foreign targeted bearer obligation** not issued by a natural person, and of the kind offered to the public, and one that has a maturity of more than one year.

Obligations issued in bearer form by the U.S. government-owned agencies of government sponsored agencies (i.e., Federal Home Loan Banks, FNMA, Federal Loan Mortgage Corporation) are not considered to meet these requirements, thus they will not qualify as "portfolio interest" exemption.

A bearer obligation must also have the following legend in English on the face of the obligation and on the interest coupons which may be detached therefrom stating: *"Any U.S. person who holds this obligation will be subject to limitations under the U.S. income tax laws, including limitations provided in IRC §165(j) & IRC §1287(a) of the Internal Revenue Code."* Without this inscription on the certificate the portfolio interest exemption will be lost on bearer obligations **not** in registered form. See the definition for **Registered Obligations** that follows.

Bearer obligations are not limited to those corporate bonds that have been registered under the Securities Act of 1933. An obligation could be issued pursuant to one of the special security exemptions of the Securities Act, such as Regulation D. This means you could float your own bond issue without paying the Commissioner of the SEC a large fee, required when registering a public bond issue. Interest on such a private type non-tradable bond is considered tax exempt. Physical delivery must be made to the purchaser outside the U.S., and a signed statement must be gotten from him saying he is not purchasing it on behalf of an U.S. person.

Lastly, it is required that interest payments be made outside the U.S. by the U.S. issuer or his agent by way of the presentation of a coupon, or upon making a demand for payment.

Registered Obligations

An obligation is in **Registered** form if it is registered as to both principle and any stated interest, and any transfer of the obligation may be accomplished only through the surrender of the old instrument and the reissuance by the issuer of a new instrument to the new holder; **or**, in a second case, if the right to the principle of, and stated interest on, the obligation may be transferred only through a book-entry system. [12]

An obligation is considered transferable only through a book entry system. Ownership of an interest in the obligation needs to be reflected by a book entry, whether or not securities are issued. A book entry is a record or ownership that identifies the owner of an interest in an obligation. The U.S. Treasury uses a book entry system.

Exceptions

Not all interest will qualify for the *portfolio interest* exemption under the Tax Reform Act of 1984. Interest effectively connected with a recipient's U.S. trade or business through a permanent establishment does not qualify as portfolio interest. Furthermore, none of the U.S. tax treaties can be relied on to exempt such "business profits".

Interest received by a 10% shareholder is not considered portfolio interest either. Unless reduced by a tax treaty such interest would be subject to the full 30% U.S. withholding. For example, under the Swiss treaty this type of interest would incur a 5% U.S. withholding tax. See tables 1 & 2 below.

The term 10% shareholder means any U.S. person who owns 10% or more of the total combined voting power of all classes of stock of such corporation entitled to vote. The offshore company might hold over 10% of the value shares in the U.S. payer, yet still qualify for the portfolio interest exemption if his voting stock participation is kept below the 10% threshold.

Another exception going against the taxpayer is that portfolio interest does not include interest received by foreign banks on the

---

12. Temp. Reg 163-1(a) & Regs. 5f.103-1(c).

extension of credit under a loan agreement entered in the ordinary course of its banking business. This exception can be circumvented by issuing a **"Registered Debt Instrument"** (as discussed, supra) to the bank, instead of entering into a normal formal loan agreement.

Another safe haven from the banking-lender restriction is provided in the treaties themselves. Article 11 of the Barbados-U.S. treaty states that "debt claims of every kind" are entitled to the reduced treaty rates. Article 11, paragraph 4 of the "new" (but now extinct) Netherlands Antilles treaty would have reduced the rate to 5%. The Swiss treaty reduces the debt claim interest rate to a 5% withholding tax, and the Netherlands-U.S. tax treaty exempts all interest of every kind from the 30% withholding. See table #1.

Table #1 (Interest on bonds issued before 7-18-84)

Country	Corporate tax rate	U.S. corporate	U.S. treasuries
Jamaica	33.3% [13]	12.5%	X
Switzerland	3.6% to 9.8%	5%	5%
Barbados (IBCs)	2.5% to 1%	12.5%	12.5%
Cayman Islands	0%	30%	30%
Bahamas	0%	30%	30%

Table #2 (Portfolio interest & "non-portfolio interest" after 7-18-84)

Country	Corporate tax rate	post 7-18-84 portfolio interest	non-portfolio debt
Jamaica	33.3%	0%	12.5%
Switzerland	3.6% to 9.8%	0%	5%
Barbados IBC	2.5% to 1%	0%	12.5%
Cayman Islands	0%	0% [14]	30% [15]

13. Jamaica applies an additional 10% income tax on companies licensed under the Banking Act and Protection of Depositors Act. Life Insurance companies are taxed at a reduced rate of 7.5% on their investment income.

14. The rate of withholding for Cayman Island companies is currently 0%, but under IRC 871(h)(5) and IRC 881(c)(3)(A)(as amended by the Tax Reform Act of 1984), the U.S. treasury **Secretary** is authorized to deny the 30% interest withholding tax exemption if he determines the exchange of information between the U.S. and the Caymans is inadequate to prevent the evasion of US income taxes. The Secretary is authorized under the Code to "publish a statement" denying the withholding exemption to tax havens like the Caymans. However, through the end of 1988 the Secretary has not issued such a statement against any nation.

Table #3 illustrates the treaty withholding rates applicable to offshore bank loans & credit & 10% voting stock shareholders.

Country	Corporate tax rate	Bank loan	10% voting stockholder
Jamaica	33.3%	12.5%	12.5%
Caymans	0%	30%	30%
Barbados IBC	2.5% to 1%	12.5%	12.5%
B.V.I. [16]	15% to 0%	30%	30%
Switzerland	3.6% to 9.8%	5%	5%
Netherlands [17]	35%	0%	0%

IRS NOTICE 87-56

Many U.S. tax treaties in force at the time the "new" BLT (Branch Level Tax) came along had "non-discrimination" provisions prohibiting the U.S. from levying the "new" branch tax. IRS Notice 87-56 was published to provide guidance as to how the BLT and the tax treaties are to interact. According to the notice residents of 28 countries, who were entitled to benefits under their U.S. income tax treaty (and who were not "treaty shopping"), would not be subject to the branch profits tax. [18]

INTERFIPOL. A document as ruthless as the Communist Manifesto fades away!

The income tax treaties entered into by the United States have all been **bilateral treaties,** meaning the agreement covered tax cooperation between just two parties. But, ten years ago the *Organization for Economic Cooperation and Development* (OECD) and the *Council of Europe* (C/E) developed a new multilateral treaty designed to combat international avoidance and

15. The Cayman Islands and Barbados do not tax capital gains. Jamaica does not tax capital gains from security transactions. Switzerland taxes capital gains.

16. The British Virgin Island low tax rate applied to Internal Business Corporations (IBCs). Other companies are taxed at 15% tax rate.

17. The Netherlands assess a flat 35% corporate tax on all profits, unless otherwise exempt by Dutch statues.

18. Nine other treaties which allow for the BLT in some circumstances were also covered in the Notice. These 9 included Canada, France, New Zealand, Trinidad & Tobago (which allowed the BLT with certain modifications), and Barbados, Poland, Rumania and the USSR which allow the branch tax without any treaty modifications.

evasion of taxes between no less than 28 nations. This new treaty was drafted in total secrecy, and the U.S. Government strongly supported the proposed multinational treaty, at least portions of it. Critics of the new treaty (which include Marshall J. Langer, the *Wall Street Journal* and more sensible people) call it INTERFIPOL. The INTERFIPOL treaty never was accepted by the industrial nations, and eventually faded away – forever we hope.

But INTERFIPOL was not really a tax treaty at all. It had no provisions for the prevention of double taxation on taxpayers, and in fact serves no benefit to taxpayers at all (hence the secrecy while it was drafted). What INTERFIPOL does provide for is the (i) exchange of information between the countries that sign the treaty (ii) cross-border assistance in the collection of taxes, and (iii) service of documents. INTERFIPOL is nothing more than a document that sought to create a new international IRS for all its members. It's really the most oppressive piece of legislation drafted since the Communist Manifesto.

The political threat was very real. If the UK decided to sign the treaty, it would extend the scope of INTERFIPOL to cover all its territories and tax havens. Bank secrecy and confidentiality would be dismantled immediately. Under **Art.29(1)** *Each State shall at the time of signature, or when depositing its instrument of ratification, acceptance or approval, specify the territory or territories to which this Convention shall apply.* [19.]

The Judicial threat is less obvious, but every bit as important. This "INTER-FIB" treaty is probably a violation of the sovereign rights of Nations and peoples everywhere, including the nations that might sign it, and the dependencies that might be affected by its ratification. **Art.11(1)** *At the request of the applicant State the requested state shall...take the necessary steps to cover tax claims of the first-mentioned State as if they were its own tax claims.*

If the treaty had ever reached the implementation stage, local courts would have been compelled to use local judicial measures to enforce a foreign tax claim, whether it agrees with the tax claims or not. Furthermore, you would have had no right of appeal against a decision,

except in the country demanding payments. In addition, all your assets would be at risk - not merely to the extent of the tax claim. Other aspects of the treaty included:

Art. 17/5 The treaty permits the use of mail to serve documents in another treaty country, and the documents need not be translated.

Art. 12 Provides for assistance in collection of taxes. The requested country must generally take steps to recover final tax claims for the applicant country, including freezing of assets and the prevention of migration of the funds sought.

Art.9 allows another country's tax officials to be present during a tax examination.

Art. 2 covers the collection of state and local taxes.

INTERFIPOL is no longer a real threat to businessmen everywhere, because as of June 1988 not one country had stepped forward to sign the "ill conceived thing", although the treaty was opened for signature on January 25, 1988. We can only hope that this threat to world liberty and freedom will end up forgotten in some dusty closet, or stashed away in some library archives, unratified, unsigned - totally abandoned.

British Government refuse to sign INTERFIPOL treaty in January, 1989.

In January of 1989, the UK Government refused to sign the much reviled multilateral tax treaty, pugnaciously referred to as INTERFIPOL by some, drawn up by the Paris based OECD and the Council of Europe (COE). This is a milestone in diplomacy and may turn out to be the single most significant tax event of the century, but surely the most important development witnessed in 1989. The following (condensed) treatise appeared in the February, 1989 issue of the *Offshore Advisor*.

"A 'sinister' manifesto"

"The specter of international master files on the tax affairs of citizens receded after the UK Government decided **not to sign** the multilateral tax treaty drawn up by the OECD and the Council of Europe.

The treaty, officially known **as the Convention for Mutual Administrative Assistance in Tax** Matters, was unofficially called "sinister", an "invasion of privacy", and a

---

[19.] *What will INTERFIPOL Mean to you?*   from OFFSHORE INVESTMENT, pg 21 (June 1988)

"document as ruthless as the Communist Manifesto" by other observers.

So reviled was the OECD's proposal, it was nicknamed INTERFIPOL, or *the bastard son of the international police force.*

The main aim of the treaty was to extricate funds held in offshore tax havens, a politically attractive idea for the U.S. Government. The repatriation to the U.S. of tax free investments held in the Caribbean would go a long way toward financing the U.S. Budget deficit, without so much as pursing the lips of President George Bush. In fact, the OECD described the U.S. as "violently in favor" of signing the treaty.

The U.S. was expected to sign it within two months and by the end of the year the OECD hoped also to receive the signatures of the Government of Japan, Denmark, Finland, Norway and Sweden. Once signed, these nations would exchange tax information on resident's affairs.

Article 29(1) of the Convention extended the scope of the treaty to offshore tax havens (including the British Commonwealth havens of the Cayman Islands, Channel Islands, B.V.I., Isle of Man, Hong Kong, Bermuda, Gibraltar, Montserrat, and Turks and Caicos Islands) within reach of jurisdictions connected by common defense or economic needs. It states: *"Each state shall at the time of the signature, or when depositing its instrument of ratification, acceptance or approval, specify the territories to which this Convention shall apply."*

According to the *Offshore Advisor*, "the British decision not to sign was greeted with relief by the Channel Islands and the Isle of Man, which might conceivably have been hit hard." **Norman Lamont, Financial Secretary to the Treasury**, said that the UK's *"extensive network of double taxation treaties and European obligations already served to unearth tax evaders in offshore centres."*

West Germany and others decide not to sign the INTERFIPOL treaty.

West Germany, known for having one of the toughest internal revenue services of all the western nations, has already said they will not sign the OECD multilateral tax treaty. Others that have indicated they will have nothing to do with INTERFIPOL include Liechtenstein, Luxembourg, Malta, and Switzerland.

Through January 1, 1999 the United States maintained a network of some 61 (+) bilateral income tax treaties with other nations as follows:

Armenia	Aruba	Australia	Austria
Azerbaijan	**Barbados**	Belarus	Belgium
Bermuda [20.]	Canada	**Cyprus**	Czech Republic
Denmark	Egypt	Finland	France
Georgia	Germany	Greece	Hungary
Iceland	India	Indonesia	Ireland
Israel	Italy	**Jamaica**	Japan
Kazakstan	Korea	Kyrgyzstan	**Luxembourg**
Malta	Mexico	Moldova	Morocco
Netherlands	Netherlands Antilles		New Zealand
Norway	Pakistan	PRC (China)	Philippines
Poland	Portugal	Romania	Russia
Slovakia	South Africa	Spain	Sweden
Switzerland	Tajikistan	Thailand	
Trinidad & Tobago		Turkey	Turkmenistan
Tunisia	Ukraine	United Kingdom	
Uzbekistan			

Estate and Gift Tax Treaties

The U.S. maintains estate, and/or gift tax treaties with many countries too:

Australia	Denmark	Austria
Canada	Finland	France
Germany	Greece	Ireland
Italy	Netherlands	Japan
Norway	Sweden	UK
Switzerland	South Africa	

Reciprocal Tax Exemption Agreements for International Shipping and/or Aviation Incomes

Under IRC §883(a) U.S. source earnings of a foreign ship or aircraft are exempt from federal taxation when the earnings are derived from the operation of a ship documented or aircraft registered under the laws of a foreign country, and the foreign country grants an **equivalent exemption** to U.S. citizens and U.S. domestic corporations. Exchange of note agreements is in force between many nations.

Argentina	Belgium	**Bahamas** *
Bolivia	Brazil	Columbia
Cyprus	Denmark	Greece

[20.] The new income tax treaty with Bermuda is a limited tax treaty dealing with income of insurance companies. It was entered into force with reservations on December 2, 1988, and (1) exempts excise taxes on insurance premiums paid to foreign insurers through December 31, 1989; (2) applies to income taxes on business profits by an enterprise of insurance; and (3) provides for exchange of tax informations and mutual assistance (with certain exceptions).

El Salvador (aviation only)		Finland
India	Jordan	**Liberia**
Panama	Peru (shipping only)	
Singapore	St. Vincent & the Grenadines	
Spain	Sweden	**Taiwan**
Turkey	Venezuela	
Mauritius	Ecuador	**Hong Kong**
Isle of Man	Japan	**Luxembourg**

* Countries with concessionary or tax haven type tax laws that exempt corporate profits are **boldfaced**.

Revenue Ruling 89-49 issued on 4/3/89 provides that the following countries not listed above qualify for the reciprocal exemption by virtue of their domestic law.

Bulgaria	Cayman Islands	Portugal
Chile (shipping only)	The Netherlands	Vanuatu
The Netherlands Antilles		

Source: Tax Management International, Andre Fogarasi, Esq.; Richard Gordon, Esq.; John Venuti, Esq.; Diane Renfroe, Esq. (Arthur Andersen & Co., Washington, D.C.)

IRS expands its powers overseas

American expatriates and multinationals beware! The IRS has broadened its powers in an effort to stop an estimated $2.3 billion in tax losses caused by the failure of some 1.1 million American expatriates living abroad who fail to file U.S. tax returns. Beginning in 1988 the State Department will be required to provide the IRS with a list of all Americans applying for passports, so that the IRS can monitor the lists in search of Americans working abroad. The IRS will be sending its agents to 65 cities in 50 countries to help Americans with their tax questions. • A recent IRS survey of 12,000 foreign owned corporations operating within the U.S. shows that most of these companies are paying only a 1% tax on their U.S. operations, while thousands pay no tax. The IRS plans to add more than 100 auditors to its staff to combat this problem.
• The number of U.S. companies owned by foreigners has risen from 6,000 in 1972 to 38,000 in 1983. While these companies gross an estimated $10.6 billion, they pay less than 1% to the U.S. Treasury in taxes. To cope with the problem, the IRS is importing tax specialists from *academia* to develop new systems of financial analysis and plan to establish a training college for its international examiners.

Source: *Offshore Investment (Isle of Man)*

In 1997, new or updated treaties were negotiated between the United States and Austria, Ireland, Luxembourg, South Africa, Switzerland, Thailand, and Turkey; a protocol was negotiated with Canada. These treaties were ratified in December 1997 and (with the exception of Luxembourg) have entered into force. Hong Kong is not covered under the tax treaty with China.

Questions on all tax treaties can be sent to

IRS, Assistant Commissioner (International), Attention: OP:IN:D:CS,
950 L'Enfant Plaza South, S.W.,
Washington, DC 20024, USA.

For details on tax treaties and conventions, get IRS Publication 54, Tax Guide for U.S. Citizens and Resident Aliens Abroad, and Publication 901, U.S. Tax Treaties, by writing to the IRS Forms Distribution Center, P.O. Box 85627, Richmond, VA 23285-5627, USA.

Capital Gains

Most treaties provide for the exemption of gains from the sale or exchange of personal property. Generally, gains from the sale or exchange of real property located in the United States are taxable.

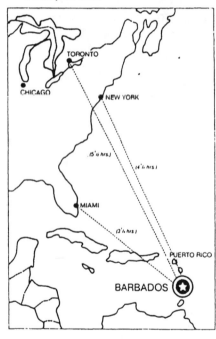

CHAPTER 14 • The Internal Revenue Code

"The Internal Revenue Code is the most complicated statute in the world. It contains the excrescence of almost 85 years of conflict between government and taxpayer. Over that time many provisions have been added by Congress to deal with perceived abuses. Some of these are so complex that great effort is required to fathom them. Quite often, the most complex provisions are fairly predictable in application once deciphered. Indeed, that is often their principal justification - that they provide a relatively clear and certain result.

Other portions of the tax law, in the Code and elsewhere, are much simpler to comprehend. In contrast to some more complex provisions however, many of these simpler tax rules are quite difficult to apply and frequently produce results which are not east to predict.

The marriage of these two sorts of provisions is probably inevitable. Predictability has a high value in economic planning; complex provisions are perhaps unavoidable in attempting to deal precisely with the vast array of sophisticated transactions structured by taxpayers, lawyers, accountants, and investment bankers. On the other hand, even a statute which became mythically prolix could not hope to deal comprehensively with the infinite verity of taxpayers' behavior. Thus, the tax law is led irresistibly to incorporate at least some of the fundamental rules to protect the system from subversion, despite the cost of lessened predictability.

Many of the Code provisions affecting foreign persons (companies, individuals, trusts, partnerships) or foreign income are of the first kind; complex, detailed, difficult to understand and grasp, but quite often fairly easy to apply in practice once the complexities are mastered. By contrast, many of the tax accounting notions applicable to foreign persons are often of the second kind, deceptively simple to understand, but often quite difficult to apply in practice. Yet accounting rules are the very earth upon which many of the most complex foreign tax towers rest." [1].

Up to now we have studied only a tiny part of **the Internal Revenue** Code relating to Controlled Foreign Corporations, Passive Foreign Investment Companies (i.e., the other Pentapus tax problems) and some of the foreign trust provisions. But, the **Code** contains many other provisions that influence offshore transactions and operations in tax havens and non-havens alike. In this chapter we will outline some of the more important **Code** provisions the tax planner should become familiar with. [2].

Income of United States Citizens in Foreign Countries

Would you like to live and work in the Bahamas or another tax haven and legally not owe Uncle Sam any taxes on your offshore earnings? Since World War II the United States has provided exemptions from Federal Income Taxes to citizens who live and work in a foreign country most of the year. In the 1940's, the first $40,000 of one's **foreign earned income** was excludable from income taxes. Due to inflation, Congress decided to increase the exclusion. The amount you can exclude for the year 2,000 is $76,000.

U.S. citizens and resident aliens of the U.S. who live outside the U.S. continue to be taxed on their worldwide incomes. However, **individuals** who live and work abroad, who meet certain requirements, may exclude up to $74,000 in year 1999 of their *foreign earned income* from their gross income. In the case of married taxpayers, each may compute the exclusion limit separately. Thus, a husband and wife with community income of $148,000 can exclude the entire amount if each works abroad and each can pass the so-called bona fide residence test or physical presence test.

---

1. - **Professor Harvey P. Dale**, with the NYU School of Law, from an article titled *"Tax Accounting for Foreign Persons"*, published by the Practicing Law Institute in Manhattan, NY in their Thirteenth Annual Institute on International Taxation (1983).

2. See Chapters 2, 3 and Chapter 12, i.e., IRC 951-58, IRC 542, 532, 552, IRC 671-679, infra.

Aside from the general $74,000 exclusion, taxpayers who live and work abroad may elect to exclude an additional amount based upon employer-provided foreign housing costs. This **housing expense exclusion** is equal to (1) the taxpayer's "housing expenses" (the excess of the reasonable cost of providing housing for the taxpayer and his family - including a second foreign household for the taxpayer's spouse and children if they do not reside with the taxpayer because of adverse conditions), over (2) "a base housing amount", computed as 16% of the yearly salary of a federal employee at grade level GS-14, step 1. For 1988 the salary is $46,649, so the "base housing amount" equals $7,464.

Example #1: George Adams is a U.S. citizen, and a calendar year taxpayer. George was a bona fide resident (tax home) of the Turks & Caicos Islands for the entire year of 1988. George as a director for the Barclays Bank in the Turks receives a $70,000 salary in 1988. Barclay's Bank provides George with housing with a fair market value of $15,000, making George's total compensation package equal to $85,000. In addition, George pays $10,000 for housing expenses. George's gross income and foreign earned income for 1988 equals $85,000, and George elects to take the foreign earned income exclusion of Code.Sec. 911(a)(2).

First, George must compute his housing cost amount exclusion by reducing his housing expenses ($25,000) by the base housing amount of $7,464, arriving at a housing cost amount of $17,536.

Next, George must compute the foreign earned income exclusion. Since George's housing cost amount ($17,536) and foreign earned income exclusion ($70,000) cannot exceed George's total foreign earned income of $85,000, George's foreign earned income exclusion for 1988 is limited to $67,464. Under IRC §911(a)(1) and (2) George is allowed to exclude a total of $85,000.

Individuals
Increased Section 911 Exclusion

For tax years beginning after 1997, the $70,000 limitation on the exclusion for foreign earned income is gradually increased to $80,000 in increments of $2,000 each year. In addition, the limitation on the exclusion will be indexed for inflation beginning in 2008.

SECTION 911 EXCLUSION INCREASES

Year	Exclusion Amount
1998	$72,000
1999	$74,000
2000	$76,000
2001	$78,000
2002 and after	$80,000

This change is important not only to U.S. citizens and residents earning foreign earned income, but also to their employers, as compensation packages for expatriate workers usually take the exclusion into account. (Act section 1172; section 911(b))

Qualified Individual

To qualify for the general foreign earned income exclusion and the additional exclusion for housing expenses, an individual's tax home must be in a foreign country and he/she must establish qualified residence either through the use of the *bona fide residence* or *physical presence test*.

Bona fide residence test: To pass the bona fide residence test a U.S. citizen must reside in the foreign country for an uninterrupted period that includes an entire calendar year (365 days). This means "settling down" in that country with some permanence. Once an individual meets the bona fide residence test he is a **qualified individual**.

Physical presence test: A citizen or resident of the U.S. whose tax home is a foreign country will be eligible for the foreign earned income exclusion if he is physically present in a foreign country for 330 days out of any 12 consecutive month period.

The physical presence time requirement of 330 full days out of any 12 consecutive month period is an important benefit to individuals who cannot meet the bona fide residence test because they were not residents for 12 months. In addition, the physical presence test allows for visits to the U.S. of up to 35 days within any 365 day period.

Example #2: George Adams undertakes a foreign assignment from June 1, 1987 to May 1, 1988. He is present in the foreign country for the entire period; thus he meets the physical presence test since he is present in the foreign country for 335 days during a 12-month period. Note, George could not meet the bona fide residence test because he was resident in the foreign country for less than 1 calendar year (365 days).

Foreign Earned Income - Defined

Foreign earned income means wages, salaries, professional fees and other amounts received as compensation by an individual for services performed in a foreign country. Note, it is the place where the services are performed that characterizes an individual's income as foreign, not the place of payment. [3.]

Foreign earned income does **not** include such items as interests or dividends, nor does it include amounts received as a pension or annuity, amounts paid by the U.S. government or its agencies to its employees, and dividends disguised as compensation. In the case of a self-employed individual where both personal services and capital are material income producing factors, the Internal Revenue Service regulations provide guidance as to what portion - not to exceed 30% - of the net profits is considered earned income.

Example #3: In 1988, **A** an architect operates his business as a sole proprietorship in which capital is not a material income producing factor. **A** receives $80,000 in gross receipts, all foreign source earned income, and incurs $40,000 of deductible business expenses definitely related to the foreign earned income. **A** elects to exclude $70,000 under IRC §911(a)(1). The expenses must be apportioned to excluded earned income as follows: $40,000 X $70,000/$80,000. Thus, $35,000 of the $40,000 in business expenses are not deductible by **A** when **A** computes his U.S. income taxes.

Ignoring any housing cost exclusion **A** might have available to reduce his taxes further, just $5,000 in taxable income would be reportable to the IRS in 1988. That is $80,000 minus $70,000 (statutory exclusion) = $10,000 gross income minus $5,000 in leftover business deductions = $5,000 taxable income.

Since **A** is permitted to claim all personal allowances and deductions common to all U.S. citizens, **A** could claim himself and his wife as dependents on his Form 1040 and deduct an additional $3,900 from the $5,000 (above), leaving just $1,100 subject to federal income tax.

Using the 1988 IRS tax tables, **A** would need to write a check for $163 by April 15, 1989 to meet his 1988 U.S. tax liability. Absent the foreign earned income exclusion cited above, A would have $36,100 in taxable income and would need to write a check for $8,405 to meet his 1988 U.S. tax liability. Note A's wife could claim her $70,000 foreign earned income exclusion for any compensation she might earn offshore too, provided she meets either the bona fide residence or the physical presence test. [4.]

Example #3 above was taken word for word from the current U.S. Treasury Regulations 1.911-6(d)(Example (1). In the Treasury's example architect A's gross receipts equaled $1,000,000 and deductions equaled $500,000. The Treasury's example did not compute the actual taxes that would have been saved by A - the U.S. taxpayer.

Tax home in tax haven AOK

The fact that the U.S. citizen's foreign country tax home is in a **no or low-tax haven** like the Bahamas or Turks & Caicos Islands is not a material factor for obtaining the foreign income and housing exclusions. **T.Reg.911-2(h)** says *"The term "foreign country" when used in a geographical sense includes any territory under the sovereignty of a government other than the U.S."*

Only foreign earned income is permitted to be excluded under U.S. Code-Section §911. Bank interest, dividends and capital gains from trading in stocks and bonds are not considered foreign earned income and are not excludable.

Persons wishing to shelter larger amounts of income and capital might investigate the use of a Bahamian holding company or trust. A properly structured Bahamian holding company can buy and sell U.S. publicly traded stocks like Exxon or Mobil free from capital gains taxes, provided no office or other business is carried-on within the United States by the company.

Deceptively Simple IRC §897

Section §897 was introduced to us with the Foreign Investment in U.S. Real Property Act of 1980 (FIRPTA). Before its enactment, shares in

---

[3.] It is immaterial whether the payer of the compensation is a resident of the United States, if services rendered are performed by the recipient in the foreign country. Consequently, U.S. source income would actually be considered foreign source income in the hands of the foreign recipient under the United States source of income rules.

[4.] Tax havens that do not tax individuals include the Cayman Islands, Bermuda, Vanuatu, the Turks & Caicos Islands, the Bahamas, Anguilla, Monaco, Campione, and Nauru. Note that while they are not tax havens, Bahrain, Saudi Arabia, the United Arab Emirates, Qatar, Oman, Uruguay, and Kuwait do not impose individual income taxes.

both publicly traded U.S. companies and privately held U.S. companies could be disposed of by a foreign person (corporation, trust or nonresident alien individual, etc.) free from all capital gains taxes. U.S. real estate holdings could also be disposed free from capital gains taxes under pre-FIRPTA law.

When you first undertake to decipher IRC §897(a), you're apt to conclude that all dispositions of *U.S. real property* are now subject to U.S. capital gains taxes. But, upon further review you learn that IRC §897(c)(3) does not purport to tax the gain on certain publicly traded stock, regularly traded on an established stock exchange, and of which is only a portfolio type holding of under 5%. Moreover, sale of closely held corporate bonds or publicly traded corporate bonds are in no way affected by IRC §897. FIRPTA did end the tax free treatment previously enjoyed by foreigners on dispositions of U.S. Real estate type holdings, and for this reason FIRPTA is a momentous piece of tax legislation.

Predictable IRC §482

The Internal Revenue Code authorizes the IRS to reallocate income between related entities if there is a deliberate attempt to shift income away from the United States. The term *entities* for purposes of IRC §482 refers to corporations, individuals, trusts, and partnerships. For the IRS to make an allocation under the Service must show that a **common control** between entities exists. Common control includes any kind of control through voting power or otherwise. Control is based on the factual evidence, and can exist without voting power. The presence or absence of the legal right to control the entity through voting shares is not needed to invoke IRC§ §482.

In the early 1970's, the IRS challenged the giant drug manufacturer Eli Lilly when Lilly's Puerto Rican subsidiary sold its offshore manufactured darvon and darvon-N products back to the parent in the U.S. at inflated prices to allow Lilly USA the lion's share of the profit. Citing IRC §482, the IRS won its case in federal court and Eli Lilly USA was required to increase its share of the profits by $12,500,000.

Ironically, the courts held that the use of the Congressionally-sanctioned tax haven Puerto Rico was not an issue, and found that had Lilly

PR sold the darvon to an independent marketer (or in PR or overseas), instead of to the parent company in the U.S., the IRS would not have been able to launch a successful challenge using IRC §482.

IRC §367

IRC §367 has been part of the Code for many years. It was originally designed to prevent foreign corporations from liquidating their U.S. subsidiaries under one of the tax free reorganization provisions of IRC §332, 351, 354, 355, 356, or 361 shrewdly transferring the profits offshore tax free. Changes and amendments to this legislation appear in almost every tax act Congress passes.

Repeal of the General Utilities Doctrine (IRC §337)

One onerous change made by the **Tax Reform act of 1986** was the repeal of IRC §337 - the **General Utilities Doctrine**. Under the new law, U.S. companies and foreign companies that liquidate after January 1, 1987 pursuant to "new" IRC §337 (12 month liquidations) will be subject to tax on any appreciation at the corporate level, and cannot shift the incidence of taxation to the shareholders, thereby reducing or eliminating all tax liability.

Prior to the repeal of IRC §337, a foreign company could simply liquidate its U.S. subsidiary under IRC §337 within 12 months of adopting a plan of complete liquidation. The foreign shareholders of a Section §337 liquidation would typically escape U.S. taxation by structuring the deal so it would happen under the protection of a U.S. income tax treaty that reduced the dividend withholding tax to 5% or 15%. For example, under the Netherlands-US Income Tax Treaty the dividend withholding tax was reduced from the statutory 30% to just 5%, which in the case of a Dutch holding company would be the only taxes paid in lieu of the "participation exemption" allowed Dutch holding companies.

While tax free liquidations under IRC §337 are no longer possible, sending dividends in large chunks, even borrowing to pay the dividend, to an offshore parent company in a country with a favorable U.S. Income Tax Treaty is a common tactic used to avoid U.S. taxes. Tax practitioners call this strategy **dividend stripping**.

U.S. Gift Taxes

The gift tax is an excise tax payable by the donor of a gift. There is no integration of the federal gift tax provisions with the federal income tax provisions, and it's technically possible for both taxes to be applied to a transfer by a foreign or domestic entity. Fortunately, the U.S. gift tax provisions don't have much reach when applied to offshore corporations and trusts because of the type of assets held, and the place where they are located.

In order for the gift tax to apply two requirements must be present. McGraw Hill writes in *International Estate* that gifts by nondomiciliaries are not taxed unless, (1) there is a transfer of property [see IRC §2511(a)(1)]; and (2) the property is situated in the U.S. at the time the transfer occurs. If both requirements are satisfied than to compute the gift the value of the property at the time of the transfer must be determined. [5.]

Under T.Regs.§25.2511-3 of the **Federal Estate and Gift Tax Code**, the gift tax applies only to transfers of real property and tangible personal property situated in the U.S. by a nonresident or citizen of the U.S. who is an expatriate. Therefore, a foreign trust can transfer stocks or bonds, as well as cash or currency, to a U.S. beneficiary free from gift tax. In fact, the only property a foreign trust is prohibited from transferring (assuming it qualifies as a non-resident alien) is U.S. real estate, and tangible personal property (cars, airplanes, personal computers, etc.) Stocks and bonds are usually considered intangible property.

U.S. Estate Taxes

One of the reasons foreigners (called *nonresident alien individuals* by the IRS - **NRAI**) often choose to engage offshore companies to hold their U.S. investments is to avoid U.S. estate taxes that they can incur should they hold U.S. investments (stocks, bonds, condominiums, real estate, raw land, etc.) directly in their own name.

Prior to the **Technical & Miscellaneous Revenue Act of 1988 (TAMRA)**, non-US citizens, whether or not they were U.S. residents, who held property interests in the U.S. (including stocks and bonds and real estate) were subject to U.S. estate taxes at rates up to 30% on estates over $2,000,000, with no marital deduction permitted. If a nonresident suddenly died, the fair market value of his U.S. assets at the time of his death would be subject to U.S. estate taxes.

TAMRA changed the applicable tax rates to 18% on property interests of $10,000 or less, and to 55% for property interests in excess of $3 million. However, the unified credit of $600,000 available to a U.S. citizen's estate is not available to the foreigner unless he lives in a country that has a favorable estate tax treaty with the U.S., and then only a portion of the unified credit is usable. If there is no treaty, the credit will exempt only $60,000 from U.S. estate taxes.

Furthermore, under the new law, nonresidents will be permitted the marital deduction only when the spouse is a U.S. citizen.

Nevertheless, as was the case under prior law, when shares of a foreign corporation are owned by a nonresident alien, they are excluded from his estate and are not subject to U.S. estate taxes, even if the only assets of the foreign corporation are U.S. real estate, condominiums, U.S. stocks and bonds. When a nonresident forms an offshore holding company in a tax haven that has no estate or income taxes he effectively sidesteps all U.S. and foreign estate taxes outright, even though the foreign company's assets might consist entirely of U.S. property. [6.]

IRS Disclosure Forms

Most people get genuinely upset when they find out about an IRS information return, fearing terrible things are in store for them once they furnish the information requested. In truth, it can probably be said that more dreadful things can happen to you if you don't file the necessary documents.

An IRS or Treasury Department information return is not an income tax return like your Form 1040. No federal income tax liability is incurred just from supplying the information requested. Frequently, the details asked for are mundane,

---

5. McGraw Hill provides two definitions of nonresident donors. The first is a person who at the date of the transfer was domiciled outside the U.S. The second is a nonresident alien who was domiciled outside the U.S. and not a citizen. Corporations, trusts or individuals can be the donor of a gift.

6. See IRC §2104(a), §2101(d).

such as your name and address, your social security number, etc. Sometimes you are requested to furnish the name of the grantor or transferor to a foreign trust.

New Treasury Form F-90-22.1

Treasury form TD F-90-22.1 is an information return that must be filed if you have a signature authority or financial interest in a foreign bank account or financial account. There is a difference between the two categories of filers, so you'll have to read the instructions on the back of the form carefully.

Treasury Form TD F-90-22.1 is the form most people want to avoid filing, fearing a paper trail will be started once the information is furnished. While this may be true, the information asked for, as in the case of a signature authority (but no financial interest) is so trifling and the fine for not filing so steep, that it is good advice to comply with the law. A complete Form TD F-90-22.1 (with instructions) is in the appendix for your convenience.

Item 26

Item 26 (United States Persons with Authority Over but No Interest In an Account) is interesting in that the information to be furnished the U.S. Treasury allows the filer to keep the real beneficial owner's name (and address) of the foreign bank account confidential.

Item 26 says, "If you complete items 27-35 for one or more accounts in which no U.S. person had a financial interest, you may state on the first line of this item, in lieu of supplying information about the owner, *No U.S. person had a financial interest in the foreign accounts.*" The form goes on to say that this statement must be based upon the actual belief of the person filing the form after he or she has taken reasonable measures to endure its correctness.

Under General definitions you are shown how you can have a financial interest in a foreign bank account. The rules for determining financial interest follow closely the rules for determining what is a Controlled Foreign Corporation under IRC §957.

Example. P.J. Roosevelt, IV owns 4% of the stock in a Turk & Caicos company. Mr. Roosevelt's job is to pick and recommend investments for the T&C Company. Being the financial advisor for the company, P.J. Roosevelt has a signature authority over the company's bank and security accounts, but because he owns less than 50% of the company's outstanding stock, Mr. Roosevelt is not deemed to have a financial interest in the accounts. [1]

NEW Form 5471 is an information return to be filed by a U.S. person who is a director or shareholder in a foreign company. A 10% or more ownership in an offshore company triggers the necessity to file Form 5471. Under pre 1997 rules, the threshold of ownership was only 5%, so the U.S. taxpayer can actually own more shares of an offshore company (today) before he has to file form 5471.

Form 5471 is filed once, when you file your U.S. tax return. It need only be filed again when you increase or decrease your holding by 10%. **A fine of $1,000 may result for failure to file.** The form states civil or criminal penalties may also result if reasonable cause for not filing cannot be established. Form 5471 is not a tax return.

Form 5471 asks for an abundance of information, but it is not an annual return and need be filed only once in most instances. Whether you have to complete all the schedules depends on the percentage of value stock held, whether the company is controlled and has subpart F income, and whether it pays you a dividend. For those going offshore a partial copy of Form 5471 is provided in the appendix. Write the IRS for the complete form, including the instructions.

New Form 3520-A (1998) for reporting transfers to foreign trusts as been updated and expanded by the Treasury Department. See the appendix of this book for some details. Contact the IRS and have them send you the instructions for this form, as they are too lengthy to include in this book.

---

1. The Roosevelts (along with other U.S. investors - including members of the Dupont family of Delaware) are known to be investors in the island of Providenciales in the Turks & Caicos Islands. Back in the early 1970's they (through a company called Provident, Limited) purchased over 4,000 acres on the island of Providenciales where a multimillion dollar resort and marina were built. The UK government later chipped in $12,000,000 for an international airport capable of landing jet aircraft, so to bring the rich, famous and other tourists into the area.

Investigating powers of the Internal Revenue Service

Congress has given the Internal Revenue Service broad powers to compel production of information it requires to ascertain tax liability or to collect tax. There are several approaches the IRS can initiate to get books and records (and other tax information) from the taxpayer. [7.]

IRC §7602(a) permits the IRS to (1) examine any books, papers, records or other data, and to take testimony under oath, and (2) summon a taxpayer or any other person, calling for him to appear, produce books and records, and give testimony. IRC §7602(a) is most often applied to summon the records of domestic taxpayers, foreign corporations doing business within the United States, and the foreign operations of U.S. companies. IRC §7602 can be used to secure information about a *U.S. shareholder's* offshore tax haven company, but in practice it is only occasionally used by the IRS's 505 international examiners.

IRC §982 (Admissibility of Documentation Maintained in Foreign Countries) allows the IRS to use its summons power to obtain records located outside the United States, so long as the summons is validly served on a person with custody or control of the records. Special procedures apply to such summons and special problems are encountered when trying to enforce them. An informal document request under IRC §982 is probably the first brush with the IRS that U.S. shareholders of a tax haven holding company will face, if they face any investigation at all.

Grand Jury Investigations. In certain criminal investigations, the IRS will seek authorization from the Department of Justice to convene a grand jury tax investigation. Where there is a grand jury in place, the summons process (above) will not be used. Instead, the grand jury will issue subpoenas for books and records.

IRS audits of domestic entities, citizens and residents could be initiated. U.S. subsidiaries of foreign corporations can also be audited.

Compelling Production of Foreign Records

To compel production of foreign based records under an IRS or grand jury subpoena, a U.S. court must have personal jurisdiction over the custodian or person in control of the documents. The fact that a corporation's records are physically located outside the U.S. does not excuse it from producing them if they are in its possession and the court has jurisdiction over the corporation.

Summons, for the most part, are only issued to domestic subsidiaries and branches of foreign parent companies operating within the United States. They can also be issued to domestic companies that have subsidiaries or branches in tax haven jurisdictions like the Bahamas, Switzerland, Bermuda or Cayman.

An IRS summons could not be issued to a foreign trustee if the trust does not have any U.S. contacts, and custody and control lie outside the jurisdiction of the U.S. courts.

Neither could the IRS use its summons power to obtain books and records from a foreign company, although the IRS could summons the production of documents from a U.S. shareholder or director of a foreign company. It is unlikely that the IRS would use its summons power as a first mode of attack. More likely, it would seek to gather information through the filing of Form 5471, or perhaps with an informal document request pursuant to IRC §682. Notwithstanding the fact that the Cayman Islands, the have strict back secrecy forbidding the disclosure of financial information by companies, banks and other professionals working in their jurisdictions, the IRS would be limited in their inquires to U.S. shareholders or U.S. directors of the offshore company.

The case of Marc Rich v. the U.S. Government

It can probably be said that the IRS will only use its summons power in cases where extreme abuse and disregard for the regulations have happened. Cases winnable in the U.S. courts and are likely to produce the largest amount of tax revenues for the government are ordinarily the first priority. This was the scenario in Marc Rich & Co., AG (a Swiss company) v. U.S., where the

---

7. IRC §7602(a) authorizes the IRS to use summons power for any *bona fide* civil audit for tax collection purpose. The IRS has no authority to compel production of documents or testimony other than that specifically granted by statues. U.S. v. Powell 379 U.S. 48 (1964), *U.S. v. LaSalle National Bank,* 437 U.S. 298 (1978).

IRS invoked IRC §482 (intercompany price transfer rules) as a foundation for their case.

Under IRC §482, when two or more organizations, trades or businesses (whether or not incorporated in the U.S.) are owned or controlled directly or indirectly by the same interests, and they conspire to shift income away from the U.S., the Secretary may distribute, apportion or allocate gross income, deductions and credits between or among such organizations to clearly reflect the income of such organization. Control, for purposes of IRC §482 is any kind of control. Voting control is not essential under IRC §482. The mere fact that the entities are somehow related is enough to show control.

In the Marc Rich case, Rich's wholly owned U.S. subsidiaries (refineries) were selling oil at bargain basement prices to Rich's offshore companies, thereby allowing the lion share of the profits to go offshore. The U.S. government grand jury subpoenaed Rich (who was a U.S. citizen), and put him under indictment to extradite him back to the U.S. to stand trial.

The Swiss never allowed the U.S. authorities to extradite Rich (who claimed Switzerland as his home), because tax evasion is not a criminal offense in Switzerland. Marc Rich became somewhat of a local folk hero in his home Canton near Zurich. Eventually, Rich's U.S. subsidiaries were forced to pay over $400,000,000 in taxes and penalties. They were than allowed to resume operations, although Marc Rich remains under Federal indictment to this day.

Naturally, the IRS was at a decided advantage here. Rich's U.S. refineries were continually at risk of being confiscated to pay the tax bill.

Is there a moral or lesson to be gleaned from the Marc Rich fiasco? Yes, there sure is. If you are operating in violation of the Internal Revenue Code's rules and regulation (as Rich's organization was), and if you have substantial assets located within the U.S. which the IRS can commandeer to pay the claim, and the dollar amount of your tax liability is large, than, yes, you probably are at greater risk than say a tax haven holding company, where assets are held offshore outside IRS jurisdiction.

Obtaining an IRS Revenue Ruling

It would be nice to be able to obtain an IRS Revenue Ruling before you go ahead with a particular offshore transaction, but rulings are not always procurable.

A Revenue Ruling is not a law passed by Congress; it is a proclamation by the Internal Revenue Service explaining the facts as they relate to a particular set of laws. Revenue Rulings are the published conclusions of the IRS concerning the application of tax law to an entire set of facts.

Revenue procedures are official statements of procedures that either affect the rights or duties of taxpayers or other members of the public, or should be a matter of public knowledge. The purpose of these rulings is to promote a uniform application of the tax laws, and therefore IRS employees must follow the rulings. While taxpayers can rely on the rulings, they can also appeal adverse return examination decisions based on the rulings to the Tax court or other Federal courts.

Rev.Proc 87-4 is a 7 page pamphlet issued by the Department of the Treasury (Internal Revenue Service). The purpose of this revenue procedure booklet is to provide guidelines for obtaining rulings, closing agreements and information letters on federal tax issues under the jurisdiction of the Associate Chief Counsel (International) and to provide information concerning determination letters under the jurisdiction of the Assistant Commissioner (International) and District Directors. The Associate Chief Council (International) is responsible for the uniform interpretation and application of the federal income tax laws and income tax treaties relating to international transactions.

The Office of Associate Chief Council (International) (hereafter called the "National Office" or "NO") generally will issue rulings on prospective transactions and on completed transactions provided, in the case of completed transactions, that the ruling request is submitted before the return is filed for the year in which the transaction occurred.

The National Office ordinarily does not issue a ruling if, at the time the ruling is requested, the identical issue is involved in the taxpayer's tax return for an earlier period, and the issue is being examined by a District Director or the Assistant Commissioner (International), or is being considered by an Appeals Office. An exception is allowed if the issue involved is subject to an IRS closing agreement.

The National Office does not issue rulings to business, trade, or industrial associations or similar groups concerning the application of tax laws to members of the group. However, it may issue rulings to these groups on their own tax status of liability if the request meets the requirements of this revenue procedure.

No rulings for hypothetical transactions.

A ruling will not be issued on alternative plans or proposed transactions or on hypothetical situations. Also, a ruling will not be issued on transactions which will not be executed within a reasonable period of time.

The **NO** ordinarily will not issue a ruling in certain areas because of the factual nature of the issues involved, or for other reasons.

No "comfort" rulings

The National Office will not issue a "comfort" ruling with respect to an issue that is clearly and adequately addressed by statute, regulations, decisions of the Supreme Court, income tax treaties, revenue rulings, or revenue procedures absent extraordinary circumstances (i.e., a request for a ruling required by a government regulatory authority in order to effectuate a transaction). However, the **NO** will respond with a general information letter which either indicates the Service's position with respect to the ruling request or directs the taxpayer to published guidance relevant to the issue.

The National Office will not issue a ruling with respect to whether a transaction has a bona fide business purpose or whether its principal purpose is the reduction of Federal Taxes.

Rulings where no regulatory guidance exists.

The National Office will consider issuing rulings involving the interpretation of statutory provision in areas in which regulatory guidance does not exist, regardless of whether there is an open regulation project. This section is inapplicable to statutory provisions requiring legislative regulations. Taxpayers are advised to contact the **NO** orally or in writing to inquire whether the **NO** will consider issuing a ruling

absent regulatory guidelines. Any preliminary decision to rule is not binding however.

Determination Letters

A **"determination letter"** is a written statement issued by a District Director or Assistant Commissioner (International) in response to a written inquiry by a taxpayer that applies the principles and precedents previously announced by the National Office to a specific set of facts. A determination letter will be issued only when a determination can be made on the basis of clearly established rules in the statute or regulations, Supreme Court Decisions, or other published revenue rulings that specifically answer the question presented. A determination letter may be issued only with respect to completed transactions. A determination letter has the same effect as a ruling, however the District Director or Assistant Commissioner (International) may modify or revoke a determination letter.

Information Letters

An **"Information Letter"** is a statement issued by either the Office of the Chief Counsel, a District Director, or the Assistant Commissioner (International) that calls attention to well-established interpretation or principle of tax law, without applying it to a specific set of facts. At the discretion of the National Office, an information letter may be issued if a request for a ruling indicates that the taxpayer is seeking general information or if the request for a ruling fails to meet the requirements of this revenue procedure. An information letter is advisory only and has no binding effect in the Internal Revenue Service.

Closing Agreements

At the discretion of the National Office, taxpayers may be asked or, at the request of the taxpayer, be permitted to enter into a closing agreement as a condition precedent to the issuance of a ruling. A *"Closing Agreement"* is an agreement between the Commissioner of the Internal Revenue and a taxpayer on specific issues or liability that is entered into under the authority in Section 7121 of the Code.

Under section 10511 of the Revenue Act of 1987, a user fee of $300 must accompany a ruling request in order for the Service to process the request.

Sing Yankee Doodle Dandy • IRS issues new reporting requirements for cash transfers to foreign corporations

The U.S. Treasury Department now requires cash transfers exceeding $100,000 to a foreign corporation during a 12 month period to be reported on Form 926. These new reporting rules are effective from February 5, 1999.

Under prior law, U.S. persons could transfer any amount in cash (in a capitalization), and there was no reporting requirements on Form 926. Taxpayers were required to report stock ownership in a foreign corporation when the shareholding exceeded 5% (value only) under old Form 5471, but Form 5471 was revised for 1998. For transactions occurring after December 31, 1997, the threshold for stock ownership of a foreign corporation that results in the reporting obligations of section 6046 has increased from 5% (in value) to 10% (of value or vote).

The IRS is going to be flooded with hundreds of thousands of Form 926s every year. The clients of every stockbroker up on Wall Street will need to be made aware of the new reporting requirements. If a client purchases over $100,000 in stock in any Canadian company or British company or Japanese company or South American company, Form 926 must be filed. There are steep fines for not reporting.

Wall Street firms trading for their own account must also file a 926 for every foreign stock purchase that exceeds $100,000 in any foreign private or public company – anywhere in the world.

Later in chapter we will show you several tax planning techniques that you can use for cash transfers exceeding $100,000. Subscribers to our newsletter can also call or email their questions and comments to me at taxman@batelnet.bs.

Background
Taxpayer Relief Act of 1997

In the Taxpayer Relief Act of 1997 (TRA 1997), Public Law 105-34 (111 Stat. 983 (1997)), Congress significantly modified the information reporting requirements with respect to foreign partnerships under sections 6038, 6038B and 6046A (and also amended section 6501(c)(8) to provide that the statute of limitations on the assessment of tax under section 6038, 6038B and 6046A does not expire until three years after the information required under those sections is reported). Certain of these modifications also affect reporting requirements with respect to foreign corporations.

Section 6038B and Transfers to Foreign Corporations

Section 6038B, as enacted in 1984, provided that United States persons that made certain transfers of property to foreign corporations were required to report those transfers in the manner prescribed by regulations. Prior to the enactment of TRA 1997, section 6038B imposed a penalty for failure to comply with the regulations equal to 25 percent of the gain realized on the exchange, unless the failure was due to reasonable cause and not to willful neglect. Thus, in the case of a transfer of cash or unappreciated property to a foreign corporation, no penalty was imposed under section 6038B if the transfer was not reported. Section 1144(c) of TRA 1997 modified the penalty applicable to the failure to furnish information required to be reported under section 6038B. The modified penalty is equal to 10 percent of the fair market value of the property at the time of the transfer.

In response to TRA 1997, Treasury and the IRS issued final regulations under section 6038B (TD 8770 at 63 FR 33568; June 19, 1998), in conjunction with regulations under section 367(a), to clarify that transfers to corporations of unappreciated property other than cash that occur on or after July 20, 1998, generally are required to be reported in accordance with §1.6038B-1(b). The preamble to the final regulations stated that rules regarding transfers of cash to foreign corporations would be provided in future regulations.

The Final Regulations

Sec. 1.6038B-1 Reporting of certain transfers to foreign corporations.

(b) Time and manner of reporting--(1) In general--(i) Reporting procedure. Except for stock or securities qualifying under the special reporting rule of paragraph (b)(2) of this section, or cash, which is subject to special rules contained in paragraph (b)(3) of this section, any U.S. person that makes a transfer described in section 6038B(a)(1)(A), 367(d) or (e)(1), is required to report pursuant to section 6038B and the rules of this section and must attach the required information to Form 926, ``Return by Transferor of Property to a Foreign Corporation.''

(3) Special rule for transfers of cash. A U.S. person that transfers cash to a foreign corporation must report the transfer if--

(i) Immediately after the transfer such person holds directly, indirectly, or by attribution (determined under the rules of section 318(a), as modified by section 6038(e)(2)) at least 10 percent of the total voting power or the total value of the foreign corporation; or

(ii) The amount of cash transferred by such person or any related person (determined under section 267(b)(1) through (3) and (10) through (12)) to such foreign corporation during the 12-month period ending on the date of the transfer exceeds $100,000.

(c) Information required with respect to transfers described in section 6038B(a)(1)(A). A United States person that transfers property to a foreign corporation in an exchange described in section 6038B(a)(1)(A) (including cash and other unappreciated property) must provide the following information, in paragraphs labeled to correspond with the number or letter set forth in this paragraph (c) and

Sec. 1.6038B-1T(c)(1) through (5).

(g) Effective dates. This section applies to transfers occurring on or after July 20, 1998, except that the first sentence of paragraph (b)(1)(i), paragraph (b)(3), and the first sentence of paragraph (c) apply to transfers occurring in taxable years beginning after February 5, 1999. See Sec. 1.6038B-1T for transfers occurring prior to July 20, 1998.

Par. 3. Section 1.6038B-2 is added to read as follows: Sec. 1.6038B-2 Reporting of certain transfers to foreign partnerships.

(a) Reporting requirements--(1) Requirement to report transfers. A United States person that transfers property to a foreign partnership in a contribution described in section 721 (including section 721(b)) must report that transfer on Form 8865 ``Information Return of U.S. Persons With Respect to Certain Foreign Partnerships'' pursuant to section 6038B and the rules of this section, if--

(i) Immediately after the transfer, the United States person owns, directly, indirectly, or by attribution, at least a 10-percent interest in the partnership, as defined in section 6038(e)(3)(C) and the regulations thereunder; or

(ii) The value of the property transferred, when added to the value of any other property transferred in a section 721 contribution by such person (or any related person) to such partnership during the 12-month period ending on the date of the transfer, exceeds $100,000.

(2) Indirect transfer through a domestic partnership--For purposes of this section, if a domestic partnership transfers property to a foreign partnership in a section 721 transaction, the domestic partnership's partners shall be considered to have transferred a proportionate share of the property to the foreign partnership. However, if the domestic partnership properly reports all of the information required under this section with respect to the contribution, no partner of the transferor partnership, whether direct or indirect (through tiers of partnerships), is also required to report under this section. For illustrations of this rule, see Examples 4 and 5 of paragraph (a)(7) of this section.

(3) Indirect transfer through a foreign partnership. [Reserved]

(4) Requirement to report dispositions--(i) In general. If a United States person was required to report a transfer to a foreign partnership of appreciated property under paragraph (a)(1) or (2) of this section, and the foreign partnership disposes of the property while such United States person remains a direct or indirect partner, that United States person must report the disposition by filing Form 8865. The form must be attached to, and filed by the due date (including extensions) of, the United States person's income tax return for the year in which the disposition occurred.

(ii) Disposition of contributed property in nonrecognition transaction. If a foreign partnership disposes of contributed appreciated property in a nonrecognition transaction and substituted basis property is received in exchange, and the substituted basis property has built-in gain under Sec. 1.704-3(a)(8), the original

319.

transferor is not required to report the disposition. However, the transferor must report the disposition of the substituted basis property in the same manner as provided for the contributed property.

(5) Time for filing Form 8865--(i) General rule. The Form 8865 on which a transfer is reported must be attached to the transferor's timely filed (including extensions) income tax return (including a partnership return of income) for the tax year that includes the date of the transfer.

(ii) Time for filing when transferor also required to report information about the partnership under section 6038. If the United States person required to file under this section is also required to file a Form 8865 under section 6038 for the period in which the transfer occurs, then the United States person must report under this section on the Form 8865 for the foreign partnership's annual accounting period in which the transfer occurred (not its own taxable year) and file with its income tax return for that year as provided in Section 6038 and the regulations thereunder.

(6) Returns to be made--(i) Separate returns for each partnership. If a United States person transfers property reportable under this section to more than one foreign partnership in a taxable year, the United States person must submit a separate Form 8865 for each partnership.

(ii) Duplicate form to be filed. If required by the instructions accompanying Form 8865, a duplicate Form 8865 (including attachments and schedules) must also be filed by the due date for submitting the original Form 8865 under paragraph (a)(5)(i) or (ii) of this section, as applicable.

(7) Examples. The application of this paragraph (a) may be illustrated by the following examples:

Example 1. On November 1, 2001, US, a United States person that uses the calendar year as its taxable year, contributes $200,000 to FP, a foreign partnership, in a transaction subject to section 721. After the contribution, US owns a 5% interest in FP. US must report the contribution by filing Form 8865 for its taxable year ending December 31, 2001. On March 1, 2002, US makes a $40,000 section 721 contribution to FP, after which US owns a 6% interest in FP. US must report the $40,000 contribution by filing Form 8865 for its taxable year ending December 31, 2002, because the contribution, when added to the value of the other property contributed by US to FP during the 12-month period ending on the date of the transfer, exceeds $100,000.

Example 2. F, a nonresident alien, is the brother of US, a United States person. F owns a 15% interest in FP, a foreign partnership. US contributes $99,000 to FP, in exchange for a 1-percent partnership interest. Under sections 6038(e)(3)(C) and 267(c)(2), US is considered to own at least a 10-percent interest in FP and, therefore, US must report the $99,000 contribution under this section.

Editor's Note: In Example 2 (above) United States brother US who only owns 1% of the partnership is considered to own the 15% partnership interest owned by his nonresident alien brother F by way of the attribution rules. US's stock ownership is considered to total 16% under the attribution rules.

Example 3. US, a United States person, owns 40 percent of FC, a foreign corporation. FC owns a 20-percent interest in FP, a foreign partnership. Under section 267(c)(1), US is considered to own 8 percent of FP due to its ownership of FC. US contributes $50,000 to FP in exchange for a 5-percent partnership interest. Immediately after the contribution, US is considered to own at least a 10-percent interest in FP and, therefore, must report the $50,000 contribution under this section.

Example 4. US, a United States person, owns a 60-percent interest in USP, a domestic partnership. On March 1, 2001, USP contributes $200,000 to FP, a foreign partnership, in exchange for a 5-percent partnership interest. Under paragraph (a)(2) of this section, US is considered as having contributed $120,000 to FP ($200,000 x 60%). However, under paragraph (a)(2), if USP properly reports the contribution to FP, US is not required to report its $120,000 contribution. If US directly contributes $5,000 to FP on June 10, 2001, US must report the $5,000 contribution because US is considered to have contributed more than $100,000 to FP in the 12-month period ending on the date of the $5,000 contribution.

Example 5. US, a United States person, owns an 80-percent interest in USP, a domestic partnership. USP owns an 80-percent interest in

USP1, a domestic partnership. On March 1, 2001, USP1 contributes $200,000 to FP, a foreign partnership, in exchange for a
3-percent partnership interest. Under paragraph (a)(2) of this section, USP is considered to have contributed $160,000 ($200,000 x 80%) to FP. US is considered to have contributed $128,000 to FP ($200,000 x 80% x 80%). However, if USP1 reports the transfer of the $200,000 to FP, neither US nor USP are required to report under this section the amounts they are considered to have contributed. Additionally, regardless of whether USP1 reports the $200,000 contribution, if USP reports the $160,000 contribution it is considered to have made, US does not have to report under this section the $128,000 contribution US is considered to have made.

(b) Transfers by trusts relating to state and local government employee retirement plans. Trusts relating to state and local government employee retirement plans are not required to report transfers under this section, unless otherwise specified in the instructions to Form 8865.

(c) Information required with respect to transfers of property. With respect to transfers required to be reported under paragraph (a)(1) or (2) of this section, the return must contain information in such form or manner as Form 8865 (and its accompanying instructions) prescribes with respect to reportable events, including--

(1) The name, address, and U.S. taxpayer identification number of the United States person making the transfer;

(2) The name, U.S. taxpayer identification number (if any), and address of the transferee foreign partnership, and the type of entity and country under whose laws the partnership was created or organized;

(3) A general description of the transfer, and of any wider transaction of which it forms a part, including the date of transfer;

(4) The names and addresses of the other partners in the foreign partnership, unless the transfer is solely of cash and the transferor holds less than a 10-percent interest in the transferee foreign partnership immediately after the transfer;

(5) A description of the partnership interest received by the United States person, including a change in partnership interest;

(6) A separate description of each item of contributed property that is appreciated property subject to the allocation rules of section 704(c)(except to the extent that the property is permitted to be aggregated in making allocations under section 704(c)), or is intangible property, including its estimated fair market value and adjusted basis.

(7) A description of other contributed property, not specified in paragraph (c)(6) of this section, aggregated by the following categories (with, in each case, a brief description of the property)--

(i) Stock in trade of the transferor (inventory);

(ii) Tangible property (other than stock in trade) used in a trade or business of the transferor;

(iii) Cash;

(iv) Stock, notes receivable and payable, and other securities; and

(v) Other property.

(d) Information required with respect to dispositions of property. In respect of dispositions required to be reported under paragraph (a)(4) of this section, the return must contain information in such form or manner as Form 8865 (and its accompanying instructions) prescribes with respect to reportable events, including--

(1) The date and manner of disposition;

(2) The gain and depreciation recapture amounts, if any, realized by the partnership; and

(3) Any such amounts allocated to the United States person.

(e) Method of reporting. Except as otherwise provided on Form 8865, or the accompanying instructions, all amounts reported as required under this section must be expressed in United States currency, with a statement of the exchange rates used. All statements required on or with Form 8865 pursuant to this section must be in the English language.

(h) Failure to comply with reporting requirements--(1) Consequences of failure. If a United States person is required to file a return under paragraph (a) of this section and fails to comply with the reporting requirements of section 6038B and this section, then such person is subject to the following penalties:

(i) The United States person is subject to a penalty equal to 10 percent of the fair market value of the property at the time of the contribution. Such penalty with respect to a particular transfer is limited to $100,000, unless the failure to comply with respect to such transfer was due to intentional disregard.

(ii) The United States person must recognize gain (reduced by the amount of any gain recognized, with respect to that property, by the transferor after the transfer) as if the contributed property had been sold for fair market value at the time of the contribution. Adjustments to the basis of the partnership's assets and any relevant partner's interest as a result of gain being recognized under this provision will be made as though the gain was recognized in the year in which the failure to report was finally determined.

(2) Failure to comply. A failure to comply with the requirements of section 6038B includes--

(i) The failure to report at the proper time and in the proper manner any information required to be reported under the rules of this section; and

(ii) The provision of false or inaccurate information in purported compliance with the requirements of this section.

(3) Reasonable cause exception. Under section 6038B(c)(2) and this section, the provisions of paragraph (h)(1) of this section will not apply if the transferor shows that a failure to comply was due to reasonable cause and not willful neglect. The transferor may attempt to do so by providing a written statement to the district director having jurisdiction of the taxpayer's return for the year of the transfer, setting forth the reasons for the failure to comply. Whether a failure to comply was due to reasonable cause will be determined by the district director under all the facts and circumstances.

(4) Statute of limitations. For exceptions to the limitations on assessment in the event of a failure to provide information under section 6038B, see section 6501(c)(8).

6501(c)(8) Failure to notify Secretary under section 6038B • In the case of any tax imposed on any exchange or distribution by reason of subsection (a), (d), or (e) of section367, the time for assessment of such tax shall not expire before the date which is 3 years after the date on which the Secretary is notified of such exchange or distribution under section 6038B(a).

(i) Definitions--(1) Appreciated property. Appreciated property is property that has a fair market value in excess of basis.

(2) Domestic partnership. A domestic partnership is a partnership described in section 7701(a)(4).

(3) Foreign partnership. A foreign partnership is a partnership described in section 7701(a)(5).

(4) Related person. Persons are related persons if they bear a relationship described in section 267(b)(1) through (3) or (10) through (12), after application of section 267(c) (except for (c)(3)), or in section 707(b)(1)(B).

(5) Substituted basis property. Substituted basis property is property described in section 7701(a)(42).

(6) Taxpayer-initiated adjustment. A taxpayer-initiated adjustment is a section 482 adjustment that is made by the taxpayer pursuant to Sec. 1.482-1(a)(3).

(7) United States person. A United States person is a person described in section 7701(a)(30).

(j) Effective dates--(1) In general. This section applies to transfers made on or after January 1, 1998. However, for a transfer made on or after January 1, 1998, but before January 1, 1999, the filing requirements of this section may be satisfied by--

(i) Filing a Form 8865 with the taxpayer's income tax return (including a partnership return of income) for the first taxable year beginning on or after January 1, 1999; or

(ii) Filing a Form 926 with the taxpayer's income tax return (including a partnership return of income) for the taxable year in which the transfer occurred.

Reporting by corporate transferor

(ii) Reporting by corporate transferor. If the transferor is a corporation, Form 926 must be signed by an authorized officer of the corporation. If, however, the transferor is a member of an affiliated group under section 1504(a)(1) that files a consolidated Federal income tax return, but the transferor is not the common parent corporation, an authorized officer of the common parent corporation must sign Form 926. See page 8 and 9 for Form 926.

Definition of intentional disregard

If the transferor fails to qualify for the exception under paragraph (f)(3) of this section and if the taxpayer knew of the rule or regulation that was disregarded, the failure will be considered an intentional disregard of section 6038B, and the monetary penalty under paragraph (f)(1)(ii) of this section will not be limited to $100,000. See §1.6662-3(b)(2).

322.

Tax Planning Techniques

First off. Transfers of any amounts over $100,000 (even single transactions involving millions of dollars) made before February 5, 1999 does not need to be reported on Form 926. Form 926 says exactly this on its first page of instructions.

For tax years beginning after February 5, 1999, one way to avoid having to file new form 926 is to transfer $99,999 or less during any 12 month period, and keep your stock ownership level below the 10% voting and non-voting stock threshold.

After the 12 month period is over, you could transfer another $99,000, and not need to report on Form 926.

You could also form a second or third offshore company (own less than 10% of its stock), and transfer $99,999 to each company, and no reporting of the cash transfers would be required under the final regulations.

Example: US person F purchases 4.5% of the nonvoting stock in Cayman company X for $95,000 on July 4, 1999. On the same day, US person F invests another $85,000 and $97,000 in two Bahamian companies, in exchange for 5% of their outstanding stock. The total transferred is $277,000, but no form 926 needs to be filed with your tax return in April, 2,000.

Furthermore, US person F could transfer the identical amounts and more ($277,000) after July 4th, 2000, and not have to file form 926 in the year 2001 either.

Transfers in excess of $100,000 by nonresidents of the U.S. to the foreign corporation, or very large loans from foreign entities and other non-US persons, would not need to be reported on Form 926.

The statute of limitation exception may be useful too. The instructions for Form 926 say "that the statute of limitations on the assessment of tax under section 6038, 6038B and 6046A does not expire until three years after the information required under those sections is reported)." This means that if you transfer $500,000 in cash into a foreign company on July 20, 1999, and fail to file 926 with your 1040 in the year 2,000, the statue of limitations for assessment expires on April 15th, 2,003 – three years after you filed your year 2000 tax return. Apparently, the IRS won't or can't assess the 10% penalty if you fail to file, and the statute of limitations runs out.

On August 5th, 1997, President Clinton signed into law the *Taxpayer Relief Act of 1997*, which along with a companion spending bill, implements a landmark balanced-budget agreement negotiated earlier this year by congressional leaders and the administration. The tax measure includes over 100 revenue-losing provisions for a net tax cut of $96 billion affecting a wide range of individual and business taxpayers.

The *Taxpayer Relief Act of 1997* provides $152 billion in tax cuts between now and 2002. While the act contains over 100 tax-reduction provisions, most of the relief is attributable to only five items. For the "middle-class" individuals there is a child credit, expanded individual retirement accounts (IRAs), and educational tax incentives. For small businesses and the moderately wealthy, there is some estate tax relief. For middle- and upper-income individuals, there is a reduction in the top rate on capital gains from 28 to 20 percent.

For a government projected to collect nearly $9 trillion in taxes over the next five years, a net tax cut of $95 billion is hardly earth shattering. Moreover, even though this is the first significant tax cut since 1981, the scope of the legislation pales in comparison with the massive broad tax cuts that marked the beginning of the Reagan administration.

Other Taxpayer Relief Act of 1979 provision

Highlighted below are some of the other major tax changes made by the *Taxpayer Relief Act of 1997* that affect offshore, foreign operations. Of particular importance is the repeal of Section 1491 Excise tax on transfers to foreign entities by U.S. persons. The analysis was prepared by tax professionals at Arthur Andersen's Office of Federal Tax Services in Washington, D.C. Andre P. Fogarasi is the Managing Director of OFTS.

The act includes changes to the international provisions that should be of interest to U.S. and foreign multinational corporations, foreign investors, U.S. and foreign individuals, and trusts. Many of the new rules are welcome simplifications of complex provisions. Other changes tighten up existing rules or clarify areas of uncertainty. While not all of these changes are favorable to taxpayers, the general thrust of the foreign provisions is to simplify and clarify several complicated rules, thus reducing compliance costs and providing greater certainty.

Tax Treatment of Transfers to Foreign Entities

Under prior law, a 35% excise tax applied to transfers of appreciated property to foreign corporations, partnerships, trusts, and estates. Various income taxes could also apply to these transfers, leading to confusion and traps for the unwary.

The *Taxpayer Relief Act of 1997* repeals the section 1491 excise tax effective August 5, 1997. Under the new law, **except as provided in regulations,** no gain or loss is recognized on the transfer of property to a foreign partnership. However, the Treasury is authorized (and has issued) regulations requiring gain recognition when the transfer results in gain, when recognized.

Securities transactions.

Earnings of a CFC that are invested in U.S. property are subject to current tax. Two exceptions are added to the definition of U.S. property: repurchase agreements and collateral or margin deposits. Investments in these assets will not create an investment in U.S. property. (Act section 1173; section 956)

Stock And Securities Trading Safe Harbor

Foreign corporations and partnerships are generally exempt from tax on income derived from trading in stocks or securities for their own account. Under prior law, to qualify for this exemption, the principal office of the foreign corporation or partnership had to be outside the United States. This limitation is eliminated for tax years beginning after 1997.

This change will give foreign entities that engage in U.S. stock and securities trading for their own account more flexibility. The economic inefficiencies of maintaining a principal office

overseas can now be eliminated. Thus, the activities set forth in "ten commandments" may be performed within the United States without risk of U.S. taxation. (Act section 1162; section 864(b)(2)(A))

Taxation of Expatriates

The act makes technical corrections to the recently adopted expatriate rules. The more important changes effect the calculation of the 10-year period following expatriation. (Act section 1601; section 877(d)(2))

Trusts and Estates

The act makes the following clarifying and technical changes to the rules for foreign trusts and estates:

a) Treasury is given authority to allow long-standing non grantor domestic trusts to elect to continue to be treated as domestic trusts despite statutory changes made in the 1996 act. (Act section 1161; section 7701(a)(30))

b) For purposes of determining whether a U.S. person's transfer to a trust is for a fair market value consideration, the obligations of any owner of the trust and certain persons who are related to any owner of the trust are disregarded. (Act section 1601; section 679(a)(3)(C))

c) In determining whether a trust is a U.S. person, (1) a trust is treated as a U.S. person if one or more U.S. persons have the authority to control all substantial decisions of the trust (and a U.S. court can exercise primary supervision over the trust), (2) a foreign trust is not considered present in, or a resident of, the United States, and (3) Treasury is given authority to allow a reasonable period of time for U.S. trusts in existence on August 20, 1996, to make modifications to comply with the new trust rules enacted on that date. (Act section 1601; sections 641 and 7701(a)(30))

Source: The source for some of the above information on *the Taxpayer Relief Act of 1997* is the *Tax Analyst* (800) 647-2883. Subscribers can obtain a CD ROM for either Macintosh or IBC compatibles.

Tax Evasion, Tax Avoidance, Tax Planning

Differentiating between tax evasion and tax avoidance is a prerequisite for successful international tax planning. **Tax evasion** is a serious crime in the United States, and in most other industrial nations, punishable by fine and imprisonment. **Tax avoidance** is not a crime. Tax avoidance is the removal of tax liability by perfectly acceptable tax planning (i.e., choosing among tax reliefs and incentives the most advantageous route consistent with normal business transactions), or even refraining from consuming a taxed product. It is not the intention of governments to combat activities harmonious with their tax laws and fiscal policies.

Action by the taxpayer, which entails breaking the law, and which moreover can be shown to have been taken with the intention of escaping payment of tax, is covered by the term **"tax evasion"**. Under U.S. law conviction of a crime calls for the government to prove *beyond a reasonable doubt* that the crime was committed. This is a heavy burden of proof for the authorities, and the government generally indicts persons for tax crimes only when it believes it will be able to win its case and get a conviction. But while the government only indicts a very small percentage of taxpayers for criminal tax offences, its success in obtaining convictions has been good.

A willful attempt by any person to evade or defeat any U.S. federal income, estate or gift tax is a felony punishable by a fine and/or imprisonment for up to five years. To win a conviction, the government must prove *beyond reasonable doubt* that each of the following three elements are present. [8.]

(1) **Willfulness** has been defined by the U.S. Supreme Court as a *voluntary, intentional violation of a known legal duty*. Willfulness requires a deliberate intention to violate the law, not simply one that is careless, accidental, inadvertent or negligent. Ignorance or mistake of law is a defense to the crime of tax evasion.

(2) The second element of criminal tax evasion is an attempt to evade tax through a willful commission of some act. The U.S. courts look for *badges of fraud,* including keeping false books or records (i.e., two sets of books); failing to keep some adequate books and records, using false names for bank accounts or safe deposit boxes; and otherwise concealing assets or sources of income through the use of such things as secret bank accounts or **"strawmen"** (i.e., foreign *nominees* own or hold property on your behalf).

(3) The third element of criminal tax evasion is that the tax actually owed is greater than the tax reported by the taxpayer. If no additional tax is due, there is no criminal tax evasion.

Instances of tax evasion includes: deliberately understating ones income; failing to file a tax or information return; failure to pay tax when due; willfully making a false oral or written statement to the government; willfully making and signing a false return; or willfully conspiring, by aiding or advising, in the preparation of false oral or written statements.

Opening a foreign bank account in itself is not tax evasion. Not reporting the interest income on your U.S. tax return is tax evasion (i.e., understating your income). The U.S. courts do not sympathize with U.S. citizen taxpayers who fail to report foreign bank interest income.

On the other hand, if 11 U.S. individuals each purchased 9% of the outstanding stock in a Cayman Island holding company, investing $1,000,000 each in their shares, there would be no tax liability for the offshore company, even if it invested the $11,000,000 in U.S. bank (i.e., Chase Manhattan, Bank of America) CDs paying 8% interest income. Such a foreign corporation would not be considered a **controlled foreign corporation** (CFC) under the United States' current tax law. For a foreign company to be a CFC, more than 50% of the voting stock or value stock must be owned by U.S. shareholders.

Under U.S. tax law none of the 11 U.S. individuals (above) are considered U.S.

---

8. From *Tax Avoidance, Tax Evasion, - United States of America* by George E. Zeitlin (Chadbourne, Park, Whiteside & Wolff, NY), chapter 10, pgs. 91 thru 102.

shareholders. A U.S. Shareholder is defined under IRC §951(b) as a U.S. person who owns 10% or more of the voting stock in the foreign corporation. U.S. persons that own under 10% are not considered when making the CFC determination. Furthermore, only a U.S. Shareholder can have offshore profits imputed to him - to be included on his income tax return. Indeed, most international tax lawyers will tell you neither the IRS nor the tax courts will attack a set-up like the one above. The reason? There are no U.S. shareholders (i.e., 10% voting stock holders) present in such a structure.

Tax Avoidance. Is it proper and legal?

There are no general provisions in the U.S. tax law that bars the availability of a tax benefit if the saving of taxes is the sole or main motive of a transaction.

"The legal right of a taxpayer to decrease the amount of what otherwise would be his taxes, or to altogether avoid them by means which the law permits, cannot be doubted." - **United States Supreme Court,** *Gregory v. Helvering,* 293 U.S. 465 (1934)

"There is a fine line between legal tax planning and illegal tax planning - tax avoidance versus tax evasion. Tax avoidance is merely tax minimization through legal techniques. In this sense, tax avoidance becomes the proper objective of all tax planning. Evasion, while also aimed at the elimination or reduction of taxes, connotes the use of subterfuge and fraud as a means to an end." - **William H. Hoffman, Jr. J.D., PhD, C.P.A.** (Professor of tax law - University of Houston, author of *West's Federal Taxation - Corporations, Partnerships, Estates and Trusts* and *Individual Income Taxes.*

"Over and over again the courts have said that there is nothing sinister in so arranging one's affairs as to keep taxes as low as possible. Everyone does so, rich or poor, and all do right, for nobody owes any public duty to pay more tax than the law demands; taxes are enforced extractions, not voluntary contributions." - **Judge Learned Hand**

Tax Planning for minimization of tax is considered a normal and prudent practice of business and finance. Businessmen large and small must always consider the tax consequences

before following through any sizeable transaction.

Legal tax avoidance covers a wide gambit. A millionaire invests his monies in municipal bonds paying 8% interest annually. **Result**: No income tax is payable, and prior to 1986, no reporting of the interest received was demanded.

Investment tax credits on industrial and business equipment were a favorite tax avoidance device in the 1970's and early 1980's. A person could invest $150,000 in a piece of machinery or airplane and receive a $15,000 tax credit against their income tax liability in the year of purchase. Credits of 6% were allowed on automobiles.

Homes make for outstanding tax shelters. A person can purchase a $100,000 home with a $10,000 downpayment. The annual mortgage payments (often greater than the initial downpayment) are deductible expenses.

Real estate ventures made for great tax avoidance schemes in the 1980's. A person could invest in a highly leveraged office building partnership and obtain more deductions then his original investment. Congress has since curbed the use of these types of tax shelters, by reason that many of them had no economic purpose other than to create tax write-offs for investors.

Other examples of legal tax avoidance scheming include tax free reorganizations, cost depletion allowances for the oil and mining industries, and acquisitions of companies with large **net operation losses** which can be carried-over and used by the acquiring company to reduce its current tax liability.

International Tax Avoidance by large MNCs.

One of the favored tax avoidance schemes of MNCs (Multinational Corporations) involves the exploitation of our U.S. income tax treaties. During the 1960's, 1970's and 1980's, the Netherlands Antilles was the preferred tax haven for the issuance of Eurodollar bonds by MNCs because interest paid to an offshore N.A. finance subsidiary was free from the U.S. 30% withholding tax under the U.S.- N.A. tax treaty. Moreover, the U.S. parent company was entitled to a deduction for the interest paid. Using a practice known as the interest spread concept, offshore finance companies paid little or no taxes to either government.

Often holding companies in zero tax havens like the Caymans, Bermuda or the Bahamas were used to make the loans to the N.A. finance company, which subsequently lent the money to the U.S. parent. Channeling interest income around into tax havens, although frowned upon by the U.S. tax authorities, was acceptable business practice offshore. Recently, the IRS has begun to crack down on *back-to-back loan schemes* involving U.S. taxpayers, but the practice is still widespread among foreigners - still supported under our current tax treaties (i.e., the Netherlands, Barbados). [9.]

Tax avoidance using tax havens can be broken down into six main categories:

1. **Emigration and shifting of residency.** The "artificial shifting of residence raises special difficulties...as company residence can be a difficult concept to define, and especially to verify where is the place of effective management of a company and whether it has been moved." To make it easier for the end user (you - the taxpayer) to use tax havens, many offshore tax haven governments have initiated laws requiring some local management participation (as in Malta and Panama), while others provide for regulated, licensed management trustee companies to help the foreigner run his company on a year to year basis. These offshore management trustee companies will take care of your books and records, provide secretarial services, directors, office space, post boxes, and tax and investment advice.

Taxpayers in countries with a relatively high level of taxation may be tempted to avoid being subject to tax in their own countries either by manipulating fiscal residency tests or by moving their residency abroad. This method of tax avoidance is better suited for some residents than for others. A UK citizen who leaves his country permanently can generally escape the reach of the Inland Revenue. Ordinarily, a U.S. citizen remains subject to U.S. income taxes (including filing of income tax returns) for up to 10 years after he exits and relinquishes his citizenship. Congress seeks to tax all United States residents regardless of their citizenship, all U.S. citizens regardless of their place of residence, and many former citizens even though they are no longer citizens or residents. Note, this is one preventive measure against tax avoidance. [10.]

Emigration to another country is not the most common form of tax avoidance as tax savings can frequently be obtained in more convenient ways.

2. **Base Companies.** Base companies are tax haven companies that shield offshore incomes from high tax country tax authorities. The most important function of a base company is to collect and shelter income that would otherwise be taxed in the taxpayer's country of residence. Base companies usually concern holding companies for asset administration and financial pivots, employing regional centres for multinational enterprises and companies formed to issue loans or bundle together other activities. Banks and insurance companies have been used as base companies to receive passive incomes from offshore finance (aside from soliciting customer deposits and insurance policies - their main line of business).

Base companies may be related to commercial, industrial or professional activities carried on outside the base company's country. The base company feeds on the offshore profits without remitting them. Base companies can also be used to obscure the real character of a transaction. Because of the difficulty in gathering information in tax havens, it is often difficult for tax authorities to prove a transaction is a sham or that a tax liability exists.

The tax advantages of a base company generally only last until the sheltered income is distributed. However, it is well recognized by the fiscal authorities that *secondary sheltering* can delay the collection of taxes indefinitely. *Secondary sheltering* embodies the use of foreign trusts, reploughing of profits back to the taxpayer or his affiliates in the form of loans, reinvesting in stocks or bonds that can thereafter

---

9. The Netherlands Antilles-U.S. income tax treaty was cancelled by the U.S. Treasury in 1987, but back-to-back loan schemes are still in use in other U.S. treaty partner nations. The Netherlands (Holland) is well-known for its finance companies and treaty network. The Dutch do not impose an interest withholding tax on monies sent outside Holland, even if the recipient is a company in a tax haven. Interest paid is a deductible expense under Dutch tax law.

10. See IRC §877 and IRC §2107.

be sold offshore tax free, or reinvesting the foreign profits in local tax haven banks where taxes are not applied.

3. **Conduit Companies.** These companies are designed to reduce source country withholding tax on dividends, interest and royalties by qualifying for tax treaty benefits

Ordinarily, tax treaty benefits only apply to the bilateral partners of the treaty. However, all U.S. bilateral treaties allow for third party exploitation of our treaties if the third (country) participant meets certain requirements. The reasoning behind this liberal approach by our treaty drafters is probably not so to discriminate against outsiders from other nations. For example, under the Barbados-U.S. income tax treaty, a third party company is entitled to the treaty benefits when its stock is regularly traded on a stock exchange.

Under the Netherlands-U.S. income tax treaty a third party outsider can obtain the same benefits reserved for Netherlands and U.S. citizens if he can meet the Netherlands requirements for residence. In Holland, this is not a terribly big obstacle to overcome if management and control of the Netherlands company is maintained in the Netherlands. Many Dutch lawyers specialize in meeting the residency requirements so third party foreigners can qualify for U.S. treaty benefits.

One drawback of using a bilateral tax treaty is the fiscal authorities of both countries can exchange tax information on companies using the treaty. The exchange of tax information is often limited by the host nation's own tax laws. In the Netherlands, information regarding the true owners of a Dutch company is not required to be disclosed to Dutch authorities. This is to say, the real shareholders of a Cayman company that owns a Netherlands company are not a matter of public record, and current Dutch law does not allow the gathering of such information by Holland's tax authorities. As much as the IRS would like to have this information, they cannot gather it under the treaty agreement.

Some conduit companies are used to channel income to base companies in tax havens. For example, a Netherlands company that invests 25% or more in a U.S. company's stock will receive a reduced dividend withholding rate of 5%. Moreover, when a Netherlands company owns 5% or more of the stock in the company paying the dividend (a.k.a. Participation Exemption), the dividend is not subject to Dutch income taxes when remitted back to Holland.

4. **Captive Insurance Companies.** A captive insurance company is usually established in a tax haven to sell insurance risks of the parent company, since no deduction is usually allowed in the source country for self-insurance. Premiums paid are often deductible, and reinvestment of premiums can be made in the tax haven tax-free.

The U.S. eliminated most of the tax advantages for captive insurance companies in the **Tax Reform Act of 1986.** Premiums paid by the U.S. company to an affiliated offshore reinsurance company are not deductible under IRC §162.

Yet, offshore reinsurance companies still flourish. There are well over 1,200 insurance companies in Bermuda alone, with a premium volume officially estimated at BD$6.2 Billion (1982). The Channel Islands, Barbados, Malta, Gibraltar, the Caymans, the Bahamas, the Turks & Caicos Islands, Western Samoa and Vanuatu also cater to offshore reinsurance companies.

5. **Shipping.** Nonresident enterprises can register ships in certain countries and carry that country's flag (*open registration,* or *flags of convenience),* although the administration headquarters is located elsewhere. The open registration country may be a tax haven, or the profits can be routed through a tax haven by leasing and chartering arrangements.

Under the new sub-part F provisions brought on by the **Tax Reform Act of 1986**, U.S. controlled foreign shipping companies must now pay U.S. tax on their offshore shipping profits. Under prior law, shippers could reinvest their profits and avoid paying U.S. taxes.

6. **Service Companies**. Service companies ostensibly perform management functions for non-trading activities in tax havens to avoid taxes, reduce operating costs, and avoid government controls. The usual technique used to shift profits from the *high* tax country to the tax haven involves payment of fees for services rendered.

A Bahamian management company that administers an offshore fund would incur no U.S. income taxes (under Sub-Part F) on fees it earns, provided the management team performs the service from within the tax haven. Such tax free operations can continue even if most of the company shareholders are U.S. persons, and even if the foreign company is classified a CFC. Non-Sub-Part F income (administration and management fees) cannot be imputed to U.S. shareholders of CFCs under U.S. tax law.

Substance over Form.

The concept of "substance over form" which, in broad terms, can be defined as the prevalence of economic or social reality over the literal wording of legal provisions, has been used to counter attempted circumvention of tax laws. This approach can be adopted by the courts as a principle of interpretation or explicitly set out in statue. In many European countries, including France, Germany, the Netherlands and Switzerland, it is embodied in the judicial concept of *abuse of law*.

Substance over form provisions and the courts' attitude to them vary from country to country. Tests used to determine if a company has real substance (not a mere *shell* holding company or extension of the sole shareholder's economic ego) take the following approach:

a) The legal personality of the base company may be disregarded;
b) The base company may be regarded as a resident in the taxpayer's country, because its place of effective control and management is situated there.
c) The base company may be found to have a permanent establishment in the taxpayer's country of residence because its management team all live and work there;
d) The sheltering of income may be disregarded because the activity of the base company or income derived from it may be regarded as an activity or income of the taxpayer himself.

Substance over form issues relating to "a" and "b" can be easily avoided if the company operates a genuine business in the tax haven, such as running a McDonalds franchise, operating an auto parts store, casino, hotel, what have you.

In the case of offshore investment vehicles, such as mutual funds and investment companies, the *substance over form* issue is looked at more carefully by the IRS and U.S. courts. If books and records are kept offshore, and the company is incorporated and run as a genuine business concern **in** the tax haven, substance over form rarely is an issue.

In the case of a Bahamian or Cayman incorporated company whose chairman and directors lived and worked in Miami, Florida, whose books and records were even occasionally kept in Florida, the IRS might try to prove that the company keeps its headquarters in the USA, thus making it subject to taxes on its worldwide income. This would be so even if all the income was generated outside the United States.

Tax avoidance - a major issue for governments

Industrial nations consider tax havens a threat to their fiscal policies and revenue raising procedures. The U.S. Treasury Department's Gordon Report concluded that banking deposits in tax havens had escalated rapidly from $11 billion in 1968 to $385 billion by 1978. Since this report is now over 12 years old, and the Caymans now claim banking deposits of over $275 billion themselves, I have to believe that the current level of bank deposits in the Caribbean havens alone easily could exceed $600 billion dollars.

Even more remarkable is the source of these deposit dollars. While no precise statistics exist, the U.S. banks in the Cayman Islands are known to hold more depositor dollars than any other nation, and are known to have more assets than any other nation. Incredibly, none of the tax havens (unless you consider Puerto Rico), belong to the United States of America.

Estimating the degree of use of tax havens to conceal illegal activities and revenue losses associated with them poses an even greater problem. Official statistics on funds flowing into and out of tax havens does not necessarily reveal many of the transactions connected with criminal activities. A report prepared in 1983 for the United States Congress' Permanent Sub-Committee on Investigations of the Committee on Governmental Affairs showed that the amount of criminal funds flowing from the U.S. into tax havens was somewhere within the range of $9 billion to $43 billion. The upper limit was determined as a proportion of the estimated size of the underground economy in the United States (estimated to be $330 billion). No one really knows the amount of monies hidden offshore. The U.S. government cannot gather adequate data from offshore companies and banks because of the strict bank secrecy laws offshore, and because they have no powers of jurisdiction.

Subpart F type provisions

This is the most significant type of tax legislation directly aimed at counteracting the tax advantages derived from the deferral possibilities offered by the use of tax haven subsidiaries. Broadly, this is achieved by taxing the subsidiary's income in the hands of its domestic shareholders. This type of legislation was first enacted in the U.S. in the 1930s (personal holding company provisions in 1934 and foreign personal holding company provisions in 1937). Then Subpart F legislation was enacted in 1962 and expanded in 1975, 1982, 1984 and 1986.

Subpart F legislation provides for the taxation of United States shareholders of controlled foreign corporations (CFC) on their pro rata share of certain categories of undistributed profits from tax haven activities and certain other activities of the foreign corporation. If the foreign corporation is not a CFC or does not have the types of income designated Subpart F; there is no immediate U.S. income tax liability.

The German "Foreign Tax Law" *(Aussensteuergesetz)* of 1972 introduced detailed rules on the attribution to resident shareholders of base companies' passive income (interest, dividends, capital gains) derived by a controlled intermediate company. Comparable provisions were enacted in Canada as part of the tax reform of 1972 *(Foreign Accrual Property Income (FAPI)* - these provisions came fully into force in 1976.

Japan introduced counteracting measures in 1978 as part of the **Special Taxation Measures Law** with an exhaustive list of 27 tax havens in three categories. France enacted legislation in 1980 (now *Article 209B of CGI)* and the United Kingdom in the **1984 Finance Act.**

Australia and New Zealand now have Subpart F provisions strikingly similar to the U.S. version.

CHAPTER 15 • Canada and Australia

Canada, with an area of 9.9 million square kilometers, is the largest country in the Western Hemisphere and the second largest country in the world (second only to the Soviet Union). Canada's 25,000,000 people enjoy a standard of living that is among the highest in the world. Some 63% of Canadian families own their own homes, the quality and size of which are among the highest in the world. Canada also ranks very high in the percentage of households owning other durable goods, such as refrigerators (99%), washing machines (77%), telephones (98%), televisions (98%), radios (99%), and video tape recorders (23.4%). [1]

Revenue Canada is a tough, tenacious tax collecting service, as formidable as the IRS. The total normal tax rate for Canadian corporations for 1990, including the 3% surtax, was almost 44%. Individual tax rates were about 32%. In 1990, individual taxpayers are required to bring into income 3/4 of capital gains net of capital losses. A lifetime capital gains exemption allows a Canadian resident individual to realize $100,000 in capital gains tax free ($500,000 if the property is a qualified farm or small business corporation).

In 1972, Canada introduced tax legislation strikingly similar to the U.S. Subpart F provisions. Corporations resident in Canada are subject to tax on their income generally on an accrued basis, from all sources inside and outside Canada, whether remitted or not. However, dividends from the *exempt surplus account* of a *non-controlled foreign affiliate* domiciled in a country that has a tax treaty with Canada, can be remitted to a Canadian company free from all Canadian income taxes.

Through 1989, Barbados, Nevis, Anguilla, Antigua, Montserrat, St. Kitts, St Lucia, St Vincent, Cyprus, Liberia (tanker haven), and Switzerland were all listed as prescribed countries for purposes of obtaining the foreign affiliate tax exemption. To receive dividends from subsidiaries domiciled in these tax havens tax free, the Canadian corporation had to own *at least 10% of the foreign affiliate's stock,* but could not own *more than 50% of the voting shares* in the foreign affiliate. The foreign affiliate privileges applied only to countries that had a tax treaty with Canada or were on the list of prescribed countries. See page 336.

Only active business income can be remitted by the foreign affiliate as a tax free dividend. Passive incomes, such as offshore capital gains, interest, dividends and royalties, are not included in the offshore affiliate's exempt surplus account, but are included instead in its taxable surplus account. Dividends from the taxable surplus account are taxable when remitted.

To better understanding how the Canadian tax system for foreign affiliates works, certain terms must be reviewed. Terms such as *Controlled Foreign Affiliate, Foreign Accrual Property Income* or *FAPI* for short, *exempt surplus, active business income* and *taxable surplus* are peculiar to the legislation.

Foreign Affiliates: A foreign corporation in which a Canadian resident (individual of corporation) owns directly or indirectly an equity percentage of at least 10% of the shares of any class of stock is defined as a **foreign affiliate** of the Canadian resident. Note, while an individual can own the requisite 10% ownership to qualify the shareholding, he/she cannot receive dividends from the foreign affiliate's exempt surplus tax free. The tax exemption is limited to Canadian corporations.

Controlled Foreign Affiliate: A foreign corporation in which a Canadian individual or corporation owns *more than 50% of the voting shares,* or a Canadian resident who owns at least 10%, and is a member of a group, wherever resident that controls the corporation, or a group of not more than five Canadians who together control the corporation (each having at least 10%) is a Controlled Foreign Affiliate. [2]

According to Subsection 91(1) of the **Canadian Tax Act,** when certain types of income (called FAPI) are earned by a Controlled

---

[1] From *Doing Business in Canada,* by Price Waterhouse (1-1-89)

[2] From *Doing Business in Canada,* by Deloitte Haskins + Sells, pgs 78-79. See also *Liquidations of Foreign Affiliates,* by Allan R. Lanthier, <u>Canadian Tax Journal</u> (March-April 1985), pgs. 245 to 249.

Foreign Affiliate, the Canadian taxpayer must include this income on his tax return, whether or not the foreign affiliate distributes the income to him. This imputation of income rule is identical to the United State's imputation of Subpart F incomes to U.S. Shareholders of Controlled Foreign corporations under IRC §951 to 958. However, there's a catch that says there is no imputation of the foreign affiliate's income that is not a controlled foreign affiliate. To derive any benefits (deferral) under the Canadian rules, you want to avoid a structure that creates a controlled foreign affiliate. [3]

Canadian case law has always found control to mean *de jure control*, meaning, ownership of more than 50% of the voting stock. However, recently a decision of the **Federal Court of Appeal** (*Queen v. Imperial General Properties, Ltd.*) was reversed by the **Supreme Court of Canada**. Here, voting rights attached to the shares were equally divided between two shareholders. The court held that the corporation was really controlled by the shareholder holding all the common shares. The corporation could be wound-up upon a vote of 50% of the shareholdings, and the controlling shareholder was found not to have relinquished control upon issuance of a second class of preference stock to the second shareholder. One can conclude that the 50% cut-off is an important one, not to be left to judicial decision. No powers (voting or otherwise) over the operation or winding-up of the corporation should be conveyed to non-voting shareholdings.

Foreign Accrual Property Income (FAPI) is defined as income from property and business other than **active businesses,** and capital gains other than capital gains arising from the disposition of property used principally for earning active business income. Property such as industrial machinery, computers, bank and office buildings, supertankers, freighters, commercial aircraft, pipelines, apartment buildings, hotels and condominiums are active business assets. Capital gains from the sale of these type assets are not FAPI.

The concept of FAPI is an important one to grasp, because FAPI type incomes are not considered to be part of the foreign affiliate's exempt surplus. Only dividends from the exempt surplus account can be repatriated tax free.

Capital gains from trading stocks or bonds, dividends (but not dividends received from another foreign affiliate), interests, royalties, certain rents and insurance of Canadian risks are non-business income, and are therefore classified FAPI.

Canadian shareholders of controlled foreign affiliates are taxed currently on their share of such affiliates' FAPI. A foreign corporation in which a Canadian corporation owns, directly or indirectly, at least 10% of the shares of any class of stock is defined as a foreign affiliate of the Canadian corporation. The FAPI rules apply to a foreign affiliate that is a controlled foreign affiliate, i.e., a foreign affiliate that is controlled directly or indirectly by the taxpayer, by the taxpayer and not more than four other persons resident in Canada, or a related group of persons, wherever resident, of which the taxpayer is a member.

The following types of income are **excluded** from the calculation of FAPI.

1) Dividends from other foreign affiliates.
2) Amounts paid to the affiliate that are deductible in computing income from active business carried on outside Canada by another foreign affiliate or related nonresident corporation.
3) Inactive income received by a foreign affiliate that is incidental to an active business, and capital gains and losses realized on assets used in an active business.
4) Foreign exchange gains or losses arising on the settlement of debt between foreign affiliates or the redemption or non-arm's-length disposition of shares of a foreign affiliate.
5) Capital gain or loss arising on the sale of shares of another foreign affiliate where substantially all the assets of the affiliate are used in an active business and the portion of a capital gain or loss that was accrued prior to the foreign corporation becoming a foreign affiliate of the Canadian taxpayer or related parties.

A deduction, computed by formula, is taken from FAPI for the foreign taxes paid on FAPI, so that Canadian tax is only paid on the net amount.

The main effect of the FAPI provision is to prevent Canadian residents from either avoiding or postponing current Canadian tax on passive or investment income that could otherwise be diverted to foreign corporations. Similar rules apply to nonresident trusts with Canadian beneficiaries. The rules are designed to bring the total current taxes, Canadian and foreign, on

---

3. Note, the Canadian and U.S. rules for **Controlled Foreign Corporations** are quite similar.

FAPI up to the effective Canadian rates.

Active Business Income is income from trading, shipping, publishing, manufacturing, or exporting. When it is earned by a non-controlled foreign affiliate in a country with a tax treaty with Canada, it is not FAPI. Active business income can be accumulated in the foreign affiliate or repatriated as dividends tax free. Active business income makes up the foreign affiliate's exempt surplus account.

Exempt Surplus: Dividends paid by a foreign affiliate are thought to come first out of the exempt surplus account of that affiliate. Dividends paid out of exempt surplus of a foreign affiliate are deductible in full in arriving at the taxable income of a Canadian corporation.

Exempt surplus generally includes all active business income of the foreign affiliate earned subsequent to the end of 1975 if the foreign affiliate is resident in a country that entered into a tax treaty with Canada and the business earnings are derived from treaty countries.

Taxable surplus: Any excess of dividend received from a foreign affiliate over available balance in the exempt surplus account is thought to come out of the taxable surplus account.

An amount computed by formula is deducted from FAPI for the foreign taxes paid on income. The net amount included in income for Canadian tax purposes is designed so that the total foreign and Canadian tax that theoretically would have been imposed if the FAPI had been earned directly by the Canadian taxpayer.

Taxable surplus includes active business income (net of underlying foreign taxes paid) by a foreign affiliate in a non-treaty country or derived from a non-treaty country after 1975. It also includes the taxable portion of capital gains derived from property and in an active business or shares substantially all of whose property is used in an active business in addition to any foreign accrual property income (FAPI).

Pre-acquisition surplus: Any remaining portion of a dividend not covered by the exempt surplus or taxable surplus accounts of the affiliate is then deemed to come out of the pre-acquisition surplus. The part of the pre-acquisition surplus is deductible in computing taxable income but reduces the adjusted cost base of the Canadian shareholder's shares in the foreign affiliate.

Canada has tax treaties with several tax havens, including Barbados, Cyprus, Luxembourg, Malta, Liberia, Singapore, Philippines, the Netherlands and Switzerland. These countries make for better foreign affiliate bases because of the low rate of taxes imposed, or other favorable tax legislation.

Barbados (Old Canadian Base)

Barbados is a low tax haven in the Caribbean. Special concessions for **International Business Corporations (IBCs)** provide for top profits tax rate of just 2-1/2%. Barbados is a prescribed country for purposes of the Canadian tax legislation herein described. Barbados also has an income tax treaty with the U.S.

Barbados is an ideal location for a Canadian foreign affiliate to organize. Barbados permits dividends paid by one IBC to another IBC or to a person not resident in Barbados to be paid free from Barbados income and withholding taxes (15% for interest income and service incomes).

Barbados is the most easterly island in the West Indies. Barbados offers tax incentives and special tax breaks for IBCs, banks and insurance companies. At December 31, 1986 there were 370 IBCs registered to operate in Barbados.

Barbados is not a particularly good tax haven for individuals. Resident individuals can pay taxes at rates as high as 50% on their worldwide incomes, but if you reside in Barbados for less than 183 days of the year, you will be liable to tax only on incomes remitted to Barbados. Moreover, capital gains are not taxed. The Central Bank of Barbados publishes a 20-page booklet titled *Barbados - A unique Offshore Business Centre.* You can receive a free copy by writing the Barbados Industrial Development Corporation at the address in the ad on page 309.

Using the chart on page 309 as a guide, a Barbados/Canadian foreign affiliate (IBC #2) could export U.S. products internationally free from U.S. income taxes using dependent or independent agents or employees (but no U.S. office), and was a publicly traded company whose shares were traded on a recognized stock exchange (like the NASDAQ or Vancouver Exchange). Affiliate #2 could pass these active business incomes to affiliate #1 for repatriation back to the resident Canadian company tax free.[4].

Interest and dividends from U.S. corporate and treasury bonds could be harbored in affiliate #2 free from tax, except Barbados's low **profits tax**es levied at a rate of 2.5 percent on incomes up to US$5,000,000, and 1 percent on incomes over US$15,000,000. Barbados' profits tax rate is on a sliding scale, decreasing as the taxable amounts increase.

Barbados-Canada Tax Treaty

The Barbados resident captive insurance company is in a unique position *vis-à-vis* companies in the other traditional offshore domiciles. As a result of the Canada-Barbados Tax Treaty, Barbados is a listed jurisdiction under section 5907(11) of the Canada Income Tax Regulations and, accordingly, dividends paid from the active business income of a Barbados captive insurance company are treated as paid out of the exempt surplus of the payer and are tax exempt in the hands of the Canadian recipient.

Barbados also is appealing to Canadian companies seeking to avoid paying Federal Excise Tax, which is not payable under a reinsurance contract. Hence, fronting by a Barbados licensed exempt insurance company, where possible, has proved to be useful.

Recent changes to the taxation of Canadian-owned foreign affiliates affect some of the Canadian companies presently licensed in Barbados, but some of the changes also clarify the rules and enable decision-making with greater certainty. Additionally, recent indications are that some income which would originally have qualified as exempt surplus and been capable of being remitted to Canada tax free might no longer be interpreted as such; however, it will only be taxable on remittance and remain capable of being redeployed into non-Canadian investment via a non-Canadian holding company.

The most recent change was in respect of the 1996 Revenue Canada technical interpretation which essentially indicated that, since exempt insurance companies were not paying tax in Barbados, their tax-free dividend status would not apply to income earned after 1995.

The response of Barbados policy makers has been amendment to the Exempt Insurance Act to allow for the taxation of exempt insurance companies by way of converting of the US $2,500 annual license fee into a tax. It was clearly a change without effective transparency and Revenue Canada did not delay in reaching this conclusion. In 1997, the Barbados policy makers took new legislative steps to remedy the amendment and recapture the lost Canadian insurance business. The draft legislation is far reaching in that it seeks to create with the necessary licensing arrangements a new category of international insurance business under the Barbados Insurance Act. It also provides that companies licensed under the legislation will pay an effective tax of 2.5 per cent on their taxable incomes and, where applicable, companies will be able to make use of the tax credit system under the relevant double-tax treaty. The purpose and scope of these amendments is to return to Canadian owned captives the ability to enjoy tax-free repatriation of dividends to Canada. The legislation was expected to be enacted by the end of 1998.

Regulation 5907(II) Country

Canada's Regulation 5907(II) names the **prescribed countries** for purposes of the *foreign affiliate* rules. Canada has tax treaties with over 50 nations. A foreign affiliate based in any of these countries could accumulate or repatriate non-FAPI profits back to Canadian corporate shareholders free of Canadian tax. The withholding rates noted are on Canadian source payments and distributions to the foreign investor.

Countries marked with a double asterisk (**) make for good foreign affiliate bases. Countries with one asterisk (*) are tax havens.

Withholding taxes

Recipient	Dividends	Interest	Royalties
Nonresident companies and individuals (no treaty)	25%	25%	25%
Australia	15%	15%	10%
Bangladesh	15%	15%	10%
Barbados *	15%	15%	10%

---

4. **Article 22(3)** of the **U.S.-Barbados tax treaty** requires that a 3rd party user (Canada) can obtain the treaty benefits only if it registered its shares on a stock exchange approved by the competent authorities (US and Barbados) to the treaty.

Belgium	15%	15%	10%
Brazil	15%or25%	15%/25%	15%/25%
Cameroon	15%	15%	10%
China	10% or 15%	10%/15%	10%/15%
Cyprus *	15%	15%	10%
Denmark	15%	15%	15%
Dominican Republic	18%	18%	18%
Egypt	15%	15%	15%
Finland	15%	15%	15%
France	10%/15%	10%	10%
Germany F.R.	15%	15%	10%
Guyana	15%	15%	10%
India	15%/25%	15%	25%
Indonesia **	15%	15%	15%
Ireland **	15%	15%	15%
Israel	15%	15%	15%
Italy	15%	15%	10%
Ivory Coast	15%	15%	10%
Jamaica **	15%	15%	10%
Japan	10%/15%	10%	10%
Kenya	15%/25%	15%	15%
Korea	15%	15%	15%
Liberia *	15%	15%/20%	10%/20%
Luxembourg *	15%	15%	10%
Malaysia **	15%	15%	15%
Malta *	15%	15%	10%
Morocco	15%	15%	10%
Netherlands *	10%/15%	15%	10%
New Zealand **	15%	15%	15%
Norway	15%	15%	10%/15%
Pakistan	15%	15%	15%
Papua New Guinea	15%	10%	10%
Philippines **	15%	15%	10%
Poland	15%	15%	10%
Romania	15%	15%	10%/15%
Singapore *	15%	15%	15%
South Africa	15%	15%	10%
Spain	15%	15%	10%
Sri Lanka	15%	15%	10%
Sweden	15%	15%	10%
Switzerland *	15%	15%	10%
Thailand	15%	15%	15%
Trinidad & Tobago **	15%	15%	15%
Tunisia	15%	15%	15%/25%
U.S.S.R.	15%	15%	10%
United Kingdom **	10%/15%	10%	10%
United States **	10%/15%	15%	10%
Zambia	15%	15%	15%

Canada's tax policy under the treaties

The usual pattern under Canada's tax treaties is that Canada may tax non-residents on gains from the disposition of direct and indirect interests in real property situated in Canada (including interests in corporations, partnerships or trusts that derive most of their value from Canadian real property).

In addition, Canada is normally permitted to tax gains on other property forming part of a permanent establishment or fixed base of a business carried on in Canada.

Furthermore, Canada is normally allowed to tax capital gains on all other types of property owned by former Canadian residents for a specified time period after they cease being Canadian residents

In general, a non-resident who "carries on business in Canada" in a year is subject to tax in Canada on that year under Part I of the Act, on the profits derived from that business.
Where only a portion of the business is carried on in Canada (e.g. a Canadian branch), the profits reasonably attributable to the activities carried on in Canada will be subject to tax on Canada.

The determination of whether or not a non-resident carries on business in Canada in a year will be based both on common law rules (mainly derived from UK tax cases; emphasizing such factors as place where contract completed) as well as deeming rules found in the Act. For example, under paragraph 253(b) of the Act, a person will be deemed to be carrying on business in Canada if that person "solicits orders or offers for sale in Canada through an agent or servant".

Branch Tax

A special tax is payable by a non-resident corporation which carries on business in Canada. This tax, which is levied under Part XIV of the Act, is usually referred to as the "branch tax". The intention of the branch tax is to put a foreign corporation which carries on business in Canada via a branch in roughly the same position as if a Canadian subsidiary were used.

In general terms, the tax is equal to 25% of the profits earned in Canada (after normal federal and provincial income taxes) that are not retained in the Canadian branch.

Barbados - Great Base for Canadian Foreign Affilates

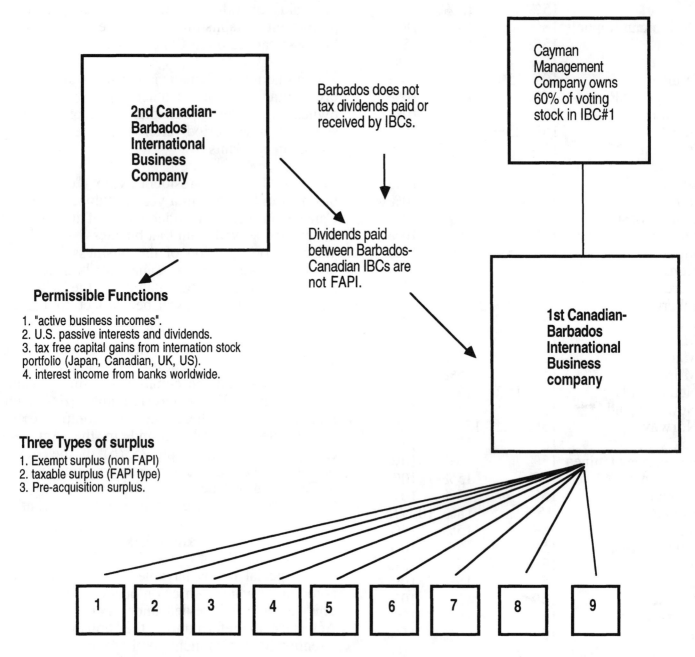

2nd Canadian-Barbados International Business Company

Barbados does not tax dividends paid or received by IBCs.

Cayman Management Company owns 60% of voting stock in IBC#1

Dividends paid between Barbados-Canadian IBCs are not FAPI.

1st Canadian-Barbados International Business company

Permissible Functions

1. "active business incomes".
2. U.S. passive interests and dividends.
3. tax free capital gains from internation stock portfolio (Japan, Canadian, UK, US).
4. interest income from banks worldwide.

Three Types of surplus

1. Exempt surplus (non FAPI)
2. taxable surplus (FAPI type)
3. Pre-acquisition surplus.

| 1 | 2 | 3 | 4 | 5 | 6 | 7 | 8 | 9 |

Up to 9 Canadian companies each owning at least 10% of the equity in Barbados foreign affiliate, but not having voting control (over 50%) could qualify to receive dividends from "exempt surplus" tax free. As few as one Canadian company owning 90% of equity but under 50% of voting stock of the IBC would qualify to receive offshore dividends from "exempt surplus account" tax free too.

FAPI = Foreign Accrual Property Income.
IBC = International Business Corporation.

Australia keeps beefing up its tax system

Australia is a high tax jurisdiction like the U.S., Canada and the U.K. Individuals resident in Australia saw personal tax rates rise to 57% in 1987. Companies pay tax at a flat rate of 36%. Individuals can pay tax rates as high as 47% for incomes over $50,000.

The normal accounting period for Australian income tax purposes is a 12 month period ending 30 June of each year.

Corporate issues that are covered by the Income Tax Assessment Act 1936 and the Income Tax Assessment Act 1997 include:

. capital gains tax provisions
. dividend imputation
. withholding tax
. carry forward of losses
. grouping of losses
. thin capitalization
. international transfer pricing
. taxation of branches as opposed to subsidiaries.

Australia's tax system has changed more in the past 15 years than in the previous forty. The information provided herein is merely a guideline for Australian tax rates.

Before 1987, interest from sources outside Australia were taxable in Australia only if they were exempt from tax in the country or origin, or were derived from the UK, New Zealand, Japan, Singapore, the Federal Republic of Germany, the Netherlands, Belgium or France. Whether the income came from a country imposing a very low rate of tax, like Barbados or Switzerland, it did not matter. The income would be exempt from Australian tax to the Australian recipient.

Recent reversals included the introduction of an accrual tax system that will input taxes to Australian corporate shareholders (but not individuals) who hold shares in offshore companies in any of 60 designated tax havens. However, if an Australian company holds less than 10% of the stock in a publicly traded tax haven company, there will be no imputation of offshore profits to the shareholder.

Judith A. Ward, an international tax partner with Price Waterhouse in Melbourne, writes:

"Australia began taxing the worldwide income of its resident individuals and corporations in earnest on July 1, 1987 when it adopted a foreign tax credit system of taxing foreign source income. Previously Australia did not tax foreign source income if it bore any tax at all in the source country; and it effectively exempted from tax dividends received by Australian companies from foreign companies (whether or not they were taxed in the source country)." [5.]

Australia's begins taxing capital gains

Prior to 1985, Australian companies and individuals did not have to worry about capital gains taxes. Australia didn't have any. New legislation ended the tax holiday on capital gains, and Australia has now joined the ranks of gains to the fullest.

Australia's capital gains taxes apply to all assets disposed of after July, 1, 1988 at the regular corporate or individual tax rates, whichever the case may be.

Aussie Tax Planning in 1990's and beyond

John Masters is an international tax partner with Price Waterhouse in Sydney, Australia. The following was excerpted from an article in PW's *International Tax Review*. It is endorsing the **offshore tax haven holding company** to hold Australian assets to avoid tax.

"Investments in post September 20, 1985 foreign subsidiaries should be through appropriate resident offshore holding companies where there is a likelihood that subsidiaries will be sold. This will shelter gain on the disposal of subsidiaries from Australian capital gains tax. And.. in addition.., foreign multinationals (MNCs), and Australian MNCs should use offshore holding companies to hold (1) Australian portfolio investments (to avoid Australia capital gains tax), and (2) intangibles (i.e., patents) used by MNC in Australia (to get a deduction in Australia and shelter the income in a low-tax or no tax haven). Unlike the growing number of industrial countries (most conspicuously the US with subpart F), Australia does not yet have tax haven legislation that would tax currently passive income of "appropriate resident" offshore subsidiaries, although planning should recognize that the possibility that Australia will institute some accrual tax system for corporations eventually."

Editor's Note: Australia's tax laws have changed so rapidly in the last 15 years that new Australian

---

5. *"International Tax Review"*, Price Waterhouse, July/August 1987 Vol 13, Number 4

tax laws could seriously undermine some of the **ideas** mentioned here.

Australia's Exchange Controls

Authority is given the **Australian Reserve Bank** to regulate and screen transactions involving tax havens. Australia has officially proclaimed the following countries to be tax havens for exchange control purposes.

The Bahamas, Bermuda British Virgin Islands, Channel Islands, Cayman, Gibraltar, Grenada, Hong Kong, Isle of Man, Liberia, Liechtenstein, Luxembourg, Nauru, Netherlands Antilles, Panama, Switzerland, Tonga and Vanuatu (certain circumstances).

Before a foreign exchange control dealer can facilitate most payments of Australian or foreign currency to these countries, the customer must obtain a tax clearance certificate from the Commissioner of Taxation stating that he is satisfied there is no purpose of tax avoidance or tax evasion behind the transaction. A tax clearance must be gotten for payments to non-tax havens when the amount exceeds $50,000, and the transaction involves loans, royalty payments and dividends. No clearance is required for equity investments, i.e., stock in Australian or foreign companies can be sold by resident or nonresidents for any amount of money without exchange control clearance.

Withholding Taxes

Australia 10% interest withholding taxes is low. Aussie companies can deduct interest charges paid to an offshore entity provided such amounts are commercially realistic.

On, 1987, Australia introduced new legislation that would restrict the **interest deduction** of foreign investors who gear their Australian investment to exceed a prescribed debt/equity ratio. The new rules apply when a foreign investor has a 15% or more interest in the Australian company, and the debt-to-equity ratio exceeds 3 to 1. **Back-to-back** "in house" loan schemes between third parties will also be challenged, but loans where the offshore parent (in a tax haven) only guarantees the loan (for example, with a bank in a non-tax haven like the Netherlands) are exonerated from these provisions.

Australian Tax Code regulates offshore tax haven companies.

Australia has **Controlled Foreign Corporation** (CFC) laws similar to those found in the United States, Canada, the U.K. and New Zealand. Income of CFCs located in designated low-tax and no-tax havens are taxed currently to the Australian shareholder under an accrual system if the income's source is tainted (i.e., passive type dividends, interest, and capital gains).

Australian shareholders are not subject to the accruals tax regime unless (1) they own 10%-or-more interest in the CFC, and (2) the income is tainted. Genuine business income of an offshore CFC is not subject to the accruals system provided that the **Tainted** income makes up *less than 5%* of total income. [6.]

Note the similarities between the Australian **Code** and the U.S. **Code**. IRC §951(b) relieves U.S. persons from the CFC provisions if they own *less than 10% of the voting stock* in the CFC. Moreover, IRC §954(b)(3) allows a CFC to accrue up to **5%** in Tainted incomes (limited to $1,000,000), much like Australian companies can.

Nonresident (foreign) companies will be CFCs if they are controlled (50% or more ownership), actually or *de facto,* by **5 or fewer** Australian residents (corporate and/or individual). Tracing rules similar to the U.S. constructive ownership rules will apply.

This Australian CFC provisions are strikingly similar to the U.S. provisions for **Foreign Personal Holding Companie**s (IRC §552(a)(2)) where ownership of *more than 50%* of total **voting or value** shares by not more than 5 U.S. persons will cause the offshore company to be treated as a FPHC. Both countries look to **de facto** control when making the CFC determination.

Loophole in Australian Code

Nonresidents are subject to Australian capital gains tax only on taxable Australian assets.

---

6. The Australian authorities are contemplating enacting new rules for **PIFs** (Passive Investment Funds), much like New Zealand's rules for **FIFs** (see page #5 & 6). PIFs are entities that are not CFCs, but derive **"passive"** income from interest, dividends, and capital gains. Accrual tax will apply to **all** Australian residents with an interest in such entities.

Shares in listed Australian companies are not taxable Australian assets unless the non-resident shareholder (together with associates) owns **10% or more** of the issued share capital.

Do the above regulations look familiar? They should. IRC §897(c)(3) of the U.S. Code allows up to **5% of the stock** in an U.S. regularly traded public stock exchange type company to be traded tax free too.

Australia's new foreign trust legislation

Following the lead of the United States - the original architect of the so-called *Controlled Foreign Corporation* legislation - the United Kingdom, Canada, Germany, Australia, Japan, France and New Zealand adopted their own versions of the CFC provisions. A few years ago, Australia enacted new non-resident trust (NRT) legislation, ostensibly similar to the legislation introduced in the United States fifteen years ago with the *Tax Reform Act of 1976 (TRA '76)*. [7.]

Australia's new non-resident trust laws can be compared with the United States' legislation under Sec. 679 - *Foreign Trusts having one or more United States Beneficiaries*.

An increasing number of Australian residents have used non-resident trusts (NRT) to hold foreign investments and accumulate foreign source income outside the reach of the Australia tax collector.

The typical structure involved a funding of a tax haven discretionary trust with a corporate or non-resident trustee. The Australian transferor to the NRT would not be subject to Australian tax on the NRT income stream, because the assets no longer belong to him, but were passed along to the foreign trustee for the benefit of certain Australian beneficiaries.

The new Australian guidelines seek to limit the advantages of using a NRT that has Australian transferors or beneficiaries by subjecting certain income earned by the NRT to Australian taxation, either on an accrual basis or with an additional tax charge.

[7.] The first Controlled Foreign Corporation provisions were introduced in the United States during the Kennedy Administration in 1962. Today, eight major territories have introduced specific anti-tax haven legislation. These 8 countries account for 90% of the world's foreign direct investment.

Transferor to NRT

Under both the Australian and United States rules the foreign trust must have a *transferor* who is a resident of that country. If there is no Australian transferor of property to the foreign trust, the provisions are not to apply.

Attributable incomes

Both the Australian and the U.S. NRT legislations rely on stock and income attribution rules as found under their Controlled Foreign Corporation provisions. The borrowing of terms and definitions from one Code-section for use in another is common practice among today's lawmakers. Legislators integrate the law - one section to the next - to unify the statutes and make them practical to apply.

Australia's (income) Attribution Rules

Whether foreign trust profits will be attributed back to the Australian beneficiary to be included with his other Australian incomes depends on whether the foreign trust is domiciled in a *listed* or *unlisted* country. The "attributable income" of a NRT is calculated for each income year of the transferor from the 1990-91 income year on up.

Once the attributable income is calculated it will be included in the assessable income of each Australian resident which transfers, or had transferred, property or services to the NRT.

Listed Countries: Australia regards 61 countries as listed countries. These include industrial nations like the U.S. and UK. Foreign trust income derived in a listed country is not attributed back to the Australian beneficiary unless the income is gotten through a tax concession offered in the listed country.

Unlisted countries: Australia's table of unlisted countries includes all the recognized tax havens, including the Cayman Islands, the Bahamas, Hong Kong, Vanuatu, Luxembourg, Gibraltar, Channel Islands, Isle of Man, Panama and the Netherlands Antilles.

Add on interest charge: The proposed legislation seeks to introduce an additional tax in the form of an *interest charge* on trust distributions to beneficiaries.

Tax and Business Planning with Ernst & Young (Australia)

Michael Whyte, principal, and Peter A. Wilson, partner, Ernst & Young (Australia) offer some tax planning tips to Australian transferors and beneficiaries of foreign trusts. They note that the accrual tax treatment apply only where the transferor is a resident of Australia. It should be possible, they say, to avoid operation of the transferor rules by structuring the plan so the transferor is non-resident. If, for example, the transferor is an Australian company it may be possible to move the residence of the company outside Australia, but only to a country that has a double tax treaty with Australia.

Another technique offered by Michael Whyte and Peter A. Wilson involves the use of a dividend trap company. Where a NRT in a listed company is getting non-portfolio dividends (i.e., dividends from a shareholding of 10% or more) from listed countries, consider inserting a dividend trap company in a no-tax haven to defer recognition of income to the NRT. There is no exemption available to a NRT in an unlisted country on non-portfolio dividends received from a listed country.

Another plan offered by Whyte and Wilson calls for the Australian beneficiary to change their residence. If arrangements are structured so that the transferor tax measures do not apply, it could still be possible for resident beneficiaries to receive the accumulated offshore income of a NRT tax free. It would be required that the corpus be distributed to the beneficiary while he/she is not a resident of Australia. For this tax free result to be gotten, the beneficiary must be a non-resident during the entire taxable year in which the distribution is made.

Before such a change in residence is undertaken, Whtye and Wilson suggest that the Australian consider the capital gains tax implications. Unless the beneficiary makes an election, he may well be found to have disposed of all non-Australian assets acquired since 19, September, 1985 (the year the Australia enacted its first capital gains tax) for their market values. The technical difficulty here is whether a beneficial interest in a foreign discretionary trust amounts to an "owned" asset.

CHAPTER 16 • Bank Secrecy • Asset Protection Trusts • Bearer Shares

Over the last few years, Asset Protection Trusts (APTs) have become the new offshore sensation. Innovative offshore legislation initiated by the governments of the Bahamas, Cook Islands, British Virgin Islands, Cayman, Gibraltar and Barbados (to name a few) have caused added excitement among lawyers, bankers, offshore practitioners and financial consultants. And while asset protection trusts appear to be a new phenomenon, they are really the same paramour in a slightly different suite.

The use of a foreign trust in an offshore no tax jurisdiction is nothing new. The U.S. tax code has dealt with the transfers to foreign trusts by U.S., taxpayers since before the 1960's. What's different about the APTs of today and the foreign trusts of twenty years ago is the type of protection provided the end user.

APTs are being marketed by lawyers, accountants and other practitioners, as effective devices for protecting ones assets from unfair litigation suits (not tax shields against the IRS), often initiated by ambitious lawyers seeking claims into the tens of millions for their clients. If the U.S. court rules against the defendant, as they so often do, his U.S. based assets are subject to forfeiture and seizure to pay the claimant and his prestigious lawyers.

Assets held by a foreign trustee in a tax haven jurisdiction that does not have an income tax treaty with the end users home country are usually not seizable. To reclaim offshore assets won in a litigation suit, the claimant and his lawyer would need to try the case in the local courts. This is usually not pursued by the claimant and his lawyer because the claimant's lawyer is usually not licensed to practice in the offshore jurisdiction.

Moreover, getting bank and financial records to divulge what assets are held by who, in what bank, in what amounts is usually impossible because of the bank secrecy codes that shield the trusts from such foreign intrusions. Plain and simple, once the assets are placed offshore they are often very difficult to seize.

APTs are used not only by folks being sued for medical malpractice, legal malpractice and recent bankrupts, but spouses in anticipation of marital collapse. Recently, one poor woman phoned to ask the addresses of banks in the Channel Islands. Why? Her husband had ferreted the family assets offshore before divorcing her. The loonier sequel to the story is that she had appointed a Gypsy clairvoyant to "pass hand over the list" to find her share of her ex-husband's hoarded cash. The effort no doubt was in vain.

Mistresses are often the direct beneficiaries of APTs. One wealthy Hong Kong businessman was sugar daddy to no less than six. Each sugar daughter was the beneficiary of her own APT. [1]

Rock solid Gibraltar trusts

Publisher tycoon Robert Maxwell's shocking death pushed his tangled web of finances into the limelight, among them vehicles established in Gibraltar to hold stock in public companies. Banks and taxmen are already picking the bones of the Maxwell Empire, and people are wondering whether Gibraltar will stand rock solid against their scrutiny or will its reputation as a confidential financial center crumble?

One source declared, "A taxman who comes here to find out what's in a Gibraltar company or trust would be told to get lost."

Chris Samuelson of offshore trust and company specialist Riggs Valmet agrees: "Maxwell's trusts and companies are clearly

---

[1.] From *"APTs: free of litigators and the law"* by Paul Ham, **Offshore Financial Review** (June 1992), pg. 9.

visible as shareholders in UK companies on the UK companies' registry. But what nobody knows is what's actually inside them." Tax authorities, creditors and even journalists have no way of discovering the nitty gritty, he adds.

It's a different story when, as John Welham of Coopers & Lybrand puts it: "Tax evasion or funny money is involved." Gibraltar has a jaundiced view on anyone trying to hide away their ill-gotten gains. A court order which allows the examination of the trust or company can be granted to investigators who can produce hard evidence of disreputable conduct (i.e., fraud, embezzlement, drug money).

So Maxwell's case is an interesting rather than a crucial test of Gibraltar's confidentiality policy.

It also highlights the scope of offshore trust and company services Gibraltar can offer. Maxwell - born in Czechoslovakia, living in the UK, with French born children, would have been a complex customer. "But trusts are useful animals because they can be tailored to suite everyone." says John Welham.

Gibraltar's Financial Services Commission discourages other firms from cashing in on APT legislation because these trusts are potential minefields.

Creating a trust or company in Gibraltar is fairly straightforward. Prestigious banks such as Barclays or Midland can do it, as can a number of lawyers and accountants. However, Riggs Valmet and Coopers and Lybrand advise against setting up a trust unless you have a spare £100,000, because of the high costs involved.

"It's really horses for courses", notes Welham. "The client may place more value on secrecy that the costs." Annual fees range from around £500 to £1,500 to administer a trust or company. In addition, it costs around £500 to establish the vehicle and more if it is a complex arrangement.

Asset protection trusts are widely available in Gibraltar, but Gibraltar's Financial Services Commission discourages other firms from cashing in because these trusts are potential minefields. Clients are strictly vetted. Coopers and Lybrand

insist on a £1 million pound indemnity insurance and the client must be certain no claims are pending against him.

According to Chris Samuelson, Donald Trump would have found it hard to set one up in Gibraltar, even a year before he ran into financial trouble. [2]

Definition of APT

Asset protection has become a "buzz phrase" according to A.R. Howard LLP of Miller & Howard Solicitors. In simple terms an Asset-Protection Trust (APT) is a trust structure, normally established offshore (in a foreign jurisdiction), comprising a limited parcel of assets set aside as a hedge against serious financial loss.

The principal whereby society will protect a basic level of assets from seizure in the event of bankruptcy recognizes a need to sustain families *in extremis*. It is no great quantum leap to argue that a modicum of comfort should also be preserved. It may be defined as a relationship which arises where property is vested in a person (the trustee), which the trustee is obliged to hold for the benefit of other persons called beneficiaries. Trust are recognized and enforced in equity. Increasingly, however, the rights of the parties to the arrangements are becoming enshrined in statute law, in some instances the point of codification.

APTs (which often involve an underlying company, an Anstalt or a partnership in addition to the trust itself) have developed as a response to certain pressures which have arisen, or which it is anticipated may arise, in respect of the assets of successful people.

While A.R. Miller believes that individuals who have suffered a loss should be recompensated in accordance with the law, he also believes because the pendulum of justice has swung too far in favor of the claimants and their attorneys, resulting in exorbitant court rewards, a need for APTs to protect ones assets is crucial.

---

[2] From *"Rock Solid Secrecy"*, by Andrea Page *(The International)* *(J*anuary 1992) pg. 14 25.

The protection of assets has always been the *raison d'etre* of trust law (coupled with the protection of individuals from others, at times, themselves), and in that sense the APT is not a new development.

EDITORIAL

APTs: Flavour of the year leaves bad taste

At a conference in Geneva in June, James Hughes, a tax partner at US law firm Jones Day Reavis & Pogue, singled out the Cook Islands as the jurisdiction most likely to revamp its laws to take quick advantage of new custom. He is right to point to the tendency, but perhaps a little unfair to single out the Cooks. All around the Caribbean and in pockets in Europe, tax havens are proposing to enact new laws on asset protection trusts (APTs). The BVI is revamping their legislation as is the Turks & Caicos Islands.

APTs are very popular with American lawyers, doctors, accountants and other high earning professionals who fear enormous costs of litigation against their practices. Business people are also placing their assets in APTs to protect themselves against prospective creditors should they go bankrupt. As one delegate at the conference said: "APTs are the perfect protection during a recession."

Marshall Langer, the Miami tax lawyer warned, "long arm" legislation such as the Racketeering Influenced and Corrupt Organization Act of 1980 (RICO) could be invoked anywhere in the world to find assets spirited off to an APT. There were also numerous criminal statutes for "aiding and abetting" the concealment of assets from the courts or the Internal Revenue; a trustee who enters into an APT aware that the assets are being concealed may be criminally charged.

Letter Rulings and Revenue Rulings

From time to time the IRS issues letter rulings and revenue rulings designed to help the taxpayer determine what tax consequences he can expect under certain situations. Below are a few Rulings that should be considered by the U.S. settlor (transferor) of a foreign trust.

IRS LTR 9332006 ™ Full Text

The use of an offshore **testamentary trust** to receive a U.S. persons assets only upon his death might afford some definite tax advantages, especially if the trusts assets are revocable by a nonresident alien individual or corporation. IRS LT. 9332006 confirms that upon his death, assets held in a foreign trust will no longer be subject to U.S. taxes, and not considered part of the U.S. person's U.S. estate, even if there are U.S. beneficiaries for the foreign trust.

LTR 9332006 -- ISSUE (4). UPON A SETTLOR'S DEATH, WILL THE PORTION OF THE TRUST TREATED AS OWNED BY THAT SETTLOR CEASE TO BE SO TREATED EVEN IF THEN TRUST BENEFICIARIES INCLUDE UNITED STATES PERSONS? Section 679(a)(2) (A) provides that the rules of section 679(a)(1) do not apply to "a transfer by reason of death of the transferor." While section 679(a)(2)(A) does not expressly address the tax consequences of the termination of foreign grantor trust status by reason of the grantor's death, the legislative history of the enactment of section 679 (H.R. Rep. No. 658, 94th Cong., 1st Sess. at 209 (1975); S. Rep. No. 938, 94th Cong., 2d Sess. at 218 (1976)) provides that "an inter vivos trust which is treated as owned by a U.S. person under [section 679] is not treated as owned by the estate of that person upon his death." Accordingly, any portion of the Trust that is treated as owned by a Settlor under the rules of section 679 shall cease to be so treated upon that Settlor's death.

LTR 9332006 ™ Full Text

ISSUE (3). IS THE TRUST A TRUST DESCRIBED IN SECTION 679? Section 679 provides (with exceptions not here relevant) that a United States person who directly or indirectly transfers property to a foreign trust shall be treated as the owner for his taxable year of the portion of such trust attributable to such property if for such year there is a United States beneficiary of any portion of such trust. Section 7701(a)(30)(A) provides in part that the term "United States person" includes a citizen of the United States. Under section 679, the term

"United States beneficiary" includes a trust beneficiary who is a United States person.

Each Settlor, a United States person, is considered to have transferred property to the Trust. Further, each Settlor and Beneficiary A is a "United States beneficiary" within the meaning of section 679. Accordingly, whether the Trust will be treated as a grantor trust under section 679 depends upon whether it is a foreign trust.

It has been represented that the Trust is a foreign trust. If that is so, the Trust will be treated as a grantor trust under section 679, and each Settlor will, for the taxable year in which the Trust is funded and in each succeeding taxable year during his or her life in which the Trust continues to have a United States beneficiary, be treated as the owner of a portion of the Trust income and corpus. That portion shall be determined in accordance with the principles of Treas. Reg. section 1.671-3, and each Settlor shall be required to take into account, in computing his or her federal income tax liability that Settlor's appropriate portion of the Trust's items of income, deductions, and credits.

Rev. Rul. 87-61 ™ Summary

FACTS. The taxpayer in this revenue ruling, a United States citizen, established a trust under the laws of a foreign country by executing a trust document and transferring certain appreciated property to a trustee, a bank incorporated in the foreign country. The trustee had legal title to the property, and the property was then located in the foreign country. Payments from the trust were to go to the taxpayer's child, with a remainder to the taxpayer's grandchild, both citizens and residents of the foreign country. The taxpayer was treated as the owner of the entire trust under Code sections 671 through 679 from the date the trust was created until he renounced his retained powers on December 31, 1984.

ISSUE. At issue is whether the taxpayer's transfer of appreciated property to a trust in a foreign country, a trust which the taxpayer is considered to own for purposes of section 671, is subject to tax under section 1491 (now repealed)

HOLDING. The Service has held that the transfer to the trust is not subject to tax under section 1491. The Service held, however, that the taxpayer will be subject to the section 1491 tax when he ceases to be the owner of the trust by renouncing his retained powers over the trust property.

ANALYSIS. The Service determined that the trust is a "foreign trust" as defined under section 7701(a)(31), a class of trusts that are "analogous to the class of nonresident alien individuals." Factors in this determination include the trust's establishment in a foreign country, the trustee's status as a foreign entity, and the corpus' location in a foreign country. Citing Rev. Rul. 77-402, 1977-2 C.B. 222, the Service held that the taxpayer in the instant ruling should be "viewed as having transferred property to [the foreign trust] only at the time [the taxpayer] ceased to be the owner of the trust" for purposes of section 671. Thus, the tax imposed under section 1491 and the reporting requirements under regulation section 1.1494-1(a) do not arise until the taxpayer renounces the powers he had retained when he created the trust.

The Service noted that its holding would not have differed if the grantor had held only a portion of the trust or if the renunciation of control had been due to an expiration or a lapse of powers.

Substance over form doctrine

The substance, rather than the form, of a transaction in which a taxpayer is involved governs the tax consequences of the transaction.[3]

A trust will be disregarded for tax purposes if it has no substance, utility, or purpose, and the income of the trust will be included in the gross income of the person who controls the trust.[4]

The sham transaction doctrine requires the IRS to examine each transaction to determine whether it has economic substance. Such analysis

---

[3] See, for example, Commissioner v. Court Holding Company, 324 U.S. 331 (1945), 1945 C.B. 58; Helvering v. Clifford, 309 U.S. 331 (1940), 1940-1 C.B. 105; Gregory v. Helvering, 293 U.S. 465, XIV-I C.B. 193 (1935).

[4] See Zmuda, supra, at page 719.

is factual in nature and can be concluded only based on the specific evidence presented in the instant cases. In *La Fargue and Stern v. Commissioner* the court held that the use of foreign trusts were not shams.

La Fargue and Stern involved taxpayers who set up foreign situs trusts and transferred property to the trusts in exchange for lifetime private annuities. In those cases, the court scrutinized the transactions and determined that the taxpayers did not have sufficient control over the trusts to justify disregarding the taxpayers' characterizations of the trusts and that any informalities in trust administration were too minor to be of any consequence. Moreover, the court determined that the taxpayers had relinquished control over the property that was transferred, and the trusts were not mere conduits for the income from that property; therefore, the transactions at issue were respected as sales. [5.]

While there are probably over 100,000 foreign trusts in tax havens like the Cayman Islands, Bermuda and the Bahamas, the U.S. tax courts have disregarded very few of them. One of the main reasons is their inability to sequester banking records and other financial details.

It seems apparent from case law and IRS rulings that before the IRS and federal tax courts will rule for or against the use of a foreign trust in a particular situation, the foreign trust must have first received a direct or indirect transfer from a U.S. person (grantor). If there is no transfer of U.S. property by a U.S. person, there is little likelihood that the foreign trust will be disregarded or ruled a sham.

ESTATE TAX PLANNING TIP

Foreigners investing in U.S. property, including U.S. real estate, stocks and bonds should always use a tax haven holding company to hold those U.S. assets. If the nonresident alien invests $5,000,000 in a Texas oil lease directly under his own name, the entire $5,000,000 would be included in his estate for purposes of computing his U.S. estate tax liability. If the nonresident alien died in 1992, the $5,000,000 lease would be subject to U.S. estate taxes at rates to 55%, and the nonresident alien would be permitted only a $60,000 tax credit.

Using the estate tax table under **IRC §2001(c)** the nonresident alien would owe $1,290,800 on amounts up to $3,000,000, and 55% of everything above that. On his $5,000,000 estate, the nonresident alien's heirs would witness the payment of ≈ $2,390,800 in estate taxes to the U.S. Treasury.

HOWEVER, under U.S. estate tax law shares of an offshore company **would not** be included in the nonresident alien's estate for purposes of calculating his **U.S. estate tax** liability, even if the only asset owned by the offshore company was the $5,000,000 U.S. oil lease. Offshore practitioners should never advise their non-U.S. clients to invest directly in the USA. A tax haven holding company should always be considered; unless the investment being planned is small - under $100,000.

---

5. See La Fargue v. Commissioner, 689 F.2d 845 (9th Cir. 1982), affg. in part, revg. in part and remanding 73 T.C. 40 (1979), and Stern v. Commissioner, 747 F.2d 555 (9th Cir. 1984)]

Bearer Shares

Bearer shares are not widely used in the United States, but are in widespread use in Europe and the rest of the world. Since their use is permitted in many popular tax havens, like Switzerland, Panama and the Caymans, it would seem appropriate to mention a few words about them here. Not all countries permit you to issue bearer shares.

Bearer shares are certificates of stock with the inscription *Payable to Bearer* written somewhere on them. Anyone holding a bearer share may present them to the company for payment. When a company issues bearer shares, there is no disclosure of the real owner's name in the shareholders register. Bearer shares are frequently used by businessmen seeking anonymity in their financial affairs. Novelists have used them to parlay motives of greed, hate and other traits of human nature into their writings, but the holder of bearer shares is no different than the holder of any brand of company shares. They're all called capitalists.

For some reason some people believe using bearer shares will exempt them from their U.S. income tax liability. Unfortunately, bearer shares themselves provide no tax advantages of any kind, and for purposes of federal income taxes they are treated the same as any other type of stock. If you own them directly or indirectly, they will (1) be included in your estate upon your demise (2) be subject to federal gift taxes if you give them away (3) liable to capital gains taxes upon their redemption or sale. In addition, dividends paid on bearer shares would be taxable income, the same as dividends on stock in any company.

Bearer shares are a tradition in some European countries. More than half of Luxembourg's companies are said to issue bearer shares. They are also widespread in the Netherlands. The following list of countries permit the use of bearer shares.

1. Austria
2. Costa Rica
3. Germany
4. Liberia
5. Malta
6. Nauru
7. Netherlands Antilles
8. Panama
9. Liechtenstein
10. Solomon Islands
11. Saudi Arabia
12. Switzerland
13. Cayman Islands (only exempt companies)
14. Turks & Caicos Islands (for companies with authorized capital of $55,000 or more).
15. British Virgin Islands
16. Bahamas

Bearer Share Warrants

Some tax havens permit you to use a hybrid type of bearer shares. These are called **bearer share warrants**. Users say they are hard to handle and deal with, and are not as well liked as true bearer shares. The following countries permit the use of bearer share warrants.

1. Bahamas
2. Vanuatu
3. Barbados
4. New Zealand

The following countries do not permit either bearer shares or bearer share warrants. Shares issued in these jurisdictions must be registered in your name or a company name.

1. Australia
2. Cyprus
3. Jamaica
4. Singapore

One of the real advantages of bearer shares is they are freely transferred from one person to another by simple delivery of the certificates. In this respect bearer shares are much like paper money. It is unnecessary to notify the company whose shares you dispose.

Bearer share certificates often come with numbered coupons you detach and redeem in much the same way you detach the coupon on a bond to collect interest.

On the negative side, bearer shares are dangerous because if you lose them or they are stolen they cannot be replaced in most cases. To vote bearer shares at a shareholders' meeting you must deposit them with a designated bank. The bank in turn will issue a document authorizing the voting stock to be cast at the meeting on your behalf. In this way the company directors and shareholders can never learn how you vote your bearer shares.

Other kinds of shares

Other less exotic sounding names for shares are issued in the offshore tax havens. These include common stock, stock with par value, stock with no-par value, preferred shares, **redeemable preferred shares**, shares that carry special voting rights or dividend rights, and shares that represent value in the company, but carry no voting privileges.

Some tax havens do not require you to issue (print) **share certificates** to shareholders. Recording the shareholder's name in the shareholders register is acceptable. This can save you the costs of printing certificates and distributing them. Switzerland and the Netherlands require only that the names of the shareholders be written in the register.

Capitalization

How does the businessperson go about capitalizing his offshore holding company? That's a common question I'm often asked to respond to. Yes, it sounds like a simple question, but is it really?

Cash or money can be exchanged for shares in a tax haven company or any foreign company, and current U.S. policy does nothing to inhibit you from displacing any amount as paid-in capital. You do not need government approval regardless of the place of incorporation or the purpose of the company.

The 35% toll tax levied under IRC §1491 was recently repealed, but the Treasury Department will probably apply a phantom tax **capital gains tax** on appreciated assets transferred to an offshore entity.

When a U.S. person transfers appreciated assets to a foreign corporation, practically speaking he is limited to cash when capitalizing his/her/a foreign company.

Registered Capital

Many tax havens charge a fee when you register your capital or buy up the shares in your holding company. Some countries, such as the Netherlands, have high paid-in capital fees. The Dutch charge a 1% nonrecurring capital appreciation tax, computed on the par value of shares or the other value of the consideration paid for the shares, whichever is the higher. Switzerland's federal stamp tax of 3% on paid-in capital is exorbitant. The Caymans charge 1/40th of 1% of the authorized share capital, subject to a maximum dollar limit.

Stamp Duties

The Stamp Act of 1765 was passed by the British Parliament to raise revenue. It required that stamps be used for all legal and commercial documents, newspapers, etc. in the American colonies. It was repealed in March 1766 because of strong colonial opposition. Whether the Stamp Act was the predecessor of the various stamp taxes (duties) that exist today in most all the tax havens and financial centers hardly seems important. What is important is to recognize their existence.

Where you sign a particular document may determine whether you are liable to stamp taxes in some tax havens. In the Netherlands Antilles the stamp tax is levied at a flat rate equal to NAf.4 per NAf.$100. This tax is due only on the transfer within the Antilles. Shares transferred by the company outside the country are not liable to the stamp tax.

The Swiss stamp tax amounts to 0.15% on the sale, transfer or purchase of shares, bonds, debentures, shares in mutual funds, bill of exchange and promissory notes in the Swiss issuer, and 0.3% if the issuer is a foreigner. The tax is applicable to registered professional security dealers, banks, bankers, management companies, depository bank of mutual funds and holding companies.

Bank secrecy in the Bahamas is alive and well

The Bahamas commitment to banking secrecy was reaffirmed by the new government on June 10th, 1993, when the Minister of Justice and Foreign Affairs, Mr. Orville A. Turnquest, stated in parliament that "....the Bahamas is not only committed to the bank secrecy laws, but to the prevention of intrusion by foreign governments."

James Smith, governor of the Central Bank, says he is committed to attracting quality not quantity.

Secrecy is strict. A fine of $5,000 applies to anyone disclosing details of accounts in breach of the confidentiality code.

The Bahamian secrecy laws are imposed on all Bank and Trust Companies, their directors, officers, and employees, attorneys, and auditors. Only with an order from the Supreme Court can a third party acquire information, in criminal matters, about any account. Tax evasion in one's home country is not a criminal matter in the Bahamas. Any offshore account in The Bahamas is protected by this strict bank secrecy law.

The Bahamas is not a party to any tax or fiscal information-sharing agreements (i.e., tax treaties) with any other country. Once you open an account in the Bahamas, you are the only one who has the privilege to access it.

In the Bahamas no minimum capital requirements are necessary for obtaining a banking or trust license, but in practice the Central Bank requires the foreign parent to guarantee the liability of the local branch or subsidiary. Because of this criterion, you seldom hear of a banking crisis in the Bahamas.

Before new banking legislation was introduced in 1966, the Bahamas had 600 banks. Many of these 600 banks were questionable, so the Central Bank pruned that number down to 90 banks. Today, the Bahamas have 404 registered banks, including Citicorp, Royal Bank of Canada, Canadian Imperial Bank of Commerce and Sumitomo.

In regards to the BCCI banking scandal that rocked the Caymans, Luxembourg and other tax havens, Governor Smith recalls: "We got rid of them before the Bank of England did."

Iqbal Singh, the banking supervisor, explains why BCCI was thrown out of the Bahamas. "We wondered how its (BCCI's) loan portfolio could grow so fast without a parallel growth in deposits."

The Central Bank subjects those seeking licenses to rigorous scrutiny: commercial and character references are required; in some cases, the FBI may be notified.

The Bahamas banking infrastructure is more developed than elsewhere in the Caribbean; 180 banks have a "physical presence" employing five or more people. Smith adds "We have a bigger supervision team here than most other countries, with 24 technical people."

Word of mouth is often the best form of policing an offshore center. "If a bank has a problem, Smith says, "We hear about it that afternoon - everyone talks."

While the number of banks in the Bahamas has fallen a bit in the 1980's, the asset base of the banks that remain has grown to an estimated $175 billion on deposit. Much of the new money is coming from Latin America, notably Costa Rica, Brazil and Argentina.

Singh says the Latin countries are very exciting. "The size of their external debt is often the same as the size of their flight capital."

The threat of taxes on Mexican banks following the North American Trade Agreement is also generating new deposits.

Tax freedom is not the only reason depositors choose the Bahamas. "We're selling efficiency, cost and secrecy - often people have trade secrets, not tax secrets," Smith says.

If fraud is suspected, the Bahamas courts will act to open accounts - "we're not impregnable," says Smith.

The Bahamas is said to employ powerful radar systems that can read the registration numbers of light aircraft. While some Bahamian banks will accept cash deposits of $50,000, the days of million dollar cash deposits by the drug cartels appears to be over.

Owen Bethel, the Bahamas Financial Secretary, says "we no longer have a drug trafficking problem - the U.S. has assisted us in cracking down on that."

The Bahamas now boast over 95,000 IBCs

In 1989 the Bahamas introduced new IBC legislation to better compete with the British Virgin Islands, the Caymans, Panama and the Turks and Caicos Islands for offshore business.

Ms. Suzanne Ducille, acting registrar general of the Bahamas Company Registrar, says "IBCs (International Business Companies) can do anything, because no one knows what they do. Your speculation is as good as mine."

"The ultimate beneficiaries may never be known - the directors may be lawyers, or there may be several layers of nominees. "

"The owners of IBCs may be divorcees, or they may not want to pay tax on dividends, or they may run international trading companies or invest in property." IBC's may overlay or underlay trusts - permutations are many and varied," comments one Bahamian banker.

One Bahamian lawyer says, "The only constraint on an IBC's activities is that the IBC may not conduct business in the Bahamas." Anything else, it seems, goes: IBC's file no annual return, and no records.

New improved real estate legislation for foreigners

The government of the Bahamas has recently made some major legislative changes to boost foreign investment:

• The repeal, due shortly, of the Removable Properties Act, which stops foreigners from buying homes without the government's permission.

The Act's repeal will mean that anyone can buy property in the Bahamas up to a maximum of 5 acres (beyond which government approval will be required).

• The imposition of a flat 7% government stamp duty on all properties, by foreigners and Bahamians, replacing the previous 12% tax which fell only on foreign buyers.

This alone has generated $35-$40 million worth of sales in Lyford Cay over the past nine months, according to local real estate agents, including the record $20 million sale of a house to Irvin Kramer, a producer of Broadway plays.

• The termination of the Investment Promotion Program (IPP), introduced by the last government, and its replacement with a policy that does not link personal residence with property.

Under the IPP, investors who bought a big enough chunk of Bahamian property were rewarded with residence status. But, this proved a disincentive to many potential investors who did not want residence.

Current residents of the Bahamas include Sean Connery, Sir John Templeton (mutual fund manager) the Barcardis (rum distillers), the Alsabahs (a branch of the Kuwaiti Royal family), Peter de Savary (the yachting entrepreneur), Nicholas Brady (former U.S. Treasury Secretary under the Bush administration), two soup fiefdoms, Tony O'Reilly (of Heinz) and John Durrant (of Campbells). [6]

[6.] From "Bahamas: Recovering the lost generation," by Paul Ham, *Offshore Financial Review,* August 1993.

New Providence Press, Ltd.
Offshore Incorporation Request Form

Name: _____

Address: _____

_____

Phone: _____   Fax:_____

THREE CHOICES FOR A CORPORATE NAME:

1. _____

2. _____

3. _____

DIRECTORS   **TRUST BENEFICIARIES**

Name: _____   Name: _____

Name: _____   Name:_____

Name: _____   Name: _____

AMOUNT ENCLOSED: _____ (Bank Cashiers check, travelers checks, international money orders for $2,100 made payable to **New Providence Press, Ltd.**) No U.S. postal money orders please. They are not negotiable outside the United States)

Send via UPS (overnight) Express carrier only to:

Thomas Azzara
New Providence Press, Ltd.   Phone/FAX: 242-327-7359
54 Sandyport Drive   Cellular: 242-359-1132 • emergencies only
P.O. Box CB 11552
Nassau, Bahamas

SIGNATURE OF REQUESTER: _____

NEW PROVIDENCE PRESS, Ltd.
(a Registered IBC in the Bahamas)
P.O. Box CB 11552
Nassau, Bahamas
Telephone/FAX 242-327-7359
Cellular 242-359-1132 (emergencies only)
WebSite: http://www.bahamasbahamas.com/
Email taxman@batelnet.bs

APPENDIX

Form TD F 90-22.1   Report of Foreign Bank Accounts

Form 3520   Creation or transfer to certain foreign trusts [1]

Form 3520-A   Annual Return of Foreign Trusts with U.S. beneficiaries [1]

Form 5471   Information Return with Respect to a Foreign Corporation [1]

Form 926   Return by U.S. Transfer of Property to a Foreign corporation. [2]

---

[1] New form 3520 A (1998) replaces old Form 3520-A. It is too long to include here. Contact the IRS and have them mail you all the forms (with their instructions) mentioned above. We've included only the first few pages here, as some of these forms and instructions are 18 pages or longer in length.

[2] Cash transfers over $100,000 are now required to be filed on form 926 beginning Feb. 5, 1999

<table>
<tr><td colspan="2">Department of the Treasury
TD F 90-22.1
SUPERSEDES ALL PREVIOUS EDITIONS</td><td colspan="2">**REPORT OF FOREIGN BANK
AND FINANCIAL ACCOUNTS**

Do **NOT** file with your Federal Tax Return</td><td>FinCEN
OMB No. 1505-0063</td><td>1</td></tr>
</table>

1 Filing for Calendar Year Y Y Y Y	2 Type of Filer a ☐ Individual b ☐ Partnership c ☐ Corporation d ☐ Fiduciary	3 Taxpayer Identification Number

Part I   Filer Information

4 Last Name or Organization Name	5 First Name	6 Middle Initial

7 Address (Number, Street, and Apt. or Suite No.)	8 Date of Birth M M D D Y Y Y Y

9 City	10 State	11 Zip/Postal Code	12 Country	13 Title (Not necessary if reporting a personal account)

14 Are these account jointly owned? a ☐ Yes b ☐ No	15 Number of joint owners	16 Taxpayer Identification Number of joint owner (if known)

17 Last Name or Organization Name	18 First Name	19 Middle Initial

Part II   Information on Financial Accounts

20 Number of Foreign Financial Accounts in which a financial interest is held	21 Type of account a ☐ Bank b ☐ Securities c ☐ Other _____

22 Maximum value of account a ☐ Under $10,000 c ☐ $100,000 to $1,000,000 b ☐ $10,000 to $99,999 d ☐ Over $1,000,000	23 Account Number or other designation

24 Name of Financial Institution with which account is held	25 Country in which account is held

26 Does the filer have a financial interest in this account? a ☐ Yes b ☐ No If no, complete boxes 27-35.	27 Last Name or Organization Name of Account Owner

28 First Name	29 Middle Initial	30 Taxpayer Identification Number

31 Address (Number, Street, and Apt. or Suite No.)	32 City

33 State	34 Zip/Postal Code	35 Country	

36 Signature	37 Date M M D D Y Y Y Y

This form should be used to report a financial interest in, signature authority, or other authority over one or more financial accounts in foreign countries, as required by the Department of the Treasury Regulations (31 CFR 103). No report is required if the aggregate value of the accounts did not exceed $10,000. **SEE INSTRUCTIONS FOR DEFINITION.** File this form with:

U.S. Department of the Treasury, P.O. Box 32621, Detroit, MI 48232-0621.

PRIVACY ACT NOTIFICATION

Pursuant to the requirements of Public Law 93-579 (Privacy Act of 1974), notice is hereby given that the authority to collect information on TD F 90-22.1 in accordance with 5 USC 552a(e) is Public Law 91-508; 31 USC 5314; 5 USC 301; 31 CFR 103.

The principal purpose for collecting the information is to assure maintenance of reports where such reports or records have a high degree of usefulness in criminal, tax, or regulatory investigations or proceedings. The information collected may be provided to those officers and employees of any constituent unit of the Department of the Treasury who have a need for the records in the performance of their duties. The records may be referred to any other department or agency of the United States upon the request of the head of such department or agency for use in a criminal, tax, or regulatory investigation or proceeding.

Disclosure of this information is mandatory. Civil and criminal penalties, including certain circumstances a fine of not more than $500,000 and imprisonment of not more than five years, are provided for failure to file a report, supply information, and for filing a false or fraudulent report.

Disclosure of the Social Security number is mandatory. The authority to collect is 31 CFR 103. The Social Security number will be used as a means to identify the individual who files the report.

INSTRUCTIONS

General Instructions

Who Must File this Report Each United States person, who has a financial interest in or signature authority, or other authority over any financial accounts, including bank, securities, or other types of financial accounts in a foreign country, if the aggregate value of these financial accounts exceeds $10,000 at any time during the calendar year, must report that relationship each calendar year by filing TD F 90-22.1 with the Department of the Treasury on or before June 30, of the succeeding year.

Exceptions

An officer or employee of a bank which is subject to the supervision of the Comptroller of the Currency, the Board of Governors of the Federal Reserve System, the Office of Thrift Supervision, or the Federal Deposit Insurance Corporation need not report that he has signature or other authority over a foreign bank, securities or other financial account maintained by the bank, if the officer or employee has NO personal financial interest in the account.

An officer or employee of a domestic corporation whose equity securities are listed upon national securities exchanges or which has assets exceeding $10 million and 500 or more shareholders of record need not file such a report concerning the other signature authority over a foreign financial account of the corporation, if he has NO personal financial interest in the account and he has been advised in writing by the chief financial officer of the corporation that the corporation has filed a current report, which includes that account.

Report any financial account (except a military banking facility as defined in these instructions) that is located in a foreign country, even if it is held at an affiliate of a United States bank or other financial institution. Do not report any account maintained with a branch, agency, or other office of a foreign bank of other institution that is located in the United States, Guam, Puerto Rico, and the Virgin Islands.

General Definitions

United States Person The term "United States person" means (1) a citizen or resident of the United States, (2) a domestic partnership, (3) a domestic corporation, or (4) a domestic estate or trust.

Financial Account Generally includes any bank, securities, securities derivatives or other financial instruments accounts. Such accounts generally also encompass any accounts in which the assets are held in a commingled fund, and the account owner holds an equity interest in the fund. The term also means any savings, demand, checking, deposit, time deposit, or any other account maintained with a financial institution or other person engaged in the business of a financial institution.

Account in a Foreign Country A "foreign country" includes all geographical areas located outside the United States, Guam, Puerto Rico, and the Virgin Islands.

Financial Interest A financial interest in a bank, securities, or other financial account in a foreign country means an interest described in either of the following two paragraphs:

(1) A United States person has a financial interest in each account for which such person is the owner of record or has legal title, whether the account is maintained for his or her own benefit or for the benefit of others including non-United States persons. It an account is maintained in the name of two persons jointly, or if several persons each own a partial interest in an account, each of those United States persons has a financial interest in that account.

(2) A United States person has a financial interest in each bank, securities, or other financial account in a foreign country for which the owner of record or holder of legal title is: (a) a person acting as an agent, nominee, attorney, or in some other capacity on behalf of the U.S. person; (b) a corporation in which the United States person owns directly or indirectly more than 50 percent of the total value of shares of stock; (c) a partnership in which the United States person owns an interest in more than 50 percent of the profits (distributive share of income); or (d) a trust in which the United States person either has a present beneficial interest in more than 50 percent of the assets or from which such person receives more than 50 percent of the current income.

Signature or Other Authority Over an Account A person has signature authority over an account if such person can control the disposition of money or other property in it by delivery of a document containing his or here signature (or his or her signature and that of one or more other persons) to the bank or other person with whom the account is maintained.

Other authority exists in a person who can exercise comparable power over an account by direct communication to the bank or other person with whom the account is maintained, either orally or by some other means.

Military Banking Facility Do not consider as an account in a foreign country, an account in an institution known as a "United States military banking facility" (or "United States military finance facility") operated by a United States financial institution designated by the United States Government to serve U.S. Government installations abroad, even if the United States military banking facility is located in a foreign country.

Filing Information

When and Where to File -This report must be filed on or before June 30 each calendar year with the Department of the Treasury, Post Office Box 32621, Detroit, MI 48232-0621, or it may be hand carried to any local office of the Internal Revenue Service for forwarding to the Department of the Treasury, Detroit, MI.

EXPLANATIONS FOR SPECIFIC ITEMS

Consolidated Reporting

A corporation which owns directly or indirectly more than 50 percent interest in one or more other entities will be permitted to file a consolidated report on TD F 90-22.1, on behalf of itself and such other entities provided that a listing of them is made part of the consolidated report. Such reports should be signed by an authorized official of the parent corporation.

If the group of entities covered by a consolidated report has a financial interest in 25 or more foreign financial accounts, the reporting corporation need only note that fact on the form in Item 20. It will, however, be required to provide detailed information concerning each account when so requested by the Secretary or his delegate.

Item 14

If the filer owns the account jointly with any other party, then yes should be marked.

Item 15

If the filer holds this account with only one (1) other party, and all accounts listed are held jointly with that party, then complete items 16, 17, 18 and 19. Otherwise, leave these items blank.

If the filer holds a financial interest in more than 25 foreign financial accounts, indicate the number in this box and do not complete any further items in Part II.

Any person who lists more than 25 foreign financial accounts in item 20 must when requested by the Department of the Treasury provide all the information called for in Part II.

Item 22
Account Valuation

For item 22, the maximum value of an account is the largest amount of currency and non-monetary assets that appear on any quarterly or more frequent account statement issued for the applicable year. If periodic account statements are not so issued, the maximum account asset value is the largest amount of currency and non-monetary assets in the account at any time during the year. Convert foreign currency by using the official exchange rate at the end of the year. In valuing currency of a country that uses multiple exchange rates, use the rate which would apply if the currency in the account were converted into United States dollars at the close of the calendar year.

The value of stock, other securities or other non-monetary assets in an account reported on TD F 90-22.1 is the fair market value at the end of the calendar year, or if withdrawn from the account, at the time of the withdrawal.

For purposes of item 22, if you had a financial interest in more than one account, each account is to be valued separately in accordance with the foregoing two paragraphs. If you had a financial interest in one or more but fewer than 25 accounts, and you are unable to determine whether the maximum value of these accounts exceeded $10,000 at any time during the year, complete Part II or III for each of these accounts.

Item 26

United States Persons with Authority Over but No Financial Interest In an Account - Except as provided in the following paragraph, you must state the name, address, and identifying number of each owner of an account over which you had authority, but if you complete items 27-35 for more than one account of the same owner, you need identify the owner only once. If you complete items 27-35 for one or more accounts in which no United States person had a financial interest, you may state on the first line of this item, in lieu of supplying information about the owner, "No U.S. person had any financial interest in the foreign accounts." This statement must be based upon the actual belief of the person filing this form after he or she has taken reasonable-measures to endure its correctness.

If you complete Part II for accounts owned by a domestic corporation and its domestic and/or foreign subsidiaries, you may treat them as one owner and write in the space provided, the name of the parent corporation, followed by "and related entities," and the identifying number and address of the parent corporation.

Item 36

Signature

This report must be signed by the person named in Part I. If the report is being filed on behalf of a partnership, corporation, or fiduciary, it must be signed by an authorized individual.

Penalties

For criminal penalties for failure to file a report, supply information, and for filing a false or fraudulent report see 31 U.S.C. 5322(a), 31 U.S.C. 5322(b), and 18 U.S.C. 1001.

Form **5471**

(Rev. January 1999)

Department of the Treasury
Internal Revenue Service

Information Return of U.S. Persons With Respect To Certain Foreign Corporations

▶ See separate instructions.

Information furnished for the foreign corporation's annual accounting period (tax year required by section 898) (see instructions) beginning , , and ending

OMB No. 1545-0704

File In Duplicate

(see **When and Where To File** in the instructions)

Name of person filing this return

A Identifying number

Number, street, and room or suite no. (or P.O. box number if mail is not delivered to street address)

B Category of filer (See page 2 of the instructions. Check applicable box(es)):

(1) ☐ (2) ☐ (3) ☐ (4) ☐ (5) ☐

City or town, state, and ZIP code

C Enter the total percentage of voting stock of the foreign corporation you owned at the end of its annual accounting period ....%

Filer's tax year beginning and ending

D Person(s) on whose behalf this information return is filed:

(1) Name	(2) Address	(3) Identifying number	(4) Check applicable box(es)		
			Shareholder	Officer	Director

Important: Fill in all applicable lines and schedules. All information **MUST** be in the English language. All amounts **MUST** be stated in U.S. dollars unless otherwise indicated.

Enter the foreign corporation's functional currency ▶

1a Name and address of foreign corporation

b Employer identification number, if any

c Country under whose laws incorporated

d Date of incorporation

e Principal place of business

f Principal business activity code number **(NEW)**

g Principal business activity

2 Provide the following information for the foreign corporation's accounting period stated above.

a Name, address, and identifying number of branch office or agent (if any) in the United States

b If a U.S. income tax return was filed, please show:

(i) Taxable income or (loss)	(ii) U.S. income tax paid (after all credits)

c Name and address of foreign corporation's statutory or resident agent in country of incorporation

d Name and address (including corporate department, if applicable) of person (or persons) with custody of the books and records of the foreign corporation, and the location of such books and records, if different

---

Schedule A Stock of the Foreign Corporation

Part I—ALL Classes of Stock

(a) Description of each class of stock	(b) Number of shares issued and outstanding	
	(i) Beginning of annual accounting period	(ii) End of annual accounting period

Part II—Additional Information for PREFERRED Stock

(To be completed **only** by Category (1) filers for foreign personal holding companies)

(a) Description of each class of PREFERRED stock (**Note:** This description should match the corresponding description entered in Part I, column (a).)	(b) Par value in functional currency	(c) Rate of dividend	(d) Indicate whether the stock is cumulative or noncumulative

---

For Paperwork Reduction Act Notice, see page 1 of the separate instructions.

Cat. No. 49958V

Form **5471** (Rev. 1-99)

Schedule B — U.S. Shareholders of Foreign Corporation (See page 4 of the instructions.)

(a) Name, address, and identifying number of shareholder	(b) Description of each class of stock held by shareholder (**Note:** *This description should match the corresponding description entered in Schedule A, Part I, column (a).*)	(c) Number of shares held at beginning of annual accounting period	(d) Number of shares held at end of annual accounting period	(e) Pro rata share of subpart F income (enter as a percentage)

Schedule C — Income Statement (See page 4 of the instructions.)

Important: *Report all information in functional currency in accordance with U.S. GAAP. Also, report each amount in U.S. dollars translated from functional currency (using GAAP translation rules). However, if the functional currency is the U.S. dollar, complete only the U.S. Dollars column. See instructions for special rules for DASTM corporations.*

			Functional Currency	U.S. Dollars
Income	**1a** Gross receipts or sales	1a		
	b Returns and allowances	1b		
	c Subtract line 1b from line 1a	1c		
	2 Cost of goods sold	2		
	3 Gross profit (subtract line 2 from line 1c)	3		
	4 Dividends	4		
	5 Interest	5		
	6 Gross rents, royalties, and license fees	6		
	7 Net gain or (loss) on sale of capital assets	7		
	8 Other income (attach schedule)	8		
	9 Total income (add lines 3 through 8)	9		
Deductions	**10** Compensation not deducted elsewhere	10		
	11 Rents, royalties, and license fees	11		
	12 Interest	12		
	13 Depreciation not deducted elsewhere	13		
	14 Depletion	14		
	15 Taxes (exclude provision for income, war profits, and excess profits taxes)	15		
	16 Other deductions (attach schedule—exclude provision for income, war profits, and excess profits taxes)	16		
	17 Total deductions (add lines 10 through 16)	17		
Net Income	**18** Net income or (loss) before extraordinary items, prior period adjustments, and the provision for income, war profits, and excess profits taxes (subtract line 17 from line 9)	18		
	19 Extraordinary items and prior period adjustments (see instructions)	19		
	20 Provision for income, war profits, and excess profits taxes (see instructions)	20		
	21 Current year net income or (loss) per books (line 18 plus line 19 minus line 20)	21		

Instructions for Form 5471

(Revised January 1999)

Department of the Treasury
Internal Revenue Service

Information Return of U.S. Persons With Respect to Certain Foreign Corporations

Section references are to the Internal Revenue Code unless otherwise noted.

Paperwork Reduction Act Notice. We ask for the information on this form to carry out the Internal Revenue laws of the United States. You are required to give us the information. We need it to ensure that you are complying with these laws and to allow us to figure and collect the right amount of tax.

You are not required to provide the information requested on a form that is subject to the Paperwork Reduction Act unless the form displays a valid OMB control number. Books or records relating to a form or its instructions must be retained as long as their contents may become material in the administration of any Internal Revenue law. Generally, tax returns and return information are confidential, as required by section 6103.

The time needed to complete and file this form and related schedules will vary depending on individual circumstances. The estimated average times are:

Form	Recordkeeping	Learning about the law or the form	Preparing and sending the form to the IRS
5471	81 hr., 19 min.	26 hr., 50 min.	32 hr., 56 min.
Sch. J (5471)	3 hr., 50 min.	1 hr., 5 min.	1 hr., 12 min.
Sch. M (5471)	26 hr., 33 min.	6 min.	32 min.
Sch. N (5471)	8 hr., 22 min.	2 hr., 47 min.	3 hr., 2 min.
Sch. O (5471)	10 hr., 46 min.	30 min.	42 min.

If you have comments concerning the accuracy of these time estimates or suggestions for making this form and related schedules simpler, we would be happy to hear from you. See the instructions for the tax return with which this form is filed.

Changes To Note

• The new principal business activity (PBA) codes beginning on page 13 of these instructions are based on the North American Industry Classification System (NAICS), which was developed by the statistical agencies of Canada, Mexico, and the United States in cooperation with the Office of Management and Budget. The NAICS-based codes replace the PBA codes previously based on the Standard Industrial Classification (SIC) system.

• The Small Business Job Protection Act of 1996 repealed section 956A, which required U.S. shareholders of controlled foreign corporations (CFCs) to include in income their share of the CFC's earnings invested in excess passive assets. This is effective for tax years of foreign corporations beginning after December 31, 1996, and for tax years of U.S. shareholders ending within which or with which such tax years of foreign corporations end.

• For tax years beginning in 1998 **only,** the Taxpayer Relief Act of 1997 ("1997 Act") provides temporary exceptions from the definition of foreign personal holding company income, for subpart F purposes, income from the active conduct of a banking, financing, insurance, or similar business, but only if the corporation is predominantly engaged in the active conduct of such business (within the meaning of section 954(h)(3)) or a qualifying insurance company. For more information, see sections 954(e)(2)(c) and 954(h) and Act section 1175. The Tax and Trade Relief Extension Act of 1998 ("1998 Act") extended the exceptions above (with modifications) to tax years beginning in 1999 **only.** For more information, see sections 954(e)(2) and 954(h), as amended, and Act section 1005.

• For tax years beginning after August 5, 1997, the 1997 Act excludes from the definition of foreign personal holding company income certain property acquired by a dealer in the ordinary course of business. See section 954(c)(2)(C). For tax years beginning in 1999 **only,** the 1998 Act provides an additional exception for certain income derived by a securities dealer. See section 954(c)(2)(C) as amended.

For more formation regarding changes to foreign personal holding company income, see the instructions for Worksheet A on page 6.

The 1997 Act also made the following changes to the tax law regarding information reporting with respect to certain foreign corporations.

• For transactions occurring after December 31, 1997, the threshold for stock ownership of a foreign corporation that results in the information reporting obligations of section 6046 has increased from 5% (in value) to 10% (of value or vote). This affects the reporting requirements for Category (2) and (3) filers. See **Categories of Filers,** on page 2.

• For taxes paid or accrued in tax years beginning after December 31, 1997, the appropriate exchange rate for translating a CFC's functional currency into U.S. dollars is the average exchange rate for the foreign corporation's tax year. See section 989(b).

• For tax years of foreign corporations beginning after December 31, 1997, and for tax years of U.S. shareholders ending within which or with which such tax years of foreign corporations end, in determining a U.S. shareholder's pro rata share of earnings of a CFC invested in U.S. property, the definition of U.S. property does not include certain assets received by dealers. See section 956(c)(2)(J) and (K).

• For tax years beginning after August 5, 1997, in computing a U.S. shareholder's pro rata share of income of a CFC, gross foreign personal holding company income includes net income from a notional principal contract (section 954(c)(1)(F)) and payments in lieu of dividends (section 954(c)(1)(G)).

• For annual accounting periods beginning after August 5, 1997, the penalty for failure to file an information return or disclose the required information under sections 6038 and 6046 increases to $10,000. An additional penalty ($50,000 maximum) may apply if the failure continues after notice from the IRS. See **Penalties** on page 3.

• For tax years beginning after August 5, 1997, the statute of limitation with respect to the period to which the information required by sections 6038 and 6046 relates does not expire until 3 years after the date on which the information is provided. See section 6501(c)(8).

• For transactions occurring after August 5, 1997, certain gains on dispositions of stock in a related corporation are treated as foreign personal holding company income, and the same-country exception of section 954(c)(3)(A) does not apply. See section 964(e).

• For dispositions after August 5, 1997, in determining a U.S. shareholder's pro rata share of subpart F income, any gains included in the gross income of any person as a dividend under section 1248 shall be treated as a distribution received by such person with respect to the stock involved. See section 951(a)(2)(B).

General Instructions

Purpose of Form

Form 5471 is used by certain U.S. citizens and residents who are officers, directors, or shareholders in certain foreign corporations. The form and schedules are used to satisfy the reporting requirements of sections 6035, 6038, 6046, and the related regulations.

Who Must File

Generally, the U.S. persons described in **Categories of Filers** must complete the schedules, statements, and/or other information requested in the chart, **Filing Requirements For Categories of Filers,** on page 2. Read the information for each of the categories of filers carefully to determine which schedules, statements, and/or information apply.

If the filer is described in more than one filing category, do not duplicate information. However, complete all schedules that apply. For example, if you are the sole owner of a CFC that is also a foreign personal holding company (i.e., you are described in Categories (1), (4), and (5)), you would complete all four pages of Form 5471 and separate Schedules J, M, and N.

When and Where To File

Form 5471 is due when your income tax return is due, including extensions. File two copies of the form and required schedules. Attach one copy to your income tax return. Send the other copy to the Internal Revenue Service Center, Philadelphia, PA 19255.

Cat. No. 49959G

Categories of Filers

Category (1) Filer

This includes a U.S. citizen or resident who is an officer, director, or 10% shareholder of a foreign personal holding company.

A **10% shareholder** is any individual who owns, directly or indirectly (within the meaning of section 554), 10% or more in value of the outstanding stock of the foreign personal holding company.

See section 552 for the definition of a foreign personal holding company.

Category (2) Filer

This includes a U.S. citizen or resident who is an officer or director of a foreign corporation in which a U.S. person (defined below) has acquired (in one or more transactions): **(1)** stock which meets the 10% stock ownership requirement (described below), or **(2)** an additional 10% or more (in value or vote) of the outstanding stock of the foreign corporation.

Stock ownership requirement. For transactions that occur after December 31, 1997, the stock ownership threshold is met if a U.S. person owns:

1. 10% or more of the total value of the corporation's stock, or

2. 10% or more of the total combined voting power of all classes of stock with voting rights.

For transactions that occurred prior to January 1, 1998, the stock ownership requirement was 5% (of value). For more information, see section 6046.

A U.S. person has acquired stock in a foreign corporation when that person has an unqualified right to receive the stock, even though the stock is not actually issued. See Regulations section 1.6046-1(f)(1) for more details.

U.S. person. For purposes of Category (2), and (3), a U.S. person is:

1. A citizen or resident of the United States,

2. A domestic partnership,

3. A domestic corporation, and

4. An estate or trust that is not a foreign estate or trust defined in section 7701(a)(31). See Regulations section 1.6046-1(f)(3) for exceptions.

Category (3) Filer

• A U.S. person who acquires stock in a foreign corporation which, when added to any stock owned on the date of acquisition, meets the 10% stock ownership requirement (discussed above) for the corporation;

• A U.S. person who acquires stock (without regard to stock already owned on the date of acquisition) that meets the 10% stock ownership requirement;

• A person who is treated as a U.S. shareholder under section 953(c);

• A person who becomes a U.S. person while meeting the 10% stock ownership requirement; or

• A U.S. person who disposes of sufficient stock in the foreign corporation to reduce his or her interest to less than the stock ownership requirement.

For more information, see section 6046 and Regulations section 1.6046-1. For the definition of a Category (3) U.S. person, see **U.S. person**, above.

Category (4) Filer

This includes a U.S. person who had control of a foreign corporation for an uninterrupted period of at least 30 days during the annual accounting period of the foreign corporation.

Filing Requirements For Categories of Filers

Required Information	Category of Filer				
	1	2	3	4	5
The identifying information on page 1 (the information above Schedule A)—see **Specific Instructions**	u	u	u	u	u
Schedule A, Part I	u		u	u	
Schedule A, Part II	u				
Schedule B	u		u	u	
Schedules C, E, and F			u	u	
Schedule H				u	u
Schedule I				u	u
Separate Schedule J				u	u
Separate Schedule M				u	
Separate Schedule N	u				
Separate Schedule O, Part I		u			
Separate Schedule O, Part II			u		

Exception. A U.S. person is not required to file for a corporation defined in section 1504(d) that files a consolidated return for the tax year.

U.S. person. For purposes of Category (4), a U.S. person is:

1. A citizen or resident of the United States;

2. A nonresident alien for whom an election is in effect under section 6013(g) to be treated as a resident of the United States;

3. An individual for whom an election is in effect under section 6013(h), relating to nonresident aliens who become residents of the United States during the tax year and are married at the close of the tax year to a citizen or resident of the United States;

4. A domestic partnership;

5. A domestic corporation; and

6. An estate or trust that is not a foreign estate or trust defined in section 7701(a)(31). See Regulations section 1.6038-2(d) for exceptions.

Control. A U.S. person has control of a foreign corporation if at any time during that person's tax year it owns stock possessing:

1. More than 50% of the total combined voting power of all classes of stock entitled to vote; or

2. More than 50% of the total value of shares of all classes of stock of the foreign corporation.

A person in control of a corporation that, in turn, owns more than 50% of the combined voting power, or the value, of all classes of stock of another corporation is also treated as being in control of such other corporation.

Example. Corporation A owns 51% of the voting stock in Corporation B. Corporation B owns 51% of the voting stock in Corporation C. Corporation C owns 51% of the voting stock in Corporation D. Therefore, Corporation D is controlled by Corporation A.

For more details on "control," see Regulations sections 1.6038-2(b) and (c).

Category (5) Filer

This includes a U.S. shareholder who owns stock in a foreign corporation that is a controlled foreign corporation (CFC) for an uninterrupted period of 30 days or more during any tax year of the foreign corporation, and who owned that stock on the last day of that year.

For purposes of Category (5), a **U.S. shareholder** is a U.S. person who:

1. Owns (either directly, indirectly, or constructively, within the meaning of sections 958(a) and (b)) 10% or more of the total combined voting power of all classes of voting stock of a CFC; or

2. Owns (either directly or indirectly, within the meaning of section 958(a)) any stock of a CFC (as defined in sections 953(c)(1)(B) and 957(b)) that is also a captive insurance company.

For purposes of Category (5), a **U.S. person** is:

1. A citizen or resident of the United States,

2. A domestic partnership,

3. A domestic corporation, and

4. An estate or trust that is not a foreign estate or trust defined in section 7701(a)(31). See section 957(c) for exceptions.

A **CFC** is a foreign corporation that has U.S. shareholders that own (either directly, indirectly, or constructively, within the meaning of sections 958(a) and (b)) on any day of the tax year of the foreign corporation, more than 50% of:

1. The total combined voting power of all classes of its voting stock; or

2. The total value of the stock of the corporation.

Form **3520-A**

Department of the Treasury
Internal Revenue Service

Annual Information Return of Foreign Trust With a U.S. Owner
(Under section 6048(b))
► Certain foreign trusts may have to issue a Foreign Grantor Trust Owner Statement(s) or a Foreign Grantor Trust Beneficiary Statement(s) (pages 3 and 4). See separate instructions.

OMB No. 1545-0160

1998

Note: *All information must be in English. Show all amounts in U.S. dollars.*

For calendar year 1998, or tax year beginning _____ , 19 ____ , and ending _____ , 19 ____ .

Part I   **General Information** *(See instructions.)*

1a Name of foreign trust

b Identification number

c Number, street, and room or suite no. (if a P.O. box, see instructions)

d City or town | **e** State or province | **f** ZIP or postal code | **g** Country

2 Did the foreign trust appoint a U.S. agent (defined on page 2 of the instructions) who can provide IRS with all revelant trust information? . . . . ☐ Yes ☐ No

If "Yes," skip lines 2a through 2e and go to line 3.

If "No," you are required to attach a copy of all trust documents as indicated below. If these documents have been attached to a Form 3520-A filed within the previous 3 years, attach only relevant updates.

Have you attached a copy of:

		Yes	No	Attached Previously	Year Attached
a	Summary of all written and oral agreements and understandings relating to the trust? . . .	☐	☐	☐	_____
b	The trust instrument?	☐	☐	☐	_____
c	Memoranda or letters of wishes?.	☐	☐	☐	_____
d	Subsequent variances to original trust documents?	☐	☐	☐	_____
e	Other trust documents?	☐	☐	☐	

3a Name of U.S. agent

b Identification number

c Number, street, and room or suite no. (if a P.O. box, see instructions)

d City or town | **e** State or province | **f** ZIP or postal code | **g** Country

4a Name of trustee

b Identification number, if any

c Number, street, and room or suite no. (if a P.O. box, see instructions)

d City or town | **e** State or province | **f** ZIP or postal code | **g** Country

5 Did the trust transfer any property to another entity during the tax year? . . . . ☐ Yes ☐ No
If "Yes," attach statement. See instructions.

Under penalties of perjury, I declare that I have examined this return, including any accompanying reports, schedules, or statements, and to the best of my knowledge and belief, it is true, correct, and complete.

Trustee's Signature _____ Title _____ Date _____

Preparer's Signature _____ Preparer's social security number _____ Date _____

1998

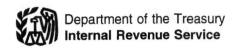
Instructions for Form 3520-A

**Annual Information Return of Foreign Trust
With a U.S. Owner**

Section references are to the Internal Revenue Code unless otherwise noted.

General Instructions

Purpose of Form

Form 3520-A is the annual information return of a foreign trust with at least one U.S. owner. The form provides information about the foreign trust, its U.S. beneficiaries, and any U.S. person who is treated as the owner of any portion of the foreign trust.

Who Must File

A foreign trust must file Form 3520-A to satisfy its annual information reporting requirements. Each U.S. person treated as an owner of a foreign trust under sections 671 through 679 is responsible for ensuring that the foreign trust files an annual return setting forth a full and complete accounting of all trust activities, trust operations, and other relevant information. In addition, the U.S. owner is responsible for ensuring that the trust annually furnishes such information (as the Secretary prescribes) to U.S. owners and U.S. beneficiaries of the trust.

Exceptions to filing Form 3520-A: Form 3520-A does not have to be filed by the following foreign trusts:

● A trust that is a Canadian Registered Retirement Savings Plan if the trust would qualify for treaty benefits under the Convention Between the United States of America and Canada with Respect to Taxes on Income and on Capital. However, if for any taxable year the trust relies on the tax treaty with Canada to avoid information reporting, the U.S. owner is required to disclose this position pursuant to section 6114. See **Pub. 901,** U.S. Tax Treaties.

● A foreign trust described in section 402(b), 404(a)(4), or 404A.

When and Where To File

File a complete Form 3520-A with the Internal Revenue Service Center, Philadelphia, PA 19255, by the 15th day of the 3rd month after the end of the trust's tax year. Furnish copies of the Foreign Grantor Trust Owner Statement and the Foreign Grantor Trust Beneficiary Statement to the U.S. owners and U.S. beneficiaries by the 15th day of the 3rd month after the end of the trust's tax year. An extension of time to file Form 3520-A (including the statements) may be granted. For details, get **Form 2758,** Application for Extension of Time To File Certain Excise, Income, Information, and Other Returns.

Definitions

A **distribution** is any gratuitous transfer of money or other property from a trust, whether or not the trust is treated as owned by another person under the grantor trust rules, and without regard to whether the recipient is designated as a beneficiary by the terms of the trust. A distribution includes the receipt of trust corpus and the receipt of a gift or bequest described in section 663(a).

A distribution also includes constructive transfers from a trust. For example, if charges you make on a credit card are paid by a foreign trust or guaranteed or secured by the assets of a foreign trust, the amount charged will be treated as a distribution to you by the foreign trust. Similarly, if you write checks on a foreign trust's bank account, the amount will be treated as a distribution.

Also, if you receive a payment from a foreign trust in exchange for property transferred to the trust or services rendered to the trust, and the fair market value (FMV) of the payment received exceeds the FMV of the property transferred or services rendered, the excess will be treated as a distribution to you.

For example:

● If you sell stock with an FMV of $100 to a foreign trust and receive $150 in exchange, you have received a distribution of $50.

● Similarly, if you receive $100 from the trust for services performed by you for the trust, and the services have an FMV of $20, you have received a distribution of $80.

If you, or a person related to you, received a loan from a related foreign trust, it will be treated as a distribution to you unless the obligation you issued in exchange is a qualified obligation.

A **foreign trust** is any trust other than a domestic trust. A domestic trust is any trust if:

1. A court within the United States is able to exercise primary supervision over the administration of the trust, and

2. One or more U.S. persons have the authority to control all substantial decisions of the trust.

A **grantor** is any person who creates a trust or transfers cash or other property to a trust. A grantor includes any person treated as the owner of any part of a foreign trust's assets under sections 671 through 679, excluding section 678.

A **grantor trust** is any trust to the extent that the assets of the trust are treated as owned by a person other than the trust. See **grantor trust rules** below. A part of the trust may be treated as a grantor trust to the extent that only a portion of the trust assets are owned by a person other than the trust.

The **grantor trust rules** are contained in subpart E of Part I of subchapter J (sections 671 through 679).

Gross value is the FMV of property as determined under section 2031 and the regulations thereunder as if the owner had died on the valuation date. Although formal appraisals are not generally required, you should keep contemporaneous records of how you arrived at your good faith estimate.

A **nongrantor trust** is any trust to the extent that the assets of the trust are not treated as owned by a person other than the trust. Thus, a nongrantor trust is treated as a taxable entity. A trust may be treated as a nongrantor trust with respect to only a portion of the trust assets. See the grantor trust rules.

An **owner** of a foreign trust is the person that is treated as owning any of the assets of a foreign trust pursuant to the grantor trust rules.

A **U.S. agent** is a **U.S. person** (defined on page 2) that has a binding contract with a foreign trust that allows the U.S. person to act as the trust's authorized U.S. agent (see instructions for Part I, **Lines 3a through 3g, U.S. agent,** on page 2) in applying sections 7602, 7603, and 7604 with respect to:

Cat. No. 25096U

- Any request by the Service to examine records or produce testimony related to the proper U.S. tax treatment of amounts distributed by, or required to be taken into account under the grantor trust rules with respect to, a foreign trust, or
- Any summons by the Service for such records or testimony.

A U.S. grantor, a U.S. beneficiary, or a domestic corporation controlled by the grantor or beneficiary may act as a U.S. agent. However, you may not treat the foreign trust as having a U.S. agent unless you enter the name, address, and taxpayer identification number of the U.S. agent on lines 3a through 3g. If the person identified as the U.S. agent does not produce records or testimony when requested or summonsed by the IRS, the IRS may redetermine the tax consequences of your transactions with the trust and impose appropriate penalties under section 6677.

The agency relationship must be established by the time the U.S. person files Form 3520-A for the relevant taxable year and must continue as long as the statute of limitations remains open for the relevant taxable year. If the agent resigns, liquidates, or its responsibility as an agent of the trust is terminated, see Notice 97-34, 1997-1 C.B. 422.

A **U.S. beneficiary** includes any person that could possibly benefit (directly or indirectly) from the trust (including an amended trust) at any time, whether or not the person is named in the trust instrument as a beneficiary and whether or not the person can receive a distribution from the trust in the current year. In addition, a U.S. beneficiary includes:
- A foreign corporation that is a controlled foreign corporation (as defined in section 957(a)),
- A foreign partnership if a U.S. person is a partner of the partnership, and
- A foreign estate or trust if the estate or trust has a U.S. beneficiary.

A foreign trust will be treated as having a U.S. beneficiary unless the terms of the trust instrument specifically prohibit any distribution of income or corpus to a U.S. person at any time, even after the death of the U.S. transferor, and the trust cannot be amended or revised to allow such a distribution.

A **U.S. person** is:
- A citizen or resident alien of the United States (see **Pub. 519,** U.S. Tax Guide for Aliens, for guidance on determining resident alien status),
- A domestic partnership,
- A domestic corporation,
- Any estate (other than a foreign estate, within the meaning of section 7701(a)(31)), and
- Any trust if it is not a **foreign trust** (defined on page 1).

Penalties

The U.S. owner is subject to a penalty of 5% of the gross value of the portion of the trust's assets treated as owned by that person at the close of that year if the foreign trust: **(a)** fails to file a timely Form 3520-A, or **(b)** does not furnish the information required by section 6048(b). See section 6677(b).
- Additional penalties may be imposed if noncompliance continues after the IRS mails a notice of failure to comply with the required reporting. See section 6677(a).
- Criminal penalties for failure to file on time and for filing a false or fraudulent return are provided by sections 7203, 7206, and 7207.

Reasonable cause. No penalties will be imposed if the taxpayer can demonstrate that the failure to comply was due to reasonable cause and not willful neglect.

Note: *The fact that a foreign country would impose penalties for disclosing the required information is not reasonable cause. Similarly, reluctance on the part of a foreign fiduciary or provisions in the trust instrument that prevent the disclosure of required information, is not reasonable cause.*

Who Must Sign

If the return is filed by:
- An individual or fiduciary, it must be signed by that individual or fiduciary.
- A partnership, it must be signed by a general partner or limited liability company member.
- A corporation, it must be signed by the president, vice president, treasurer, assistant treasurer, chief accounting officer, or other corporate officer (such as a tax officer) who is authorized to sign.

The paid preparer must complete the required preparer information and:
- Sign the return, by hand, in the space provided for the preparer's signature (signature stamps are not acceptable).
- Give a copy of the return to the filer.

Identification Numbers and Addresses

Identification numbers. Use social security numbers or individual taxpayer identification numbers to identify individuals. Use employer identification numbers to identify estates, trusts, partnerships, and corporations.

Address. Include the suite, room, or other unit number after the street address. If the Post Office does not deliver mail to the street address and the U.S. person has a P.O. box, show the box number instead of the street address.

Foreign address. Enter the information in the following order: city, province or state, and country. Follow the foreign country's pratice for entering the postal code, if any. Please do not abbreviate the country name.

Specific Instructions

Part I, General Information

Line 2. If the trust did not appoint a U.S. agent, attach the following documents to Form 3520-A:
- A summary of the terms of the trust that includes a summary of any oral agreements or understandings you have with the trustee, whether or not legally enforceable.
- A copy of all trust documents (and any revisions), including the trust instrument, any memoranda of wishes prepared by the trustees summarizing the settlor's wishes, any letter of wishes prepared by the settlor summarizing his/her wishes, and any similar documents.

Lines 3a through 3g, U.S. agent. If a foreign trust with a U.S. owner does not have a U.S. agent, the Secretary may determine the amounts required to be taken into account with respect to the foreign trust by the U.S. owner. See section 6048(b)(2). In order to avoid this result, a U.S. owner of a foreign trust should ensure that the foreign trust appoints a U.S. person to act as the foreign trust's limited agent for purposes of applying sections 7602, 7603, and 7604 with respect to a request by the Secretary to examine records or produce testimony, or a summons by the Secretary for such records or testimony. Any U.S. citizen, resident alien, or domestic corporation (including a U.S. grantor or U.S. beneficiary of a foreign trust) may act as the U.S. agent of the trust.

In order to authorize a U.S. person to act as an agent under section 6048(b), the trust and the agent must enter into a binding agreement substantially in the format that follows on page 3. Attach a copy of the authorization to Form 3520-A.

Return by a U.S. Transferor of Property
to a Foreign Corporation
(under section 367)

OMB No. 1545-0026

Part I   U.S. Transferor Information (see instructions)

Name of transferor	Identification number (see instructions)

Number, street, and room or suite no. (If a P.O. box, see instructions.)

City or town, state, and ZIP code

1 The following questions apply only if the transferor is a corporation:

a If the transfer was a section 361(a) or (b) transfer, was the transferor controlled (under section 368(c)) by 5 or fewer domestic corporations? . . . . ☐ Yes ☐ No

b Did the transferor remain in existence after the transfer? . . . . ☐ Yes ☐ No
If not, list the controlling shareholder(s) and their identification number(s):

Controlling shareholder	Identification number

c If the transferor was a member of an affiliated group filing a consolidated return, was it the parent corporation? . . . . ☐ Yes ☐ No
If not, list the name and employer identification number (EIN) of the parent corporation:

Name of parent corporation	EIN of parent corporation

2 If the transferor was a partner in a partnership that was the actual transferor (but is not treated as such under section 367), list the name and EIN of the transferor's partnership:

Name of partnership	EIN of partnership

Part II   Transferee Foreign Corporation Information (see instructions)

3 Name of transferee (foreign corporation)   **4** Identification number, if any

5 Address (including country)

6 Place of organization or creation   **7** Foreign law characterization (see instructions)

8 Is the transferee foreign corporation a controlled foreign corporation? . . . . ☐ Yes ☐ No

For Paperwork Reduction Act Notice, see separate instructions.   Cat No. 16982D   Form **926** (Rev. 10-98)

Part III **Information Regarding Transfer of Property** (see instructions)

9 Date of transfer	10 Type of nonrecognition transaction (see instructions)

11 Description of property transferred:

_____

_____

_____

_____

_____

_____

12 Did this transfer result from a change in the classification of the transferee to that of a foreign corporation? ☐ **Yes** ☐ **No**

13 Was the transferor required to recognize income under Temporary Regulations sections 1.367(a)-4T through 1.367(a)-6T (e.g., for tainted property, depreciation recapture, branch loss recapture, etc.)? . . ☐ **Yes** ☐ **No**

14a Was intangible property (within the meaning of section 936(h)(3)(B)) transferred pursuant to the transaction? . . . . ☐ **Yes** ☐ **No**

b If yes, describe the nature of the rights to the intangible property that was transferred in the transfer:

_____

_____

_____

Please Sign Here	Under penalties of perjury, I declare that I have examined this return, including accompanying schedules and statements, and to the best of my knowledge and belief it is true, correct, and complete. Declaration of preparer (other than taxpayer) is based on all information of which preparer has any knowledge.		
	⎸ _____ Signature	Date	⎸ _____ Title
Paid Preparer's Use Only	Preparer's ⎸ signature	Date	Check if self-employed ' ☐	Preparer's social security no.
	Firm's name (or yours ⎸ if self-employed), and address		EIN ' ZIP code '

⊛

Bibliography

ABN Bank, **Netherlands Antilles Companies**

Bagley R. and Moore, M., **U.S. Tax Aspects of Doing Business Abroad**

Bischel J. & Feinschreiber, R., **Fundamentals of International Taxation,** Practising Law Institute, 1983.

Bischel, J.E., **Income Tax Treaties**

Bittker, B. & Eustice, J., **Federal Income Taxation of Corporations and Shareholders**

Central Bank of Barbados, **Off-Shore Business in Barbados**

Commerce Clearing House, **Federal Estate & Gift Taxes: Code & Regulations (1996)**

Commerce Clearing House, **1998 Master Tax Guide**

Curacao International Trust Co., N.V., **An Introduction to Taxation of Offshore Companies in the Netherlands Antilles**

Deloitte, Haskins & Sells, **Taxation in Panama**

Hoffman, W.H., **West's Federal Taxation of Corporations, Partnerships, Trusts & Estates**

Kroll, A., **Thirteenth Annual Institute on International Taxation (1983)**

Langer, Marshall, J., **Practical International Tax Planning**

Malone, Midas, **How to do Business Tax Free**

Panel Publishers, Inc., **International Tax Journal**

Peat Marwick, **Investing in Bermuda**

Prentice-Hall, Inc., **Federal Treasury Regulations**

Prentice-Hall, Inc., **Complete Internal Revenue Code of 1986**

Price Waterhouse, **Doing Business in the Caymans • Doing Business in Bermuda • Doing Business in the Bahamas • Doing Business in the Channel Islands • Doing Business in the United States • Doing Business in Hong Kong • U.S. Citizens Abroad • Corporate Taxes - A Worldwide Summary (1995) •**

Starchild, Adam, **Tax Havens for Corporations**, Gulf Publishing Company

Touche Ross International, **Tax & Investment Profile (Bermuda, Bahamas, Jamaica, Cayman Islands)**

Virgin Islands Government, **United States Virgin Islands Business Guide (1998)**

Warren, Gorham & Lamont for Research Group, **Journal of Taxation**

UBS Publications, **Founding a Company in Switzerland**

Offshore Manual & Directory (1999 • 7th edition)

Published by Dr. Kim F.B. Weiss

Carlton Press is proud to be the oldest and continuous provider and publisher of asset protection, offshore, privacy and tax haven products and services in the world, founded in 1972.

Never before has anyone, anywhere put together such a comprehensive, thorough and in-depth manual. This easy to read and use report was five years and thousands of research-hours in the making. It is the new recognized and indispensable authoritative guidebook of the experts. It gives you the inside track to the offshore world community.

In this directory you'll find literally thousands of names, addresses, numbers and contact information for virtually everything you could want to know about asset protection, anonymous and offshore banking, mail drops, offshore, privacy, PT, tax avoidance and tax haven related matters - and much much more!

IF YOU CAN'T FIND IT HERE, DON'T BOTHER LOOKING ELSEWHERE!!

Never before has anyone, anywhere put together such a comprehensive, thorough and in-depth manual. This easy to read and use report was five years and thousands of research-hours in the making. Now offered for the first time. The 252-page fact-filled 6th edition of the 'PT Offshore Manual & Directory' is expanded and kept right-up-to-date on a daily basis. It is the new recognized and indispensable authoritative offshore manual of the experts. It gives you the inside track to the asset protection, expatriate, offshore, privacy and tax avoidance product and service providers.

In the TABLE OF CONTENTS you can read which areas of essential information have been covered and revealed in this unsurpassed source book. A short introduction sets out and explains in detail the basic advantages, opportunities, practices, principles and uses of each group, where relevant.

With "PT Offshore Manual & Directory" you will have access to 1,100+ of the world's leading providers of asset protection, anonymous banking, expatriate, mail drops, offshore, privacy, PT, second passports, tax avoidance and tax haven products, services and expert advice - many of whom your accountant, financial advisor or lawyer keep to themselves, or don't even know about!

ORDER THE 'PT OFFSHORE MANUAL & DIRECTORY' NOW for US$97 - an GET AN (UN)FAIR ADVANTAGE OVER BIG BROTHER!

TABLE OF CONTENTS:

Offshore Manual & Directory

Investment Opportunities.

10. Maildrops and Serviced Offices.
Andorra-Virtual Offices (82 Countries and Territories).
   Business Center Office Networks.
11. Miscellaneous.
   Cheque Cashing Facilities.
   Divorce Services.
   Financial Services.
   Miscellaneous.
   Secrets Revealed.
12. Offshore Companies.
   Banks.
   Offshore Company Formation and Registration Services.
   Trusts.
13. Orders of Chivalry.
   Various Orders of Chivalry.
14. Press Passes.
15. PT Service Providers.
16. PT Newsletters, Publications and Websites.
   Newsletters.
   Newspapers and Magazines.
   PT Information and Reference Websites.
   Various Publications and Publishers.
17. Real Estate.
   Commercial.
   Distinctive Properties and Estates.
   Residential.
   Wanted.
18. Registration of Aircrafts, Cars and Vessels.
   License Plates for Tax Free Cars.
   Registration of Aircrafts.
   Registration of Vessels.
19. Second Passports and Dual Nationality.
   Immigration.
   Second Passport and Dual Nationality.
   Visas.
20. Tax Advisors and Offshore & PT Consultancy.
   Offshore and PT Consultancy.
   Tax Advisors.
21. Tax Free Cars.
22. Tax Havens and Offshore Financial Centers
   Andorra-Wyoming (75 Countries and Territories).
   23. Telecommunications
Anonymous Email, Remailing and Telephone.
   Callback Services.
   Email Autoresponder Services.
   Email-To-Fax Services.
   Encryption Software: PGP
   Fax-On-Demand Services.

Fax Services.
Internet Links to Search Engines and Resources.
Internet Management and Publishing Services.
Internet Domain Name Registration and Service Providers.
   Miscellaneous.
   Personal Telephone Numbers.
   Telecommunication Service Providers.
24. Titles of Nobility.
   Attached to Land.
   Available for Promotion of Commercial Products and Services.
   Through Adoption/Marriage.
Through Brokers/Intermediaries/Transfer from a Noble/Princely Family.
   Through Genealogy Tracing.
   Through Patent Letters.
25. Travel Agent Status.
   Travel Agent Status with IATA ID.
26. Travel Discount and Benefit Cards.
27. University Degrees.
Degrees by Mail: Through Distance-Learning/Life- and Academic-Experience.
   Doctoral Degrees.
   Honorary Awards.
28. Websites.
Useful News, Offshore, PT and Related Websites.

Published by Dr. Kim F.B. Weiss.

To order send check or money order for $97 + $5 ($102 = total) shipping and handling to:

Tax Haven Reporter
P.O. Box CB 11552
54 Sandyport Drive
Nassau, Bahamas 242-327-7359
242-327-7359
fax: 242-327-7359
e-mail - taxman@batelnet.bs

The Offshore Manuel and Directory is priority mailed to customers inside the U.S. on the day a customer's check, MO or travelers checks is received. Add an additional $10 for airmail delivery to areas outside the United States, Canada or Mexico.

Asset Protection 2000

by Mark Nestmann

You don't have to be a criminal to lose your property to forfeiture. I know this first-hand. My wife and I once owned a house in Florida. We rented it through a property manager. One day, the local police told me that they were going to seize it. They even said they could seize the rent checks, since I had supposedly "laundered the proceeds of crime." Although the police later backed off (my tenants had wrecked the house so badly that it wasn't worth seizing), ever since, I've been researching these Nazi-like laws.

Later, I found out that the manager had rented the house to tenants that police claimed were drug dealers. And that if we had owned the house through a corporation, we might not have even been allowed to make a claim to get it back! I didn't know that my tenants might be drug dealers. But mere innocence--or ignorance--isn't enough to avoid forfeiture. If you're a professional or own a business--or just your own home--your wealth and property are at risk.

Confiscations have increased 500% since 1984

In 1984, Congress changed the forfeiture laws to allow police and government agencies to keep all or most of whatever property they can seize. And it made the procedure for doing so much more favorable to the government. In the most common procedure--civil forfeiture--prosecutors don't accuse you of a crime, but instead file a lawsuit against your property. Prosecutors can seize property if they believe it's connected in some way to a crime--virtually any criminal offense. Once they do, it's up to you to prove your property is innocent. Otherwise, you lose it!

Your property is presumed guilty. I know it sounds insane--it is insane--but it's the law. Since the new procedures came into effect, government confiscations have increased 500%. More than $5 billion has been deposited into the U.S. Justice Department's Asset Forfeiture Fund. It's only the largest such federal fund--and state and local forfeiture funds account for billions more in seized assets.

Attack of the Forfeiture Squads

Forfeiture is such a great deal for police and government agencies that they have every incentive to seize property. Since it's so easy and profitable, it's no wonder forfeitures are soaring! No doubt, you've read headlines like these-- "Court orders prominent San Diego physician to forfeit every dollar he's ever earned" "Feds seize second mortgage from innocent lien holder and refuse to make payments" "Authorities seize Washington, D.C. car dealership due to alleged illegal acts by salesman"

Can You Prove Your Property is Innocent?

These examples may sound like something from a horror movie. But they happen more than 5,000 times/week in the United States, when you combine federal, state and local forfeitures. If you have a business, can you guarantee that every customer that you've ever served has received everything he or she was promised? If not, prosecutors could conceivably confiscate every dime you've ever earned.

Have you ever deposited or withdrawn a large quantity of cash into your bank account? Or made a large deposit, then transferred the proceeds elsewhere? If so, you've committed a "suspicious transaction." The government can seize it all, then make you prove that you had legitimate motives to get it back. If you can't-- kiss your account goodbye.

Need to know more, order a copy of *Asset Protection 2000* at U.S.$75/each plus $7.50 North American shipping; $15 outside North America. Don't forget my free bonus reports listing the attorneys and banks in the single country whose laws were designed to repel government confiscation.

Send check or money order made payable to *Tax Haven Reporter* or Tom Azzara to:

Thomas Azzara
54 Sandyport Drive
P.O. Box CB 11552
Nassau, Bahamas
tele: 242-327-7359
fax: 242-327-7359

New Providence Press, Ltd.
Offshore Incorporation Request Form

Name: _____

Address: _____

_____

Phone: _____   Fax:_____

THREE CHOICES FOR A CORPORATE NAME:

1. _____

2. _____

3. _____

DIRECTORS   **TRUST BENEFICIARIES**

Name: _____   Name: _____

Name: _____   Name:_____

Name: _____   Name: _____

AMOUNT ENCLOSED: _____ (Bank Cashiers check, travelers checks, international money orders for $2,100 made payable to **New Providence Press, Ltd.**) No U.S. postal money orders please. They are not negotiable outside the United States)

Send via UPS (overnight) Express carrier only to:

Thomas Azzara
New Providence Press, Ltd.
54 Sandyport Drive   Phone/FAX: 242-327-7359
P.O. Box CB 11552   Cellular: 242-359-1132 • emergencies only
Nassau, Bahamas

SIGNATURE OF REQUESTER: _____

NEW PROVIDENCE PRESS, Ltd.
(a Registered IBC in the Bahamas)
P.O. Box CB 11552
Nassau, Bahamas
Telephone/FAX 242-327-7359
Cellular 242-359-1132 (emergencies only)
WebSite: http://www.bahamasbahamas.com/
Email taxman@batelnet.bs

Forming a company in the Bahamas

by Thomas P. Azzara (aka The Tax Haven Reporter) • **http://www.bahamasbahamas.com/**
http://maxpages.com/tax6planning/Home

Offshore fiscal paradises

Nearby tax havens like the Cayman Islands, the British Virgin Islands, Panama, Barbados, and **The Bahamas** have become prominent financial centers rivaling the industrial cities of Los Angeles, Chicago, London, Tokyo and New York for business. The pint-sized Cayman Islands now boast more commercial banks (over 530) in the commercial registrar than in all California. The dollars on deposit in these Cayman banks exceeds $410 billion dollars, and that's more dollars on deposit than in all (≈ 450+) of California's commercial banks.

The Bahamas, just 50 miles off the coast of Florida, were once the third largest financial center in the World - behind New York and London. Today the Bahamas still rank in the top ten, right behind the Caymans in depositor dollars and offshore company formations. There are more than 390 banks and trust companies registered here in Nassau.

The Bahamas, the Cayman Islands and Bermuda have no personal income taxes, no corporate income taxes, no capital gains taxes, no withholding taxes, no estate, gift or inheritance taxes, no sales taxes, no employment taxes, no death duties, and no probate fees. Guarantees against future taxes are provided by these governments for periods up to 50 years. **Exempt trusts** can receive a guarantee up to 100 years.

Question: Do you have contacts in the Bahamas who are trustworthy? What costs will I incur in setting up a company in the Bahamas?

THR: My partners include a mid-size Law firm with an office here in downtown Nassau and a U.S. tax consultant. These lawyers have over 40 years of business experience here in the Bahamas.

The **total** costs for forming an IBC (International Business Company) with us here in the Bahamas is as follows:

Costs to form IBC (includes company memorandums; shareholder and director meetings; government and other formation fees) = $ 1,000
Cost for registered agent (i.e. the legal address for company); A registered office (P.O. Box # and Telephone #) + trustees and asset protection trusts .... = $ 800
My advice for steering you to the right people + coordinating your company formation + opening up the company's bank accounts...... = $300
Total costs (first year) = **$2,100**

Annual maintenance costs
(registered office + trustee fee + registered agent fee, i.e., P.O. Box, telephone #) (Paid annually 12 months from the date that appears on the company's = $600 pa
Annual government fee for $50,000 authorized capital for IBC (paid by April 30th - every year) = $250 pa
Our advice to these entities on annual basis + free newsletter....... = $200 pa
Total cost (2nd year) = $1,050 pa [1].

Our law office will be the registered office <u>and</u> registered agent for the IBC (i.e., we will provide you with a street address, P.O. Box #, telephone # + FAX & office in downtown Nassau).

We usually use two asset protection type trusts in a business plan with a non-U.S. person to act as trustee. If you have access to the internet go to **http://maxpages.com/tax6planning/Home**

Banks ordinarily charge substantially more ($1,000+ additional) to act as your trustee, and this expense isn't necessary in many cases. Unnecessary administrative fees at the larger Nassau banks can cause costs to skyrocket.

---

[1]. If more active participation is required, employing nominee directors, presidents, etc., fees will run $500 to $1,000 additional. Using nominees isn't recommended, and isn't necessary in our opinion.

We provide the trust instruments to the foreign trustee of the foreign trusts. The fee for this is included in the total costs ($2,100). Our trust deeds are more suited for the U.S. taxpayer. See **Revenue Rul 69-70 & IRS Letter Ruling 9332006** in Tax Havens of the World for details.

It is our opinion that most trusts for Americans drawn up by foreign banks, lawyers and trust companies are all but worthless to the U.S. taxpayer. They simply are not trained or knowledgeable in U.S. tax law. When a U.S. taxpayer is involved, trust documents should be drafted by someone who has studied the Internal Revenue Code sections for grantor and non-grantor trusts (i.e. IRC §671 thru §679).

Question: How long does it take to form a company in the Bahamas?

THR: If a client wants to form a company through the mail he/she should UPS overnight $2,100. (cashiers check or money orders) to my address here in Nassau. We'll prepare all the documents, forward the appropriate fees to the Government Registrar, etc. A company can be registered without the client even coming to Nassau. The total turn around time is about 4 days - total.

When you are ready to incorporate, contact me at 242-327-7359 and I'll fax you the details; or go to my webiste at **http://www.bahamasbahamas.com/offshore thr.html** for our **OFFSHORE REQUEST FORM**. Just sent it overnight with a bank cashiers' check, MOs or travelers checks, and your company will completed in a few days, and I'll UPS you bank application forms + ATM Master Card forms, so you can open accounts without even coming to Nassau. We've formed over 900 IBC's in the last nine years here in Nassau.

Question: What forms must I file with the IRS after the company is formed?

THR: If properly managed, a Bahamian IBC and trust will have no income tax returns to file with the IRS, and will not be a CFC (Controlled Foreign Corporation). Neither you nor the offshore managers should have to file Forms 3520, 3520-A, Form 5471, or other information return with the IRS.

Question: Is it necessary to use a trust and holding company in a business plan?

THR: We think so. It is our opinion that you should try to circumvent the United States CFC provisions (IRC § 957 (a)). If you are fortunate to find a foreign partner who can own 50% of your offshore company that is one recognized plan. Eleven U.S. shareholders each owning 9% of the offshore company is also a legal and approved structure for avoiding the CFC status. For the U.S. taxpayer who wants to remain independent (without partners), his plan probably should include a company and a trust as outlined in my book.

Question: Do you open the bank and securities accounts for the IBCs?

THR: The client opens the bank accounts and controls the affairs of the company. We provide officers for brokerage accounts in the U.S., but many clients trade right through the offshore bank.

We have arrangements with several of Nassau's better banks. We can provide you with the bank's application forms, signature cards, bank brochures etc., so you can open your account without physically flying into the Bahamas. You can obtain a VISA and/or debit card from the Bahamas largest bank, too. You will need one or two reference letters from your local U.S. bankers + photocopy of your passport picture ID – which most offshore banks want notarized now; but these are easy to obtain.

The Bahamian banks we work with have been in operation here in Nassau for over 30 years. These banks have subsidiaries in all the other tax havens, including the Caymans, Hong Kong, Monaco, Zurich, Gibraltar, the British Virgin Islands and Jersey in the Channel Islands. One is a giant British bank, with more than 2,000 offices worldwide. One of the banks has no offices inside the United States, and is wholly owned by a $20 billion dollar South African bank – the parent co.

370.

You can choose whichever bank you want. With either bank, clients can trade with broker's anywhere in the world, under the guise of the Bank's name. The client's IBC does not appear on the stock certificates, and anonymity is totally preserved. This is a traditional way of doing business in the Bahamas and the other tax havens.

Masking a client's Stock Market trades is a traditional way of doing business here in the Bahamas and in the other tax havens. It's done by most all the major bank and trust companies. Banks in the Bahamas do not have to file tax returns with the IRS.

The *Bahamian Bank Secrecy Code* forbids any bank executive or advisor from giving information to any outside tax collector, attorney or foreign court.

Question: What can I invest in offshore?

THR: There are few restrictions as to what an IBC can invest in. U.S. stocks, bonds and mutual funds, futures, options and commodity contracts are frequently bought through offshore companies because they are not liable to U.S. capital gains taxes. Treasury bonds, bank CDs are also purchased through offshore companies. No U.S. withholding taxes are payable on interest incomes as long as the IBC does not open an office or carry on other business inside the U.S.

Using offshore banks, customers can usually trade on any stock exchange anywhere in the world at costs more or less equivalent to the costs you would incur with discount broker Charles Schwab.

You can, of course, call your own shots on what stocks and bonds or mutual funds the IBC purchases. You'll pay only the broker's commission (≈ 1¢ to 3¢ a share + a nominal fee for having the stock certificates put in the Bahamian bank's name (instead of IBC's name). Call 242-327-7359 for more details.

Question: You live in the Bahamas. Who are some big names using that haven as a tax shelter?

THR: Business people from around the globe use the Bahamas as a tax haven. There are currently over $390 billion dollars on deposit in Bahamian banks. Former U.S. citizen Sir John Templeton (knighted by the Queen Elizabeth II of England) lives in Nassau. Templeton managed over $20,000,000,000 for clients worldwide. He gave up his U.S. citizenship years ago, probably to escape the USA's 55% estate tax on estates over $2.6 million dollars. U.S. Treasury Secretary Nicholas F. Brady (P.O. Box N-7776) has a home in Lyford Cay. Remember it's his branch of the Federal Government that was responsible for writing the Treasury Regulations under IRC §951 thru §958 for CFCs back in 1962! There are forty or fifty Bacardi's (the rum distillers) living in Nassau. Incidentally, the Lyford Cay area is a millionaire's row here in Nassau.

Question: How can investors learn more about these tax havens?

THR: My new book, *Tax Havens of the World ($75) (7h edition),* and newsletter would be most useful in helping you develop your offshore plan. Customers that order a 12 month subscription to our newsletter get a copy of the new 7th edition **FREE**. To order *Tax Havens of the World ($75)* or the newsletter - the *Tax Haven Reporter ($150/yr./12 issues)* write **Tax Haven Reporter**, P.O. Box CB 11552, Nassau, Bahamas • Telephone/Fax • 242-327-7359 • e-mail taxman@batelnet.bs Check or money orders bring immediate airmail service. No credit cards - sorry. Three day priority mail delivery on all U.S. orders - guaranteed.

> *Tax evasion is not illegal in the Bahamas, since we do not have income, capital gains or inheritance taxes. Tax evasion is not considered suitable grounds for ordering access to information about an account.* - from **Welcome Bahamas,** - Our #2 Industry Banking, pg 71.

> *"While a Bahamian company may offer tax advantages to non-Bahamian beneficial owners under certain circumstances, it is essential that the laws of their own country be carefully considered before action is taken. Unless adequate planning is undertaken, the tax advantages may ultimately be lost to the owner. Consideration must be given to the ultimate disposition of accumulated funds."* - **Touche Ross International (Bahamas).**

IRS Letter Ruling 9332006 shows how America's wealthiest taxpayers can save millions (even billions) in taxes, but you must include it in your estate tax plan and your WILL.

IRS –LTR 9332006 ™ Full Text

The use of an offshore testamentary trust to receive a U.S. persons assets only upon his death might afford some definite tax advantages, especially if the trusts assets are revocable by a nonresident alien individual or corporation. IRS LT. 9332006 confirms that upon his death, assets held in a foreign trust will no longer be subject to U.S. taxes, and not considered part of the U.S. person's U.S. estate, even if there are U.S. beneficiaries for the foreign trust.

LTR 9332006 -- ISSUE (4). UPON A SETTLOR'S DEATH, WILL THE PORTION OF THE TRUST TREATED AS OWNED BY THAT SETTLOR CEASE TO BE SO TREATED EVEN IF THEN TRUST BENEFICIARIES INCLUDE UNITED STATES PERSONS? Section 679(a)(2) (A) provides that the rules of section 679(a)(1) do not apply to "a transfer by reason of death of the transferor." While section 679(a)(2)(A) does not expressly address the tax consequences of the termination of foreign grantor trust status by reason of the grantor's death, the legislative history of the enactment of section 679 (H.R. Rep. No. 658, 94th Cong., 1st Sess. at 209 (1975); S. Rep. No. 938, 94th Cong., 2d Sess. at 218 (1976)) provides that "an inter vivos trust which is treated as owned by a U.S. person under [section 679] is not treated as owned by the estate of that person upon his death." Accordingly, any portion of the Trust that is treated as owned by a Settlor under the rules of section 679 shall cease to be so treated upon that Settlor's death.

In 1970 the IRS issued the following ruling (only part of the ruling is included here, but the IRS' entire Revenue Ruling 69-70 is in my book - Tax Havens of the World) to study...

Revenue Ruling 69-70 states: "An individual beneficiary who is resident of the United States is not taxable on a distribution from a foreign trust considered to be owned by a nonresident alien grantor under subpart E of subchapter J of the Code" - these are the exact words of the Internal Revenue Service tax writers - i.e., tax lawyers working for the Treasury department writing your tax law. They are people from Harvard, Stanford, and other big name institutions.

For more details on how to apply the IRS's advice, contact the Tax Haven Reporter at 242-327-7359 or email me at taxman@batelnet.bs

I've formed over 900 of these foreign testamentary asset protection trusts for client already. But, if you don't instruct someone (in your U.S. WILL) to transfer the U.S. assets offshore to the foreign trustee, you'll be missing the boat to the tax heaven. You must include this information, and be very specific as to the amount you want transferred to the foreign trustee, and this information must be in your U.S WILL – before you die!

Under current U.S. estate tax law. U.S. estates over $21,000,000 pay a flat 55% estate tax duty. What' left over will be taxed every year, unless you implement a tax strategy before you die. But, smalle estates (under $20,000,000) can take advantage of this tax planning too.

Thousands of Offshore Banks trade the NYC Stock Markets tax free – legally! How?

http://www.bahamasbahamas.com/offshore.html

Interested in finding out more about the world's leading tax havens and financial centers? Want to learn about the U.S. tax laws governing foreign investment by U.S. taxpayers? Try a 12 month subscription to the *Tax Haven Reporter* ($150/12 issues) and receive **FREE** a copy of our 350 page new, 7th edition - *Tax Havens of the World* (regular price by itself = $75).

• Trade NYSE stocks, bonds, options and commodities - **TAX FREE** - offshore like thousands of offshore banks do! Find out how Big "8" accounting firms exploit IRS Revenue-Ruling 69-70 to pass *foreign source income* on to U.S. beneficiaries free from Federal Income taxes! It's totally legal to do.

• Two summers ago, **Michael Jordan** of the Chicago Bulls purchased the Bahamian island known as Crab Cay for $3.9 million. Business people from around the globe use the Bahamas as a tax haven. Former U.S. citizen Sir John Templeton lives in Nassau. Templeton managed over $20,000,000,000 for clients worldwide. He gave up his U.S. citizenship years ago, probably to escape the USA's 55% estate tax on estates over $2.6 million dollars. U.S. Treasury Secretary Nicholas F. Brady has a home in Lyford Cay. There are forty or fifty Bacardi's (the rum distillers) living in Nassau.

• Tom Azzara, the author of *Tax Havens of the World,* lives and works in sunny **Nassau** in the tax free **Bahamas.** Over the last 9 years, Tom has registered more than 900 **International Business Companies** (IBCs) at a total cost of $2,100 per company (each IBC comes with 2 Bahamian trusts, trustees, registered agent, registered office in Nassau, etc.). The Bahamas are the ideal no-tax haven, just 3/4 hour from Miami. There are more than 400 banks in the Bahamas with over $390 billion dollars on deposit. Offshore companies can trade in the U.S. Stock Market free of capital gains taxes. An IBC or foreign trust can receive US bank CD interest or treasury bond interest 100% free from all taxes - U.S. and other. Americans who live offshore can exclude up to $72,000 in *foreign earned income* too.

• Over 20 tax havens are covered in my book *TAX HAVENS OF THE WORLD* ($75) including, the Bahamas, Caymans, Switzerland, Vanuatu, Bermuda, Barbados, Hong Kong, Singapore, Channel Islands & the Isle of Man (famous havens used by modern British businessmen), Campione, Panama, Anguilla, Antigua, Liberia, Gibraltar, Cyprus (shipping tax havens), and little Nauru (3rd smallest nation in the world), and many more. Also covered are the Exempt Companies, the International Business Corporation (IBC), the Foreign Trust, the Foreign Personal Holding Company, Exempt Shipping Companies, Exempt Offshore Banks, Exporting U.S. products tax free, the important U.S. Income Tax Treaties, and Australian & Canadian tax havens. Americans planners must learn how to avoid the USA's "Controlled Foreign Corporation" (CFC) legislation.

• Don't miss out. This book and newsletter is an invaluable reference source. One international tax lawyer (graduate from NYU School of Law) with offices in Geneva and London (Imperial House) writes: *"I would like to repeat that I find your analysis of the Tax Code to be excellent. I enjoy each and every issue of the **Tax Haven Reporter.** I commend you on your jurisprudential reasoning and treatment of international tax matters discussed in your newsletter."*

ORDER FROM:

Tax Haven Reporter
P.O. Box CB 11552
Nassau, Bahamas
Tele/fax: 242-327-7359
cellular 242-359-1132
E-Mail taxman@batelnet.bs

SEND me a copy of **TAX HAVENS OF THE WORLD** plus a 12 month subscription to the **Tax Haven Reporter.** I'd like to learn how to operate virtually tax free too. **Enclosed is $150.00** for both the book and the newsletter.

(Check or money order only please - no credit cards - sorry)

NAME_____ _____

ADDRESS_____ _____

CITY_____ _____

STATE_____ ZIP_____

Reviews and Acknowledgments

One U.S. educated international tax lawyer (graduate of the NYU School of Law*) whose law firm has offices in Geneva, London (Imperial House) and the United States writes:

"I would like to repeat that I find your analysis of the Tax Code to be excellent. I enjoy each and every issue of the _Tax Haven Reporter_. I commend you on your jurisprudential reasoning and treatment of international tax matters discussed in your newsletter. Please let me know if you would be interested in receiving articles for publication dealing with other specific areas of international tax law and/or estate planning such as e.g., Swiss Banking Secrecy, use of trusts, doing business in Russia, or tax haven related topics of interest."

* The NYU School of Law produces some of the best, well trained international tax lawyers of any University in the United States.

"Your book is better than Marshall Langer's _Practical International Tax Planning._" (over $200/copy) • John S. from Southwick, Mass.

"Best book on tax havens I've ever read." • C. Brooks, CPA, Pennsylvania

"I'd like to meet you since you've taken the time and effort to pass this useful information along to me. How about being my guest on a cruise sometime in the future?" - Captain Mike Burke, Windjammer Barefoot Cruises, Ltd. (Miami, Florida)

"I don't know where to begin describing my happiness with the purchase of **Tax Havens of the World.** I have devoured every word of the book already, twice. What shocks me is the detail and accuracy of your book. I have asked tax lawyers everywhere the same topics, and the only answer I get is that ... offshore is not possible ... and I don't do any. Great Answer." • comments from a Certified Public Account, with offices in Newton, Mass., and Providence R.I.

About the author

Tom Azzara grew up on Long Island, New York, but has lived the last ten years in the sunny, tax free Bahamas. In addition to his book, _Tax Havens of the World,_ Tom publishes a newsletter, the _Tax Haven Reporter_. In addition to publishing, he currently acts as a consultant to over 900 International Business Companies (called IBCs), which he helped organize. Tom works independent of/with a Bahamian bank owned by a $20 billion dollar parent bank from South Africa. Most of his companies end up with them.

http://www.bahamasbahamas.com/

http://maxpages.com/tax6planning/Home

http://www.endtaxes.com/

NASSAU ESTATE TAX PLANNERS
P.O. Box CB 11552
Nassau, Bahamas
tele/fax: 242-327-7359
e-mail • taxman@batelnet.bs